EARLY FAMILIES OF
HERKIMER COUNTY
NEW YORK

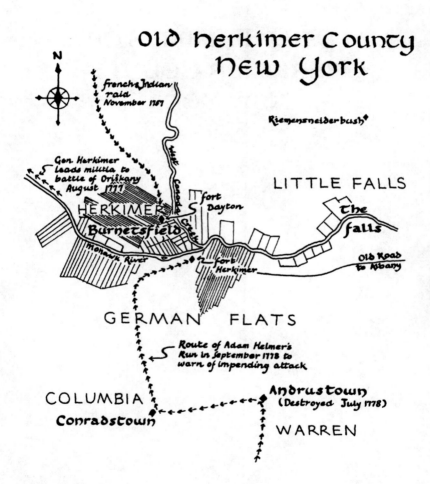

Old Herkimer County New York

N

French & Indian raid November 1757

Riemensneiderbush

Gen. Herkimer leads militia to battle of Oriskany August 1777

HERKIMER

Burnetsfield

Mohawk River

fort Dayton

fort Herkimer

LITTLE FALLS

The Falls

Old Road to Albany

GERMAN FLATS

Route of Adam Helmer's Run in September 1778 to warn of impending attack

COLUMBIA
Conradstown

Andrustown
(Destroyed July 1778)

WARREN

EARLY FAMILIES OF HERKIMER COUNTY NEW YORK

Descendants of the Burnetsfield Palatines

BY WILLIAM V.H. BARKER

Illustrations by Mrs. Lesley Nowakowski

CLEARFIELD

Reprinted for
Clearfield Company, Inc. by
Genealogical Publishing Co., Inc.
Baltimore, Maryland
1999, 2001

CONTENTS

- Acknowledgements -

This book presents original genealogical research and analysis on families living in the Herkimer County, New York area from about 1720 to 1799. A major information source was the collected genealogical material of the Herkimer County Historical Society, including family files, cemetery inscriptions catalog, probate summaries, and, in particular, their recently published books on the Bellinger, Harter, and Petrie families. Navy Cmdr. Lyle F. Bellinger's lifelong research on the Bellingers was an early inspiration for this present book and use was made of his working papers which have been kept by the Herkimer Historical Society. All such material has been generously made available to this researcher through the assistance of that organization's staff, with special thanks due for the review by Mrs. Hazel Patrick and the priceless aid and encouragement of the Herkimer Society's president, Mrs. Jane Spellman.

For those periods for which church records have been preserved, the principal sources of information were Vosburgh's transcripts of the Churchbooks of German Flats, Herkimer, & Stone Arabia, New York, plus the early New York Lutheran church records of Rev. Kocherthal (presented in MacWethy's Book of Names). In addition, the names of many individuals who provided informaton on one or more families have been noted in the book at the point where their additions or corrections appear. Of these persons, special note is due to Mr. Hank Jones of Universal City, California for his contributions and review. Only a small part of Mr. Jones' findings are included in this work and reference is made to his book for more on the German origins of the early Mohawk Valley Palatines (see Bibliography).

Introduction

Herkimer County, in north central New York's Mohawk Valley, received its name in 1791 in memory of General Nicholas Herkimer, the Revolutionary War militia commander who died as a result of wounds received at the Battle of Oriskany in 1777. The county is nearly at the geographic center of the state, shares about the same latitude and climate as central Michigan or Massachusetts, and spans about 30 miles from north to south and 15 miles east to west. The west to easterly flowing Mohawk River cuts Herkimer County approximately in half, with the towns of Fairfield, Herkimer, Little Falls, Manheim, Newport, Norway, Ohio, Russia, Salisbury, and Schuyler lying to the north of the river and Columbia, Danube, Frankfort, German Flats, Litchfield, Stark, Warren, and Winfield being south of the Mohawk. The county seat is at Herkimer, a town of about nine thousand people in 1970 which is readily accessible to the modern day motorist at Exit 30 of Interstate 90, some sixty miles due west of Albany on the New York Thruway. To either side of the flats adjoining the Mohawk River the terrain rises to thickly wooded low rolling hills, made fertile and smoothed by centuries under water at the bottom of an enormous post ice-age lake which apparently covered the better part of northern New York some four to eight thousand years ago.

The Mohawk River, some two to three hundred feet in width, is key to the region's early development. This river, drops about 400 feet in altitude in its course to Albany, was navigable for barge traffic from earliest times, although the presence of a few falls necessitated the establishment of "carrying places" for short distance overland portage of goods. The valley, cut by the Mohawk River, runs essentially from the river's source in the highlands north of Rome, New York to about the town of Amsterdam, just west of Schenectady; while the river itself continues on to empty into the Hudson River just north of Albany. Further details on the topography, resources, and early history of the region may be pursued through references listed in the Bibliography on page 349 (especially recommended are the books by Beers, Greene, Hardin and Hislop).

Of its early inhabitants, the Mohawk Valley was under the control of the Iroquois Indian nation when Europeans began to enter the region in the early 1600's. The Iroquois called themselves Onkweonweke, meaning "the only real men" (Hislop, page 22), and were recognized as the most intelligent of the new world Indians, as well as the most formidable, being capable of organized and sustained warfare (Cookingham's History of Oneida Co.). About the year 1550, under the leadership of the philosopher Dengiwidah and the orator Hiawatha, the Iroquois had organized themselves into a confederation of five nations, these being the Mohawks (known as flesh eaters, supposedly resorting to occasional cannibalism of enemies), the Senecas, the Onandagas, the Cayugas, and the Oneidas. A sixth nation, the Tuscororas, was added about the early 1700's. There were probably in excess of 15,000 Indians in the region about the year 1700, but by the time of the American Revolution their population had eroded to about 10,000 (NY Gov. Tryon's estimate in 1774), due in part to lack of resistance to European diseases. Their numbers then fell sharply during and just after the Revolution as a result of migrations to Canada and points westward, the exodus being necessitated by the fact that most of the Iroquois, except for the Oneidas, took the British side during the War of Independence. The most important Indian leader of the latter 1700's was the Mohawk chief Joseph Brandt. Brandt was born in 1742, educated in English at Dr. Wheelock's school in Lebanon, Connecticut, and was an ally of the colonists during the mid-18th century era of Britain's Mohawk Valley Indian administrator Sir William Johnson (Sir William's second wife was Brandt's sister). However, during the Revolution, Brandt joined forces with Sir John Johnson, Col. Guy Johnson, Capt. Walter Butler, and others in waging the most terrifying sort of warfare against the Mohawk Valley settlers. Since the Indian culture lacked written records, genealogical information is scarce and thus not treated in this book, except for mention of an occasional intermarriage with the white settlers (see for example the Dacksteter and Deny families on pages 291-3).

As to the early Europeans, the Dutch traders of Fort Orange (now Albany) initiated commerce with the Mohawk Valley Indians in the early 1600's and by 1634 surgeon Myndert Van Der Bogart had explored the Mohawk region (Hislop's Mohawk book). The Dutch traded alcoholic beverages, firearms, tools, and fabrics, in exchange for land and beaver hides. In 1664 the British took control of New York State and the Mohawk Valley area came under the jurisdiction of Albany County from that time until about 1774 when it became Tryon County (in 1784 the area was renamed as Montgomery County, the western portion of which was set off in 1791 as Herkimer County). In modern times, Herkimer County is bounded by Oneida County on the west and by Montgomery and Fulton Counties on the east. Prior to 1760 there was only limited settlement by the Dutch or English to the west of Schenectady, since the Mohawk region was vulnerable to incursions of the French and their Indian allies from Canada. The perilous condition of being an outpost settlement was shown in 1690 when Schenectady, only 15 miles west of Albany, was largely destroyed in a midwinter's night raid by a French and Indian war party.

With the exception of a few families, such as the Fondas, Schuylers, and Van Slykes, the Dutch and English seem to have been little induced to settle the Mohawk Valley, and so the opportunity fell to a group of immigrant Germans from the Palatinate, or lower Rhineland, area in central Europe. Several thousand of these Palatines had left their German homelands, being much reduced in circumstance after years of warfare with France, and had gone to England at Queen Anne's invitation in 1709 (Professor Knittle's book, cited in the Bibliography, treats in detail this historic migration). The English temporarily housed many of these people in tents outside London and early in 1710 about two thousand were placed aboard ships for passage to the American colonies, being promised land in New York in exchange for work in Hudson River camps, to be set up for the production of pitch for use in sealing naval vessels. There were delays in embarking and the Palatines were crowded into undersized and ill provisioned ships so that the Atlantic Ocean crossing itself became a tragedy in which, by New York Gov. Hunter's account, some 466 of them perished. From 1710 to 1712 the German immigrants required government subsidy, and the payment records by Gov. Hunter to heads of households survive (as in Knittle) and are referred to throughout this book as the NY Palatine Subsistence List. The pitch operations having failed, the Germans had to fend for themselves, moving for a while to contested lands in the Schoharie Valley west of Albany.

The Palatines remained a displaced people without land entitlement until September 1721 when the Albany City Council endorsed their petition to purchase Mohawk Valley land, not closer to Albany than 40 miles west of Ft. Hunter. Then on October 16, 1721, New York Governor William Burnet, presumably wishing to see buffer settlements of a friendly population in the central Mohawk area, granted the appropriate license, which allowed the Palatines, in 1722, to purchase land from the Indians in the vicinity of where the West Canada Creek flows into the Mohawk River. Upon completion of the survey of these lands in 1723, and in response to the request of Palatine leaders Joseph Petrie and Conrad Richert, the deeds were prepared under the designation of the Burnetsfield Patent. At about the same time, other Palatines received land grants at Stone Arabia and elsewhere in the Mohawk Valley. However, for purposes of this book, we are concerned mainly with the Burnetsfield Patentees as their lots were wholly within the present county of Herkimer, New York (see appendix pages 328-9 for list of names and lot

assignments). Most of the Burnetsfield Patentees apparently settled on their
lands between 1723 and 1725, with the exception of the Rickerts, who the Bellinger
book says remained in the Schoharie Valley, and Adam Michael Smith and son Ephraim
(listed in Pearson's Schenectady book as early residents of that city). Initially
called Burnetsfield, in the Kingsland district, the early Herkimer County area was
variously referred to as Stone Ridge, The Flats, The Falls, and most commonly as
German Flats. Prior to the American Revolution, German Flats encompassed both the
present town of Herkimer (north of the Mohawk River) and the county area south of
the Mohawk. However, by the time of the 1790 census, the town of Herkimer had
become a separate entity and German Flats was limited to the area south of the
river.

From 1723 onwards, until the French & Indian Wars commenced, German Flats was
generally at peace and the residents prospered to the extent that some writers
have termed the community almost utopian. Wheat grew abundantly in the fertile
soil and the accumulation of livestock and goods was extensive. Within the 1725
to 1755 time frame the Burnetfield patentees were joined by some of their 1710
Palatine kinsman from the Bashor, Christman, Getman, Hilts, Pfeiffer, and Steele
families, and also by later German immigrants such as the Clapsaddles, Eysamans,
Franks, Moyers, Rasbachs, Schells, Seghners, and Witherstines. Some of the
Patentee surnames, such as Coens and Poenradt, are not seen in later German Flats
records, so it is possible that, like the Lant family, a few may have moved back
eastward to more populuous areas prior to the 1750's. In addition to being
farmers, occupations of the early German Flats residents included magistrate (Jost
Petrie), schoolteacher (F. Bell), trader (G. Kast), blacksmith (J. Hess), butcher
(A. Bauman), miller (J. Weaver, D. Steele) and weaver (L. Harter). The first
known minister was Rev. George Michael Weiss, who served from 1735 to 1742 but for
whom no records remain (Vosburgh's GF churchbook). Weiss was followed by the
Elder Rosencrantz in 1751, who was suceeded in 1752 by his son Rev. Abraham
Rosencrantz, the latter serving until his death in 1796. No actual church records
survive for the years prior to 1760, except for the brief note of visiting
minister Sommer as to marriages in 1748 of Petrie's son and Bell's daughter,
Swinterman's daughter (groom not named), and Acus Van Slyck & Maria Petrie, and
the marriages in 1749 of Johannes Bell & Elisabeth Pfeiffer, and Frederick Miller
& Margaret Wohleben.

At 3 AM on November 12, 1757, disaster struck German Flats in the form of a
surprise raid by a French & Indian war party under the command of Lt. M. de
Bellestre, whose later report indicated 40 killed, 150 prisoners, and much booty
taken (appendix pages 331-2 give a projection of the population at the time of
this raid). No listing of the casualties of that raid exists, however the absence
of certain names afterwards permits speculation as to the identity of some of the
forty persons who lost their lives that November morning (it seems particularly
plausible that families such as Coens, whose property was on the northern edge of
the town, were hard hit). Sir William Johnson's papers note an investigation into
why the neighboring Indians had failed to warn the settlers in advance of the 1757
raid (friendly Indians did for example awaken Rev. Rosencrantz and take him safely
away), and perhaps the reason can be found in the account therein of the murder of
two Oneida Indians in September 1757 by a Thomas Smith, trader at German Flats at
that time. After the 1757 devastation there were periods of relief such as the
negotiated return of some prisoners in 1758 and the building, in that same year,
of Ft. Stanwix as a protective outpost about 35 miles west of German Flats. With
the French surrender to English forces at Montreal in 1760, relative peace was
restored to the Mohawk Valley, although occasional difficulties with the Indians
required that the settlers maintain a more vigilant militia than had been required
in earlier years. A group of later German immigrants appeared about 1766 with the

establishment of Peter Hasensclever's settlement at New Germantown (also called New Petersburg), located just west of the German Flats area in the present area of Schuyler, NY. Rev. Rosencrantz's church at German Flats, destroyed in the 1757 raid, was restored about 1760 and from then on we have the first records of baptisms and marriages, which are preserved to modern times. There remain annoying gaps in these church accounts, such as the absence of data for the period from 1770 through 1775, the limited amount of marriage records prior to 1781, and the total lack of information on deaths in the Herkimer County area prior to 1800. These difficulties notwithstanding, the church records from 1760 on, not only at German Flats but at St. Johnsville, Stone Arabia, and points eastward, form the major basis for the genealogies of families presented in this book. Of particular note to the modern-day researcher is the fact that many of the early German Flats families both moved and visited up and down the Mohawk Valley, thereby necessitating the search of church records over a wide geographic area for the presence of relevant marriage and baptism entries. Of note also is the information value of the baptismal sponsors, as those individuals were usually of the same generation (except when a grandparent would be sponsor for a grandchild of the same given name) and most often were brothers or sisters of the parents.

The second devastation to fall upon German Flats and the surrounding pre-Herkimer County area came from the alignments brought about by the American War of Independence. The British enrolled most of the area Indians, plus several Mohawk Valley settlers as well, to the Tory cause, and in August 1777 the bloody battle of Oriskany pitted former neighbor against neighbor and resulted in the estimated loss of some forty or so German Flats militiamen (see more details under Nicholas Herkimer profile on page 127). Oriskany turned the British back to Canada momentarily, but a year later they were back in a more nefarious form of military tactic, that of the hit and run assault on isolated settlements. From 1778 through 1782, the British waged a war of attrition in the Mohawk Valley, with members of raiding parties paid eight dollars for each scalp taken, regardless of the victim's combative status, sex, or age. For the German Flats residents it was a nightmare, with most forced to live continuously within the protective enclosures at Fort Dayton and Fort Herkimer. They were most vulnerable when out gathering food and tending crops, as was the case with the Bell family who were massacred during an outing at the Andrustown settlement in July 1778. Sometimes the settlers had to scramble quickly into the forts, as happened in September 1778 when the surviving scout, Adam Helmer, outran Indian pursuit to warn of the approach of Brandt's force (the attackers, numbering about 450, burned most of the German Flats structures and carried away livestock, but desisted from attacking the fortifications in which the residents had taken refuge).

By the end of the American Revolution, the Herkimer County region was severly depleted in manpower and resources and a new phase in its rebuilding began with the expansion westward of New Englanders, who were lured by the open lands of northern New York which had become available with the departure of the Indians. The resultant shift in population base was evident in the 1790 census when about a third of the Herkimer area people appear to be new arrivals of English extraction (compared to a negligable percentage in the 1778 German Flats relief list). We have pretty much limited ourselves in this book to the earlier families, primarily of German background, who were established in the region by the time of the Revolution, and in most cases have not attempted to trace individuals born after the year 1800.

FAMILY GROUPS - Families are arranged alphabetically by surname within this book and by earliest generation first within a section. A section begins with a banner of the form ****** **SMITH** ******** which will appear at the top of a new page and correspond to an entry in the book contents. An exception to the surname order has been made for scattered individuals and families who were not present in the area for very long or for whom information is not extensive enough to warrant a separate section. Those people are listed in alphabetical order in the "Other Families" section at the end of the book.

GENERATION ORDER - Each generation will normally begin with a banner of the form "SMITH - 2nd Generation" (this may not appear for the first generation) and will end with a delimiter line of the form "--------------------". Individuals of the first two generations are highlighted in **bold** print if they are believed to be of the family of interest. Also we have in many sections provided the names of other, generally non-related persons, who share the same or similar surname. These others are important from the standpoint of the records researcher's task in sifting through similiar names.

NUMBERING - An identifying number (ID#) is used to distinguish between persons of the same name and to link an individual as a child in one generation to their appearance as an adult in the next generation. However, the order of adult individuals within a generation is by their given name rather than their ID# (to permit comparison between similarly named persons).

CHILDREN - A parent will have his or her name in full and starting near the left margin, while a child's name appears indented and without the surname. The qualifier "pr." before a child's name indicates that there is probable likelihood based on some analysis, but not supportable evidence, to associate that child with the parent indicated. The qualifier "ps." on the other hand indicates only the possibility of the parent-child relationship and is normally used to temporarily place a child until enough data can be obtained to make an analysis. A plus ("+") sign preceding the identifying number of a child indicates that more information exists on the child in the following generation.

SPELLING - The same person may appear in the early 18th century records with their name spelled differently on each occurence! Consequently, in order to save space and avoid complications of identity, we have frequently standardized names to their modern day or anglicized form (such as JOHN SMITH for JOHANNES SMIDT). We have also tended to drop the German ornamental "Johan" which frequently preceded a boy's given name and, on occasion, have shortened women's names where the ornamental prefix Anna or Maria was apparent (i.e. ANNA ELISABETH and MARIA ELISABETH are both just ELISABETH).

Abbreviations Used

```
----        ----------------------------------------------------------
 b          born (birthyear known)
 b ca       born about (birthyear approximately known)
 b say      birthyear is a guess only
 bp         baptised (or baptismal)
 d          died
 d y        died young
 E&N        Enterprise & News (Raney Library, St. Johnsville NY)
 FPL        Ft. Plain NY (Reform Dutch Church)
 FR         Fonda NY (Reform Dutch Church)
 GF         German Flats NY or German Flats Reform Dutch Church
 HK         Herkimer NY or Herkimer Reform Dutch Church records (Vosburgh)
 HCH        Herkimer Co. Historical Society, 400 N Main, Herkimer NY 13350
 LDS        Latter Day Saints Computer Index (CFI)
 m          married
 ms.        manuscript
 pr.        probably
 ps.        possibly
 SA         Stone Arabia (Montgomery Co.) NY
 SAL        Stone Arabia Lutheran Church records (Vosburgh)
 SAR        Stone Arabia Reform Dutch Church records (Vosburgh)
 SCH        Schenectady NY
 sp         sponsor at baptism (godparent of a child)
 spf        sponsor for baptism (person acting as godparent)
 SHH        Schoharie NY (St. Paul´s Lutheran Church records, Vosburgh)
 SHR        Schoharie Reform Dutch Church records (Vosburgh)
 SJ         St. Johnsville NY (as a place)
 SJR        St. Johnsville Reform Dutch Church records (Vosburgh)
 WCL        West Camp (NY) Luth. Church (Kocherthal Records <Book of Names>)
 WHS        Whitestown Protestant Church (Utica NY, Vosburgh)
 wit.       witness at marriage
```

Special Lists of Individuals

1710-12 NY (Hunter) Palatine Subsistence List (Knittle, see Bibliography)
      <format (2A,3Y) means 2 adults or adolescents, 3 youngsters under age 10>

1717 Simmendinger Register (census of NY Palatines, see Knittle)

1723 Burnetsfield Patent (see appendix pages 327-329)

1751 Stone Arabia Testimonial for Rev. Wernig (Vosburgh´s FPL churchbook)

1753 Burnetsfield Church Building Subscribers (Vosburgh´s GF churchbooks)

1757-69 German Flats Militia Lists (MacWethy´s Book of Names, pages 8-14)

1771 Burnetsfield Minister´s Support List (Vosburgh´s GF churchbooks)

1778 German Flats Relief (MacWethy´s Book of Names, pages 116-7)

1790 Montgomery Co. NY Census (extract in this book, pages 337-348)
      <census 3-digit format: (#men - #boys under age 16 - #women)>

********** ARMSTRONG **********

101: **ARCHIBALD ARMSTRONG** - pr. born in England ca 1730 to 1740; pr. died ca
1787; m1 ca 1761 ELISABETH STAHRING dau of NICHOLAS STAHRING & ANNA; m2 at German
Flats 11 Mar 1784 ELISABETH CRIM (Krembs) dau of PETER CRIM & ELISABETH EMIGE and
a widow of Maj. JOHN EISENLORD (died at Oriskany battle 1777). Archibald came to
America as a soldier in the 46th British Regiment stationed in New York about 1761
and, upon completion of his military duty, he elected to remain in the Mohawk
Valley in the community of his wife's kin. In 1767 he was a Corporal in Capt.
Conrad Frank's German Flats militia company and during the American Revolution he
served in Col. Bellinger's 4th Tryon Co. Regiment. Around the time of the
Revolution he seems to have been the only Armstrong in the German Flats area, so
there is little doubt that the "pr." children, born during the early 1770's gap in
GF church records, belong to him. He may have died by 1787 when reference is made
to a widow Armstrong (in shopkeeper James Van Horne's records as found in Beers
History of Herkimer Co.), which would make the daughter Gertrude born in July 1788
a posthumous child (but the church record does not so state). Another hint of his
possible demise by 1790 is his absence from the census then.

surname ARMSTRONG

+102: JOHANNES b 11 Jan 1761 (bef. parent's marriage); ps. d. young
 103: MARIA b 5 May 1764 (sp Maria Stahring, Con. Orendorf); pr. d y
 104: CATHERINE b 26 Apr 1765 (sp. Cath. Folts, Joh. Eysaman)
 105: ANNA b GF 27 Jun 1766 (sp Cath. Staring, Adam Staring)
+106: ELISABETH bp SA 11 Aug 1767; ps. m 1802 JOHN WALLRATH
+107: HENRY bp SAR 24 Sep 1768 (sp Adam Steele & w. Eva <Staring>)
+108: NICHOLAS b say 1770; m 1797 EVE CUNINGHAM
+109: pr. ADAM b say 1772; m 1793 SARA H. SARJE
+110: pr. ARCHIBALD b say 1774; m by 1795 LYDIA ...
 111: pr. DOROTHEA b say 1775; m 1795 Johan GEORGE BAUMAN
 112: MARIA bp GF 18 May 1777 (sp. Cath. Dietrich, Hen. Staring)
 113: MARGARETA bp German Flats 19 Dec 1779 (sp. Fred Fox & Elis.)
         by second wife (Elis. Krems)
+114: GERTRUDE b SA 20 Jul 1788 (sp Peter Schuyler & w. Gert.)
         m at Minden NY 2 Nov 1808 JOHN NELLIS

115: **ELEAZER ARMSTRONG** - born 2 Mar 1757 and bp as an adult at GF 5 Oct 1789 (sp
Geo. Staring, Elisabeth Armstrong). Most likely he was an English relative of
immigrant Archibald and came to America after the Revolution.

ARMSTRONG - 2nd Generation

109: **ADAM ARMSTRONG** - pr. born ca 1770 to 1773; died by 1813; m at Herkimer 25
Dec 1793 SARA H. SARJE (wife given as "Eva" on 1795 bp rec.) pr. dau of a HENRY
SALJE, who was ps. the Henry Sallier of Frankfort NY whose widow Catherine
<Steele> m2 1805 John F. Getman. In 1813 the Herkimer Church records show a
confirmation of Marie Armstrong, age 17 of Frankfort NY, dau of Adam dec'd.

 116: ELISABETH bp GF 7 Jul 1793 (sp Jac. Brodhack & Doro.)
         pr. m by 1813 MOSES SAEGER
 117: ARCHIBALD bp GF 15 Jan 1795 (sp Arch. Armstrong & Laddy)
 118: MARIA b ca 1796; liv. 1813 (age 17 at HK Ch. Confirm.)

-3-

110: ARCHIBALD ARMSTRONG - pr. born ca 1770 to 1775; m by 1795 LYDIA ... We assume, but cannot be certain, that this was an Archibald Jr. (rather than a 3rd marriage for the immigrant Archibald). Archibald and wife Laddy were sponsors for bp of Archibald, son of Adam Armstrong.

       119: LYDIA bp GF 9 Jul 1795 (sp Mich H Meyer, Elis. Armstrong)

107: HENRY ARMSTRONG - b Stone Arabia NY 22 Sep 1768; m at German Flats NY 26 Jan 1796 DOROTHEA BAUMAN (bp 1778) dau of FREDERICK BAUMAN & DELIA FOLTS Children were Caroline (b 1804), Catherine (1811), & Sally Ann (1813), possibly others.

102: JOHN ARMSTRONG - born 1761 to 1763 (there was definitely a John Armstrong born 1761, but that one may have died young and another John subsequently born of the same parents ca 1763); m MARIA ... Served in Col. Bellinger's 4th Tryon NY Regiment during the Revolution. John Armstrong appears on the 1790 German Flats census (1-2-1).

       120: JOHN b 19 Mar 1784 (bp GF Oct 1789, sp Nic Starin & Elis.)

108: NICHOLAS ARMSTRONG - pr. born ca 1770 to 1775 (son of Archibald as given in DAR vol 140 page 185); m 1797 EVE CUNINGHAM (b 1780, d 1821). DAR #139595 has Nicholas as the son of the Archibald Armstrong who died in Oneida Co. NY and who married Nancy Sterling (i.e. should be Elisabeth Staring). Was a sponsor for Aug 1794 bp of Border child.

       121: ARCHIBALD 1816-1855 m DIANA HUBBARD

106: ELISABETH ARMSTRONG - born 7 Aug 1765; ps. m Palatine NY 7 Nov 1802 JOHN WALLRATH. She had a daughter Helena born out of wedlock in 1785 (bp GF 4 Aug, sp Samuel Dorn & Helena), relative to which the Rev. Rosencrantz made the following entry in the baptismal register "... Armstrong's wanton daughter has given birth to a child and the same day brought it to be baptized, but as such dissolute creatures can hardly be relied upon, I have not put down any father" (translation by Vosburgh, Records of GF vol 1 page 100).

********** AYER (Eyer, Oyer) **********

201: FREDERICK AYER - born in Holland ca 1747; died at the Battle of Oriskany 6 Aug 1777; m ELISABETH ... Immigrated in Oct 1764 with his four year old stepson JOHN FINSTER and was in Peter Hasenclever's group that settled at the New Petersburg camp (now East Schuyler, on the Mohawk River just west of Herkimer NY). He may have stayed a while at Hasenclever's works in New Jersey prior to coming up the Hudson River in a flat-bottomed boat about 1765 ("Frederick Oyer and His Descendents" by Phyllis Smith Oyer, copy at Herk. Co. Hist. Soc.). Pr. related to the **MARGARET AYER** (Oyer) who married by 1777 PETER MULTER Sr. Frederick's widow Elisabeth appears on the 1790 Herkimer census (1-0-3).

surname AYER

  202: GEORGE b ca 1766; prisoner of war 3 Apr 1780
+**203:** JACOB 1767-1815 m MARGARET BEKKER
+**204:** FREDERICK 1768- m 1789 ELISABETH HOCKSTATTER
+**205:** pr. JOHN b say 1770; m by 1790 ANNA ...
  206: PETER 1771-1853 m ELISABETH CLARK
  207: CHRISTIAN b say 1773; pr. d. young
  208: LORENTZ b 15 Jun 1776 (sp Lorentz Rinckel & Cath.); pr. d. y.
  209: CATHERINE b 3 Jul 1777 (sp Lorentz Rinckel & Cath.)

AYER - 2nd Generation

204: FREDERICK AYER - born SAR 29 Feb 1768 (sp. Geo. Sneck & Barbara; DAR #55358 has b 1769); died at Springville (Erie Co.) NY; m 29 Dec 1789 ELISABETH HOCKSTATTER (b 1767, d 1866) dau of CHRISTIAN HOCKSTATER & MARIA CATHERINE WITRIG. Had a son PETER (b GF 20 Feb 1793, sp. Peter Riema, Cath. Hockstater).

203: JACOB AYER - born 26 Mar 1767 (sp. Geo. Schnek jr & Barbara); died Schuyler NY Sep 1815; m 29 Feb 1790 MARGARET BEKKER pr. a dau of DIBOLD BEKER. His widow m2 ca 1815 John Finster. Was taken prisoner in the Revolution on 3 Apr 1780 (Book of Names page 113).

  210: pr. CHRISTIAN b say 1790 (bp GF Feb 1791)
  211: DIETRICH b GF 22 Jan 1791 (sp. Clem McGnot & Elis. Barb.)

205: JOHANNES AUER (Ayer?) - pr. born ca 1760 to 1773; m by 1790 ANNA ... Living at New Deutschland (New Petersburg) in 1790. Surname Auer pr. variant of this Ayer family (but not mentioned in P.S. Oyer's Oyer book).

  212: CHRISTIAN b GF 15 Oct 1786 (sp. Christn Hockstater & Cath.)
  213: VALENTIN bp SJR 30 May 1790 (sp Val. Miller & Maria)

206: PETER AYER - born New Petersburg NY 5 Dec 1771; died Schuyler NY 6 Jun 1853; m 9 Feb 1799 ELISABETH CLARK (b Nine Partners, Dutchess Co., NY 9 Dec 1782, d 14 Jan 1853). Had 13 children including John P. (1799-1872 m Charity Frank), Jacob (1801-1868 m Mary Riema), Margaret (b 1802, m Peter Multer), Elizabeth (b 1804, m Fred. Riema), James (1806-1893 m1 Martha Jane Burrill), Solomon (1808-1858 m Christina Redman), Henry (1809-1880 m Cath. Clemens), Eve (b & d 1810), Catherine, Peter jr (b 1814, d 1821), Hannah (b 1816 m Jacob Clemens), Rachel (1821-1889 m Michel Clemens), Daniel (twin, 1821-1883 m Mary Lintz).

********** BARSH (Bretsch, Borsch) **********

301: LUDWIG BARSH - pr. born ca 1678 (Ludwig Buers on NY City sick list, age 32 in 1710); m CATHERINE ... (b ca 1682, age 28 in 1710). Pr. the Ludwig Bresch with wife & 1 child on the 1709 London Palatine list (sailed from Holland to England 15 Jul 1709). Ludwig Borsch was on the NY Palatine Subsistence list in 1710 (2A,1Y) & in 1712 (3A,2Y) and ps. was related to JONAS BORSCH on that same list in 1710 (3A,2Y). In 1723 Ludowick Pears drew Burnetsfield lot #27 (north of Mohawk River) & his wife Catherine got lot #23 (south of the Mohawk).

surname BARSH
302: CATHERINE b ca 1707 (age 3 in 1710)
303: ANNA MARIA b 3 Jan 1711 (sp. Conrad Fredrich)
+304: LUDWIG b WCL 31 Mar 1713 (sp. Joh. Cuntz & w. Maria Cath.)

BARSH - 2nd Generation

304: Mr. BARSH - (ps. LUDWIG, born NY Camps Mar 1713); pr. died before 1760; m ... (ps. a Hess). Need a Mr. Barsh here as the father of the Maria who married in 1763 Adam Helmer Jr.

+305: ps. ADAM b say 1735; m1 ANNA EVA ...; m2 1768 MARGARET ...
306: pr. MARIA b say 1744; m 1763 ADAM HELMER Jr.
+307: ps. LUDWIG 1748-1832 m MARGARET

305: ADAM BARSH Sr. - pr. born ca 1714 to 1735 (son or grandson of immigrant Ludwig); died ca 1777 (ps. at Oriskany); m1 by 1760 ANNA EVA ... ; m2 SAR 14 Nov 1768 MARGARET ... a widow of Mr. HELMER (pr. Godfrid). Adam Bers was on the 1771 Burnetsfield Minister´s Support List and pr. his widow was the Margaret Barsh with 1 adult & 4 children on 1778 GF relief.

+308: pr. ADAM jr. b say 1754; m by 1776 ANNA EIGNEBROD
309: ps. ELISABETH (Barsh?) b say 1757; m JOST FOX
+310: LUDOLPH b SA 4 Sep 1760 (sp Ludolph Shoemaker & Gertr.)
           (pr. RUDOLPH ca 1758-1828 m 1782 MARGARET FOX)
           by 2nd wife
311: MARIA b SAR 14 May 1769 (sp John Wike & Doro.)
312: pr. CATHERINE b ca 1774 (age 81 in 1855); spf 1793 Helmer bp
           m1 1796 ARCHIBALD GIBSON; m2 1830 JOST WAGGONER
313: JACOB b GF 6 Mar 1776 (sp. Ludwig Campbell, Cath. Spohn)
314: ps. MARGARET ca 1777-1813 m PHILIP P. HELMER

BARSH - 3rd Generation

308: ADAM BARSH jr - pr. born ca 1750 to 1758; m by 1776 ANNA EIGENBROD (her surname fr. 1789 St. Johnsville church rec.). Pr. the Adam in Klock´s Revol. Reg. (listed with Ludolph) and on the 1790 Palatine NY census (2-2-2).

+315: ADAM b GF 9 Aug 1776 (sp. Ludwig Barsh)
+316: pr. GEORGE A. b say 1780; m by ca 1800 NANCY SHULTZ
           children cont. next page -->

-6-

children of Adam jr. cont.
```
317: pr. ABRAHAM AD.  b GF 21 Apr 1783 (sp Jost Fox & Elisabeth)
318: CATHERINE  b GF 5 Aug 1786 (son of Adam & Anna)
             (bp sp Geo. Hen Glock, Cath. H. Weber)
319: JACOB  bp SJR 5 May 1789 (sp. John Hess, Maria Eigenbrod)
320: EVA  bp SJR 8 May 1791 (sp John Hess & Anna <Fox>)
321: JOHN  bp SJR 24 Feb 1793 (sp Wm Nellis & Magdalena)
322: TIMOTHY  1799-1872  m 1821 MARGARET SMITH (1798-1873)
```

307: LUDWIG BARSH - born ca 1748; died Herkimer NY 17 Jun 1832 (age 84-5-22); m by
1783 MARGARET ... Ludwig Barsh & Margaret Campbell were sponsors for Jan 1768 bp
of Margaret, dau of Adam Helmer & Maria (Barsh). A Ludwig Barsh and Margaret Fox
were sponsors for Apr 1782 bp of Margaret, dau of Jost Fox & Elisabeth. Ludwig &
Margaret sponsored 1786 bp of Gertrude, dau of George Steel & Dorothy. Ludwig was
in Bellinger's 4th Tryon Co. Revol. Regiment and had 2 adults & 1 child on 1778 GF
relief. He appears on the 1790 GF census (1-1-2) listed next to George Steele.

```
+323: pr. GEORGE  ca 1773-1838 m by 1797 ELIZABETH UTTERMARK
 324: SIMON  b GF 21 Mar 1783 (sp Simon Nicols & Anna)
+325: ps. ADAM  b say 1787; m by 1809 CATHERINE HUYK
```

310: RUDOLPH BARSH ("Ludolph" on mar. rec.) - born ca 1758; died Little Falls NY
Apr 1828 (age 70); m German Flats NY 17 Sep 1782 MARGARET FOX (b ca 1762, d 26 Nov
1823 age 61) ps. dau of PHILIP FOX. In Col. Bellinger's Revol. Regiment.
Presumably moved east to Brunswick, Co. Renselaer, NY during the Revolution. On
1790 Palatine NY census (1-1-2), next to H. Klock & David Hess.

```
 326: ADAM R.  bp Brunswick NY 6 Jun 1782; pr. d. young
+327: ADAM  b SJR 21 Nov 1790 (sp Geo. Barsh, Maria Reuter)
```

BARSH - 4th Generation

315: ADAM BARSH - pr. born ca 1770 to 1788 (pr. son of Adam jr.); m by 1809
CATHERINE HUYK. Children include Adam (b ca 1809; m Herk. NY 1831 BARBEL CONR.
MAUER), Elisabeth (b 2 Feb 1809, sp. Elis. Hauck, widow of Manlius NY), Dalia (b
1814), Louisa (b 1816, sp. Gerrit Hawk), & John (1819).

327: ADAM R. BARSH - bp St. Johnsville NY 25 Dec 1790 (son of Rudolph & Marg.); m
by 1813 MARIA ... Had sons Hiram (b SA 7 Mar 1814) & George (bp Minden NY 1821).

316: GEORGE A. BARSH - pr. born ca 1760 to 1780; m by ca 1800 NANCY SHULTZ. Had
son Nathaniel (married in 1828 Margaret Helmer).

323: GEORGE BARSH - born ca 1773; died 1838 age 65; m ELIZABETH UTTERMARK (b ca
1777, d 1854 age 77). Living at Minden NY 1810 to 1812 . Had George Geo. (m 1821
EVA NIC. WOHLEBEN); Margaret (1808-1889 m JOHN PETRIE); Charles (bp Minden NY Aug
1810; ps. m MARIA EYSAMAN); Elisabeth (bp 1812, sp Rev. John J. Wack & w. Helen;
m by 1834 FREDERICK J. HELMER), Melinda (1818).

```
 328: pr. ANNA GEO.  b ca 1797; liv. 1815 (age 18, Ch. Confirm)
             pr. m 1820 PETER J. FOX
 329: pr. PETER G.  b ca 1799; d HK 1817 age 18
```

********** BASEHORN (Bashar, Passage) **********

401: JACOB BOSHAAR - pr. born in Germany before 1665; died by Nov 1719; m1
Brietenbach Germany 20 Jan 1681 GERTRUDE MEYERS (d 1693); m2 30 Jul 1693
CHRISTINA MAURER (aka CHRISTINA WEVER) dau of GEORGE MAURER (see Jones´ "The
Palatine Families of New York" for more on German family origins). Widow
Christina m2 Kingston NY Nov 1719 WILJEM BOLK (b England, widower of PIETERNELLA
SMIT). Jacob was on the NY Palatine subs. list in 1710 (6A,2Y) & in 1712
(5A,2Y) and naturalized at Albany NY 22 Nov 1715.

                        surname BASHAR
     +402: JACOB   bp Nov 1681; m before 1717 ANNA CATHERINE ...
     +403: GEORGE bp Jun 1694; m 1716 MARIA ELISABETH WENRIG
      403A BARENT bp May 1698; liv. 1733 (spf Hen. Beem bp)
     +404: MARGARET bp Feb 1701; m 23 Aug 1721 ALBERT BEEM
     +406: MAGDALENA bp Jun 1706; m 1735 JOHANNES DE GRAFF

                        BOSHAAR - 2nd Generation

402: Johan JACOB BOSHOOR - bp Germany 10 Nov 1681; m Anna CATHERINE ...   On
NY Palatine subsistence list in 1710 (2A,0Y) and in 1712 (3A,0Y). Naturalized
at Albany NY 31 Jan 1716. On 1717 Simmendinger census with wife Anna Catherine
& 2 children. Pr. sponsored, with Magdalena Wendrig, Feb 1716 bp of Magdalena,
dau of Christofel Denmarken & Christina Bernhart.

     +407: GEORGE (HENRY) b 17 Mar 1717 (sp. Geo. Stump & wife)
      408: ps. dau b say 1720; ps. m son of JOHANNES CHRISTMAN Sr.
      408A pr. SUSANNA b say 1724; d 1754; m by 1746 CHRISTIAN JANI
     +409: pr. JACOB   ca 1728-1804 m by 1747 MARGARET KOCH
      410: ps. PETER   b say 1734; prisoner in Canada 1758
                (i.e. "Peter Bachoren" as given in Book of Names page 112)
      410A ps. MARIA ELISABETH (Bashor?)   m by 1761 NICHOLAS WOHLEBEN

403: GEORGE BOSHAAR (Yuriann Pesor) - born in Germany pr. ca 1685 to 1698; m
at Kingston NY 7 Aug 1716 MARIA ELISABETH WENRIG (b in Germany ca 1693, age 17
in 1710) dau of BALTHASAR WENNERICH. Children baptised at Kingston NY (KNR).

      411: JACOB   bp Kingston 22 Jun 1718 (sp. Jacob Pesor, Doro. Beems)
      412: BALTUS bp 31 Jul 1720 (sp. Baltus Wenrig, Magdal. Wenrig)
      413: MATHEUS bp KNR 26 Dec 1721 (sp. Math. Wendel, Cat. Snyder)

404: MARGARET PEESHAR - bp Feb 1701; m Kingston NY 23 Aug 1721 ALBERT BEEM. Had
a child (b before 21 Aug 1721), MAGDALENA (bp Jan 1723, sp Geo. Beem, Magd.
Peshar), CHRISTINA (bp 1725, Wm Bolk, Christina Boshar), ANNA (bp 1728, Wm
Dowdie, Anna Beem), HENDRICK (bp Mar 1733, sp Barent & Magd Peshar), MARGAREt
(bp 1736, Tam Zeetiwik, E. Sevel), & ALBART (bp 1738, sp Jan Maklein, Eva Smit).

406: MAGDALENA PEESHAR - bp Jun 1706; m Kingston NY (KNR) 9 Aug 1735 JOHANNES DE
GRAFF of Albany. She had a daughter JOHANNA (father not named, bp KNR Jun 1724
<sp Jury Beem, Elis. Beem>, pr. m Gerrit Teerpenink). Magdalena & John De
Graaf had JAN (bp KNR Dec 1735, sp Jan van Aaken, Marg. DeGraaf), MARIA (bp
1738, sp. Jurian Tappen, Blandina Parsen), MARGARET (bp May 1746, sp Joh.
Schraam, Catrina Weysing), & ANNATJE (bp Jan 1749, sp. Hen. & Ann Beem).

409: JACOB BASHAR - born ca 1728 (pr. son of Jacob & Cath.); died Herkimer NY
13 Jul 1804 (age about 76); m by 1746 MARGARET KOCH (liv. 1778). Jacob &
Margaret sponsored the 1746 SAL bp of Christian, son of Christian Jani &
Susanna, but that record may refer to a baptism in Monmouth Co. New Jersey,
since Jani traditions have Jacob Boshar adopting his orphaned nephew Henry Jani
about 1754 and then moving to the Mohawk Valley (Cuyler Reynolds, Hudson-Mohawk
Geneal., page 966). Jacob was in Mark Petrie's 1757 GF militia and in Capt.
Conrad Frank's 1767 GF militia, suggesting that he lived south of the Mohawk
River prior to the Revolution. A Jacob Boeshorn was named as an executor on the
1773 will of Nicholas Wohleben of Burnetsfield, and we assume this would have
been the older Jacob (b 1728). At Fonda NY Jacob & Margaret sponsored the 1774
bp of Peter, son of Jacob Kitts & Eva, the Nov 1776 bp of Margaret, dau of Henry
Yanney (Jani), the Nov 1777 bp of Philip, son of Lucas Feeter, and the May 1778
bp of Conrad, son of Thomas Moore & Catrina. If Jacob's birthyear of 1728 is
correct, then he would seem a bit young to produce all the Bashors who appear as
married adults in GF and SA records of the 1760's (our guess is that orphaned
children of George Bassage & Sophia of Greenbush NY came to live near their
uncle Jacob at Burnetfield ca 1756 to 1762). Pr. this Jacob was the one with 5
adults & 3 children on 1778 GF relief and on the 1790 Herkimer census (2-1-2).

```
+415: pr. JACOB  b say 1745; m by 1761 CATHERINE ...
+416: pr. HENRY b say 1747; m by 1764 ELISABETH KITTS
 417: pr. ANNE EVA (Boshar?)  b say 1755; m by 1776 HENRY MILLER
+417A ps. JOHN  b say 1757; m by 1778 ANNA SPANNENBERG
 418: CHRISTINA  bp Fonda NY 6 May 1759 (sp H. Crim, Cristina Emich)
 419: ANNA  bp Fonda NY 4 Jul 1762 (sp Hen. Crim & Cristina)
```

407: GEORGE HENRICH BASHAR (aka Henrich Passage/Bassache) - pr. the George
born 17 Mar 1717 (son of Jacob); ps. died ca 1756-60; m SOPHIA MAGDALENA
CASSELMAN (b 1718) dau of CHRISTIAN CASSELMAN & MARIA JUDITH. George lived in
Albany Co. and Greene Co. NY and may have died during the French War, as it
seems that many of children appear about then in the area of German Flats NY.

```
 420: HENDRICH  bp Schoharie/Greenbush NY 25 Aug 1736; pr. d.y.
+421: CHRISTIAN  b Greenbush NY 1739
+422: MARGARITA  b 1741; ml 1760 JOHN J. RADCLIFFE
+423: Hannes GEORGE  bp Loonenburg NY 1 Oct 1741
 424: JOHANNES  bp Loonenburg NY 4 Oct 1742; pr. d. young
 425: JOSEPH  b Greenbush NY 1746; pr. d. young
 426: MARIA  b Greenbush NY 6 Apr 1748; d 1826; pr. m JACOB FULMER
+427: JOHN  b Greenbush NY 1749;  pr. m MARGARET CRIM
 428: MARY  bp Mohawk NY 24 May 1752
 429: HENRY  b Greenbush NY 1754
+430: JOSEPH  b Rhinebeck NY 16 Sep 1755; pr.  m ANNA
```

BASEHORN - 4th Generation

421: CHRISTIAN PASSAGE (Peshause) - pr. born Greenbush NY 1739; m by 1763
MARGARETHA ... In Capt Conrad Frank's militia company in 1767.

```
 431: child  b SAR 25 Apr 1763 (child of Christian & Margaret)
 432: CATHARINA  bp SA 13 Feb 1765 (sp Joh. Frank, Cath. Getman)
 433: MARGARETHA  bp SA 27 Jan 1771 (sp Christian Ittig & Marg.)
 434: JOHANNES  bp GF 14 Mar 1777 (sp John Passage & Marg.)
```

423: GEORGE PASSAGE - ps. the George born at Loonenburg NY 1741 (son of George Hendrick & Sophia Magdalena); died 1778; m say 1771 MARGARET CRIM (b 1755, d 1845) dau of PAUL CRIM & MAGDALENA STEELE. Widow Margaret Passage had 1 adult & 4 children on 1778 GF relief. Possibly his widow was the Margaret Bosharr on the 1790 Caughnawaga (Fonda) NY census (2-0-2) next to John and Philip Miller.

+435: ps. GEORGE b say 1771; m 1788 LEA OSTRANDER
+436: ps. JACOB b say 1776; m by 1804 CATHERINE SHOEMAKER

416: HENRICH BOSSART - pr. born ca 1740 to 1747 (pr. an early son of Jacob & Margaret); m by ca 1763 ELISABETH KITTS (aka GOETZ). Henry apparently moved to Caughnawaga (Fonda) NY by ca 1772 and pr. remained there.

437: pr. ELISABETH b SAR 8 Mar 1764 (dau of ... Bashar & Elis.)
pr. m FR 1787 JAMES BECK (or BURK)
438: GERRIT b SAR 9 Jul 1770 (sp Gerrit Van Brake, Anta Gotzin)
439: MARGARET bp Fonda NY 1 Oct 1772 (sp Hans Neff & Anna) pr d y
+440: ps. HENRY b say 1773; m by 1793 ELISABETH CLAUS
441: MARGARET bp Fonda 1775 (sp Christian Jani, Christina Boshar)
+442: ps. JACOB b say 1777; m by 1803 ANNA

415: JACOB BOSHAR - pr. born before 1746 (presumably son of Jacob & Margaret); m by 1761 CATHERINE ... Jacob and wife Catherine sponsored the Jan 1761 SAR bp of Jacob, son of Nicholas Wohleben & Maria Elisabeth, assuming 1761 was too late for the immigrant Jacob (bp 1681, also had a wife named Catherine). Jacob & Catherine sponsored the Nov 1776 bp of Jacob, son of Frantz Frieba & Margaret, the Aug 1779 bp of Jacob, son of Henrich Miller & Eva (pr. Boshar), the 1780 bp of James, son of James Yuel & Margaret (Christman), the Dec 1787 bp of Jacob, son of Conrad Eigenauer & Anna (Spohn), and the Oct 1791 bp of Catherine, dau of James Yuel & Margaret. Finally in Apr 1793 Jacob & Catherine sponsored the bp of Catherine, dau of Jacob Christman & Maria (Small). It seems strange that this Jacob was not called jr. and no children are known for this couple.

417A JOHN BASHOR (BUSSERT) - m by 1778 ANNA SPANNENBERG.

443: JACOB b FR 26 Sep 1778 (sp Jac. Bussert & Margaret)
444: JOHN b Fonda NY 6 Mar 1782 (sp. Hen. Janney, Christina **)

427: JOHN PASSAGE - bp Greenbush NY (also rec. Ft. Herkimer NY) 19 Nov 1749; m MARGARET CRIM possibly the Margaret (bp Dec 1751) dau of HENRICH CRIM. A John Passage had 2 adults and 2 children on 1778 German Flats relief.

+445: CHRISTIAN bp Greensbush NY 27 Mar 1770
+446: HENRY bp Greensbush NY 17 Jul 1775; m ANNA HELMER
447: JACOB bp GF 24 Feb 1778 (sp Jacob Fulmer & Maria <Boshar>)
448: LENA C. bp Albany NY 21 May 1780 (sp. Joh. & Marg. Redly)
d 20 Mar 1839 (age 58-11-18); m 1799 NICHOLAS SHOEMAKER
449: CATHERINE bp Greensbush NY 11 Oct 1781
+450: GEORGE bp Greensbush NY 1785; pr. m MARGARET HELMER

430: JOSEPH BASSAGE (Passage) - pr. the Joseph born at Rhinebeck NY 16 Sep 1755 (son of Hendrick & Sophia Magdalena); m ANNA ... Was sp. for bp at Albany Apr 1779 of Johannes son of John Redlif & Margaret Passage.

451: SOPHIA bp GF 18 Nov 1783 (sp John Schall & Salome)
pr. m by 1805 FREDERICK FOX

422: MARGARITA PASSAGE   born 1741; m1 18 Oct 1760 JOHN J. REDLIF (RADCLIFFE, pr. the John Jac. b 1734, d ca Jun 1780); she m2 at Albany 7 Aug 1780 JAMES PHILIPS. Margaret, wife of John Redlif, had children Jacob (bp 1761), Henry (b 1763), Nicolase (1765), John (1768), Wilhelm (1770), Sophia (b 1773) and John (bp Albany Apr 1779). She sponsored the May 1780 bp of Lena Passage.

PASSAGE - 5th Generation

445: CHRISTIAN PASSAGE - pr. born ca 1765 to 1778; m ELISABETH MOORE

    452: CHRISTIAN bp Palatine NY 13 Jan 1798
    453: EDWARD   bp Herkimer NY 1804
    454: DAVID bp 1 Jan 1809
    455: ANNA bp Minden NY 27 Mar 1813
    456: BENJAMIN bp Minden NY 11 Aug 1816

435: GEORGE PASSAGE Jr - pr. born ca 1755 to 1767; m Schenectady NY 10 Feb 1788 LEA OSTRANDER. At Normanskill in 1788 (Pearson's Schenectady book, page 134).

    457: MARY b 6 Oct 1788
    458: GEORGE b 14 Oct 1790
    459: JOHANNES b 23 Feb 1793
    460: EVA b 15 Jun 1797 (bp Schenectady 23 Jul)
    461: ELISABETH bp Schenectady 14 Sep 1799
    462: MARGARIETA b 5 Jan 1802

450: GEORGE PASSAGE - born ca 1785; died 1852 (age 67); m ANNA MARGARET HELMER (b 1778, d 1845) dau of Lt. ADAM HELMER & ANNA BELLINGER. Apparently lived at Columbia (Herk. Co) NY between 1811 and 1821. Children included HENRY (b 1806), EVA (b 1809, m MR. FOX), MARIA (bp Columbia NY 13 Jan 1811), PETER (b Herkimer NY 1812, m HARRIET WARD), JOHN (b 20 Jun 1818), ADAM (bp Columbia NY 9 Mar 1821; d 1876) and LANY (m SIMON SPOHN).

440: HENRY PASSAGE - pr. born ca 1750 to 1770; m ELISABETH CLAUS

    463: ELISABETH b Albany 5 Sep 1793 (sp. Hen. & Elis. Class)
    464: PETER bp Stone Arabia NY 12 Apr 1801
    465: HENRY bp Stone Arabia NY 16 Oct 1803; pr. d 1849

446: HENRY PASSAGE - born 1775; died 1835; m ANNA HELMER (b 1781) dau of Lt. ADAM HELMER & ANNA BELLINGER. Children were Margaret (b 13 May 1799, d 1875), John (b Jun 1801), Anna (b Warren NY 1803), Adam (1805), Joseph (1808), & Maria (1810).

442: JACOB BOSSERT - pr. born ca 1760 to 1780; m by 1803 ANNA ... Had sons JACOB (b Aug 1803) and HENDRICK (b 16 Aug 1805) and probably lived near Palatine NY from 1803 to 1805 as children were bp at Stone Arabia Lutheran Church.

436: JACOB PASSAGE - pr. born ca 1760 to 1780; m CATHERINE SHOEMAKER. Living at Endrichstown in 1803 when dau Margaret born (b Jan 1803, sp John Aclar & w. Margaret); also had son CHRISTOPHER (bp HK Jul 1804, sp Christopher Shoemaker & Elis.) & Magdalena (b HK 30 Dec 1805, sp Nicholas Shoemaker & Magdalena).

481: **ABRAHAM BAUM** - bp Albany NY 1 Jan 1742 (son of JOHN BAUM & ANNA BURGER); died Utica NY 1797; m DOROTHY CUNINGHAM sister of John and Andrew Cuningham (F. Deuel notes) and presumably a dau of WILLIAM CUNINGHAM. In 1767 he was a private, along with his brother Samuel, in the militia co. of John M. Veeder. Based on the fact that daughter Gertrude was the last of the children to be baptised at Albany, Deuel estimated that Abraham moved his family into the Mohawk valley about 1774 although he returned during the war years to Normanskill. Abraham Baum was listed on the 1790 German Flats census (2-1-4), apparently living near William Salis, Peter Dygert, and John Cuningham. Most information comes from the F. Deuel notes on Baum at the Oneida Historical Society in Utica NY. The will of Abraham Bome of German Flats, dated 15 Mar 1796, mentions wife Dorothy, sons John and William, and daughters Ann Dygert, Margaret Weber, Elisabeth Dygert, Gertrude Dygert, Chardarien Myer, Mary Bome, and Eva Bome.

surname BAUM

    482: ANNATJE b 6 Dec 1763; m WILLIAM DYGERT jr.
    483: MARGARET b 21 Apr 1765; m 1786 JACOB JAC. N. WEAVER
+484: JOHN b 1 Jan 1767; m MARGARET JAC. CHRISTMAN
    485: CATHERINE b ca 1768; m HENRY JAC. MEYER
    486: ELISABETH b 8 Sep 1769; m PETER P. DYGERT
    487: MARIA bp Albany 30 Oct 1771
    488: GERTRUDE b 4 Jul 1773; m 1791 SEVERINUS P. DYGERT
+489: WILLIAM 1783-1868 m SARAH BUTTERFIELD
    490: EVA b GF 16 Jul 1786 (sp Wm Cuningham & Margaret)

490A HENDRICK BAUM - pr. born ca 1715 to 1740. Hendrick was in Dygert's 1757 militia unit and his family appears to have lived east in the Canajoharie and Palatine NY areas. Pr. had a son Philip Baum who married by 1764 Catherine and had children bp at Stone Arabia NY 1764 to 1768. No tie is seen between these Baums of Montgomery Co. and the family of Abraham Baum of Herkimer Co.

BAUM - 2nd Generation

484: JOHN BAUM - born Albany NY 1 Jan 1767 (bp sp Nich. Brower, Maritje Boom); m 26 Jan 1789 MARGARET JAC. CHRISTMAN (b 21 Aug 1768) dau of JACOB CHRISTMAN & ERNESTINA BELLINGER.

    491: CATHERINE b 6 Oct 1793 (sp Fred. Christman, Cath. Baum, unm)
    492: ABRAHAM b 16 Aug 1795 (sp Peter Christman, Maria Baum, unm)
    493: JOHN b Port Leydon, Black River, NY 3 Oct 1807
              (sp Jacob Weber & Gertrude of Frankfort)

489: WILLIAM BAUM - born Oct 1783; died 23 Mar 1868 (age 86); m SARAH BUTTERFIELD (b 1783, d 1852) ps. a dau of the LEVY BUTTERFIELD who was listed on the 1790 Herkimer census (1-1-2).

********** BAUMAN (Bowman) **********

501: **Johan PETER BAUMAN** - pr. born at Bacharach on the Rhine, Germany ca 1617
(son of PETER BAUMAN & CHRISTINA ROSSLER); liv. 1665 but died before 19 Jun 1678;
m at Bacharach Germany 6 Oct 1652 ANNA MAGDALENA SOMMER dau of HANS WILHELM SOMMER
& SOPHIA CONRADT. Reference for this family is "BAUMANN/BOWMAN FAMILY of the
Mohawk, Susquehanna, and Niagara Rivers" by Maryly B. Penrose (Liberty Bell
Associates, P.O. Box 51, Franklin Park NJ 08823; pub. 1977). More on the German
Baumann ancestry can be found in "The Palatine Families of New York" by Mr. Hank
Jones (P.O. Box 8341, Universal City 91608).

surname BAUMAN
+502: ADAM bp Bachar. Germ. 1665; m1 SUSANNA CATHERINA DRESCH

BAUMAN - 1st Generation

502: **ADAM BAUMAN** - bp Bacharach Germany 8 Oct 1665 (son of PETER BAUMAN & ANNA
MAGDALENA SOMMER); liv. 1717; m1 at Bacharach 17 Feb 1688 SUSANNA CATHERINE DRESCH
(d 1710) dau of NICHOLAS DRESCH; m2 (as widower from Bacharach on the Rhine) at NY
6 Mar 1711 ANNA MARGARETHA ..., widow of JOHAN KUGEL (of Unter-Oetisheim, Commune
Maulbroner, duchy of Wuerttenberg). Was a butcher and appears on the NY Palatine
subsistence in 1710 (4A,2Y) and 1712 (3A,2Y) and on the 1717 Simmendinger census
at New Queensberg with wife Maria Margaretha & 5 children. Pr. the Johan Adam
Bauman who had lot #14 on the Burnetsfield Patent. Pattern of baptism
sponsorships in the 1760 to 1785 time frame indicates close connection with the
family of Johan George Smidt, probably arising from marriage of one or more of
following children with Smiths.

surname BAUMAN
503: MARGARET ELISABETH bp 12 Jan 1690
504: ANNA MARGARET bp 9 Nov 1692; ps on NY list in 1712 (3A,0Y)
505: ELISABETH CATHERINA bp 4 Apr 1695
ps. (Bauman?) m PHILIP BELLINGER
506: HENRICH PETER bp 27 Jul 1698; pr. d y (or rem. in Germany)
507: MARIA SYBILLA bp 12 Sep 1700
508: MARIA MARGARET bp 11 Feb 1703
+509: JACOB b in Germany say 1705; m ELISABETH ...
+510: ADAM b in Germany say 1707; m ELISABETH ... (ps. Smith)
by 2nd wife
511: SUSANNA b say 1715; m Schoharie 1732 ROBERT FLINT
512: MARIA CATHERINE b SH 9 Jun 1717 (Hen. Spoon & w.<C Wohleben>)
ps. (Bauman?) m FREDERICK BELL jr.

513: **HEINRICH BAUMAN** - pr. born ca 1680 to 1690; pr. died 1710; his widow ANNA
MARIA m2 25 Oct 1710 JOHAN ADAM SOELLNER. Widow Anna Maria was from Upstatt, near
Brustel, commune Speyer, Germany (mar. rec. in "Book of Names" page 42).

+514: ps. JACOB m GERRITJE WYNGARDT (bp 1710)

BAUMAN - 2nd Generation

510: ADAM BAUMAN - pr. born ca 1703 to 1716; living Nov 1771 ("at the Falls" as under Albany list of freeholders) and pr. liv. 1778 (German Flats Relief); pr. m ELISABETH ... (ps. ELISABETH SMITH, b 1715, dau of GEORGE SMITH). Town lots at Burnetsfield went only to adults, so we think the father, rather than this Adam, was the patentee on lot #14. However, this Adam probably inherited that property and later passed it to his son John A. (i.e. a John Bauman owned lot #14 in 1791). Adam Bauman had 5 adults and 2 children (under 16) on 1778 GF relief, which could be this Adam if his household then included married son George Adam´s family.

```
+515: pr. GEORGE ADAM  b say 1738; m ELISABETH ... (pr. Weaver)
 515A ps. PETER  b say 1740; in 1769 GF militia (after Adam Bauman)
 516: ps. ELISABETH  1742-1808  m HENRY WALLRATH
+517: pr. JACOB   1745-1802  m ANNA FOLTS
+518: pr. FREDERICK  1750-1823  m DELIA FOLTS
 519: ps. CATHERINE  b say 1752; liv. 1769 (spf Jacob Smidt bp)
 520: JOHN A.  b say 1756; on 1790 census (4-0-2)
 521: ADAM A.  b say 1760; on 1790 census (1-2-1)
+522: pr. CHRISTOPHER  bp 8 Mar 1764 (sp. Adam Smidt)
```

509: JACOB BAUMAN - pr. born ca 1700 to 1709 (son of Adam); died 1770; m ELISABETH
Prior to 1757 Jacob moved from Burnetsfield to Canajoharie NY and subsequently many in this branch of the family moved to Pennsylvania. Two sons (George Adam & Jacob) and a grandson were Tory soldiers in the infamous Butler´s Rangers, which terrorized the Mohawk Valley during the American Revolution. The children listed below were named in his will, prepared 6 Jan 1757.

```
523: GEORGE ADAM  b say 1731; pr. m ANN MARIE CONRAD
524: CATHARINA  b say 1732; m ABRAHAM WARTMAN
525: MARILIS  b say 1734; pr m JOHANNES LIPE
526: JOHN  b say 1735; pr m ELISABETH FLINT
527: SUSANNA  b say 1736; m JOHN FLINT (b 1726)
528: JACOB  b 1 Jan 1738; m ELISABETH
529: PETER  b say 1742; d Oriskany 1777; m 1767 CATHERINE HELMER
530: MARGREDA  b say 1747; m 1767 JOST CONRAD
531: ANNA  b say 1749; m 1768 CORNELIUS FLINT
```

532: JACOB BOWMAN - pr. born ca 1700 to 1710; m GERRITJE WYNGARDT (bp 1710) dau of GERRIT LUCASE WYNGARDT & SARA VISSCHER of Albany. Was perhaps a relative of the Henrich Bauman whose widow married Adam Soellner in 1710. Children bp at Schenectady include GERRIT LUCASE (bp Mar 1738), ANDRIES (bp Jul 1742), LUCAS (bp Sep 1744) and possibly JOHN (m at Schenectady Dec 1767 EVA BARHEYT).

BAUMAN - 3rd Generation

518: FREDERICK BAUMAN - born ca 1750; died Utica NY 1 Sep 1823 (age 73); m DELIA FOLTS (b 1752, d 1824) dau of JACOB FOLTS & ANNA CATHERINE PETRIE. A Frederick Bauman had 2 adults and 1 child (under 16) on 1778 German Flats relief.

```
533: CATHERINE  b Dec 1774; d 1841; m Johan DIEDERICK STEEL
534: DOROTHEA  bp GF 10 Dec 1778 (sp Conrad Folts & Anna)
        m HENRY ARMSTRONG
535: ADAM  bp GF 28 Mar 1784 (Adam Bauman ..); m APPOLONIA WEAVER
536: ELISABETH  bp GF 20 Jan 1788 (sp John DeMuth & Elis. <Folts>)
        m HENRY V.R. WEAVER
```

515: GEORGE ADAM BAUMAN - pr. born ca 1730 to 1738; m ELISABETH ... (Bauman book
has her as ELISABETH WEAVER dau of NICHOLAS WEAVER based on multiple appearance of
Weavers at bp of Bowman children). Wife Elisabeth sponsored, with Joh. Nich.
Weaver, Jan 1762 bp of Catherine, dau of Frederick Bellinger & Catherine (Weaver).
George A. was in Bellinger's Revol. Regiment (Book of Names, page 166).

    +537: ADAM   1758-1834   m BARBARA H. HARTER
    +538: Johan NICHOLAS   b SAR 11 Apr 1761 (sp John Weaver & Ernestina)
          m CATHERINE HERWIG
    +539: Johan GEORGE   bp 1766 (sp. Geo. Smid, Appolonia Weaver)
          m DOROTHY ARMSTRONG

517: JACOB BAUMAN - born ca 1745; died 23 Jul 1802 (age 57 years 4 months); m at
Palatine NY 20 Feb 1770 ANNA FOLTS (b 1750) dau of JACOB FOLTS & ANNA CATHERINE
PETRIE. Jacob was in 17769 GF militia and had 2 adults & 4 children (under 16) on
1778 GF relief. Children, except Catherine, named in his will (26 Jun 1802).

    540: ANNA   bp Stone Arabia 14 Jun 1770; m HENRY WALLRATH
    541: PETER   ml ca 1795 ELISABETH HERWIG
    542: JACOB   b 8 Jun 1777; liv. 1802 (HK Ch. Confirm.)
    543: ELISABETH   bp Herkimer 7 Jun 1785; m CHRISTIAN HARTMAN
    544: CATHERINE   bp St. Johnsville 15 Jan 1792; pr. d. young

520: JOHN A. BAUMAN - pr. born ca 1747 to 1760; A John Bauman served in Col.
Bellinger's Revol. Regiment and a John A. appears on the 1790 Herkimer census
(4-0-2), along with an Adam A. Beauman.

BAUMAN - 4th Generation

537: ADAM BAUMAN - born Canajoharie NY 1758; died Herkimer NY 1834; m at Herkimer
21 Sep 1786 BARBARA HEN. HARTER (b 1766, d 1836) dau of HENRY HARTER & CATHERINE
PFIEFFER (DAR vol. 83, page 100). Children - Henrich (bp St Johnsville 1790),
Peter (bp 1793), Catherine (b 1797), Adam (b 1800), & Elisabeth (b 1804).

522: CHRISTOPHER BAUMAN - bp as "Stophel" 8 Mar 1764 (son of Adam & Elis.; sp.
Adam Smidt and Margaretha Hen. Weaver); m ca 1790 MARIA ... (b ca 1767, liv. 1850
age 83). Despite Bauman book placement of him as son of George Adam & Elisabeth,
the church record has father as only "Adam" so we assume he was a late son of the
elder man. Children Elisabeth (b GF 1792, sp. George Bauman, Cath. Bauman) and
John (b 1801, sp John Bauman, Cath. Petry).

539: GEORGE BAUMAN - born German Flats 2 Aug 1766; died Herkimer NY 19 Jun 1808;
died by 1813; m Herkimer NY 1795 DOROTHY ARMSTRONG. His wife was listed as widow
Dorothy Bauman when she sponsored 1813 bp of a child of Moses Saeger & Elisabeth
(Armstrong). Children include Frederick (1800), Elisabeth (bp 1803, m Peter L.
Harter), Henry (1806), George (1808).

538: NICHOLAS BAUMAN - bp Palatine NY 23 Apr 1761 (son of George Adam & Elis.); m
at Herkimer 14 Sep 1794 CATHERINE HERWIG. Children - John (bp HK 1795), Elisabeth
(1798), Susanna, Adam (1804), Peter, Magdalena, and Nicholas.

********** BELL **********

601: Johan **FREDERICK BELL** - pr. born in Germany ca 1687 to 1692 (ps. son of a
Jacob as that was the name given his first son, see Hank Jones "Palatine Families
of New York" for Bell origins in Germany); killed as aged widower at Andrustown
massacre 18 Jul 1778 (as given in Simms´ Frontiersmen of New York); m ca 1711 Anna
Maria, who is believed to have been ANNA MARIA HELMER a dau of PHILIP HELMER (this
premise seems supported by proximity of Philip Helmer at their naturalization at
Albany in 1715 and on the Burnetsfield map). His name was not on the NY Palatine
subsistence list, perhaps due to being in the household of ELISABETH BELL, who was
on that list in 1710 (2A,0Y) & in 1712 (4A,1Y). Frederick lived at the Hunterstown
camp in 1711 when he was a volunteer for the Canadian expedition and at the time of
the 1717 Simmendinger he was at New Queensbury. He and his wife received
Burnetsfield lots 15 & 16 on the east side of the West Canada Creek and he
apparently was the schoolteacher at German Flats (1760 SAR mar. rec. of dau
Gertrude). In 1725 he was listed as executor and friend on the will of Melchert
Folts and in 1753 a Frederick Bell witnessed a land deed of Jacob N. Weber.

As to the children of this Frederick, the only birth appearing in church
records is that of Jacob in 1712 (Book of Names page 23). Simms gives Thomas as a
son of immigrant Frederick and the will of George Henry Bell (born 1730, which
seems too early to be a grandson) lists a brother Deitrich, so that makes for four
sons at least. To this we add a Frederick Jr. and the John who married in 1749
Elisabeth Pfeiffer (Vosburgh´s German Flats church records, vol. 1). Simms also
says this Frederick Bell had a daughter who married Lawrence Frank, but the
earliest available Lawrence Frank (born 1749) seems spoken for with a wife named
Maria Meyer. However we note the Hatch papers assumption that Lawrence Frank may
have had a first wife named Margaret Bell, who, if she existed, was most likely a
granddaughter, rather than a daughter, of immgrant Frederick Bell. We have tried
to salvage something from the Simms account by presuming an early daughter
Elisabeth (pr. named after the immigrant Frederick´s mother) who may have married a
Frank. The family of Frederick Bell suffered great loss of life in both the French
& Indian War and the Revolution. The moderate number of children identifiable in
the next generation, as grandchildren of immigrant Frederick, may especially have
been due to more being lost in the 1778 Andrustown massacre than has been recorded.

surname BELL
+602: JACOB   b WCL 28 Jul 1712 (sp. Mich. Harter, Jac. Weber)
 603: ps. ELIZABETH (Bell?) b say 1714; may have married a Frank
+604: ps. PHILIP b say 1716; in militia 1757; ps. unm
+605: FREDERICK   b say 1718; pr. m by 1740 ...
+606: ps. ADAM   b say 1721; killed at Andrustown 1778
+607: THOMAS   b say 1723; m by 1760 ANNA ELISABETH (pr. Hilts)
 608: GERTRUDE   ca 1725-1808   m 1760 JOHN LEON. HELMER
+609: JOHANNES   b say 1728; m 11 Jun 1749 ELISABETH PFEIFFER
+610: GEORGE HENRY   1730-1806   m CATHERINE HERKIMER
 611: pr. MARIA b say 1731; m 1748 JOST PETRIE jr.
+612: DIETERICH   ca 1733-1812; unm brother of George Henry

613: HENRY BELL - pr. born ca 1705 to 1730; Naturalized 1755 (Book of Names page
5). Probably of a different Bell family and possibly an ancestor of the MICHAEL
BELL who married at Schoharie NY 22 Jul 1789 MARIA TRUEX.

BELL - 2nd Generation

606: ADAM BELL (existence questionable) - ps. born ca 1715 to 1735; supposedly killed at the Andrustown massacre in July 1778; m ...   The Hatch Papers say that the Bells lived on the south side of the Andrustown settlement, which was the first part hit in the Tory raid of July 1778, and that Adam Bell was captured, scalped alive, and then had his head crushed with a stone. Hatch has Adam´s daughter as Margaret Bell, wife of Lawrence Frank (born 1749 and apparently married to Maria Meyer by 1776) and Adam´s son as the Frederick who was son-in-law of PAUL CRIM. However, no such Adam can be seen in the militia or church records of the 1760 to 1778 time frame and the name is rare among Bell descendents (mainly an Adam Fr., born in 1772). We think the Hatch account may be more correct in the description of events than in the assignment of names and we suggest as an alternative that perhaps three Frederick Bells were killed at the Andrustown massacre - these being Frederick Sr. (the immigrant, shot while climbing a fence to get to his horse), Frederick Jr. (perhaps Hatch´s "Adam" who was scalped alive), and a younger Frederick (the one shot through the window while fetching his rifle).

612: DIETERICH BELL - born ca 1733; died unmarried at Herkimer NY 24 Aug 1812 at age 79. Presumably the brother Dietrich listed in George Henry Bell´s will in 1804. Was a sponsor for Nov 1760 bp of Thomas, son of Thomas Bell & Elisabeth, also a sponsor (with Sara Hilts) for Sep 1763 bp of Dietrich, son of John L. Helmer & Gertrude (Bell), and for 1764 bp of John, son of Nicholas Hilts. A Dietrich Bell was a Tory (United Empire Loyalist List) which might explain why this man was not on the Revolutionary period military or relief lists. Another Dietrich Bell was a Revol. War prisoner (Book of Names page 114) and that may have been the younger Dietrich, baptised 1770 (son of a Frederick Bell).

605: FREDERICK BELL jr. - pr. born ca 1715 to 1722 (son of Frederick Sr. and brother of Thomas as given in Simms); pr. died at Andrustown 1778; m ...   Probably the senior of the two Frederick Bell´s on militia lists in 1767.

        +614: ps. MELCHERT b say 1740; d by 1762; m CATHERINE SHOEMAKER
                    in Capt. Petri´s militia Feb 1757
         615: pr. ANNA ELIZABETH FR. b say 1745; liv. 1762 (spf M. Bell bp)
        +616: JACOB F. b say 1747; liv. 1775 (GF resident)
                    pr. d 1777; m 1768 MARIA MEYER
        +617: pr. FREDERICK b say 1751; m by 1776 DOROTHY CRIM
         618: ps. MARGARET b say 1753; liv. 1770 (spf Helmer bp)
                    ps. m ca 1770 LAWRENCE FRANK

610: Capt. GEORGE HENRY BELL - born ca 1730; died 9 Feb 1806; m 1753 CATHERINE HERKIMER (b say 1735) dau of Johan JOST HERKIMER (b 1695, d 1775) & CATHERINE PETRIE. Served at Battle of Oriskany in 1777 (Petrie book page 5). His will dated 10 Feb 1804 mentions brother Richard and nephews Lawrence Bell, George Rosencranz, and Henry Uhle, but not his wife who presumably died between 1793 and 1804. Also mentioned were a son and four daughters, plus grandchildren Catherine Bell and Han Yost Bell; see John B. Potter´s 1963 ms. on "HERKIMER SCHUYLER & Allied Families". The Petrie book lists two other children (Jost & Catherine, both born after 1780) but we feel they belong instead to his son Nicholas.

        +619: JOSEPH b say 1754; pr. d bef 1780; m MARIA SMITH
        +620: NICHOLAS b say 1756; d 1781; m CHRISTINA TEN BROECK
         621: ANNA 1759-1840 m Lt. PETER WAGGONER
         622: MARIA b SAR 26 Mar 1762; m 1783 HENRY JOHN WALLRATH

-17-

602: JACOB BELL - born NY camps 28 Jul 1712 (sp. Michael Harter, Jacob Weber, & Anna Eva Thomas). No further record, so perhaps he died young.

609: JOHANNES BELL - pr. born ca 1720 to 1730; died by 1761; m 11 Jun 1749 ELISABETH PFEIFFER. His widow m2 SAR 13 Dec 1761 THEOBALD NELLIS a widower. Simms (Frontiersmen of New York, vl, p 344) says the Tories Frederick and Thomas Bell were brothers. Other children may be John & Matthew Bell in Campbell´s Revol. Regiment (ps. raised in Montgomery Co. due to Nellis adoption).

> 623: ps. MARIA b say 1750; m 1768 MARTIN SEYBERT
> 624: ps. ANDREW b say 1752; on 1790 GF census (1-2-3)
> +625: ps. FREDERICK (the Tory) b say 1754; d 1781; m LENA SEEBER
> 625A: ps. THOMAS b say 1756; Tory in Revol. (Simms)

604: PHILIP BELL - pr born ca 1713 to 1738; pr. died in French & Indian War. In Feb 1757 Philip was in the German Flats militia and we suspect he may have died soon afterwards as there is no sign of him in the 1760´s church or militia records, or later. The fact that in 1769 Jacob Bell & Maria (Meyer) named a first son Philip, suggests a close connection (but we think that the 1769 father was Jacob F. and thus pr. a nephew rather than a son of this Philip).

607: THOMAS BELL - pr. born ca 1715 to 1728; m by 1760 ANNA ELISABETH ... (pattern of baptism sponsorships and property transactions strongly suggest that wife was ELISABETH HILTS, pr. dau of SIMON JACOB HILTS). Deuel (E&N 12 Jun 1929) has the widow Elisabeth Bell who m2 in 1766 ANDREW MCKOOM as formerly the wife of this Thomas and Simms ("Frontiersmen of New York" page 384) has Thomas as brother of Frederick and son of immigrant Frederick Bell, whose wife was Anna Mary. Support for the assumption that he probably died soon after 1760 lies in the absence of his name in church records after 1760 (including the 1771 Burnetsfield Minister´s support list which names other elder Bells such as George Henry, Jacob, Frederick and Frederick jr.), nor does he appear on the 1767 or 1769 GF militia rosters, or on the 1778 GF relief list. Pr. his son Thomas was the Revolutionary soldier (and perhaps briefly a Tory) to whom Simms refers (ibid.).

> +626: pr. FREDERICK b say 1742; ml ... m2 MARIA EVA HAACK
> +627: pr. JACOB ca 1745-1838 m ELISABETH ... (b 1754, pr. Weaver)
> +628: ps. ELISABETH b say 1747; liv. 1763 (spf Dornberger bp)
> 629: ps. LAWRENCE b say 1758; liv. 1804 (Geo. H. Bell´s will)
> +630: THOMAS b SAR 25 Oct 1760 (sp Diet. Bell, Sara Sim Jac Hilts)
>   d 1813; ml 1782 ANNA DORNBERGER

BELL - 3rd Generation

617: FREDERICK BELL - pr. born ca 1745 to 1759; killed at Andrustown 18 Jul 1778; m DOROTHY CRIM (pr. born 1760) dau of PAUL CRIM & MAGDALENA STEELE. An Indian reportedly thrust his gun through a window and shot Frederick as he was reaching for his rifle which was kept suspended from the rafters (Herkimer Evening Telegram article of 7/16/1977, page 4). His widow was probably the Dorothy Bell with 2 children on 1778 German Flats relief and apparently she m2 CONRAD SCHAEFER.

> +631: ps. FREDERICK b say 1775; captured 1778
>   pr. m GF 1795 MARIA PETRIE
> 632: MAGDALENA bp 9 Jun 1777 (dau of Fred & Dor. Grimm)

802: JOHANNES BELLINGER <B1> - bp Rodenbach Germany 17 Nov 1664; died upstate New York after 1725; m at Huttengesas nr Langenselbold Germany 24 Apr 1690 ANNA MARGARETHA KUHN (bp Langenselbold 1661) dau of HANS KUHN & CATHARINA. Letter and number designation in angle brackets <B#> is provided to permit reference to Cmdr. Bellinger´s numbering in the "Genealogy of the Mohawk Valley Bellingers and Allied Families" (by Cmdr. Lyle Frederick Bellinger, index by Hazel Patrick, published 1976 by Herkimer Co. Hist. Soc.). A carpenter, Johannes came to New York with the family of Nicholas Bellinger in the British-sponsored Palatine immigrations of 1710. Appears on NY Palatine Subsistence List in 1710 (4A,0Y) and 1712 (5A,0Y) and on the 1717 Simmendinger census as a resident at New Queensberry with wife Anna Maria Margaretha and two children. Had Burnetsfield lot #20, which later passed to his son Philip.

> +819: FREDERICK 1691-1766 m ANNA ELIZABETH FOX
> +820: PHILIP bp 16 Dec 1695; liv 1766; m ... (ps. a Bauman?)
> +821: Johan PETER bp 30 Apr 1697; d 1786; m1 MARGARET ...
> +822: ADAM bp 15 Jan 1699; m APPOLONIA ...

809: MARCUS BELLINGER <B3> - pr. born ca 1682; m1 ANNA CONRAD; m2 1737 MARIA MARGARETHA ZEH dau of JOHANNES ZEH Sr. & MAGDALENA. On NY Palatine subsistence list (4A,0Y) and 1712 (4A,1Y) and on Simmendinger Census of 1717 with wife Anna and 5 children. Lived at Schoharie NY and later moved to Huntersfield NY. Bellinger book (page 8) repeats Cady assumption that child Anna was b ca 1705, but more likely she was at least 10 in 1710 (see subsistence list).

> 823: ps. child b say 1699 (ps dependent over age 9 in 1710)
> 824: ANNA b say 1700; pr d 1736; m MATTHYS WARNER
> 825: MARIA BARBARA b say 1711; m 1737 MATTHYS WARNER
> 826: MARIA E. b say 1713; m JOHANNES ZEH jr
> 827: ANNA CATHARINA b say 1716; m 1738 JOHANNES ZEH jr
>   by second wife
> 828: JOHANNES 1738-1820 m ANNA MARIA RICKERT
> 829: ANNA 1739-1766 m JACOB SCHAEFER
> 830: ps. HENRY bp 14 Oct 1740 (Cady record only)
> 831: MARCUS 1742-1822 m MARIA BORST

BELLINGER - 2nd Generation

822: ADAM BELLINGER <B7> - bp Germany 15 Jan 1699 (son of John, H. Jones findings); died by 1750; m APPOLONIA ... Widow Appolonia m2 FELIX MEYER. The will of widow Appolonia (No. 2 in book 1 at Fonda NY) mentions daughters Catherine and Appolonia (Bellinger book page 28).

> 832: CATHARINA 1726-1812 m MARCUS COUNTRYMAN
> 833: ANNA MARIA b say 1730; m by 1750 PETER KILTS
> 834: ANNA EVA 1732-1797 m GEORGE SNELL
> 835: APPOLONIA b say 1733; m by 1754 FREDERICK HARTER
> 836: dau (pr. MARGARET or "Beggi") m by 1756 FREDERICK COUNTRYMAN
> 837: ANNA ELISABETH ca 1736-1822 m ADAM SNELL
> 838: ERNESTINA b say 1738; m JOHN WEAVER
> +839: ADAM 1740-1824 m MARIA ELISABETH PETRIE
> +840: JOHN b say 1746; m ANNA KRAUSS
> +841: FREDERICK b say 1747; d 1781; m CATHARINA PUTMAN

819: **FREDERICK BELLINGER** <B2> - bp 13 Sep 1691 (H. Jones findings); died ca 1766; m ca 1713 ANNA ELIZABETH FOX (bp 1695) dau of JOHN PHILIP FOX & CATHERINA NEITZERT. Vol. for Canada expedition 1711. He was born too late to have been the father of Capt. Peter, as assumed by Bellinger book, and the NY Palatine subs. lists of 1710 and 1712 show him as a single adult (no dependents). On 1717 Simmendinger census with w. Anna Elis. & 3 children. Lived at Palatine NY.

    +842: FREDERICK   pr b say 1713; m by 1742 ANNA ROSINA WALLRATH
    843: ELIZABETH   b say 1715; m Col. JACOB KLOCK
    844: CATHERINE   b say 1717; m CHRISTOPHER FOX
    +845: JOHANNES   1719-1777 m MAGDALENA KLOCK (he d at Oriskany)

816: JOSEPH BELLINGER <B41> - born 4 Feb 1712 (son of Henrich & Anna Maria); d 7 Nov 1794; m 20 Oct 1733 SOPHIA LAWYER (b 1714, d 1798) dau of JOHN LAWYER & ELISABETH. Children´s births rec. at Schoharie NY.

    846: SOPHIA   1734-1759   m 1750 CHRISTIAN ZEH
    847: ELISABETH   1741-   m 1759 GEORGE HILTS
    848: JOHANNIS LAWYER 1746-1825   m MARGARET KLOCK
    849: CATHERINA   1748-   m 1766 GEORGE KLOCK
    850: ANATIA   1750-   m 1769 ADAM DIETZ

821: Capt. **PETER BELLINGER** <B11> - pr. the Johan Peter bp Langenselbold Germany 30 Apr 1697 (son of John & Margaret); died 1786; m1 before 1723 MARGARET ... (Margaret received Burnetsfield lot #48; doubt Bellinger book assumption that she was a Weaver); m2 by 1750 (he was widower at May 1760 bp of Col. Peter´s son) ANNA MARGARET HORNING pr. dau of NICHOLAS HORNING & MARIA. Naturalized at Albany NY Jan 1716 . Capt. in French & Indian War; declared too old for service in 1762, but reinstated later and served in Revl War. Children below as given in Bellinger book.

    +851: PETER   1726-1813 m DELIA HERKIMER; Col. in Revl
    852: CATHERINE 1732-1843   m 1775 ABRAHAM LEITHAL
    853: Anna ELIZABETH 1739-1803   m Lt. TIMOTHY FRANK
    854: ps. dau   b say 1741; m Mr. FOX (Vera Eysaman notes)
    +855: JOHN P.   1743-1820 m MARIA DYGERT
    856: Anna MARGARET   1750-1837 m1 1767 CHRISTIAN SCHERER
                      by 2nd wife (Margaret Horning, Spinner Rec.)
    +857: Anna MARIA   1751-1848 m GEORGE SMITH
    +858: FREDERICK   1752-1829 m MAGDALENA WOHLEBEN
    859: DOROTHEA   1755-1847 m ABRAHAM WOHLEBEN
    860: ANNA   1757-1841 m Johan ADAM HELMER

820: **PHILIP BELLINGER** ("Lips") <B6> - bp Germany 16 Dec 1695 (H. Jones findings); liv. 1766; m ... (ps. Cath. Bauman ? <a guess based on date and neighborhood proximity>).

    +861: FREDERICK   1727-1781   m CATHERINE WEAVER
    +862: PHILIP   1728-1802   m 1749 ELISABETH FINK
    +863: JOHN   b say 1732; m ELISABETH BARBARA FOLTS
    864: ELISABETH   b ca 1742; m JACOB DEVENDORF
    865: ps. ERNESTINA   ca 1745-1819 m JACOB CHRISTMAN
    866: MARGARETHA   b say 1747; m 1767 Johan JOST FOLTS (b 1742)
    +867: PETER   b say 1749; m CATRINA PUTMAN
    +868: Johan JOST   b say 1751; m ELISABETH PUTMAN

839: Lt. ADAM BELLINGER <B68> - born 1739 (son of Adam & Appolonia); died 2 Jan 1824 age 84; m MARIA ELISABETH PETRIE (b Feb 1740, d 16 Dec 1808 age 68-10) dau of MARCUS PETRIE & ANNA EVA KESSLER. Served as Lieut. at Battle of Oriskany.

    869: MARIA ELISABETH b SAR 23 Mar 1765 (sp. Elis. & Lipps Bellinger)
                         d 1831; m WILLIAM FEETER
    870: ADAM jr. ca 1766-1822 LENA G. ZIMMERMAN Sneidersbush 1792
    871: ANNA EVA b 29 Mar 1767; m 1787 JOHN DIET. PETRIE
    872: Johan HENRY b SAR 15 Jan 1768 (sp Hen Bellngr, Elis Scholl)
                    m ANNA EVA COUNTRYMAN
    873: PETER 1769-1825 m ELISABETH ZIMMERMAN
    874: APPOLONIA 1770-1846 m HENRY H. ZIMMERMAN
    875: CHRISTOPHER b say 1771; m ELMA
    876: MARCUS 1772-1837 m DOROTHY P. LAUX
  +877: PHILIP 1773-1855 m JULIANNA BREITENBACHER
    878: MARIA b say 1775; m 1795 JOHANNES JOH. PETRY
    879: JOHN b GF 9 Apr 1779 (sp John M. Petrie & Doro.)
                   d 1841; m ANNA EVA ZIMMERMAN
    880: ANNA b 7 Apr 1782 (sp Geo. Snell & Eva)

841: FREDERICK A. BELLINGER <B69B> - pr. born ca 1740 to 1750; died 12 Jul 1781 (from wounds at Battle of Sharon on 9 Jul 1781); m 26 Oct 1766 CATHARINA PUTMAN.

    880A ps. JACOB F. b say 1770; m by 1791 SOPHIA ... (SJR bp rec)
    881: JOHN b 10 Jan 1775; m 1795 MARY LAWRENCE
    882: ELISABETH b say 1776; m 1795 DAVID FANCHER.

842: FREDERICK BELLINGER <B12> - pr. born ca 1713 to 1725 (son of Fred.); m by 1742 ANNA ROSINA WALLRATH dau of HENRICH CONRAD WALLRATH & CHRISTINA. Bellinger book, page 11, advises caution as children placed here are not a certainty.

  +883: ps. JOHANNES F. b ca 1742; m CATHERINE P. BELLINGER
  +884: FREDERICK ca 1746-1834 m CATHERINE ... at Yukersbush
    885: MARIA b 1748; m 1768 JOHN J. WALLRATH
  +886: Johan HENRY b ca 1750; m 1771 MARGARETHA WINDECKER
    887: MARIA MARGARET bp SA 14 Sep 1752 (sp Geo Klock & w. Marg.)
    888: CATHERINE b ca 1756; m 1776 HENRY HEES
    889: ELISABETH b 1760; m bef. 1782 Johan GEORGE LAUX
    890: DELIA b ca 1762; liv. Jan 1786 (spf Laux bp, SAR)

858: FREDERICK BELLINGER ("Hoffrich") <B78> - born 1752 (son of Capt. Peter); died 14 Jul 1833; m ca 1773 MAGDALENA WOHLEBEN (b 1755, d 1829) dau of NICHOLAS WOHLEBEN and a granddaughter of NICHOLAS FELLER. After the 1778 burning of German Flats, he moved with his parents to Ft. Plain where his wife's family lived.

    891: ELISABETH 1774-1847 m ANDREW JAC. PFEIFFER
    892: MARGARET 1776-1817 m 1813 LORENTZ TH. SHOEMAKER
    893: FREDERICK 1780-1863 m 1802 ELISABETH TH. SHOEMAKER
    894: ANNA b GF 5 May 1783 (sp John Fox & Anna)
                 d 1874; m FREDERICK BELL
    895: PETER F. 1785-1863 m 1808 ELISABETH HEN. CRANTZ
    896: CATHERINE 1789-1846 m MELCHIOR REESE (b 1784)
    897: MAGDALENA b GF 26 Apr 1792 (sp Stphl Shomaker, Lena Bell)
                 d 1880; m 1812 ADAM NIC. SPOHN

861: Lt. Col. FREDERICK PH. BELLINGER <B51> - born 1727 (son of Philip); liv. May 1781 but died before 1783; m CATHERINE WEAVER dau of NICHOLAS WEAVER. Apparently in 1769 he was the Frederick P. Bellinger, clerk of Capt. Petrie's GF militia unit, and during the Revolution became a high ranking officer serving in the 4th Tryon Co. Regiment. He became a prisoner of war in 1777 and was listed as age 50 when parolled in Canada by Gen. Haldimand. His parentage as son of Philip was established in a land transaction of his son Christopher (see Herk. Co. Deed Book 28 page 478 and E&N article of 20 Nov 1929 "By their deeds shall ye know them").

```
+898: JOHANNES   b say 1755; killed 1780; m 1780 ERNESTINA HARTER
 899: MARGARETHA   b ca 1756; d 1836 (age 80); m JOHN POST
+900: PETER F.   1759-1815   m ELISABETH HARTER
 901: CATHARINE   b SAR 27 Nov 1761 (sp Elis. Bauman, Nic Weber)
                  d 1819; m JOHN DOCKSTADER
+902: CHRISTOPHER F.   1763-1839 m ANNA L. HARTER
```

845: Lt. JOHANNES F. BELLINGER <B14> - born ca 1719 (son of Fred.); died along with his sons John & Frederick at Oriskany 6 Aug 1777; m ca 1744-7 MAGDALENA KLOCK (b ca 1725, bp 1728) dau of HENRY KLOCK   He inherited 1311 acres of his father's Harrison Patent land at St. Johnsville NY (Bellinger book page 13).

```
+903: JOHN jr   ca 1747-1777   m 1766 ANNA FOX
+904: FREDERICK   ca 1749-1777   m ...
 905: MARGARETHA   b 3 Jan 1751; m1 1766 PHILIP HELMER (the Tory)
                   she m2 1783 PHILIP L. HELMER (the Patriot)
 906: ps. CATHERINA   1754-1788   m 1787 CHRISTIAN SCHEPPERMAN
 907: ANNA   ca 1758-1838   m 1785 JOHN P. GREMPS (CRIM)
 908: ELISABETH   b 25 Jan 1760; m 1790 MICHAEL P. STOWITZ
 909: MAGDALENA   b 17 Mar 1762; liv. Jul 1786 (spf Gremps<Crim> bp)
+910: HENRY   b SAR 30 Jun 1764 (sp Hen. Klock & Anna)
                   d 1836; m MARGARETHA NELLIS
 911: DELIA   b SAR 20 Dec 1768 (sp Anna & John Hess)
                   d 1841; m JOHN EHLE (son of Christian)
```

855: JOHN P. BELLINGER <B74> - born 28 Apr 1743; died 26 Feb 1820 (age 76-10); m1 1 Feb 1767 MARIA DYGERT dau of WERNER DYGERT & LENA HERKIMER; m2 7 Mar 1793 the Petrie widow CATHERINE BELLINGER (b 1750, d 1842) dau of Col. PETER BELLINGER.

```
 912: PETER   b SAR 22 Jan 1768 (sp. Peter Bellinger, Cath. Dygert)
                   d 1844; m DOROTHY STEEL
 913: LANY   1769-1821   m CHRISTOPHER P. BELLINGER
 914: MARIA CATHERINE   b 1770; m1 CHRISTOPHER T. SHOEMAKER
                   m2 CHRISTOPHER P. BELLINGER
 915: LUCINDA   b ca 1770; killed 1778 by being shot out of a tree
                   (by Indian chief Plat Kopf, Simms page 212)
 916: pr. ELISABETH J P   b say 1772; liv. Mar 1786 (spf Shoemaker bp)
 917: JOHN   1772-1843   m CATHERINE PETRY
 918: GEORGE   b GF 2 Dec 1779 (sp Geo. Rosencrantz, Maria Frank)
                   m 1803 DELIA JAC. G. KESSLER
 919: JOST   b GF 20 Jun 1783 (sp Jost Herkimer & Cath.)
                   m1 CHRISTINA CAMPBELL m2 DELIA N. CASLER
 920: MARIA MARGARET   b 7 Feb 1786 (sp Sev W Dygert, Marg. Scherer)
                   by 2nd wife
 921: STOPHEL   b GF 2 Jan 1795 (sp Col. Pet. Bellinger & Delia)
 922: DANIEL   ca 1796-1877 m MARGARET LOTTRIDGE
```

863: JOHN PH. BELLINGER <B53> - pr. born ca 1720 to 1732 (son of Philip); m
ELISABETH BARBARA FOLTS ps. dau of MELCHIOR FOLTS. Bellinger book puts his birth
about 1735, but we suspect an earlier date, of say 1725, as we think that his
father (Philip, b 1695) would name a son after his father (John, b 1664) before
naming a son Philip after himself. He moved to Minden NY after the 1777 Oriskany
battle and was pr. the Hannes, who with Hannes jr. & Peter, was at the 1779 GF
auction of Nicholas Smith's estate. His son Major John Bellinger jr of Utica was
foster father to Col. Nich. Smith (who called him "uncle"). We thus conclude that
the Margaret, who married in 1769 Nicholas Smith Sr., was a daughter of this John
Ph. Bellinger (which fits naming patterns of Smith descendents and relieves Capt.
Peter Bellinger of having two living daughters named Margaret, as given in
Bellinger book), and discount the Bellinger book notion that Bellinger sisters
(Maria & Margaret) had married Smith brothers (George & Nicholas).

    +923: pr. MARGARET ca 1748-1779 m 1769 NICHOLAS SMITH
     924: pr. CATHERINE b say 1756; liv. 1779 (spf Weaver bp)
     925: GEORGE b ca 1758; pr. d. young
           (bp 1760, sp. Geo. Herkimer & Elisabeth Conr. Folts)
    +926: JOHN b ca 1760, d Utica NY 1815; m CATHERINE WEAVER
     927: GERTRUDE b ca 1761; m by 1779 FREDERICK WEAVER
     928: PETER b SAR 27 May 1763 (sp. John DeMuth, Elis. Ritman)
     929: GEORGE b 20 Mar 1765 (sp. George DeMuth & w. Anna)

840: JOHN BELLINGER <B69A> - born ca 1746; m ANNA KRAUS (b 1746) dau of JACOB.

     930: GEORGE b SA 8 Sep 1766 (sp Geo. Krauss & Cath.)

868: JOST BELLINGER <B58> - born ca 1751; m ELISABETH PUTMAN of Randall NY (wife
had a brother David Putman who was age 26 in Nov 1782, Bellinger book page 27).
Taken prisoner on 7 Sep 1781. Children apparently bp at Fonda NY (rec. not seen).
Bellinger book feels this Jost might be the one on Mohawk NY census of 1790
(1-3-2) "with Putmans and Yates all around".

     931: FREDERICK b 8 Nov 1777 (sp Jury Putman, Barber Divendorf)
     932: PETER JOS. b ca 1780; age 79 in 1860; m CATHERINE SHEAL
     933: JOHANNES (twin) b 13 Sep 1781 (sp John Dievendorf & w.)
     934: DAVID (twin) 13 Sep 1781 (no sponsors legible)
    934A GEORGE bp SJR 4 Mar 1792 (sp. Fred Bellinger & Cath.)

851: Col. PETER BELLINGER <B71> - born 1726; died 26 Mar 1813; m Jan 1750 DELIA
HERKIMER (b 1728, d 1804) dau of Johan JOST HERKIMER & CATHERINE. Noted for his
heroic leadership at the Battle of Oriskany (Book of Names page 164) and Commander
of 4th Tryon Co. militia regiment during the American Revolution.

     935: CATHERINA b Sep 1750; d 1842; m1 RICHARD M. PETRIE
             m2 1793 JOHN P. BELLINGER (Petrie book page 14)
     936: MARGARET ca 1758-1830 m MARKS D. PETRIE
    +937: Johan PETER 1760-1851 m CHRISTINA TEN BROECK
     938: HELENA b 18 Sep 1762 (sp Magd., w of Wnr Dygert); pr. d y
     939: GERTRUDE 1764-1821 m NICHOLAS CASLER
     940: Johan JOST 1766-1804 m1 ANNA EVA CAMPBELL
     941: JOHANNES 1767-1819 m NANCY STARING
     942: CHRISTOPHER P. b SAR 21 Nov 1770 (sp Joh Bellingr, Eva Petri)
             d 1837; m1 LANY BELLINGER
     943: DELIA b ca 1772; m JOHN NICHOLAS HERKIMER TEN BROECK

867: PETER BELLINGER <B57> - born ca 1749; m Fonda NY CATRINA PUTMAN. Hero of the
ham string cutting and escape on a plough horse story (connected with the Sharon
Battle 9 Jul 1781, see Frothingham's "History, Montgomery Co." page 47). On 1790
Palatine NY census (1-0-3).

    944: PETER b 15 Apr 1786 (sp Pet. Yates)

862: PHILIP BELLINGER <B52> - born 1728 (son of Philip); died 1802; m 25 Jun 1749
ELISABETH FINK (b ca 1728, d 1808 age 80-6-16) pr. a dau of CHRISTIAN FINK &
CATHERINE although Bellinger book (page 24) has her as a dau of WILLIAM FINK &
MARGARET SNELL. On 1790 GF census (2-0-2).

    945: ps. Johan JOST b say 1752; killed ps. 15 Oct 1781
   +946: ADAM P. b ca 1753; m ELISABETH
   +947: PETER ca 1755-1778 m ELISABETH CAMPBELL
   +948: WILLIAM 1759-1833 m HANNAH MATTICE
   948A CATHARINA b 25 May 1760; liv. Dec 1784 (spf J. Bellinger bp)
   +949: PHILLIP III b 22 Sep 1761; m MARGARET
   +950: CHRISTIAN 1764-1838 m BARBARA DIEVENDORF
   951: John FREDERICK b 6 Jun 1766; killed 9 Jul 1781
   952: ANDREW b 12 May 1768; m 1792 CATHARINE GROS

857: ANNA MARIA BELLINGER - b 14 Sep 1751; d 27 Jan 1848 (age 96, buried Herkimer
Reform. Church); m 16 Jul 1771 GEORGE SMITH (b 1744, d 1809) son of MARTIN SMITH.
Notes of Mrs. Vera Eysaman say she had a sister who married a Fox and was aunt of
Mrs. Adam Spoon & Peter Alder (alias Peter Bellinger), which fits for children of
Frederick Bellinger & Magdalena Wohleben.

BELLINGER - 4th Generation

946: ADAM P. BELLINGER <B291> - born say 1753 (son of Philip); m by 1782 ELISABETH
...(ps. an Ecker or Snell?). Lived at Canajoharie Castle 1792 and pr. the Adam B.
on 1790 Canajoharie census (1-2-3) living near Wallraths, Kilts, & Adam Ecker.

    954: MARGARET b 18 Feb 1782 (sp Jac. Eaker & Marg. <Fink>)
    955: PHILIP b GF 7 Oct 1783 (sp Adam Snell & Elis.<Bellingr>)
    956: ADAM jr. b say 1785; m by 1804 BARBARA
    957: JOST bp SJR 2 Jan 1791 (sp Jost Folts & Marg.)
    958: ABRAHAM b SJR 27 Nov 1792 (sp Christn Bellinger & Barb.)
    959: ELISABETH b 2 Mar 1794 (sp Dienes Flanders)

950: CHRISTIAN BELLINGER <B295> - born 15 Jan 1764; m 1784 BARBARA DIEVENDORF (b
1763, d 1838) dau of JACOB D. DIEVENDORF & ELISABETH BELLINGER.

    960: JACOB b 1 May 1785; m 1808 MARIA SMITH (b 1787)
    961: CATHERINE b say 1787; m 1805 PETER SHARP
    962: ELISABETH b say 1788; m 1808 CONRAD MOWERS of Stark NY
    963: MARGARET bp SJR 5 Sep 1790 (sp Jost Folts & Marg.)
           d 1858; m CONRAD SNELL
    964: BARBARA bp SJR 12 Aug 1792; m1 JOHN EYGENBRODT
    965: PHILIP C. 1800-1872 m CATHERINE ZIMMERMAN
    966: MARY m ABRAHAM SNELL of Minden NY
    967: FANNY   m Ft. Plain NY 1819 JAMES BAXTER

902: CHRISTOPHER F. BELLINGER ("Stophel") <B285> - born 24 Nov 1763; died of cancer 9 Jan 1839; m 28 Nov 1786 ANNA L. HARTER (b 5 Aug 1768, d 1830) dau of LORENTZ HARTER jr. & CATHERINE DOCKSTADER. On 1790 HK census (1-1-2).

> **968:** FREDERICK C. b 9 Sep 1787; ml STELLA COOK
> **969:** ELIZABETH b SJR 11 Nov 1791 (sp Pet. Bellinger & Elis.)
> **970:** ANNA b SJR 2 Oct 1793 (sp Henry Wallrath & Anna)
>   m FREDERICK HELMER
> **971:** CHRISTOPHER C. 1796-1868 m ANNA MARGARET WEAVER
> **972:** DAVID b 7 Apr 1803
> **973:** JOHN 1805-1871 m ELISABETH EDICK
> **974:** MARGARET b say 1807; m 1826 WILLIAM TALCOTT
> **975:** MADLENA b Sep 1810

884: FREDERICK BELLINGER <B82> - born ca 1746; m CATHERINE ... (ps. Fox or Wallrath). On 1790 Palatine NY Census (2-2-3) near Ulrich Bauder & Yukers.

> **976:** JACOB b ca 1768; m SOPHIA KLOCK
> **977:** JOST b ca 1770; m ELISABETH ...
> **978:** ANNA b ca 1772; m ANDREW SHEFFER
> **978A** ps. JOHN F. b say 1775; m HK 1802 ELISABETH G. SMITH
> **979:** ELISABETH b May 1779; d 1831; m HENRY HEES

904: FREDERICK BELLINGER <B102> - born ca 1749; killed at Oriskany 6 Aug 1777;

> **980:** JOHN FRED. b 11 Jun 1775; m ELISABETH YOURAN (b 1775)

886: HENRY BELLINGER <B84> - born say 1750; m 22 Jan 1771 MARGARET WINDECKER

> **981:** ANNA b 22 Oct 1772; m 1792 JOHN C. HOUSE
> **982:** FREDERICK H. b say 1773; m ELISABETH KLOCK
> **983:** JOHN H. b say 1782; d 1824; m LENA WALLRATH (dau of Adam A)
> **984:** PETER H. 1788-1874 m MARGARET AUSMAN
> **985:** MARIA b say 1792; m JACOB AUSMAN
> **986:** ELISABETH b say 1796; m HENRY AUSMAN

910: HENRY BELLINGER <B107> - born 30 Jun 1764; died 33 Apr 1836; m 14 Jul 1785 MARGARET NELLIS dau of CHRISTIAN H. NELLIS. Lived at Palatine NY in 1794. Of two Henries on the 1790 Palatine NY census this one pr. had the smaller family (1-2-4).

> **987:** MAGDALENA b say 1787; m 1805 JOSEPH NELLIS
> **988:** NANCY b say 1789
> **989:** JOHN H. bp SJR 17 Nov 1791 (sp John Ehle & Delia)
>   m 1814 POLLY CRANE
> **990:** pr. ELISABETH bp SJR 26 Jan 1794 (sp Jac. Klock, Elis. Nellis)
>   ml CASPER LODOWICK
> **991:** CATHERINE bp 4 Oct 1795; ml TRUMAN FULLER
> **992:** DAVID b say 1797

883: JOHANNES F. BELLINGER <B81> - born ca 1742 (son of Fred. F.); m by 1770 CATHERINE P. BELLINGER ps. dau of Philip (Bellinger book). John & Cath. sponsored Jul 1770 bp of Catherine, dau of Jacob Christman & Ernestina Ph. Bellinger.

> **993:** JOHN b say 1763; m LENA W. FOX Clockville (Sullivan) NY
> **994:** ps. ANNA b say 1765; liv. Jun 1782 (spf John Hess bp)

898: JOHANNES F. BELLINGER <B281> - born ca 1755 (son of Col. Fred.); attacked and killed by Indians while mowing hay 24 Jul 1780; m May 1780 ERNESTINA HARTER (b 1761) dau of Capt. HENRY HARTER and former wife of Lt. JOHN MEYER (Beers "Herkimer Co." page 151). His widow m3 1784 ADAM STAHRING. He refused to run for his gun when stalking Indians approached and was thus slain while Harter brother-in-law got away (Harter book page 9).

     995: JOHN b 8 Mar 1781; m EVA CLEPSATTLE desc. in Neb.

903: JOHN BELLINGER jr. <B101> - born ca 1747 (Bellinger book page 43); killed at Oriskany 6 Aug 1777; m 2 Dec 1766 ANNA FOX ps. dau of PHILIP FOX. His widow pr. m2 ADAM NELLIS jr.

     996: FREDERICK b say 1768; m ELISABETH
     997: GEORGE b SAR 25 Nov 1770 (sp John Bellinger & Maria Lena)
     998: JOHN F. b say 1773; m MARY (of Canajoharie)

926: Maj. JOHN BELLINGER <B302> - born ca 1760 (son of John); died 9 Oct 1815; m1 GF 29 Nov 1785 CATHERINE P. WEAVER (b 29 Aug 1765, d 12 Dec 1812) pr. dau of NICHOLAS JAC. WEAVER (Bellinger book page 54; Catherine´s middle initial "P" is pr. an error in church rec.). In 1788 he brought his family, including stepson Nicholas Smith, to settle at Utica NY, where he subsequently managed a tavern and built the first frame house.

     999: CATHERINE b GF 6 Jul 1786 (sp ... Weaver, Cath. Christmn)
                d 1830; m 1809 JOSHUA OSTROM
    1000: ELISABETH b GF 12 Mar 1788 (sp Joh Christman, Elis. Weaver)
    1001: ANNA b GF 8 Oct 1790 (sp Anna Joh. N Weaver, Fr. Christman)
    1002: HANNAH b 1792
    1003: MARGARET b 1794
    1004: MARIA b 1795; pr. d. young
    1005: DEBORAH
    1006: JOHN b 1798; d 1841 (or 1844) left estate to Nich. Smith
    1007: MARIA 1800-1825 m SMITH MOTT

900: Capt. PETER F. BELLINGER <B283> - born 22 Feb 1759; died 1815; m ELISABETH HARTER (b 1764, d 1823) dau of HENRY HARTER & CATHERINE PFEIFFER. On 1790 Herkimer census (2-1-5), near Harters (Nich., Lawrence, & Henry), and still living at Herkimer NY in 1802 when daughter Anna was confirmed.

    1008: CATHERINE b 16 Dec 1782; m Col. JACOB P. WEAVER
    1009: ANNA b GF 4 Aug 1784 (sp. Stophel Bellingr, Appol. Harter)
               m GEORGE A. CLEPSATTLE
    1010: ERNESTINA b GF 2 Jan 1786 (sp Adam Staring & Ernestna); d y
    1011: ERNESTINA b GF 16 Dec 1787 (sp Philip Harder & Cath.)
    1012: ELISABETH b 27 Apr 1790 (sp John Dockstader & Cath.)
    1013: FREDERICK P. b 15 Mar 1792 (sp. Fred. Bauman & Delia)
               m MARY BARBARA WEAVER
    1014: ANNA MARGARET b 23 Jul 1794; m FREDERICK G. WEAVER
    1015: HEINRICH b 24 Mar 1796; m ELISABETH CAMPBELL
    1016: MARIA b 7 Mar 1799; m JOHN H. MYERS
    1017: ELISABETH b 4 Jul 1803; d 7 Jan 1824 (age 20-6)

937: PETER BELLINGER jr. <B504> - born 21 May 1760; died 8 Aug 1851; m 12 Sep 1784
CHRISTINA TEN BROECK (bp 1760) widow of NICHOLAS BELL. Lt. and Q.M. in Revol.
service from 1779-82, succeeding Lt. Rudolph D. Steele. Pr. the Peter on 1790
Canajoharie NY census (1-2-2) listed next to Hen. Bell.

    1018: PETER P. b GF 25 Jun 1785 (sp Stophl Bellnger, Delia Petri)
                    d 1858; m CATHERINE EIGHNEY (or Amey)
    1019: JACOB b GF 4 May 1789 (sp Jost Bellingr, ...); d 22 May 1807
    1020: NANCY 1792-1830 m ROBERT McCHESNEY

947: PETER BELLINGER <B292> - born say 1755 (son of Philip & Elis.); killed on a
scouting expedition 29 Jun 1778; m ELISABETH CAMPBELL.

    1021: NICHOLAS b GF 28 Aug 1776 (sp. Rud. Shoemaker jr & Doro.)
    1022: DANIEL b 22 Nov 1777 (sp Jacob Piper, Marg. Rosencrantz)

877: PHILIP BELLINGER - born 1773; m JULIANNA BREITENBACHER dau of BALTUS
BREITENBACHER.

    1023: BALTUS b GF Apr 1792 (sp. Balt. Breitnbacher & Juliana)

949: PHILIP BELLINGER (pr. BELLANGER or BETTINGER) <B294> - Bellinger book has
born 22 Sep 1761 (son of Philip); ps. m1 by 1778 MARIA ...; m by 1784 MARGARET ...
He looks to be the Philip Bellanger naturalized 8 Mar 1773 with the Hasenclever
men (Book of Names page 7) which suggests that he was perhaps a later immigrant,
rather than one of the German Flats Bellingers. The 1784 bp record has him as
Philip "Bettinger". On 1790 Herkimer census (1-4-1) near Moulder, Jos. Klock,
Jos. Koch, & John Finster. See Bettinger on page 284.

    1024: pr. PHILIP b 19 Jul 1778 (sp Nic. Kolsch & Maria Frederica)
    1025: pr. GEORGE b GF 12 Sep 1784 (sp Mich Witrig & Elis.)
    1026: CATHERINE b 13 Dec 1786 (sp Deo. Bekker & Cath.)
    1027: PETER b 9 Nov 1794 (sp John Finster & Maria <Schnek>)

948: WILLIAM BELLINGER <B293> - born 6 Oct 1759; died 13 Jun 1839 (age 74 <gives
birthyear ca 1765!?>); m HANNAH MATTICE (b 1751, d 1825). Was in Revol. service
and his pension says he had a brother killed in Jul 1781 (pr. Frederick). William
Bellinger was on 1790 Canajoharie NY census (2-4-5).

    1028: MARGARET 1781-1844 m 1801 JACOB DIEVENDORF
    1029: ELISABETH b GF 6 Oct 1782 (sp Wm Fink); m CORNELIUS RUNKLE
    1030: JOHN 1784-1816 m MARGARET MITCHELL
    1031: PHILIP b 27 Jan 1787; m ELISABETH RUNKLE
    1032: MARIA m1 WILLIAM CHRISLER m2 1810 PETER HENNIS
    1033: CATHERINE b 18 Mar 1789; m JACOB LASHER
    1034: ANDREW W. 1790-1859 m ELISABETH LIPE
    1035: CONRAD b 17 Mar 1794; m HELEN KELLER

923: MARGARET BELLINGER - pr. born ca 1745 to 1752 (Bellinger book has her as dau
of Capt. Peter but we think she was dau of John Bellinger & Barbara Elisabeth, as
indicated in the naming pattern of the children of Col. Nicholas Smith); killed
along with her husband and others at German Flats NY 10 May 1779; m SAR 20 Nov
1769 NICHOLAS SMITH (d 1779) pr. son of MARTIN SMITH.

BRODHACK - 1st Generation

1101: BARTHOLOMEW BRODHACK - pr. born ca 1735 to 1762; pr. m1 by 1779 ANNA MARIA ...; m2 by 1786 ELISABETH KESSLER (her Kessler identity seems likely from the sequence of bapt. sponsorships and the location of the 1790 residence for this couple). Bartholomew was ps. related to the "Nicholas Broadhauer" who, with wife Margaret, was sponsor for Jun 1764 bp of Nicholas, son of John Wirth & Dorothy. Bartholomew & Anna Maria sponsored Feb 1779 bp of Maria, dau of Frederick Getman & Catherine. Then he was a sponsor, with Elizabeth Kessler, for Aug 1779 bp of Adolph, son of John Kessler and sponsored, with wife Elisabeth, Aug 1787 bp of Lena, dau of George Hausman & Maria Elisabeth (Kessler). He also sponsored, with Elisabeth, Sep 1790 bp of Elisabeth, dau of Conrad Kessler & Cath. (Crim). Appears on 1790 German Flats census (2-1-3) adjacent in list to John Kessler Sr. and other Kesslers (Casler).

surname BRODHACK
    1101A ps. ANNA b say 1780; m by 1802 GEORGE BRIETENBACHER
    1102: BARTHOLOMEW b 17 Apr 1786 (sp Geo. Hausman & Maria Elis.)

1103: JACOB BRODHACK - pr. born ca 1740 to 1758; m pr. by 1777 DOROTHY STAHRING dau of NICHOLAS STAHRING (Dorothy Brodhack, wife of Jacob, was identified as Nicholas Staring's daughter in a 1788 property transfer <Oneida Co. Deed Book #3, page 329>). Listed with Bartholomew Brodhack and John Brodhack in Col. Bellinger's 4th Tryon Co. Revolutionary Regiment (Book of Names page 166). Jacob & wife Dorothy were sponsors for Apr 1789 bp of Dorothea, dau of Peter Jos. Staring & Maria. Jacob Broadhack was listed with 2 adults & 1 child (under age 16) on 1778 German Flats relief. On 1790 Herkimer census (1-3-4), in list just before Philip F. Helmer and Fred. Getman.

    1104: child b say 1774 (under age 16 in 1778)
    1105: JACOB b SAL 9 Feb 1778 (sp Barth. Brdhk, Maria Staring)
    1105A ps. POLLY b say 1782; m 1801 GEORGE P. DOCKSTADER
    1106: HENRICH b GF 18 Jul 1787 (sp Nic. A. Staring & Elis.)
    1107: ANNA b 11 Dec 1789 (sp. Phillip Helmer & Anna)
               m 1811 ABRAHAM DYGERT
    1107A pr. NICHOLAS b say 1791; liv. 1811 (wit. Anna Brodhack mar.)

1108: JOHN BRODHACK - pr. born ca 1750 to 1764; m by 1789 MARIA ... In Revolutionary service. On 1790 Herkimer census (1-1-1), next in list to Godfried Riegel.

    1109: BARTHOLOMEW b GF 4 Nov 1789 (sp Barth. Brodhk & Elis.)
    1111: MARIA bp SJR 28 Oct 1792 (sp. Henry Sallie & Mary)

1110: MARY CATHERINE BRODHACK - pr. born ca 1740 to 1758; m by 1775 FREDERICK GETMAN pr. a son of Capt. FREDERICK GETMAN & MARGARET (see Getmans on pages 103-5).

********** CAMPBELL (Gemmel) **********

1201: JAMES CAMPBELL - pr. born ca 1700 to 1720; m ... . A James Campell
was at German Flats by Jun 1768, when church records (Vosburgh's GF Vol.
2 page 137) show he received a payment for services and a "Cimmi Cemmel" appears on
the 1771 Burnetsfield Minister's Support List. Probably he was related to
Thomas Campbell whose name appears as the clerk noting receipt of church
payments from August 1767 through March 1768 (ibid. page 138). Possibly he was
related to the James (Jeems Gimmel) of Kingston NY who married by 1720 MARTHA
BIER and had son John baptised at Kingston 23 Oct 1720. Based on the
appearance of name James amongst the sons born between 1770 and 1790 to John,
Ludwig & Patrick Campbell, we presume this James to have been the head of the
Herkimer area family and also the father of Maria Elisabeth Campbell whose
marriage record at Stone Arabia in 1761 gives her as a daughter of a James (her
husband George Hauss is probably the person of that name on the 1771
Burnetsfield Minister's Support List).

surname CAMPBELL

+1202: pr. JOHN b say 1738; m1 by 1763 SARA MONTURE
 1203: ps. CATRINA m Schenectady NY 7 Mar 1758 JOHN SIMSON
+1204: MARIA ELISABETH b say 1742; m 1761 GEORGE HOUSE
+1205: pr. PATRICK 1750-1796 m by 1775 CATHERINE BELLINGER
 1206: pr. MARGARET b say 1750; liv. 1768 (spf Barsh bp)
           ps. m LUDWIG BARSH
+1207: pr. LUDWIG ca 1756-1813 m by 1777 MARIA PETRIE

1208: ALEXANDER CAMPBELL - pr. born ca 1725 to 1735; m1 CATHERINE ... (b ca
1734, d 12 Jul 1767 age 33); m2 at Schenetady NY 23 May 1768 MAGADALENA VAN
SEYSE dau of JOHANNES VAN SEYSE. Possibly the Alexander who went to Canada as
a Tory (United Empire Loyalist list). No apparent tie to the German Flats
family.

 1209: CATRINA bp Schenectady NY 27 Jul 1769
 1210: MARGARITA bp 31 May 1771
 1211: MARGARITA bp Schenectady NY 27 May 1776

1212: DANIEL CAMPBELL - born ca 1731; died 16 Aug 1802 age 71-10-28; m Albany
NY 14 Apr 1760 ELISABETH BRADT (pr. Engeltje, dau of ARENT SAMUELSE BRATT, died
28 Sep 1812). Pearson's "Schenetady" says he was from Ireland. Possibly the
Daniel Sr. who, with Daniel Jr., went to Canada as a Tory (United Empire
Loyalist list).

 1213: ps. ELISABETH b say 1757; m PETER BELLINGER (ca 1755-1778)
 1214: DAVID bp 15 Nov 1768; died 29 Jun 1801

1215: Col. SAMUEL CAMPBELL - born ca 1738 (son of James Campbell & Margaret
<Lindsay>); died 1824 age 86; m JANE CANNON as given in Comp. of Amer. Gen. v 1
page 56. His father James came from Scotland to Boston MA in 1728 and came to
Cherry Valley NY ca 1741 with other families from New Hampshire. His wife and
four children were prisoners of war in the Revolution. Prob. related to the
Elisabeth Campbell who married at Cherry Valley in 1752 WILLIAM DICKSON, and
the John, Nathaniel, & Samuel Campbell in Col. Fisher's Revol. Regiment. Had
son James (1772-1870, m Sarah Elderkin).

1202: Major **JOHN CAMPBELL** - pr. born ca 1728 to 1740; died ca 8 Aug 1790 (son Ludwig´s bp record of Sep 1790 says the father Johannes died seven weeks earlier); m1 by 1763 SARA MONTURE; m2 SAR 28 Feb 1769 BARBARA ELISABETH WEAVER. His widow BARBARA ELISABETH CAMPBELL m2 at Herkimer NY Dec 1792 JOHN SMITH, a widower.   John Campbell was at Fort Stanwix in 1763 (son Christian´s bp rec.) and was pr. the John in Capt. Conrad´s militia unit in 1767. A John Campbell is listed, with Ludowick Campbell, as having 4 adults & 3 children on the 1778 German Flats relief. Widow Barbara on 1790 GF census (2-3-3).

    1216: CHRISTIAN bp Palat. NY 3 Mar 1763 (sp Lt Brown, Lt Abbot)
  +1217: PATRICK JOH. b say 1768; m 1790 GERTRUDE JAC. MEYER
         by 2nd wife
  +1218: JOHN JOH. b 10 Feb 1770; m 1792 MARIA JOSEPH MEYER
    1219: ps. JACOB b say 1775; unm 1804 (spf Jacob Campbell bp)
    1220: MARIA b GF 14 Nov 1777 (sp John V Slyke & Margaret)
    1221: ADAM b GF 15 May 1779 (sp Adam Staring & Cath.)
    1222: pr. JAMES bp Fonda NY 11 Mar 1782 (of Joh. & Barb.)
    1223: GEORGE HENRICH b GF 9 May 1784 (sp G. Hen Bell & Cath.)
    1224: ANNA EVA b GF 23 Jul 1786 (sp Adam Weaver & Cath.)
    1225: LUDWIG b 13 Sep 1790 (posthum.)

1207: **LUDWIG CAMPBELL** - born ca 1756; died German Flats NY 3 Jan 1813 (age 57); m by 1777 MARIA PETRIE (b ca 1757, d 24 Nov 1821 age 64). Listed with John Campbell on 1778 GF relief. Sponsored 1788 bp of John, son of Lt. John Schmid & Elisabeth, and, with Maria Elisabeth (wife?), Sep 1790 bp of Ludwig, son of John Chample. On 1790 GF census (1-4-2).

    1226: JOHN b GF 5 Feb 1777 (sp Joh Chample & Barb. Elis.)
    1227: JAMES L. b GF 17 Oct 1779 (sp. Patrick Gimmel & Cath.)
           m by 1801 ANNA STARING
    1227A pr. JACOB L. (see James!?) m by Nov 1804 ANNA (spf Davis bp)
    1227B ps. MARIA b say 1783; m by 1803 THOMAS DAVIS
  +1228: TIMOTHY b GF 17 Jul 1784 (sp And. Piper, M. Cath. Frank)
    1229: PETER b GF 25 Dec 1786 (sp Pet. Orendorf & Cath.<Piper>)

1205: General **PATRICK CAMPBELL** - born 1750; died 1796 (DAR); m CATHERINE STAHRING dau of NICHOLAS STAHRING (Staring tie given in Oneida Deed Book #3 page 329 despite claim in Harter book, page 20, that wife was a Bellinger). Listed at Lt. and as just "Patrick Camples", with Ludwig & John Campbell, in Bellinger´s Revol. Regmt. On 1790 GF census (2-2-6).

    1230: ANNA EVA b say 1772; m GF 1792 JOST BELLINGER (b 1766)
    1231: ADAM P. b say 1774; m 1 Jan 1795 MARGARET JOH. FRANK
    1232: JAMES (Ciems) b GF 11 May 1778 (sp Ludwig Cample & Maria)
    1233: ps. JACOB b say 1780; m by 1802 ELISABETH FRANK
    1234: CATHERINE b GF 8 Jan 1783 (sp Adam Nic. Staring & Cath.)
           pr. m by 1803 PETER RATH
    1235: CHRISTINA b 4 Jul 1785 (sp Pet. Bellinger & Christina)
           d 1808; m 1803 JOST BELLINGER (b 1783)
    1236: MARIA b GF 18 Nov 1787 (sp. Nic. N. Staring & Maria)
           d 1863; m LAWRENCE HARTER
  +1237: PATRICK b 1 Jun 1790 (sp Hen. N. Staring & Elis.)
           m by 1808 SUSANNA WEBER

CAMPBELL - 3rd Generation

1218: JOHN JOH. CAMPBELL - born 10 Feb 1770; m 31 Jan 1792 MARIA MEYER dau of
JOSEPH MEYER & CATHERINE CLAPSADDLE.

> 1238: ANNA EVA b 14 Sep 1792 (sp Adam Chample, Anna Eva Meyer)
> 1239: JOHANNES b 16 Apr 1794 (sp Pat. Chample & Gertrude)
> 1240: MARIA b 31 May 1802 (sp Andrew & Cath. Meyer)

1217: PATRICK JOH. CAMPBELL pr. born ca 1760 to 1773; m 12 Aug 1790 GERTRUDE
JAC. MEYER pr. dau of JACOB MEYER & MARGARET. Children born after 1800 include
John (1801), Jacob (1804), Wilhelm (1807), Isaac (1810), Peter (1814), and
Angelina (1817).

> 1241: MARGARET b 20 Dec 1790 (sp Joh Gimmel & Margaret)
> 1242: DELIA b GF 1 Jan 1793 (sp Joh. Lud. Campbell, Cath Jac. Meyer)
> 1243: MARIA CATHERINE b 16 Feb 1795 (sp Mich Meyer, Cath. Chample)
> 1244: JOHN b Warren NY 20 Oct 1801 (sp Jacob Meyer)
> 1245: JACOB b HK 2 Feb 1804 (sp Jac Gemmel, Dor. Cranz, unm)

1237: PATRICK CAMPBELL jr. (PATRITIO) - born German Flats NY 1 Jun 1790 (son of
Patrick); liv. 1814; m by 1808 SUSANNA WEBER pr. dau of NICHOLAS WEAVER &
BARBARA KELLER. Children Catherine (b 1808, bp sponsors Nicholas Weber &
Barbara, ...), Elisabeth (1810, bp sp. John Staring & Cath.), and Jeremias
(1812).

1228: TIMOTHY CAMPBELL - pr. the Timothy born German Flats NY 17 Jul 1784 (son
of Ludwig & Maria, with bp sp And. Piper, M. Cath. Frank); m by 1807 EVA
STARING (b 1785) dau of NICHOLAS STARING & MARIA (S. Kimball notes). Children
Hans Dietrich (b 1807, sp Elis. Staring & Dietrich Casler), Daniel (1812),
Alpert (1814), Lewis (1817), Caroline Elisabeth (1819), and Catherine Lisba.

********** CHRISTMAN **********

1301: JOHANNES CHRISTMAN (Hannes) - born ca 1668 (age 41 in 1709); m ANNA
GERTRAUD ... The 1709 London list of Palatines (Book of Names page 103) has him a
Menonite with sons ages 7 & 5, and girls ages 9 & 2. Next he is on the NY
Palatine subs. list of 1710 (3A,3Y) and in 1712 (5A,3Y). Perhaps one child was
lost between London and New York so that count of children, which was four in 1709
(say before birth of Jacob that year), remains four in New York in 1710. John
was a sponsor, with Dorothy Shoemaker, at 1716 bp of Henrich Schneider. Wife
Gertraud sponsored the 1717 bp of Gertraudt Sixt. Naturalized at Albany NY 17 Jan
1716 and appears on 1717 Simmendinger census with wife Anna Gertraud & 6 children.

                        surname CHRISTMAN
        1302: dau b ca 1700 (age 9 in 1709)
       +1303: pr. JOHN b ca 1702 (son age 7 in 1709)
        1304: son b say 1704 (age 5 in 1709); ps. died 1710
        1305: dau b ca 1707 (age 2 in 1709)
       +1306: JACOB ca 1709-1790 m 1738 CATHERINE ...
       +1307: pr. son (guess name of FREDERICK) b say 1711
        1308: child b say 1714

1309: ELIZABETH CHRISTMAN - On NY Palatine subs. list in 1710 (1A,2Y) & in 1712
(3A,0Y). Pr. a widow with 2 children who reached age 10 by 1712. Placement of
daughter Margaret comes from H. Jones´ "Palatine Families of New York".

        1310: MARGARET b say 1702; m MICHAEL SMITH (b 1707)

                    CHRISTMAN - 2nd Generation

1307: FREDERICK CHRISTMAN (?) - pr. born ca 1702 to 1717; m ... (pr. a
Catherine, and ps. a Bashor, as suggested by bp sponsors of grandchildren). He is
needed as there are three John Christmans of the following generation. The name
Frederick was given to early sons of the John & Nicholas assigned below as ps.
children. Pr. this man moved to German Flats with his brother John before 1757.

        1311: ps. CATHERINE (Christman?) b say 1741; m MARC DEMUTH
       +1312: pr. FREDERICK 1748-1832 m EVA MEYER
       +1313: pr. JOHN b say 1752; m by 1778 ELISABETH
       +1314: ps. NICHOLAS ca 1755-1846 pr. m 1780 MARY CHRISTMAN

1306: JACOB CHRISTMAN - pr. born ca 1709 (Deuel´s notes at Oneida Hist. Soc., as
taken from death record); died Stone Arabia NY 29 Apr 1790; m 1738 CATHERINA ...
Ps. the Jacob in Lt. Severinus Dygert´s 1763 militia company. Living at
Canajoharie NY in 1744 (son´s bp rec., Book of Names page 62) and probably he
remained in that area.

       +1315: JOHN   b say 1740; m 1764 CATHERINE DOCKSTADER
        1316: ps MARGARET (Chrstmn?) b say 1742; m by 1763 GEORGE SCHACO
       +1317: JACOB bp Canajoharie 13 Aug 1744 (sp Jac. Fehling & Magd.)
                     d 1811; pr. m by 1774 ANNA ... (Deuel´s notes)
        1317A ps MARIA EVA (Chrstmn?) b say 1746; m by 1764 HENRY FRITSHER
        1317B pr. ELISABETH b say 1748; m 1764 CIEMS BILLINGTON
       +1318: ps. NICHOLAS b say 1755; m by 1779 ANNA EVA ...
        1319: ps. MARY b say 1759; m 1780 NICHOLAS CHRISTMAN

                            -36-

1303: JOHN CHRISTMAN - pr. born ca 1702 to 1710; m by 1734 MARGARET FELLER dau of NICHOLAS FELLER & ELISABETH.   Son Nicholas was mentioned in the will of father-in-law Nicholas Feller (May 1734).   Probably the Christman branch which escaped capture in the Nov 1757 French & Indian raid on German Flats (The Palatines of New York State, page 81).

        1320: ps. ELISABETH (Christman?)   ca 1726-1806 m GEORGE NELLIS
    +1321: NICHOLAS   b say 1732; m by 1766 SUSANNA ... (b ca 1733)
    +1322: JACOB   1741-1826   m ERNESTINA BELLINGER
        1323: MARGARETHA JOH.   b say 1743; liv. 1760 (spf Marg. Demuth bp)
                    pr. m 1764 WILLIAM CUNINGHAM
    +1325: ps. JOHN   b say 1747;   m 1769 CATHERINE FOLTS (b 1748)

                        CHRISTMAN - 3rd Generation

1312: FREDERICK CHRISTMAN - born Herkimer NY Aug 1748; died Columbia NY 24 Oct 1832 (age 84-2); m by 1783 (pr. ca 1774) EVA MEYER (b 1752, d 1828) dau of HENRY MEYER & MARIA GETMAN (Getman book page 15 and DAR vol 158 page 279).   Was a sponsor for Sep 1782 bp of Frederick, son of Henrich Miller & Eva.   In Col. Bellinger's Reg. in Revol.   On 1790 German Flats census (1-1-5).

    +1326: JACOB BASHOR   1775-1849   m MARY ELISABETH SMALL
        1327: MARGARET   b GF 23 Feb 1777 (dau of Fred.)
                    (sp. Marg. Christman, a Meyer <first name not given>)
        1328: pr. MARIA   b say 1780; m by 1801 JACOB BELL
        1329: FREDERICK   bp GF 4 Jan 1783 (sp. Fred. Getmen & Marg.)
        1330: CATHERINE   bp GF 28 Mar 1784 (sp Wm Folmer & Cath. Meyer)
        1331: MARIA ELISABETH   b GF 30 Jul 1786 (sp. John Smidt & M. Elis.)
    +1332: BARENT   b GF 17 Aug 1788 (sp Fred. Meyer & Marg.)
    +1333: GEORGE F.   1790-1871   m 1811 MARY BELL (dau of Philip)
        1334: HENRICH   b GF 1 Jun 1793

1322: JACOB CHRISTMAN - born 1741; died 1826 (Deuel notes); m SAR 18 Feb 1766 ERNESTINA BELLINGER (b 1745, d 1819) dau of PHILIP BELLINGER (Bellinger book page 26).   Had 2 adults & 5 children on 1778 GF relief and was at Whitestown in 1808.

    +1335: JOHANNES   bp SA Apr 1767 (sp Joh Christman jr & w Marg.)
                    d 1851; m CATHERINE CUNINGHAM (d Utica NY 1808)
    +1336: MARGARETHA   b 21 Aug 1768 (sp. Wm Cuningham & w Marg.)
                    m 1789 JOHN ABR. BAUM
        1337: CATHERINA   b 3 Jul 1770 (sp Joh. F Bellingr, Cath. P Bellngr)
                    m 1790 GEORGE DEMUTH
        1338: FREDERICK   b say 1772; d Ellisburg NY 31 Mar 1853
    +1339: JACOB jr   b ca 1774; d Utica NY 1843; m KEZIAH MAYER
    +1340: PETER   b 5 Apr 1776 (sp. Peter Weber & Maria Cath.)
                    d 1843; liv. 1794 (spf Hiser bp)
        1341: NICHOLAS   b 2 Jun 1779 (sp Joh. Bellinger, Cath. Weaver)
                    m MARGARETHA CAMPBELL
        1342: GEORGE   b 7 Jan 1782 (sp. Geo. Weber & Marg.)
        1343: ELISABETH   b GF 29 Oct 1783 (sp Chrsphr Bellngr, Cath. Demuth)
                    m by 1810 GEORGE WEAVER
        1344: MARIA   b GF 4 Oct 1786 (sp. Geo. G. Demuth, Cath. Cuningham)
                    m JOHANES WIDRICK (son of Geo.)
        1345: GERTRAUT   b 24 Oct 1789 (Mark DeMuth & Cath); m JOHN WEAVER

                                -37-

1317: JACOB CHRISTMAN - bp Canajoharie NY 13 Aug 1744; died Stone Arabia NY 25 Aug 1811 (age 66-11-5); m ANNA ... (pr. Laux, judging from bp sponsors below). Deuel notes place the Jacob (b 1763) who married Helena Dygert as a son of this Jacob & Anna, but no church or bible record is known to support this and we feel that the Jacob born 1784 is the right one for this couple. Jacob & Anna sponsored Jan 1781 bp of Thomas, son of George Smith & Anna. Pr. the Jacob on 1790 Palatine NY census (1-5-3) near Eliz. Prime, Conrad Kitts, & Henry Louks (Laux).

      1346: Anna MARIA b SAL 9 Nov 1774 (sp Hermanus Crommel & Cath.)
                m 1795 HEINRICH WILLIAMS
      1347: ADAM bp 4 Oct 1778 (sp Adam Empie & Maria)
                m by 1809 NANCY
      1348: JOHANNES b 15 Jun 1781 (sp. Sev. Koch & Cath.<Laux>)
                m by 1807 MARGARET GARLOCK (Gerlach)
    +1349: JACOB bp GF 27 Jan 1784 (sp Jacob Laux & Elis.<Koch>)
      1350: JOSEPH b say 1785; m by 1807 EVA DE HORSE
      1351: CATHERINE b say 1787; m by 1808 WILLIAM OWEN
      1352: FREDERICK b 15 May 1789 (sp. Caspar Koch & Cath.<Laux>)
      1353: WILLIAM b say 1792; m by 1813 NANCY
      1354: ANNA bp SAL 1 Jan 1795 (sp. Peter Fuchs & Anna)
      1355: SARA bp St. Arabia 21 Oct 1799

1315: JOHN CHRISTMAN - pr. born ca 1735 to 1745 (son of Jacob, as given on mar. rec.); m at Palatine NY 5 Feb 1764 Anna CATHERINE DOCKSTADER dau of CHRISTIAN DOCKSTADER & CATHERINE NELLIS. Pr. the John on 1790 Palatine NY census (2-3-3) near Nicholas Chalkgo, James Pellendom (pr. Billington), David Weber, D. Van Vleet, and Henry A. Louks.

      1356: MARIA b SA 19 Apr 1764 (sp Maria Eva wife of H. Fritscher)
      1357: JOHANNES b SAR 14 Jun 1765 (sp Geo. Schacko & Margaret)
      1358: CATHERINE b SAR 14 Sep 1766 (sp Cath Laux, Jac. Christman)
    +1359: JACOB b SAR 18 Sep 1768 (sp. Wm Merckel & w. Engel)
              pr. m 1789 CATHERINE BETSINGER
      1360: HENRICH b SA 8 Oct 1769 (sp. Hen. Nellis & w. Marg.)
              d Stone Arabia NY 2 Jul 1790
      1361: ps. ELISABETH b say 1771; m by 1789 CHRISTOPHER DAVID WEBER
     1361A pr. ISAAC b say 1773; liv. 1793 (spf Christman bp)
      1362: pr. GEORGE bp GF 16 Jun 1776 (Adolph Kesler, M. Elis Nellis)
      1363: PETER bp Albany 28 Nov 1780 (son of John & Cath. Dockstdr)

1325: JOHN CHRISTMAN - pr. born ca 1740 to 1748; liv. 1823 (spf Christman bp); m1 26 Aug 1769 CATHERINE FOLTS (b 1748) dau of CONRAD FOLTS & CATHERINE DEMUTH; m2 27 Sep 1780 CATHERINE HILTS. Pr. the John Jr in 1769 GF militia in 1769. Pr. the John J. Christman with 2 adults & 3 children on 1778 GF relief (the other John, who m Cath. Dockstader, had more than 3 children alive then). John of Fairfield NY had sons George and Jacob confirmed in 1802 (HK Ch. rec.).

    +1364: pr. JOHN b say 1772; m 1794 MARGARET NIC. HILTS
      1365: pr. CATHERINE b say 1774; m 1796 GEORGE NIC. HILTS
             pr. by 2nd wife
    +1366: GEORGE b say 1782; liv. 1802 (HK Ch. confirm.)
          George Joh. m 1806 MARIA NIC. HILTS
    +1367: JACOB b GF 29 Nov 1785 (sp Melch. Folts & Cath. Smith)
          d 1842; m by 1809 REBECCA SMITH
      1368: ANNA bp GF 4 Mar 1788 (sp Thomas Bell & Anna)
          liv. 1805 (HK confirm.); pr. m HK 1809 CONRAD FULMER

1313: **JOHN CHRISTMAN** - pr. born ca 1740 to 1757; m ELISABETH ... Pr. the John
on 1790 Canajoharie NY census (1-2-3).

    +1369: Johan FREDERICK b 28 Jan 1778 (sp Fred. Christman & Eva)
     1370: JAMES bp GF 7 Nov 1779 (sp James Juel & Marg.)
     1371: CATHERINE bp 26 Sep 1781 (sp Nic Jordn & Anna); pr d young
     1372: MARIA ELISABETH b GF 27 May 1783 (sp Jac Christmn, Elis. Nellis)
     1373: CATHERINE bp Minden NY 6 Mar 1796

1318: **NICHOLAS CHRISTMAN** - pr. born ca 1730 to 1750; m by 1779 ANNA EVA ... In
Capt. Conrad Frank´s GF militia co. in 1767, next to Hen. Miller.

     1373A ps. SUSANA b say 1777; liv. 1794 (spf Ryan bp)
     1374: MARIA bp GF 27 Jan 1779 (sp Hen. Miller & Anna Eva)

1321: **NICHOLAS CHRISTMAN** - born say 1732; m SUSANNA ... (Widow Sus., b ca 1733,
d 1811 age 88). In Van Alstine´s Canajoharie militia co. in 1763.

     1375: MARGARET 1759-1837 m JAMES YUEL (Yule)
    +1376: ps. JACOB b 1763; in Revl 1781; m HELENA DYGERT
     1377: CATHERINE b SAR 16 Nov 1767 (sp Cath. & George Wever)
     1378: ps. JOHN b 1771; died 1855

1314: **NICHOLAS CHRISTMAN** - pr. born ca 1755; died Stone Arabia NY 2 Aug 1846
(age 94); pr. the same Nicholas who m at Albany NY 10 Apr 1780 MARIA CHRISTMAN.

     1379: FREDERICK bp Albany Dec 1780 (sp F Raff, Elis. Pillington)
     1380: Johan JOST bp GF 9 Nov 1787 (sp Jost Snell & Cath. Forth)
         pr. m by 1807 EVA DE HORSE
    +1381: ANDREAS bp 18 Oct 1789; pr. m 1812 MARIA WARMUTH
     1382: JOHN b SAL 10 Nov 1791 (sp. Geo. Saltsman & Sabina)
     1383: SAMUEL b Stn Ar. 12 Apr 1793 (sp Sam. Gray, Lena Loeschr)
     1384: DANIEL b SAL 3 Feb 1795 (sp Jac Schako & Cath.); pr. d. y.
     1385: MARIA bp 1 Jan 1797
     1386: ELISABETH b 19 Feb 1799
     1387: DANIEL b 3 Feb 1800
     1388: ANN bp Palatine NY 9 May 1802
     1389: HENRY b 27 Apr 1804; m 1823 LEA JAC. SMITH

CHRISTMAN - 4th Generation

1381: ANDREAS CHRISTMAN - bp St Johnsville 18 Oct 1789 (son of Nich. & Maria); pr.
m at Herkimer 1812 MARIA WARMUTH. Son Andrew bp at Columbia NY 26 Sep 1813.

1332: BARENT CHRISTMAN - born 17 Aug 1788; m by 1814 MARGARET ... They were
sponsors for Jan 1814 bp of Anna Elisabeth, dau of Jacob Christman & Maria Small.

1369: FREDERICK CHRISTMAN - bp 1778; pr. m by 1798 JOHANNA ... and had children
John (bp 30 Jul 1798) & Elisabeth (bp Minden NY 26 Aug 1800).

1333: GEORGE FR. CHRISTMAN - born GF 23 Sep 1790 (son of Fred. on mar. rec.); died
28 Jul 1853; m 16 Jun 1811 MARY BELL (b 1791, d 10 Oct 1833, cem. rec.) dau of
PHILIP BELL & DOROTHY HILTS. Lived at Warren and Columbia NY. Had children Philip
(b 1811, sp Jac. Bell & Maria), William (1820), & Maria Elis. (1823).

1390: GEORGE CHRISTMAN - m by 1811 MARIA BODMAN (b ca 1787, d 6 Oct 1833 age 46-10-). Son John G. (b 1811, m 1833 MARIA JAC. BELL), a blacksmith.

1366: GEORGE JOH. CHRISTMAN - pr. born ca 1775 to 1785; m 11 May 1806 MARIA HILTS (pr. b 1776, d 28 Jul 1806 age 37-8-4 <sic. but age should read 31-6-6>) dau of JOHN NICHOLAS HILTS and once wife of JACOB BELL. Had son David (b 20 Jun 1806, sp. John Imhof & w. Cath.)

1367: JACOB J. CHRISTMAN - born 29 Nov 1785; died Fairfield NY 22 Nov 1842 (age 57 less 6 days); m by 1809 REBECCA SMITH (pr. b ca 1783, d 19 Jul 1853 age 70 as wife of "Jacob L. Christman"). In 1825 they, and co-owners Adam & Marg. Smith, sold Burnetsfield lot #1 (Mary Cath. Coens land). Children Simon (b Jan 1809), Zimbri (m 1827 Sus. Folts), Lehman (m 1829 Cath. Jac. Smith), Jacob (b Mar 1813), Lewis (b 14 Oct 1815, m 1835 LUCINDA KAST), Rebecca, John, and ps. Louise (dau of Jacob Christman & REBECCA STEVENS<?>., m 1844 JOSEPH M. SMITH). Was a farmer.

1326: JACOB FR. CHRISTMAN - pr. the Jacob Bashor Christman born 1775 (DAR vol 158 page 279); died 1849; m GF 23 Dec 1792 MARIA JAC. SMALL (Maria Elisabeth b 25 Apr 1771, d 4 Oct 1842) dau of JACOB SMALL.

    1391: CATHERINE bp GF 21 Apr 1793 (sp Jacob Boshar & Cath.)
    1390A JACOB bp GF 26 Apr 1795 (sp Jac Small, Mar. Christman)
    1392: WILLIAM bp Herkimer 3 Jan 1803
    1393: ANNA ELISABETH b 3 Jul 1812 (bp 1814)

1359: JACOB CHRISTMAN - pr. bp 18 Sep 1768 (son of John & Cath.); m at Stone Arabia NY 26 Nov 1789 CATHERINE BETSINGER. Living Palatine NY 1793.

    1394: HENRICH bp SAL 25 Sep 1790 (sp. Hen. Laux & Maria)
    1395: JOHN b say 1792; m 1822 RACHEL FR. EIGENBRODT
    1396: JACOB bp SJR 14 Jul 1793 (sp Isaac Christman, Maria Snell)

1339: JACOB CHRISTMAN Jr. - born ca 1784 (son of Jacob & Ernestina, Bellinger book page 26); m at Fred. Meyer's house Herkimer NY 31 May 1803 CESIA MEYER dau of NICHOLAS MEYER of Fort Schuyler. Lived at Whitestown NY.

1349: JACOB CHRISTMAN - pr. born ca 1770 to 1785 (ps. the son of Jacob bp German Flats 27 Jan 1784); m at Minden NY 1806 MARIA GRAY

1376: JACOB CHRISTMAN - born 1763 (Deuel notes); m by 1795 HELENA DYGERT dau of PETER P. DYGERT & BARBARA KOCH. Enlisted Apr 1781 and served in Capt. Henry Van Derwerken's Co. (Deuel notes). Had children Jacob (b 19 Dec 1795), Catherine (b Oct 1799, m Harry Jaks), Patrick (b Aug 1801), Nicholas (b Oct 1802), Betsy (b Sep 1803), George (Mar 1812), & Nelson (Oct 1815).

1335: JOHN CHRISTMAN - bp SA 29 Apr 1767; died Ellisburg (Jeff. Co.) NY 11 Mar 1851; m GF 24 Jun 1792 CATHERINE CUNINGHAM dau of WILLIAM. Had JACOB J. (b GF 20 Oct 1793, sp Jac. Chrstmn, Eva Cunnghm; m CATH. SWARTZFEGER)

1364: JOHN CHRISTMAN - pr. born ca 1765 to 1775; m GF 4 May 1794 MARGARET J. NIC. HILTS (Peggy) dau of Johan NICHOLAS HILTS & ELIZABETH FOX. Children Catherine (bp GF 14 Oct 1794), John (m CATHERINE SCHELL <b 8 Feb 1803>), Nicholas (1802, 1830 ANNA WOHLEBEN), Jacob (1805) & Philip (1809).

1340: PETER CHRISTMAN - pr. born 1776; m by 1795 MARIA ...(Campbell?). Sponsored May 1795 bp of Peter Joh. Bellinger and Sep 1795 bp of Abraham Joh. Baum.

1401: ANDREW CLAPSADDLE - pr. born ca 1705 to 1715; m ... (pr. a EVA).
Supposedly three Clepsattle brothers immigrated to America with one remaining in
Pennsylvania and the other two moving to the Mohawk Valley in New York. Our
subject Andreas may have been the one who arrived at Philadelphia from Germany on
the ship Eliza on 27 Aug 1735 (age 22 at the time). Andrew was naturalized 16 Dec
1737 (Book of Names page 5) and about 1748 children Johannes, Augustinus, & Johan
Jost were listed with him as early members of the Lutheran church (Book of Names
page 61). If we assume Andrew married after coming to America then the reported
1727 birthyear (DAR #55358) for son Augustinus seems a bit early. Pr. the Andrew
Cibsadle in Capt. Conrad Frank´s 1767 GF militia company, listed next And. Weavor
& Deitrick Stehl (Book of Names page 12). Andrew sold Burnetsfield lot #9 to
Augustinus on 24 Sep 1769.

surname CLAPSADDLE

```
  1402: JOHANNES   b say 1737; liv. ca 1748 (Book of Names page 61)
 +1403: AUGUSTINUS  b say 1739; d 1777; m 1763 BARBARA WENTZ
  1404: Johan JOST  b say 1745; liv. ca 1748 (Book of Names page 61)
 +1405: CATHERINE   1748-1839  m pr. by 1769 JOSEPH MEYER
 +1406: pr. GERTRUDE  b say 1751; m 1769 HENRY FRANK
 +1407: pr. ANDREW   ca 1755-1809  m by 1776 MARIA DYGERT
 +1408: WILLIAM     1758-1827  m 1781 MARIA ELISABETH HAENER
  1409: ps. JACOB    b say 1760; in Col. Bellinger´s Revol. Regiment
```

CLEPSATTLE - 2nd Generation

1407: ANDREW CLAPSADDLE - born ca 1755; died 27 Jun 1809; m1 by 1775 MARIA
DYGERT dau of WILLIAM DYGERT & MARIA ELISABETH ECKER; m2 GF 6 Jan 1795 MARGARET
DYGERT step-sister of his first wife; m3 widow PHOEBE ROLLIN widow of Mr. INGHAM
(Duell notes from Jane Bellinger, HCH). Andrew had 2 adults & 2 children on 1778
German Flats relief. Supposedly had brothers Augustinus, Wilhelm, George, John,
and Jost, and a sister Catherine (HCH Clepsattle file). His will, probated 1809,
gave Burnetsfield lot #10 to his son John and mentions a brother William, but not
a son of that name.

```
  1410: MARGARET  b GF 25 Apr 1776 (sp. Wm Klepsttle, Marg. Dygert)
                  m RUDOLPH J. SHOEMAKER
 +1411: ANDREAS   b GF 21 Dec 1777 (sp Wm Dygert & Maria)
                  m ELISABETH FR. WEAVER
 +1412: JOHN A.   b 1779; m 1804 ANNA PIPER
  1413: MARIA     b SA 24 Feb 1780 (sp And. Reeber & Maria)
  1414: EVA       1781-1874  m JOHN BELLINGER (b 1781)
 +1416: GEORGE A. ca 1782-1859  m by 1805 ANNA BELLINGER
  1416: ELIZABETH  b 22 Aug 1786 (sp John Campbell & Barb.); pr. d.y.
  1417: HENRICH   b GF 8 Jul 1788 (sp Hen. Frank & Gert.); pr d young
  1418: MARIA ELISABETH  b 18 Aug 1789; m 1809 GEORGE HILTS
  1419: WILLIAM   b 13 Nov 1791 (sp Wm Helmer, Eva Dygert); pr d young
  1420: GERTRUDE (Cattrout) b ca 1794; m 1815 ANDREW JOSELYN
                  poss. by 2nd wife
  1421: REBECCA   b say 1796; mention in will of father
                  by 3rd wife
  1422: HENRY     b 9 Aug 1800; d 1826;  m LUCY PADDOCK
  1423: DANIEL    b say 1801; m DELIA SMITH of Schuyler
```

1424: HARRIET   b 21 Feb 1803; m NICHOLAS STEELE
1425: EUNICE   b 23 Sep 1808 (mother Phoebe Rollin); died young

1403: Major **AUGUSTINUS CLAPSADDLE** (Denis) - DAR #55358 has him born in Germany
1727 but a birthyear of 1735 to 1743 fits other information better; killed at
Battle of Oriskany 6 Aug 1777; Augustinus Klebbsattel m SAR 28 Jun 1763 BARBARA
WENTZ pr. dau of GEORGE WENTZ.   In 1767 GF militia co. of Capt. Conrad Frank and
listed as Major Enos Clepsattle in 1777 (Book of Names page 131).   His widow
Barbara had 3 adults & 7 children on 1778 GF relief. He lived on Burnetsfield lot
#9, which went to his son George.

        1426: CATHERINE AUG.   b 24 Dec 1763 (sp. Cath. Hess, Jac. Wentz)
                        d 7 Feb 1823 (age 59-1-4); m 1786 PETER WILH. DYGERT
        1427: ANNA EVA   b 6 May 1766 (sp. Fred Orendorf & Eva <Getman>)
       +1428: GEORGE   b 12 Sep 1767; m 1786 ANNA W. DYGERT
        1429: MARGARET   ca 1769-1827   m 1791 PETER JAC. PFEIFFER
        1430: ANNA ("Nancy")   ca 1772-1843   m GEORGE M. EDICK
        1431: AUGUSTINUS jr.   1774-1842   m by 1803 ELISABETH FRANK
       +1432: JOHN   1777-1848   m BARBARA HELMER

1402: **JOHN CLAPSADDLE** - pr. born ca 1735 to 1743 (pr. son of Andrew); m by 1791
ANNA ...   Listed as a child of Andreas on the Manheim Church records (early
membership list in Book of Names page 61). A John Clepsattle and Maria were
sponsors for Apr 1795 bp of John, son of Peter Dygert & Catherine.

        1433: JOHANNES   b 24 Jan 1791 (sp John Dygert, Anna Clepsattle)

1408: Col. **WILLIAM CLAPSADDLE** - born German Flats NY 1758 (DAR #55358 has b
1762); died 9 Jul 1827; m GF 30 Dec 1781 MARIA ELISABETH HAENER (b ca 1758, d GF
19 Feb 1837 age 78-8-)

        1434: CATHERINE   b GF 11 May 1783 (sp Pet. Lambert, Cath. Apeal)
                        d 29 Jun 1810; m 1808 PETER CHRSTPH. ECKLER
       +1435: JOHANNES WILHELM   b Jul 1785 (Pet. W Dygert, Cath Clpsttle)
                        WILLIAM jr   m 1805 ANNA DOCKSTADER
        1436: AUGUSTINUS   b GF 1 Feb 1787 (sp Geo Klepsttle & Anna)
                        d 20 May 1871; m ELIZABETH HESS
        1437: DOROTHY WILH.   b say 1788; liv. 1802 (Herk. Ch. Confirm.)
       +1438: ELISABETH   1790-   m JOSEPH CON. FOLTS
        1439: MARIA   b SJR 8 Aug 1792 (sp And. Clsattle, Maria Dygert)
                        m 1816 GEORGE JOS. HESS
        1440: ANNA   b GF 23 Aug 1795; age 16 at 1811 Herk. Confirm.
                        d 1863;   m 1826 ICHABOD TANNER
        1441: MARGARET   b ca 1797; liv. 1815 (age 18 at Confirm.)
                        m 1820 MARTIN MCKOOM
        1442: PETER   b ca 1799; age 16 at 1815 Herk. Confirm.
                        d 1888; m MARIA STEELE

1406: GERTRUDE CLAPSADDLE - pr. born ca 1745 to 1752; m 1769 HENRY FRANK jr..
Children in probable order of birth were Henry (pr.), John (pr.), Jacob (pr.),
Gertrude (1782), Anna Eva, Elizabeth, Catherine, Andries, & Dorothy.

1405: CATHERINE CLAPSADDLE - born 18 Nov 1748 (sister of Major Augustinus); died 3
Apr 1839 age 90-4-9; m by 1769 JOSEPH MEYER. Children John (1769), Maria (?),
Andries, Eva, Jacob, Elis., Joseph, John, Gertrude & Dorothy.

1411: ANDREW CLAPSADDLE jr. - born German Flats NY 21 Dec 1777; m by 1799 ELISABETH FR. WEAVER (pr. the Elisabeth, bp 1781, dau of FREDERICK WEAVER & GERTRUDE BELLINGER). Had Gertrude (1799-1814), Daniel (b & d 1803), Maria (b 1805, sp Fred. Weaver & w. Maria of Warren), Margaret (1809), Anna Eva (1812), and Andrew Frederick (1818-1884).

1431: AUGUSTINUS CLAPSADDLE jr. - born 3 May 1774 (family bible of Dr. C.J. Clepsattle); died 19 Jan 1842 (age ca 68, not 89 as seen in some records); m by 1803 ELISABETH FRANK (b 19 Jun 1772, d 28 Jun 1862) dau of LAWRENCE FRANK. Had Lawrence (1801-1886, m MARGARET HESS), Denus (b 1803), Stephen (1806), Michael (1811), Eva (1822) and Henry (1827-1905, m ELISABETH N. CROSS)).

1428: GEORGE CLAPSADDLE - born 12 Sep 1767; m 5 Dec 1786 ANNA W. DYGERT dau of WILLIAM DYGERT & MARIA ELISABETH ECKER. On 1790 GF census (2-2-5).

> **1443: ELIZABETH** b GF 3 May 1787 (sponsors not shown)
> **1444: AUGUSTINUS** b GF 20 Sep 1789 (sp Geo. Dygert, Mar. Clepsttl)
> **1445: JOHN** b 24 Jan 1791; liv. 1810 (age 18 at Confirm.)
> **1446: CATHERINE** b 1 Aug 1794 (sp Peter Dygert & Cath.)
> **1447: WILLIAM** b 1796 (sp. William Dygert & Marg.)
> **1448: ANNA** b 1799
> **1449: GEORGE** b 6 Oct 1805 (sp John Clepsattle & w. Anna)
> **1450: NICHOLAS** b 29 Dec 1809

1415: GEORGE A. CLAPSADDLE - b ca 1782; d Columbia NY 23 Dec 1859 (age 77-8-23); m 23 Dec 1804 ANNA BELLINGER ("Nancy", b 1784, d 10 Sep 1838 age 54-1-6) dau of PETER F. BELLINGER & ELISABETH HARTER. Children Elisabeth (b 1805, m Miles Terpening), Jacob (1808), Marie, Peter G. (1817-1886), George Henry (b 1821, m Clarissa Snook), Andreas (1824), Fred (1827) & Anna (1829); most went to Illinois.

1432: JOHN CLAPSADDLE - born 21 Apr 1777 (sp. John Hess & Margaret); died 8 Sep 1848 (age 70); m BARBARA ELISABETH HELMER (b ca 1782, d Columbia NY 12 Jul 1853 age 71) (see Compend. of Amer. Genealogy, vol. 4, page 323) dau of GEORGE F. HELMER & MARGARET MEYER. Children were John (b 1803), Margaret (1805, sp Geo. Helmer & w. Marg.), Anna, Peter (1810, sp Peter F. Helmer & Gert. Shoemaker), Margaret (1812, sp Geo. Ittig & w. Anna), and Caroline (1819, sp Jacob Helmer & w. Elis.).

1412: JOHN CLAPSADDLE - born 1779 (son of Andrew); m 7 Jul 1805 ANNA PIPER dau of JACOB PIPER & ELISABETH FOLTS. Had Andreas (b 1805, sp Andrw Clepsttle & w. Phoebe), David(1807), Margaret (1809), Elisabeth (1811, sp Peter P. Pfeiffer & w. Marg.), Jonas (1814, sp Geo. Harter jr, Gert. Clepsattle, unm), Maria Catherine, John Peter, Anna, Peter N., & Wilhelm Rudolph (1828).

1435: WILLIAM CLAPSADDLE - born GF 26 Jul 1785 (son of Col. William); m 27 Jan 1805 (wit. Aug. Clepsattle, brother of groom, & Fred Dockstader, bride's brother) ANNA DOCKSTADER (b 1788) dau of JOHN DOCKSTADER & CATHERINE BELLINGER. This Johan Wilhelm Clepsattle was not "John" or "John R." as some accounts indicate. Had Catherine (b 1806, sp. Cath. Clepsattle & Fred. Dockstader, unm), Elisabeth (b Mar 1815), Magdalena (1818, sp Anna Clepsattle, Christopher Bellinger).

********** COENS (KUNTZ) **********

1601: JOHANNES COENS - pr. born ca 1680 to 1690; died by 1723; m MARIA CATHERINE
... (pr. the Maria Catherine Contz living ca 1745, on list of early Lutheran
church members, Book of Names page 61). Johannes appears on NY Palatine list in
1710 (1A,1Y) & in 1712 (4A,1Y) and was pr. the Johannis Coens naturalized at
Albany 31 Jan 1716. On 1717 Simmendinger census with wife Maria Catherine & 4
children. His widow was presumably the Maria Catherine Coens who received
Burnetsfield lot #1 and it looks like her land was passed through Hilts to the
Smith and Christman families.

surname COENS

1602: ps. ANNA (Coens?) b say 1703; liv. 1710 (NY subsist. list)
presumed to have m by ca 1725 SIMON JACOB HILTS
+1603: LUDWIG b 6 Dec 1711 (sp. Ludwig Bersch); liv. 1722
1604: ps. ELISABETH (Coens?) b say 1715; m PETER FOLTS Sr.

1605: Johan CHRISTOPHER KUNTZ - On NY Palatine subsistence list in 1710 (2A,2Y)
and in 1712 (2A,2Y). Also on the NY list was a JACOB KUNTZ in 1710 (2A,0Y) & 1712
(2A,0Y). We mention these Kuntz men due to the similar sounding name to Coens,
however neither they, nor the family of Mattheus Kuntz below, are seen as related
to the Johannes Coens family of German Flats.

1606: MATTHEUS KUNTZ (Mathias) - pr. born near Nassau-Saarbruecken Germany ca 1660
to 1685; m ANNA MARGARETHA ... On NY Palatine subsistence list in 1710 (5A, 1Y)
and in 1712 (3A, 1Y). Naturalized at Albany on 17 Jan 1716 (next in list to John
George Smith). Possibly related to another Matheus Kuntz on the NY Palatine
subsistence list in 1710 (3A, 0Y), but not in 1712 (poss. died by then). On 1717
Simmendinger census with wife Anna Margaretha and 5 children.

surname KUNTZ

+1607: Johan JACOB b say 1691; m 1714 SUSANNA MICHEL
+1608: PHILIP HENDRICK b say 1695; m 1717 MARIA ELISABETHA MAEMIG
1609: child b say 1701 (under 10 in 1710)
1610: Johan DAVID b 24 Jun 1711 (sp. Dav. Ifland, Barb. Shoemaker)
1611: pr. child b say 1714

COENS - 2nd Generation

1603: LUDWIG COENS - pr. the Ludwig born 6 Dec 1711 (son of Johannes). In 1722
he received Burnetsfield lot #2, in the dependents area south of the Mohawk River
(now Ilion NY area).

1607: JACOB KUNTZ (Cuntz) - pr. born ca 1685 to 1693 (son of Mattheus as seen on
mar. rec.); m 2 Nov 1714 SUSANNA MICHEL dau of HENRICH MICHEL from commune
Weisenheim, district of Zweibruecken. Ps. the JACOB KUNTZ on NY Palatine list
(2A,0Y) say in 1712. On 1717 Simmendinger census with wife Susanna and 1 child.

1608: PHILIP HENDRICK KUNTZ (Cuntz) - pr. born ca 1690 to 1696 (son of Mattheus,
as on mar. rec.); m 25 Jun 1717 MARIA ELISABETHA MAEMIG dau of FERDINAND MAEMIG of
Ansberg NY & from Wollberghofwen (Cologne) Germany. Naturalized 14 Feb 1716. No
indication of descendents in the Mohawk Valley.

********** CRIM (Cremps, Gramps, Grimm, Kremps) **********

1701: JOHANNES KREMBS <J> - born in Germany ca 1680 (Gramps family bible, NY
State DAR, v 12, p 101); died 1770; m by 1710 APPOLONIA ... Pr. the John living
at Stone Arabia NY 1751 (Wernig testamonial, Vosburgh's Ft. Plain Church rec.).
Came to New York on the ship Midfort. Was on NY Palatine subsistence in 1710
(2A,0Y) & in 1712 (2A,2Y), and on the 1717 Simmendinger census at New Queensberg
with wife Appolonia & 1 child. JOHANNES (descendents designated by <J>) headed
one of two early families named Crim in the Mohawk Valley, the other being that
of PAUL Crim, who came up from Pennsylvania about 1750 and established the
ill-fated Andrustown settlement (Paul's line designated by <P>).

                     surname CRIM
        1702: WILLIAM   b at sea, bp WCL Jun 1710 (sp ship Capt. Fowles).
       +1703: PETER   b say 1716; m by 1739 ELISABETH EMIGE
        1703A ps. DOROTHY (Crim?)   b say 1720; m by 1739 JACOB SCHULTZ
        1704: HENRICH   b say 1722; m by 1745 CHRISTINA EMIGE
        1705: pr. MARIA MARGARETHA   b say 1725; m by 1745 WILLIAM LAUX

                     CRIM - 2nd Generation

1704: HENRICH CRIM <J> - born 1722; died Aug 1808; m by ca 1745 CHRISTINA EMIGE
(b ca 1718, d SAR 22 Aug 1796 age 78, her surname on Fonda bp rec. of Jacob
Bashar's children 1759-62). Was in Lt. Sev. Dygert's militia in 1757 and
sponsored Apr 1755 bp of Christina, dau of Ludwig Heinrich & Rosina Elis.

        1706: ps. BARBARA   b say 1744; m 1762 ISAAC N. EMIGE
        1707: MARIA ELISABETH   b say 1746; liv. 1760 (spf Sprecher bp)
                     pr. m by 1768 PHILIP KILTS
        1708: MARGARET   bp 29 Dec 1751; pr. m by 1770 JOHN PASSAGE
       +1709: pr. JOHN   b say 1753; m 1787 SYBILLA KRATCENBERG
       +1710: HENRICH H.   b say 1755; m by 1783 ANNA NELLIS
        1711: ANNA EVA   b SAL 9 Jul 1756 (Christ. Schults & w. Eva<Emige>)
        1712: CHRISTINA H.   b say 1758; m 1778 CARL ALEX. WERNER
        1713: ps. CATHERINE   b say 1760; m by 1788 HENRICH BRODT
        1714: ANNA   b SAR 19 Mar 1763 (sp Marg., w. of Jac. Boshaar)

1703: PETER CRIM <J> - pr. born before 1717; m by 1739 ELISABETH EMIGE (b ca
1716, d 8 Feb 1793 age 76-4-8) pr. a dau of Stone Arabia patentee JOHN EMIGE.
Peter was a sponsor for baptisms in 1751 & 1755 of sons of Adam Laux & Cath.
Elis. (Snell), and pr. for 1772 bp of Peter Eisenlord. Ps. the Peter in Col.
Klock's Regiment at the Oriskany battle in 1777.

        1715: MARGARET bp SA 14 Oct 1739 (H. Crim, Marg Crim, Chrstna Emig)
                     m by 1764 JOHN KAYSER
       +1716: DOROTHEA   b SA 1740 (sp. Jacob Shultz & w.)
                     m SA 26 Mar 1761 PHILIP W. FOX (son of Wm Sr.)
        1717: ANNA EVA   bp 23 Oct 1743 (sp Stofel Schulz & w. Eva)
       +1718: CATHERINE   b say 1745; ml HENRY LANDMAN; m2 1779 E. LEHMAN
        1719: ELISABETH   b say 1748; ml by 1768 JOHN EISENLORD
        1718A PETER jr.   b say 1752; m by 1778 CHRISTINA WARMOUTH
       +1720: JOHANNES   b 29 Jun 1756 (sp. Hannes Emigre & w. Elis.)
                     pr. m ANNA BELLINGER

                     -45-

1721: **PAUL CRIM** <P> - born in Germany 1730; died at Warren NY 1813; m 1750
MAGDALENA STEELE (d 1802) ps. a dau of ADAM STEELE. Hatch Papers (page 30) say he
came from Hesse Cassel Germany to Pennsylvania ca 1722 <sic., ps. Paul´s father
may have immigrated before 1730). Pr. before 1750, Paul purchased 1000 acres in
the Henderson Patent, then called by the Germans "Andrustown" and now in Warren
NY, in southern Herkimer County. By 1753 Paul Crim supposedly built the first log
house at Andrustown, where he had settled along with Frederick Bell, Frederick
Bell jr., Stephen Frank, George Hoyer, Fred Lepper, John Osterhout, George
Staring, & Jacob Wohleben (Paul Draheim article, Herkimer Evening Telegram,
7/16/1977). Due to French & Indian incursions about 1757, Paul withdrew to the
German Flats fort, but later returned to Andrustown, along with Adam Reese & John
Schaeffer. In 1767 Paul was in Capt. Conrad Frank´s GF militia unit, listed next
to Caspar Boner & Frederick Bell. John Powers, an Englishman and early Andrustown
resident, fled to Canada in the spring of 1778 and in July 1778 he may have guided
Joseph Brandt´s Tory raiding party in the infamous Andrustown massacre (Paul Crim
& his family narrowly escaped death by hiding in the woods).

    +1722: JACOB   1751-1830   m ELISABETH FRANK
     1723: MARIA CATHARINE   b say 1753; m by 1779 CONRAD KESSLER
    +1724: MARGARET   1755-1845   m GEORGE PASSAGE
    +1725: DOROTHY   1760-   m1 FRED BELL; m2 CONRAD SCHAEFFER
    +1726: HENRY   b 1762 (sp Nic. Wohlebn); m MARGARET KESSLER
    +1727: ADAM A.   b 1763 (bp Jan 1764, sp Adam Steele, Eva Staring)
                d 1844, m ELIZABETH HOOVER (1761-1836)
     1728: GERTRUDE   b GF 16 Jun 1765 (sp Gert. Steel, Died. Wohleben)
                liv. 1784 (spf Gert. Schaeffer bp)

CRIM - 3rd Genereation

1727: ADAM A. CRIM <P> - born 1763 (bp 31 Jan 1764); died 1844; m ELIZABETH HOOVER
(b 1761, d 1836). Ref. DAR vol 146 page 141.

    1728A ANNA   b SJR 6 Dec 1790 (sp John Huber & Gertrude)
    1729: JACOB ADAM   1795-1887   m CHRISTINA GARNER

1710: HENRICH H. CRIM <J> - pr. born ca 1745 to 1757; m by 1783 ANNA NELLIS. Was
sponsor for Feb 1783 bp of John, son of John Nellis & Anna.

    1730: ANNA   bp SA 30 Mar 1794 (sp Hen. Krems Sr. & Christina)

1726: HENDRICK P. CRIM <P> - born 12 Jan 1762; m before 1784 MARGARET KESSLER (b
ca 1763, d 1806 age 43). Pr. the Henrich on 1790 GF census (1-3-1).

    1730A pr. MAGDALENA   b say 1782; liv.1813 (spf Ang. Crim bp)
               pr. m by 1806 NICHOLAS SHOEMAKER
    1731: PETRUS   bp GF 8 Feb 1784 (sp Conrad Kessler & Cath.)
    1732: CATHERINE   b GF 5 Oct 1786 (sp. Adam Crim & Anna Kessler)
    1733: pr HENRY jr   1788-1858   m 1809 CATHERINE KESSLER (b 1789)
    +1734: pr. PAUL H.   b say 1790; m by 1812 MARIA BARBARA HELMER
    1735: ADAM   b GF 5 Feb 1791 (sp Adam Ries ...)
    1736: JOHANNES   b GF 19 Apr 1793 (sp John Osteroth & Cath.)
    1737: PHILIP   b GF 8 Apr 1795 (sp Phil. Kauder, Lena Passage)
    1737A MARGARET   b HK 7 Aug 1803 (sp John Eckler & Margaret)

1722: JACOB CRIM <P> - born Andrustown NY 1751; died 1830; m ELISABETH FRANK (b 1754, d 1813, DAR vol 129 page 80). Had 3 adults & 5 children on 1778 German Flats relief and was on 1790 GF census (1-3-4). At Warren NY in 1806.

    1738: pr. GERTRUDE JAC. b say 1770; m 1787 JOHANNES HEN. HUBER
  +1739: PAUL b GF 3 Jul 1776 (sp Fred Bell & Dorothea <Crim>)
    1740: MARIA CATHERINE b 6 Mar 1778 (sp Fred Harter, M. Cath Crim)
             m 1796 PHILIP PETER KAUDER
    1741: MARIA b May 1783 (sp John Wohlgmuth); m HENRY H. HARTER
    1742: JACOB jr 1787-1874 m EVE STAHRING (b 1797, d 1878)
    1743: GEORGE b GF 20 Mar 1792 (sp Geo. Fred. Haoyer & M. Elis.)
    1744: ANNA b 6 Dec 1794 (sp Johan .. Bell, Anna Osteroth)
    1745: EVA b GF 27 Oct 1795 (sp Hen. Bassage, Eva Osteroth)

1720: Sgt. JOHN P. GREMPS <J> - pr. the John born 29 Jun 1756 (son of Peter & Elisabeth, Bellinger book has him born 1758); died 3 Aug 1819; m ANNA BELLINGER (b 1758, d 1838) dau of Lt. JOHANNES BELLINGER & MARIA MAGDALENA KLOCK. In Col. Klock's Regiment at Oriskany battle 1777 (Bellinger book page 44).

    1746: ELIZABETH b GF 20 Dec 1783 (sp Geo. Laux & Elis.<Bellingr>)
    1747: MAGDALENA b 31 Jul 1786 (sp John Eisenlrd, Lena Joh Bellngr)
    1748: ANNA b SAR 6 Nov 1788 (sp Hen. Krems & w. Anna)
             (Bellinger book has sp. Hen. Kraus, Anna Laux)
    1749: CATHERINE b ca 1793; m AARON VEDDER
    1750: MARGARETHA b 30 Aug 1792 (sp Jac. Snell, Maria Scholl)
    1751: PETER moved to Van Buren Co., Michigan
    1752: MARY m JOHN REESE

1709: JOHANNES GREMS <J> - pr. born ca 1743 to 1755; m 1787 SYBILLA KRATCENBERG. Called "John Krems Sen." at bp of son John in 1787, so pr. not the John born ca 1762 (age 15 at Oriskany 1777, as in Bellinger HCH note# 1.28).

1718: CATHERINE CRIM - pr. born ca 1730 to 1760; ml HENRICH LANDMAN m2 Stone Arabia Luth. Church 21 Mar 1779 John EDWARD LEHMAN son of JOHN EDWARD LEHMAN.

1725: DOROTHY CRIM <P> - born 1760; died 26 Apr 1852 age 72 (sic., Petrie book page 24, pr. should read age 92); ml by 1776 FREDERICK BELL (killed at Andrustown 1778); m2 by 1782 CONRAD SCHAEFFER. A daughter by her second marriage was CHARITY SCHAEFFER (b 18 Feb 1784, d 1857, m JOSEPH PETRIE <1775-1821>)

CRIM - 4th Generation

1734: PAUL H. CRIM <P> - pr. born ca 1775 to 1791; m by 1812 MARIA BARBARA HELMER dau of ADAM HELMER & ANNA BELLINGER. Children born at Brutus, Cayoga Co., NY include DANIEL (b 5 Jan 1812, sp Joh. Adam Helmer & Anna), ANGELINA (b 7 Dec 1813, sp Magdal. Crim, Fred Hoyer), TIMOTHY (b 14 Nov 1815, sp Hen Crim jr & w Cath, Warren NY), and ANNA (b 15 Oct 1817, sp John Crim & Eva Helmer, Warren NY).

1739: PAUL JAC. CRIM <P> - born 1776 (Hatch Papers page 34); m Mar 1802 MARGARET FOX (b Dec 1782) dau of JOHN FOX. Was a shoemaker. Children were Jacob Paul (1802), John (1804), Henry (1805), Elizabeth, Paul P. (1809), Mary Katherine (1811), Hannah (1813), Stephen, Frederick, Eva Marie, Jeremiah, Margaret, & Chester.

1801: **WILLIAM CUNINGHAM** - pr. born ca 1700 to 1720; pr. m by 1737 MARGARET ...
(her name presumed from grand-daughter naming patterns). Pr. father of Dorothy,
Andreas, & John Cuningham, who were sister and brother as given in Deuel's notes
(Oneida Hist. Soc.). Later baptismal sponsorships suggest a relationship also
with William, Barbara (wife of Patrick Delaney), & Maria Cuningham (wife of Henry
Dygert). Wiliam was pr. related to the Henry Cunningham, who had a daughter
Margaret bp at Albany in 1747. There is a William Cuningham Patent shown on early
Burnetsfield maps and a tradition that Cuninghams were descended from a lord mayor
of Dublin Ireland.

surname CUNINGHAM

+1802: ps. MARGARET ca 1737-1807 m 1770 WILLIAM DYGERT
+1803: pr. BARBARA b say 1739; m by 1760 PATRICK DELANEY
+1804: pr. WILLIAM b say 1741; m by 1764 MARGARET CHRISTMAN
+1805: ANDREAS b say 1743; m 1766 BARBARA ELISABETH DOCKSTADER
 1806: DOROTHY b say 1745; m by 1763 ABRAHAM BAUM
+1807: JOHN b say 1747; m 1769 ANNA MARIA FOLTS
+1808: pr. MARIA b say 1749; m 1768 HENRICH DYGERT
+1809: ELISABETH b 1752; m by 1778 PETER DOCKSTADER

1810: HENRY CUNINGHAM - pr. born ca 1700 to 1727; m by 1747 MARGARET ... Living
at Albany NY in 1747.

 1811: MARGARET bp Albany NY 13 Dec 1747 (sp Wm & Cat. V Den Berg)
 1812: ps. CATHERINE b say 1749; m by 1769 GERRIT STAATS of Albany

----

CUNINGHAM - 2nd Generation

1805: **ANDREAS CUNINGHAM** - pr. born ca 1730 to 1750; died at Oriskany battle 6
Aug 1777; m Palatine NY 7 Jan 1766 BARBARA ELISABETH DOCKSTADER dau of GEORGE
DOCKSTADER & MAGDALENA WEAVER. In Capt. Petrie's GF militia co. in 1769.

 1814: CATHARINA b GF 27 Jul 1766 (sp Cat. Dckstdr, John Cuninghm)
+1815: WILLIAM b 18 Jan 1768; m FPL Nov 1791 MARY HOUSE
 1816: ELISABETH b SAR 10 Aug 1769 (Pet. Dockstdr, Elis. Cuninghm)
       ps. m 1786 DIETRICH M. DEMUTH
 1817: pr. ANDREW jr. b say 1773; liv. Aug 1791 (joined SA church)
 1818: ANNA MARGARETHA bp GF 14 Sep 1777 (sp John Dckstdr, Cath. Weber)

1807: **JOHN CUNINGHAM** - pr. born ca 1730 to 1750; m 28 Feb 1769 ANNA MARIA FOLTS
(b 1745, d Manlius NY 1802) dau of JACOB FOLTS & CATHERINE PETRIE. Sponsored,
with Cath. Getman, Nov 1765 bp of John, son of Marcus Edick & Barbara (Weaver).
In Capt. Mark Petrie's 1769 GF militia unit and was an early settler of Utica
(Deerfield) along with George DeMuth, Jacob Christman, & Abraham Baum. On 1790 GF
GF census (2-0-5) near Ab. Baum, W. Salis, Peter Dygert, & F. Bowman. He sold his
land there in 1793 and moved to Manlius NY.

+1819: pr. ANNA JOH. b say 1769; m 1785 DIETRICH STEELE
 1820: MARGARET b SA 1 Feb 1770 (sp Marg Cuningham, Conrad Folts)
           m by 1792 HENRY DYGERT (son of Peter)
+1821: ps. JOHN b say 1771; m REBECCA SCHNEIDER

1804: WILLIAM CUNINGHAM - pr. born ca 1725 to 1743; liv. 1790 (attested to will of George Demuth Mar 1790); m by 1764 MARGARET CHRISTMAN (Duell notes). He sponsored, with Anna Toll, 1760 bp at Schenectady of Annetje, dau of Jacob Ittig & Cath.(Frank). William & wife Margaret sponsored Aug 1768 bp of Margaret, dau of Jacob Christman & Ernestina (Bellinger), and Oct 1783 Albany bp of Margaret, dau of John Helmer & Catherine (Miller). At Palatine NY in 1764 (bp rec.) and later at Utica (Bellinger file# 4.45). On 1790 GF census (2-0-5) near F. Bowman, Salvea, Anna Demuth, ...

+1822: ps. JOHN b say 1761; m by 1790 MARGARET ...
1823: ANNA b SAR 6 Apr 1764 (sp Marg. Cuningham, Jacob Christman)
1824: MARIA b GF 5 Jul 1766 (sp Maria Cuninghm, John Christman)
1825: child b SAR 15 Nov 1768
+1826: MARGARET b Jan 1770 (sp Marg. & Fred. Getman)
m GF 20 Jun 1791 JOHANNES HISER
1827: CATHERINE b say 1774; d 1808; m 1792 JOHANNES CHRISTMAN
1828: EVA bp GF 4 Jan 1778 (sp Geo. Dygert & Anna)
ps. m 1797 NICHOLAS ARMSTRONG

1803: BARBARA CUNINGHAM - pr. born before 1745; m by 1760 PATRICK DELANEY. Children Anna (bp SCH 1760), Catherine (1763), & John (1765, sp John Cuningham).

1809: ELISABETH CUNINGHAM - born 1752; died 1829 age 52; m by 1778 PETER DOCKSTADER son of GEORGE DOCKSTADER & MAGDALENA WEAVER. Children were Catherine, George, William, John, Peter, Elisabeth, & Elijah.

1808: MARIA CUNINGHAM - m at Palatine NY 25 Oct 1768 HENRICH DYGERT (Teughardt). Had Jane (1768), Margaret (b 1770, sp. Wm & Marg. Cuningham), Maria, ...

1802: MARGARET CUNINGHAM - born ca 1737; died Herkimer NY 7 Nov 1807 (age 70); m SAR 1770 WILLIAM DYGERT (b 1723).

CUNINGHAM - 2nd Generation

1821: JOHN CUNINGHAM - pr. born ca 1760 to 1772; m by 1793 REBECCA SCHNEIDER. Had children Elisabeth (bp SJR 25 Aug 1793, sp. Thomas Young & Elisabeth) and Clarion (son, bp GF 24 Nov 1806). Lived at Canajoharie in 1793 (SJR bp rec.).

1822: JOHN CUNINGHAM (Konnikum on 1790 church rec.) - pr. born ca 1765 to 1772; m by 1790 MARGARET ... Ps. the John on 1790 Canajoharie census (1-2-3).

1829: RACHEL bp SJR Jul 1790 (sp Nic. Killes & Eva)

1815: WILLIAM CUNINGHAM - bp Palatine NY 19 Jan 1768 (son of Andrew); m at Minden NY 1 Nov 1791 MARY HOUSE dau of JOHN JOST HAUS. Had Cath. (b SAL Mar 1792).

1819: ANNA JOH. CUNINGHAM ("Johanna") - m German Flats NY 3 Nov 1785 Johan DIETRICH STEELE (Stahle). Sponsored 1779 bp of George, son of Marc DeMuth.

1826: MARGARET CUNINGHAM - pr. the Margaret born Jan 1770 (dau of Wm); had a child James (b GF 31 Jul 1790, sp Deit. Demuth & Elis.) by John Shutler of Schenectady.

********** DAVIS (DEVI) **********

1903: THOMAS DAVIS - pr. born ca 1670 to 1680, (ps. a son of DAVID CHRISTOFELSE who died in French & Indian raid on Schenectady NY 9 Feb 1690 as seen in Pearson´s "First Settlers of Albany"); liv. 1724; m Schenectady 14 Dec 1701 CATARINA KLEIN dau of JOHANNES KLEIN (Pearson´s Schenectady book, pg 53).

surname DAVIS
```
    1904: MARGARITA  bp Schencectady NY 18 Oct 1702
    1905: JOHANNES   bp 29 Apr 1705; ps. m by 1750 HANNAH HARRIS
   +1906: THOMAS  bp 16 Oct 1707
   +1907: LUDWIG (LEWIS) bp 4 May 1710; m 1731 MARIA CLEMENT
    1908: MARIA  bp 9 Oct 1715
    1909: WILLEM  bp 3 Sep 1721
   +1910: PETER  bp Schenectady NY 31 May 1724; m MARIA SALTSMAN
```

DAVIS - 2nd Generation

1911: JAMES DAVIS ("Ciems") - pr. born ca 1705 to 1723; m by 1742 MARIA ... Pr. father of the Capt. John James Davis (killed at Oriskany in 1777) and head of the Fonda NY branch. Other Davis men in Col. Fischer´s Revol. Regiment from the Fonda area were Isaac, Martinus, James jr, John, & Thomas. James & Maria sponsored May 1773 Fonda NY bp of Martinus, son of John Davis & Janitje.

```
    1915: pr. ELISABETH  b say 1740; m by 1763 PETER QUACKENBOSH
   +1916: JAMES bp SAR 1742;  m SAR Feb 1766 REBECCA VAN PRAAKEL
   +1917: JOHN JAMES  b say 1744; m 1763 JANITJE VEEDER
              a Capt. John James was killed at Oriskany 6 Aug 1777
    1918: pr. ISAAC  b say 1748; liv. 1768 (spf Davis bp)
    1919: pr. ABRAHAM  b say 1750; m by 1771 CATHERINE ROGERS
    1920: pr. CATHERINE  b say 1752; liv. 1768 (spf Davis bp)
              m by 1772 HENRICH LEWIS (bp 1744)
    1921: MARTINUS  b say 1756; killed at Oriskany 6 Aug 1777
    1922: pr. BENJAMIN  b say 1758; killed at Oriskany 6 Aug 1777
```

1923: JOHN DAVIS - pr. born ca 1700 to 1730; pr. m ELISABETH ... John & Elisabeth sponsored Jul 1768 SAR bp of John, son of Sander Luwis. Ps. the John Devi at Canajoharie NY ca 1742 (Book of Names page 60).

```
   +1925: ps. ADAM  b say 1755; m by 1782 CATHERINE ...
    1926: ps. MARIA  b say 1760; m by 1778 HENRY LEWIS (b ca 1758)
```

1907: LUDWIG DAVIS - bp Schenectady NY 4 May 1710; m Schenectady 14 May 1731 MARIA CLEMENT dau of PETER CLEMENT & ANNA RUYTING. Ps. his son Thomas was the Capt. killed at Oriskany in 1777.

```
    1927: CATHERINE  bp Schenectady NY 19 Sep 1731
    1928: ps. ANNETJE  b say 1733; m by 1754 FRANTZ PRUYN
    1929: THOMAS  b say 1737 & bp Ft. Hunter NY 27 May 1741
              (sp. John Clement, Lewis Clement, Elis. Powel)
    1930: JOHN  bp Ft. Hunter NY 19 Jul 1741 (sp John Quakenbos,
              sp. also Will Printup jr., Gertruy Quakenbos)
   +1930A ps. JACOB  b say 1750; m by 1781 CATHERINE RIEMENSNEIDER
```

1910: **PETER DAVIS** - bp Schenectady NY 31 May 1724; m by 1753 MARIA SALTSMAN dau
of GEORGE SALTSMAN & MARGARET. Peter was in Lt. Dygert´s 1757 militia, listed
next to Balt. Dillenbach & John Hecki, and he & his wife belonged to the Stone
Arabia Lutheran church in 1770. On 6 Feb 1781 Dr. William Petry´s records show he
treated three of Peter Davis´ daughters, who had been wounded by Tory Indian
raiders. Some trouble arises from a 1769 SAL church record recaping birthdates
for Catherine as 1749 (should be 1759 as SAL footnote fixes), Margaret as 1760
(should be 1761 to avoid overlap with Thomas) & Maria as 1763 (ps. 1753?).

    +1931: JOHN pr. b 5 Oct 1751 (bp 1757); ps m 1769 DOROTHY SNEIDER
     1932: MARIA bp SAL Apr 1753 (sp Mich. Saltsman & w. Maria); ps. d y
    1929A MAGDALENA b SAL Sep 1754 (sp Ludwig Devi & w Maria)
     1933: CHRISTINA b SAL Oct 1756 (sp And. Dillnbach, Christna Sltsmn)
      ps. m by 1780 MICHAEL CRANTZ
    +1934: pr. PETER b say 1758; m by 1781 ELISABETH SPOHN
     1935: CATHERINE pr. b SAL 2 Feb 1759 (sp Andr. Fink & w.)
     1936: THOMAS b SAR 3 May 1760; died 13 Jan 1769 (SAL)
      (1760 sp Tho. Davis widower, Otila w. of Tho. Gilly)
     1937: MARGARET pr. b 15 Apr 1761 (rec. has 1760 but is doubtful)
      (SAL bp sp. Wm Caselman & w. <Marg Saltsman>)
     1938: GEORGE b SAR 12 May 1762; in Revol. service
     1939: pr. MARIA b SAL 9 Apr 1763 (sp Mich. Saltsman & w.)
     1940: WILLIAM b SAR 5 Feb 1764 (sp Wm Nellis & M. Doro.<Saltsmn>)
     1941: ELISABETH b SAR 13 Oct 1765; liv. 1783 (spf Davis bp)
     1942: HENRICH P. b SAR 6 Mar 1768 (sp Barb Shults, Hen. Dillenbch)
     1943: ANNA P. b SAL 2 Jul 1769 (sp Wm Nellis jr, Marg. Dillenbach)
      m 1785 PETER WALTZ (WALS)
     1944: THOMAS P. b 9 Jan 1772 (sp Wm Gutbrod, Maria Schultz)
      pr. m by 1805 MARIA CAMPBELL
     1945: MICHAEL P. b 15 May 1773 (sp Bern. Kaiser, Barb. Emigin)

1906: **THOMAS DAVIS** - ps. the Thomas bp SCH 16 Oct 1707; m RACHEL PICKARD. Ps.
the widower Thomas who sponsored May 1760 bp of Thomas, son of Peter Davis.

     1945A EVA T. b say 1734; liv. 1760 (spf Wallrath bp)
   +1945B JOHN 1739-1780 m by 1763 MARIA ... (pr. HELMER)
   +1946A ps. JOST HENRY b say 1750; m by 1787 CATHERINE BARTRAM
     1946B ps. DANIEL b say 1754; at Oriskany in 1777 (Book of Names)

DAVIS - 3rd Generation

1925: ADAM DAVIS - pr. born ca 1745 to 1757; m by 1782 CATHERINE ... An Adam
Davis sponsored, with Anna Haus, Sep 1770 SAL bp of Adam, son of Geo. Fred. Knaus.
An Adam, Jacob, & Joseph Davis were in Col. Klock´s Revol. Regiment.

     1947: JOHANNES b GF 14 Jan 1782 (sp Pet. Lambrt, Lena Zolngr)
     1948: DANIEL b GF 11 Oct 1784 (sp Leon. Horning, Elis. Brockman)

1946A JOST HENRY DAVIS - ps. born ca 1750 & died 1836 (age 86, as seen in Petrie
book, pg 36); m by 1787 CATHERINE BARTRAM. Jost Henrich Debus was on a Tryon Co.
census ca 1776, apparently living near Fairfield or Sniedersbush with wife & 1
girl under age 16 (Mohawk Valley in the Revolution, pg 154). He was probably the
same man as called HENRY DEBUS (see page 291). Had son Christian (bp Schenectady
NY 25 Feb 1787).

1930A JACOB DAVIS - pr. born ca 1740 to 1754; m CATHERINE RIEMENSNEIDER (Pearson´s
Schenectady book) pr. dau of HENRY RIEMENSNEIDER. The dates and wife fit the man
whom the Petrie book (page 36) calls JOST HENRY DAVIS (b 1750, d 10 Feb 1836 age
86) & says m Cath. Riemensneider (b ca 1758, d 10 May 1839 age 81); but there was
a separate Jost Henrich Davis (m Catherine Bartram) and another man called the
late Jost Davis (with Jacob in Klock´s Revol. Reg.) when his daughter was a POW ca
1780 (Book of Names, pg 114). Jacob Davis was a German Flats resident in May 1775
and on 1790 Palatine NY census (1-5-1). Called Jacob DeBus in the GF church
records. If we add boys Jacob (bp 1778) & Ludwig (bp 1785), we obtain the 1790
census count of five (see DEBUS on page 291 of this book).

      1949: ROBERT BOHANNAN bp Schenectady NY 13 Oct 1781
      1950: HENDRICK bp Schenectady NY 13 Oct 1781
      1951: pr. DANIEL 1788-1862 m CATHERINE RITTER
      1952: JOHN JAC. b say 1790; m 1814 MARGARET MEYER

1917: JOHN DAVIS (called Johan Jost in Mohawk Valley in the Revol., page 234) -
pr. born ca 1730 to 1745; m SAR 4 Jun 1763 JANITJE VEEDER dau of JOHN VEEDER &
ELISABETH (from 1803 will of John Veeder).

      1953: MARIA b SAR 1 Nov 1768 (sp. Cath. Davis, Isaac Davis)
      1954: MARTINUS b FR 23 May 1773 (sp James Davis & Maria)
      1955: JOHN VEEDER b FNR 18 Oct 1775; m 1798 NANCY QUACKENBOS
      1956: SARAH b FNR 25 Oct 1777

1931: JOHN DAVIS - ps. the John (son of Peter & Maria) born SAL 5 Oct 1751; m SAL
21 Jan 1769 DOROTHEA SYBILLA SCHNEIDER. A John Davis sponsored, with Eva Emige,
Jan 1771 SAL bp of Anna Eva, dau of John Casselman. A John Davis & Sara (sic)
sponsored Sep 1781 GF bp of Annatje, dau of Jacob Bottman.

1945B JOHN DAVIS (DAVY) - born 4 Jan 1739; died 29 Oct 1780 (Dr. Beatrice Gram
notes and Book of Names page 168); m by 1767 "MARIA WELMER" who was pr. ANNA
MARIA HELMER dau of ADAM HELMER & MARGARET. Pr. the John in Bellinger´s 4th Tryon
Co. Regiment, along with a George & Peter Davis. John Davis had 2 adults & 6
children on 1778 GF relief and his widow was pr. the Mary Davy on the 1790
Canajoharie NY census (0-1-5).

      1957: MARGARET b GF 3 Mar 1767 (sp. Marg. Meyer, Joh. Helmer)
      1958: CATHERINE b SAR 15 Aug 1768 (sp. Fred. Reigel & Cath.)
      1959: JOHANNES b GF 26 Jun 1776 (sp. Philip Helmer & Anna <Meyer>)
                m1 1801 BARBARA MOYER
      1960: ANNA b GF 2 Sep 1779 (sp. John Kessler & Gertrude <Helmer>)

1934: PETER DAVIS - pr. born ca 1750 to 1759; ml by 1781 ELISABETH SPOHN dau of
NICHOLAS SPOHN & ELISABETH DIEVENDORF; m2 GF 30 Dec 1792 MARIA HILLER dau of JOHN
HILLER. Sponsored 1785 bp of Elis., dau of Conrad Eigenauer & Anna (Spohn). On
1790 Herkimer Census (1-1-5) near Nich. Spohn.

      1961: CATHERINE b GF 27 Oct 1781 (sp John Dvndorf & Cath. Spohn)
      1962: GEORGE b 24 Sep 1783 (sp Nic. Spohn & Elis. Davis)
      1963: SUSANNA P. b 12 Jun 1785 (sp. Hen Davis, Anna Moog)
                m 1807 JACOB HILTS
      1964: ELISABETH b 17 Mar 1787 (sp Hen. Spohn, Cath. Nellis)
      1965: MARIA b GF Aug 1792 (sp Nic. Spohn & Cath.)
                by 2nd wife
      1966: ANNA b GF 29 Dec 1793 (sp Pet. Hiller, Anna Joh. Hess)

********** DEMUTH **********

2001: **JACOB DEMUTH** - pr. born ca 1650 to 1665; ps. m1 ... ; pr. m2 in NY MARIA
THONIUS (Maria "Deunes" widow of Jacob DeMot m2 at Kingston NY 1723 Peek DeWit).
Was on the NY Palatine subs. list in 1710 (4A,2Y) & in 1712 (5A,0Y) and was pr.
the Jacob Dimouth in the 1710 West Camp list with 1 boy (age 9-15) & 2 girls (age
9-15). The counts for adults and dependents don't seem to quite square with the
kids below, even with Cordelia off in the Petrie househdold. A guess that this
Jacob was the one at at Beckmansland on the 1717 Simmendinger census, with a wife
& 3 children. Also seen on NY Palatine subs. list were Anna Maria Demuth (single
adult in 1710) and Agnes Demuth (two adults in 1710, one was ps. the PETER DEMOTT,
age 13 in 1711, who was bound out to Cornelis Wyckoff of the Flatlands in Apr 1711
<and the Peter DeMuth at Hackinsack on the 1717 Simmendinger census>).

                         surname DEMUTH
     2002: CORDELIA   b say 1688; m by 1710 Johan JOST PETRIE
    +2003: pr. DEITRICH   b say 1696; liv. 1712 (first communion)
     2004: ps. DOROTHEA   b say 1698; m 1717 JOHAN FREDERICK
    +2005: ps. JOST   b say 1700; liv. 1723 (got Burnetsfield lot)
     2006: ps. ANNA   b say 1702; liv. 1715 (spf P. Meyer bp)

2007: **ANNA CATHERINE DEMUTH** - A widow, pr. of Alexander Demuth, she was on NY
Palatine subsistence list in 1710 (4A,0Y) & 1712 (4A,0Y) with son George.

    +2008: GEORGE   b say 1691; pr. m 1714 MARGARETHA DOPF
    +2009: ps. JACOB   b say 1693; at Hackensack 1717 (Simmendinger list)
                       m Elisabeth ... (they had 3 children in 1717)
     2010: ps. FREDERICK   b say 1700; liv. 1714 New Town (1st communion)
                       ps. m CHARLOTTA ... (had Conrad & Elis. bp NYC 1733-6)

                      DEMUTH - 2nd Generation

2003: **DIETRICH DEMUTH** - pr. born ca 1695 to 1699 (had first communion at
Queensberg in 1712, Book of Names page 39); liv. 1742 (early GF Luth. Church list,
page 61 of Book of Names); pr. m a GERTRUDE ... (her name a guess based on
descendent naming patterns, ps. a Petrie judging from names of supposed children
below). In 1723 "Tegrigh Timuth" got Burnetsfield lot #17 and he was pr. married
by then as his lot was in the heads of household area.

     2011: ps. ELISABETH (Demuth?)   b say 1725; m JOHANNES PETRIE
    +2012: pr. JOHANNES   b say 1728; m1 1766 ELISABETH FOLTS (b 1741)
     2013: ps. JOST   b say 1730; liv. 1757 (Petrie's GF militia unit)
                      pr. d ca 1757-61; m DELIA ... (she m2 1762 F. Lepper)
    +2014: pr. MARCUS   b say 1733; m by 1760 CATHERINE ...
    +2015: pr. DIETRICH   (Marcs' broth.) b say 1737; m by 1776 APPOLONIA
    +2016: pr. GEORGE   b say 1740; m ANNA ... ; in Revol. service
     2017: pr. GERTRUDE   b say 1743; m 1764 NICHOLAS J. WEAVER

2008: **GEORGE DEMUTH** - m (as son of the late Alexander) 26 Oct 1714 MARGRETHA DOPF
dau of PETER DOPF. On 1717 Simmendinger census at Heesberg with wife & ch.

     2018: ELISABETH   bp Kingston NY 3 Jul 1714 (sp. Joh. & Elis. Lamet)
     2019: Johan PETER   bp Rhinebeck NY 25 Mar 1720

                              -53-

2005: **JOST DEMUTH** - pr. born ca 1690 to 1705; m ... (ps. an Elisabeth, viewing Folts children´s names). In 1723 he may be the Jost who got Dietrich DeMuth´s dependent area lot #12 at Burnetsfield, but that seems a bit unusual as most patentees assigned their second lot to a son or a wife. If the Burnetsfield Jost was a son of Dietrich, perhaps we should question the Folts tradition that a Jost was father of Conrad Folts´ wife (Catherine, b 1722). The John Jost DeMuth in Petrie´s 1757 GF militia was ps. a son of this Jost or of Dietrich (if Johan Jost).

```
        2020:  pr. CATHERINE  1722-1765  m CONRAD FOLTS
        2020A  ps. JOHN JOST  b say 1732; in 1757 GF militia
        2020B  ps. JOST  b say 1736; m by 1784 SARA ... (spf Demuth bp)
       +2020C  ps. FREDERICK  b say 1740; m by 1776 ...
```

DEMUTH - 3rd Generation

2015: DIETRICH DEMUTH - pr. born ca 1740 to 1755; m by 1776 APPOLONIA ...

```
        2021:  DIETRICH  bp GF 3 Nov 1776 (sp Adam Bellngr & Mar. Elis.)
        2022:  child  bp GF Jul 1784 (bp Feb 1785, sp Jost DeMuth & ...)
        2023:  CATHERINE  bp 15 Jan 1788 (sp Fred DeMuth, Cath Riegel)
        2024:  SARA  bp GF 17 Feb 1790 (sp Jost DeMuth & Sara)
```

2020C FREDERICK DEMUTH - pr. born before 1755; m by 1776 ... Appears on Tryon Co. census ca 1776 next to George Demuth in northeast Herkimer area, with 1 male & female (age 16-50) and 1 boy & 1 girl (Mohawk Valley in the Revolution, pg 155).

```
       +2024A  ps. JOHANNES  b say 1775; m 1794 ANNA J. NIC. WEAVER
```

2016: Capt. GEORGE DEMUTH - pr. born before 1745; died ca 1789; m by 1766 ANNA ... (pr. a Weaver). Adjutant of Bellinger´s Revol. Regiment. In his will dated 1788 he calls himself "George Deamewood" and names wife Hannah and grown daughters Gertrude & Catherine, plus (minors) Anna, Elisabeth, Maria, & Margret. Also named were "eldest son George, second son Nicholas, third son John, & fourth son Richard", plus his loving friends John Smith & Melger Folts (wit. by Wm Cuningham, John Christman, & Elija Freeman). Descendants in Perth Amboy New Jersey (Book of Names page 170). Widow Anna on 1790 GF census (1-3-5).

```
        2025:  DIETRICH  bp GF 4 Aug 1766 (John Demuth, Elis. Folts); pr d y
        2026:  GERTRUDE  bp 19 Jan 1768; m 1786 JOHANNES DIET. PETRIE
       +2027:  GEORGE  bp 7 Feb 1769; pr. m 1790 CATHERINE JAC. CHRISTMAN
        2028:  NICHOLAS  bp Palatine NY 7 Jul 1770 (sp Nich. Weber & Marg.)
        2029:  CATHERINE  1770-1850  m FREDERICK REALS (Riegel)
        2030:  RICHARD (Dietrich)  b say 1774; liv. 1788 (father´s will)
        2031:  ANNA  bp GF 14 Jul 1776 (sp Pet. Weber, Gert. Bellngr)
                     dau of Geo. & "Elisabeth"; liv. 1803 (Herk. Ch. Confirm.)
        2032:  PETER  b GF 20 Jun 1780 (sp John Kessler & Cath.<Shoemkr>)
        2033:  JOHANNES  b GF 28 Jul 1782 (sp John Dockstr & Cath.<Bellngr>)
        2034:  ELISABETH  b 6 Mar 1784 (sp Diet. Petrie & Elis); liv. 1788
                     m 1802 PETER JOH. MEYER
        2035:  MARIA  b say 1786; liv. 1788
        2036:  MARGARET  b 21 Sep 1787 (sp Marc. DeMuth & Marg.); liv. 1788
```

2012: JOHANNES DEMUTH - pr. born before 1742; died HK 17 Nov 1810; m1 1766
ELIZABETH FOLTS (b 1741) dau of JACOB FOLTS & CATHERINE PETRIE; m2 after Aug 1777
ELISABETH DYGERT (b 1749, d 1815) dau of WILLIAM DYGERT & ELISABETH ECKER and
widow of FRED. HELMER. John was in 1769 GF militia, had 3 adults & 2 children on
1778 GF relief, and was on 1790 HK census (1-1-2). He held Diet. Demuth's
Burnetsfield lot #17 in 1791.

>   2037: pr. PETER J. b say 1768; m FR 1786 SARAH PUTMAN

2014: Capt. MARCUS DEMUTH - pr. born ca 1743 (DAR v 16, page 8, says born on Long
Island NY); living 1789 (spf Oct 1789 bp of Gertrude, dau of Jacob Christman); m
CATHERINE ... (liv. Oct 1789). Sgt in 1769 GF militia and Captain of Rangers in
Bellinger's Regimen (he was shot in the arm and taken prisoner at German Flats in
1780). Marc had 5 adults & 6 children on the 1778 GF relief and was on 1790
Herkimer census (3-2-3), near Deerfield area Riegel & Weavers.

>   2039: MARGARET b 12 Apr 1760 (Jost C. Folts, Marg. Joh Christmn)
>   2040: ps. MARCUS b say 1762; soldier in Col. Bellinger's Regiment
>   2041: FREDERICK b SAR 5 Sep 1764 (sp Joh. Demuth, Marg. Christmn)
>   +2042: CATHERINE 1766-1811 m NICHOLAS HARTER
>   (Dec 1766 bp sp Maria Elis. & George Nellis, married)
>   +2043: DIETRICH M. b say 1768; m 1786 ELISABETH CUNINGHAM
>   2044: GERTRUDE b say 1772; m 1791 SAM ROCHELLE (or Russell)
>   2045: GEORGE b 8 Feb 1779 (sp. Geo. Mich. Weber, Anna Cuningham)
>   +2046: ps. PHILIP 1790-1884 m1 MARY DEMUTH

DEMUTH - 4th Generation

2043: DIETRICH M. DEMUTH (Richard) - pr. born ca 1755 to 1769; m 28 Feb 1786
ELISABETH CUNINGHAM (b 1769) dau of ANDREW CUNINGHAM (Deuel notes). Joh. Diet.
Demuth & Elisabeth were sponsors for 1792 bp of Nicholas, son of Nicholas Harter &
Cath. Demuth. In Col. Bellinger's Revol. Regiment.

>   2047: CATHERINE b GF 18 Jan 1788 (sp Capt Marc DeMuth & Cath)
>   2048: ELISABETH b GF 16 Sep 1789 (sp Joh Christman, Cath. Cuninghm)
>   2049: EVA bp 15 Aug 1792; d 1825; m GEORGE FOLTS jr.
>   2050: MARIA b GF 22 Oct 1794 (sp Nic. Staring & Maria)
>   2051: GEORGE R. b 1809; m CORNELIA HARVEY

2027: GEORGE DEMUTH - bp SAR 7 Feb 1769 (sp Johan Nich. Sm..<Smith>, Maria Elis.
Dockstader); pr. m 2 Oct 1790 CATHERINE JAC. CHRISTMAN (b 1770) dau of JACOB
CHRISTMAN & ERNESTINA BELLINGER. Had daughters ANNA (bp GF 21 Oct 1794, sp. Pet.
Christman, Anna DeMuth) and MARIA (b HK May 1808).

2024A JOHANNES DEMUTH - born say 1775; m 14 Jan 1794 ANNA J. NIC. WEAVER pr. dau
of NICHOLAS WEAVER & GERTRUDE DEMUTH. Children include GERTRUDE (b GF 2 Jul
1795, sp. Diet. DeMuth, Marg. Weaver) and ALLEN (b HK 1 Aug 1808, sp. Nich. Weaver
& w. Gertrude).

2046: PHILIP DEMUTH - born 21 Apr 1790; died nr. Sac City Iowa 1884; m1 his cousin
MARY DEMUTH; m2 CATHERINE MOWER. Letter of granddaughter Katherine Demuth Voth in
1941 to Cdmr. L. Bellinger said her great-grandfather was supposedly a captain and
scout in the Revolution and had a friend named Adam Helmer.

2101: GEORGE DOCKSTADER <D1> - pr. born in Germany ca 1679 (on Jun 1709 London list of Palatines as George Tachfetter, Lutheran farmer aged 30, with son age 3, as in Book of Names page 109 <H. Jones reads son's age as 1/3>); living Aug 1734 (minister's visit to GF, Vosburgh's HK Church Rec. vol 3, page 46); m ANNA ELISABETH ...   On NY Palatine subsistence list in 1710 (2A,1Y) & 1712 (2A,2Y) and on 1717 Simmendinger census with wife Anna Elisabeth & 4 children. About 1723 he drew Burnetsfield lot #18 and in 1730 purchased lot #21 from Leonard Helmer. Designations in brackets, such as <D1>, are a cross reference to an individual's assigned number in the Dockstader book ("The Dockstader Family" by Doris Dockstader Rooney, 1918 La Mesa Drive, Dodge City, Kansas 67801; pub. 1983).

surname DOCKSTADER

```
+2102: GEORGE ADAM  b ca 1709; m by 1728 CATHERINE STAHRING
+2103: CORNELIUS  b say 1711; m an Indian squaw
+2104: HEINRICH  1714-1774  m CATHERINE VAN ANTWERPEN
+2105: CHRISTIAN  b say 1715;  m CATRINA NELLIS
+2106: FREDERICK  b 14 May 1717; m ANNA ELISABET STAHRING
 2107: ps. DIRKJE  b say 1719; m ALBERT VAN DEWERKEN
 2107A ps. ANNA (Dockstader?)  m by ca 1738 NICHOLAS STAHRING
 2108: pr. PETER  b ca 1723; died Adams NY 1 Dec 1813 age 90
 2109: BARBARA ELISABETH  ca 1724-1812 m 1750 Johan PETER WAGNER
 2110: pr. JOHN  b say 1726; liv. 1754 (sold land to Jac. N. Weber)
          a John Dockstader was deeded Burnetsfield lot #21
          by George Dockstader in 1753 and sold one acre
          thereupon to Jacob N. Weaver in 1754.
 2111: ps. CATHERINE (Dockstader?)  b say 1729; m JACOB N. WEAVER
 2112: pr. LEONARD  b say 1732; liv. ca 1743 (Book of Names page 61)
          as a child of a Jurgen Dachstater "at the Fall";
          pr. died by 1760 (no Leonard G. seen post-1760)
```

DOCKSTADER - 2nd Generation

2105: CHRISTIAN DOCKSTADER <D8> - pr. born ca 1715 to 1725; m CATHERINE NELLIS dau of WILLIAM NELLIS & MARGARET KLOCK. On 1790 Canajoharie census (1-1-3).

```
 2113: ANNA SABINA  b say 1743; m 1760 JACOB C. LEIPER
 2114: CATHERINE CHR.  b say 1746; liv. 1760 (spf Cath. Nellis bp)
          m 1764 JOHN CHRISTMAN
 2115: MAGADALENA  bp Palatine NY 26 Jan 1755; m 1772 JOHN BACKUS
 2116: BARBARA (twin)  b 20 Jan 1760 (sp Barb. Dygert, Jac. Lepper)
          m 1783 JOHN M. COUNTRYMAN
 2117: MARIA   (twin)  b SAR Jan 1760 (sp Hen. Merckel, Adam Emgie)
          pr. m GF 1782 JACOB KELLER
 2118: JOHN  b SAR 25 Dec 1763 (sp Hen. Nellis & Marg.); m CATHERINE
          (pr. m GF Jan 1786 CATHARINE H. ECKER)
 2119: ps. (?) WILLIAM  b say 1780; m by 1812 CATHERINE CHRISTMAN
          (pr. Wm was a son of John Chr. rather than a brother)
          (Rev. Spinner's "avunculus" was sometimes a grandfather!)
```

2103: CORNELIUS DOCKSTADER <D3> - pr. born ca 1710 to 1717; m ..., a Mohawk or Oneida Indian woman. His sons George & Joseph were Indians of influence in the Oneida tribe as well as patriot soldiers in the Revolution (cont. on page 291).

2106: FREDERICK DOCKSTADER <D5> - born Schoharie NY 14 May 1717 (sp. Fred.
Schaester & wife); m ANNA ELISABETH STAHRING. Ref. for dau Barbara is "The Van
Derwerken Family" by Paul W. Prindle (1966) page 87.

+2120: FREDERICK b say 1745; m 1767 MARIA CATHERINE J. WALLRATH
 2121: BARBARA b say 1749; m SAR Dec 1767 ALBERT J. VANDERWERKEN
+2122: JOHN F. 1751-1839 m BARBARA ELISABETH WEAVER
+2123: NICHOLAS b 1752; m by ca 1780 MARGARET ... at Oppenheim NY
 2124: ANNETJE b ca 1754; liv. 1772 (spf VanDerWerken bp)
 2125: CATHERINE b SAL 14 Mar 1756 (sp Jerg Adam Dckstdr & Cath)
        m JACOB REESE (Reis)
 2126: GERTRUDE b ca 1758; m by 1775 JACOB WALLRATH
 2127: GEORGE bp SAR 3 Jan 1762 (sp. Geo Adam Dockstdr & w. Eva)
        m 1781 MAGDALENA REESE
 2128: LEONARD F. b say 1763; liv. 1791 (spf Dockstadr bp)

2102: GEORGE ADAM DOCKSTADER (aka ADAM) <D2> - pr. born ca 1709 (age 1/3 then);
died 6 Jun 1791 (rec. Christ Church, Montreal Canada); m CATHERINE STAHRING (b
say 1713) pr. dau of NICHOLAS STAHRING & MARIA CATHERINE. Sponsored Feb 1754 SAL
bp of Henrich, son of Andries Franck. We assume George Adam had no children
before 1728 when his age was ca 18 and his wife pr. ca 15-16.

+2129: GEORGE 1728-1808 m pr. by 1747 MAGDALENA WEAVER
+2130: ps. HENDRICK b say 1732; m 1758 MAGDALENA WEAVER
 2131: ABRAM b say 1735 (b 1726, Dkstdr ms.); m EVA
+2132: GEORGE ADAM b say 1740; m 1760 EVA BERLETHS
+2133: MARCUS G. b say 1742; m 1761 ELISABETH SCHULTZ
+2134: NICHOLAS b say 1744; m 1765 CATHERINE VANDERWERKEN
 2135: MARIA ELISABETH b say 1746; liv. 1760 (spf John G Dckstdr bp)
        m 1763 JOHN ECKER
 2135A ps. MARIA b say 1748; m SAR 1768 JOHN DUNN
 2136: SARAH b say 1750; m 1773 THOMAS WHITAKER
 2137: CATHARINE bp SAR 18 Jan 1752 (sp. Hen. Dockstdr & w. Cath.)
        m 1775 JACOB Y. TRUAX
 2138: FREDERICK b SAL 29 May 1755 (son of George Adam & Cath.)
        (sp. Fred. Dockstader & w. Elisabeth)

2104: HENRICH DOCKSTADER <D4> - pr. born 1714; died 1774 (birth & death dates
from family tradition, Dockstader book page 10); m 1732 CATHERINE ANTWERP (b 1714,
d 1789 <Prindle's The Van Derwerken Family>); ps. m2 CATHERINE WEAVER. A Henrich
& wife Catherine sponsored the 1752 SAR bp of Cath. (G. Ad.) Dockstader and the
1756 SAL bp of Cath. (Joh.) Leder, but neither record tries to further identify
sponsor Henrich (we think a Sr. or Jr. would be in order if another couple named
Henrich & Cath. <Weaver> were also living then).

 2139: JELLIS H. 1732-1787 m 1748 MARY FELTER (d 1797)
+2139A pr. ADAM (aka GEORGE ADAM) b say 1734; liv. 1762
        (spf 1762 G A Dockstdr jr bp); m by 1774 MARIA PHILIPS
 2139B pr. HERMANUS b say 1736 (Dockstader book has b ca 1746)
+2140: ps. HENRICH <diff. man?> m by say 1745 CATHERINE WEAVER
 2143: pr. BARBARA H. b say 1744; liv. Nov 1761 (spf Galinger bp)
+2144: ps. NICHOLAS b ca 1746; m 1772 DOROTHY VANDERWERKEN
 .... ps. also George, Jacob, Cath., Fred., ... <see #2410 next gen.>

2139A ADAM DOCKSTADER - pr. born ca 1730 to 1752; m MARIA PHILIPSE

    2146: PHILIP b Fonda NY 14 Mar 1774 (sp Geo. Fyles & Anna)

2120: FREDERICK F. DOCKSTADER <D26> - pr. born ca 1740 to 1747; m SAR 15 Sep 1767
MARIA CATHERINE J. WALLRATH pr. dau of JOHN WALLRATH. Pr. the Fred. F. Dockstader
on the 1790 Caughnawaga (Fonda) NY census (3-0-2).

    2147: JACOB b 8 Sep 1768; d 1844; ml MARIA ECKER
    2148: LENNERT b SAR 5 Sep 1770 (sp Lennert Dockstader & Anna)
    2149: ELISABETH bp Fonda 21 Nov 1772 (sp H. Dockstdr jr & Elis.)
           m 1795 HERMANUS M. EHLE
    2150: JOHN b FR 2 May 1775 (sp John Dckstdr & Barbara)
    2151: FREDERICK b 24 Aug 1777; pr. d. young
    2152: AMALIA b 7 Nov 1779; m 1823 JOHN FOX
    2153: FREDERICK b 12 Jan 1782; m SARAH WEMPLE
    2154: JOHN b 25 Oct 1784; m 1814 MARIA CASSELMAN
    2155: HERMANUS b say 1790; m 1817 HANNAH VAN EPS

2129: GEORGE DOCKSTADER <D13> - born Stone Arabia NY 1728 (son of George Adam,
birthdate calc. from age at death); died Jefferson Co. NY 29 Feb 1808 at age 80; m
pr. by 1746 MARIA MAGDALENA WEAVER pr. a dau of NICHOLAS WEAVER & BARBARA (as
suggested by children names below, while Dockstader book has her a dau of JACOB
WEAVER). George was living at German Flats by 1757 when his children were
captured in the French & Indian raid (E&N 9/9/1936). The Indians were reluctant
to kill his eccentric son George and instead assigned him to watch over their
children (which he is said to have put onto pieces of wood and pushed off to drown
in a lake). George was the only Dockstader in the 1769 GF militia and on the 1778
GF relief (with 4 adults). In a 1774 document he appointed his brother Hendrick
as agent to recover money from his brother George Adam (Dockstader book page 17).
Pr. was the George taken prisoner in arms at German Flats (Book of Names page 166)
and released in 1782 at age 65 (Dockstader book, but we the age seems overstated
by 12 years or so!). His household on the 1790 Herkimer census (4-6-6) not doubt
includes the families of his married sons John & Peter.

    2156: GEORGE b say 1746; liv. 1757 (eccentric or mentally retarded)
    2157: BARBARA ELISABETH b say 1748; m 1766 ANDREW CUNINGHAM
    2158: CATHERINE 1749-1824 m LORENTZ HARTER
  +2159: PETER ca 1750-1842 m ELISABETH CUNINGHAM
    2160: ps. MARY b say 1752; ps. m MICHAEL HARTER (?, E&N 9/9/1936)
    2161: pr. ELISABETH b say 1754; liv. 1769 (spf Demuth bp)
    2162: pr. FREDERICK b say 1756; ps. d. y. (no further record)
  +2163: JOHN b SA 13 Aug 1760 (sp. Fred., Elis. Dockstdr)
           pr. d 1815 and m CATHERINA BELLINGER
    2164: GERTRUDE bp 16 Jul 1763 (sp Ger. DeMuth, Nicol <Jac.> Weber)
    2165: Johan NICHOLAS bp GF 1765 (sp. George Smidt, Marg. Weber)

2132: GEORGE ADAM DOCKSTADER <D14> - pr. born ca 1732 to 1742 (son of George
Adam); m at Stone Arabia 2 Dec 1760 EVA BERLETHS (Eva aka Ballantine) dau of JOHN
WOLFGANG BERLET & ANNA BARBARA. He went to Canada as a Loyalist in the Revolution
and as a result his lands at Caughnawaga NY were confiscated.

    2166: GEO. ADAM b SAR Feb 1762 (Dockstdrs- Geo Adam H, M Elis G A)
           children cont. next page -->

```
               children of George Adam & Eva, cont.
   2167: MARGARET   b SAR 6 Mar 1764 (sp Elis. .., Nic. Dockstader)
                    m 1783 THOMAS SULLIVAN
   2168: JOHN   b SA 4 Aug 1766; pr. d Canada 1854 age 94 (sic.)
              pr. this John m Montreal Can. ca 1790 CECILIA LEROY
   2169: CATHERINE   b ca 1767
   2170: FREDERICK   b FR 24 Mar 1774 (sp Fr. Dckstdr & Cath); d 1792
   2171: HENRY   (HENDRIK)   bp Fonda NY 9 Mar 1777
   2172: MARY   b 29 Aug 1779; m 1796 Montreal Can. JOHN TEASDALE
   2173: LENA   b Montreal Canada 3 Apr 1785
```

2140: HENRICH DOCKSTADER <D10> - Dockstader book gives no birth or death dates and
we strongly suspect this was the same man as the earlier Henrich (#2104, m Cath.
Antwerp); pr. died bef. 1790 (not on Mont. Co. census); m CATHERINE WEAVER, who
the Dockstader book calls a dau of JACOB WEAVER & ELISABETH, but we lean to
placing as a dau of NICHOLAS WEAVER & BARBARA (as we feel Jacob's Catherine went
to Peter Pfeiffer). Dockstader researchers may have assumed this man was the
Henrich J. Dockstader, who with wife Catherine, sponsored the Aug 1791 FNR bp of
Catherine, dau of Fred H. Dockstader & Maria (Ecker), but we think the 1791 Henry
J. was the son of a John (ps. of John & Maria <Service>?).

```
   2174: HENRY H.   b ca 1740; liv. 1761 (spf Everson bp)
                    m 1767 ELISABETH ECKER (had son Jacob b 1768)
  +2176: pr. GEORGE H.   b say 1742; d 1808; m 1765 BARBARA SCHULTZ
   .... ps. also ... Barbara, Nicholas <see #2104 prior gen.>
   2178: JACOB H.   b ca 1748
   2179: CATHERINE   b 1750; m 1771 DANIEL SERVICE
  +2180: FREDERICK H.   bp 6 Jul 1751 (sp. Fred. Docksdr & w. Elis.)
                    m 1773 MARIA ECKER
   2181: LEONARD H.   b say 1754; m 1775 ANNA REIS
   2182: JOHANNES   1756-1786   m Sep 1774 MARIA SERVICE
   2183: ANNETJE   b 1757; m SAMUEL REESE
   2184: MAGDALENA H.   b SAR 13 Dec 1761 (sp Magd., w of H. Dockstdr)
```

2130: HENRY DOCKSTADER <D24> - pr. born before 1742; m 10 May 1758 MARIA MAGDALENA
WEAVER. Was a Tory and moved to Canada ca 1782 with sons Geo. Adam, John, Fred.,
Henry & Joseph (all were Tory soldiers in the Revolution).

```
   2185: GEORGE ADAM   b ca 1759; d 1793;   m CATHERINE ... Tory soldier
   2186: JOHN   b SAR 4 Dec 1760 (sp John Glaser & w. Elis.); d by 1801
                    Tory Capt. in Butler's Rangers; m SARAH ... (an Indian)
   2187: FREDERICK   b ca 1761; d 1781; m ca 1780 ELISABETH STEVENS
   2188: JOSEPH   bp SAR 25 Mar 1763 (sp Fr. Dockstdr & M. Elis.); d 1763
   2189: CATHERINE   b Schenectady 18 Sep 1765; m ISAAC JACOB TRUAX jr
   2190: HENRY   b SAR 17 Nov 1767 (sp Hen. Seever & Fraena)
                    liv. 1812 (militia Lt. in Lincoln, Canada)
   2190A JOSEPH   b 9 Oct 1772; m HANNAH HODGE
```

2122: JOHN F. DOCKSTADER <D28> - bp SAR 1 Aug 1751; died Palatine NY 1839; m by
1777 BARBARA WEAVER, pr. Barb. Elisabeth (b May 1755 <Dockstader book has b 1757,
d 1825>) dau of PETER WEAVER. DAR (vol. 88, pg 28) has a John Dockstader m
BARBARA EAKER (1757-1835) with son FREDERICK I. (1790-1835, m DORCUS GARDINER).
John & wife Barbara Elis. sponsored Jul 1794 SAR bp for a dau of Nicholas Weaver &
Elis. (Zoller) and a 1797 bp for a son of Jacob Blank & Cath. (Weaver). Children
(see Dockstader book, pg 37).

2133: MARCUS G. DOCKSTADER <D15> - born ca 1738 (son of George Adam); died 21 Aug 1821; m SAR 13 Aug 1761 ELISABETH SCHULTS (b 1739, d 1821) dau of JACOB SHULTS & DOROTHEA (Shults book page 13). On the 1790 Caughnawaga (Fonda) NY census (2-0-2).

    2195: CATHERINE bp SA 9 Dec 1761 (sp Mar. Elis. Dockstdr ...)
                  d 1831; m PETER ABR. YATES (b 1752)
    2196: JACOB bp 19 Feb 1763; d 1807; m ELISABETH GROFF
    2197: MARIA bp SA 25 Mar 1765; m1 HENRY AD. LAUX
                m2 by 1797 CORNELIUS H. SMITH
    2198: MARCUS b SA 15 Mar 1770 (sp John Dkstdr, Anna Eva Schults)
                d 1839; m1 1791 SARAH BROWER
    2199: JOHN b ca 1777; d Stone Arabia 1778 (age 1 year)

2123: NICHOLAS DOCKSTADER <D29> - b 1752; m by 1780 MARGARET ... at Oppenheim NY. Had MARGARET (m 1796 Henry Zoller), CATRINA (b GF 11 Sep 1781, sp Debald Jung, Marg. Getman), & NICHOLAS (b GF 1 Mar 1786, sp John H Walrath, Lena Zoller).

2134: NICHOLAS DOCKSTADER <D16> - pr. born ca 1730 to 1745 (son of George Adam); m at Stone Arabia 17 Oct 1765 CATHERINE VANDERWERKEN (b ca 1744) pr. dau of JOHANNES VANDERWERKEN & CHRISTINA LYNN. Ran a hotel and farm at Sand Flats, near Fonda NY, as in Comp. of Amer. Genealogy (vol. 6 page 152) and "The Van Derwerken Family" page 75. Pr. the Nicholas on the 1790 Caughnawaga NY census (2-2-5).

    2200: ELISABETH 1766-1794 m RIAL BINGHAM
    2201: JACOB b Stone Arabia 1 Mar 1769; pr d young
    2202: JOHN N. b 6 Dec 1771; m MARGARET HACKNEY
    2203: JACOB N. b 11 Feb 1774; m ANGELTE HANSEN
    2204: NICHOLAS N. b 23 May 1776; m 1798 SARAH YATES
    2205: GEORGE ADAM b 31 Oct 1779; m1 SARAH VEEDER
    2206: FREDERICK b 28 Nov 1782; pr. d young
    2207: DERKJE b 27 Feb 1786; m WILLIAM YOST
    2208: HENRY b 1788; pr. d Chittenango NY Jan 1810 age 22
    2209: CATHERINE AMELIA b ca 1793; m ADAM V. SNYDER

2144: NICHOLAS DOCKSTADER <D25> - pr. born ca 1745 to 1751 (son of Henry); m SAR 11 Oct 1772 DOROTHY VANDERWERKEN (aka DIRKJE VANDERWERKEN) pr. dau of JOHN VANDERWERKEN & CHRISTINA LYNN (Prindle's The Van Derwerken Family, page 81).

    2211: CATRINA b Fonda NY 20 Nov 1774 (sp Thomas VDwerkn & Elis.)
    2212: CASPAR b say 1778; m by 1802 MARGARET WALLRATH
    2213: HENRICH b GF 2 Jul 1780 (sp Hen Dockstdr & Elis.)
    2214: ABRAM b Fonda NY 20 Aug 1783 (sp Abhm VDwerkn, Cath Dockstdr)
    2215: NICHOLAS b Fonda 29 Dec 1785 (sp Nic Dockstdr & Cath.)

DOCKSTADER - 4th Generation

2180: FREDERICK H. DOCKSTADER <D60> - bp Palatine NY 6 Jul 1751 (son of Henrich & Catherine <Weber>); m at Stone Arabia NY 4 May 1773 MARIA ECKER dau of ADAM ECKER & ELISABETH NELLIS. Had 14 children (see Dockstader book page 64).

2127: GEORGE F. DOCKSTADER <D33> - born 27 Dec 1761; died 12 Jul 1840; m 1781 LENA REESE dau of MARCUS RIES. Had 11 children incl. Elisabeth (b GF 8 Aug 1781, sp Elis. Reis, Jac. Dockstdr), Marcus, Magdalena, Frederick, George, Nicholas, Catharina, Nancy, Gertrude, Margaret, & Leonard.

2176: GEORGE H. DOCKSTADER <D56> - pr. born ca 1735 to 1745; liv. 1802 (will prep.); m at Palatine NY 9 Jun 1765 BARBARA SCHULTS (b ca 1743, liv. 1837 age 94) dau of JACOB SHULTS & DOROTHEA. Was a private in the Revolution and later lived at Sand Flats NY.

      2217: HENRY b 20 Apr 1766; m ca 1788 CATHERINE BAYER
      2218: DOROTHEA b 18 Dec 1767; m 1784 ADAM EVERSON
      2219: CATHERINE b SAL 4 Apr 1770 (sp Joh. Schuls); m HENRY ECKER
      2220: ELISABETH b 26 May 1776; ps. m JOHN ECKER

2221: Col. GEORGE DOCKSTADER (ps. the Indian Docksteter, see page 291) - m by 1787 DOROTHEA ... and had a son PETER (bp GF 31 Dec 1787, sp Maj. Peter Schuyler).

2163: JOHN DOCKSTADER <D73> - pr. the John born 1760 (son of George <Bellinger book says born 1756>); died 1815; m by 1780 CATHERINA BELLINGER (b 1761, d 1819) dau of Lt. Col. FREDERICK P. BELLINGER & CATHERINE WEAVER (Bellinger book page 52 and Beers˜ "Herkimer County" page 164). At Oriskany according to MacWethy˜s "Book of Names", page 166. Descendents in Phelps NY. Rev. Spinner˜s note on 1802 Herkimer Church bp record was that Lawrence was this couple˜s third child in order to be born blind.

      2223: CATHERINE bp Herkimer NY 26 Nov 1780
      2224: GEORGE b GF 26 Dec 1782 (sp Jac Weber & Cath.)
               (Bellinger book says George was born blind)
      2225: ELISABETH b GF 28 Feb 1785 (sp Stophl Bellinger, Anna Harter)
    +2226: FREDERICK b 14 Mar 1785 <?>; m by 1812 CATHERINE WEAVER
      2227: ANNA (Nancy) b GF 30 Jan 1788 (sp Stof. Bellinger & Anna)
          m Herk. NY Jan 1805 WILLIAM CLEPSATTLE (not "JOHN R.")
      2228: JOHN bp SJR 18 Jul 1790; m1 (Harter) m2 Ms. VAN BUREN
      2229: PETER b say 1792; m Apr 1810 EVA GEO. NELLIS
      2230: MARIA 1794-1872 m GEORGE H. BELL
      2231: NICHOLAS b SJR 7 Jan 1794 (sp Fr. Weber, Cath. Harter)
      2232: LAWRENCE b 12 May 1802 (blind, sp. Lawr. Harter)

2159: PETER DOCKSTADER <D69> - born 25 Dec 1751 (son of George); died Adams NY 1 Feb 1842 (age 92); m1 Sep 1776 ELISABETH CUNINGHAM (b 1752, d 15 Sep 1829 age 77); m2 SUSANNA ... (b ca 1772, d 28 Apr 1835 age 63); see Enterprise & News of 9/9/1936 and Dockstader book (page 72). In 1757 Peter was a captive in Canada, being held there for three years before being returned. He was in Col. Bellinger˜s 4th Tryon Co. Regimeint (with George & John Dockstader) and reportedly saw service at Oriskany. Pr. the Peter on settlement list of Nicholas Smith˜s estate at German Flats in 1779.

      2232A JOHN b say 1777; pr. m GF 1795 ANNA H. STAHRING
      2233: CATHERINE bp GF 1 Feb 1778 (sp Lor. Harter & Cath.)
           pr. m 1795 GEORGE H. STAHRING
      2234: GEORGE b GF 29 Jun 1780 (sp Geo. Jac. Hilts & Cath.)
          m Utica NY 1801 POLLY BRODHAWK
      2235: WILLIAM b 19 Jun 1782; m 1810 BETSY BURCH
      2237: ANNA b GF 9 May 1785 (sp John Delaney, Anna Harter)
      2238: ELISABETH bp SJR 7 Mar 1790 (sp John Dckstdr & Cath.)
          m 1810 ELIJAH WRIGHT
      2239: PETER b SJR 30 Dec 1793 (sp Peter Harter & Cath.)
          m 1816 LORANEY BLACKSTONE
      2240: ELIJAH

********** DORNBERGER **********

2251: **FREDERICK DORNBERGER** - pr. born ca 1725 to 1740 (son of Nicholas of
Somershausen, dec´d by 1760); liv. 1790 (HK census); m Stone Arabia NY 7 Apr
1760 ELISABETH HILTS dau of CHRISTOFEL HILTS of the Falls (SAR mar. rec.).
Fred. Dornberger listed on 1790 Herkimer census (1-0-3).

surname DORNBERGER
2252: ELISABETH b 17 Jan 1762 (sp Elis. Con. Folts, Geo. Hilts Sr.)
        m by 1787 WILLIAM WABEL
2253: ANNA b 1763 (sp Stofel Hilts, Elis. Bell); m THOMAS BELL
2254: GEORGE b 13 Nov 1765 (sp. Geo. Hilts Sr. & Mar. Elis.)
+2255: LORENTZ b 1767; m 1793 CATHERINE KAST (b 1765)
+2256: MARIA b SAR 29 Jan 1770 (sp Geo. Folts, Maria Hilts)
+2257: CATHERINE b say 1771; m 1792 PETER FR. KAST
2258: MARGARET b say 1773; m 1791 JOHN J. HILTS
+2259: WINA bp GF 14 Jul 1776 (sp. Thomas Fulmer & Cath.)
        SABINA liv. 1792 (spf Hilts bp)
2260: JOHANNES b GF 13 Sep 1778 (sp John Hilts, Christina Folts)

DORNBERGER - 2nd Generation

2255: **LORENTZ DORNBERGER** - born 4 Oct 1767 (SAR, bp sp Lorentz Hilts, Cath.
Hilts); m German Flats NY 19 Nov 1793 CATHERINE KAST - pr. the Catherine (b
1765) dau of FREDERICK KAST & ELISABETH HELMER

2260: THOMAS b GF 24 Dec 1795 (sp Thomas Bell & Anna)

2253: **ANNA DORNBERGER** - born 6 Jul 1763; died Herkimer NY 13 Oct 1809 (age
46); m THOMAS BELL. Was sponsor, with John Hilts, for May 1779 bp of Wiena,
dau of George Hilts & Elisabeth.

2257: **CATHERINE DORNBERGER** - pr. born ca 1760 to 1772; m 1792 PETER FR. KAST
(b 1770, d 1849) son of FREDERICK KAST. According to the treatment records of
Dr. William Petry, a Catherine Dornberger was scalped and wounded with a spear
in five sundry places on 9 Jul 1779. We think that to sustain such injury and
survive would suggest that Dr. Petry´s patient was a grown woman, so an early
birthyear of say 1760-61 seems in order. However another possibility is that
this Catherine was a younger child (consistent with first sponsorship
appearance and marriage dates) and that the 1779 scalping victim was the mother
"Elisabeth" (see discussion under Christofel Hilts Sr.). Catherine was a
sponsor, with John McKoom, for Sep 1790 bp of Catherine, dau of Godfrid Hilts &
Maria.

2256: **MARIA DORNBERGER** - born SAR 29 Jan 1770; pr. m by 1790 JACOB LASSEN.
Assumption of marriage comes from sponsors at baptism of Lassen girls Sara (b
1790, bp GF Feb 1792, sp. Lorentz Dornberger & Sara McKoom) and Elisabeth (b
Feb 1792, sp. Jacob Folts & Sabina Dornberger).

2259: **SABINA DORNBERGER** - pr. born ca 1771 to 1775; m by 1800 SEVERINUS KAST.
Had dau Maria (b New Germany Oct 1800, sp M. Elisabeth Witrig, parents listed
as Sev. Cass & "Abinae" Dornberger). Sabina was sponsor for a Hilts bp in
1792.

********** DYGERT (Diewehert, Tygert) **********

2281: WARNER DYGERT - pr. born near Huttengas Germany before 1665 (son of Hans & Gertrude, as in H. Jones' "The Palatine Families of New York); liv. 1730 (got Mohawk Valley land from Wm Copernol); m ANNA CATHERINE ... Werner was on the NY Palatine subs. list in 1710 (5A,2Y) & in 1712 (6A,3Y), naturalized at Albany 11 Oct 1715, and on the 1717 Simmendinger census at New Queensberg (Schoharie) NY with wife Catherine & 6 children. In 1723 he got lots 1 & 47 on the Stone Arabia Patent. Most info is from charts of Dygert genealogist Frank D. Deuel.

surname DYGERT

+2281A ps. (?) WARNER 1689-1760 m ...
2281B MAGDALENA bp Langenselbold Germ. 25 Feb 1691; d Jun 1691
2281C ELISABETH bp Langenselbold Germ. 11 Jan 1694 (H. Jones' book)
+2282: Johan PETER bp 9 Aug 1696; m ANNA ELISABETH FOX
2284: SABINA bp 5 Jan 1698
+2285: SEVERINUS bp 3 Oct 1700; m MARIA AGNES ...
2286: MARGARET bp 1 Nov 1701; m by 1722 FRED. STATEN, Schenectady
2286A OTTILA bp 18 Feb 1705 (H. Jones' Palatine Families of NY)
2286B CONRAD bp Langenselbold Germ. 4 Dec 1707; d Aug 1708

DYGERT - 2nd Generation

2282: PETER DYGERT - bp Langenselbold Germany 9 Aug 1696; living Apr 1753 (spf Laux bp); m ANNA ELISABETH FOX as in Bellinger book page 15 (source for children's birthyears <many seem a bit early>). Naturalized at Albany 31 Jan 1716 and on 1717 Simmendinger census with wife Anna Elisabeth.

+2287: DAVID b at sea 1710; m MARIA KUNGUNDA LOUCKS
2288: DELIA b say 1714; m JOHN REEBER
2289: MARGARETHA b say 1716; m1 PETER WEAVER m2 WILLIAM FINK
+2290: SEVERINUS b say 1718; m GERTRUDE ECKER
2291: ps. CATHERINE b say 1720; m by 1743 GERRIT AUSER. MARCELIS
        (Marcelis of Schenectady, they had son Wm bp 1747)
+2292: PETER P. b say 1721; m by 1755 ANNA BARBARA KOCH
+2293: WILLIAM 1723-1802 m1 MARIA ELISABETH ECKER
+2294: HENRY b say 1725; m ANNA MARGARETHA ...
2295: GERTURDE b say 1726; m by 1753 GEORGE LOUCKS (Laux)
2296: BARBARA b say 1728; m 1760 BEATUS KOCH
2297: ELISABETH b say 1730; ps. m CONRAD KLOCK (Bellinger book)

2285: SEVERINUS DYGERT - bp Germany 3 Oct 1700; m MARIA AGNES ... . Naturalized at Albany 31 Jan 1716 and drew lot #18 on the 1723 Stone Arabia Patent. Was a Lt. of the Stone Arabia NY militia in 1757 and commissioned Captain in 1758. Still in military service in 1763, as was Peter Bellinger (bp 1698) who also headed a militia unit at about that time. Severinus & wife Maria Agnes sponsored Feb 1752 bp of Severinus, son of Rudolph Koch & Elis. (Dygert).

+2298: WARNER 1719-1780 m MAGDALENA HERKIMER
+2299: PETER S. b say 1721; father-in-law of Gen. Herkimer
2300: ELISABETH b say 1723; m by 1752 RUDOLPH KOCH
2301: MARGARET b say 1726; ps. m NICHOLAS SNELL
2302: ps. CATHERINE b say 1728; m by 1745 HENDRICK HERKIMER
2303: ps. LANY (Bellinger book has m Gen. Herkimer)
2304: MARIA b say 1732; ps. 1st wife by 1760 of NICHOLAS HERKIMER
+2305: JOHN S. b say 1735; m1 by 1756 CATHERINE FINK

2281A: WARNER DYGERT jr. (?) - "Daughters of the American Colonists Lineage Book"
page 202-3 has a Warner jr. as born 1689 (son of immigrant Warner), died 1760,
and with son Severinus (b 1715, d 1794) who married an Anna Maria in 1738 and
was the father of PETER S. DYGERT (Lineage book says b 1740, d 1801, m SARAH
SCHUYLER). We question this account as no Werner "jr." can be seen on the
1715/16 Albany naturalizations or on the 1723 Stone Arabia Patent. Nor can we
find a Severinus to fit the dates 1715-1794, there being an earlier Severinus
(naturalized 1716) and the later Severinus P. (who had a son Peter born in 1759).
As to Peter S. Dygert, we think it likely he was born by the mid 1720's (to be
Ensign in 1763) and thus pr. a son of the earlier Severinus.

DYGERT - 3rd Generation

2287: Ens. DAVID DYGERT (David also called DEBALT, DEWALD, or THEOBALD) - born at
sea 1710; liv. 1786; m MARIA KUNIGUNDA LOUCKS (aka KINGET). In 1763 he was a
Sgt. in Capt. Goshin Van Alstein's Canajoharie militia, along with Severinus,
Peter, & Henry Dygert, and in 1767 an ensign in Jost Herkimer's Grannadiers. He
& Kunigunda sponsored the Jan 1771 bp of Kunigunda, dau of Dietrich Wohleben, and
the Mar 1786 FR bp of Theobalt, son of Jacob Seeber.

          2306: PETER   bp 27 May 1744 (sp. Jacob Wallrath, Barb. Laux)
         +2307: HENRY   bp SA 3 Jul 1746; m 1768 MARIA CUNINGHAM (Deuel notes)
          2308: DAVID   b say 1751; killed at Oriskany 1777 (Deuel)
          2309: pr. ELISABETH b say 1753; ml 1770 DIETRICH WOHLEBEN (d 1777)
                         m2 by 1779 JACOB SEEBER
         +2310: ps. GEORGE b say 1757; m by 1778 ANNA ...
          2311: MARGARET b SAR 17 Jul 1762 (sp Marg., wife of Wm Fink)

2294: HENRY P. DYGERT - born 1725; m ANNA MARGARET ... (Bellinger book page 15).

          2312: ELISABETH b 1749; m by 1767 NICHOLAS THUMB
         +2313: PETER H.   1751-1808 m by 1782 ANNA DYGERT (or SAERT)
         +2314: WILLIAM H. 1753-1791 m 1777 AGNES THUMB
          2315: SEVERINUS H. b say 1755; killed in Revol. (Klock's Regiment)
         +2316: ps. HENRY b say 1760; m by 1796 ELISABETH ...

2305: Capt. JOHN S. DYGERT - pr. born ca 1730 to 1740 son of Severinus & Maria
and grandson of Warner & Maria Catherine (Petrie book page 11); killed at
Oriskany 6 Aug 1777; ml by 1756 CATHERINE FINCK dau of ANDREAS FINCK & ANNA
MARIA; m2 29 Nov 1759 DOROTHY SHOEMAKER dau of RUDOLPH SHOEMAKER & GERTRUDE
HERKIMER. John & wife Catherine sponsored 1756 bp of John, son of Johannes Leder
& Elisabeth.

         +2317: SEVERINUS bp 1760 (sp Sev Dygrt & w Maria) m 1782 ANNA SUITS
          2318: ELIZABETH bp 1762 (Gert& Rud. Shoemakr) d 1815; m ROBERT GRAY
          2319: ANNA MARIA b 28 May 1763; d 1766
          2320: JOHANNES   b SAR 11 May 1765 (sp. John Snell & w. Elis.)
         +2321: WARNER b 1766; m SUSANNA REISS
          2322: PETRUS b SAR 7 Jul 1768; ps. d. young
         +2323: RUDOLPH b 28 Jul 1769; m 1795 ELIZABETH EHLE
          2324: MARIA b say 1771; m 1789 GEORGE WAUFEL
          2325: GERTRUDE b say 1773; m 1796 ABRAHAM HEES
          2326: CATHERINE b say 1775; ml 1795 JOHN GERHARDT WALLRATH

2292: PETER P. DYGERT - born 1721 (son of Peter); m ANNA BARBARA KOCH (b 1732)
dau of CASPER KOCH & FRENA MULLER (i.e. Veronica Miller).

    2327: PETER   b 11 Aug 1755 (sp Peter Tygrt, Vrena Koch); pr. d y
    2328: CATHERINE   b 6 Oct 1756; m SAL 1778 HENRICH DICKHAUT
    2329: PETER   b 13 Jun 1758; m 1786 ELISABETH BAUM
    2330: VROENA   b 21 Jun 1760 (sp. Cath., wife of Hen. Wallrath)
    2331: SEVERINUS P.   b SAR 8 Jun 1762 (sp. Sever. Koch, Cath. Frey)
          m 1791 GERTRUDE BAUM
    2332: ELISABETH   b SAR 22 Feb 1764 (sp Elis. Ecker, John Koch, unm)
    2333: CASPER   b SAR 20 Feb 1766 (sp Sev. P Dygert & Gertr.)
  +2334: HENRICH   b SAR 17 Mar 1768 (sp Hen. Gilly, Marg. Snell)
          m by 1792 MARGARET CUNINGHAM

2299: Capt. PETER S. DYGERT - pr. born ca 1715 to 1725, despite DAC (Daughters of
American Colonists Lineage Book, pg 202-3) which has him born 1740 (see comment
above under #2218A); died 1801; ps. ml ...; m by ca 1758 SARAH ...(DAC has b
1742, d 1820). We think the DAC´s calling her SARAH SCHUYLER was a guess only
and our inclination would be to consider SARAH MATTICE a stronger possibility
(see Rex Mattice´s book regarding unplaced dau of NICHOLAS MATTICE). Peter S.
Dygert was noted as a "father-in-law" in the 1777 will of Gen. Nicholas Herkimer,
so possibly Peter had an earlier wife (before Sara) who was the mother of Mrs.
Maria (Dygert) Herkimer. Peter served in the militia under Severinus Dygert´s in
1757 and he was an Ensign in 1763 (pr. then a middle aged man). Children are
from a Frank Duell´s E&N article (10/30/1935). Cdmr Bellinger notes (HCH file
#3.08) say that Peter Dygert liveds near Haus (John House) & Freymeyer (pr. John,
formerly of Schoharie, whose wife was a Mattice) and that Peter had a daughter
who married Adam Mayer (pr. Catherine).

  +2335: MARIA   b say 1756; m as 2nd wife Gen. NICHOLAS HERKIMER
  +2336: NICHOLAS   b 1760 (sp. Nich. Herkimer & w. Maria <Dygert?>
          d 1806; m MARIA ABEEL
    2337: GERTRUDE   b 14 Jun 1761 (sp. Gert., wife of Jacob Snell)
    2338: ELISABETH   b SAR 20 Nov 1762 (sp Elis., w. of Hen. Frey jr.)
    2339: DOROTHY b 15 Mar 1764 (Dor. & John Dygrt) m ABRAHAM HERKIMER
    2340: CATHERINE   b 27 Aug 1765 (sp. Cath. wife of Hen. Herkimer)
    2341: ANNA (NANCY)   b 15 Jan 1767; d 1 Jan 1841; m DAVID MOYER
  +2342: HENRICH   b 3 Mar 1769; m 1791 MARGARET FREYMEYER
    2343: ELIZABETH   b 14 May 1771 (sp. Elis. Dygert, w. of Rud. Koch)
    2344: PETER P.   b say 1773; a minor in 1777 (Gen. Herkimer will)

2290: SEVERINUS P. DYGERT - pr. born ca 1718 (Bellinger book) to 1737 (DAR
#329456); m by 1759 GERTRUDE ECKER.

    2345: ps. ANNA   b say 1755; m by 1780 PETER H. DYGERT
    2346: ELISABETH   b say 1757; m by 1780 JOHN SILLEBACH
  +2347: Johan PETER   b 24 Nov 1759 (sp. Peter Dyg, Geo. Ecker)
          m 1790 MARIA SNELL
    2348: CATHERINE   b SAR 4 Nov 1762 (sp Cath., w. of Hen. Walrath)
          m 1784 PETER W. NELLIS
    2349: SEVERINUS S.   b SAR 25 Jan 1765 (sp. Wm Dygert & M. Elis.)
          m 1792 APPOLONIA SNELL
    2350: GERTRUDE   b 12 Nov 1767 (DAR #329456)
    2351: MARGARET (twin)   1769-1826 m HAN YOST SNELL
    2352: DELIA (twin)   b SAR 12 Nov 1769 (sp Delia & John Reeber)
          m 1797 HENRY WALLRATH

2298: WARNER DYGERT - born 1719 (DAR vol 49 page 92); killed by Indians at Fall
Hill in Little Falls NY in 1780; m MAGDALENA HERKIMER dau of Johan JOST HERKIMER
& CATHERINE PETRIE. In 1757 a Warner was in Lt. Sev. Dygert´s militia company
and in the Revolution he held a key position in the Committee of Safety for
Canajoharie (Book of Names page 181). He was apparently held prisoner a while by
a Tory raiding party. Children from Petrie book page 5.

+2353: Johan JOST b say 1743; d 1813; m 1777 ELIZABETH MOYER
 2354: MARIA b say 1746; m 1767 JOHANNES P. BELLINGER
 2355: CATHERINE 1749-1837 m HENRICH JOH. FAILING
 2356: ANNA 1749-1813 m1 CONRAD JAC. FOLTS
 2357: ELIZABETH b say 1754; m by 1775 Joh. DIETERICH PETRIE
 2358: MAGDALENA b 5 Jan 1763; pr. m 1784 HENRICH UHLE
 2359: MARIA CATHERINE b 1764 (sp. Mar. & Joh. Jost Herkimer);
                m 1784 PETER WALRATH
+2360: SEVERINUS W. 1766-1849 m 1790 MADALINE HERKIMER
                (1766 bp sp. Sev.Dygert & Elis. Barbara Schuyler)
 2361: ps. PETER W. b say 1768; m GF 1786 GERTRUDE GEO. WEAVER

2293: Capt. WILLIAM DYGERT - born Schoharie NY 2 Oct 1723 (Bellinger book page
15); died Frankfort NY 28 May 1802 (age 78-7-24); m1 MARIA ELISABETH ECKER (d ca
1769, name from Nov 1752 bp rec.); m2 SAR 21 Aug 1770 MARGARET CUNINGHAM (b 1737,
d 4 Oct 1807). Had 7 adults & 6 children on 1778 German Flats relief and was on
1790 GF census (3-0-4).

 2362: PETER b ca 1748; died young
 2363: MARIA ELISABETH b Jun 1749; d 26 Jun 1815
                m1 by 1777 FRED. F. HELMER; m2 JOHN DEMUTH
+2364: WILLIAM jr. b Dec 1750; m 1782 ANNA BAUM
 2365: MARIA bp 13 Nov 1752 (sp. Elis. Dygert, Adam Ecker)
                d by 1795; m ca 1772 ANDREW CLEPSATTLE
+2366: GEORGE 1754-1808 m CATHERINE STEELE
+2367: PETER 1757-1821 m CATHERINE AUG. CLEPSATTLE
 2368: CATHERINE b say 1763; m 29 Nov 1785 MARCUS GRANTS
 2369: ANNA b say 1765; m 5 Dec 1786 GEORGE AUG. CLEPSATTLE
 2370: GERTRUDE b SAR 2 Jun 1767 (sp. Gert. Steele, ...)
                d 1851; m 1785 NICHOLAS G. WEAVER
 2371: EVA W. b say 1769; m GF 1795 MICHAEL JOH. MEYER
                by 2nd wife
 2372: MARGARET b say 1773; m 1795 ANDREW CLEPSATTLE widower
 2373: MAGDALENA 1775-1851 m JOHN PIPER (Pfeiffer)
 2374: DOROTHEA b GF May 1777 (sp. John Cuningham & Dor.)
 2375: WERNER b GF Aug 1778 (Pet. Dockstdr & Elis.); m EL. MYER
 2376: MARIA b 9 Jul 1784 (sp. And. Clepsattle & Maria)

DYGERT - 4th Generation

2366: GEORGE DYGERT - born 26 Sep 1754; died HK 26 May 1808 (age 53-8-); m
CATHERINE STEELE. Children <Deuel notes> were Elizabeth (m a Steele), Gertrude
(b 1806, m a Willett), Catherine (m Michael Myers), and George.

2310: GEORGE DYGERT - born ca 1753 to 1759; m by 1778 ANNA ... George & wife
Anna were sponsors for Jan 1778 GF bp of Eva, dau of William Cuningham.

2307: HENRY D. DYGERT - pr. born ca 1740 to 1750; m Palatine NY 25 Oct 1768 MARIA
CUNINGHAM pr. a dau of WILLIAM CUNINGHAM.

      2377: KUNIGUNDA (JANE) b say 1769; m 1793 NICHOLAS H. STARING
      2378: MARGARET b SAR 8 Nov 1770 (sp Marg. & Wm Cuningham)
      2379: MARY b say 1772; m 1788 HENRY ACKLER (Eckler)
      2380: DAVID b say 1773; m 1795 CATHERINE STARING
      2381: WILLIAM b say 1775; m CATHERINE MILLER
      2382: HENRICH b say 1777; m 1795 ELISABETH H. STAHRING Coln.

2316: HENRY DYGERT - pr. born ca 1750 to 1775; m ELISABETH ... Had a daughter
Maria bp at Minden 9 Oct 1796 (mother given as Elisabeth).

2334: HENRICH DYGERT - born 1768; m MARGARET CUNINGHAM (b 1770) dau of JOHN
CUNINGHAM & MARIA FOLTS. Lived in Herkimer Co. in 1793.

      2383: MARIA b 19 Sep 1792 (bp SJR 1793, sp John Cuninghm & Maria)

2342: HENRICH P. DYGERT - pr. born ca 1750 to 1771; m 1791 MARGARET FREYMEYER.
Lived at Canajoharie Castle in 1792 (SJR bp rec.).

      2384: ELISABETH b SJR 8 Mar 1792 (sp Pet. Dygert, Elis. Schuyler)
      2385: PETER bp St Johnsville 16 Jun 1793 (sp Peter Dygert & Sara)
      2386: ANNA bp GF 11 Mar 1795 (sp Tim. Hess, Anna Schuyler)

2353: Johan JOST DYGERT - born say 1743; died 1813; m 12 Apr 1777 MARIA ELISABETH
MOYER (aka MARILIS MOYER, b 1763, age 74 in 1837) dau of JOHN MOYER of Manheim NY.
His widow m2 1824 JOHN TOCKEY. Jost was an militia Ensign in 1767.

      2387: WERNER b GF 23 Dec 1782 (sp John Brower, Debora Brower)
      2388: JOHANNES b GF 14 Apr 1785 (sp Sev. W Dygert, Marg. Rosncrnz)

2336: NICHOLAS DYGERT - born 22 Jun 1760; died 31 Mar 1806; m 21 Oct 1782 MARIA
ABEEL dau of JOHN ABEEL & MARY KNOUTS and widow of JACOB RADNOR (E&N of 30 Oct
1935). In the Revolution Nicholas was taken prisoner to Canada and forced to run
the Indain gaunlet. A Nicholas, with Engel Van Slyke, sponsored Jun 1781 bp of
Nich., son of John Smith & Anna Eva.

      2389: PETER b 26 Aug 1783 (sp John Appeal & Maria)
              m GERTRUDE DIEFENDORF
      2390: CATHARINE b 10 Jan 1785; m NICHOLAS GROS (son of Lawr.)
      2391: JOHN b 17 Feb 1788; m BETSY DUBOIS

2313: PETER H. DYGERT - born ca 1751 (DAR# 227009); m 778 ANNA DYGERT or ANNA
SAERT (DAR). Was a private in Revol. service.

      2392: HENRICH b GF 4 Aug 1780 (sp Sev Dygrt, Jac Zerr, Cath Dygrt)
              d 1859; m MARIA YERDON
      2393: SUSANNA b GF 30 Sep 1782 (sp Chrstn Hufngel, Sus. Stamm)
      2394: PETER b 26 Apr 1787 (sp Peter Dygert jr., Barb. Stamm, unm)

2329: PETER DYGERT - pr. born ca 1750 to 1770 (son of Peter & Barbara); m 1786
ELISABETH BAUM dau of ABRAHAM BAUM & DOROTHY CUNINGHAM.

      2395: CATHERINE bp SJR 19 Feb 1792 (Caspar Dygert, Cath Konikum)
      2396: PETER b GF 28 Feb 1793 (sp Peter Dygert & Barbara)
      2397: DOROTHY b GF 30 Apr 1795 (sp Hen. Dickhaut & Cath.<Dygert>)

2347: PETER S. DYGERT - born Palatine NY 1759; died there 1841; m SAR 10 Apr 1790
MARIA SNELL (b 1769) dau of GEORGE SNELL & ANNA EVA BELLINGER as given in Martin's
Snell book (page 36) and DAR (vol 130 page 220).

    2398: SEVERINUS bp SAR 8 May 1791 (sp Sev. Dygert & w Gertr.)
                m ANNA EVA KAISER (dau of Henry)
    2399: ELIZABETH b 1794; m PETER EHLE (1792-1808)
    2400: GEORGE bp SAR 3 Jan 1796 (sp Geo Snell, Marg Dygert, unm)
    2401: GITTY bp SAR 29 Nov 1801 (sp John Fink, Dor. Fox)
    2402: MARGARET b SAL 30 Apr 1804 (sp Jost Snell & Marg.)
    2403: ANNA EVA b 24 May 1809

2367: PETER WM. DYGERT - born 1757; died 1821; m 1786 CATHERINE AUG. CLEPSATTLE (b
1763, d 1823) dau of AUGUSTINUS CLEPSATTLE & BARBARA WENTZ. Children <from Deuel
notes> were William (b GF 8 Jul 1787), Elizabeth (b 24 Jul 1790), Peter (b 8 Aug
1792), John (b 20 Apr 1795), Daniel, Warner, Dennis, & Mary.

2323: RUDOLPH DYGERT - born 28 Jul 1769; m Palatine/Stone Arabia NY 28 Jun 1795
ELISABETH EHLE (b 1774) dau of PETER EHLE & MARY MADDALENA DOUW.

    2404: MARIA bp Palatine NY 3 Apr 1796 (sp Peter Ehle & w Delia)
    2405: JOHN b 1 Apr 1798; d 1 Mar 1865
    2406: CATHERINE b 3 Dec 1803
    2407: HARRIET JANE b 3 Aug 1806
    2407A JAMES HENRY b 16 Jun 1810
    2408: ABRAHAM b 11 Aug 1816

2317: SEVERINUS JOH. DYGERT - born Tryon Co. NY 1760 (age given as 71-11-21 on
Revol. service pension application of 1 Sep 1832); died Steuben Co. NY 1849; m
German Flats NY 13 Dec 1782 ANNA SUITS (aka "Nancy", b 1763, d 1829, as in DAR vol
136 page 101) pr. a dau of JOHN SUTZ & ELISABETH. In his pension application, he
notes that his father substituted for him on the Oriskany call-up and was slain in
battle. Pr. the Severinus I. Tygert on 1790 Palatine NY census (2-2-4) listed
next to John Wick.

    2409: JOHN b GF 4 May 1783 (sp Adam Sutz, Elis. Dygert)
    2410: ELISABETH b GF 1 Jan 1785 (sp W. Dygert, Elis. Spalsberg)
    2411: SEVERINUS b SAR 16 Feb 1789 (sp Jost Snell, Betsy Koch)
    2412: CATHERINE b 1791 (sp. Hen. Sutz, Cath. Dygert)
              d 1868; m JOSEPH A. WARNER (1793-1867)

2331: SEVERINUS P. DYGERT - born 8 Jun 1762 (son of Peter P., as given in Deuel
notes at Oneida Hist. Soc.); m GF 8 Mar 1791 GERTRUDE BAUM (b 1773) dau of ABRAHAM
BAUM & DOROTHY CUNINGHAM.

    2413: CATHERINE b GF 26 Jul 1792 (sp Hen. Dickhaut & Cath.)
    2414: ABRAHAM bp GF 21 Oct 1794 (sp Abraham Baum & Dorothy)

2349: SEVERINUS S. DYGERT - pr. born ca 1750 to 1770; m 1792 APPOLONIA SNELL (b 26
Mar 1770) dau of ADAM SNELL (b 1736) & ANNA ELISABETH BELLINGER (b 1736) as in
Bellinger book (page 30). Snell book (page 41) gives children as Delia,
Elisabeth, Adam, Werner, John S., George, & Elijah.

    2415: DELIA b Sep 1792
    2416: ELISABETH bp Palatine NY 22 Mar 1795

2360: SEVERINUS WER. DYGERT - born 1766 (son of Warner); died 1849; m GF 8 Aug
1790 MAGDALENA HERKIMER dau of HENRY HERKIMER.

    2417: WERNER bp SJR 2 Oct 1791 (sp Nic. Herkimer & Marg.)
    2418: ANNA bp GF 24 Feb 1793 (sp H. Rosencrant, Anna H. Herkimer)
    2419: HENRICH b GF 11 Jan 1795 (sp Hen. Uhly & Dorothea)
    2420: GERTRUDE b GF 9 Oct 1801
    2421: ISAAC b GF 26 Feb 1806

2321: WARNER DYGERT - born 1766 (sp. uncle Warner Dygert); m SUSANNA REISS

    2422: MAGDALENA b 18 Sep 1791 (sp. Rud. Dygert, Barb. Nestel)
         m JOHN EYSAMAN
    2423: MARIA b SAR 27 Nov 1793; pr. d. young
        (sp. John Reiss, Elis. Koch, unm)
    2424: MARIA bp Palatine NY 14 Jun 1795 (sp Nic. Dygert and Maria)
        m NICHOLAS KILTS

2364: WILLIAM DYGERT jr - pr. born ca 1753 to 1759 (jr implies son of William);
died 26 Jun 1818; m ANNA BAUM dau of ABRAHAM BAUM (Comp. of Amer. Genealogy, vol
7 page 68). On 1790 Herkimer census (1-3-3).

    2425: ELISABETH b 3 Apr 1783; m ADAM STEELE (b 1 Mar 1779)
    2426: WILLIAM 1784-1849 m CATHERINE FOLTS (1788-1871)
    2427: DOROTHEA 1786-1864 m SYLVANUS FOLTS (1784-1852)
    2428: ABRAHAM b GF 19 Dec 1787 (Adam Staring, Cath); m ANNA BRODHACK
    2429: HENRY 1789-1833 m MAGDALENA FOLTS (b 1796)
    2430: JOHN B. bp SJR 19 Feb 1792 (sp Johm Boom & Margaret)
        d 1854; m ELISABETH DIEVENDORF
    2431: ANNA b 12 Feb 1795 (Joh Demuth & Elis.); m F. ISAAC CLUTE
    2432: GEORGE 1797-1850 m1 MARY ARBUTHOUT m2 ALMIRA DORRILL

2314: WILLIAM H. DYGERT - born 8 Jul 1753; died Ft. Plain NY 7 Aug 1791; m 1777
AGNES THUMB pr. sister of immigrant ADAM THUMB (b 1734). Identified as William H.
on 1785 bp record of son Severinus.

    2433: MARGARET b SAL 6 Oct 1778 (sp. Nic. Thum & Elis.)
        m PETER P. HELMER
    2434: HENRICH b GF 15 Apr 1781 (sp Nic. Van Slyke & Gertr.)
        m1 HK 1804 BARBARA SCHELL m2 1822 POLLY WHEELER
    2435: WILHELM b GF 9 May 1783 (sp Chrstn Hufngel, ... Frankin)
        m 1801 ANNA PET. SCHUYLER
    2436: SEVERINUS b GF 10 Aug 1785 (sp Sev S Dygrt, Anna Huffnagel)
        d 1803; m CHARITY ... (had dau Doro. b Utica NY 9 Jul 1803)
    2437: ADAM b 23 Aug 1787 (sp. Adam Thom & w. Christina Meyer)
        m JANE DUSLER
    2438: PETER b say 1790; m 1810 ELISABETH GEO. P. HELMER

2335: MARIA DYGERT - pr. born ca 1735 to 1758 (dau of Peter S.); m by 1760, as
his second wife, Gen. NICHOLAS HERKIMER. In his will dated Feb 1777 Gen. Nicholas
Herkimer names his wife Maria, father-in-law Peter S. Dygert, and minor brother
(of his wife) named Peter. Nicholas Herkimer & "wife Maria" were sponsors for bp
in Jun 1760 of Nicholas, son of Peter S. Dygert & Sara (Schuyler) and in Aug 1762
of Nicholas, son of John Roof & Anna Marie (Leonard). In Jul 1766 Maria, wife of
Nic. Herkimer, was sponsor for bp of Maria, dau of John Seuffer & Maria.

********** ECKLER (Ackler) **********

2451: HENRY ECKLER - born 16 Oct 1711; m 1738 MARGARET YOUNG whom we suspect
was pr. a dau of HENRICH YOUNG & MARGARET, although Eckler book presumed she was
the Margaret (b 1716) dau of THEOBALD YOUNG & MARIA CATHERINE, as given in "The
Eckler Family of the Mohawk Valley" by A. Ross Eckler jr. (1949, 3643 Brandywine
St, Wash. 8, DC). He settled near Canajoharie NY by 1739 and was naturalized 11
Sep 1761, along with an Augustus Eckler (relation to Henry uncertain).

```
                         surname ECKLER
        +2452: HENRY  1739-  m CHRISTINA ...
         2453: MARIA  b 13 Nov 1740; d 4 Aug 1743
         2454: JOHN   b 12 Oct 1742; d 8 Aug 1743
         2455: CHRISTOPHER  b 12 Aug 1744 (sp Jung & w Marg.); pr d young
         2456: ELIZABETH  b 17 Sep 1746; m MICHAEL SCHNEIDER
        +2457: CHRISTOPHER  b 1748; m pr. by 1783 CATHERINE
        +2458: JOHN   ca 1751-1812  m MARGARET HOOVER
        +2459: PETER  b 2 Jul 1754; ml 1782 CHRISTINA KRAMER
         2460: JACOB  b 30 Oct 1757
        +2461: LEONARD  1760-1838  m CATHERINE YOUNG
```

ECKLER - 2nd Generation

2457: CHRISTOPER ECKLER - born 25 Dec 1748; died Warren NY 5 Jun 1838; m
CATHERINE ... (b Apr 1752, d Warren NY 20 Feb 1835). Enlisted May 1776 in Capt.
Henry Eckler´s company (Morrison´s "Index of Revolutionary War Soldiers" page
43). Had children baptised 1794-6 at St. Paul´s Lutheran (SPL), Minden NY.

```
         2462: PETER  b say 1783; m 1808 CATHERINE CLEPSATTLE (d 1810)
         2463: NICHOLAS  b GF 19 Nov 1788 (sp Stephen Eysaman & Anna Eva)
         2464: JOHN  b 27 Aug 1790 (sp John Fink & Doro.<Fox>)
         2465: CHRISTOPHER  b SPL 2 Jun 1794 (sp Ch. Eckler, Elis. Contryman)
         2466: MARIA  b SPL 6 Nov 1796 (sp John Eckler & Marg.)
```

2452: Capt. HENRY ECKLER jr - born 11 Aug 1739; m CHRISTINA ... (b Oct 1746, d
21 Jan 1841 age 94) who was possibly a Springer or Shaul (Eckler book).
Supposedly Henry attended school in the Mohawk Valley with Indian Chief Joseph
Brant and would usually win in wrestling matches between them. In May 1776,
Henry was appointed a Capt. in the Tryon Co. militia and he was on the 1790
Canajoharie census (1-3-5). He lived most of his life on his farm at Chyle
(pronounced "kile") near the Otsquago Creek in Warren (Herkimer Co.) NY. Two of
his young daughters were killed during a Tory Indian raid in 1781.

```
         2467: HENRY  b 24 Jan 1766; m 1788 MARIA DYGERT
        +2468: JACOB  b ca 1773; m ca 1796 CHRISTINA ...
         2469: MARGARET  b ca 1775; m ca 1794 GEORGE VETTERLY
         2470: dau  b say 1776; killed 1781
         2471: dau  b say 1778; killed 1781
         2472: ELIZABETH  b say 1782; m ca 1800 NICHOLAS SMITH
        +2473: JOHN  b 22 Jun 1783; m SOPHIA VAN HORNE
         2474: EVA  b ca 1784; m ca 1804 JAMES HOUSE
         2475: DAVID  b 11 Jun 1788; m 1811 MARIA SPRINGER
         2476: BENJAMIN  1790-1877  m MARY COLE (ca 1791-1864)
```

2458: JOHN ECKLER - born 26 Jun 1751; died 1812 (age ca 61); m before 1780 MARGARET HOOVER (Hardin & Willard's Herkimer Co. History). On 1790 Canajoharie NY census (1-6-2), living near Henry Eckler and Jacob Hoover.

    2477: HENRY b say 1777
    2478: JOHN b GF 2 Oct 1782 (sp Dan. Ullendorf & Cath.)
    2479: CHRISTIAN b Oct 1785
    2480: MARGARET b 18 Oct 1794 (sp Conr. Haus, Marg. Eckler)
    2481: DANIEL b SPL 19 Jul 1797-8; m ca 1820 CATHERINE ...
    2482: CATHERINE b SPL 5 Apr 1798 (sp Wm Ecker, Christina Knautz)

2461: LEONARD ECKLER - born 22 May 1760; died 10 Jan 1838; m 1787 CATHERINE YOUNG pr. dau of JACOB YOUNG & DOROTHY RICKERT. Leonard was on the 1790 Canjoharie NY census (1-1-2) living near John H Wallrath, Hendrick Eckler (pr. son of Capt. Henry), and Adam Young.

    2483: MARGARET b 28 May 1788; m CHRISTIAN CLAUS
    2484: JACOB bp SJR 12 Jul 1790 (sp Jac. Young, Eva Young)
                  d 1889; m CATHERINE PHIL. BELL
    2485: GEORGE b 28 Dec 1791; d 1862; m ELISABETH PHIL. BELL
    2486: HENRY b 26 Mar 1793; d 1827
    2487: ADAM b 9 Jun 1795 (sp Geo. Schall); m CATHERINE HELMER
    2488: LEONARD b SPL 12 Feb 1797; d 1860; m MARGARET PHIL. BELL
    2489: JOHN b 1803; d 1835

2459: PETER ECKLER - born 2 Jul 1754; m1 1782 CHRISTINA KRAMER (d 1811); m2 ca 1818 HANNAH SCHAEFFER (b ca 1772). Was on the 1790 Canajoharie census (1-3-3). His first wife was ps. related to the Henrdrick Cramer who appears to be living not far from Peter Eckler on the 1790 census. Information on children John and Margaret seen in E. Hallenbeck's "Our Van Horne Kindred" page 49.

    2490: PETER b GF 18 Sep 1783 (sp Hen. Aekler & Christina)
    2491: pr. MARGARET b say 1787; m 1808 PHILIP VAN HORNE
    2492: JOHN E.   1789-1859 m 1810 MAGDALENA VAN HORNE
    2393: MARIA b SPL 3 Mar 1794 (sp Hen. Eckler & w. Maria)
    2394: HENRICH b SPL 6 Jan 1797 (sp. Hen. Eckler jr., Marg. Eckler)

ECKLER - 3rd Generation

2468: JACOB ECKLER - pr. born ca 1770 to 1775; m ca 1796 CHRISTINA ... He moved to Penfield, Monroe Co., NY and had children Henrich (1798), Elizabeth (1799), Maria (1801), Jacob (1802), John (1804), Susanna (18059, Benjamin (1808), Sophia (ca 1819), and perhaps another dau.

2473: JOHN ECKLER - born 22 Jun 1783; m 6 Dec 1804 SOPHIA VAN HORNE (b 1786, d 1853) dau of THOMAS VAN HORNE & MARIA FREDERICKS. Held the Eckler homestead at Chyle and was living there in 1854 (age 71) when visited by the historian Nathaniel Benton, who wrote "No alienations out of the family had taken place since the first grant by the patentee <over about one hundred years>. This is an occurence so unusal, that I have deemed it worthy of particular notice. ... (John) had a brother Henry living in Sharon, aged 88 years.". Children were Henry (1805), Thomas (1808), Christina (1809), John (1810), & Mary Ann (1815).

********** EDICK (Ittig) **********

2501: **Hans MICHAEL ITTIG** - pr. born in Germany ca 1670 to 1680; tradition puts his death at German Flats NY ca 1734-35 and a grave marked only "M I" found below the floor of the Ft. Herkimer church (built ca 1760) pr. marks his remains; m1 ANNA MARIA ...; m2 pr. ca 1711 EVA ... (liv. 1713 as mother of Margaret). His wife was ps. the Eva living ca 1745 (see listing of early Lutheran church members in Book of Names, page 61). Appears as Johan Michael Jttich on NY Palatine subsistence in 1710 (1A,2Y) & in 1712 (3A,2Y) and at Albany NY for naturalization on 14 Feb 1716 with Hans Michiel Edich Jr. Sponsored, with Maria Christina Mendes, 1716 bp of Michael, son of Johan Ludwig Wanner & Agnes Barbara. Most likely he was the "Michel Stig" listed, with wife & 4 children, on the 1717 Simmendinger census at New Ansberg and the Johan Michael who in 1723 received Burnetsfield lot #33.

surname EDICK

+2502: MICHAEL   b say 1700; natur. 1716 with father
+2503: JACOB MIC. b say 1704; m 1725 MARGARET VAN SLYCK
 2504: MARGARET bp Schenectady NY 1 Feb 1713 (dau of Mich. & Eva)
 2505: ps. ELIABETH (Edick?) ca 1714-1776 m CONRAD FRANK
 2505A ps. daughter b say 1718; ps. m a Kessler (George or Henrich)

2506: **CHRISTIAN STTICH** - pr. born before 1685; m by 1711 ANNA MARGARET ... The wife of Christian Sittig sponsored, with Hans Henry Hammer, Nov 1711 bp of Margaret, dau of Albrecht Schreiber & Eva (Book of Names, pg 20). Appears on 1717 Simmendinger census at New Ansberg, with wife Anna Margaret & 2 children.

EDICK/ITTIG - 2nd Generation

2503: **JACOB MICHAEL ITTIG** - pr. born ca 1702 to 1708; m Schenectady NY (Dutch Reform Church, 1st marriage for both parties) 29 Dec 1725 MARGARET VAN SLYCK pr. dau of MARTEN VAN SLYCK. In 1723 he received Burnetsfield lot #21, probably as the dependent assignee of his father Michael.

2505B JOHANNES bp Schenectady NY 28 Apr 1726
2506A ps. MARIA BARBARA b say 1727; m by 1760 GEORGE N. WEAVER
2507: pr. MARGARET b say 1729; m 14 Jan 1748 NICHOLAS LIGHTHALL
+2508: JACOB jr 1730-1770 m CATHERINE FRANK
+2509: CHRISTIAN b say 1734; m MARGARETHA ...

2502: **MICHAEL ITTIG** - pr. born ca 1695 to 1701; pr. died before 1775 (undated tombstone in Ft. Herkimer churchyard); pr. m1 by 1723 ELISABETH ... (ps. a Demuth or Wohleben); pr. m2 by 1762 MARIA ... (Parson's Edick book). Michel jr. was naturalized 1716 and received Burnetsfield lot #20 (dependent lot strip on south side of the Mohawk) between Jacob Edich & Conrad Fulmer in 1723. At the same time, Elisabeth Edick, pr. wife of this Michael, received Burnetsfield lot #5 in a dependent area north of Mohawk River Pr. the Michael who, with Maria, sponsored 1762 bp of Elisabeth, son of Michael Ittig & Catherine.

2509A ps. BARBARA (Edick?) b say 1722; m GEORGE WENTZ
+2509B pr. JACOB Sr. b say 1724; m by 1755 SARAH ...
+2510: pr. MARCUS b say 1730; m1 MARGARET ; m2 1762 BARBARA WEAVER
+2512: MICHAEL 1734-1806 m CATHERINE ORENDORF

2509: CHRISTIAN ITTIG - pr. born ca 1730 to 1740; m by 1758 MARGARET ... (we
suspect she was a Frank even though Parson's Edick book has her a Weaver <basis
uncertain>); m2 by 1776 ANNA EVA ... His wife Margaret sponsored Jul 1761 bp of
Margaret, dau of Joh. Petrie & Elisabeth. Christian was a corporal in the 1767 GF
militia and a Sgt. when taken prisoner at the Little Falls mill battle June 1782
(he was returned after the Revolution). He had 4 adults & 6 children on 1778 GF
relief and was on 1790 Herkimer census (2-4-3). Edick book has son George listed
before Conrad & Christian on land deed in Herk. Co. Book #3 page 225 (not seen).

    2515: ELISABETH ca 1758-1846 m CHRISTOPHER SHOEMAKER
+2516: GEORGE C. b say 1760; pr. m 1783 DELIA PETRIE
+2517: CONRAD b SAR Feb 1762 (sp. Conrad C Frank, Elis Stphl Fox)
        d 1846; m1 CATHERINE DIETRICH; m2 NANCY FIKES
+2518: JACOB CHR. b 1764 (sp. Jacob Ittig & wife Catherine)
        d 1844; m1 EVA JO. FRANK m2 SUSAN WOOLABER
+2519: CHRISTIAN b 22 Sep 1766 (sp. Chr. Scherer & Anna Eva Frank)
        m ELISABETH EMPIE
    2520: CATHERINE CHR. b SAR 22 Nov 1770 (sp Acus Folmer, Cath Piper)
        m 1789 HENRICH WERNER
    2521: ANNA CHR. b say 1772; m 29 Jan 1793 GEORGE FRIBA
        by second wife
    2522: JOHANNES b 27 Mar 1776 (sp John C Frank & Appolonia <Weber>)
    2523: MARGARETHA b 5 Jan 1778 (sp. John Hess & Marg.<pr. Fulmer>)
        pr m 1795 RUDOLPH J. SHOEMAKER
    2524: Johan JOST b 5 Jan 1781 (sp. Jost Herkimr & Cath.)
    2525: DIETRICH b 29 Sep 1783 (sp. Joh. Petrie & Doro.<Kessler>)
    2526: MARCUS b 10 Aug 1785 (sp. Marcus Kessler, Cath. Petrie)
    2527: Johan JOST b 14 Oct 1787 (sp. John Smith & Maria Elis.)
    2528: ANNA EVA b 6 Mar 1790 (sp. Johannes Kassel & Anna)

2511: JACOB ITTIG Sr. - pr. born ca 1720 to 1732; m SARAH ... Pr. the Jacob Edick
Sr. on roster of Oriskany heroes.

    2528A ps. MARIA b say 1750; liv. 1779 (spf Geo J. Ittig bp)
        pr. the Maria 1748-1825; m 1780 PETER JAMES WEAVER
+2529: pr. JACOB J. 1755-1821 m 1777 ELISABETH WEAVER
    2529A ps. CATHERINE (Edick?) b say 1757; m by 1784 FRED. G. WEAVER
+2530: pr. GEORGE JAC. 1761-1838 m ANNA MARGARET SCHERER
    2531: GEORGE MICHAEL b 2 Sep 1763 (sp George Wentz & Barbara)

2508: JACOB ITTIG jr - born 1730 (son of Jacob Michael, vital dates from Parson's
Edick book); died 1770 from lockjaw arising after stubbing toe in a jumping match;
m CATHERINE FRANK (b 1731, her surname on 1758 bp rec.) dau of STEPHEN FRANK
(Edick book, which tells of plaque in Deposit NY cemetery saying Stephen Frank,
son of Conrad, was father of Catherine). His widow Catherine m2 1772 NICHOLAS H.
WEAVER son of HENRY WEAVER. Jacob & wife Catherine sponsored Jul 1764 bp of
Jacob, son of Christian Ittig & Margaret.

    2532: ELISABETH bp SCH 28 May 1758 (sp Van Slycks, Peter & Elis.)
    2533: ANNETJE bp SCHenectady 1 Jun 1760 (sp Wm Cuningham, Anna Toll)
+2534: CONRAD b 20 Sep 1763 (sp. Conrad Frank & Cath. Getman)
+2535: JACOB JAC. b 24 Oct 1765 (sp. John Frank, Eva Frank)
        d 1807; m 1787 MARGARET YORK
    2536: CHRISTIAN b SAR 16 Jun 1768 (sp Christian Ittig & Marg.)

2510: MARCUS ITTIG - pr. born ca 1720 to 1738; killed in action 2 Sep 1779 (in Bellinger's Regiment, Book of Names page 167); m1 MARIA MARGARETHA ...(d 1762, ps. Getman?); m2 at German Flats 14 Sep 1762 ANNA BARBARA WEAVER dau of ANDRIES WEAVER. He & wife Maria Margaret sponsored Nov 1760 bp of Geo. Michael, son of Geo. Nich. Weaver & Barbara. In Dygert's militia in 1757 (listed next to Geo. Getman & John Shoemaker) and 1767 and had 6 adults & 5 children on 1778 GF relief.

```
      2538: CATHERINE   b SAR 23 Feb 1760 (Cath. F Orendrf, Mich. M Ittig)
      2539: FREDRICH   b 23 Mar 1762 (sp. Fred. C. Frank, Marg. H. Meyer)
      2540: MARGARETHA   b 14 Jul 1764 (sp. Marg. Weber unm, Frd Haack)
      2541: JOHANNES   b 19 Nov 1765 (sp. Joh. Cunningham, Cath. Getman)
      2542: BARBARA ELISABETH   b SAR 8 Feb 1768 (sp. Stofel Strobel & Elis.)
                    m 1785 JOHANNES DINGES
     +2543: HENRICH   b SAR 4 Apr 1770 (sp Jac. Ittig & Cath.)
      2544: ANNA   b 22 Jul 1775 (sp Jac. Brdhaus, Anna Kunick)
      2545: PETER   b SAL 26 Mar 1778 (sp Pet. Getman, Elis. Pfeiffer)
```

2512: Capt. MICHAEL ITTIG - born German Flats 1734; died there 9 Mar 1806 (age 71-9-5/church rec. or 71-8-25/tombstone); m SAL 20 Nov 1760 CATHERINE ORENDORF (b ca 1741, d 2 Jun 1812 age 70-8-2) dau of FREDERICK ORENDORF. He inherited Burnetsfield lot #33. In Revol. service (Book of Names) but Bellinger book says he did not go with his company to Oriskany. He & Cath. sponsored 1760 bp of Cath., dau of Marcus Ittig, and 1764 bp of son of George N. Weaver & Barbara. Had 4 adults & 4 children on 1778 GF relief and was on 1790 GF census (3-0-4).

```
     +2546: FREDERICK   b 30 Mar 1761 (sp. Fred. Orendorf & Eva)
                    m1 CATHERINE DELANEY; m2 1802 ELISABETH HARTER
      2547: ELISABETH   b SAR 23 Jul 1762 (sp Hans Michael Ittig & w Maria)
                    d 1815; m 1785 JOST HESS
     +2548: GEORGE   b SAR 8 Oct 1765 (sp. Geo. Ohrndrff & Marg. Weber)
                    m by 1805 ANNA CLEPSATTLE
      2549: MICHAEL   1771-1846 m DOROTHY FLAGG (1773-1853) DAR V19 pg 33
      2550: pr. CATHERINE   b say 1775; liv. 1790 (spf C. Hess bp)
                    m by 1802 WILLIAM MILLER of Warren
      2551: EVA   b Aug 1778 (sp Eva Orendorf & George Hess)
                    d 1808; m FREDERICK HESS
      2552: ps. MARY   (Edick book)
      2553: ps. ANNA   b say 1786; m by 1816 MARCUS L. SHOEMAKER
```

EDICK (Ittig) - 4th Generation

2519: CHRISTIAN EDICK - born 22 Sep 1766; died Palatine NY 16 Apr 1814 age 48-7-; m 6 Jul 1794 ELISABETH EMPIE. His widow Elisabeth m2 1815 JOHN SNELL a widower. Ps. lived at Fonda NY after 1800 as children were bp there from 1800 to 1808. He had three sons and three daughters still living at time of his death.

```
      2554: MARGARET   b SAL 30 Jun 1795 (sp. Fred Getmen, Maria Empie)
      2555: DANIEL   b 18 Mar 1797 (sp Philip Empie & w. Elis.)
      2556: WILHELM   b 24 Mar 1799 (sp. Wm Frederick, Cath. Empie)
      2557: ELISABETH   b 22 Sep 1800 (FR sp Christina Yany & Gert.)
      2558: CHRISTIAN   1802-1882   m CATHERINE FREDERICK
      2559: PHILIP   b 31 Aug 1804 (FR sp Philip Philips, Elis. Casler)
      2560: GEORGE   b Fonda NY 25 Jul 1806 (sp Geo. Frederick, Cat Gage)
      2561: MARIE   b 22 Apr 1808 (sp Isaac Seaver & Christina)
```

2517: CONRAD ITTIG - born German Flats 1 Feb 1762; died W. Frankfort NY 1846; m1
at GF 28 Feb 1785 CATHERINE DIETRICH ; pr. m2 NANCY HANNAH FIKES. Ref. for second
wife is DAR vol. 49, page 328 and DAR vol. 151, page 48. Ps. the Conrad listed in
4th Tryon Co. Regiment and in Ranger unit in Revol.

    2562: NICHOLAS b GF 4 Feb 1787 (sp Joh. Nich. Staring, Cath. Edig)
    2563: JACOB b 7 Jul 1788 (sp. Jacob Ittig & Elisabeth)
    2564: CHRISTIAN b 30 Sep 1789 (sp. Christian Ittig & Marg. Fr. Fox)
    2565: MARIA b 7 Jun 1791
    2566: STOPHEL b GF Nov 1792 (sp Stophel Shoemaker)
    2567: ELISABETH b GF Mar 1794 (sp John Frank, Marg. Ittig)
            by 2nd wife
    2568: BARBARA 1817-1886 m JOSEPH BORDEN

2534: CONRAD ITTIG - pr. born 1763 & bp 20 Sep 1763 (son of Jacob Jr); died
Deposit NY 1845; m 1787 MARGARET WHITAKER (b 1770, d 1798, as in DAR Vol 87 page
137) dau of Squire WHITAKER & MARGARET; pr. m2 ELIZABETH SNEEDEN (DAR vol 99 page
11), or perhaps ELIZABETH SUYDEN. On 1790 Harpersfield NY census (1-1-2) next to
Squire Witacer. Children Jacob & Margaret Elis. were by 1st wife.

    2569: JACOB C. 1790-1859 m 1810 SALLY DURFEE
    2570: MARGARET ELIZABETH m THOMAS GARDNER ROGERS

2546: FREDERICK EDICK - born 30 Mar 1761 (son of Michel); died 20 Jun 1829 (age
68-3-20, bur. Myers Park); m1 CATHERINE DELANEY; m2 16 May 1802 ELISABETH HARTER
(b 1781, d by 1815) dau of LAWRENCE HARTER & CATHERINE (Dockstader). Children by
second wife were Catharina, Anna, & Elisabeth (Harter book page 13). Pr. the
Frederick in Revol. service with 4th Tryon Co. militia regiment. On 1790 GF
census (2-0-3) next to A. Wohleben & Jost Hess.

    2550: ELISABETH b GF 19 Jul 1785 (sp Jost Hess & Elis.<Edick>)
    2552: MICHAEL b SAR 13 Oct 1796 (sp Mich. Ittig & Dorothy)

2530: GEORGE JAC. EDICK - born ca 1761; died 5 Aug 1838 age 77; m 2 Dec 1787 ANNA
MARGARET SCHERER (Peggy, b ca 1767, d 1821) dau of CHRISTIAN SCHERER & ANNA
MARGARET BELLINGER (Bellinger book page 36). Pr. the George in Revol. service and
ps. the George F. (ps. error on mid. initial?) who m Marg. Scherer and had dau
Maria bp 1811. On 1790 GF census (1-3-2).

    2571: Johan PETER b 13 May 1788 (sp Pet. Fox & Anna <Scherer>)
            d Columbia NY 16 Sep 1832 (age 44, tombstone)
    2572: JACOB b GF Jul 1789 (sp. John Bellinger & Cath. Scherer)
            m EVA STEELE (b 1790)
    2573: CHRISTIAN b 5 Dec 1790 (sp. Conrad Getman & Maria)
    2574: MARGARETHA b 10 Sep 1792 (sp. Peter Scherer, Elis. Bellinger)
    2575: JOHN b Hkm 19 Jan 1794 (sp Joh. Cassel & Anna); d 22 Jun 1840
            m1 DIANA VAN DEUSEN m2 SARAH STERNBERG
    2576: ELISABETHA b Warren NY 16 Jan 1804
    2577: ABRAHAM b 17 Jul 1805 (sp. Conrad Getman & w. Maria)

2516: GEORGE EDICK - we side with Edick book that this George was a son of
Christian (despite minister's entry of George Michael on 1783 mar. record); m GF 9
Jan 1783 DELIA PETRIE pr. dau of MARCUS PETRIE jr. Land bequest in 1793 (HCH
Frank file, orig. not seen) has Delia, wife of George Ittig, as a Conrad Frank
descendent, which is possible if Delia was a grand-daughter rather than a
daughter. George was on 1790 HK census (1-1-3) near Witherstine, Schells, et al.

children of George & Delia

2578: DELIA G.   b GF 7 Aug 1784 (sp. Conrad Ittig, Elis. Petrie)
2579: JACOB G.   b GF 13 Apr 1787 (sp. Jacob Ittig & Cath. Petrie)
2580: MARIA G.   b 19 Aug 1789 (sp John Chamble, Maria Marc. Petrie)
2581: JOHANNES G. b 25 Sep 1791 (sp. Joh. Ittig, Appol. Bellinger)
2582: MARGARET   b 23 Jan 1794 (sp. Joh. Widerstein & Marg.)

2548: GEORGE MIC. ITTIG - born ca Sep 1765 (son of Michel, birthdate calc. from death info); died Columbia NY 4 Jul 1830 (age 64-9-6); m by 1805 ANNA CLEPSATTLE (Nancy, b ca 1772, d 4 Oct 1843 age 72-1-6). Clepsattle wife is only one mentioned in Parson's Edick book, thus we presume another George Michel was husband of Delia Petrie. A George M. Ittig appears on 1810 census at Warren NY. Edick book gives children as John J., George L., Michel, Betsy (Elisabeth, b Warren NY Jun 1805, sp. Jos. Hess & w. Elis.<Edick>), & Catherine.

2529: JACOB J. EDICK - born German Flats 21 Jul 1755; died Deerfield NY 23 Feb 1821; m 1777 ELISABETH WEAVER (b 1760, d 1847) dau of GEORGE WEAVER (as in E&N 10 Jul 1929 and DAR vol 114 page 311). For children Jacob and John, see DAR vol 101 page 244 and DAR vol 96 page 31 (other children's dates from HK church rec.). Prob. the Jacob J. (son of Jacob) in 4th Reg. Tryon militia. Two of his sons (George & Christ. Bellinger Ittig) moved to Russel Ohio ca 1830.

2583: GEORGE   b GF 16 Oct 1779 (sp Joh. Nicol Weber & Maria Ittig)
                  d 1864; m1 REBECCA SMITH m2 OLIVE BASS
2584: JACOB jr   1782-1859 m ISABEL LEAVENWORTH
2585: ELISABETH   1784-1864 m PHINEAS SHERMAN
2586: MARCUS   b 27 Feb 1786 (sp. Fred Meyer & Anna Marg.)
                  d 1860; m ELIZA PEEK
2587: CATHERINE   b 4 Feb 1788 (sp. Fred. Weaver & Cath.)
                  d 1876; m EVERETT PEEK
2588: HENRICH   b 9 Nov 1789 (sp. Henrich Saljc & Barbara)
2589: JOHN   b GF 15 Nov 1791 (sp. Marc Ittig, Elis. Meyer)
                  d 1823; m LOVINA SHERMAN
2590: MARGARET   b 23 Feb 1794 (sp. Michael Weaver & Elisabeth)
                  d 1876; m JOHN CAVANA (son of Peter)
2591: CHRISTOPHER B. 1796-1875 m CYNTHIA EATON
2592: THOMAS   b 8 Jan 1801; d 2 Apr 1807 unm

2535: JACOB ITTIG - pr. born 24 Oct 1764 (son of Jacob jr & Cath., birthyear in DAR vol 147 page 278); died Deposit NY 1807; m 1787 MARTHA YORK (b 1768).

2592A SUSANNA b Albany NY 30 Sep 1790 (sp. Fr Ittig, Cath Weaver)
2593: ERASTUS   1804-1886 m CATHERINE F. COGSWELL

2518: JACOB C. EDICK - pr. the Jacob born 30 Jul 1764 (son of Christian & Marg.); died Spinnerville NY 12 Oct 1844 age 81; m1 1792 EVA JOH. FRANK dau of JOHN FRANK; m2 SUSAN WOHLEBEN (b 1771, d 1820) dau of PETER WOHLEBEN. Enlisted as private in Revolutionary service in 1779 (DAR vol 65, page 102 and Vol 49, page 329).

2594: BETSY   m ISAAC FITCH
2595: BENJAMIN   1804-1890 m2 JANE WILLIAMS
2596: SUSAN   1809-1906 m JAMES PADDOCK

2543: HENRICH ITTIG - born 4 Apr 1770 (son of Marcus); pr. m CATHERINE KAISER (another Henry apparently m DOROTHEA MILLER <see Getman book>). Ps. the Henrich on 1800 census at Warren NY.

EYSAMAN - 1st Generation

2601: **HANES EYSAMAN** (John) - pr. born ca 1705 to 1720; killed by Tory Indians on
9 Jun 1779; m ... (wife's name unknown, she was slain also on 9 Jun 1779). He
presumably immigrated to America between 1725 and 1745, as the Eysaman name does
not appear on any of the earlier NY Palatine records, and is mentioned, with his
children, as being amongst the initial members of the Manheim Lutheran Church,
probably about 1745-50 (Book of Names page 61, dates are a guess). He was in
Capt. Mark Petrie's German Flats militia company in 1757. As he seems to be the
only one of this surname in the area, the young adults in the 1760's (i.e.
Anthony, John, & Maria) are assumed to have been his children (without the "pr."
qualifier) and link to son Stephen, who survived the attack in which his parents
were butchered, as provided in Beers "History of Herkimer Co." (page 180).

```
                        surname EYSAMAN
      +2602: ANTONIUS    b say 1740;  m by 1763 JANNETJE
       2603: ELISABETH   b say 1742; m 1762 PAUL SEGHNER
      +2604: JOHN    1744-1828   m 1766  ELISABETH KESSLER
      +2605: pr. STEPHEN    1761-1844 m2 ANNA EVA PETRIE
```

EYSAMAN - 2nd Generation

2602: Johan **ANTHONY EYSAMAN** - pr. born ca 1730 to 1745; m by 1763 JANNETJE ...
Possibly killed at the same time as his parents on 9 Jun 1779 (Cdr. Bellinger's
notes #3.15.2). Anthony & wife Jannetje were sponsors for bp Jan 1763 of Anthony,
son of Paul Segner & Maria Elisabeth (Eysaman).

2604: **JOHN EYSAMAN** jr. - born ca 12 Mar 1744; died Herkimer NY as widower 24 Aug
1828 (age 84-5-16, Church rec.); m 26 Oct 1766 ELIZABETH KESSLER (b ca 1747, d 24
Jun 1824 age 77) pr. dau of JACOB KESSLER & CATHERINE STEELE. Pr. the "John
Iceman" on 1790 Herkimer NY census (2-2-6) living near Petries, M. Kessler, John
Kessler, Farmer, & H. Klock..

```
      +2606: pr. JACOB   ca 1769-1816; m 1794 ANNA EVA MEYER
       2607: ANTONIUS   bp May 1770 (sp Stephen Eysaman, Marg. Kessler)
       2608: DOROTHEA   b 6 Jun 1776 (sp. Joh. Petrie & Dorothea <Kessler>)
                        pr. m ADOLPH KESSLER
      +2609: PETER   b 7 Jun 1778 (sp. Joh. Kessler & Elisabeth)
                        m by 1800 CATHERINE KLOCK
       2610: MARY ELIZABETH   b 23 Aug 1780 (sp. Jacob Kessler & Elis.)
                        m RICHARD PETRIE
       2611: MARY CATHERINE   b 11 Jan 1782 (sp. Conrad Kessler & Maria Cath.)
                        m 1804 JOHN TH. SHOEMAKER
      +2612: JOHN   b 1784 (sp John Kesslr & Cath); m MARIA ELIZ. PETRIE
      +2613: ANNA   b 11 Oct 1785 (sp Jac. Petrie & w Maria)
                        m 1803 MARCUS M. PETRIE
       2614: DELIA   b 24 Dec 1790 (sp Dan. Jac. Petrie & Anna Segner)
                        m 1812 JOHN J. SCHELL
       2615: LENA   b 21 Mar 1792 (sp. Jac. Kessler & w. Delia)
```

2605: **STEPHEN EYSAMAN** - born Mar 1761; died Little Falls NY 15 May 1844 age 83 years; m1 ... (first wife, name unknown, reportedly killed by Indians 9 Jun 1779); m2 by 1780 MARIA ... (bp sponsorships noted below suggest she was a Kessler); m3 by 1785 ANNA EVA PETRIE (b 1768, d 1823) dau of JOST M. PETRIE & CATHERINE KESSLER (Petrie book page 18). Stephen sponsored, with Maria Orendorf, Apr 1767 bp of Magdalena, dau of Paul Seghner & Elisabeth (Eysaman). Beers History has him taken prisoner to Montreal after the June 1779 Tory Indian attack (in which his parents, first wife, and infant were killed) and not released until December 1782; but that story doesn't quite fit with an April 1780 birth of his child, by wife "Maria", and Stephen Eysaman appearance, with wife Maria, sponsor for Apr 1780 bp of Maria, dau of Jacob Kessler & Maria Catherine <Petrie>. On 1790 German Flats census (1-1-3).

       2616: child   killed by Indians 9 Jun 1779
                     by 2nd wife
       2617: MARGARET b GF 2 Apr 1780 (sp Nic. Rsncrantz, Marg. Kessler)
                     by 3rd wife (Anna Eva)
    +2618: ELISABETH b 2 Apr 1785 (sp Geo.H. Bell, Elis. Segner)
                 m 1805 PETER B. KESSLER (son of Nich.)
    +2619: JOSEPH 1787- m ANNA KESSLER (had 3 sons)
       2620: CATHARINE bp 16 Oct 1789 (sp. Cath. J. Petrie, widow)
                 m 1810 WILLIAM N. STAHRING
       2621: JOHN S. b 30 Sep 1791 (sp John Eysaman & Elisabeth)
                 m 1812 POLLY YOUNG (dau of Barent)
       2622: GEORGE b 31 Dec 1793 (sp. Geo. Hausman & Maria Elis.)
       2623: ANNA STEPH. b say 1794; m 1813 MELCHIOR RINCKEN
    +2624: JACOB 1796-1879 m MARIA BELLINGER
       2625: PETER b say 1798; m 1826 MARIA LEPARD
    +2626: HENRY b 21 Aug 1801; m MARGARET BELLINGER
       2627: ANNA EVA b HK 17 May 1806 (sp Peter Eysaman & Cath.)
                 m 1827 ADAM JOH. KESSLER

EYSAMAN - 3rd Generation

2626: Ensign HENRY EYSAMAN - born 21 Aug 1803; m 9 Dec 1823 MARGARET BELLINGER (b 1803) dau of CHRISTOPHER P. BELLINGER & MAGDALENA BELLINGER (b 1769 dau of John P. Bellinger). Five children, incl. Delia Maria (m. John W. Bellinger) and Philo (b 1843, m Mary Rankin).

2606: JACOB EYSAMAN - pr. the Jacob born ca 1769 (birthyear from death figures); died 30 Apr 1816 (age 47); m Jul 1794 ANNA EVA MEYER dau of JOSEPH MEYER. Lived at Warrentown in 1805 (HK bp rec.)

       2628: JOHANNES b 9 Apr 1795 (sp Joh. Diet. Petrie & Dor. Eysaman)
                 m 1816 ELISABETH OXSENER (dau of John)
       2628A MOSES b HK 20 Jul 1805 (sp Peter Eysaman & w. Cath.)

2624: JACOB EYSAMAN - born 15 Jun 1796; died 13 Jan 1879; m 21 Jul 1816 MARIA BELLINGER (b 1795) dau of JOHN BELLINGER & CATHARINE PETRIE.

       2629: MARY CATHERINE b 4 Feb 1819
       2630: PHILO ELIJAH b 27 Apr 1822; d 29 Dec 1827
       2631: JAMES 1826-1905 m ELVIRA PARKS

2612: JOHN ESYAMAN (jr.) - pr. born ca 1780 to 1785; m 11 Nov 1804 MARIA ELIZABETH PETRI dau of JOHN PETRIE & BARBARA KLOCK. Petrie book (page 22) notes two children, Barbara Elisabeth and John (b HK 4 Apr 1805, sp John J. Petri & w. Maria).

2619: JOSEPH EYSAMAN - born 25 Oct 1787 (bp sp. Joh. Dietrich Kessler & Marg. Petrie); m ANNA KESSLER.

```
        2632: JOSEPH   b 11 Sep 1806
        2633: WILLIAM  b 9 Feb 1808
        2634: FRANCIS    m MARIA CASLER
```

2609: PETER EYSAMAN - born ca 1778 (age 72 in 1850, pr. son of John jr.); m CATHERINE KLOCK (b say 1775) dau of HENDRICK KLOCK & MARGARET WAGNER (Dockstader book page 157). Was sponsor for bp in 1806 of Anna Eva, dau of Stephen Eysaman.

```
        2635: PETER jr.  b say 1798; m 1819 MARIA SMALL (dau of Melch.)
      +2636: ABRAHAM  b 1800-1864  m DOROTHY FEETER
        2637: BARBARA ELISABETH  b ca Jan 1805; d 10 Sep 1805 (age 0-8-28)
        2638: HENRY P.  b HK 16 Jul 1806; m MARY ANN ...
        2639: JOHN P.  b ca 1808; m 1830 MARGARET WOHLEBEN
        2640: CATHERINE  b HK 30 Aug 1809; m GEORGE RASBACH
        2641: SANFORD  b 25 Dec 1812; m MARY PETRIE (dau of John & Barb.)
```

2613: ANNA EYSAMAN - born 11 Oct 1785 (sp. Jacob Petrie & w. Maria); m HK 14 Aug 1803 MARCUS M. PETRIE. Mar. witnesses were John J. Eysaman & John T. Shoemaker. Daughter Catherine b HK 30 Oct 1803 (sp Peter Eysaman & w. Cath.).

2642: ELIZABETH S. EYSAMAN - born 1785; m 1805 PETER B. CASLER (son of Nicholas). Had 11 children (Bellinger book page 60).

EYSAMAN - 4th Generation

2636: ABRAHAM EYSAMAN - born 15 Feb 1800; died 29 Feb 1864; m DOROTHY FEETER (b 1798) dau of Col. WILLIAM FEETER & MARIA ELIZABETH BELLINGER as in Petrie book page 40. Identified as son of Peter on confirmation in 1815 (Herk. Church rec.).

```
        2643: WILLIAM   1819-1883  m CORNELIA SOPHIA CASLER
        2644: JOHN PETER  b 19 Jan 1821; d 12 Apr 1826
        2645: MARY CATHERINE  b 19 Feb 1825; d 7 Mar 1830
        2646: GEORGE FEETER  b 11 Jul 1827; d 16 May 1850 unm
        2647: MARGARET  b 2 Aug 1829; d 12 Jul 1856
        2648: ELIZABETH HELEN  b 12 Apr 1831; d 10 Apr 1835
        2649: DELIA ANN  b 27 Mar 1832; d 17 Jan 1839
        2650: HORACE  1834-  m MARY E. SMITH
        2651: CYNTHIA ELIZA  b 1 Nov 1836; d 26 Mar 1837
        2652: ABRAHAM JAMES  b 18 May 1839; d 13 Apr 1861
```

********** FELLER **********

FELLER - 1st Generation

2701: NICHOLAS FELLER - pr. born in Germany ca 1660 to 1675; m ELISABETH ...
From Guntersblum, earldom Leinig-Hartenburg, Germany (son Philip´s mar. rec.). On
NY Palatine subsistence list in 1710 (2A,2Y) and 1712 (4A,2Y). On 1717
Simmendinger census at Queensburg with wife Elisabeth and 6 children. Drew lot# 7
(property descended to Hilts family) on 1725 Burnetsfield Patent and lived at
German Flats 1723 to 1734. His will dated 8 May 1734 (published in Enterprise &
News 4 Mar 1931) mentions leaving his place in Church to Nicholas Christman, son
of Hanes Christman (see also Vosburgh, Herkimer Ch. Records vol. 3, page 44).
Supposedly he had two daughters named Catherine (Enterprise & News 31 May 1939).
His only son Philip remained in the Hudson River area of eastern New York and we
observe that the Feller name no longer appears in the Mohawk Valley after the
passing of Burnetsfield Patentee Nicholas.

surname FELLER
+2702: Johan PHILIP   b say 1696; m 1717 CATHARINA ELISABETH RAUH
2703: pr. CATHERINE   b say 1700; m 1732 LAMBERT STARENBERG
2704: pr. CATHERINE   b say 1702; m NICHOLAS WOHLEBEN
2705: MARGARET   b say 1710; m by 1726 JOHANNES CHRISTMAN Jr.
2706: MARIA ELISABETH   b 26 Jul 1712; m GEORGE HILTS

FELLER - 2nd Generation

2702: Johan PHILLIP FELLER - pr. born ca 1690 to 1697; died 1768; m 18 Sep 1717
CATHARINA ELISABETHA RAUH dau of NICHOLAS RAUH of Oppenhiem in the Palatinate in
Germany ("Book of Names" page 46). Philip´s sons left descendents at Rhinebeck NY,
some of whom took the surname "Fellows".

+2707: NICHOLAS   b 21 Jul 1717 (sp. Johan Niclaus Rau)
            m ANNA MARIA NIER
2708: JOHN   1719-1791   m ANNA BARBARA DIETER
2709: PHILIP   1723-   m 1748 SUSANNA ELISABETH SCHAEFER
2710: ELISABETH   bp Kinderhook NY 1727
2711: JACOB   bp Rhinebeck NY 17 Feb 1734
2712: Johan WILHELM   bp Rhinebeck NY 27 Apr 1736

2703: CATHERINE FELLER - born Guntersbum Germany 31 May 1700; m at Schoharie NY
1732 LAMBERT STARENBERG (pr. b 1695)

********** FOLTS (Voltz) **********

2801: **MELCHERT FOLTS** - pr. born in Germany 1676; died 1759; ml by 1711 ANNA EVA
... ; m2 by 1717 MARGARETHA ...; and m3 by 1725 ANNA CATHERINE ... (named in his
will). Melchert appears on the NY Palatine subsistence list in 1710 (2A,0Y) and
1712 (2A,1Y). Melchior Voltz & wife Anna Eva sponsored Nov 1711 bp of Anna Eva,
dau of Michael Freymeyer & Elisabeth. Pr. arrived directly at New York in 1710,
rather than via Philadelphia (as in 1974 ms. "The Descendents of Peter Folts" by
Charles P. Brown, Box 416, R.D. 2, Altamont NY). Listed at Livingston Manor, NY
1710-11 by Rupp (book of early Germans) and at Haysbury camp in 1711 when
enlisting for Canada expedition (Book of Names, page 125). Melchert was
naturalized at Albany 3 Jan 1716, on the 1717 Simmendiger census with wife
Margaret & 3 children, and ca 1723 drew Burnetsfield lot #2. His will prepared
Jan 1725 (Beers "History of Herkimer Co., New York", pages 247-8) mentions wife
Anna Catrina, sons Jacob, Peter, Conrad, & daughters Anna Margaret & Elizabeth
Catrina; executors were Fred. Bell, George Kast, & Lawrence Harter (will wit. by
George S. Smidt, John Williams, & Anna Bell).

                    surname FOLTS
    +2802: JACOB MELCHOIR   1711-1807 m CATHERINE PETRIE
    +2803: PETER   1714-1777   m ELISABETH ... (ps. COENS)
     2804: JOHANNES   b 28 Mar 1716; pr. d. by 1725
    +2805: Johan CONRAD   1719-1779   ml CATHERINE DEMUTH
     2806: ANNA MARGARET b 29 Oct 1721; liv. ca 1725 (father's will)
                 (ps. Margaret married a Kessler or Bell)
     2807: ELIZABETH CATRINA b 17 Dec 1723; d Mar 1807; m DANIEL PETRIE
                 (Elis.'s age at death <85-3-3> gives birthdate ca Dec 1721)
    +2808: ps. ELISABETH BARBARA   b say 1728; m JOHN BELLINGER

2809: MICHAEL FOLTS - Naturalized at Albany NY May 1755; pr. different family.

                    FOLTS - 2nd Generation

2805: **CONRAD FOLTS** - born 7 Jan 1719; died 6 Jan 1779; ml ANNA CATHERINE DEMUTH
(b 1722, d 1765) dau of Johan JOST DEMUTH; m2 SAR 16 Jun 1767 MARIA CATHERINE
HILTS as in 1983 Folts ms. by Jane Bellinger (HCH, Herkimer NY). Pr. the Conrad
Folts with 4 adults & 2 children on 1778 GF relief.

    +2810: JOSEPH   1740-1833   m 1767 MARGARETHA BELLINGER
    +2811: ELISABETH   1744-1827   m JACOB PFEIFFER (PIPER)
    +2812: MELCHERT   1746-1829 ml MARIA EVA STAHRING; m2 MARY GETMAN
     2813: CATHERINE   b 26 Aug 1748; m JOHANNES CHRISTMAN
     2814: ANNA   b say 1750 (#36 in J. Bellinger Folts ms.)
    +2815: GEORGE   b 19 Feb 1753; m CHRISTINA ...
     2816: HANNES   b say 1756 (#38 in Folts ms.)
    +2817: CONRAD   bp SAR 7 Aug 1760 (sp. Peter Foltz & w. Elisabeth)
                 d 1828; m 1784 CATHARINE LENTZ
     2818: JACOB   b 8 May 1765 (sp Dan Petrie & Elis.); pr d. soon
                 by second wife
    +2819: ANNA MARGARET   b SAR 12 Apr 1768 (sp. Christian Riegel & Marg.)
                 d 1822; m CONRAD FR. HELMER
     2820: JACOB   b SAR Jun 1770 (sp. Jacob Petrie, Maria Hilts)
                 d 1814; m by 1804 CATHERINE HEES

2802: **JACOB FOLTS** - pr. born ca Nov 1711 (Brown´s "Descendents of Peter Folts"), died Frankfort NY 30 Jan 1808 (age 96-1-26, Duell); m ANNA CATHERINE PETRIE (b 14 Jul 1714, d 11 Jun 1799) dau of Johan JOST PETRIE & CORDELIA DEMUTH. About 1723 he received Burnetsfield lot #3, south of the Mohawk River (in the present area of Frankfort NY), and apparently sometime before the Revolution he purchased adjacent lot #2 from Martin Smith. In 1767 Lt. Jacob Folts was in the GF militia and both he and his son Conrad were wounded at the Battle of Oriskany in 1777 (DAR #55358). Jacob Folts had 4 adults & 5 children on 1778 GF relief and was on the 1790 GF census (1-0-2) as "Jacob Sr.". Jacob was blind from his 80th year of age and spent his last years in second childhood (Beers "Herkimer Co." pages 246-248).

> 2821: ANNA MARIA b say 1734; d 1737
> 2822: ANN MARGRET b 29 Dec 1736; m ADAM JAC. GARLOCK (Folts ms.)
> +2823: JACOB jr. b say 1738; liv. 1763 (non-militia status)
> 2824: ELIZABETH b 25 Jan 1741; m 1766 JOHANNES DEMUTH
> 2825: CATHERINE 1744-1815 m 1766 JOHN J. KLOCK
> 2826: ANNA MARIA b 1745; m 1769 JOHN CUNNINGHAM
> +2827: CONRAD 1747-1793 m ANNA DYGERT
> 2828: ANNA b 7 Mar 1750; d by 1793; m 1770 JACOB BAUMAN
> 2829: DELIA b 20 May 1752; m FREDERICK BAUMAN
> 2830: DOROTHEA b 21 Oct 1754

2803: **PETER FOLTS** - born 22 Aug 1714 (Brown´s Folts book); killed at Oriskany 6 Aug 1777; m ELISABETH ... ps. a dau of JOHANNES COENS & CATHERINE which we feel offers a better age and name fit than the say a dau of JOHANNES RASBACH & MARGARET. His widow may lived after 1777 with son-in-law George Hilts and, as we suspect she was born before 1724, we do not think she was the Elisabeth (d 1808 age 84) who married by ca 1786 FREDERICK HARTER. Peter was in Capt. Petrie´s 1757 GF militia, listed just before Hanes foltz (pr. his son). Family tradition says that during the Revolution his children John & Catherine were taken up a hill and killed by Tory Indians (pr. at Schellsbush in East Herkimer).

> 2831: JOHN b say 1740; in militia 1757; pr. killed ca 1779
> +2832: CATHERINE b say 1742; killed by Indians pr. ca 1779
> ps. m JOHN J. FOX (tradition, origin uncertain)
> 2833: ELISABETH P. b say 1746; liv. Mar 1762 (spf Stahring bp)
> m 1769 GEORGE HILTS
> +2834: CONRAD P. ca 1748-1829 m MARIA HILTS
> +2835: PETER 1750-1827 m BARBARA RASBACH
> 2836: ps. CHRISTINA b say 1753; liv. Jul 1776 (spf Hilts bp)
> +2837: ps. MELCHERT ca 1755-1816 m by 1788 MARGARET ...

2808: **ELISABETH BARBARA FOLTS** (or Barbara Elisabeth) - pr. born between 1725 and 1742; m before 1760 JOHN BELLINGER son of PHILIP BELLINGER. Had a son George Bellinger, born before 1760, and we believe a daughter Margaret born in 1748 (later wife of Nicholas Smith). On the basis of the 1748 child, we feel she was probably born before 1732 and thus would not have been a daughter of Conrad Folts (b 1719), leaving by default for her to have been a daughter of immigrant Melchior (but born at a later date than the preparation of his will in 1725). Thus we finds ourselves at odds with the tradition, seen in the Bellinger book, that Elizabeth Barbara was a sister of Joseph C. Folts (who married in 1767 Margaret Ph. Bellinger). On the basis of their marriages to offspring of Philip Bellinger, Elisabeth Barbara would have been a sister-in-law as well as an aunt (more likely than a sister) to Joseph C. Folts.

2817: CONRAD C. FOLTS - bp 7 Aug 1760 (son of Conrad); died 1828; m GF 20 Jun 1784 CATHARINE LENTZ. Present when his brother Jost fought the Indians in the West Canada Creek on 9 Jul 1779 and pr. the Folts who later, when a prisoner of war in Canada, accused the Tory Hilts of scalping his sister, Mrs. Dornberger (Simms Frontiersman of New York, vol 2 page 281). Conrad C. was on the 1790 GF census (1-3-1), along with Jacob Sr. & Conrad J. in the Frankfort NY area.

    2838: MELCHIOR b GF 22 Oct 1785 (sp Melch. Folts & Maria)
    2839: MICHAEL b GF 9 May 1788 (sp Mich. Witrig & Elis.)
    2840: JOHANNES bp SJR 5 Sep 1790 (sp Philip Lentz, Cath. Folts)
    2841: CATHERINE b 17 Dec 1791 (sp Pet. Riema, Cath. Piper)

2827: Capt. CONRAD J. FOLTS - born 7 Dec 1747 (Petrie book page 9); drowned in the Mohawk River at Frankfort NY 7 Jun 1793; m ANNA DYGERT (b ca 1754, d Frankfort 20 May 1813 age 59-10-) dau of WARNER DYGERT & MAGDALENA HERKIMER. Widow Anna m2 1805 TIMOTHY FRANK son of CONRAD FRANK. Possible child Anna, born May 1783 (dau of Conrad or Peter, no mother listed) pr. does not belong to Conrad P. Folts (who had a child born Feb 1783) or to the unmarried Conrad Jr. (who m 1784 Cath. Lentz). Conrad I. Folts was on 1790 GF census (2-4-3).

   +2842: JACOB C. b 1775; m ELIZABETH STEELE
    2843: WARNER 1777-1837 m MARY GETMAN
    2844: MARY b 8 Feb 1779 (sp Jost Dygert & M. Elis.)
    2845: JOSEPH b 9 Feb 1782; m ELIZABETH CLEPSADDLE
    2846: ps. ANNA b GF 31 May 1783
   +2847: SEVERENUS b 23 Mar 1784 (sp Diet. Petrie & Elis.<Dygert>)
               m DOROTHY DYGERT
    2848: JOHANNES b 20 Feb 1786; m ELIZABETH HARTER
    2849: CATHARINA b 27 Jun 1788 (sp Adam Garlock)
              m WILLIAM W. DYGERT
    2850: ABRAHAM b GF 31 Jan 1791 (sp Hen. Uhly & Lena)
              d 22 Oct 1823
    2851: DANIEL b GF 3 May 1793 (sp John Getman & Elisabeth)

2852: CONRAD P. FOLTS - born ca 1748 (son of Peter); died Herkimer NY 14 May 1824 (age 76); m by 1776 MARIA HILTS (b ca 1750, d 1834) pr. dau of CHRISTOFEL HILTS (the Kilts <"Giels"> sponsors below were pr. in-laws of Maria Hilts via her sister Catherine who married Nicholas Kilts). Pr. the Conrad Vols in Capt. Petrie´s 1769 GF militia, listed just following Peter Vols (Folts) and Christian Schell. Conrad Folts & wife Maria were sponsors for Jul 1778 bp of Peter, son of Peter Foltz & Barbara (Rasbach), and for Jul 1782 bp of Lorentz, son of Lorentz Hilts & Barbara. Pr. the Conrad, who with Peter, had 5 adults & 5 children on 1778 German Flats relief (Book of Names, page 117). Conrad was on the 1790 Herkimer census (1-1-3) in the East Herkimer area, listed near Marc Raspach, Peter Folts, and Michael Myer.

    2853: STOPHEL b GF 25 Mar 1777 (sp. Lorentz Hilts & Maria)
    2854: pr. PETER C. b say 1778; m CATHERINE ... (ca 1787-1825)
    2855: JACOB b GF 12 Aug 1780 (sp Godfrid Hilts & Maria)
    2856: ELISABETH b GF 20 Feb 1783 (sp Peter Giels, Magdal. Stamm)
    2857: MARIA CATHERINE b 28 Oct 1785 (sp Nic. Spohn, Cath. Giels)
    2858: JOHANNES b GF 8 Mar 1788 (sp John Hilts, Maria Gils)
    2859: FREDERICK b GF 21 Aug 1790 (sp F Dornberger & Elis.)
    2860: ANNA b GF 9 Mar 1793 (sp Thomas Bell & Anna)

2815: GEORGE FOLTS - born 19 Feb 1753; died Newfane NY ca 1839-40; ps. ml by 1776 MARGARET ...; m by 1782 CHRISTINA ... (ps. a Bender or a Bell?). In February 1802, three of his daughters died from drinking the same bad water as killed Mrs. Sarah (Hilts) Smith. George & Christina sponsored Dec 1804 HK bp of Daniel, son of Jacob Folts & Catherine (Hees). George was on the 1790 Herkimer census (2-2-3).

    2861: CONRAD b 18 Dec 1782 (sp Conrad Helmer & Marg. <Folts>)
          m MARGARET ORENDORF
    2862: CATHERINE b GF 5 Feb 1785 (sp Tho. Bell & Anna); d 17 Feb 1802
    2863: GEORGE b GF 13 Sep 1787 (sp Jacob Smidt & Cath.)
          m EVA DIET. DEMUTH
    2864: ELISABETH b GF 30 Nov 1789 (Melc. Fols & Maria); d 10 Feb 1802
    2865: ANNA b Oct 1792 (sp. Jacob Folts, Cath. Christman)
          d 13 Feb 1802 (age 9-3-27)

2823: JACOB FOLTS jr - Capt Klock´s delinquent list 1763 (Book of Names pg 11)

2867: JOHN FOLTS - pr. born ca 1732 to 1741 (pr. son of Peter). Hans Folts listed just after Peter Folts in Capt. Petry´s 1757 GF militia co.

2810: Johan JOST FOLTS - pr. born 13 Aug 1740 (Bellinger book page 26 has him as brother of Barbara Elisabeth Folts, wife of John Bellinger Sr.); died Pamelia, Jefferson Co., NY 15 Apr 1833 age 93; m SAR 6 Jan 1767 MARGARETHA BELLINGER (b 16 Apr 1752, d 26 Apr 1824, family bible) dau of PHILIP BELLINGER. Simms (Frontiersman of New York, vol 2 page 281) tells of the attack on Folts and others picking berries near the West Canada Creek on 9 Jul 1779 in which Jost Folts felled three Indians with a single shotgun blast and then fought others off in hand to hand combat although his arm was shattered and cut by their tomahawks. Joseph had 5 children on the 1778 GF relief and was on the 1790 Herkimer census (2-2-4).

    2868: ELISABETH b say 1770; m 1789 GEORGE MCKOOM (b 1768)
    +2869: MELCHERT JOST b say 1772; m CATHERINE SMITH
    2870: Johan JOST b 7 Jun 1777 (sp. Wm Bellinger...)
    2871: CATHARINE m ISAAC HURLBUT
    2872: MARGARET b 5 Mar 1780 (sp. Conrad Folts, Cath. Harter)
          m JAMES STREETER
    2873: JOHN b 3 Oct 1785; d Pamelia NY Oct 1860; m 1812 KATHERINE
    2874: ANNA b 7 Dec 1789; m SMITH SCOVILLE

2875: MELCHERT FOLTS - pr. born ca 1755; died Herkimer NY 1816 (age 60-11-28, buried Frankfut NY); m by 1785 MARGARET ... Melchert and Margaret were sponsors for Apr 1788 bp of Polly Maria, dau of Jacob Petrie & Maria.

    2876: JOHN b GF 3 Oct 1785 (sp John Christman & Cath.)

2812: MELCHERT FOLTS jr - born 5 May 1746 (son of Conrad); died 2 May 1829 (age 83); ml 1769 MARIA EVA STAHRING (scalped 1779); m2 pr. ca 1780 MARY GETMAN aka "Liz" (d Jun 1829) dau of FREDERICK GETMAN & MARGARET (Getman book) and widow of FREDERICK STEPHENS (d Aug 1777). As "McLeod" Folts he had 1 child under 16 on the 1778 GF relief and on the 1790 Herkimer census (1-3-2), Melchert appears listed next to brother George. Melchert Folts was the town clerk of Herkimer in 1789, as noted in Benton´s "History of Herkimer Co." (Albany 1856)

    2877: pr. ANNA MEL. b GF 13 Aug 1776 (sp. Geo. Folts & Margaret)

children of Melchert cont.
2878: JOHN b 19 Jun 1778 (son of Melchior & Maria); pr. d. y.
         (bp sp John Demuth & wife <Folts>)
            by second wife
+2879: CONRAD b GF 8 Aug 1783 (sp Conrad Folts, Cath. Weaver)
            d 1853; m 1803 SUSANNA COLE
+2880: MARGARET b GF 24 Mar 1786 (sp John Getman, Margaret Folts)
            d 1878; m ADAM SMITH
2881: MELCHERT b GF 9 Oct 1788 (sp. Melc. Jos. Folts, Dor. N. Hilts)
            m KATY ...
2881A JOHANNES b GF 10 Sep 1790 (sp Marc Raspach, Cath. Pfeifer)
2882: PETER b 1792; pr. d. young
+2883: PETER b GF 8 Nov 1795 (sp Pet. Piper & Marg.); m ANNA COLE

2835: PETER P. FOLTS - born 15 Sep 1750; died 16 Nov 1827; m 6 Nov 1776 BARBARA
RASBACH (b 1759, d 1841) dau of MARX RASBACH & SOPHRONIA MOAK. "Klock Genealogy"
by Mrs Dan F. Williams (Helen Laura Clock) has daughter Nancy Folts marrying
Christian Petrie son of JOHANNES PETRIE & BARBARA KLOCK (b 1751, d 1807). Ps.
sponsored Stone Arabia bp 1769 of Peter, son of John Schell. On 1790 HK census
(1-2-3) next to Conrad Folts.

2884: PETER b 6 Jul 1778 (sp Conrad Folts & Maria)
            Peter died 6 Oct 1779
+2885: JOHN 1780-1867 m 1802 CATHERINE CASLER (Jacob's dau)
2886: NANCY (ANNA) b GF 31 May 1783 (sp Conr. Ittig, Anna Moog)
            m 1806 CHRISTIAN PETRIE
2887: CATHERINE b GF 16 Feb 1786 (sp Marc Raspach, Cath. Hilts)
            m JOHN NELLIS
2888: PETER b GF 19 Jul 1788 (sp. Peter Schell, Marg. Raspach)
            m ELIZABETH YOUNG
2889: MARKS b GF 16 Oct 1790 (sp John Hiels, Marg. Dornberger)
            d 1850; m ELIZABETH SPARKS
2890: FROENA (FANNIE) b 2 Jul 1792 (sp Geo Harter, Ann Raspach)
            d 24 Oct 1814
2891: ELIZABETH b 26 Nov 1794 (sp Nic. Spohn & Elis.)
            m JOHN CASLER
2892: JACOB 1797-1883 m1 MARY SCHERER

2832: CATHERINE FOLTS - pr. born ca 1735 to 1745 (dau of Peter); supposedly m
JOHN J. FOX (b 1741, d 1810) but that John has not been found so far in Fox family
(ps. a son of Wm Fox & Margaret <Kast>?).

2825: CATHERINE FOLTS - apparently born Jan either 1744 or 1749 (depending on how
tombstone is read); died 18 Mar 1813 (or 1815) at age either 64-2-20 (gives
calculated birth date of 28 Jan 1749) or possibly 69-2-20 (gives 1744 birth year
as noted in Petrie book).

2811: ELISABETH FOLTS - born 1744; died 1827; m after 1760 JACOB PIPER. Poss. the
Elisabeth who was sponsor at bp 1760 of George Bellinger son of John Bellinger &
Elisabeth Barbara Folts.

2819: ANNA MARGARET FOLTS - born 10 Apr 1768 dau of Conrad Folts & Maria Catherine
Hilts; d 10 Feb 1822; m CONRAD HELMER (b 1766, d 1841) son of FREDERICK A. HELMER
& BARBARA ELIZABETH HOMAN (Bellinger book page 121).

2861: CONRAD G. FOLTS - born 18 Dec 1782; m by 1807 MARGARET ORENDORF. Had son George (d 13 Nov 1807).

2879: CONRAD FOLTS - born 8 Aug 1783; died 28 Aug 1853; m 12 Apr 1803 SUSANNA COLE dau of ESAU COLE & SUSANNA. Had children Catherine (1804), Almira (1806), Melchior (1807), Susanna (1809), Aaron (1810), John Adam (1812), Elizabeth (1814), William N. (1816), Joseph (1817), and Anna Mary (1820).

2842: JACOB FOLTS - pr. born ca Jul 1773 (calc. from age at death); pr. the Jacob who died at Herkimer NY 9 Feb 1814 (age 40-7-); m ELIZABETH STEELE (b 1776, d 1854) dau of GEORGE STEELE & DOROTHY SHOEMAKER. See "The Herkimers and Schuylers" by Phoebe Strong Cowen (Albany 1903) and Petrie book which lists him as JOHANN JACOB C. FOLTS and has his dates as born 1775, died 1831 (basis not given).

      2893: pr. ELISABETH JAC. b ca 1796; liv. 1810 (HK confirm. age 14)
      2894: pr. JACOB JAC. b ca 1802; d HK 14 Oct 1812 age 10-9-20
      2895: JOHN b ca 1810; d HK 1824 (age 14, son of Jacob dec'd)

2885: JOHN FOLTS - born Herkimer NY 22 Jul 1780 (son of Peter, bp sp John Rasbach & Maria Elis.); died Ft. Herkimer NY 28 Oct 1867; m 9 Mar 1802 CATHERINE CASLER (b 18 Apr 1782, d 7 Aug 1856) dau of JACOB KESSLER & CATHERINE PETRIE.

      2896: SOLOMON b HK 15 Nov 1803 (sp Chrphr Casler, Anna Folts)
      2897: JOHN m EMILY BULLARD of Newport
      2898: JONAS b say 1807; m CATHERINE KESSLER
      2899: DAVID 1810-1875 m SUSAN SMALL (d 1888)
      2900: MARY m WILLIAM FOLTS
      2901: JACOB m MARGARET SMITH of Shells Bush
      2902: FANNY m MR. WORMER
      2903: LUCINDA m EDWIN GILBERT
      2904: VERONICA (SUSAN) m 1843 WILLIAM SMALL
      2905: WILLIAM b 1823; d 1825
      2906: PETER m MALINDA SCHELL

2869: MELCHERT J. FOLTS - pr. born ca 1765 to 1770 (son of Jost); m by 1790 CATHERINE SMITH dau of ADAM SMITH. Melchior was sponsor, with Catherine Smidt, for Jan 1786 bp of Jacob, son of John Christman & Catherine <Hilts>. Children were Catrina (b 15 Jan 1791), Margaret (1792, bp sp. Jost Folts & Marg.), Maria (1794), Maria (1805), Elizabeth (1807), David (1810), and Melchior (b 10 Nov 1812, bp Watertown NY 1 Mar 1813). Ref. Duell article in Enterprise & News 15 May 1929.

2883: PETER FOLTS - born GF 8 Nov 1795; died 25 Sep 1875; m 3 Oct 1819 ANNA COLE dau of ESAU COLE & SUSANNA. Had children Mary Ann (1822), Lydia (1823), William F. (1825), Catherine (1827), Susannah (1829), Adelaid (1832), and Judson Lafayette (1835), as given in 1984 Folts family notes of Mrs. Jane Bellinger (HCH).

2847: SYLVANUS FOLTS - born 1784; died 2 May 1852 (age 68-1-9); m DOROTHY DYGERT (b ca 1786, d 14 Apr 1864, age 78).

2880: MARGARET FOLTS - born 24 Mar 1786; died 8 Nov 1758 (or 1878); m 3 Dec 1803 ADAM SMITH (b 1779, d 1857) son of ADAM SMITH & SARAH HILTS

********** FOX (Fuchs) **********

3001: **PHILIP FOX** (Johan Philip Fuchs) - pr. born in Germany ca 1650 to 1663 (son of Christoffel <b ca 1608, d 1698 age 90> & Maria); living in NY 1738 (he and wife Eva were sponsors at 1738 bp of of Henrich Frey´s daughter); ml at Niederbieber Germany 22 Mar 1683 CATHARINA NEITZERT dau of Johan WILHELM NEITZERT; m2 also at Niederbieber 7 Jul 1707 EULALIA (Anna Eva)... widow of SEBASTIAN BERNER. He was listed as a miller when appearing as sponsor at 1699 baptism of Georg Fredrich Neff´s child at Neuwied Germany. Emigrated to America and seen on NY Palatine subsistence list in 1710 (8A, OY) and in 1712 (7A, OY) and on 1717 Simmendinger census with wife Anna Eva and 4 children. Pr. related to the ANNA ELIZABETH FOX (b ca 1680) who married PETER DYGERT son of immigrant Werner. Material on the Fuchs ancestry in Germnay is quoted, with permission of the author, from "The Palatine Families of New York" by Mr Hank Jones (P.O. Box 8341, Universal City, Ca 91608).

                    surname FOX
  +3002: Johan CHRISTOPHEL 1684- m JOHANNA ELISABETH KORSING
   3003: ANNA ELSA   1685-1691
   3004: Joh. MATTHIAS bp 19 Jun 1687; d 1689
   3005: CHRISTINA bp 21 Apr 1689; liv. 1716 (spf Christina Sixt bp)
   3006: Johan NICHOLAS bp 15 Mar 1691; d 1692
   3007: ANNA MARGARETHA bp 25 Sep 1692; d 1693
   3008: ANNA MARGARETHA bp 4 Mar 1694
   3009: ANNA ELISABETH bp 2 Dec 1695; m FREDERICK BELLINGER
  +3010: pr. WILLIAM b say 1697; m2 MARGARET KAST
   3011: ANNA CATHARINA bp 31 Oct 1700
   3012: Johan ANDREAS bp 1702; pr. d young (not seen 1710).

                    FOX - 2nd Generation

3002: Capt. **CHRISTOPHER FOX** - bp Niederbieber Germany 6 Jan 1684 (sp. Joh. Christopher Neitzert, his mother´s brother, ...); ps. died by 1717 (not on Simmendinger census then); m by 1710 JOHANNA ELISABETH KORSING (b 1688) dau of RUDOLPH KORSING & DELIA. On NY Palatine subsistence list in 1710 (2A, OY) and in 1712 (3A, OY). Was a miller and listmaster at the NY Camps ca 1710 and described as capable but brusque (Bellinger book page 14). We suspect the Bellinger book errs in assuming that this Christopher later married Catherine F. Bellinger.

     +3013: PHILIP b 31 Jul 1712 (sp Ludolph Curring, Philip Fox)
               pr. m DOROTHY PETRIE
      3014: EVA b 11 Oct 1714; ps. m JACOB STERNBERG (Cady)
      3015: CATHERINE b say 1717; m 1735 ANDREW W. NELLIS

3016: **PETER FOX** - pr. born in Germany ca 1680 (age 31 in 1710); m ANNA MARGARET ... (b ca 1686, age 24 in 1710). Prob. related to immigrant Philip Fox & children. On the NY Palatine list in 1710 (2A, 1Y) and in 1712 (3A,1Y). Poss. the Peter who appears in 1720 Raritan church item.

      3017: ps. PETER b say 1708; in Van Alstein´s militia 1763
      3018: ps. ANNA MARGARET   b ca 2 Dec 1712; d 14 Jan 1800 (age 87-1-11)
               m by 1737 JOHANNES H. KLOCK
     +3019: ps. CHRISTOPHER b say 1716; m CATHERINE BELLINGER
      3020: ps. MAGDALENA b 1725; m 1747 JACOB WALLRATH

3010: **WILLIAM FOX** Sr - pr. born at Neiderbieber Germany ca 1695 to 1700; ml ...
; m2 in NY MARGARET KAST (b 1707, d 1791) dau of GEORGE KAST. Naturalized at
Albany NY 31 Jan 1716.

    3021: ANNA EVA   ca 1725-1768 m 1743 JACOB STERNBURGH
    3022: CHRISTINA   b say 1727; m 1748 PHILIP BERG
  +3023: Johan GEORGE   bp 20 Mar 1732; m 1766 MARY ENDERS
  +3024: PHILIP W.   ml BARBARA ... m2 1761 DOROTHY P. GREMPS
  +3025: WILLIAM jr   1732- m CATHARINE TIMMERMAN
    3026: MARIA   bp 1 Feb 1734; m JOHN GEORGE SNELL
  +3027: CHRISTOPHER W.   1744-1820 m ELIZABETH HESS
    3028: DOROTHY b say 1746; m 1764 DIETRICH LAUX
    3029: ANNA b say 1747; m 1768 JOHANNES HESS (b 1745)

FOX - 3rd Generation

3019: CHRISTOPHER FOX (Stofel) - pr. born ca 1710 to 1720; ps. died 1766 (Comp.
of Am. Gen. vol 7 page 6); pr. ml CATHERINE BELLINGER (b say 1717, d by 1763) dau
of FREDERICK BELLINGER & ANNA ELIZABETH FOX (bp 1695 dau of Philip Fox); m2 1763
ELIZABETH WALLRATH (b 1716, d Ft. Plain NY 1793) dau of HENRICH WALLRATH and widow
of GEORGE WINDECKER. Pr. the Stofel Fox who received Burnetsfield lot #26, and,
based on the lot assignment patterns, we suspect that in 1723 he was a minor and a
dependent in the household of Frederick Bellinger & Elisabeth (Fox). We think the
Bellinger book (page 14) didn't allow for more than one Christopher in this
generation and so tried to have Capt. Christopher (bp 1684) as the husband of
Catherine F. Bellinger (but that requires marriage to a niece some 33 years his
junior and is otherwise without support). Conceivably this Stofel was a son of
Capt. Christopher, and it may be a bad guess for us to put Peter & Margaret as his
parents just in order to avoid a first cousin relationship with his first wife.
Presence of a Stofel Fox in Capt. Mark Petrie's 1757 German Flats militia unit is
seen as support for existence of this younger Christopher, though possibly the
1757 Stoffel was a son of Philip (b say 1737 to 1741).

  +3030: ps. PETER b Mar 1738; d 29 Sep 1822 age 84-6
    3031: ELIZABETH b 1739; m 1762 FREDERICK FRANK
  +3032: FREDERICK b ca 1741; m 1763 ELIZABETH FRANK
  +3033: JOHN b ca 1744; m ANNA FRANK
    3034: MARY b ca 1747; m 1767 NICHOLAS OXNER

3027: Maj. CHRISTOPHER W. FOX - born Palatine NY 1744; died there 1820; m SAR 24
Mar 1768 ELISABETH HESS (liv. 1795) dau of JOHN HESS jr. Christopher was at
Oriskany with his brother Philip and was wounded during the Revolution.

  +3036: JOHN b SAR 24 Oct 1769; d 1832; m ELISABETH DIEVENDORF
    3038: PETER C. b SAR 10 Jan 1771 (sp Jacob Sternberg & Marg.)
        a General in 1821; d 1859; m 1793 ANNA NELLIS
    3039: CHRISTOPHER C. 1774-1852 m by 1795 MARGARET GRAMPS (Crim)
    3040: JACOB b 19 May 1776; d 28 Dec 1776
    3040A DANIEL C. 1777-1847 m ELISABETH LAMPMAN
    3041: MARGARET b GF 10 Apr 1781 (sp. Geo. Salsman, Marg. Snell)
        m THEODORE CHAPIN
    3042: ANNA b GF 2 Aug 1783 (John Hess & Anna <Fox>); m ADAM LAUX
    3042A MARY b 5 Feb 1786; m PETER B. COOK

3013: PHILIP FOX - born 31 Jul 1712 (son of Christopher); ps. m1 EVA ... (Leetham ms.) or DOROTHY PETRIE dau of JOST PETRIE & CORDELIA DEMUTH (Petrie book page 3). Bellinger book has him as father of Peter Fox (ID #3030, b Mar 1738).

```
        3043: CATHERINE   b say 1737; m 1756 JOSEPH BORST
        3044: RUDOLPH   1739-1806   m CATHERINE ELIZABETH MILLER
      +3045: CHRISTOPHER PHILIP   b say 1741; m1 1760 MARGARETHA KLOCK
        3046: ELIZABETH   b say 1743; m 1760 NICHOLAS HILTS
        3047: DELIA   b say 1745; m 1767 ARNAULT PUTMAN
        3048: ANNA   b say 1746; m 1766 JOHANNES BELLINGER
      +3049: Johan JOST   b say 1748; pr. m by 1782 ELISABETH
      +3050: DANIEL   b 1752; d 1819; m CATHERINE FOX
      +3051: PHILIP P.   b say 1754; m GF 25 Sep 1781 CATHERINE ACKERSON
        3052: ps. MARGARETHA   b 8 Nov 1760 (dau of Philip & Dor.)
```

3024: PHILIP W. FOX ("Lipps Fox") - pr. born ca 1725 to 1738; m1 BARBARA ... ; m2 SAR Mar 1761 DOROTHY P. GREMPS (Crim, b 1740) dau of PETER CRIM.

```
      +3053: ps. WILLIAM PH.   b say 1755; m by 1782 MARGARET WARMOUTH
        3054: MARIA   b 22 Apr 1760 (sp G Snell); pr. m by 1781 DANIEL HESS
        3055: ps. PETER PH.   b say 1765; liv. 1793 (spf Hess bp)
        3056: ANNA MARGARET   b SA 29 Oct 1770 (sp Pet. Crim, Cath. Laux)
        3057: JOHANNES   b GF 2 Aug 1781 (sp. John Wagner, Elis. Lambman)
        3057A GEORGE   b GF 7 Jun 1784 (sp Geo. Fox & ...)
```

3025: WILLIAM FOX jr - born 17 Oct 1732; liv. 1795; m CATHERINE ZIMMERMAN. Will in 1795 names children as William, Christopher, Peter, Catherine, Nancy, Lena, Elisabeth, Eve, & Delia (Col. Bell adds Maria & Jacob W., Bellinger book page 15).

```
        3058: CATHERINE   b 12 Jun 1753; m DANIEL FOX (son of Philip)
      +3059: WILLIAM W. jr   b say 1755; m ANNA EVA LOUCKS
      +3060: CHRISTOPHER W.   b 3 Aug 1757; m MARGARET NELLIS
        3061: PETER W.   b 3 Sep 1759; m MARIA RICHTER
        3062: NANCY   b say 1761; m by 1782 JOHN C. NELLIS
                       (appar. not the Anna b 11 Feb 1774)
        3063: LENA   b say 1763; m JOHN BELLINGER of Clockville
        3064: DOROTHEA   b say 1765; m by 1782 JOHN FINK
        3065: MARGARET   d 1829; m JOHN FLANDERS
        3066: ELIZABETH   m JACOB ABEEL
        3067: EVE   m LUDWIG NELLIS
        3068: DELIA   b SAL Aug 1771; d 1854; m ADAM SUITS widower
```

FOX - 4th Generation

3045: Capt. CHRISTOPHER PHILIP FOX - pr. born before 1742; died St. Johnsville NY 27 May 1804; m1 SAL 15 Apr 1760 MARGARET KLOCK dau of Henry; m2 ca 1777 CATHERINA HESS dau of JOHN HESS jr & widow of JACOB WEAVER. Was in Revol. service.

```
        3069: LENA   b SA 15 Aug 1760 (sp Magdalena, w. of John Bellinger);
                     m TEUNIS FLANDERS
        3070: PETER C.   b SAR 9 Aug 1762; m 6 Aug 1782 CATHERINE FRAEST
        3071: CATHERINE b 23 Aug 1764; m JACOB FLANDERS
        3072: JOHN b 5 May 1766; d FPL 24 May 1813 (46-10-16) pr. m MARIA CLAS
        3073: ELIZABETH   b SAR 9 Jan 1769 (sp Cath Klock, Daniel Fox)
```

                    children of Christopher Ph. cont. (by 2nd wife)
        3074: CHRISTOPHER C. b ca 1774; d 29 Nov 1852 age 78
        3074A pr. JACOB C. b say 1776; liv. 1794 (spf Fox bp)
        3075: pr. DANIEL b GF 25 Aug 1782 (sp. Daniel Fox & Cath.)
        3076: DAVID b 15 Aug 1783 (Simon Nicholson & Anna); m NANCY HESS
        3077: pr. ELISABETH b GF 15 Apr 1786 (J Bellinger, Cath. H Klock)
        3078: FREDERICK b SJR 18 May 1788 (Fred Getman & Eva); m ANNA FOX

3060: CHRISTOPHER W. FOX - born 3 Aug 1757; m MARGARET NELLIS dau of LUDWIG
NELLIS. Pr. on 1790 Palatine NY census (2-3-1), near William W. Fox.

        3079: pr. JOHN b GF 18 Mar 1781 (sp. John Nelles & Marg. Fox)
        3080: DANIEL b GF 23 Mar 1783 (sp Daniel Fox & Cath.)
        3081: JACOB b SJR 15 Mar 1794 (sp. Jac. C. Fox, Delia W. Fox)

3050: DANIEL FOX - born 1752 (son of Philip II); died 1819; m CATHERINE FOX (b
1755) dau of WILLIAM FOX jr & CATHARINE. On 1790 Palatine NY census (2-2-*).

3032: FREDERICK FOX - born ca 1741; pr. died by 1802; m 1763 ELISABETH FRANK (b
1747, d 1815) dau of Capt. CONRAD FRANK (Comp. of Amer. Gen. vol 7 page 6). On
1790 GF census (2-3-5) next to John Frank and John Shoemaker.

        3082: FREDERICK b SAR 17 Oct 1764 (John Bellingr, M. Cath. Frank)
        3083: ELISABETH b GF 13 Sep 1766 (sp Fred Frank & w. Elis.<Fox>)
        3083A ELISABETH bp SAR 22 Sep 1768 (sp Tim. Frank & w. Elis.)
       +3083B PETER FR. b say 1770; m 1787 ANNA SCHERER
        3084: pr. MARGARET b say 1772; liv. 1789 (spf Ch. Ittig bp)
        3085: LENA b GF 30 Jan 1778 (sp. John Frank & Anna Eva)
                    pr. m by 1804 MICHAEL MCLAUCLON
        3086: GEORGE 1780-1834 m ELISABETH HESS (dau of Fred.)
        3087: JAMES (Jacob James) b GF 8 Mar 1784 (sp James Yuel & Margaret)
                    liv. 1802 (HK conf.); m HK 1807 DOROTHY JOS. HERKIMER
       +3088: MICHEL FR. b GF 18 Dec 1785 (sp Fred P Bellinger & Lena)
                    d 1818; m CATHERINE ORENDORF
        3089: MARIA b 25 Jan 1789 (Abm Rosencrnz); m 1811 DANIEL MEYER
        3090: CATHERINE b GF 23 Oct 1792 (sp Jost Herkimer & Cath.)
                    m 1810 JOHN STAHRING

3023: GEORGE FOX - pr. born ca 1735 to 1750; m Schoharie NY 6 Oct 1766 MARIA
ENTIS. On 1790 Palatine NY census (3-0-3), next to Peter Wagner.

        3090A PETER b SAR 3 Nov 1767 (sp Wm Fox & Margaret)
        3091: JACOB b SA Oct 1770 (sp Stophel Fox & Elisabeth)
        3092: MARIA b GF 14 Jul 1781 (sp. Peter Wagner, Maria Landman)

3033: JOHN FOX - pr. born ca 1744; m ANNA FRANK (b 1750, d 1830) dau of CONRAD
FRANK. On 1790 German Flats census (2-2-5) next to Bellingers & T. Shoemaker.

        3093: FREDERICK b GF 15 Nov 1777 (sp. Fred Frank & Elis.)
        3094: MARIA b GF 5 Dec 1780 (sp. Fred. Bellinger & Maria)
        3095: MARGARET b 4 Dec 1782 (John Hess & Marg.); m 1802 PAUL CRIM
        3096: JOHANNES b GF 15 May 1785 (sp John Smith & Mar. Elis.)
        3097: pr. MARIA CATHERINE JOH. b say 1787; m 1805 PETER MARTZ
        3098: LAURENTZ JOH. b GF 15 May 1789 (sp Lor. Shoemakr, Lena Fox)
                    liv. 1805 (wit. Cath. Fox mar.); m 1811 BOLLY LINK
        3098A JACOB b GF 17 Aug 1792 (sp Maj Jacob Petri & Maria)

3049: Johan JOST FOX - b say 1748; m by 1782 ELISABETH ... (ps. Kraus or Barsh)

       3099: MARGARET b GF 7 Apr 1782 (sp. Lud. Barsh & Marg. Fox)

3030: PETER FOX - born Mar 1738; died 29 Sep 1822 (age 84-6). Pr. the Peter on 1790 Canajoharie NY census (4-3-4) and father of Philip P. (m FPL 1792 MAGDALENA P. FEHLING).

3051: PHILIP P. FOX - pr. born ca 1740 to 1755; m 25 Sep 1781 CATHERINE ACKERSON. On 1790 Palatine NY census (1-1-2) and was living there in 1793.

       3100: DANIEL b GF 25 Aug 1786 (sp Daniel Fox & Cath.)
       3100A JOST bp SJR 28 Nov 1790 (sp. Jost Fox, Elis. Fox)
       3101: ANNA bp SJR 8 Sep 1793 (sp. Peter Fox, Anna Nellis)

3053: WILLIAM PH. FOX - pr. born ca 1745 to 1758; died 4 Dec 1804; m 20 Aug 1776 MARGARET WARMOUTH (b 1758, d 1836, surname on 1790 bp rec.) dau of PETER WORMWOOD & ANNA FEHLING (Martin's Fehling book, page 38).

       3102: DANIEL b GF 2 Feb 1782 (sp. Daniel Hess & Maria); d Nov 1848
       3103: ELISABETH b GF 2 May 1786 (sp Pet. Ph Fox, Ellis. Ommerstetr)
       3104: JOHN bp SJR 9 May 1790 (sp Peter Knieskern & Lea)
       3105: GEORGE bp SJR 21 Mar 1793 (sp. Geo. Diefendorf & Cath.)

3059: WILLIAM FOX - pr. born ca 1750 to 1760; m by 1781 ANNA EVA LOUCKS. William W. on 1790 Palatine NY census (2-2-3).

       3106: WILLIAM b GF 10 Jan 1781 (sp Pet. Fox, Maria Hen. Laux)

FOX - 5th Generation

3072: JOHN CH. FOX - born 24 Oct 1769; died 1832; m FPL 23 Aug 1791 ELISABETH DIEVENDORF dau of JOHN JACOB & CATHERINE of Canajoharie (Francis Marion Fox ms., 1896). Had Cath. (b GF Feb 1802, sp John Jacob Dievendorf & Cath.).

3088: MICHEL FOX - born ca 1785; died German Flats NY 24 Dec 1818 (age 33); pr. the Michel (son of Frederick Fox Esqr. dec'd) who m 1808 CATHERINE F. ORENDORF.

3083B PETER FR. FOX - pr. born by 1770; m 1787 ANNA SCHERER (b 1769, d 1845) dau of CHRISTIAN SCHERER. Sponsored May 1788 bp of Peter G Edick.

       3107: CHRISTIAN b GF 15 Apr 1788 (sp Pet. Joh. Bellngr, C. Sherer)
       3108: MARIA CATHERINE b GF 15 Mar 1791 (sp Pet. Schrer, C Bellngr)
       3109: FREDERICK b GF 16 Oct 1795 (sp Geo F Fox, Anna Joh. Fox)

3110: PETER FOX - pr. born ca 1735 to 1760; m CATHERINE ... Pr. the Peter on 1790 GF census (1-0-3) listed near H. Staring, G. Witrig, etc. in New Schuyler area.

       3111: MAGDALENA b GF 22 Apr 1781 (sp. John Jordan, Elis. Hess)
       3112: MARGARET b GF 2 Aug 1785 (sp Joh. Fox, Anna James Thompsn)
       3113: CATHERINE b GF 29 Feb 1788 (sp Jac. Molter, Cath. H. Staring)

3044: RUDOLPH FOX - m ELISABETH MILLER. Had dau ANNA MARIA (b SAR 7 Sep 1766, sp. Maria & Daniel Miller).

********** FRANK **********

Two or three Frank families appear to have settled at German Flats before the time of the French & Indian devastation in 1757 and only one of these, that of 1763 militia Capt. CONRAD Frank, potenially descend from a 1710 Palatiner (i.e. from Johannes, the only Frank seen on the 1710 NY subsistence lists). The other two families, those of HENRY and STEPHEN, reportedly immigrated from Germany about 1750 (History of Chatuaqua Co. NY page 235+) and were presumably unrelated until the 1766 marriage of Henry's daugther Eva and Stephen's son John. An alternate view is expressed in a large plaque at the Revolutionary Cemetery in Deposit NY which says that Stephen was the son of Conrad (born 1698) and also the father of the Catherine (born 1731) who married Jacob Ittig Jr. This sequence is possible but the dates seem to cut things a bit close so we have left the issue open by showing the Stephen Frank line as if it were a separate family. Because of their propinquity, we treat the three German Flats Frank families together below, using a letter in brackets to designate probable lines of CONRAD <C>, HENRY <H>, and STEPHEN <S>.

Another Frank family, headed by ANDRIES Frank, was living at Canajoharie NY by about 1742 (Book of Names page 60) and had children born between 1735 and 1760 with names Eva, Catherine, Christofel, Adam, John, Henry, Jacob, and possibly Elisabeth (who married by 1776 Frederick Staring). During the Revolution we see probable descendents of Andries in Col. Fisher's Regiment from the Fonda NY area which lists Henry, Adam (at Oriskany), Albert, Andrew (wounded), John (killed at Oriskany), and Jacob (killed). A DAVID Frank, born in Germany in 1745 (as given in Pearson's "First Settlers of Schenectady") was living at Schenectady by 1762 and is not placable with any of the other Franks.

3201: JOHANNES FRANK <C> - pr. born in Germany ca 1660 to 1680; m1 ... m2 as a widower at the NY camps 10 Jul 1711 MAGDALENA ... widow of LUDWIG STREIT (b ca 1666, as stated age 42 in 1708 London list, of Westhofen, commune Alzey). On NY Palatine subsistence list in 1710 (1A,0Y) and in 1712 (3A,2Y). If the Conrad of German Flats were a son by his first marriage, then Conrad's apparent absence on the 1710 subsistence list (ie. immigrant John is listed without dependents) may be explained by Conrad's being out then in the care of another family. Not seen at naturalization but on Simmendinger census of 1717 with wife Magdalena and 2 children. Johannes' wife Magdalena apparently had children from her first marriage (ie sons born ca 1700 & 1702 and daughters born 1703-1708) which may account for presence of a William Streit in Capt. Petrie's GF militia co. in 1757. Johannes Frank was a sponsor for the Feb 1712 bp of John, son of Wilhelm Brandeau.

surname FRANK
+3202: ps. CONRAD 1698-1772 m ANNA ELISABETH ... (ca 1714-1776)

3203: MICHAEL FRANK - born ca 1689 (age 20, unm Catholic, on 1709 London list, Book of Names page 91). Probably was the Michael who returned to Holland in 1709 (Knittle's "The Early Palatine Emmigration" page 276).

FRANK - 2nd Generation

3202: Capt. **CONRAD FRANK** <C> - born ca 1698; died 1772 age 74; ps. ml by 1720
... (existence of first wife assumed to permit earlier children); m say ca 1735
ANNA ELISABETH ... (b ca 1714, d 1776 age 62, see Bellinger book page 34). Conrad
Frank (nor any Frank for that matter) did not receive property on either the
Burnetsfield or Stone Arabia Patents, and our first known evidence of him in this
country is when he and Andrew Clepsattle were naturalized on 16 Dec 1737. In
German Flats militia in 1757 and the Capt. in command of a militia company
1764-67. He and his wife were sponsors for Jan 1762 bp of Conrad Melchior, son of
Adam Thumb & Christina Meyer. A deed of 25 Feb 1793 conveying land of this
Conrad, names his sons born after 1739 (as listed below) and daughters as Maria
Catherine, wife of Peter Weaver; Elisabeth, wife of Frederick Fox; Anna, wife of
John Fox; Delia, wife of George Ittig; and Eve, wife of Frederick Getman. No
earlier children are mentioned (see Frank file at Herk. Co. Hist. Soc.).

    +3204: ps. MICHAEL b say 1726; m 1744 CATHERINE FINK
     3205: ps. GEORGE MICHAEL b say 1729; in GF militia 1757
     3206: ps. MAGDALENA (Frank?) b say 1733; m CONRAD FULMER jr.
               pr. by 2nd wife
    +3207: FREDERICK   1740-1830 m 1762 ELIZABETH FOX
    +3208: TIMOTHY b 1741; m 1764 ANNA ELIZABETH BELLINGER
    +3209: CONRAD jr b say 1744; m 1765 GERTRAUDT MEYER
     3210: ELIZABETH 1747-1815 m 1763 FREDERICK FOX
     3211: MARIA CATHERINE b ca 1748; died 1825 (age 77)
             m at Palatine NY 1769 PETER J. WEAVER
    +3212: ANNA 1750-1830 m JOHN FOX
     3213: ANNA EVA b say 1752; m by 1771 FREDERICK GETMAN
     3214: DELIA b say 1754; m GEORGE ITTIG (in father's will)
    +3215: JOHN 1756-1840 m by 1779 APPOLONIA WEAVER

3216: **HENRY FRANK** Sr.<H> - pr. born ca 1710 to 1723; pr. m CATHERINE ...
Supposedly Henry immigrated with his brother Christopher before the French &
Indian War, landing at Philadelphia and remaining in that area a few years before
moving to the Mohawk Valley near the present town of Frankfort NY. In the 1757
French & Indian raid on German Flats the wife of Henry Frank, her 18-month old
son, and five daughters were captured and taken Canada, where they were held
prisoner several years (Eva was repatriated in 1760 but Mary, who was sick with
smallpox then, was kept a fourth year <account of John Joh. Myers, grandson of
Henry Frank>). In Capt. Conrad Frank's militia co. in 1767, where his name
follows that of Jacob & Marc Ittig; Henry Frank Jr. appears separately later in
same militia list (Book on Names page 12). Presumably was the Henrich Frank who,
with Maria Catherine (reads like wife), was sponsor for 1767 bp of Maria
Catherine, dau of John Frank & Anna Eva. Henry Frank & Catherine were sponsors for
GF Dec 1789 bp of John, son of Joseph Meyer & Catherine (Clepsattle). The History
of Chautauqua County NY (page 235) gives his children as Henry, Lawrence (b 1749),
Jacob, Eva, Mary, & Margaret. We have added daughter Elisabeth (m Staring) here
even though Stone felt she was a descendent of Stephen Frank (the Elisabeth who
married Jacob Crim seems a better choice for daughter of Stephen).

     3217: MARIA b ca 1743 (twin); m Palatine NY 1766 JOHN MEYER
     3218: EVA b ca 1743 (twin); m 1766 JOHN STEPH. FRANK
     3219: ps. ELISABETH ca 1746-1835 m FREDERICK PH. STAHRING
    +3220: HENRY jr b say 1747; m 1769 GERTRUDE CLEPSATTLE
    +3221: LAWRENCE 1749-1813 m MARY MEYER (Myers)
     3214: MARGARET
     3222: JACOB b say 1756; died in Revolutionary action

3223: **STEPHEN FRANK** <S> - pr. born before 1717; m ... and, either this Stephen
or a son of that name, pr. married by 1777 SOPHIA ... (see Sep 1777 Stephen Justus
Frank bp). Settled early at Andrustown with Paul Crim and taught school there in
the German language (Herkimer Evening Telegram 7/16/1977). We believe this
Stephen was born in Europe, came to New York with relative Conrad Frank (ps. his
father), re-visited Germany in 1749 (to deliver letter of neighbor Johannes
Miller) and was naturalized in New York 11 Sep 1761 (same day as a Fred. Frank).
Had 2 adults & 1 child on 1778 GF relief.

> 3224: pr. CATHERINE 1731-1824 m1 JACOB EDICK m2 NICHOLAS H. WEAVER
> +3225: pr. FREDERICK b say 1737; m pr. by 1760 SUSANNA
> +3226: pr. STEPHEN b say 1741
> +3227: JOHN STEPH. b ca 1743; (sp. 1761 bp Jacob Weber´s son)
>   m 1766 ANNA EVA BARBARA FRANK (dau of Henry)
> +3228: pr. NICHOLAS b say 1752; liv. 1777 (spf Nic. Weaver bp)
>   pr. m1 by 1777 MARGARET ...; m by 1783 ELIZABETH FONDA
> 3229: ps. ELISABETH 1754-1813 m JACOB CRIM

FRANK - 3rd Generation

3209: CONRAD FRANK Jr. <C> - pr. born ca 1735 to 1745; m SAR 26 Aug 1765 GERTRAUDT
MEYER dau of HENRY MEYER & ANNA MARIA GETMAN. Pr. the Pvt. Conrad in GF militia
in 1767. Conrad´s Revolutionary service included duty at Fort Stanwix in 1777,
the Battle of Amboy (where he was wounded in the right arm), Sullivan Indian
campaign, and in 1778 a winter trek on snowshoes with Capt. Bleecker´s troop whose
mission was to burn British shipping on Lake Ontario.

> 3230: ANNA b GF 24 Dec 1765 (sp. Anna Eva Frank, Conrad Orendorf)
> 3231: LENA bp GF 14 Jul 1777 (sp Conrad Folmer & Lena)

3207: FREDERICK FRANK <C> - born Jun 1740 (son of Conrad and older brother of Lt.
Timothy); died 2 May 1830 age 89-6-26; m 16 Nov 1762 ELISABETH FOX (b 1739, d
1814) pr. dau of CHRISTOPHER FOX & CATHERINE BELLINGER. Fred. & Eliz. sp. bp Sep
1766 of Elizabeth dau of Frederick Fox & Elisabeth. Pr. the Frederick in GF
militia in 1757 and the Capt. who succeeded to Capt. Michael Ittig´s Co. after
Oriskany. Poss. the Frederick with 2 adults & 4 children on 1778 GF relief.
Children from Bellinger book page 46.

> 3232: ANNA ELISABETH bp Oct 1763 (sp. Elis Bellinger); m PETER GETMAN
> 3233: FREDERICK jr b say 1765; d 1815
> 3234: MARIA CATHERINE bp 7 Feb 1769; m 1793 JOHN U. MCKOOM
> 3235: ANNA EVA FR. b say 1771; liv. 1789 (spf Dan. Hess bp)
> 3236: pr. FREDERICK b GF 7 Jan 1787 (son of Fred & Elis.)

3225: FREDERICK FRANK <S> - pr. born before 1735; m by 1762 SUSANNA ... Pr. the
Frederick naturalized with Stephen Frank on 11 Sep 1761. Frederick & Susanna
sponsored the Jun 1763 bp of Susanna, dau of Fred Miller & Eva, and the Feb 1779
bp of Jacob, son of Henry Huber & Elisabeth.

> 3237: ps. MARGARET b say 1753; m 1770 VALENTINE BEYER
> 3238: ps. SUSANNA b say 1758; m by 1777 HENRY GARTER
> 3239: ps. MARIA b say 1760; liv. 1777 (spf Garter bp)
> 3240: MARIA CATHERINE bp SAR 17 Feb 1762 (sp Con. Frank & wife)
> +3241: ps. HENRY b say 1770; m MARIA MILLER

3227: JOHN STEPH. FRANK <S> - pr. born ca 1743 (age ca 7 ca 1750); ps. died
Frankfort NY 1833 (other accounts have him dying at Gallapolis Ohio in 1817 or
dying as late as 1853); m Palatine NY 16 Feb 1766 ANNA EVA BARBARA FRANK dau of
HENRY FRANK. Stone in the "Starin Family" (page 36) says that in 1837 this John
Frank told Col W. L. Stone (father of author Stone) of his role on the committee
of safety for German Flats during the Revolution and of his partaking in the
pursuit of Brandt as far as the Tory Young´s settlement after the Andrustown
massacre <the reader is advised here that Stone was much better with the
ingredients of stories than with the identities and dates of participants>. John
Frank was listed in Capt. Conrad Frank´s German Flats militia in 1767, near in
list to Jost Dygert, Christian Passage, John Moyer, & Hendrick Frank Jr (Book of
Names page 13). John Steph. Frank & Anna Eva were sponsors at Dec 1777 bp of Anna
Eva, dau of John Osteroth & Catherine, which fits the Andrustown residence. John
Frank & Anna Eva were sponsors at Dec 1765 bp of Jacob, son of Jacob Ittig and
were sponsors at Jan 1778 bp of Lena, dau of Fred Fox & Elisabeth (Frank). "John
(Stephen) Frank" was sponsor, with Eva, for 1787 bp of Johannes, son of John
Getman & Maria Cath.(Frank). Probably the John who had 3 adults & 5 children on
1778 German Flats relief and the John S. Frank on the 1790 German Flats census
(3-1-7).

>   3242: MARIA CATHERINE b 2 Mar 1767 (sp. Maria Cath. & Hen. Frank)
>   3243: STEPHANUS NICHOLAS bp GF 23 Jun 1770 (of Eva Barb.)
>   (1770 bp sp. Stephen Nicel ... & Anna Paschas)
>   ps. the Nich. (son of John Steph.) who m THANKFUL LANDON
>   3244: pr. MARGARET JOH. b say 1772; m GF 1791 JACOB WEAVER
>   3245: pr. EVA JOH. b say 1774; m 1792 JACOB CHR. EDICK
>   3246: STEPHANUS JUSTUS bp GF 28 Sep 1777 (of John & Eva)
>   (sp. Stephen Frank & Sophia)
>   3247: ELIZABETH bp GF 13 Jan 1779 (dau of John & Eva)
>   (sp. John Bellinger & Elis. Harter)
>   3248: ANNA MARIA b GF 2 Jun 1788 (dau of John Steph. Frank)
>   (sp Lorentz Frank & Anna Maria)
>   +3249: JOHANNES bp St. Johnsville 7 Jan 1791 (son of John & Eva)

3215: Judge JOHN FRANK <C> - pr. born 1756 (son of Conrad); died 18 Apr 1840 (age
84); m APPOLONIA WEAVER (b ca 1753, d GF 18 Mar 1817 age 64) dau of JACOB WEAVER &
MARGARET. John Frank & Appolonia were sponsors for Mar 1776 bp of John, son of
Christian Ittig & Anna Eva. John was clerk in his father´s militia company and in
August 1783 helped defend Ft. Herkimer in the last battle of the American
Revolution `as stated in his pension S23664 and in Bellinger book page 38). In
1791 he was commissioned a justice of the peace for Montgomery Co. and his house
was located south of the Mohawk River a few rods west of the old fort (notes in
Frank file at HCH). John Frank appears on the 1790 German Flats census (3-1-8)
near to Frederick Fox, Shoemakers, & Frederick Frank. Probate record of John
Frank (d by Apr 1844) list kin as Conrad Frank, Margaret Campbell, Sarah McCombs,
Elisabeth Campbell (admin. Fred F. Myers, Mic. F. Myers, & George H. Fox).

>   3250: pr. MAGDALENA b say 1775; m 1795 JOHN A. MCKOOM
>   3251: MARGARET JOH. b say 1776; m 1795 ADAM P. CAMPBELL
>   3252: MARIA CATHERINE bp GF 7 Jun 1778; pr. died young
>   (sp. Peter Weber & Maria Cath.)
>   3253: CONRAD b GF 10 Nov 1779 (sp. Tim. Frank & Anna)
>   3254: CATHARINA b GF 6 Oct 1781 (sp Peter Orendorf & Cath.<Piper>)
>   3255: ANNA bp GF 14 Jun 1783 (sp John Fox & Anna <Frank>)
>   3256: APPOLONIA b GF 8 Jun 1785 (sp Stophl Bellngr, Cath Demuth)
>   m 1804 FREDERICK F. MEYER

3220: HENRY FRANK jr. <H> - pr. born ca 1740 to 1750; m at Palatine NY 20 Nov 1769
GERTRUDE KLEBSATTEL pr. dau of immigrant ANDREW CLEPSATTLE. In Capt. Conrad
Frank's militia co. in 1767.

    3257: pr. HENRICH HEN.   b say 1772; m GF 1793 ELISABETH BOTTMAN
  +3258: pr. JOHN   b say 1774; m 1795 MARGARET GERLACH
    3259: pr. JACOB   b Palatine NY 21 Oct 1777 (son of Hen.)
             (sp. Jacob Folts & Cath.)
    3260: GERTRUDE   b GF 7 Jan 1782 (sp. Joh. Dinges, Gert. Bellinger)
    3261: ANNA EVA   bp GF 12 Mar 1786 (sp John Frank & Anna Eva)
    3262: ELIZABETH   bp GF 17 Dec 1787 (sp Nic. Frank & Elis. Meyer)
    3263: MARIA CATHERINE   b GF 28 Apr 1790 (sp Wm Clepsattle & Maria)
    3264: ANDRIES   bp St. Johnsville 20 Feb 1792
              pr. m by 1812 CATHERINE BIRCKY (Parkie)
    3265: DOROTHEA   bp GF 10 Mar 1795 (sp Michel Myers & Anna Eva)
             m 1811 JACOB BIRCKY (Bargy)

3221: LAWRENCE FRANK <H> - born Frankfort NY 1749; died Busti NY 1813; m MARY
MYERS (b 1753, d 1831) pr. dau of Lt. PETER MEYER. Pvt in Col. Van Renselaer's
Revol. Regiment. See DAR. vol. 68 page 208, vol. 110 page 100, and vol. 157 page
218. He seems the only candidate age-wise for Hatch Papers allegation of a
Lawrence Frank marriage to a daughter of Adam Bell, but we see no other indication
of a first (Bell) wife for this Lawrence (see Bell family for other doubts
regarding Adam Bell account).

  +3266: HENRY LAW.   b say 1770; m 1805 MARGARET DEMUTH
    3267: ELISABETH   1772-1862 m by 1803 AUGUSTINUS CLEPSATTLE jr.
  +3268: LAWRENCE   1774-1830 m1 ELIS. PFEIFFER m2 1802 ANNA BELL
    3269: MARGARET   bp GF 18 Jul 1776 (sp Mich. Meyer & Marg. Meyer)
             m by 1803 STEPHEN FRANK
    3270: JOHN L.   1786-1875 m LUCRETIA CHAPMAN
    3271: MARIA   b GF 29 Nov 1786 (sp John Jac. Weber & Maria)
    3272: MICHAEL   1788-1869 m BETSY STEWARD
         (1788 bp sp Mich. Meyer & Cath.)
    3273: MATTHEW b SJR 30 Aug 1792 (sp John & Eva Frank)
           pr. died young
    3274: MATTHEW   1798-1867 m BARBARA ANN LOY

3204: MICHAEL FRANK - pr. born ca 1718 to 1725; m 1744 CATHARINA FINK. Pr. the
Migell Franck in Lt. Sev. Dygert's militia in 1763 (Book of Names, page 9).

    3275: ps. CATHERINE   b say 1745; m 1765 ADAM KILTS
  +3276: ps. MICHAEL   b say 1765; m by 1789 CATHERINE
  +3277: ps. GEORGE MICHAEL   b say 1770; m by 1799 MARIA COUGHNET

3228: NICHOLAS FRANK - pr. born ca 1745 to 1760; m by 1783 ELISABETH FONDA (b
1766) dau of JAN J. FONDA of Albany NY. Had children AEGIE (bp WSL <West Sand
Lake Ch.> 8 Aug 1783), Stephen (bp WSL 17 Jul 1785, sp. Nich. Weber & w. Cath.),
JOHN (bp Albany NY Jul 1787, sp. Wouter & Wyntje Fonda), CATHERINE (bp Albany May
1790, sp. ... John Fonda), MARGARET, POLLY, MARIA, GEERTRUY, JAMES, and ABRAHAM.
Lived at Greenbush (now Renselaer) NY.

3226: STEPHEN FRANK - pr. born before 1760; m ... Father of Elisabeth.

    3278: ELISABETH STEPH.   b say 1776; m 1796 JOHN HILLER

3208: Lt. TIMOTHY FRANK <C> - pr. born ca 1735 to 1745 (son of Conrad); died after 19 Jul 1818 (will prepared) and before 3 Dec 1822 (will probated); m1 5 Jul 1764 ANNA ELIZABETH BELLINGER (b 1739, d 1803) dau of Capt. PETER BELLINGER; m2 ANNA DYGERT (b ca 1753, d 1813 age 59-10-) dau of WARNER DYGERT & LENA HERKIMER (Bellinger book page 34). Timothy Frank had 2 adults & 5 children on 1778 German Flats relief. He was living at Warren NY in 1818.

> 3279: MARIA b 25 May 1765 (sp. Mar. Cath. Frank); m CONRAD GETMAN
> 3280: ANNA MARGARET b 5 Mar 1767 (sp. Peter Bellinger & w. Marg.)
>   m 1788 CONRAD AUG. HESS
> 3281: ANNA ELIZABETH 1769-1805 m JOHN GETMAN
> 3282: ANNA EVA b 1770 (sp. Anna Eva Frank); m JACOB WEAVER
> 3283: LENA b 12 Mar 1777; d 1817; m FREDERICK GETMAN jr
> ... supposedly many other children

3212: ANNA FRANK - born Dec 1750; died Jan 1830 age 79 yrs 1 month; m by 1777 JOHN FOX (b ca 1745). Sponsors at baptism of their first child were Fred Frank & Eliz. Fox (Bellinger book page 47).

3284: EVE FRANK - pr. widow of a Frank. Given as 1 adult & 5 children on 1778 German Flats relief.

FRANK - 4th Generation

3277: GEORGE MICHAEL FRANK - pr. born ca 1750 to 1775; m MARIA COUGHNET.

> 3285: GERTY bp Fonda NY 1799

3266: HENRY FRANK <H> - pr. born ca 1765 to 1785 (son of Lawrence as indicated on 1805 mar. rec.); m 25 Dec 1805 MARGARET DEMUTH dau of GEORGE DEMUTH deceased. Living at Frankfort NY in 1805.

3241: HENRY FRANK <S> - pr. born ca 1760 to 1775; m pr. by 1795 MARIA MILLER. They were probably the Henry & Maria who sponsored Nov 1795 bp of Maria, dau of Henry H. Frank & Elisabeth (Bottman). They had a son Frederick who m 1821 ANNA RINCKEL dau of LAWRENCE RINCKEL & CATHERINE YUKER.

3257: HENRY H. FRANK <H> - pr. born ca 1770 to 1775 (son of Henry); m 30 Apr 1793 ELISABETH BOTTMAN.

> 3286: JOHN b 26 Nov 1793 (sp John Frank & Marg. Gerlach)
> 3287: MARIA b 4 Nov 1795 (sp Henry Frank & Maria)

3258: JOHN FRANK <H> - pr. born ca 1750 to 1775; m German Flats 20 Dec 1795 MARGARET GERLACH. Apparently was living at Frankfort in 1810.

> 3288: WERNER b 13 Feb 1808 (sp Warner Folts, Elis. Getman)
> 3289: MARIA ELISABETH b 29 Jan 1810
>   (sp Abhm Folts, Maria Frank of Frankfort)

3249: JOHN FRANK jr <S> - ps. the John bp 1791 (Chautauqua Co. History has John jr. as son of John Steph.); m ELISABETH DIEVENDORF dau of JOHN DIEVENDORF & MARGARET PH. FOX.

3268: LAWRENCE L. FRANK <H> - pr. born the Lawrence born 1774 (Herk. Cemetery rec.); died 4 Jan 1830; ml 21 Jun 1795 ELISABETH PFEIFFER (b ca Apr 1778, d 27 Jan 1802 of neglect in childbirth) dau of JACOB PFEIFFER ; m2 as a widower 1802 ANNA BELL (pr. b ca 1771, d 1844) dau of JACOB BELL. Lived at Frankfort NY in 1802 and marriage was witnessed by Henry Frank, a brother of the groom, and by a Frederick Bell. Cemetery records at Herkimer Co. Hist. Soc. show Lawrence (b 1774, d 1830) along with a Nancy (ie. pr. Anna) whose dates are born 1771 and died 3 Aug 1844. It looks like the Nancy born 1771 and the Anna Jac. bp GF Feb 1783 may be the same person, which, although it presents an unusual delay in baptism, seems at least more likely than a third wife (also named Anna) for Lawrence or another Jacob Bell with daughter Anna. His estate papers mention wife Nancy and other heirs including Jacob Frank, Isaac Frank, Martin Chrysler & Mary (Frank), John Hilts & Eliz. (should be Margaret Frank), Jacob Bell & Elisabeth (Frank), Barbara Frank, Lawrence Frank, Nancy Frank, and George M. Frank.

        3290: pr. MARGARET b say 1796; m JOHN HILTS
        3291: ELISABETH b ca 1799 (bp Dec 1801); d 1 Feb 1802 age 2-6-20
        3292: ps. MARY (ps. a twin?) 1799-1827 m MARTIN CHRYSLER
                    by 2nd wife
        3293: ELISABETH b say 1803; m 1820 JACOB BELL
        3294: JACOB b 11 Dec 1804 (sp Jacob G. Weber & Marg.)
        3295: ABRAHAM b 2 Dec 1806 (sp Henry M. Myer & w. Maria)
        3296: ISAAC b 11 Dec 1808
        3297: HENRY b 14 Aug 1810 (sp Geo. H. Bell unm, Barb. Weber unm)
        3298: LUCIA b Apr 1812 (sp Pet. Helmer, Cath Bell, unm); d Nov 1812
        3299: MARIA BARBARA b 10 Jan 1814 (sp Fred. Dockstader & w. Cath.)
        3300: LAWRENCE b 5 Apr 1816 (sp Fred. Stevens & w. Anna)
        3301: ANNA b 22 May 1818 (sp John Myer & Marg. Weber)
        3302: CATHERINE b 22 May 1820; pr. d 21 Jun 1822
        3303: GEORGE MICHEL b 12 Aug 1823 (sp Geo. F. Myers & w. Cath.)
        3304: PETER b 7 Sep 1825 (sp Geo. L. Harter & w. Elis.)

3276: MICHAEL FRANK - pr. born ca 1745 to 1754; m CATHERINE ... Lived at "Klesberg" in 1789 (SJR rec.)

        3305: GEORGE bp St. Johnsville 8 Feb 1789 (sp Geo. Ocher)

3243: NICHOLAS FRANK <S> - pr. son of John Stephen and perhaps the Stephen Nicholas born 1770; m by 1801 THANKFUL LANDON ps. dau of REUBEN LANDON (b 1757).

        3306: WILHELM b 15 Nov 1801 (sp John Frank, uncle)
        3307: ANDREAS b 17 Dec 1803 (sp. Fred. Stevens & w. Anna)
        3308: DAVID b 21 Sep 1807 (sp. Paul Crim & w. Marg.)

3309: STEPHEN FRANK <S> - pr. born ca 1765 to 1780; m by 1803 MARGARET FRANK dau of LAWRENCE FRANK (Chautaqua Co. History page 237). Had children Nicholas, Matthew, Polly (pr. the Maria bp Columbia NY 15 Aug 1803, m Jacob Loy), Stephen (b 1806, sp Nic. Frank & w. Thankful), Denus (Augustinus b 1808, sp Aug. Clepsattle & w. Elis.), Hiram (b 1810, sp Elis. Meyer a widow), Eve, Solomon, Elizabeth, Jacob (twin), Joseph (twin); the last three being born after family moved south.

********** FULMER (Volmer) **********

3401: CHRISTIAN FULMER - pr. born ca 1680 to 1695; pr. m ... Ps. he was the "Christian Former" naturalized at Albany NY 22 Nov 1715, otherwise no mention has been found of this surname in the various NY Palatine lists from 1709 to 1717. Pr. this Christian was the patentee who received Burnetsfield lot #18 on the south side of the Mohawk, although some maps show that lot held by a Christina Folmer (pr. an error rather than a wife of this Christian) in what appears to be the dependents area of the Patent. In 1725 Christian's house was located by the plank saw mill, which was half owned by Melchert Folts (will of Melch. Folts). We presume, but have no proof, that Christian was the father of the three Folmers (Conrad, Thomas, & Augustus) who were in the Capt. Frank's 1767 GF militia.

surname FULMER

+3402: pr. CONRAD   b say 1718; m by 1761 HELENA...
3403: ps. ELISABETH b say 1720; m Schoharie NY 1739 MICHAEL WARNER
+3404: pr. THOMAS   b say 1730; m by 1761 CATHERINE ... (pr. Hilts)
+3405: ps. AUGUSTUS b say 1744; in 1767 GF militia
+3406: ps. JACOB b say 1746; m MARIA BASHAR (b ca 1748)
           (ps. Jacob and/or Augustus were early sons of Conrad)

3407: JACOB FULMER - pr. born ca 1720 to 1740; m ROSINA ... Had a daughter Margaret (bp Schoharie NY Dec 1765) and ps. a son Jacob (m at Fonda NY 1800 MARGARET MARTIN). There seems little to tie this or remaining first generation Fulmers to those at German Flats.

3408: JOHN FULMER - pr. born ca 1720 to 1735; m by 1753 CATHERINE STRAAT. Naturalized 3 May 1755 (name follows that of Johan Hess in list as given in Book of Names page 5). Pearson (First Settlers of Schenectady page 70) has a Catherine also for this couple but birthdate in 1802 seems unlikely.

3409: MARGARET bp Rhinebeck NY 10 Feb 1754
3410: JACOB bp Rhinebeck NY 23 Jul 1758
3411: GEERTJE ("Gertrude") bp Rhinebeck 5 Oct 1760
3412: MARIA MAGDALENA b Rhinebeck NY 8 Jan 1763
3413: ANNETJE bp Schenectady NY 6 Feb 1778

3414: ANNA CATHERINE FULMER - pr. born ca 1700 to 1708; m by 1726 DAVID GARLOCK (i.e. Thewalt Keurlack as given in Pearson's Schnectady book, page 99).

FULMER - 2nd Generation

3405: AUGUSTUS FOLMER (Acus, ps. Jacob) - In 1767 Augustus was in the GF militia listed next to Jacob Wentz & Fred Jost Shoemaker (Book of Names, page 13). Acus Folmer, with Elis. Shoemaker, sponsored Nov 1770 SAR bp of Margaret, dau of John Hess, and Nov 1770 bp of Catherine, dau of Christian Ittig & Margaret.

3402: Sgt. CONRAD FULMER - pr. born ca 1715 to 1722; pr. died before 1790 (not on census then); ps. m1 ... (ps. Shoemaker?); m by 1761 HELENA ... (ps. a Hilts or a Frank). Conrad received Burnetsfield lot #19 and may have been the Conrad Sr. who settled in Columbia NY (Wm U. Smith letters). Sgt. Conrad was in the 1767 GF militia but a younger Conrad was pr. the one in Col. Bellinger's Revol. Regiment. He was probably the Conrad Fulmer with 3 adults & 3 children (under age 16) on the 1778 German Flats relief (noted as living distant from Fort Dayton).

children of Conrad & Lena

3415: pr. MARGARET (Fulmer?) b say 1752; m by 1776 JOHN HESS
3416: pr. ELISABETH (Fulmer?) b say 1754; m by 1776 GEORGE ORENDORF
3417: pr. LANY BARBARA 1756-1830 m by 1778 FREDERICK ORENDORF jr.
+3418: ps. CONRAD b say 1758; m 1783 ELISABETH HILTS (b 1766)
+3419: Anna MARIA bp 13 Sep 1761 (sp. Maria Marg. Weber, Frd Frank)
      "Maria Conr." m 1788 FREDERICK HESS
+3420: Johan WILLIAM bp GF 10 May 1764 (sp Thomas Fulmer & w. Cath.)
      m ELISABETH PETRIE
+3421: CATHERINE bp SAR 29 Apr 1767 (sp Cath. Shoemaker, * Dygert)
      pr. m 1789 JACOB M. HISER
3422: ps. JOHN b say 1771; liv. 1792 (spf J. Fulmer bp)

3406: JACOB FULMER - pr. born ca 1740 to 1752; m by 1778 MARIA BASHAR (b ca Apr 1748, d Herkimer NY 12 Sep 1826 age 78 as widow of Jacob Fulmer). Possibly this was the same person as the above "Acus" (nickname for Jacob) and/or "Augustus" (1767 GF militia). Jacob & Maria sponsored Feb 1778 GF bp of Jacob, son of John Passage & Margaret (Crim) and also Aug 1795 bp of Lena, dau of William Fulmer & Elisabeth (Petrie). Jacob played the fiddle at the June 1782 engagement ceremony of Fred Smith (Hatch Papers).

3404: THOMAS FULMER - pr. born ca 1725 to 1743; m pr. by 1761 CATHERINE ..., pr. CATHERINE HILTS ps. dau of GEORGE HILTS & MARIA ELIZABETH FELLER (Hilts wife inferred from bp sponsors and child names below). Thomas was an Indian interpreter and was in the 1767 GF militia and in Col. Bellinger's Revol. Regiment. Thomas had 3 adults & 5 children on the 1778 German Flats relief and was on the 1790 Herkimer census (3-3-5).

+3423: ps. CATHERINE b say 1760; liv. 1777
+3424: CHRISTIAN bp 27 Oct 1762 (sp Nic. Hilts & w. Elisabeth)
      m 1784 ANNA EVA MISSELSUS
3425: MARGARET (twin) b GF Oct 1764 (sp. Fred. Helmer & w. Sabina)
3426: MARIA ELISABETH (twin) bp 16 Oct 1764 (Maria Wentz, Geo. Hilts)
3427: Johan GEORGE bp 25 Nov 1766 (sp. Geo. Hilts & Elis.)
      pr. died young
3428: GERTRUDE TH. b say 1770; m 1790 GOTTFRID CHR. RIEGEL
+3429: Johan GEORGE bp 1777 (sp. Geo. Jac. Hilts & Cath.)
3430: THOMAS b GF 26 Sep 1780 (sp John Christman, Cath. Hilts)

FULMER - 3rd Generation

3424: CHRISTIAN FOLMER - bp 27 Oct 1762; m at German Flats 22 Jul 1784 ANNA EVA MISSELSUS. In Col. Bellinger's Regm.

3431: CATHERINE bp GF 9 May 1785 (sp Thomas Fulmer & Cath.)
      pr. d young
3432: MARIA bp GF 11 Mar 1787 (sp Geo. Hilts & Maria Volmer)
3433: GEORGE bp GF 13 Mar 1789 (sp Jac. G Weaver & Maria)
3434: CATHERINE bp GF 17 Apr 1791 (sp Conrad Volmer & Elis.)
3435: GERTRUDE bp GF 31 May 1792 (sp Godf. Riegel & Gertr.)
3436: THOMAS bp GF 8 Nov 1795 (sp John Helmer, Elis. Fulmer)
3437: ANNA EVA bp Stone Arabia 6 May 1798
3438: CHRISTINA bp Minden NY 14 Sep 1800
3439: PETRUS bp Herkimer NY 12 May 1805 (sp H. Beyer & Sara)

3418: CONRAD FULMER - pr. born ca 1750 to 1760; died by Jan 1806; m at German
Flats 15 Jul 1783 ELISABETH HILTS (b 1766) dau of NICHOLAS HILTS & ELISABETH FOX.
Probably the Conrad Fulmer who was on the 1790 Herkimer NY census (1-3-1), listed
next to Nicholas Hilts and Hezekiah Talcott.

> +3440: JACOB C. bp GF 5 Sep 1784 (sp Jacob G Weaver & Maria)
> m 1804 MARY CATHERINE RASBACH
> +3441: Johan GEORGE bp Feb 1787 (sp Geo. Hilts, Gertr. Fulmer)
> m 1806 CATHERINE WIEDERSTEIN
> +3442: CONRAD bp 1789 (sp Philip Bell & Dor.<Hilts>)
> pr. m 1809 ANNA CHRISTMAN
> +3443: JOHANNES bp GF 16 Jul 1792 (sp John Fulmer, Marg. Hilts)
> m 1814 EVA HARTER

3429: Johan GEORGE FULMER - bp 1777 (son of Thomas, bp sp. Geo. Jac. Hilts &
Cath.); m MARIA WARTENBACH pr. dau of ANDREW WARTENBACH of Albany Co.

> 3444: pr. CATHERINE b say 1800 (dau of George);
> m1 by 1822 HENRY WEAVER; m2 1845 SOLOMON MAIN
> 3445: ANDREAS b HK 25 Jan 1805 (sp Hen. F Helmer, Maria Fulmer)
> 3446: MARIA bp 25 Jan 1807
> 3447: GEORGE bp GF 10 Apr 1814
> 3448: JACOB bp GF 8 Mar 1818

3420: WILLIAM FOLMER - bp German Flats 10 May 1764; died by Jul 1817; m German
Flats NY Dec 1788 ELISABETH PETRIE (b SAR 29 Mar 1766) dau of MARCUS PETRIE & ANNA
MARIE. His widow m2 Jul 1817 THOMAS T. SHOEMAKER son of THOMAS SHOEMAKER &
ELISABETH HARTER. In Col. Bellinger's Regm. in Revolution. Wilhelm Folmer &
Elisabeth Fox were sponsors for bp Jan 1784 of Elisabeth, dau of Lorentz Harter &
Barbara Delaney. Probably the William on the 1790 German Flats census (1-1-5),
but to be recently married and have that large a household suggests that he may
have picked up the surviving dependents of his father (Sgt. Conrad) who was
presumably deceased by then.

> 3449: MARIA bp GF 31 May 1789 (sp .. Shoemaker, Maria Grantz)
> 3450: CONRAD bp GF 2 May 1791 (sp Stofel Shoemker & Gertr.)
> 3451: MARCUS bp GF 30 Jun 1793 (sp Aug. Hess & Marg.)
> 3452: LENA bp GF 10 Aug 1795 (sp. Jacob Fulmer & Maria)
> 3453: ANNA b HK 30 Jul 1808 (sp. Lor. Shoemaker & w. Cath.)

3419: Anna MARIA FULMER - born 27 Jun 1761 and bp 13 Sep 1761 (dau. of Conrad; bp
sp. Maria Marg. Weber dau of Andries and Fred Frank son of Conrad); pr. the Maria
Conr. Fulmer who m at German Flats 15 Apr 1788 Joh. FREDERICK HESS.

3421: CATHERINE FULMER - bp Stone Arabia NY 29 Apr 1767; ps. the Cath. who m at
German Flats 5 Feb 1789 JACOB M. HISER ("Huysser")

3423: CATHERINE FULMER - pr. born ca 1755 to 1762; In 1777 she had a child named
Margaret (born 6 Aug, sp John Hess & Margaret <pr. Folmer>).

3428: GERTRUDE TH. FULMER - pr. b ca 1768 to 1773 (dau of Thomas); m at German
Flats 24 Nov 1790 GOTTFRID CHR. RIEGEL. She is poss. the Gertrude who has son
Gerrit bp at Herkimer 21 May 1788.

FULMER - 4th Generation

3442: CONRAD FULMER - pr. bp at German Flats 24 Nov 1789 (son of Conrad & Elis.); ps. the Conrad who m at Herkimer 23 Jul 1809 ANNA CHRISTMAN. Presumably this was the Conrad (brother of Jacob) who lived along North Creek near the bridge where the creek empties into the west creek at Herkimer NY (That Conrad had one son living in 1903 as mentioned in Wm U. Smith's letters).

> 3454: PHILIP   bp Herkimer NY 8 Apr 1810
> 3455: CATHERINE   bp 17 May 1812 (sp Jac. Christman & w. Marg.)
> 3456: son   b say 1825; liv. 1903

3440: JACOB C. FULMER - pr. the Jacob bp at German Flats 1 Sep 1784 (son of Conrad and had a brother Conrad); m 27 May 1804 MARIA CATHERINE RASBACH dau of JOHN RASBACH (pr. the John b 1764) and sister of Marcus. He was a carpenter and moved to the town of Steuben NY (Wm U. Smith's letters).

> 3457: ELISABETH   b HK 14 Nov 1804 (sp John Christman jr & Marg.)
> 3458: ANNA   b Herk. 26 Dec 1806 (dau of Jac. & Cath.)
> 3459: CATHERINE   b HK 18 Feb 1809 (sp. Geo. Fulmer & w. Cath.)
> 3456: AARON   1812-1898   m MARGARET SMITH

3441: Johan GEORGE C. FULMER - bp German Flats 27 Feb 1787 (son of Conrad & Elis.); pr. the Geo. C. Fulmer who m at Herkimer 5 Jan 1806 CATHERINE WIEDERSTEIN

> 3460: CATHERINE   bp HK 3 Aug 1806 (sp Jac. Volmer & Cath.)
> 3461: ELISABETH   bp Herkimer 17 Sep 1809
> 3462: MARIA   bp 23 Aug 1812

3443: JOHN FULMER - bp German Flats NY 16 Jul 1792 (son of Conrad); m 1814 EVA HARTER (b 1793) dau of PHILIP H. HARTER & CATHERINE PHILIPS (Harter book page 24). Children were Conrad, Peter Philip (b 1816, sp Jacob Fulmer & Maria Catherine), John, Wilhelm, Lawrence (bp Mar 1826, sp. Benj. Smith & Maria), Catharina, Elizabeth, Anna, and Frederick (b 1838, sp Conrad Folmer & Anna).

********* GETMAN (Goedman) **********

3501: **FREDERICK GETMAN** - born in Germany in 1693 (son of CASPAR GETMAN & MARIA BARBARA); died 1781; m by 1721 MARY BIERMAN dau of JOHANNES BIERMAN as in the Getman book ("The Getman Family Genealogy 1710-1974" by William Laimbeer, copy at Herk. Co. Hist. Soc.). Believed to have come to New York in 1710 and was pr. a dependent on the NY Palatine subsistence listing for his mother, Barbara Getman, who was on that list in 1710 (2A,0Y). A Maria Barbara Getman was also on NY list in 1710 (2A,0Y). Pr. he was the Frederick Kietman naturalized at Albany 22 Nov 1715 (name alongside Johannis Beerman). The Getman book birthyear estimates seem late for son Frederick and daughter Eva, and should thus be verified for each child.

                    surname GETMAN
+3502: ANNA MARIA   1721-1811 m HENRY MEYER
+3503: GEORGE   1723-1789   m UTILIA SHOEMAKER
+3504: FREDERICK   b say 1726; m by 1760 MARGARET ...
+3505: JOHN   b 1728; m 1762 ANNA MARIE MARKLE   to Canada as a Tory
 3506: ANNA EVA   b 1731 (?); m FREDERICK ORENDORF
            (Orendorf dates suggest earlier birth for Eva, say 1725)
 3506A ps. MARGARET (Getman?) b say 1732; m by 1760 MARCUS ITTIG
+3507: CHRISTIAN   1734-1821   m ANNA EVA ZIMMERMAN
 3508: CATHERINE   ca 1737-1806   m JOHN SHOEMAKER

                    GETMAN - 2nd Generation

3507: Capt. **CHRISTIAN GETMAN** - born 1734; died 1821; m 8 Jul 1760 ANNA EVA ZIMMERMAN (b 1743, d 1822) dau of ADAM ZIMMERMAN & CATHERINE NELLIS and widow of JOHN MERCKEL. See Martin's Zimmerman book for story of his wife's loss of her first husband and child to Indians. Was in Lt. Dygert's militia co. in 1757 and on 1790 Palatine NY census (3-2-3). Children from Getman book (page 220).

    3509: CATHERINE   b 27 Sep 1761 (sp. Joh. Getman); m LUDWIG RICHARDS
               (sp. also Cath. dau of Adam Zimmerman)
    3510: PETER   b SAR 1764 (sp Geo. Getman & w Ottila)
                           d 1845; m ELISABETH RICHTER
    3511: ANNA   b 16 Nov 1765; died soon
    3511A ANNA EVA   b 19 Dec 1767; m SAR 1788 JOST SCHOLL a widower
    3512: JOHN   b 16 Jan 1769
    3513: CHRISTIAN   b 17 Jan 1771; m MARY EACKER
    3514: JACOB   b 13 Feb 1773; m SUSANNA JOSLIN
    3515: FREDERICK   b 5 Jan 1780; d 1867
    3516: ADAM   b 28 Jun 1783; m MARY VAUCHE
    3517: ELISABETH   b SAR 27 Jan 1787 (sp Hen. Crim & Anna <Nellis>)

3504: Capt. **FREDERICK GETMAN** - pr. born ca 1715 to 1732 (Getman book has born 1736, but a reference for that date is not given and it seems late, given daughter Catherine's birthyear of ca 1748); supposedly died 1792/3 (ibid.); m by 1761 MARGARET ... (her name on 1761 SAR bp rec., pr. a Frank or Ittig); pr. m2 GF 15 May 1787 MARGARET JOH. MILLER. This man may have died by 1790 presuming the Frederick Getman on the 1790 Herkimer census was a younger Frederick. His will dated 7 Apr 1788 mentions sons Peter, Conrad, John and Frederick, and daughters Catherine, wife of Geo. Weaver, Maria, wife of Melchert Folts, and Margaret, wife of Gershom Skinner. Laimbeer's Getman Genealogy explains the appearance in church

                            -103-

records of parents Frederick & Margaret (1761 & 1766) and Frederick & Catherine
(child Conrad, b 1763 & bp 1764, and 1775 to 1793) as one couple only, with this
Capt. Frederick marrying by 1763 MARY CATHERINE BROADHACK (Getman book has
Catherine Brodhack as his only wife but Margaret, rather than Catherine, appears
as wife of Frederick on bp records in both 1761 and 1766). We think the 1763
church bp record incorrectly lists the wife as Maria Catherine instead of Margaret
(ps. minister was thinking ahead to sponsor's name <Maria Catherine Frank>) and we
feel a Frederick Jr. (pr. son of Capt. Frederick) was the husband of Maria
Catherine Brodhack and father of the children born from 1775 onwards. It makes
more sense for Fred Jr., not Sr., to have a daughter Catherine bp in 1789 (see
further justification under Fred. Jr. in next generation). Ps. the Frederick in
Capt. Conrad Frank's militia co. in 1767. Additional references noted are Ilion
Sentinel article "Getman Family" August 17/24, 1939 (not seen) and Cdmr.
Bellinger's HCH file #1.7.

<pre>
                        Children of Capt. Frederick
    +3518: pr. FREDERICK b say 1746; m by 1775 CATHERINE BRODHACK
    +3519: CATHERINE F.   b say 1748; m by 1776 GEORGE WEAVER
     3520: MARIA   b say 1757; m1 by 1776 FRED. STEVENS; m2 M. FOLTS
    +3521: PETER   1760-1826 m ELISABETH FRANK
     3522: MARIA MARGARETHA b 21 Jul 1761; m GERSHOM SKINNER
                (1761 sp. Maria Margaret And. Weber, Jacob Geo. Wentz)
    +3523: CONRAD b SAR 9 Dec 1763 (sp. Con. Orendorf, Cath. Frank)
                d 1836;   m MARIA FRANK
    +3524: JOHN b 1766 (sp John Cuningham, Anna Folts)
                m1 CATHERINE FRANK; m2 ANNA ELISABETH FRANK
</pre>

3503: GEORGE GETMAN - born 1 May 1723; died 1 Sep 1789; m by Rev. Peter Nicholas
Sommer in Jun 1750 UTILIA SHOEMAKER (b say 1725, liv. Dec 1783) pr. dau of THOMAS
SHOEMAKER. Helmer book page 116 has Utilia as dau of John Shoemaker, but no
evidence is offered and only Thomas seems of right age to be father (seems
supported by order of children's names below). In Lt Dygert's militia co. in 1757
and in Col. Klock's regiment at Battle of Stone Arabia in the American Revolution.

<pre>
    +3525: FREDERICK b 1751; m ANNA EVA FRANK
    +3526: THOMAS 1752-1820 m ELISABETH HELMER
    +3527: JOHANNES b 2 Jul 1754 (sp John Shoemaker, Cath. Getman)
                m MARGARET LOUCKS
    +3528: Johan GEORGE b 11 Jul 1756 (sp. Fred Getman & Wife)
     3529: ANNA MARIA b 11 Jul 1756 (sp. Christian Getman)
                m 1782 HANS LUDWIG KRING
</pre>

3505: JOHN GETMAN - born 1728 (unm son of Frederick as given on mar. rec., with
birthdate from Getman book); m 1762 ANNA MARIE MARKLE; ps. m2 by 1771 MARIA
MARGARET .... Bp of a Henry (b 1771, as below), John, & George Getman, children
of a John Getman & Maria Margaret are grouped together in the Stone Arabia Reform
Dutch Church records and pr. they belong to the John & Margaret (Loucks) of the
next generation. John was in Dygert's militia in 1757 but took the Tory side
during the American Revolution and went to Canada.

<pre>
     3530: PETER b SAR 29 Aug 1763 (sp Jac Merckel, Cath. Fink)
     3531: MARGARET b SAR 14 Nov 1764 (sp Marg. wife of H. Merckel)
                ps. by 2nd wife (?)
     3532: ps. HENRICH b SAR Oct 1771 (sp Caspar Koch & w. Cath.<Laux>)
</pre>

3523: CONRAD GETMAN - born SAR Dec 1763 (son of Fred.); died 29 Mar 1836; m 8 Nov
1785 MARIA FRANK (b 1765) pr. dau of TIMOTHY FRANK (Bellinger book page 62).
According to German Flats churchbook entry Conrad had a child, GEORGE MICHEL ITTIG
(born 13 Feb 1786) by ANNA CHRIST. ITTIG but married Maria Frank nonetheless.
Lived at Columbia, Herkimer Co., NY. His 7 children were Margretha, Anna
Elisabeth (b 1788), Timothy (b GF 16 Jul 1790, sp. Tim Frank & Elis.), Permelia,
Maria, Daniel, and Catharina (b 1803).

3518: FREDERICK GETMAN jr. - pr. born ca 1735 to 1753; m by 1775 MARY CATHERINE
BROADHACK. Probably the Frederick Jr. in Col. Bellinger's Revol. Regiment and the
Frederick Getman on 1790 Herkimer census (1-2-3) living near the Brodhacks (John &
Jacob), Philip F. Helmer, & Gershom Skinner. Lambier's Getman book says this man
was the same person as Capt. Frederick (son of immigrant Frederick), however that
would have him choosing the name Catherine for a daughter born in 1789 while an
older daughter of the same name was still apparently alive (as wife of George
Weaver). Amongst the Mohawk Valley Palatines, baptism sponsors were often selected
to match the first name of the child and most likely to be of the parent's
generation, usually close relatives such as the parents' brothers and sisters (and
less frequently just friends or neighbors). An exception to the same generation
rule was made in the case of sponsors who were the child's grandparents. In 18th
century German Flats we do not have parents selecting older children as sponsors
for younger ones! Thus with three children of Capt. Frederick included amongst
the bp sponsors below (i.e. Mrs. Maria Stevens, Mrs. Margaret Skinner, & Peter
Getman), we feel those sponsors must be sisters and brothers of Fred jr., himself
a separate person from Capt. Frederick.

  +3535: FREDERICK Jr 1775 (sp Fred. Stevens & Maria)
      d 1841; m LENA FRANK
  3535A pr. MARIA b SAL 31 Dec 1778 (dau of "Dieterich" Gtmn & Cath.)
      (sp. Barth. Brodhack & Anna Maria)
  3536: ELISABETH   m MR. SHARP (Nath.?)
  3537: POLLY (MARY) b 18 Jul 178x; m GEORGE J. GETMAN
  3538: MARGARET b 24 Mar 1784 (sp Con. Getman, Maria Meyer)
      m 1805 JOHN AUG. HESS
  3539: GEORGE F. b 4 Apr 1787 (sp. Geo. Weaver & Cath.)
      m HK 1804 MARGARET W. HANER
  3540: CATHERINE b GF 13 Dec 1789 (sp Gers. Skinner & Marg.); pr d y
  3541: BARTLETT BROADHACK b 22 Nov 1790 (sp Bar. Brodhack & Elis.)
      m ELIZABETH GRANT
  3542: CATHERINE b GF 26 Aug 1793 (sp Pet. Getman & Mar. Elis.)

3525: FREDERICK GETMAN - born 1751 (son of George, as given in Getman book); died
Mar 1812; m ANNA EVA FRANK dau of CONRAD FRANK & ELISABETH. Deacon of Stone
Arabia Church 1784 and member of NY Senate 1797-1800.

  3543: ELISABETH b 26 Dec 1771
  3544: FREDERICK b 1775
  3545: CATHARINE b GF 26 Aug 1783 (sp Isac Paris, Cath. Bayer)
  3546: DELIA (OTTILIA) b 17 Aug 1786 (sp Thom. Getman & Elisabeth)
  +3547: DANIEL b SAR 18 Jan 1791 (sp Peter Weber & Maria Cath.)
      d 1881; ml DELIA ZIMMERMAN

3528: GEORGE GETMAN - born 11 Jul 1756 (son of George); died 1828; m1 25 Dec 1781
ELISABETH P. HOUSE dau of PETER HOUSE; m2 1800 DELIA ... On 1790 Palatine NY
census (1-3-3).

> 3548: GEORGE b GF Mar 1783 (Fr. Getman & Eva); m ELIZABETH EMPIE
> 3549: PETER b 26 Mar 1785; m MARIA SHULL
> 3550: MARY b 17 Mar 1787 (Ludw. Kring & Maria); m WILLIAM NELLIS
> 3551: JOSEPH b 31 May 1789; m1 ELIZABETH RICHARDS
> 3552: DELIA b 1790
> 3553: BENJAMIN b 1791; m MARITJE VAN ANTWERP
> 3554: CHRISTOPHER b SAR 20 Nov 1793 (sp Geo. Getman, Elis. Haus)
>   m POLLY MILLER
> 3555: WILLIAM b 1796; m CATHERINE CHARLESWORTH
>   by 2nd wife
> 3556: MARGARET b 1801
> 3557: NICHOLAS b 1807

3527: JOHANNES GETMAN - born Stone Arabia NY 2 Jul 1754; m 13 Feb 1776 MARGARET
LOUCKS. Suspect mar. date may have been earlier (say by 1771, with Henrich bp SAR
1771 son of a John & Marg.). On 1790 Palatine NY census (1-6-4) and later moved
to Columbia, Herkimer Co., NY and was living at Conradstown in 1802 (son Henry's
mar. rec.). See earlier John Getman (the Tory who m 1762 Maria Merckel).

> 3558: pr. JOHN b SAR 6 Mar 1776 (sp Hen. Laux, Elis. Dygert)
>   d 20 Aug 1794 unm
> 3559: pr. GEORGE b SAR 7 Mar 1778 (sp Geo. Getman, Elis. Dygert)
>   m POLLY GETMAN
> 3560: HENRY b 9 Oct 1779; m 1802 CATHERINE A. MILLER
> 3561: MARY ELISABETH b 2 Jan 1781; m WARNER FOLTZ
> 3562: JACOB b 22 Jan 1783; m ELIZABETH BARRINGER
> 3563: FREDERICK b 1784; m RUTH PANGBORN
> 3564: MARIE b 17 Jun 1786; m ANDREW MILLER
> 3565: RICHARD b SAR 6 Jun 1788 (sp Diet. Laux, Elis. Koch)
>   m GERTRUDE MEYER
> 3566: UDELIA b 24 Apr 1790; m MICHAEL MEYER
> 3567: MARGARET b SAR 4 Apr 1794 (sp Wm Fox & w. Anna Eva)
>   m JOHN CARNER
> 3568: ANNA b 5 Nov 1795 (sp Diet. Laux & Anna)
>   m JOHN K. RITTER no issue

3524: JOHN FR. GETMAN - born 13 Aug 1766; pr. m1 5 Dec 1786 MARIA CATHERINE FRANK
ps the dau (b 1762) of FREDERICK FRANK & SUSANNA ... (Bellinger book page 62);
m2 ca 1789 ANNA ELISABETH FRANK (b 1769, d 1805) dau of TIMOTHY FRANK; m3 18 Sep
1805 CATHERINE STEELE widow of HENRY SALLIER of Frankfort NY. Lived next to his
brother Peter Getman in Frankfort NY (Bellinger book page 34). Children as given
in Getman book page 367 were Katherine, Johannes, Elisabeth, Frederick, Timothy,
Anna, Warner, Jacob, Henry, Eve, George (b 1806), Rudolph, and Lydia.

> 3569: JOHANNES b 21 Jun 1787 (sp. John <Stephen> Frank & Eva)
>   m KATHY HOUSE
> 3570: KATHERINE b say 1788; m JACOB HOUSE
>   by second wife
> 3571: ELISABETH b 1790; m CONRAD PETRIE
> 3572: FREDERICK b 2 Feb 1792; m MARY OXNER
> 3573: TIMOTHEUS b GF 11 Jun 1793 (sp Con. Hess & Cath.)
> 3574: ANNA b GF 17 Apr 1795 (sp Warner Folts, Marg. Fox)

3521: PETER GETMAN - Peter born 11 May 1760 (son of Fred.); died 26 Dec 1826; m at
German Flats NY 9 Jan 1783 ANNA ELISABETH FRANK (bp 1763) dau of FREDERICK FRANK &
ELISABETH FOX. Same Peter seen separately as son of Capt. Frederick (pr. more
likely) or son of George. Living at Frankfort NY in 1802 (dau Elisabeth's HK
church confirmation record).

            3575: MARY CATHERINE b GF 13 Sep 1783 (Con. Getman, Cat. Frank) d y
            3575A ELISABETH 1785-1831 m HENRY F. MEYER
            3576: CONRAD b 17 Aug 1787 (sp Conrad Getman & Maria)
                       died 5 Jul 1843
            3577: JACOB b GF 31 Aug 1789 (sp Jac. Ittig, Cath. Flack)
                       will prep. 1843; m ANNA SCHELL
            3578: CHRISTOPHER b 9 Feb 1792 (sp Con. Folts & Anna)
            3579: ANNA MARGARET b 1 May 1793; m MICHAEL F. MYERS
            3580: CATRINA b 24 Oct 1795; m JOSHUA MADISON
            3581: ANDREW b 24 May 1796/7; m ELIZABETH EDICK
            3582: pr. DOROTHEA b 2 Feb 1801; m PETER G. GETMAN
                       (called sister in Jacob Getman's will)
            3583: pr. ROBERT b 28 Apr 1804; m MARGARET PIPER

3526: THOMAS GETMAN - born 17 Nov 1752 (son of George); died 25 Dec 1820 (bur. at
Getman homestead, Ephratah NY); m ELIZABETH HELMER (b 1753, d 6 Oct 1837) ps. a
dau of GODFRID HELMER (as in Helmer book page 116) but our guess for her parents
would be LEONARD HELMER & CATHERINE NELLIS. On 1790 Palatine NY census (1-3-3).

           +3584: GEORGE T. 1774-1834 m MARGARET COOK (Koch)
            3585: KATHERINE b 1778; m RICHARD SUTS
            3586: THOMAS b 1780; m ELIZABETH SHULL
            3587: JOHN T. b GF 9 Mar 1782 (sp John Getman & Marg.)
                       m MARY NELLIS

3519: CATHERINE GETMAN - pr. b ca 1745 to 1755; living 1788 (ment. in father's
will); m by 1776 GEORGE JAC. WEAVER

3520: MARY GETMAN - pr. born ca 1740 to 1757; died Jun 1829; m1 FREDERICK STEVENS
(died 1777); m2 ca 1780 MELCHERT FOLTS (b 1746, d 1829) son of CONRAD FOLTS & ANNA
CATHERINE DEMUTH.

GETMAN - 4th Generation

3547: DANIEL GETMAN - born 18 Jan 1791; died 7 Dec 1881; m1 1813 DELIA ZIMMERMAN
(b 1794, d 1828) dau of Lt. HENRY ZIMMERMAN & MARGARET BELLINGER; m2 14 Nov 1834
LANY ZIMMERMAN. Children were Elijah, Jeremiah, Frederick, Ann Eliza (b 1819, m
Adam Smith), Henry (b 1822, m Eunice Barnes), and Catherine (b 1824, m Nelson
Burdick).

3535: FREDERICK GETMAN Jr - born 18 May 1775; died 10 Nov 1841; m LENA FRANK (b
1777) dau of TIMOTHY FRANK & ANNA ELISABETH BELLINGER

3584: GEORGE T. GETMAN - born 1 Jan 1774; died 23 Jun 1834; m MARGARET KOCH
(Cook). Children as given in Helmer book page 117 include CASPER (b 1799, m
Elisabeth Bauder), Robert (1805), John, Thomas, Catherine, Elizabeth, Hannah.

********** GRAY (Krahe) **********

3601: **ANDREW GRAY** - pr. born in Great Britain ca 1685 to 1705; pr. died near
Stone Arabia NY after 1750; m ... (tradition says a girl of Dutch descent). He
is said to have moved with two brothers from Scotland to Ireland and thence to
New York in 1735 (Greene's "History of The Mohawk Valley / Gateway to the West"
vol. III, Chicago 1925). About 1750 he built the Gray homestead at Stone Arabia
and supposedly had four sons (of these only Adam seems identifiable, other
possible sons are Robert, John & Samuel). Notes of Mrs. M. Bach, in the
Enterprise & News of 28 Jan 1928, say Andrew had two wives and, by the first
wife, had son Adam (who married in 1746 Elisabeth Horning), and, by the second
wife, had son Samuel (no evidence provided). Greene's version seems more likely
to us than an account in Reynolds' Hudson-Mohawk Geneal., which has the Grays
descending from a John Gray who married at Beverly Mass. in 1704 Ruth Hubbard.
One researcher (Dunckle) says a Catherine Gray, presumably daughter of Andrew,
was wife of Peter Wohleben (but that Peter's wife in 1765 was Catherine Flagg).

surname GRAY

        +3602: pr. ADAM   b say 1722; m 1746 MARIA ELISABETH HORNING
        +3603: ps. ROBERT b say 1725;

3607: **ARCHIBALD GRAY** - pr. born before 1732; m ELISABETH GREEHAM. Ps. related
to the above Andrew, Archibald & Elisabeth had a daughter CATHERINE (bp
Schenectady 11 Aug 1751). A later Archibald Gray of Dunoon Scotland (died there
1803) came to New York in 1794 with a son Daniel (Reynolds H-Mohawk Geneal.).

GRAY - 2nd Generation

3602: **ADAM GRAY** - pr. born in Scotland or Ireland ca 1715 to 1725; died ca
1776 of consumption; m at Canajoharie NY 21 Oct 1746 MARIA ELISABETH HORNING (b
ca 1720, d 1807 age 87) presumably a dau of NICHOLAS HORNING & MARIA. Adam came
to New York as a youth, about 1730, from Ballibag (Co. Monehan) Ireland,
according to Mrs. Margaret M. Bach of Bath NY, a descendent of this Adam thru
his son Andrew (see St. Johnsville E&N 28 Jan 1928). We believe the indications
good enough to assign as early (undocumented) children of Adam at least Nicholas
(named for grandfather Horning), Maria (named for grandmother Horning), Samuel
(naming order of his children fits for a son of Adam), and Adam, that we place
them below, without a "pr." (qualifier normally used in absence of a church or
family birth record).   "Adam Krah" was on the 1751 Stone Arabia minister's
support list, being listed alongside Dietrich Horning. Adam Gray & wife
sponsored the Oct 1771 bp of George, son of Andreas Heintz & Maria (Gray).

        3610: NICHOLAS   b say 1748; killed at Oriskany Battle in 1777
       +3611: SAMUEL   1751-1831 m CATHERINE SUTZ
       +3612: pr. CATHERINE 1752-1825   m JOHN M. SMITH
        3613: ps. ANNA   b say 1753; died in infancy
        3614: ANNA MARIA b say 1755; m SAR Jul 1771 ANDREW HINES (HEINTZ)
        3614A: ADAM b say 1757; liv. 1823 (brother Andrew's will)
       +3615: ANDREW 1759-1823 m CATHERINE SNELL
       +3616: JOHN (twin) b SAR 14 Feb 1762 (sp John Laux, Elis. Krem, unm)
                  d 1800; m MARIA SNELL
       +3617: ROBERT (twin) 1762-1816 m ELISABETH DYGERT

3603: ROBERT GRAY - pr. born before 1730 (ps. a son of immigrant Andrew?)

      3617A ps. ADAM b ca Jun 1749; d Minden NY 5 Dec 1813 age 64-6 unm
    +3617B ps. ROBERT b say 1753; m Albany NY 1777 SUSANNA LAGRANGE

GRAY - 3rd Generation

3611: Capt. **SAMUEL GRAY** - born 23 Jan 1751 (Greene´s History of The Mohawk
Valley); died Palatine NY 19 Mar 1831 (age 80, E&N 1/29/1928); m 28 Apr 1776
CATHERINE SUTZ (b 31 Aug 1753, d 10 Mar 1825 age 71-6-0, her full name on 1797
bp rec.) pr. dau of JOHN SUTZ. Samuel served in Col. Klock´s Regiment during
the Revolution and was at the Battle of Oriskany. Another Samuel was bp at
Southeast Twp (Putnam Co.) NY 1754 son of EDWARD GRAY & MARY PADDOCK (LDS CFI).
Samuel & Catherine had 9 sons and 2 daughters (E&N 1/28/1928) as seen below
(list provided 1985 by researcher Joan S. Szablewski, 88 Skyway Dr., Scotia NY
12302). The will of Samuel of Palatine, dated 6 Apr 1826, names 10 children
(all those below except Jost).

      3617C ADAM b say 1777; liv. 1840 Erie Co. NY
    +3618: SAMUEL   b say 1779; m 1798 LENA OBEDS
     3619: JOHANNES   bp GF 18 Feb 1781 (sp. John Glock & Margaret)
     3620: NICHOLAS b GF 8 Apr 1783 (sp John Grey, Christina Smidt)
                  d Montgomery IL 1875 age 92; m CATHERINE MARKELL
    +3621: ANDREW S. bp GF 16 May 1785 (sp. And. Grahe, Cath. Snell)
                  m 1808 ELISABETH SCHULTZ(dau of John)
     3622: MARY b SAR 17 Jun 1787 (sp. Hen. Koch & w. Maria Young)
                d 1863; m 1806 GEORGE G. LOUCKS
     3622A JOST b SAR 8 Apr 1789 (sp. Jost Fink & Maria)
     3622B WILLIAM b SAR Apr 1791; d 1862; m 1810 ANNA G. SALTSMAN
     3623: JACOB S. b SAR 4 Apr 1793; d 15 Apr 1862; m HANNAH EVERSON
     3623A DANIEL b SAR 23 Jan 1795 (sp. Maria Elisabeth Gray, widow)
               d Montgomery IL 1855; m MARGARET SHAVER (or SLOVER)
     3624: CATHARINE b SAR 26 Feb 1797 (sp. John Schultz & w. Cath.)
                d Kanona NY 1854; m 1815 WILLIAM SNELL

3615: Col. ANDREW GRAY - born Palatine NY ca 27 Feb 1759 (son of Adam, as in
Mrs. Bach´s notes); died Minden NY 19 Dec 1823 (age 64-9-21); m GF 9 Jul 1786
CATHERINA JOH. SNELL (b ca 1766-7, died 15 Dec 1843) dau of GEORGE SNELL & MARIA
FOX (DAR vol 141, page 161). Will of Andrew Gray of Palatine NY, dated 27 Nov
1823, mentions wife Catherine, sons Adam A., George, Charles, & James; daughters
Sally Gray, Nancy Loucks, Mary Kyne, & Catherine Devoe; brother Adam.

     3625: MARIA b SAR 21 Mar 1787 (sp Jacob Snell & w. Maria Merkel)
              m JOHN KEYSER
    +3626: ADAM bp SAR 24 Sep 1789 (sp. Adam Gray, Betsy Snell)
              m1 MAGDALENA LOUCKS
     3627: GEORGE b SAR 25 Feb 1792 (sp. Geo. Laux & w. Elis.)
              m CATHERINE COOK
     3628: NANCY b 20 Jun 1794; m PETER G. LOUCKS
    +3629: CHARLES 1796-1871 m 1826 ELISABETH PETRY
     3630: CATHARINA bp Palatine 13 Dec 1798; m CHARLES DEVOE
     3631: JAMES b 6 Jun 1801; m MARY ANN STRAYER
     3632: SALLY b SAL 24 Aug 1804 (sp. Peter Koch & Eva)
              m1 MR. BAUDER m2 ANDREW EIGENBRODT

3616: JOHN GRAY - pr. the Johannes born 14 Feb 1762 (son of Adam and twin of Robert); died May 1800; m MARIA SNELL (b 17 Oct 1768, d Jan 1845) dau of GEORGE SNELL & MARIA FOX and sister of the Catherine Snell who married Andrew Gray (Mrs. Bach's notes). Some info on children from Martin's Snell book (page 45).

> 3633: MARIA   b SAR 13 Jul 1787 (sp Mar. Elis. Grey (born Horning))
>   ps. m Minden NY 9 Mar 1806 JACOB CHRISTMAN
> 3634: JACOB   b SAR 19 Jun 1789 (sp. Jac. Schnell & w. Maria)
> 3635: child   b SAR 1 Aug 1791
> 3636: NICHOLAS bp SAR 19 Jan 1794 (sp Joh. Smith & w. Cath.)
>   m1 1813 MARIA EVERSON; m2 by 1825 SOPHIA ... (b 1800)
> 3637: GEORGE J.   b say 1796; m 1815 ANNA SCHULTZ (dau of Jacob)
> 3638: JOHN J.   b say 1798; m Ft. Plain NY 1820 ELECTA TRUMBULL

3617: ROBERT GRAY - born Palatine NY (SAR) 14 Feb 1762 (son of Adam, bp sp. Andrew Weymar & wife Veronica); died Minden NY 16 Aug 1816 (age 54-7-); m GF 30 Jun 1783 ELISABETH JOHANNES DYGERT (b ca 1762, d Minden NY 25 Oct 1815 age 53 years 7 mos 20 days) dau of JOHN DYGERT & DOROTHY SHOEMAKER (Petrie Geneal. page 11). Robert was from Tillenbergh, near Ephrath, NY, and a son of Adam. He had four sons and one daughter (Mrs. Bach notes).

> 3639: JOHANNES   b GF 7 Oct 1784 (sp. Joh. Gray, Maria Tyghart)
> 3640: CATHERINE bp SJR 11 Mar 1789 (sp Jac. Frisch, Cath. Dygert)
> 3641: ADAM R.   bp SJR 18 Mar 1792 (sp. Adam Gray, Anna Spayer)

3617B ROBERT GRAY - pr. born ca 1740 to 1760 (ps. a grandson of immigrant Andrew?);m at Albany NY 1777 SUSANNA LAGRANGE. Another entry at Albany has a ROBERT GRAY with wife ELISABETH DRUMMER (they had a son John bp Albany 29 Apr 1779).

3612: CATHERINE GRAY - pr. born between 20 Apr 1751 and 19 Apr 1752; died Herkimer NY 19 Apr 1825 age 73; m by 1776 JOHN M. SMITH (b 1748, d 1822) son of MARTIN SMITH. She is presumed to be the sister of Andrew Gary, who married Cath. Snell, as Charles Gray (b 1796) and Smith children are styled as "cousins". Her first known child, born in 1776, was Adam Smith (probably named for her father).

GRAY - 4th Generation

3626: ADAM GRAY - bp Palatine NY 4 Oct 1789 (son of Andrew); m1 MAGDALENA LOUCKS; m2 PHEBE GUILE. Was a farmer.

3621: ANDREW S. GRAY - pr. the Andrew bp German Flats NY 16 May 1785; m at Minden NY 6-13 Nov 1808 ELISABETH SCHULTZ (ps. later m ELISABETH PHILLIPS?)

3629: CHARLES GRAY - born 20 Sep 1796 and bp Palatine NY 2 Oct 1796; died 1871; m at Herkimer 20 Sep 1826 ELIZABETH PETRY (b 1805 d 1898) dau of JACOB WILLIAM PETRY & MARY SMITH. Was a lawyer (Petrie book, page 121).

3618: SAMUEL GRAY - pr. born ca 1776 to 1780; m at Fonda NY 1798 LENA OBEDS (aka MAGDALENA OBITS). Children include Catarina (b SAL 18 Mar 1800, sp. Samuel Gray & Catarina),'Ann (b SAR Dec 1801, sp. Peter Ehle, Elis. Obits), Elleage (b SAL 1803), John (bp Palatine NY May 1807).

********** HAGER (Haeger) **********

3701: Rev. Johan FREDERICK HAEGER - bp Seigen Germany 1684 (son of Henry Haeger & Catherine Friesenhagen); m in NY 13 Nov 1717 ANNA CATHERINE ROHRBACH. Rev. Haeger was a Reform Dutch Church minster who immigrated with the Palatine Germans in 1710 and, although the records of the Lutheran minister Kochtheral survive (printed in Book of Names), the contemporary account of marriages and baptisms, which Rev. Haeger surely kept, are lost. He was Chaplain with the troops who went to Canada in 1711 under Col. Nicholson. His name appears on the NY Palatine subsistence list in 1710 (1A,0Y) and 1712 (1A,0Y). He was a sponsor, with Johann Muller & Margartha Marten, for the Feb 1712 bp of Fridrich, son of Heironymus Weller & Anna Juliana and again a sponsor for the Mar 1712 bp of Fridrich, son of Johan Conrad Marten & Maria. No children known.

3702: HENRY HAGER - pr. born ca 1670 to 1685; m by 1702 MARIA JACOBI. His widow Maria was on the NY Palatine subsistence list as Maria Hagerin in 1710 (1A,1Y) & 1712 (2A,0Y) and m2 JOHANNES MULLER. Possibly she was a sister-in-law of Rev. Johan Frederick (Petrie book page 3). See John Miller family for more.

                        surname HAGER
    +3703: HENRY   1702-1796 m1 DOROTHY KAST m2 GERTRUDE PETRIE

                        HAGER - 2nd Generation

3703: HENRY HAGER - born 1 Sep 1702 (son of Henry, birth & death dates from DAR <not seen> as cited in HCH Kast ms.); died Breakabeen (Schoharie Co.) NY 13 Jul 1796; m1 DOROTHY KAST (b 1715) dau of GEORGE KAST Sr. & ANNA ; m2 GERTRUDE PETRIE (b 1715) dau of JOST PETRIE & CORDELIA DEMUTH. Received Burnetsfield lot #8, located on the north side of the Mohawk River next to Ponradt property, probably in light of his status as a dependent of Johannes Miller. He was naturalized 3 May 1755 and in 1768 he received a grant of 900 acres at Fulton in Schoharie County and probably moved there about that time (1984 notes of Mr. D. L. Haverly, 23 Wedgewood Dr., Albany NY 12211). Henry & wife Gertrude sponsored Oct 1777 bp of grandson Henrich, son of Matheis Brown.

                        by 1st wife
    3704: ANNA MARIA b 4 Oct 1732; m JACOB MEYER
                        by 2nd wife
    3704A pr. CATHERINE b say 1734
                        m Albany NY 1758 JOH. MAURITIUS GOETSCHIUS
    3705: ANNATIE b say 1735; m by 1759 FREDERICK BECKER
    3706: ELISABETH b say 1736; m 1760 CHRISTIAN BRAUN
    3707: EVA   b say 1738; m 1766 CONRAD MATTICE
    3708: DELIA b say 1740; m 1767 JONAS VROOMAN of Schoharie.
    3709: JOHANNES b say 1742; m 1769 MARIA SWART
    3710: JACOB b say 1743; m by 1765 CORNELIA VROOMAN
    3711: HENRICH Jr b say 1745; d ca 1770; m MARIA LARROWA
    3712: PETER bp 1746; m by 1773 MARIA LARROWA (wid. of Henr. Jr.)
    3713: GERTRUDE bp 1748; m 1771 MATHEIS BRAUN
    3714: SARA b 5 Nov 1749 (sp. Joh. Fink & Maria Eva)
    3715: DOROTHEA bp 3 May 1751; m HANNES MATHEES
    3716: DAVID b 14 Oct 1753;
    3717: JOST b 18 Apr 1762

********** HARTER (Herder) **********

HARTER - 1st Generation

3801: Johan NICHOLAS HARTER - pr. born in Germany ca 1660 to 1680; died by Sep 1711; m ANNA ... On NY subsistence lists in 1710 (3A,2Y). Then Anna Harterin, without Nicholas, on NY list in 1711 (1A,1Y). Descendents in Herkimer Co. area are mainly from "The Mohawk Valley Harters" by Marion Kofmehl and Hazel Patrick (their ident.# for Harters are given below in brackets, ie. <H#>).

surname HARTER
+3802: LORENTZ 1698- m APPOLONIA ...

3803: Johan MICHAEL HARTER - pr. born before 1685 (pr. a relative of Nicholas); died NY ca 1716; m MARIA ... His widow m2 27 Nov 1720 JACOB ESCHWYN. On NY subs. list in 1710 (3A,3Y) and 1712 (4A,2Y). The last record for Michel is naturalization at Albany in Jan 1716, then his widow & 4 children are on the 1717 Simmendinger census. His children Jacob, Peter, Michel jr, & William (as per Hank Jones in Harter book page xvii) settled at Columbia Co. in the Hudson Valley.

HARTER - 2nd Generation

3802: LORENTZ HARTER Sr.<H1> - born 14 Oct 1698; pr. liv. 1778; m by 1723 APPOLLONIA ... (b 1702, liv. 1776). Harter book has his wife as APPOLONIA SCHUT, but evidence seems lacking and the descendent naming and association suggest a possible Helmer connection. Lorentz was naturalized at Albany 28 Feb 1716 and a patentee at Burnetsfield on lot #37 in 1722. He wrote the birthdates for himself, his wife, and his children in his family bible, which is now preserved at the Herkimer Co. Hist. Society. In this "Herrther Bible", Lorentz stated he had 8 sons and four daughters, but gave the names and dates for only the five sons and four daughthers now known. Perhaps he purchased the bible after the last child was born and entered all data at one time, which might account for omitting details on children that had died young (see Bellinger book page 94 for a full transcript, in the original German, of his bible entries). His will dated 1 Jul 1776 mentions wife Abelonia, eldest son Nicholas (who got 20 shillings for his birthright), and three other sons, Fredrich, Hendrix, & Lorentz, who were to inherit his property, including lot# 12. Also mentioned were daughters Catherine, Elisabeth, and Margaret and an "Abelonia Schuttin", who was to receive his loom (she was probably his granddaughter, age about 10 then). Probably the Lorentz Sr who had 3 adults and 1 child (under 16) on 1778 German Flats relief.

```
+3804: NICHOLAS  1723-1801  m ANNA MARIE
+3805: Johan FREDERICK  1726-1812 m APPOLONIA BELLINGER
+3806: PHILIP  b 13 Nov 1729; pr. m GERTRUDE ... (or CATHERINE)
+3807: HEINRICH  1731-1820 m CATHERINE PFIEFFER
 3808: CATHERINE  b 2 Apr 1733; pr. m 1764 WILLIAM SCHUTT
 3809: ANNA MARGARETHA  b 1735; d 21 Sep 1822 unm
 3810: ELISABETH  b 29 Jul 1737; d 1805; m THOMAS SHOEMAKER
 3811: MARIA BARBARA  b 9 Oct 1740; pr. d. before 1776
+3812: LAWRENCE  1743-1815 m2 CATHARINA DOCKSTADER
```

HARTER - 3rd Generation

3805: FREDERICK HARTER <H3> - born 8 Nov 1726; died Herkimer NY 28 Jul 1812 (age 86); m1 APPOLONIA BELLINGER (b 1733) pr. dau of ADAM BELLINGER & APPOLONIA; m2 by 1786 ELISABETH ... (b ca 1724, d HK 24 Oct 1808 age 84, wife of F. Harter - some accounts have Elisabeth as a Rasbach and widow of Peter Folts, but our guess is that she was a Hilts and the widow of Thomas Bell & Andrew McKoom). After the 1757 French & Indian raid, he and his family were taken as captives to Canada, the men being kept there in a separate prison camp a mile or more removed from that of the women and children. While there in 1759, he built a birchbark coffin for his just deceased son Frederick and used the opportunity, while transporting it to the women's camp, to make good his escape and return on foot to German Flats (Harter book page 130). Frederick had 5 adults & 4 children on 1778 GF relief and lived on the east bank of the West Canada creek. Frederick & Maria Elisabeth sponsored Oct 1786 bp of Catherine, dau of Philip Helmer & Anna (Meyer), and Jan 1788 bp of George, son of George Mich. Weaver & Cath. (Harter). On 1790 HK census (4-0-3).

```
    +3813: LORENTZ F.   1754-1830  m CATHERINE WEAVER
    +3814: Johan ADAM  b Sep 1756; m ELISABETH HELMER
     3815: FREDERICK  b 3 Aug 1757; d Canada Mar 1759
    +3816: FREDERICK  b 1 Jul 1760; d 1804 unm
    +3817: Johan NICHOLAS  b 8 Mar 1762; m CATHARINE DEMUTH
     3818: HENRICUS  b 12 May 1763; killed 10 May 1779
    +3819: PHILLIP    1764-1802  m ELISABETH MYERS
     3820: CATHARINA b 17 Nov 1765; m GEORGE MICHAEL WEAVER
    +3821: Johan GEORGE  b 25 Feb 1767 (sp Geo. Helmer, Elis. Folts)
                         m CATHARINA PFEIFFER
    +3822: Johan JACOB  b 14 May 1768; m HELENA MCKOOMS
    +3823: Johan THOMAS  b Feb 1770; m ANNA RASBACH
```

3807: Capt. HENRY HARTER <H5> - born 17 Feb 1731; died Warren NY 12 Apr 1820 as a widower (age 90-1-25); m 5 Oct 1756 CATHERINE PFIEFFER (b 23 Dec 1734, d Herkimer 31 Dec 1802). Hendrick was captured when the French burned German Flats in 1757 and had to run Indian gaunlet. Had 5 adults & 6 children on 1778 GF relief.

```
     3824: CATHERINE   1759-1840 m MICHAEL MYERS
    +3825: CHRISTINA (ERNESTINA)   1760-1837  m1 1776 JOHN F. MEYER
    +3826: PHILIP H.   1762-1848  m CATHERINE PHILLIPS
     3827: ELISABETH  b 19 Oct 1764; m 1781 PETER BELLINGER
     3828: MARIA BARBARA  b 1766; d 1836 (age 70); m ADAM HARTMAN
     3829: APPOLONIA  b 22 Oct 1767; liv. 1784 (spf Meyer bp)
    +3830: LORENTZ  b 1768; m ANNA EVA ... (pr. Frank)
     3831: ANNA  b 2 Feb 1770 (sp Lor. Ph Harter, Cath. Pfeifer)
     3832: ANNA MARGARET  1773-1859  m 1794 ADAM F. HELMER
    +3833: HENRY H.   1774-1813  m1 GERTRUDE SCHEURMAN
```

3812: LAWRENCE HARTER jr <H9B> - born 26 Dec 1742; died Herkimer 15 May 1815 (age 72); m1 LANY MCKOOMS; m2 1768 CATHARINA DOCKSTADER (b ca 1749, d Herkimer 27 Feb 1824 age 75 as widow of Lorentz) dau of GEORGE DOCKSTADER & MARIA MAGDALENA WEAVER. A Lawrence Harter jr had 2 adults and 3 children on 1778 German Flats relief. Lawrence & Catherine were sponsors for Jan 1778 bp of Catherine, dau Peter Dockstader & Elisabeth (Cuningham). Children were by 2nd wife.

```
     3834: ANNA  1768-1830  m 1786 STOPHEL FRED. BELLINGER
    +3835: PETER L.   1770-1852  m 1793 CATHERINE HEN. MEYER
                      (1770 sp Peter Dockstader, Marg. Harter)
    +3836: PHILIP L.  1772-1841  m1 SARA MCKOOMS m2 MARIA BELL
     3837: LAWRENCE L.  1773-1850  m MARGARET JAC. PFEIFFER
```

3838: GEORGE L. 1779-1866 m 1805 ELISABETH WEAVER
3839: ELISABETH 1781- m 1802 FREDERICK EDICK (Ittig)
3840: NICHOLAS 1783-1860 ml CATHERINE PETRY
3841: CATHERINE b 16 Aug 1785 (sp Jac Weaver & Cath.)
3842: JOHANNES 1787-1857 m 1814 MARGARET PFEIFFER (b Feb 1794)
3843: APPOLONIA b 26 Jul 1789; m BENJAMIN SHULTZ
3843A ps. MICHAEL b GF 21 Dec 1790 (sp. Mich. Meyer & Cath.)
3844: FREDERICK b GF 19 Jul 1793 (sp Fred Harter & Marg.)

3804: NICHOLAS HARTER <H2> - born 25 Aug 1723; died 9 Jun 1801; m ANNA MARIE ...
He appears to have inherited his mother's Burnetsfield lot (#7, south of the
Mohawk River, now Ilion NY) which he sold to Dietrich Steele, probably before the
Revolutionary War. Nicholas had 6 adults on 1778 relief and deeded land in 1797
to his children Lawrence N., Abigail Smith, and Barbara Crouch (wife of Francis).

+3845: ps. PHILIP b 1740; d 1830; m ...
3846: APOLLONIA (ABIGAIL) 1750-1827 m JOSEPH SMITH
+3847: LAWRENCE N. b say 1753; m DOROTHY ...
3848: MAGDALENA
3849: MARIA BARBARA b 8 Aug 1762 (sp. Geo. Helmer, M. Barb. Wholben)
         m 1789 FRANK KREID (CROUCH)

3806: PHILIP HARTER <H4> - born 13 Nov 1729 (family bible); pr. died between 1758
and 1763 (not in father's will in 1776); ps. m CATHERINE (Harter book page 3) but
we suspect his wife was the widow Gertrude Harter who m SAR 28 Nov 1763 PETER
HUNT. Philip was captured in the 1757 French attack on German Flats and was
apparently the Philip Arter, prisoner, whose release was secured September 1758
(Book of Names, page 112). All Harter brothers except this Philip are listed in
the 1769 GF militia (Book of Names pages 13-14).

3850: MARIA b say 1750; prisoner in Canada 1757-8
3851: ELISABETH b say 1752; prisoner in Canada 1757-8
+3852: LORENTZ PHIL. ca 1755-1843 m BARBARA DELANEY

HARTER - 3rd Generation

3814: ADAM F. HARTER <H22> - born Sep 1756; died Herkimer NY 7 Dec 1837 age
81-2-2; m 5 Jul 1785 ELISABETH HELMER (b 1765, d 1838) dau of Philip F. & Anna.

3853: APPOLONIA b 2 Jun 1788; m 1836 PETER PIPER (1790-1855)
3854: HENRICH A. 1790-1854 m MARIA ELISABETH PETRIE
3855: ANNA b 11 Oct 1792; m ABRAHAM PETRIE
3856: CATHERINE b 20 Oct 1794 (sp Jac. Harter & Lena)
         m MELCHERT FOLTS jr.
3857: ELISABETH b 1797; m 1817 ASAHEL HANCHETT
3858: EVA b say 1801; m 1820 MARC A. COUNTRYMAN
3859: MARGARET b 3 Apr 1805; d 3 Sep 1817 age 12
3860: ADAM b 22 Jul 1807; d 6 Nov 1808 age 1

3816: FREDERICK HARTER <H24> - born 1 Jul 1760 (sp. Fred Young, unm, & Elisabeth,
unm dau of Adam Bellinger); died unm Herkimer NY 8 Jun 1804 age 43-11-7. Pr.
sponsored, with Cath. Crim, 1778 bp of Catherine, dau of Jacob Crim & Elis. Frank.

3821: GEORGE F. HARTER <H29A> - born German Flats 25 Feb 1767; m there 18 Aug 1793
CATHERINE PFEIFFER (b 1775, d 1851) dau of JACOB PFEIFFER & ELISABETH FOLTS.

      3861: JACOB b 1 Nov 1795 (sp Jac. Harter & Lena); d HK 1803
      3862: GEORGE G. b 15 Mar 1797; m CATHERINE PH. HILTS
      3863: HENRY G. ca 1799-1846 m DOROTHY PH. HILTS
      3864: PETER 1803-1855 m MAGDALENA PH. HILTS
      3865: ELISABETH 1809-1894 m MELCHERT C. FOLTS

3833: HENRY H. HARTER <H49B> - born 1774; died 1813; m1 GERTRUDE JOH. SCHEURMAN (b
1779, d Warrentown NY 1805 of neglect in childbirth); m2 at Herkimer NY 26 Oct
1806 MARIA CRIM (b May 1783, d 1880) dau of JACOB CRIM & ELISABETH FRANK.
Children Anna (b 1799), Elisabeth (b 1801, d 1804 age 2-10-), Henry (1803),
Catharine (1807), Elisabeth (1809), Gertrude (1811).

3822: JACOB F. HARTER <H29B> - born SAR 14 May 1768; died Herkimer NY 14 Oct 1828
age 59-7-5; m GF 12 May 1789 HELENA MCKOOMS (b 1766, d 1833) dau of ANDREW MCKOOMS
& ANNA ELISABETH (earlier a Bell widow, pr. a Hilts).

      3866: ELISABETH b SAR Jun 1789 (Jacob G. Weber & Maria <McKoom>)
      3867: APPOLONIA b GF 8 Aug 1790 (sp. Tho. Harter, Sara McKoom)
                  m by 1811 MICHAEL L. HARTER
      3868: CATHERINE b 15 May 1792; m LEONARD H. HELMER
      3869: THOMAS b 4 Mar 1794 (sp Thomas Bell & Anna)
                  m 1815 ELISABETH JAC. SMITH
      3870: ADAM b 9 Mar 1799; m DELIA JAC. HERKIMER
      3871: FREDERICK
      3872: ANDREAS b 9 Apr 1802; m CATHERINE AD. COUNTRYMAN
      3873: PHILIP 1804-1896 m ALMIRA FOLTS
      3874: MARIA b 4 Apr 1806; m 1825 JOHN LIVINGSTON
      3875: JOHN b 14 Mar 1811; m 1832 MARY HELMER

3813: LAWRENCE F. HARTER <H21> - born Mar 1754; died 26 May 1830 (age 76 yrs 2
months); m pr. ca 1778 CATHERINE WEAVER (b 1764, d 1802 age 37) dau of JACOB
WEAVER & CATHERINE. Was a farmer and appears on 1790 Herkimer census (1-2-3),
next to Fred. Harter Sr.

      3876: ELIZABETH b GF 11 Feb 1781 (sp Barb. Herder, Phil. Herder)
      3877: HENRICH b 12 Jul 1783 (sp Adam Harter, Anna Harter)
      3878: APPOLONIA b 14 Sep 1785 (sp Jost Smid & Appolonia)
      3879: FREDERICK b 22 Jun 1787 (sp Fred Harter, Barb. Harter)
      3880: CATHERINE 1789-1875 m JOHN JOSEPH SMITH
      3881: LAWRENCE b SJR 1 Jan 1792 (sp Jac Weber & Maria)
      3882: JACOB L. 1793-1895 m CATHERINE HELMER
      3883: MARIA 1795-1834 m CONRAD HARTER
      3884: EVA b 4 Sep 1802; m JABEZ SMITH

3830: LAWRENCE H. HARTER <H47> - born 1768; ps. died by 1800 (if wife m2 Jac.
Weaver); m ANNA EVA ... pr. a dau of TIMOTHY FRANK despite apparent later marriage
of Eva Tim. Frank to Jacob Weaver and Harter book suggestion of a Getman wife (no
good candidate there). Sons Henry & Timothy were named in the will of their
grandfather Henry in 1820.

      3885: HENRY b 25 Feb 1793 (sp Hen. Harter, Magd. Frank)
      3886: TIMOTHY b GF 9 Mar 1795 (sp Con. Getman & Maria <Frank>)

3847: LAWRENCE N. HARTER <H11> - pr. born before 1765; liv. 1816 (Herk. Deed book #16 page 239); m by 1810 DOROTHY ... In Bellinger's Revol. Regiment. In 1810, he & Dorothy sold land in Petrie's Patent (Harter book page 2).

3852: LORENTZ PHIL. HARTER <H33> - born ca 1755; died Manlius NY 1843 (age 88); m BARBARA DELANEY (d 1823-8) dau of PETER DELANEY. On 1790 GF census (1-2-5).

      3887: GERTRUDE b ca 1775; liv. 1853; m 1793 ANDREW MILLER
      3888: PHILIP b GF 26 Apr 1776 (sp. Stofel Shoemaker & Cath.)
      3889: MARGARETHA b 8 Jul 1778 (sp. Geo. Leithal & Marg.)
      3890: LAWRENCE 1781-1866 m MARIA CAMPBELL
      3891: ELISABETH b GF 9 Dec 1783 (sp Wm Folmer, Elis. Fox)
                      d 1843; m JOHN FOLTS
      3892: BARBARA 1786-1863 m ABRAHAM SHOEMAKER
      3893: CONRAD b 1789 (sp. Wm Delaney, Gert. J. Hess)
                   d 1823; m ELISABETH DELANEY
      3894: LENA b 30 Mar 1792 (sp. Augus. Joh. Hess, Lena Tim. Frank)
      3895: CATHERINE b Jul 1794 (sp Pet. Delaney, Maria Leithal)
                      d 1852; m GEORGE F. REALS (Riegel)
      3896: HENRY 1796-1863 m 1821 HANNAH F. REALS (Riegel)

3817: NICHOLAS F. HARTER <H25> - born 8 Mar 1762; died Deerfield NY 26 Jul 1854; m 13 May 1788 CATHERINE DEMUTH (b 1766) dau of MARCUS DEMUTH & CATHERINE. Was a shoemaker and moved to Deerfield in 1784. On 1790 Herkimer census (3-0-2).

      3897: APPOLONIA b 27 Mar 1789 (sp. Geo. Harter, Gert. DeMuth)
                      m Mr. ... CARL STEVENS
      3898: NICHOLAS b GF 3 Mar 1792 (sp. Diet. Demuth & Elis.)
                     d 1822; m HANNAH ...
      3899: CATHERINE b ca 1793; m AMOS CUTER
      3900: ELISABETH 1794-1877 m GEORGE HICKS
      3901: RICHARD 1797-1883 m RACHEL LEWIS

3835: PETER L. HARTER - born 9 Apr 1770; died 6 Oct 1852 (in 84th year, bur. Myers Pk, Herk.); m GF 4 Aug 1793 CATHERINE HEN. MEYER (b ca 1773, d 1832 in 59th year) pr. dau of HENRY MEYER & MARGARET.

      3902: FREDERICK b 4 Aug 1793 (GF sp Wm Helmer, Elis. Meyer)
      3903: CATHERINE b ca 1797; d 10 Aug 1832 age 35
      3904: LAWRENCE P. b 20 Feb 1798 (SAR sp L. Harter, Marg. Meyer)
                       m 1821 ELISABETH G. BAUMAN
      3905: MARGARET b 1 Jan 1802 (sp F. Meyer); m ADRIAN BROWN
      3906: EVA b Nov 1804 (sp Geo. Meyer & Cath.); m GEORGE G. WITRIG
      3907: CHRISTOPHER b 17 Jan 1807; m 1829 ANN BROWN
      3908: WILHELM b Mar 1813 (sp uncle F. Harter, Anna Meyer); d 1814
      3909: ANNA RHODE b 11 May 1815 (HK sp Isai Dalkert, Anna Bellinger)

3845: PHILIP HARTER - born ca Jul 1740; died a widower at Herkimer NY 8 Jun 1830 (age 90 yrs minus 1 month); m ... (ps. ANNA). A Philip Harter sponsored, with Anna McKoom, Jun 1785 GF bp of Elisabeth, dau of Jacob G. Weaver & Maria (McKoom). Then in 1786 a Philip Harter & Anna were sponsors for Apr 1786 GF bp of Daniel, son of John Meyer & Alita (Nebie). Ps. had son FREDERICK who may have married by 1789 ELISABETH ... (a Frederick & Elisabeth Harter <ps. married?> sponsored Jan 1789 SJR bp of Elisabeth, dau of David Meyer & Anna Dygert).

3819: PHILIP F. HARTER <H27> - born 27 Jul 1764 (death rec.); died Herkimer 24 Sep 1802; ml EVA ... ; m GF 13 Jan 1793 ELISABETH MYERS dau of HENRY MEYER (Harter book page 6). Was a blacksmith at Deerfield NY.

>   3919: EVA   b GF 4 Dec 1791 (sp. Phil. H. Harter & Cath.)
>   liv. 1808 (Fred. Harter's will)

3826: PHILIP H. HARTER <H43> - born 1762; died Warren NY 1848; m Columbia Co. NY Feb 1785 CATHERINE PHILLIPS (b 1765, d 1853 age 88-6-5). Pr. the Philip on 1790 Herkimer census (1-1-2) listed next to Adam Hurder.

>   3910: PETER P.   b GF 27 Jan 1787 (sp. Pet. F Bellinger & Elis.)
>   d 1876; m ELISABETH AD. MEYER
>   3911: ANNA   b SJR 21 Oct 1788 (sp Wm Philips, Marg. Harter)
>   d 1838; m DANIEL CRAMER (son of Henry)
>   3912: CATHERINE   1791-1854   m JOHN J. WITHERSTINE
>   3913: EVA   b 25 Aug 1793; m 1814 JOHN CON. FULMER
>   3914: HENRICH   1795-1875   m 1816 ANNA SCHELL
>   3915: ELISABETH
>   3916: LAWRENCE   b 18 Dec 1803; d 11 Apr 1804
>   3917: PHILIP   b say 1806; m by 1826 MARY CATHERINE GARDINIER
>   3918: MARIA   b 21 Feb 1808; m 1825 BENJAMIN JAC. SMITH

3836: PHILIP L. HARTER - born 30 Dec 1772; died 7 Dec 1841 (age 70 yrs less 23 days); ml GF 23 Dec 1792 SARA MCKOOM (b 1770, d Apr 1839 age 70) dau of ANDREW MCKOOM & ANNA ELISABETH; m2 MARY BELL (b ca 1772, age 78 in 1850) widow of THOMAS BELL (d 1813). Children Jacob P. (b 1793), Elisabeth, Lawrence, Mary, Andrew, Conrad, David, Daniel, Catherine, Philip, Anna, and Magdalena.

3823: THOMAS F. HARTER <H29C> - born SAR Feb 1770; died 19 Feb 1847 age 76-11-28 (bur. Myers Park, Herk.); m GF 24 Nov 1793 ANNA MARC. RASBACH (Nancy, b ca 1773, d 1855 age 82) dau of MARCUS RASBACH & SOPHRONIA MOAK. Son Jacob listed apparently was adopted by Thomas, as child's natural parents were stated in 1823 as Jacob F. Harter & Anna M. Rasbach, wife of Thomas (Harter book page 20).

>   3920: LENA   b GF 17 Nov 1794 (sp Jacob Harter & Lena)
>   m ADAM STAHRING   moved to Michigan
>   3921: ps. JACOB   b 27 Jun 1797; m 1823 CATHERINE DYGERT
>   3922: ANNA   b 8 Jun 1803; m MARTIN RULISON
>   3923: BENJAMIN   b 12 Oct 1805; m MARY BALDE
>   3924: JOSEPH   b 1806; liv. 1823 (age 17, Herk. Ch. dismissal)
>   3925: MOSES   b 20 Jul 1808; unm
>   3926: EVA   b ca 1812; d 1870 age 58 (bur. Myers Park)

3825: ERNESTINA HARTER - born 1 May 1760; died 6 Jun 1837; ml 7 Jun 1776 JOHN F. MEYER (supp. killed 1778, see Henry Meyer family for his story); m2 May 1780 JOHN BELLINGER; m3 ADAM STAHRING (d 1815).

********** HARTMAN **********

HARTMAN - 1st Generation

3901: **Johan ADAM HARTMAN** - born in Edenkober Germany ca Sep 1743; died German
Flats NY 5 Apr 1836 (age 92-7); m1 MARIA CATHERINE ...; m2 MARIA BARBARA HARTER (b
1760, 1836) dau of HENRY HARTER & CATHERINE PFEIFFER. Was a soldier in the
American Revolution and was wounded on 29 Oct 1781 as indicated from treatment
records of Dr. William Petry. William Smith letters (1903) tell of an incident
after the cessation of Revolutionary fighting in which Adam Hartman offered to
accompany on a trip an Indian, who had been boasting earlier that same evening in
a tavern of his killing of civilians during the war and of his fabricating of a
pouch from a victim's hand. The dead body of the Indian was later found, in the
spring of 1784, and Adam was arrested; but he was not convicted due to lack of
evidence . Adam appears on 1790 German Flats census (1-5-2). In Book of Names,
page 170, is comment that descendents of Adam Hartman married into the family of
John Shoemaker. Children living in 1847 were Conrad, Christopher, Jacob, Michael,
Catherine Garner, Elizabeth McGinnis, Nancy Wilder.

                      surname HARTMAN
      +3902: JACOB   b 11 Jun 1777 (sp. Jacob Hiller & Elisabeth)
       3903: CATHERINE b say 1780; m Mr. GARDNER
      +3904: ADAM   b 17 Jan 1782 (sp. John Dinges & Maria Marg. Schiff)
      +3905: CHRISTIAN b 8 Mar 1784 (sp. Christn Hochstater & M. Cath.)
       3906: CONRAD   b 7 Dec 1785 (sp Jac Dietrich, Cath. Rinckel); pr d y
       3907: THEOBALD   b 1 Oct 1787 (sp. Theob. Bekker & Cath.)
      +3908: CONRAD   b 30 Mar 1791 (sp Con Witrig, Cath. Ad. Staring)
              m DELIA SCHELL
       3909: MICHAEL   b 22 May 1793 (sp. Mich. Witrig & Elis.)
       3910: ELIZABETH   b say 1795; m Mr. MCGINNES
       3911: ANNA   (Nancy)   m Mr. WILDER

HARTMAN - 2nd Generation

3904: **ADAM HARTMAN** - born 17 Jan 1782; m by 1804 ANNA MUNTERBACH. Had children
Anna (b HK 1 Apr 1804, sp. John F. Weber & Anna Dockstader, unm) and Cahterine (b
Dec 1805, sp. Fred. Dockstader & Cath. Weber, unm).

3905: **CHRISTIAN HARTMAN** - born GF 8 Mar 1784; m Herkimer NY 6 Apr 1806 ELISABETH
BAUMAN (b 1785) dau of JACOB BAUMAN. Children were Jacob (b 1806), John (1808), &
Anna Maria (1815) as given in Bauman book, page 68.

3908: **CONRAD HARTMAN** - born German Flats NY 30 Mar 1791; m DELIA SCHELL dau of
PETER SCHELL & CATHERINE HILTS (Wm U. Smith notes). Had sons David (d at Herkimer
ca 1891) & Peter (moved to Coartland Co.).

3902: **JACOB HARTMAN** - born 11 Jun 1777; m Herkimer NY 6 Jun 1802 ANNA GATSIN dau
of SEVERINUS GATSIN

********** HELMER **********

4001: **PHILIP HELMER** - bp vic. of Nieustadt Germany 20 Mar 1659 (see H. Jones´
"The Palatine Families of New York" for more); died before 1741; m 1685 ELISABETH
MOCKLER (ibid.). On 1709 London list with wife & 6 children and on NY subs. list
in 1710 (5A,3Y) and 1712 (7A,1Y). Philip Kelmer in 1710 was at West Camp NY with
4 sons (1 mature, 2 age 9-15, 1 under 9) & 2 daughters (Book of Names, pg 124). A
PETER HELMER was also on the NY subs. list in 1710 (2A,2Y) & 1712 (2A,2Y). Philip
was naturalized at Albany 11 Oct 1715, listed next Fred Bell, and was on the 1717
Simmendinger census with wife Elisabeth & 5 children. In 1723 he got Burnetsfield
lot #25, north of the Mohawk River (next to Fred Bell). Info on children mostly
from H. Jones´ book and P. Williams´ "The Helmer Family".

> surname HELMER
> 4001A MARIA BARBARA   bp (Neustadt?) Germany 14 Mar 1688
> +4002: LEENDERT (LEONARD)   bp 5 Feb 1690; m by 1715 ELISABETH...
> 4003: ps. MARIA (Helmer?)   b say 1691; m ca 1711 FREDERICK BELL
> 4004: CATHERINE ELISABETH   bp 27 Apr 1692; (ps. m by 1715 Riegel?)
> 4004A JOHANNES   bp 25 Jul 1694 (The Palatine Families of New York)
> 4004B MELCHIOR   bp 5 Apr 1696 (The Palatine Families of New York)
> +4005: ADAM   bp 24 Aug 1700; m by 1723 ANNA MARGARET ...
> 4006: MARGARET bp (Neustadt?) Germany 31 Oct 1700; liv. 1710
> 4006A APPOLONIA bp 30 Mar 1703; ps. m by 1723 LORENTZ HARTER
> +4007: GEORGE FREDERICK   bp 9 Jun 1706; m MARIA BARBARA KAST

HELMER - 2nd Generation

4005: **ADAM HELMER** Sr. - bp in Germany 24 Aug 1698; m by 1723 MARGARET ...   In
1723 Adam got Burnetsfield lot #6 (north of the Mohawk) and his wife received lot
#12 (south of river). In 1791 lot #6 was held by his sons Fred & Henry.

> +4009: FREDERICK ADAM   1725-1804 m BARBARA ELIZABETH HOMAN
> +4010: PHILIP b say 1728; pr. m SAR 1762 MARIA PHILLIPINA ECKER
> 4010A ps. LEONARD b say 1730 (Helmer book has m CATH. ZIMMERMAN)
> +4011: Johan ADAM jr b say 1733; m 1763 MARIA BARSH
> 4012: ELIZABETH MARGARET b say 1737; m 1760 ICABOD BANY
> 4013: CATHERINE b say 1739; m 1759 FREDERICK RIEGEL
> 4014: pr. MARIA ("Welmer") b say 1741; m by 1767 JOHN DAVIS
> 4015: MARGARET b say 1743; m 1763 CHRISTIAN RIEGEL
> 4016: GERTRUDE b say 1744; m 1763 JOHN KESSLER
> +4017: JOHN A. b say 1747; m 1767 MARGARET MEYER
> +4018: HENRY A. 1749-1815 m by 1777 MARIA ELISABETH ...

4007: **FREDERICK HELMER** - bp in Germany 9 Jun 1706; m MARIA BARBARA KAST dau of
GEORGE KAST & ANNA . In 1723 he received Burnetsfield lot #1. George Kast´s will
notes that Frederick had 8 children but does not name them (Helmer book, pg 30).

> 4019: pr. ANNA MARIA b say 1729; m 1750 PETER HOYER
> 4020: pr. CATHERINE (Helmer?) b say 1732; m by 1752 ADAM STARING
> +4021: FREDERICK F. ca 1735-1777 m1 SABINA ..; m2 ELISABETH DYGERT
> 4022: ps. ELISABETH b say 1737; m by 1758 FREDERICK KAST (b 1727)
> +4023: GEORGE F.   1739-1815   m MARGARET MEYER
> +4024: PHILIP F.   1740-1830   m ANNA MEYER
> +4025: Johan ADAM   1754-1830   m ANNA BELLINGER (b 1757)

4002: **LEONARD HELMER** - bp in Germany 5 Feb 1690; living 1781 (will dated 27 Jun 1781 <in which he mentions brother Adam>, probated 1791); m ELISABETH ... (ps. Poonradt <children´s names> or Riegel <first child´s bp sponsor>). Naturalized at Albany 11 Oct 1715. In 1723 he had Burnetsfield lot #21, which in Sep 1730 he & his wife (Elisabeth Helmer signed separate endorsement) sold to George Dockstader. About 1730 Leonard moved his family from German Flats to Stone Arabia NY.

   +4026: GODFRID b WCL 1715 (sp Gotf Ruehl & w.); m MARGARET ...
   +4027: PHILIP b say 1717; liv. 1751
   +4028: Johan LEONARD b say 1720; m ca 1749 CATHERINE NELLIS
    4029: GERTRUDE b say 1728; m by 1751 JACOB KROUS (son of Jac.)
    4030: ANNA MAGDALENA b say 1730; m by 1751 PHILIP PIER
   +4031: JOHANNES LEON. b say 1735; m 1760 GERTRUDE BELL
    4032: ELIZABETH b say 1740; m 1761 PETER EYGENBRODT (b 1738)
   +4033: ps. ADAM b say 1742; m by 1782 MARIA ELISABETH ...
    4034: MARIA MARGRED b say 1745; m 1766 JOHN HATCOCK

HELMER - 3rd Generation

4033: ADAM HELMER - pr. born ca 1730 to 1745; m by 1782 MARIA ELISABETH ...   Ps. the Tory Adam Helmer whose farm was confiscated in 1777 (Helmer book).

    4035: GERTRUDE b GF 28 Sep 1782 (sp Hen Flander, Gert. Kraus)

4011: ADAM HELMER jr - pr. born ca 1725 to 1738 (son of Adam); died 6 Aug 1777 at the Battle of Oriskany; m 1763 MARIA BARSH. In militia 1757

    4036: JOHANNES b 19 Mar 1763 (sp Joh. Helmer, Elis. Ritmans)
    4037: ADAM b GF 21 Aug 1765 (sp. Hen. Helmer, Elis. Folts)
    4038: ANNA MARGARET b 9 Jan 1768 (sp Marg. Campbell, Ludwig Barsh)
    4039: MARIA b SA 3 Mar 1770 (sp Philip Helmer & M Philipina)
    4040: ANNA b ca 1771; d Herkimer NY 19 Oct 1845 (age 74-5)

4025: ADAM F. HELMER - born at German Flats 1754; died Brutus NY Apr 1830; m 27 Feb 1776 ANNA BELLINGER (b 1757, d 1841) dau of Capt. PETER BELLINGER & MARGARET, as given in Bellinger book. His words "Flee for your lives, the enemy are not an hour behind" saved many lives on 17 Sep 1778 when he outran Indian pursurers to warn German Flats residents of an impending attack by Chief Joseph Brandt´s war party. Pr. the Adam on 1790 GF census (2-1-5).

    4041: FREDERICK b 6 Feb 1777 (sp. Fred F. Helmer & Elis. Dygert)
   +4042: MARGARET bp 12 Sep 1778 (sp Geo. Smidt & Maria <Bellinger>)
               m GEORGE PASSAGE
    4043: ANNA b 3 Oct 1781 (sp And. Gray, Anna Fox); m HENRY PASSAGE
    4044: ADAM b ca 1783
    4045: PETER b 25 Jul 1786 (sp. Joh. Joh. Shoemaker & w. <Fox)
    4046: ANNA ELISABETH b 1788; m JAMES MOORE
    4047: CATHARINE b 14 Oct 1790 (Peter Staring, Maria Bellinger)
               m JOHN HILTS
    4048: DAVID b GF 7 Jan 1793 (sp. Fr. Bellinger & w. Magdalena)
               m by 1812 MARIA CATHERINE FOX
    4049: MARIA BARBARA b ca 1795; m PAUL H. CRIM
    4050: EVE b 24 Aug 1800 (sp. Gradus Bohlson & w. Elis.)

4009: FREDERICK ADAM HELMER - born ca 16 Aug 1726 ; died 5 Mar 1805 (age 78-6-19);
m BARBARA ELISABETH HOMAN (came to America 1754) pr. sister of PETER HOMAN. In
1769 GF militia and had 2 adults & 3 children on 1778 GF relief. He was on the
1790 HK census (3-1-2), pr. with brother Henry on their father's Burnetsfield lot.

```
     4051: MARGARET  b 28 Oct 1763 (sp John Kessler & Gertr.)
                     d HK 30 Nov 1831 (age 68-1-2); m by 1798 JACOB G. WEAVER
    +4052: CONRAD  b SAR 28 Jan 1766  (sp Phil. Helmer & w.)
                   d 1841; m MARGARET FOLTS (Helmer book, page 19)
     4053: PETER  b 7 May 1768 (sp Peter Homan)
                  pr. m by 1800 ANNA STAHRING (Helmer book page 19)
    +4054: ADAM F.  1770-1854  m 1794 ANNA MARGARET HARTER
```

4021: Johan FREDERICK HELMER jr - pr. born ca 1730 to 1740; died 6 Aug 1777 at the
Battle of Oriskany; m1 pr. before 1760 SABINA ... (aka Wina) who was pr. SABINA
HILTS and ps. dau of GEORGE HILTS; m2 by 1773 MARIA ELISABETH DYGERT (b 1749, d
1815) dau of WILLIAM DYGERT & MARIA ELISABETH ECKER. Was in 1757 GF militia. His
widow was pr. the Elisabeth Helmer with 1 adult & 8 children on 1778 GF relief,
and she m2 JOHN DEMUTH. Helmer book says 10 children.

```
     4055: GEORGE  b 13 Nov 1760 (sp Nic. Hilts & Elis. <Fox>); pr d y
    +4056: FREDERICK  b 14 Apr 1763 (sp Geo. Helmer, Maria Meyer unm)
    +4057: JOHANNES  b SAR 3 Sep 1765 (sp Joh. Hilts,Anna Weber); d 1829
    +4058: GEORGE  b SAR 14 Nov 1767 (sp Geo. Hilts, Appol. Harter)
                   ps. the George Fred. who m by 1802 ELISABETH THUM
     4059: ANNA  b SAR 22 Jan 1769 (sp Anna & Philip Helmer)
     4060: ps. DOROTHY  b say 1770; liv. 1787 (spf Jac. Helmer bp)
     4061: SABINA FRED.  b say 1772; m 1792 PETER ADAM STARING
                         pr. by second wife
     4062: WILLIAM FR.  b 19 Jul 1773; m 1794 CATHERINE FR. MEYER
    4062A ELISABETH  b say 1774 (Deuel ms. on Dygerts)
    4062B PETER F.  b 1776 (Deuel ms. on Dygerts)
     4063: HENRICH  b GF 30 Dec 1777 (posthum.) (sp Wm Dygert & Marg.)
                    pr. the Hen. F. who m HK 1806 EVA FR. MEYER
```

4023: GEORGE F. HELMER - born Oct 1739; died Columbia NY 23 Mar 1823 (age 82-5); m
SAR 8 Jan 1770 MARGARET MEYER (b ca 1752, d Columbia NY 1818 age 66) pr. a sister
of JACOB MEYER. Pr. the Ensign in 1767 grenadier unit of Jost Herkimer (Book of
Names page 12). George had 2 adults & 4 children on 1778 GF relief and appears on
1790 German Flats census (3-2-5) near in list to Adam Helmer. Living at
Conradstown in 1802 and at Warren in 1815. Helmer book says he had 8 children.

```
     4064: ADAM  b SA 13 Nov 1770 (sp Adam Helmer, Anna Marg. Bell)
     4065: JACOB  b 25 Feb 1778 (sp Jacob Meyer & Marg.)
                  pr. m 1806 ELISABETH H. KLOCK
     4066: BARBARA  b GF 25 Dec 1780 (sp Lorentz ... & M. Barb.)
                    m HK 1802 JOHN CLEPSATTLE (b 1777)
     4067: MARGARET  b 28 Jul 1783 (sp Jost Bellngr, M. Barb. Harter)
                     pr. m HK 1806 JOHN H. KLOCK
     4068: PETER G.  b GF 20 Jun 1786 (sp. Adam Staring & Cath.)
                     m HK 1809 GERTRUDE SHOEMAKER
     4069: ANNA  bp SJR 6 Mar 1790 (sp Joseph Mayer & Cath.)
                 m by 1818 HENRY J. MEYERS
     4070: EVA  b GF 28 Nov 1792 (sp Thom. Shoemaker & Anna Eva)
                m HK 1815 MARC CRANTZ jr.
```

4026: GODFRID HELMER - born Dec 1715 (sp. Godfrid Riegel & wife); pr. died ca 1765; ml 6 Apr 1737 MAGDALENA ... (Ehle surname in Helmer book, no other support seen); m2 by 1764 ANNA MARGARETHA ... His widow was ps. the Margaret Helmer who m 1768 ADAM BARSH. His will dated at Canajoharie 14 Mar 1765 mentions 5 sons and 4 daughters (one of whom, Margaret, he made special provision for) and left 50 acres in NY granted to George Klock (Daniel Miller and Jacob Krous were executors).

    4071: LEONARDT   b say 1740; no furth. rec. (ps Tory?)
    4072: MARGARETHA   b say 1745; liv. 1765 (ps. an invalid)
    4073: CATHERINE   b say 1747; ml 1767 PETER BOWMAN (d 1777)
            m2 ADOLPH WALLRATH
    4074: CHRISTINA   1749-1827 m HENRY NELLIS (1746-1829)
    4075: ELISABETH   b say 1753; liv. 1765 (will)
            ps. m SAR 1770 THOMAS YOUNG
  +4076: JOHANNES   b 15 Jan 1758 (sp John Helmer, Marg. Hilts)
            m MARGARET EHLE
    4077: GODFRID jr.   b 31 Jan 1760; ps. died at Oriskany 1777
            (bp sp. Godfrid Shoemaker & beloved finance)
    4078: JOSEPH   b 8 Feb 1762; m 1788 SUSANNA FLINT (dau of Sander)
            by second wife
    4079: HENRY   b 20 Aug 1764 (sp Hen. Nellis & wife Elis.)
            m 1792 CATHERINE MCCAFFERY (b 1770, d 1837)

4018: HENRICK A. HELMER - born ca 1749; died Herkimer NY 15 May 1815 (age 66);   m MARIA ELISABETH ... (b ca 1752; d Herkimer 14 Apr 1819, age 67). Had seven children. On 1790 Herkimer census (1-4-4), next to Fred. A. Helmer.

    4080: pr. ELISABETH   b GF 3 May 1777 (sp Nich. Hilts & Elis.)
    4080A MARGARET   1778-1844   m JACOB SMITH (son of Adam)
    4081: JACOB H.   b say 1780; m HK 1810 SALLY SPEEFEN
    4082: HENRY H.   b 8 Dec 1784 (Ad. Harter, Marg. Helmr); conf. HK 1802
    4083: MARIA ELISABETH   b GF 13 Nov 1786 (sp Jacob Bell & Elis.)
    4084: JOHN H.   b GF Sep 1788 (sp. Geo. Helmer, Anna Eva Folts)
            m HK 1814 DOROTHY FALK
    4085: LEONARD   b GF 16 Sep 1791 (sp Adam Helmer, Cath. Riegel)
            m 1809 CATHERINE HARTER

4017: JOHN HELMER - pr. born ca 1740 to 1745 (son of Adam); m 11 Aug 1767 MARGARETHA MEYER dau of HENRICH MEYER & ANNA MARIA GETMAN. In the Revolution one or two John Helmers were Tories and another a patriot who was taken prisoner (some of the those Johns pr. remained in Canada as relatively few can be seen on the 1790 Montgomery Co. NY census).

    4086: HENRY   b 13 Apr 1768 (sp. Hn Helmer, Maria Meyer)
    4087: Johan ADAM   b 8 Feb 1770 (sp. Fred Meyer, Cath. Getman)
    4088: ps. CONRAD   b GF 24 Apr 1776 (son of John)
            (sp. Conrad Orendorf & Catherine)

4031: JOHANNES LEON. HELMER - pr. born ca 1717 to 1737 (son of Leonard); m at Stone Arabia 7 Feb 1760 GERTRUDE BELL (b ca 1725, Gertrude, widow of Leonard Helmer, d Herkimer 23 May 1808 age 83) dau of FREDERICK BELL.

    4089: Han YOST   b say 1760; Pvt. in Van Schaick Reg. in Revol.
    4090: DIETRICH   bp SAR 25 Sep 1763 (sp. Dietrich Bell)
    4091: ELISABETH   b SAR 25 Jul 1765 (sp Elis. Hess, Leonard Helmer)
    4092: LEONARD   b 15 Jul 1766 (see Helmer book, page 10)

4028: Johan LEONARD HELMER jr. - pr. born ca 1715 to 1730; died by 1766; m ca 1749
CATHERINE NELLIS (b 1724, d 1805) dau of CHRISTIAN NELLIS & BARVALIS KLOCK and
widow of ADAM ZIMMERMAN (Bellinger book page 12, Helmer book page 13, & Zimmerman
book). Pr. sponsored, Barbara Elis. Dockstader, 1743 SA bp of JOHN ERNESTUS PIER
son of PHILIP PIER & MAGDALENA (Helmer). Widow Catherine m2 1766 JACOB KLOCK.

    +4093: ps. PHILIP (Tory) b say 1749; m 1766 MARGARETHA BELLINGER
    +4094: JOHN bp 17 May 1751 (sp Joh. Helmer, Cath. Zimmerman); a Tory
    +4095: Johan LEONARD bp 8 Aug 1752 (sp. Leon. Helmer & w. Elis.)
    4095A ps. ELISABETH b ca 1753; m THOMAS GETMAN

4010: PHILIP HELMER - pr. born ca 1725 to 1735 (son of Adam); m SAR 4 May 1762
MARIA PHILLIPINA ECKER. Wife Phillipina sponsored, with "Freidrich Helmer Aug
1769 bp of Fred, son of Fred Riegel & Catherine (Helmer). He & Phillipina
sponsored Mar 1770 SAR bp of Maria, dau of Adam Helmer & Maria. Ps. the Philip on
1790 Palatine NY census (2-4-4), near John P. Helmer, Fred Bome, & Jacob Cross.

    +4096: ps. PHILIP (Patriot) b say 1757; m 1783 MARGARET BELLINGER
    +4097: ps. JOHN PH. b say 1760; m by 1783 ANNA DUSSLER
    4098: ps. GEORGE b 25 Mar 1763 (birthdate seen in Helmer book)
    4099: ps. child b SAR 2 May 1764 (dau of Philip)
              (sp. Christina Helmer, Jacob Merckel, unm)
    4100: ps. ELISABETH PH. b say 1765; m GF 1784 FREDERICK BAUM

4024: PHILIP F. HELMER - born ca Jul 1740; died 8 Jun 1830 age 90 years less 1
month; m SAR 17 Jul 1763 ANNA MEYER (b ca 1747, d 1829 age 82) dau of Lt. PETER
MEYER. Helmer book says he lived at Stone Arabia NY and had 5 children, but we
feel that he was pr. the Philip with 3 adults & 7 children on 1778 GF relief and
the Philip F. on the 1790 Herkimer census (3-3-6).

    +4104: pr. JOHN PH. 1757-1833 m 1786 MARIA WOLF
    4105: ELIZABETH b GF 11 Sep 1765 (sp. Elis. Folts, Adam Helmer)
              m ADAM F. HARTER
    4106: FREDERICK b SAR 17 Feb 1767 (sp Fred. Helmer & Wina)
    +4107: GEORGE b 9 May 1769 (sp. George Helmer, Marg. Majer)
    4108: MARIA BARBARA b SA Jan 1771 (sp Cath. & .. Staring)
    4109: PHILIP P. b say 1774; m MARGARET BARSH (b ca 1777)
    4110: ps. PETER P. b ca 1776; d HK 1821 age 45; a blacksmith
    4111: FREDERICK PH. ca 1778-1826 unm
    4112: ANNA MARGARET b 19 Nov 1780 (sp. Pet. Weber & Anna Maria Ittig)
    4113: ANNA b 1 Jan 1783 (sp. Geo. Stahring & Barbara Harter)
              m 1804 HENRY J. MEYER
    4114: CATHERINE b 24 Mar 1785 (sp. Mich. Meyer & Cath.); pr. d y
    4115: CATHERINE b 18 Oct 1786 (sp. Joh. Fred. Harter & Maria Elis.)

4027: PHILIP HELMER - pr. born ca 1715 to 1720 (son of Leonard); sponsored, with
Marg. Nellis, 1751 SA bp of ANNA SOPHIA PIER dau of PHILIP PIER & MAGDALENA
HELMER. Ps. the Philip L. on 1790 Palatine NY census (1-2-4) near Jacob J Klock.

4116: PHILIP J. HELMER - pr. born ca 1720 to 1740; m by 1760 ELISABETH HERRIS.
Middle initial "J" seen on bp records of the Fonda Dutch Reform Church which has
children as Jannetje (bp FR 25 Feb 1760, sp Jacob & Cath. Herris) & Aaron (bp FR 9
Aug 1775, sp. Sam Rees & Mar. Runner). A Philip Helmer & wife (ps. an Elisabeth?)
sponsored May 1771 SAL bp of Elisabeth, dau of George Schwarn & Catherine.

4054: ADAM HELMER - bp SA Jul 1770; died 1854; m 9 Mar 1794 ANNA MARGARET HARTER
(b 1773, d 1859, bur. Helmer Cem.) dau of HENRY HARTER & CATHERINE PFEIFFER
(Harter book page 10). Children Anna (b 1795, m Han Thomas Helmer), Henry A.
(1797-1868 m Fanny Rasbach), Barbara Elisabeth (1799-1825 unm), Lorentz, Cath.
(1804-1868 unm), Frederick A. (m Eliza Getman), Peter (unm), & Margaret.

4052: CONRAD HELMER - born 28 Jan 1766; died 1841; m ANNA MARGARET FOLTS (b 1768,
d 10 Feb 1822 age 53-10-) dau of CONRAD FOLTS. At Herkimer NY in 1802.

    4117: PETER C. b 9 Sep 1789; m 1812 ANNA RASBACH
    4118: CONRAD   b 16 Apr 1792 (sp Adam Helmer, Cath. Christman)
               m 1815 CATHERINE SCHELL
    4119: BARBARA ELISABETH b say 1795; m 1815 MARCUS RASBACH
    4120: CATHERINE b 24 Mar 1801 (sp Geo. Folts & Christina)

4056: FREDERICK F. HELMER - born 14 Apr 1763; liv. 1790. On 1790 Herkimer census
(2-1-3) next to John F. Helmer.

4058: GEORGE FREDERICK HELMER - pr. born ca 1760 to 1780; m GF 1796 ELISABETH THUM
dau of MELCHIOR THUM & ELISABETH. Lived at Conradstown in 1802. Had child
MELCHIOR (b HK 28 Apr 1802, sp Nic. Thum & w. Marg.).

4107: GEORGE PH. HELMER - pr. the George born 9 May 1769 (son of Philip F.); died
14 Sep 1849; m 11 May 1790 CATHERINE H. STAHRING (E&N 4/22/1929). Had 12 kids.

    4121: HENRICH b GF 26 Jun 1790 (sp Col. H. Staring & Elis.)
               m HK 1810 ELISA MAYER (dau of Wm)
    4122: pr. PHILIP G. b GF 23 Apr 1792 (sp Ph. Helmer & Anna)
    4123: ELISABETH b GF 5 Sep 1794 (sp Peter Helmer, Elis. Staring)
               m HK 1812 PETER WM. DYGERT
    4124: CATHERINE 1797-1869 m NICHOLAS SMITH

4125: JOHN HELMER - pr. born ca 1730 to 1760; m by 1779 MARIA ...

    4126: ADAM b GF 6 Jun 1779 (sp Adam Vorrer & Margaret)

4057: JOHN F. HELMER - born ca 1765; died Herkimer 26 Nov 1829 (age 64-9-23); pr.
m by 1794 MARGARET MUNTERBACH (her surname on 1803 bp rec.). On 1790 HK census
(1-0-0). Children pr. PETER (b GF 6 Jul 1794, sp Hen. Harter, Marg. Helmer) &
Anna (bp HK Feb 1803).

4076: JOHN G. HELMER - born 15 Jan 1758 (son of Godfrid); died 5 Aug 1837; m
MAGDALENA EHLE (b 1760) dau of HARMANUS EHLE. Pension says he had a brother
killed at Oriskany (pr. Godfrid jr.). Had 6 children including Elisabeth (bp SJR
1788), Christina (bp 1791), & Godfrid (bp SJR Dec 1793). On 1790 Palatine NY
census (1-1-3), next to Hanyost Helmer (pr. brother Joseph).

4094: JOHN HELMER - bp 17 May 1751 (son of Leonard jr); ps. m CATHERINE MILLER and
had son JOHN (b SAL 30 nov 1780, sp. Leonard Helmer) and dau MARGARET (bp Albany 3
Oct 1783, sp. Wm Cuningham & Marg.). Was a Tory in the Revolution and ps. the
John Helmer captured 12 Apr 1777.

4097: JOHN PHIL. HELMER - pr. born ca 1740 to 1766; m by 1783 ANNA DUSSLER. Ps. the John P. on 1790 Palatine NY census (1-3-3), listed near Philip Helmer, Fred. Bome, Jacob Cross, & John Nellis. Children pr. included JOHN (b GF 5 Jan 1783, sp Jac. Huber, Anna Helmer), JACOB (b GF 23 Nov 1787, sp. Jacob Smith & Dorothy Helmer), and ANNA (bp SJR 23 Dec 1789, sp Jacob J Klock & Anna).

4104: JOHN PH. HELMER - pr. born ca 1757 to 1764 (Helmer book page 11 has b 7 Jul 1757 son of a Philip); died Manheim NY 20 Jan 1833; m 15 Jan 1786 MARY WOLF (b 1768) dau of MICHAEL WOLF & ELISABETH. Had eight children. Pr. the John Helmer on 1790 HK census (1-1-3), near Mark DeMuth & Fred Riegel at Deerfield.

    4127: PHILIP   b GF Jun 1787 (sp Con. F. Helmer, Marg. Scherer)
    4128: pr. MARGARET b GF 28 Feb 1789 (sp Jac. W Petri, Marg. Helmr)
    4129: GERTRUDE b GF 3 Apr 1790 (sp. Fritz Riegel, Gert. DeMuth)
    4130: LENA   b GF 15 Nov 1791 (sp Godf Riegel, Lena Dygert)
    4131: JOHN   b GF 15 Dec 1793 (sp Ph. Kelsch & Marg. <Wolf>)
    4132: ANNA   b 1802 (sp Fred. Petrie, Cath. Thum)

4095: LEONARD HELMER - pr. the Leonard born 1752; m by 1777 ELISABETH KOCH (her surname on 1792 bp rec.) pr. the Elisabeth (b 1756) dau of RUDOLPH KOCH & ELISABETH DYGERT. On 1790 Palatine NY census (1-3-4), near Getmans.

    4133: pr. JOHN b SAL 9 Feb 1778 (sp Suf. Koch, Elis Finkin)
    4134: pr. RUDOLPH b SAL 30 Mar 1780 (sp Rud. Koch, Maria Schell)
    4135: CATHERINE b GF 1 Feb 1783 (sp Jac. Mohr & Maria Cath.)
    4136: ANNA b SAR 14 Oct 1787 (sp Caspar Koch & w. Cath.)
    4137: HENRICH b SAR 3 May 1792 (sp Jac Getman, Cath Getman, unm)

4093: PHILIP HELMER ("The Tory") - pr. born ca 1749 (son of Leonard jr & Cath.); died by 1783; m 14 Sep 1766 MARGARET BELLINGER (b 1751, d 1837) dau of JOHN BELLINGER & MAGDALENA KLOCK. About 1776, he went to Canada as a Tory with Jacob J. Klock. Had 5 daughters born 1769 to 1775 and his widow m2 1783 another PHILIP HELMER ("The Patriot", Bellinger book page 44).

    4139: CATHERINE PH. b SAR 14 Sep 1766 (sp. Cath. Hess, Joh. Kraus)
                m GF 1786 JACOB GRASS (Kraus)
    4140: DELIA (twin) b SAR 20 Apr 1769 (sp Sophia Pier, Jac Krous)
    4141: MARGARET (twin) b 20 Apr 1769 (sp Elis Helmer, Diet. Merkel)

4096: PHILIP HELMER ("The Patriot") - ps. born 11 Jun 1757 (son of a Philip, as given in the Helmer book page 12); m GF 4 May 1783 MARGARET BELLINGER (b 1751, d 1837) widow of PHILIP HELMER ("The Tory").

    4141A ps. PHILIP PH. b say 1784; m 1806 MARGARET LUD. PARIS
    4142: JOHN b GF 21 Mar 1786 (sp. Henrich Joh. Bellinger & Marg.)
    4143: CATHERINE bp SJR 9 May 1790 (sp Jac. J Klock, Delia Bellngr)
    4144: pr. ELISABETH bp SJR 16 Dec 1792 (sp. Pet. Young & Mar. Lisa)
    4145: LEONARD b SAR 14 Aug 1795 (sp Geo. Getman & w. Marg.)

4109: PHILIP P. HELMER - pr. born ca 1770 to 1775; m MARGARET BARSH (b ca Oct 1777, d HK 21 Apr 1813 age 35-6-3). Identified as parents of Ludwig on Herkimer NY 1832 mar. record of son Ludwig to Phoebe Kast.

4201: GEORGE HERKIMER - pr. born in Germany ca 1650 to 1670; m MAGDALINE ...
George Herchemer was on the NY Palatine subsistence list in 1710 (2A,1Y) and in
1712 (4A,0Y) and was naturalized at Albany NY 11 Oct 1715. George drew lot #44 on
the 1723 Burnetsfield Patent.

surname HERKIMER
+4202: Johan JOST b say 1695; d 1775; m CATHERINE PETRIE
4203: ps. HANES JURY naturalized at Albany NY 31 Jan 1716

HERKIMER - 2nd Generation

4202: JOST HERKIMER ("Joseph") - pr. born in Germany ca 1690 to 1700; died 1775;
pr. m before 1723 CATHERINE PETRIE (d 1775) dau of JOHANNES PETRIE & ANNA GERTRUDE
VON RINGH as in Petrie book pages 1-6 and "The Herkimers and Schuylers" by Phoebe
Strong Cowen (Albany 1903). Jost received Burnetsfield lot #36.

```
4204: GERTRUDE   ca 1722-1806 m RUDOLPH SHOEMAKER
4205: MAGDALENA  b say 1724  ml by 1745 WARNER DYGERT; m2 N. SNELL
4206: ELISABETH BARBARA  1726-1800  m 1743 PETER D. SCHUYLER
+4207: NICHOLAS  1728-1777  ml LANY DYGERT m2 MARIA DYGERT
4208: DELIA  1728-1804  m Col. PETER BELLINGER
4209: CATHERINE  b say 1729; m 1753 GEORGE HENRY BELL
+4210: HENDRICK  1730-1779  m CATHERINE DYGERT
+4211: Johan JOST  ca 1732-1775  m MARIA VAN ALLEN
4212: ANNA   b say 1734; m 1750 PETER TEN BROEK
4213: ELIZABETH  b say 1737; d 1820; m by 1756 HENRY FREY
4214: MARIA  b say 1739; m 1758 Rev. ABRAHAM ROSENCRANTZ
+4215: GEORGE  1744-1786/8  m ALIDA SCHUYLER
4216: JOHN  b ca 1745; d 20 Apr 1817 (age 72) unm
```

HERKIMER - 3rd Generation

4215: GEORGE HERKIMER - born 1744; died 24 May 1788; m Aug 1775 ALIDA SCHUYLER (b
1752, d 1830) dau of DAVID P. SCHUYLER & ANNA BRATT. He inherited Burnetsfield
lot #36 from his father (Jost Herkimer will of 1771). In Nov 1775 George was
degraded from militia Captain due to striking sub-ordinate G. McGinnis. George
and Alita sponsored Apr 1780 bp of George, son of Lt. John Smith & Elisabeth.
Widow Alida Herkimer appears on 1790 Canajoharie NY census (2-1-6).

```
4217: JOHN   1775-  m 1795 POLLY (or Sara)
4218: JOSEPH  1776-1824  m EUNICE TROWBRIDGE
4219: MARGARETHA  b 5 Sep 1777 (Marg. Rosencranz, Abm Wohlebn); d y
4220: CATHERINE  b 26 Mar 1779 (sp. Jost Herkimer & Cath.)
            m PETER STERNBURG
4221: MARGARETHA  b 19 Mar 1781 (sp Philip Steinmetz & Maria)
            m JOHN McCOOMBS
4222: MAGDALENA  1782-1859  m H. FELIX GREEN
4223: Johan NICHOLAS  b 1 Feb 1787; pr. d. young
4224: GERTRUDE  1788-1873 m JACOB EACKER
```

4210: HENDRICK HERKIMER - born 1730; died 1 Aug 1779; m pr. ca 1748 CATHERINE
DYGERT. Info on their descendents seen in a 1963 manuscript (at Herkimer Co.
Hist. Soc.) entitled "HERKIMER/SCHUYLER & Allied Families" by John B. Potter jr
(61 E. Main Street, Mohawk NY).

      4225: ps. CATHARINE b say 1749; m by 1777 PETER SCHUYLER
   +4226: JOSEPH b Oct 1751; m CATHERINE SCHUYLER
      4227: NICHOLAS m G. Flats 19 Feb 1782 MARGARETHA GEO. SNELL
   +4228: ABRAHAM b say 1757; m by 1788 DOROTHEA DYGERT
      4229: MAGDALENA b say 1760; m 1790 SEVERINUS WER. DYGERT
   +4230: GEORGE H. 1763-1829 m MARY LOUX
                  (1763 bp sp. Geo. Herkimer, Cath. Shoemaker, unm)
      4231: ELIZABETH b 3 Nov 1764 (sp Cath. Dygert, John Smidt)
                  m 1784 NICHOLAS SCHUYLER
   +4232: HENRY b 23 Jan 1766; m 1789 CATHERINE ZIMMERMAN
      4233: ANNA b say 1772; pr. m 1795 ABRAHAM BUR

4211: Col. JOST HERKIMER - born ca 1732; died Kingston Canada 16 Aug 1795; m by
1759 MARIA VAN ALLEN (b ca 1735) dau of LAURENS VAN ALEN (1703-1740) of Albany and
Kinderhook. He was a Tory and took his family to Canada during the Amer.
Revolution. Descendents remained in Canada (op. cit.).

      4234: GEORGE bp Palatine NY 12 May 1761; killed at Detroit (Revl)
      4235: ARRIANC b 11 Jun 1763; ps. m Capt GLEASON
      4236: CATHERINE b 3 Aug 1765; m THOMAS MARKLAND
      4237: LORENTZ bp Palatine NY 30 Jul 1767; m ELISABETH ...
      4238: MARIA bp Palatine NY 13 Apr 1769 (of Jost & Marytje)
                  she ml NEIL MCLEAN; m2 ROBERT HAMILTON
      4239: NICHOLAS b 24 Jan 1771; m CHARLOTTE PURDY
      4240: JOSEPH KERBY m CATHERINE MARKLAND
      4241: JACOB drowned in Lake Ontario Oct 1804; m ...
      4233: JANE m Capt. JOSEPH ANDERSON

4207: Gen. NICHOLAS HERKIMER - born German Flats NY 1728; died 10 Aug 1777 from
effects of leg amputation after the Battle of Oriskany; suposedly ml a dau of
SEVERINUS DYGERT (LANY or MARIA?) & sister of PETER S. DYGERT; and m2 MARIA DYGERT
dau of PETER S. DYGERT (Gen. Herkimer's will refers to Peter S. as his father in
law). Gen. Herkimer has been described as a moderately wealthy landowner of short
slender build, dark complexion, black hair, and bright eyes (Ward's The War of the
Revolution, pages 480-3).

    In July 1777 he mobilized all Mohawk Valley men between the ages of 16 and 60
to prepare to repel the British force of about 1500 troops under Col. Barry St.
Leger which was approaching Ft. Stanwix. Yielding to the impetuousness of his
colonels, Gen. Herkimer led his force of some 800 men into the Oriskany creek
ravine on the morning of August 6th 1777, where about half of St. Leger's men,
mostly Indians under Chief Joseph Brant, waited in ambush. At the onset of the
battle, Herkimer was shot in the leg and a sizable number of his militiamen were
killed (estimates place patriot fatalities on that day at from 150 to 200 men).
Nonetheless, he helped rally his troops and is credited with turning the battle
into a victory of resistence which twarted British goals of dividing the colonies
at New York in the American Revolution. He apparently had no children (at least
none are mentioned in his will prepared in February 1777). His home is still
standing at the south bank of the Mohawk River at Danube, near Little Falls NY.

4228: ABRAHAM HERKIMER - pr. born ca 1750 to 1767; m by 1788 DOROTHEA DYGERT (b 1764) dau of PETER S. DYGERT. Descendents moved to Penn.

    4242: HENRICH   b 29 Mar 1788 (sp. Hen. Dygert, Lena Herkimer)
    4243: PETER   bp SJR 9 May 1790 (sp Peter Dygert & Sara)
    4244: NICHOLAS   b 30 Jan 1792 (sp. Nich. Herkmr & Marg.)
    4245: CATHERINE   b 1 Feb 1794 (sp. Hen. Uhly & Lena)

4230: GEORGE H. HERKIMER - born German Flats 15 Feb 1763; died 1829; m MARY LOUX. Children were Caty, Elisabeth (b 1788), Hannah (1789), Henry (b Feb 1792), Catrina, Margret, Mary, George, William, Timothy, Delaney.

4232: HENRY HERKIMER - born German Flats 23 Jan 1766 (son of Hen. & Cath.); died 1813; m 1789 CATHERINE ZIMMERMAN (b 1768, d 1854) dau of HENRY ZIMMERMAN & pr. CATHERINE FOX. They settled at Shuyler Lake and had children Anna (bp SJR 1790), Catherine (b SJR 18 Aug 1793, sp. Jacob Snell & Elisabeth), Joseph, Henry, Robert, Alonzo, Jacob, Margaret, Mary, Hannah, and Delia. Lived in Otsego Co. NY in 1793 (SJR bp rec.).

4226: JOSEPH HERKIMER - born Oct 1751; m by 1777 CATHERINE ELISABETH SCHUYLER (b 1751, d 1800 or 1836) dau of PETER D. SCHUYLER & ELISABETH BARBARA HERKIEMR.

    4246: NICHOLAS   b 13 Sep 1777 (Nic. Schuyler, Marg. Rosencrantz)
    4247: MARY   1778-1798   m WILLIAM DYGERT
    4248: CATHERINE   b GF 25 Aug 1780 (sp Nich. Schuyler, Marg. Getman)
                 d 1847;   m1 ELIJAH STRONG m2 SAMUEL LORD
    4249: GEORGE   b 26 Jan 1783 (Geo. Herkimer & Alita)
    4250: ANNA (NANCY)   b 6 Feb 1784 (Fred Fox & Elis. <Frank>)
                  1784-1851   m JAMES CAMPBELL   no children
    4251: Johan JOST   b 21 Mar 1786 (sp. Joh. Smidt & M. Elis.)
    4252: DOROTHEA   1788-1867   m JAMES FOX
    4253: ELIZABETH   b 20 Jan 1790 (sp Fred. Frank & Elis. <Fox>)
    4254: HENRICH   b 21 Jul 1792 (Fred. Fox & Elisabeth <Frank>)

********** HESS **********

4301: **JOHANNES HESS** - born in Germany 1692 (if son of John, age 16 on 1709
London list); liv. 1749; m WCL (NY camps) 19 Aug 1711 CATHERINE KORSING (b 1694)
dau of RUDOLPH KORSING (aka "Ludolph" or "Lilof") & DELIA of Hellstein Isenberg
Germany. A blacksmith, Johannes emigrated from Bleichenbach Hanau Germany to New
York in 1710 and was on the NY Palatine subsistence list in 1710 (1A,0Y) & in 1712
(2A,0Y). He was naturalized at Albany NY 17 Jan 1716 and in 1723 got Burnetsfield
lot #31. Sponsored, with wife Cath., Jul 1744 bp of granddaughter Cath. Hess.
Hess info in St. Johnsville E&N 3 Oct 1928.

surname HESS
```
     4302: ANNA EVA   b 1713; ps. (Hess?) m ANDREW CLEPSATTLE
     4303: ANNA MARIA  b 19 Apr 1715 (sp. Marg. Burckhard)
                 ps. Maria (Hess?) m by 1745 GUSTAV OSTERHOUT
     4304: ANNA CATHERINE  b 25 Mar 1717 (sp. Cath. Conrad)
    +4305: AUGUSTINUS  1718-1782  m1 CATHERINE KAST m2 ANNA SCHELL
    +4306: JOHANNES  b 1721; m ANNA MARGARETHA JUNG
    +4307: FREDERICK  b 1722; liv. 1745 (spf Joh. Hess bp)
     4308: DOROTHY  b 1724; m by 1753 ADOLPH WALLRATH
```

4309: **NICHOLAS HESS** - On NY Palatine list in 1710 (2A,3Y) and in 1712 (2A,3Y) and
naturalized at Albany NY 17 Jan 1716.

4310: **JOSEPH HESS** - On 1717 Simmendinger census with wife Catharine & 1 child.
Also on that 1717 census was a WILLIAM HESS (with wife).

HESS - 2nd Generation

4305: **AUGUSTINUS HESS** - born Schoharie NY 21 Dec 1718; killed near Ft. Herkimer
15 Jul 1782; m1 by 1743 CATHARINE KASS (b 1721, d 1754) dau of GEORGE KAST; m2
ANNA SCHELL pr. a sister of CHRISTIAN SCHELL Sr. In a pension application
Christian Schell jr (b 1758, son of Christian Sr.) was called a cousin by Jost
Hess (Petrie book page 10). Drew Burnetsfield lot #10 (Little Falls). Augustinus
was a miller, blacksmith, and owner of a ferry boat. In a Tory Indian raid near
Ft. Herkimer in 1782, he and Valentin Staring were killed while providing a
rearguard defense as residents fled to the fort.

```
     4312: ELISABETH  b 1 Jul 1743; m 1764 HENRICH J. STAHRING
     4313: CATHERINE  b 27 Jul 1746; d 1838; m 1768 JOHANNES DIEVENDORF
    +4314: JOHN  b 1747; m by 1770 MARGARET ... (pr. FULMER)
    +4315: FREDERICK  1749-1795 m1 MARIA STAHRING
    +4316: GEORGE  b 1750; liv. 1776
    +4317: AUGUSTINUS jr.  b Oct 1752; m by 1776 MARIA SHOEMAKER
     4317A ANNA  b 24 Dec 1754; pr. m by 1784 JAMES NESCH
                 (Kast ms. says this Anna  m John Waft)
                 pr. by 2nd wife
    +4318: CHRISTIAN  b Mar 1756; m Apr 1775-6  ELISABETH KAST
    +4319: JOST  b 1758; d 1844; m 1785 ELISABETH EDICK
     4320: Johan NICHOLAS  bp 7 Aug 1760 (sp. Nich. Weber & Marg.)
    +4321: CONRAD  bp 3 Apr 1762 (sp. Conrad Frank); m MARG. T. FRANK
     4322: HENRY (bp John)  b SAR 25 Apr 1764 (sp Joh. Schell & w. Barb.)
     4323: DANIEL  b GF 19 Apr 1766 (sp. Dan. Miller & Anna Maria)
     4323A ANNA EVA  b SAR 27 May 1768 (sp Anna Eva & Fr. Orendorf)
```

4306: **JOHANNES HESS** jr. - pr. born ca 1715 to 1725; m 10 Nov 1743 ANNA MARGARET JUNG (YOUNG) we think dau of DEBALT JUNGu (tradition has dau of FREDERICK JUNG, while Martin´s Zimmerman book suggests she was the Margaret Hen. Jung (born WCL 1716)). John pr. lived at Palatine or Canajoharie NY.

 +4325: CATHERINE 1744-1821 m1 JACOB WEAVER; m2 CHRISTOPHER P. FOX
 +4326: JOHANNES b 27 Oct 1745; m 1768 ANNA FOX
 4327: ELISABETH b 12 Aug 1747; m SAR 1768 CHRISTOPHER W. FOX
 4328: ANNA b 25 Mar 1749 (sp. Aug. Hess & w. Cath)
   m 1770 Lt. JACOB JA. KLOCK (Bellinger book, page 42)
 4329: Johan FREDERICH b 10 May 1751; m ANNA CATHERINE NELLIS
 +4330: DEBALT b 1753 (sp Debalt Jung & w. Cath.); m MARJORY ...
 4323: DANIEL b 16 Mar 1756; d 11 Apr 1758
 +4331: DANIEL 1758-1842 m MARIA FOX
 4332: AUGUSTINUS JOH. b say 1760; liv. 1792 (spf Hiser bp)

4307: **FREDERICK HESS** - born ca 1724 (Vosburgh); pr. living 1767. Sponsored Jun 1745 bp of the dau of Gustavus Osterod & Anna Maria (Book of Names page 62) and for Oct 1745 bp of John, son of John Hess & Margaret (Jung). Pr. the Frederick listed just after Augustinus & John Hess in Capt. Frank´s 1767 GF militia.

HESS - 3rd Generation

4317: AUGUSTINUS HESS jr. - born 10 Oct 1752; pr. died Mar 1833 age 80; m MARIA SHOEMAKER (b 1757) pr. dau of JOHN SHOEMAKER & CATHERINE GETMAN (Bellinger book pg 47). He escaped after temporary capture at Oriskany. On 1790 GF census (1-5-4).

 4333: CATHERINE b GF 28 Apr 1776 (sp Joh. Shoemakr & Cath.<Getman>)
 4334: ELISABETH (twin) b 11 Sep 1779 (sp Stfl Shoemkr & Elis.)
   m JOHN EDICK
 4335: DOROTHEA (twin) b 11 Sep 1779 (sp Fr Ittig, Dor. Shoemkr)
   m JOHN BURGHDORF
 4335A JOHANNES AUG. b GF 1 Jul 1782 (sp John Hess & Marg.)
   m 1805 MARGARET GETMAN
 4336: AUGUSTINUS III (?, Bellinger book) pr. same as above John
 4337: ANNA MARGARET
 4338: FREDERICK b GF 9 Nov 1785 (sp Fred. Hess & Maria)
   m MARIA SKINNER
 4339: CONRAD b GF 26 Oct 1787 (sp Conrad Hess & Marg. Frank)
 4340: HENRY b 26 Nov 1789 (sp John Jac. Kessler & Cath.)
   m AMY SKINNER
 4341: MARY b 1794; d 21 Apr 1846

4318: CHRISTIAN HESS - pr. born ca 1750 to 1760; m ELISABETH KAST (b 1758) dau of FREDERICK KAST & ELIZABETH HELMER. On 1790 GF census (1-2-3).

 4341A ps. GERTRUDE (Hess?) b say 1776; m by 1794 ADAM H. WEAVER
 4342: ELISABETH b GF 16 Jul 1777 (sp. Gert. Kast & Conrad Hess)
 4343: AUGUSTINUS b GF 8 Nov 1781 (sp Fr. Kast & Elisabeth)
 4344: JOST b 11 Mar 1784 (sp Jost Hess & A. Elis. Fox)
 4345: CONRAD b GF 19 Jul 1786 (sp Peter Fr. Fox, Cath. Kast)
 4345A ELISABETH b GF 29 May 1788 (sp Geo. Kast, Elis. F Bellinger)
 4346: MARIA b GF 5 Apr 1791 (sp Dan. Hess, Cath. Scherer)
 4347: JOST b GF 27 Jun 1793 (sp .. Kast, Maria Osteroth)
 4348: EVA b GF 12 Aug 1795 (sp Phil. P Kauder, Eva Osteroth)

4321: Johan CONRAD HESS - born SAR 27 Mar 1762 (bp 3 Apr, son of Augustinus & Anna); died 10 May 1839 (Kast book); m German Flats NY Jan 1788 MARGARET TIM. FRANK (b 1767) dau of Lt. TIMOTHY FRANK. On 1790 GF census (2-1-3).

> 4349: DANIEL b GF 26 Oct 1789 (sp Dan. Hess, A. Eva Fr. Frank)
> > m 1811 MARGARET ORENDORF
> 4350: ELIZABETH b 25 Jul 1792; m 1812 JOHN N. SPOHN
> 4351: DAVID b GF 7 Aug 1794 (sp Pet. Joh. Bellinger & Doro.)
> 4351A MARGARET b say 1802; m 1823 ADAM NELLIS (Leetham ms.)

4331: DANIEL HESS - born 1758 (son of John & Margaret); died 1842; m by 1781 MARIA FOX pr. a dau of PHILIP W. FOX. On 1790 Palatine NY census (1-2-4) next to John Hess & Adam Barsh. Lived in Otsego Co. NY in 1794.

> 4352: JOHANNES b GF 13 Jun 1781 (sp John Hess & Anna <Fox>)
> 4353: MARGARET b GF 4 Jan 1786 (sp Wilhelm Fox & Margaret)
> 4354: MARIA (twin) bp SJR 15 Apr 1790 (sp Adam Barsh & Anna)
> 4355: ANNA EVA (twin) bp Apr 1790 (sp Daniel Weber, Cath. Klock)
> 4356: JOSEPH b SJR 2 Aug 1793 (sp. Peter Ph. Fox, Marg. C. Fox)
> 4356A BENJAMIN b SAL 8 Nov 1795 (sp Christ. Fox & Elis.)

4330: DEBALT HESS (David) - born 22 Sep 1753 (son of John & Margaret, died 1841; m MARJORY ... (Bellinger book page 43). Theobald Hess & Margaret sponsored Feb 1795 bp of Margaret, dau of Nicholas Forbes & Sara. David Hess was on 1790 Palatine NY census (2-3-4) next to Rudolph Barsh.

> 4357: ps. TIMOTHY b say 1775; liv. 1795 (spf A. Dygert bp)
> 4338: ELISABETH b GF 8 Dec 1783 (sp Stphl Fox & Elis.<Hess>)
> 4338A PETER SCHUYLER b GF 23 Jun 1785 (sp Maj. Pet. Schuyler)

4315: FREDERICK HESS - born 1749 (son of Augustinus & Catherine); died 1795; m1 before 1776 MARIA STAHRING (aka "Bally", d before 1788) dau of JOST STAHRING (son of Nich.); pr. m2 15 Apr 1788 ANNA MARIA FULMER (b ca 1762, d 1830) dau of CONRAD FULMER. See Comp. of Amer. Genealogy vol. 6 page 499 and Bellinger book page 73. Pr. the Frederick on 1790 German Flats census (2-2-4) next to Conrad Hess.

> 4358: FREDERICK b GF 6 Jul 1777 (sp. Fred. Fox ...)
> > pr. m by 1802 EVA ITTIG (b 1778, d 1808)
> 4359: ELISABETH b GF 13 Aug 1779 (sp. Con. Hess, Sus. Flack)
> > d 1830; m 1802 GEORGE F. FOX
> 4360: HENRICH bp GF 8 Sep 1782 (sp Nich. Hess & Maria Frank)
> 4361: MARIA b GF 17 Nov 1784 (sp Augustin Hess & Maria)
> 4362: ANNA b Gf Aug 1786 (sp Lor. Shmkr, Susanna Wohleben)
> > by 2nd wife
> 4363: MAGDALENA bp SJR 26 Mar 1789 (sp Christphr Fox & Elis.)
> 4364: MARIA CATHERINE b 26 Apr 1790 (sp Con. Hess & Margaret)
> 4365: CONRAD b GF 1 Jan 1792 (sp Fred. C. Frank & Elis.)

4329: Johan FREDERICH HESS - born 10 May 1751 (son of John, sp. Fr. Jung, Marg. Nellis); died 1806; m ANNA CATHERINE NELLIS (Bellinger book page 43). Pr. the Frederick on 1790 Palatine NY census (2-3-4) near John Nellis & Fox family. Family moved to Otsego Co. and married with Schremlings (Book of Names page 10).

> 4365A pr. JOHN F. b say 1775; liv. 1794 (spf Schremling SJR bp)
> 4366: ANNA bp GF 23 Oct 1781 (sp Dan. Fox & Cath.)
> 4367: ps. CATHERINE b GF 2 Feb 1794 (sp Jost H. Herkimer & Cath.)

4316: GEORGE HESS - pr. born ca 1750 to 1760; George Hess was sponsor, with Anna Maria Fulmer, for bp Nov 1776 of Anna Maria, dau of John Hess & Margaret.

4326: JOHANNES HESS - born 27 Oct 1745 (sp. Fred Hess, Eliz. Jung); m SAR 23 Feb 1768 ANNA FOX dau of WILLIAM FOX Sr. & pr. MARGARET KAST. Sponsored Aug 1783 bp of Anna, dau of Christopher Fox & Elisabeth and was pr. the John on 1790 Palatine NY census (2-0-1) listed near Daniel Hess & Adam Barsh.

4314: JOHANNES HESS - born 1747 (pr. son of Augustinus and not an extended marriage for the older John Hess <b 1721> who married Margaret Young); m by 1776 MARGARET ..., pr. MARGARET FULMER ps. dau of CONRAD FULMER. On 1790 German Flats census (1-5-4) next in list to Augustinus Hess.

       4368: MARIA MARGARET b SAR 21 Oct 1770 (sp Acus Folmr, Elis. Shmkr)
       4369: pr. GEORGE J. b say 1772; liv. 1789 (spf G. Hess bp)
       4370: pr. GERTRUDE b say 1774; liv. 1788 (spf Harter bp)
                  Gertrude Joh. m GF 1794 MARTIN MARVEL
       4371: ANNA MARIA b GF 1 Nov 1776
                  (sp. Geo. Hess, Anna Maria Fulmer)
       4372: CONRAD b GF 5 Sep 1780 (sp Conrad Fulmer & Lena)
       4373: JOST b GF 26 Sep 1783 (sp Jost Hess, A. Elis. Frank)
       4374: FRIEDRICH b GF 31 Mar 1785 (sp Fred. Frank & Elis.)
       4375: CATHERINE b GF 26 Oct 1787 (sp Wm Fulmer, Cath. Orendorf)
       4376: HENRICH b 12 Mar 1790 (sp Fr. Christman & Anna Eva)
       4377: RUDOLPH b 24 Jan 1793 (sp Conrad Orendorf & Cath.)

4319: Johan JOST HESS - pr. born ca 1750 to 1765; m German Flats NY 12 May 1785 ELISABETH EDICK (Ittig, b ca 1762, d HK 8 Jun 1813 age 51) dau of MICHEL ITTIG & CATHERINE ORENDORF. On 1790 GF census (1-2-3).

       4378: ANNA b GF 20 Sep 1785 (sp James Nasch & Anna)
       4379: GEORGE b GF 18 Dec 1788 (sp. Geo. J. Hess, Gert. Dievendorf)
       4380: CATHERINE bp SJR 30 May 1790 (sp Dan Petrie, Cath. Ittig)
       4381: ELISABETH b GF 12 Mar 1792 (sp Fred. Edick & Cath.)
       4382: EVA b GF 9 Mar 1793 (sp Fred Hess jr, Eva Ittig)

4328: ANNA HESS - b 25 Mar 1749 (sp. Aug. Hess & w. Cath); m 27 Sep 1770 JACOB JAC. KLOCK (b 1750, d bef 1792) son of Col. JACOB KLOCK & ELISABETH BELLINGER

4325: CATHERINE HESS - born 16 Jul 1744 (sp. Joh. Hess Sr. & w. Cath.); m1 JACOB WEAVER; m2 ca 1777 CHRISTOPHER PHILIP FOX (d 1804) son of PHILIP FOX.

4327: ELISABETH HESS - b 12 Aug 1747 (sp. Jacob Staring, Dor. Elis. Jung); m 1763 CHRISTOPHER W. FOX son of WILLIAM FOX Sr.

4401: CHRISTOFEL HILTS (Stofel or Christopher) - pr. born near Marth Germany ca 1670 to 1680; m there by 1698 EVA CATHERINA ... See Jones´ "The Palatine Families of New York" for more on German origins (H. Jones, P.O. Box 8341, Universal City, Ca 91608). Christofel appears on the NY Palatine subsistence list of 1710 (4A,1Y) & 1712 (4A,2Y) and on the 1717 Simmendinger census at New Heidelburg, with wife Eva Catherine & 5 children. He seems to have settled in the Schoharie NY area and remained there with his son Theobolt, while his younger sons moved to German Flats, perhaps as early as 1730. By February 1757 he was presumably deceased or too old for military service, thus the Stofel Hilts Sr. & Jr. in Capt. Petrie´s German Flats militia unit then were pr. a son and grandson.

surname HILTS

+4402: THEOBOLT (MATTHYS) bp Jul 1698; m by ca 1724 EVA MERKELSE
+4403: SIMON JACOB bp Dec 1700; "Jacob Sr." in 1757 militia
  4403A HANS LEONARDT bp Neiderkirchen im Osteral, Germ. 7 Aug 1703
  4403B EVA CATHERINE bp Niedrkrhm Ger. 24 Mar 1706 (H. Jones´ note)
  4404: MARGARET bp Marth Germany 28 Dec 1708 (sp Andr. Tromb)
+4405: GEORGE b say 1711; m MARIA ELISABETH FELLER (b 1712)
  4406: pr. MARIA ENGEL b say 1714; liv. Apr 1731 (spf Hilts bp)
+4407: pr. CHRISTOPHEL b say 1717; "Stofel Sr" in 1757 militia
  4408: pr. ADAM b say 1722; in 1757 GF militia; pr. d before 1760
  4409: ps. MARIA CATHERINE b say 1725; m 1767 CONRAD FOLTS (b 1719)

HILTS - 2nd Generation

4407: CHRISTOFEL HILTS Sr. - pr. born ca 1710 to 1720; died by 1769; m ... (ps. a Catherine). In Petrie´s GF militia in Feb 1757 and ps. the Stofel Els on list of 1757 GF captives in Canada (Book of Names). Simms "Frontiersman of New York" (Vol 2 page 281) tells of a Tory raider named Hilts who in July 1779 scalped his sister, a Mrs. Dornberger. She was no doubt Mrs. Elisabeth (dau of this Stofel Hilts) Dornberger, not the Catherine Dornberger whom Dr. William Petry treated for injuries, along with Jost Folts, at that time (Herkimer Democrat, 17 Feb 1875). Potential son Joseph (born ca 1760) may have been this unnamed Hilts Tory who supposedly scalped either his sister (Elisabeth) or his niece. Canadian descendents notes (from the line of the Hilts who married a daughter of Jost Petrie Jr.) imply that the earlier Hilts and his wife were both deceased by June 1779.

  4409A ps. EVA (Hilts?) b say 1737; m by 1760 JOST PETRIE jr.
+4410: pr. CHRISTOFFEL b say 1739; ps. the Jr. in Feb 1757 GF militia
       Stofel (son of Stof. dec´d) m 1769 THORATHEA SNYDER
  4411: ELISABETH b say 1741; m 1760 FREDERICK DORNBERGER
  4412: CATHERINE STOF. b say 1743; liv. Mar 1760 (spf Miller bp)
         (ps. the Cath. captive in Canada Nov 1757 - Apr 1759)
         Cath. Stof. m SAR Sep 1760 NICHOLAS KILTS
  4413: pr. MARIA 1750-1834 m by 1777 CONRAD P. FOLTS
  4414: son (name unk) b say 1752; d ca 1779; m ELISABETH JOS. PETRIE
         (infant son Jos. Hilts went to Canada Jun 1779 with Jos. Petri)
+4415: pr. LORENTZ b say 1754; ml by 1776 MARIA ...
+4416: pr. FREDERICK STOPH. b say 1756; m 1792 JULIANA MEYER
  4416A ps. JOSEPH b ca 1760; liv. in Canada 1851 (age 91)

4405: GEORGE HILTS Sr. - pr. born ca 1702 to 1712; pr. died before 1790 (not on census); m MARIA ELIZABETH FELLER (b 1712) dau of NICHOLAS FELLER & ELISABETH. George Sr. was in the 1769 GF militia and had 4 adults on the 1778 GF relief. Pr. the George & wife Elizabeth who sponsored 1766 bp of George, son of Thomas Folmer & Catherine. The property of his father-in-law Nicholas Feller (Burnetsfield lot# 7) was owned by George's son Nicholas Hilts in 1791.

+4417: Johan NICHOLAS 1733-1809 m 1760 ELIZABETH FOX
4417A ps. EVA (Hilts?) b say 1736; m by 1760 FREDERICK MILLER
4418: pr. CATHERINE (Hilts?) b say 1738; m by 1762 THOMAS FULMER
4419: ps. SABINA b say 1740; m by 1760 FREDERICK HELMER
4420: ps. MAGDALENA b say 1742; m 1766 HENRY WITHERSTINE
+4421: JOHN G. 1744-1820 m 1785 MARIA MEYER
4422: ps. ELISABETH (Hilts?) ca 1745-1828 m MELCHIOR THUMB
+4423: GEORGE b say 1748; m 1769 ELISABETH FOLTS

4403: SIMON JACOB HILTS (Jacob Sr.) - bp Marth Germany 12 Dec 1700 (Jones' "Palatine Families"); liv. Feb 1757 (GF militia) but pr. died soon after (no Jacob appears in 1760's church or militia records); m ... (Anna?), ps. a dau of JOHANNES COENS & MARIA CATHERINE to explain passing of Widow Coens Burnetsfield lot #1 to Sarah (Hilts) Smith. Ps. both he and Jacob jr. were killed in the Nov 1757 French & Indian raid from the north (attackers would have hit Coens property early). By 1755, land in the Peter Winne Patent, near the West Canada Creek, was deeded to this Simon Jacob by Timothy McGinnes and by 1812 portions of that land were held by Thomas Bell jr, son of Thomas Bell & Elisabeth (Hilts?).

+4424: ps. CHRISTOFEL b say 1725; pr. died 1756-7
4425: pr. ELISABETH (Hilts?) b say 1727; ml pr. by 1745 THOMAS BELL
m2 1765 ANDREW MCKOOM
4426: pr. JACOB Jr b say 1737; in GF militia Feb 1757
+4427: ps. JOHN b ca 1742; died Herkimer NY 12 Mar 1830 age 87
+4428: SARAH 1743-1802 m Dec 1764 ADAM SMITH
4429: pr. CATHERINE ca 1746-1837 m 1780 JOHN CHRISTMAN
(Cath. was spf 1766 bp of Anna, dau of Adam Smith & Sara)
+4430: GEORGE JACOB b say 1748; m by 1776 CATHERINE

4402: Hans THEBAL HILTS (aka Deobald or Matthys) - bp Marth Germany 28 Dec 1698 (H. Jones findings); died by 1769 (dau Elisabeth's mar. rec.); m by 1734 ANNA EVA MERKELSE. While his brothers moved to German Flats, he stayed at Schoharie and his children's bp rec. are in the Dutch Reform Church there (SHR) (1984 notes of Hugh U. Hilts, Box 5, Dewberry, Alberta, Canada).

4431: MARIA MAGDALENA b say 1724; liv. 1740 (joined SHR ch.)
m SHR 1749 ADAM JOH. SCHAEFFER
4432: pr. MARIA ENGEL bp SHR Apr 1731 (dau of Matthys & Anna Eva)
4433: ANNA DOROTHEA bp SHR 1 Feb 1734 (sp Thom. Shoemaker & Dor.)
m 1757 JOST CHP. WARNER (had Jost, Eve, Peter, Matth., Jacob)
+4434: GEORGE bp SHR 13 Mar 1737 (sp Jurian Timmer & M. Elis.)
m 1759 ELIZABETH BELLINGER
+4435: CHRISTOFFEL bp Nov 1738 (sp Jerri Sybel & w Mar. Engel Hilts)
m 1773 MARIA BORST (dau of JOST BORST)
4436: CATHERINE ELISABETH bp 24 Nov 1740 (sp Joh. Finck, Ballin)
4437: ELISABETH bp 17 Apr 1742 (sp Jacob Jo. Sneider & w Elis.)
m Oct 1769 JOHANNES H. SCHNEIDER
4438: ps. MARGARET b say 1745; liv. 1761 (spf Sophia Hilts bp)

4424: CHRISTOFEL HILTS - pr. born ca 1723 to 1730 (pr. son of Jacob, although George is a possibility also); m ... This was the Stovel Hilts who, along with his family, was captured by ten French Indians (presumably Hurons) in 1756, as given in Henry I. Wendel´s letter of 3 May 1756 to Sir William Johnson (Sir William Johnson papers, vol. 9). We suspect that this captured Stofel was either killed soon or held prisoner awhile and thus not likely to have been either the Stophel Hilts Sr. or Jr. who were in the Feb 1757 GF militia. Family traditions (Mr. Hugh U. G. Hilts, 1983 correspondence to W. Barker) tell of Godfrid Hilts who was supposedly about age 12 when captured ca 1756-7 and whose family were all killed by Indians, except for a sister Elisabeth (who would seem to be the Elisabeth Hilts mentioned as being held at Onondanga in Sir William Johnson´s letter to Thomas Butler, dated 9 Apr 1757). If Christofel was indeed father of that Godfrid then Christofel´s wife was perhaps a Riegel (note that Godfrid was sponsor at Riegel baptisms 1766-67) and, if Godfrid´s birthyear was about 1744 (as family tradition has him about age 12 when captured by Indians), then an early birth year for father Christofel of say 1727 is suggested (which places Jacob as the most likely father for this Christofel).

+4439: pr. GODFRID b say 1744; m 1777 MARIA MILLER
4440: pr. ELISABETH b say 1748; captive of Indians (Apr 1757)

4410: CHRISTOFEL HILTS Jr. - pr. born ca 1735 to 1750 (given as son of Stofel dec´d of the Flats on 1769 mar. rec.); m at Schoharie NY (SHR) 15 Jan 1769 THORATHEA SNYDER (b Zurich Switzerland). If this was the same Stofel Hilts jr., of Capt. Petry´s GF militia co. in Feb 1757 then an early birthyear (say 1739) is suggested, along with a rather late marriage age of 30 in 1769. We suspect this was the same Stofel who was sponsor for the 1763 bp of Anna, dau of Frederick Dornberger & Elisabeth Stof. Hilts, and the Stofel Hilts in the 1769 GF militia.

4435: CHRISTOFEL HILTS - bp Schoharie Dutch Reform Church 23 Nov 1738 (son of Theobalt & Anna Eva, sp Jerri Sybel & w Mar. Engel Hilts); m there (as son of deceased Deobald) on 10 Oct 1773 MARIA BORST dau of JOST BORST. His will dated 23 Oct 1797 (Schoharie courthouse, extract courtesy of Mr. Hugh U. Hilts 1983) mentions children George, Dewald, Margreda, and Catharina; executors named were George Hilts, Peter Snider and William Mann.

4441: GEORGE b Schoharie NY 17 Dec 1774
4442: DEWALD b Oct 1777; m MARGARET STUBENRACK
4443: MARGARET b say 1780; liv. 1797 (father´s will)
4444: CATHARINA b 17 Oct 1789

4416: FREDERICK STOPH. HILTS - pr. born ca 1750 to 1757; m Herkimer NY 14 Feb 1792 JULIANA MEYER dau of JACOB MEYER. Frederick was a sponsor for Sep 1790 GF bp of Godfrid, son of Godfrid Hilts & Maria. Apparently he moved to Canada after 1800 and lived near Godfrid Hilts, where in 1817 Frederick, referring to himself as "old", protested a land rental decision.

4445: BARBARA b GF 11 Mar 1795 (sp. Hen. Meyer & Barbara)
4446: ps. ADAM b ca 1800, liv. 1820 (confirm., Markham Canada)

4423: GEORGE HILTS Jr. - pr. born ca 1738 to 1749 (pr. son of George Sr. &
Elisabeth, as he was called "Jr."); died 1 Feb 1813; m SAR 1 Mar 1769 ELISABETH
P. FOLTS dau of PETER FOLTS & ELISABETH RASBACH; m2 GF 22 Jul 1784 ANNA MARGARETH
STARING a widow, pr. Margaret Rasbach, widow of Valentine Staring (d 1782).
George Hilts jr. had 5 adults & 2 children on the 1778 German Flats relief,
although that seems short by one or two children under age 16. George appears on
1790 HK census (2-1-4) near Schells & John Hilts jr. His will written 26 May 1809
(executors Nic. Thumb & Rud. Dievendorf) names wife Margaret, sons John (oldest) &
George, and daughters Catherine, wife of Peter Schell, Elizabeth, Suffenth, wife
of Jacob Helmer, and grandsons Jacob & Solomon, sons of John G.

> 4447: CATHARINA G.   bp 1770 (sp Conrad Folts, .. rina Hilts)
>   d 1822; m 1790 PETER JOHN SCHELL
> +4448: JOHN G. b say 1772; m by 1803 MARGARET DORNBERGER
> +4449: ps. MARCUS b say 1774; m by 1795 MARGARETH ...
> 4450: ELISABETH G.   b GF 7 Mar 1777 (sp Melc. Thum & Elis) unm 1809
> 4451: WIENA b 2 May 1779 (sp. Joh. Hilts, Anna Dornberger)
>   pr. m JACOB HELMER
> 4452: GEORGE b 10 Jul 1781 (sp. Georg Hiels, Cath. Hiels)

4430: GEORGE JACOB HILTS - pr. born ca 1740 to 1753; pr. died ca 1781; m by 1776
CATHERINE ... (pr. a Bell or a Bauman). His wife was pr. the widow Catherine
Hilts who m ca Jun 1782 Frederick Smith. George Jacob was in the 1769 GF militia.
George Jac. & Catherine were sponsors for 1777 bp of George, son of Thomas Folmer,
and for Nov 1778 bp of Frederick, son of Jacob Bell & Elisabeth.

> 4453: Johan ADAM bp 1776 (sp. Adam Smith & Sara)
> 4454: pr. MARIA BARBARA b 6 Aug 1778 (dau of George & Catherine)
>   (sp. Johannes Kessler & Gertrude <Helmer>)
> 4455: Johan GEORGE b 10 Dec 1780 (sp. Geo. Hilts jr & Elis.)

4434: GEORGE HILTS - bp Schoharie NY 13 Mar 1737 (son of Deobald); m 3 Jan 1759
ELIZABETH BELLINGER dau of JOSEPH BELLINGER & SOPHIA LAWYER. We believe this
George was a son of Theobalt of Schoharie despite the Bellinger book claim that he
was a son of George Sr. of German Flats (page 50, implies a church rec.<not
seen>). Our basis lies in the naming of an early child Eva and his continuous
residence at Schoharie NY, plus the fact that George Jr. at GF is never seen as
George Stof. (which by default he would been if the Schoharie George was the son
of George Sr.). George of Schoharie in a will dated Aug 1808 mentions children
John, Peter, David, Sophia, Eva, Catherine, and Elisabeth.

> 4456: CHRISTOFFEL b SHR 1760 (sp Christofel Hilts, Elis. Snyder)
> 4457: SOPHIA b Nov 1761 (sp. Christn Zee, Anna Margaretha Huls)
> 4458: EVA   b SHL 1 Sep 1763 (sp Lorentz Schulkraf & w.)
> 4459: CATHARINA b SHL 1 Jan 1766 (sp Christoph Huls, Cath. Bellinger)
> 4460: JOHANNES b 22 Jul 1770; ps. m by 1796 ...
> 4461: PETER b SHR 11 Dec 1772; ps. m CATHERINE
> 4462: ELISABETH b say 1776; liv. 1808 (George's will)
> 4463: DAVID b 9 Apr 1779 (SHH sp David Zeh, Elis. Fins)

4427: JOHN HILTS - born ca 1743 (ps. son of Jacob); died Herkimer NY 12 Mar 1830
age 87; m ... (ps. MARGARET DUNBAR, not Dornberger). A John Hilts appears on the
1790 Herkimer census (1-2-3) near John Christman, Thomas Bell, Philip Bell, & Adam
Smith. Ps. had a son John Joh. who m 1791 Margaret Dornberger (they had kids b
1792-94 with Dornberger sponsors); but if so, that John jr. must have died by 1803
when John G. Hilts was married to Margaret Dornberger.

4421: JOHN G. HILTS - born ca 1744; died Herkimer NY 3 Nov 1820 (age 76); m 10 May
1785 MARIA MEYER (b ca 1743, d 1830) dau of HENRICH MEYER & ANNA MARIA GETMAN and
widow of JACOB BELL. Pr. the John who sponsored Sep 1765 bp of John, son of
Frederick Helmer & Sabina. Will of John Hilts, written Feb 1813 (probated 1821),
names wife Mary, son George J. and daughter Anna (executor Christoper Bellinger;
witnesses David Folts, Jacob Bell, & Peter M. Myers). Pr. the John Hilts on 1790
GF census (1-1-3) listed near H. Uhle & Kesslers.

+4464: ANNA b say 1786; liv. 1813 (in father's will)
+4465: GEORGE b say 1788; m 1817 ELISABETH SMALL
 4466: MARIA b GF 3 Jun 1790 (sp. John McKooms, Maria Meyer)

4415: LAWRENCE HILTS - pr. born ca 1745 to 1755; m1 by 1776 MARIA ... (wife's pr.
mistakenly listed as Catherine on 1778 bp rec.); m2 by 1782 BARBARA ... Lorentz
was most likely a son of Stofel Sr. or Jr., with two or three wives (the 1776 and
1778 wives may be same person, perhaps Maria Catherine). He sponsored 1767 bp of
Lorentz, son of Frederick Dornberger & Elisabeth (Hilts). Lorentz & Barbara
sponsored May 1791 bp of Barbara, dau of Jacob M. Hiser & Cath. (Fulmer). On 1790
Herkimer census (1-5-2) in the Deerfield area next to Nich. J. Weaver & Geo.
Michael Weaver. He held land in Vaughn Canada by 1811 and his son Christopher L.
served for Canada in the War of 1812.

 4467: CHRISTOPHER b 28 Jul 1776 (son of Lawrence & Maria)
          (sp. George Miller & Christina Vols)
 4468: LAWRENCE b 28 Jun 1778 (son of Lawrence & "Catherine")
          (sp Godfrid Hiels)
          by 2nd wife (Barbara)
+4469: LORENTZ b GF 26 Jul 1782 (sp. Conrad Folts & Maria <Hilts>)
 4470: CHRISTINA b GF 1 Nov 1784 (Christn Reigel jr, Cath. Demuth)
 4471: GEORGE b 22 Jan 1787 (sp. Geo. Mich. Weaver)
 4472: ADAM b 24 May 1789 (sp. Adam Riegel & Sara McKoom)

4417: Johan NICHOLAS HILTS - born ca 1733 (son of George, Bellinger book page 16);
died 15 Dec 1809 (age 76-8-); m 15 Apr 1760 ELIZABETH FOX dau of JOHN PHILIP FOX
(b 1712) & pr. DOROTHY PETRIE (Petrie book page 3). Nicholas had 3 adults & 7
children on 1778 GF relief and was on the 1790 Herkimer census (3-1-3). His will,
probated May 1819 (executor John M. Smith), lists sons John, Nicholas, George (who
got 100 acres of Burnetsfield lot #7), & Philip.

+4473: Johan GEORGE NIC. b 1762; pr. m 1796 CATHERINE CHRISTMAN
+4474: JOHANNES   bp 1764 (sp. Sara Hilts, Deitrich Bell)
          m SUSANNA MILLER
 4475: ELISABETH b SAR 12 Feb 1766 (sp. Jost Petri & w. Maria Eva)
          m 1783 CONRAD FULMER
 4476: DOROTHEA b 18 Jan 1768; m 1789 PHILIP JACOB BELL
 4477: MARIA b 6 Feb 1770 (sp John Hilts, Mar. Petri); pr d young
 4478: NICHOLAS b say 1772; liv. 1809
 4479: MARGARET (PEGGY) b say 1774; m 1794 JOHN CHRISTMAN
 4480: MARIA b 22 Jan 1776 (sp Mar. Miller, Joh. Tho. Shoemakr)
+4481: PHILIP b 13 Sep 1778 (sp Lor. Hilts & Mar.); m ELISABETH HESS
 4482: CATHERINE b 5 Feb 1781 (sp. Joh. Christman & Cath.)
          m by 1809 JOE. EMHOFF (Imhof)

4465: GEORGE HILTS - pr. born 1796 (son of John G.); and pr. the George J. who died at Little Falls NY 1859 (surv. by wife Polly <b 1802, d 1864>); m Herkimer NY 17 Aug 1817 ELISABETH SMALL dau of MELCHIOR SMALL. Had dau MARY (b 2 Jan 1818, sp. Veronica Rasbach, Jacob Small), who pr. d 10 May 1828 <dau of Geo. & Elis.>)

4473: GEORGE NIC. HILTS - pr. the George born 1762 (son of Nich. & Elis.); m 1796 CATHERINE CHRISTMAN. Children were pr. NICHOLAS (ca 1795-1856 m 1816 ANNA WM. SHUTT), JOHN (b ca 1799, m 1831 ANNA G. CHRISTMAN), CATHERINE (b ca 1801, d HK Oct 1823 age 22), & PHILIP (b HK Dec 1804, sp. Philip Hilts; d 1824 age 20)

4439: GODFRID HILTS - pr. born ca 1744 to 1754; died Markham (Ontario) Canada 1835; m 1777 MARIA MILLER (d ca 1801) dau of FREDERICK MILLER & MARIA EVA (Mr. Hugh Hilts notes). Descendent traditions are that Godfrid´s family was captured and massacred about 1756, and that he was raised for some time by the Indians. By 1766 Godfrid was a sponsor, with Maria Helmer, for bp of Maria Riegel and he was again a sponsor for 1768 bp of Godfrid, son of Christian Riegel & Margaret. In 1778 he and his wife Maria sponsored bp of Maria, dau of Melchior Thum & Elisabeth. Was on 1790 HK census (1-3-3). In 1800 Godfrid sold Glens Purchase lot #26, in the Schellsbush area of Herkimer, and ca 1801-02 he moved to Canada.

> +4483: JACOB   b 10 Sep 1778 (sp. Jac. Kessler & Elis. <pr.Miller>)
> 4484: MARIA   b 6 Jan 1781 (sp. Thomas Bell & Susanna Miller)
> 4485: STOPHEL   b 17 Jan 1783 (sp. Lorentz Hilts & Barbara)
> 4486: ELISABETH GODF.   b say 1784; m ca 1801 CHRISTIAN STICKNEY
> 4487: FREDERICK   b 10 Dec 1785 (sp. Fred. Schell & Anna Eva Miller)
> 4488: MARGARET   b 15 Dec 1787 (sp. Marcus Schell & Marg. Thum)
> 4489: GODFRIED   b 23 Sep 1790 (sp. Fred Hilts & Elis. Thum)
> 4490: CATHERINE   b 23 Sep 1790 (sp. Joh. McKoom & Cath. Drnbrger)
> 4491: GEORGE   b 7 Aug 1793 (sp. George Hilts & Maria)
> 4492: JOHANNES   b 19 Jan 1796 (bible rec.); m MAGDALENA HEISE

4448: JOHN G. HILTS - born 1 Jan 1772 (son of George Jr., 1984 notes of Kath. Wheelock, 215 Crawford St, Boone, Iowa 50036); pr. m GF 17 Dec 1791 MARGARET DORNBERGER (b ca 1772; a Margaret, wife of John Hilts, died HK 30 Jan 1836 age 64). GF 1791 mar. rec. has groom as "Johannes Joh." which is either an error or Margaret Dornberger had two husbands named John Hilts. Wheelock notes have wife as MARGARET DUNBAR (b 20 Jul 1774) but 1803-4 HK bp rec. of Jacob & Margaret (Peggy) and 1822 HK mar. rec. of Solomon Hilts list parents as John G. & Margaret Dornberger. Only sons Jacob & Solomon were named in the 1809 will of their grandfather George Hilts. Wheelock notes list children as GEORGE (b 6 May 1792 <GF sp. Geo Hilts & Sabina Dornberger>), m ELIZABETH SMALL), NANCY (b 1 Jan 1794, m JACOB SCHELL), BETSY (b Jul 1795, m WILLIAM SPINK), JOHN (b Jun 1797, d 1873 <pr.m 1817 MARGARETHA FRANK>), CATHERINE (b Mar 1799, m 1819 HENRY FOLTS), SOLOMON (b 19 Apr 1802 <GF ch. has b 15 Apr>), JACOB (b May 1803), PEGGY (b Sep 1804, m ALEX HALL), FRED. (b Mar 1806, d Apr 1806), ADAM (b Jan 1807, m EVA FOLTS), EVA (b Sep 1808), THOMAS M. (b May 1811, unm), POLLY (b Feb 1812), JOSEPH (b Oct 1814, m MARY LADD), & CAROLINE (b Aug 1815 <HK sp. Pet. P. Schell, Marg. Hilts, unm>, m WILLIAM B. HAILLE).

4474: JOHN J. NIC. HILTS - bp 1764 (son of Nicholas); died ca 1813; m GF 26 Feb 1784 SUSANNA MILLER (b 1763, d 18 Aug 1843 age 80-2-3, was 30 years a widow) dau of FREDERICK MILLER & ANNA EVA. John Nic. & Susanna sponsored Sep 1803 bp of Maria, dau of Daniel Helmer & Elis. (Hilts). Pr. the John Jr. on 1790 HK census (1-2-3) in East Herkimer area listed near Schells & Geo. Hilts.

                    children of John N. & Susanna
  4493: ELISABETH b GF 29 Sep 1784 (sp. Con. Volmer & Elis.)
        ps. m by 1803 DANIEL HELMER
  4494: ANNA EVA b 3 Nov 1785 (sp. Philip Bell & Anna Miller)
 +4495: Johan GEORGE b 14 Jan 1787; pr. m 1809 ELISABETH CLEPSATTLE
        (sp. Joh. Georg J. N. Hilts & Cath. W Petrie)
  4496: GODFRIED b GF 16 Dec 1789 (sp. Godfrid Hilts & Maria)
  4497: JOHANNES b 27 Oct 1791 (sp. Joh. Hilts & Marg. Dornberger)
  4498: MARGARET b 6 Sep 1793 (sp. Joh. Christman & Marg. Hilts)
  4499: CATHERINE b 17 Jul 1803 (sp Jac. Volmer, Cath. Rasbach, unm)

4469: LAWRENCE HILTS - pr. born 26 Jul 1782 (son of Lawr. as shown on mar. rec.);
m 18 Feb 1806 MARGARETHA WARTENBACH dau of ANDREW WARTENBACH of Albany Co.
Marriage witnesses were John Armstrong of GF and Christopher Hilts of Manlius.
Had dau MARGARETHA (b GF 30 Oct 1811, sp. George Volmer & w. Maria)

4449: MARCUS HILTS - pr. born ca 1755 to 1775; m by 1795 MARGARETH. Had dau
ELISABETH (b 8 Jul 1795, sp. John P. Folts & Elis. Hilts).

4481: PHILIP N. HILTS - born 13 Sep 1778; m ELISABETH HESS. Children were
ELIZABETH (b say 1797; m1 JACOB PIPER m2 ADAM SMITH), DOROTHY (b 10 Apr 1802, sp.
Philip & Dorothea Bell, pr. m HENRY G. HARTER as in Wm U. Smith notes), MARIA (b
19 Dec 1803, sp. Daniel Helmer & w. Elis.), pr. JOHN PH. (b ca 1804; d 25 Jun
1812 age 8), ANNA (b 14 Mar 1806, sp. Nich. Hilts, Ann Hess unm), MARIA MAGDALENA
(m PETER G. HARTER), CATHERINE (m GEORGE G. HARTER), AARON (b 27 Nov 1813, sp.
Geo. Hilts & w. Cath.), HARVEY (b 20 May 1816), and PHILIP (b 25 Jul 1822).

                          HILTS - 5th Generation

4495: GEORGE J. HILTS - pr. the Johan George born 14 Jan 1787 (son of John on
mar. rec.); died 13 Jun 1863 (age 75-5-16); m 22 May 1809 ELISABETH CLEPSATTLE
(pr. b ca 1791, d 1863) dau of ANDREW CLEPSATTLE. Mar. wit. were Thomas Bell &
Rudolph J. Shoemaker Esq. His wife was pr. the Elisabeth Hilts, who died at
Herkimer NY 3 Jun 1863 (age 71-11-15, survived by husband George). Children
MARIA (Feb 1810; d Jan 1830 age 18, bp sp. John Sillebach, Maria Bell, unm),
MARGRETTE (1814-1901 m JACOB M. HARTER), WILLIAM (b Jul 1818, sp. Joh. Bellinger
& w. Anna Eva), CHRISTOPHER (b Jul 1821, sp. Geo. Hilts & w. Cath.; m 1843 MARY
HARTER), DIANA (b Nov 1823, sp. Fred. Helmer & w. Elis.), CATHERINE (b 27 Jan
1826, sp. Geo. A. Clepsattle & w. Anna), & GEORGE J. (liv. 1835)

4496: GODFRID HILTS - born 1789 (son of John N.); m 18 Mar 1810 WILHELMINA FALK
dau of BALTHASARIS FALK. Mar. wit. were John Nich. Hilts jr (pr. brother) and
John Volmer, unm. Children SALLY (b 27 Nov 1810, sp. Joh. Nich. Hilts & w.
Magdal.), & ps. NICHOLAS G. (b say 1813; m by 1834 GERTRUDE HELMER & had dau
ELISABETH b Jun 1834, sp. Math. Smith & w. Elis.)

4483: JACOB GODF. HILTS - born 10 Sep 1778; m HK 10 Sep 1807 SUSANNA DAVIS (b
1785) dau of PETER DAVIS. Marriage wit. were John Nicholas Spohn & Jacob Folts.
Lived at Markham, Ontario, Canada.

4500: JOHN J. HILTS - b say 1797 (son of John G.); m HK 2 Jul 1817 MARGARETHA
FRANK dau of LAWRENCE FRANK jr. Children include WILHELM (b ca 1819), ELISABETH
(b 15 Jun 1823, sp. Jacob Hilts), PETER (b 27 May 1825, sp. Jacob Frank), &
LUCINDA (bp 27 Jan 1829, sp. John G. Hilts & w. Marg.)

                                -139-

HISER - 1st Generation

4601: HENRY HISER - pr. born ca 1715 to 1725; died by 1787 (when his widow remarried); m by 1760 ANNA MARIA RASBACH (b ca 1739, d 17 Jun 1822 age 83) dau of JOHANNES RASBACH & MARGARET BIERMAN. His widow m2 1787 HENRY WITHERSTINE (see death record of Anna Maria, Herk. Reform Ch. Rec., vol 1 page 283). Neither the name Hiser nor close variants such as Hyser appears on early Palatine lists, although there is a PETER HEUSER on the NY Palatine subsistence list in 1710 (3A,0Y) and in 1712 (2A,2Y) and on the 1717 Simmendinger census with wife Anna Elisabeth and 5 children. More likely the Hiser family immigrated later than 1725 as the name is not seen on the 1725 Burnetsfield Patent. Pr. the Heinry Heufer in Capt. Mark Petrie's 1769 GF militia unit, next to Frederick Rasbach. Henry appears on a Tryon Co. census ca 1776, listed next to Jost Schmit & Frederich Rasback, with 1 male (over age 50), 1 female (age 16-50), and 1 boy (under age 16) & 4 girls (Mohawk Valley in the Revolution, page 153).

surname HISER
4602: MARGARET   b SAR 31 Dec 1760 (sp Geo. F Helmer, Marg J. Raspe)
ps. the Marg. liv. 1792 (spf Lena Hiser bp)
+4603: JOHANNES   b SAR 23 Oct 1762 (sp John Rasbach & w.)
m 1791 MARGARET CUNINGHAM
4604: MARIA H.   b say 1766; m 1785 HENRICH LEIMBACH
+4605: CATHERINE   b SAR 14 May 1768 (sp. Peter Wohleben & Cath.)
d 9 May 1822; m 1786 CHRISTIAN SCHELL
4605A pr. dau   b say 1770; liv. 1776 (census)
+4606: Johan HENRICH   b 30 Jan 1779 (sp. Peter Folts & Barbara)
d 1834; m MAGDALENA SMITH

4607: MARTIN HYSER - pr. born ca 1730 to 1750; m ... A Martin Hyser was in Col. Bellinger's Revol. Regiment (Book of Names, page 167). His marriage seems established by existence of Elisabeth, dau of Martin, who married Christain Riegel, and had a son named Martin (Riegel book).

+4608: ps. JACOB M.   b say 1766; m 1789 CATHERINE FULMER
+4609: ps. RUDOLPH   b say 1768; prisoner in Revol.
4610: ELISABETH   b say 1777; d 1863; m by 1797 CHRISTIAN RIEGEL jr.

4611: MATHEIS HISER (Huyser, ps. same man as above Martin) - pr. born ca 1730 to 1755; m by 1777 BARBARA ... Ps. his wife was the Barbara Hausser who sponsored, with John Kessler, Jun 1788 GF bp of John, son of George Carl & Margaret. Different birth dates for daughters named Elisabeth may distinguish this Matheis from Martin Huyser. But, given the uncertainty about Mrs. Elisabeth (Hiser) Riegel's birthdate (supposedly 22 Feb 1770 or 1777), we should not exclude the possibility that she may have been the Elisabeth below (b 1780, dau of Mathew).

4612: CATHERINE   bp 16 Aug 1777 (sp. Conr. Orendorf & Cath.)
pr. m 1796 ADAM RIEGEL
4613: ELISABETH   b GF 25 Jan 1780 (sp. Geo. Orendorf & Elis.)

HISER - 2nd Generation

4606: HENRY H. HISER - born 30 Jan 1779 (son of Henry, as given on mar. rec.);
died 1 Dec 1834 (age 55-10); m 16 Apr 1802 MAGDALENA SMITH (b 1782) dau of ADAM
SMITH & SARAH HILTS. William U. Smith's notes refer to a Henry son of Henry Hiser
who is presumed to be this person. Ref. for daughter Mary Ann is Harter
Genealogy. Presumably this is the Henry listed as close friend and executor of
the will of Sgt George Smith (son of Martin) in 1809 at Herkimer NY. Mentioned in
his estate papers, dated Apr 1835, were son Henry jr, wife Lany, Eva (Emelinee)
Hanchet, and Hysers as follows - Adam, Jacob, Sarah Ann, Aaron, Mary Ann, &
William.

      4614: HENRY   b 7 Jan 1803 (sp. Christian Schell & Cath. Schell)
                     d 1872; m 1827 SARAH SMITH (b 1806, dau of Adam)
      4615: DAVID (ps. ADAM?) b 30 Nov 1805 (sp Adam Smith & Marg.)
      4616: EVA b 7 Jan 1809 (sp. John Shell & w. Anna Eva)
                 apparently m Mr. HANCHET
      4617: JACOB b 2 Sep 1811; m 1835 EVA HELMER
      4618: SARAH ANN b 12 Jun 1814 (sp. Marcus Rasbach & Elis. Helmer)
      4619: AARON b 11 Sep 1816; m 1843 LAURA THUMB
      4620: MARY ANN 1821-1907 m 1841 ISAAC HARTER.
      4621: WILLIAM b 11 Sep 1826 (sp. Fred. Small & w. Marg.)

4608: JACOB M. HISER - pr. born ca 1755 to 1770; m German Flats 5 Feb 1789
CATHERINE FULMER ps. the Catherine (bp Apr 1767) dau of CONRAD FULMER & HELENA.
He was listed as a prisoner, along with Rudloph Hiser, in the Amer. Revolution
(Book of Names page 114). He appears on the 1790 German Flats census (1-0-2) in
the Columbia area near William Fulmer, Philip Ausman, Conrad Orendorf and Timothy
Frank.

      4622: CATHARINA b 24 Sep 1789 (sp John Hiser, Eva Sev. Orendorf)
      4623: BARBARA b GF 23 May 1791 (sp Lor. Hilts & Barbara)
      4624: LENA b 9 Sep 1792 (sp Aug. Joh. Hess, Marg. Hiser)
      4625: LUDOLPH b GF 6 Nov 1794 (sp Ludolph Hiser, Cath. G. Weaver)

4603: JOHANNES HISER - born 23 Oct 1762 (sp. John Raspe & wife); m German Flats NY
20 Jun 1791 MARGARET CUNINGHAM (b 1770) dau of WILLIAM CUNINGHAM & MARGARET
CHRISTMAN.

      4626: WILHELM b 6 Sep 1792 (sp. Lud. Huyser & Eva Cuningham)
      4627: ELISABETH b 26 Nov 1794 (sp. Peter Christman & Elis. Huyser)

4609: RUDOLPH HISER (Ludolph) - pr. born ca 1750 to 1775; He was listed, along
with Jacob M. Hiser, as a prisoner during the Revolution (Book of Names page 114).
Ludolph Huyser, sponsored, with Eva Cuningham, Sep 1792 bp of Wilhelm, son of John
Huyser & Marg. (Cuningham).

4605: CATHERINE H. HISER - born 14 May 1768; m German Flats NY 8 Aug 1786
CHRISTIAN JOH. SCHELL (b 1763) son of JOHN SCHELL & BARBARA RASBACH. Naming of her
Schell children demonstrates pattern consistent for a daughter of Henry & Maria
(see Schell).

HOCKSTATTER - 1st Generation

4701: CHRISTIAN HOCKSTATTER - pr. born ca 1730 to 1740; died Schuyler NY 14 Jan 1834; m1 ... (this first wife died enroute to America in 1764); m2 ca 1766 MARIA CATHERINE WITRIG dau of MICHAEL WITRIG as in Arnold's Ayer book page 14. Came with Hasenclever workmen to America and resided at New Petersburg (now E. Schuyler area of Herkimer Co). He was naturalized on 8 Mar 1773. He and his wife were sponsors for Mar 1794 bp of Christian, son of Adam Hartman & Maria Catherine. Christian Hofstader appears on 1790 German Flats census (with 1-4-2). Served in Col. Bellinger's 4th Tryon Co. milita regiment (Book of Names page 167).

surname HOCKSTATTER

```
+4702: ELISABETH  1767-1866 m 1789 FREDERICK AYER
 4704: HENRICH  b 5 Aug 1770 (sp Hen. Bekker, Elis. Frank)
+4705: MARIA CATHERINE  b GF 3 Jan 1776 (sp. Mich. Witrig & Amelia Cath.)
 4706: JACOB  b GF 27 Dec 1778 (sp. Jacob Wietrich & )
 4707: CHRISTIAN  b 28 Jan 1782 (sp. Thomas Jung & Maria Elisabeth)
 4708: GEORGE  b 15 Oct 1784 (sp. Geo. Riema & Cath. Elis. Rinckel)
 4709: MICHAEL  b 11 Dec 1787 (sp. Mich. Witrig & Elis.)
 4710: THEOBALD  bp SJR 7 Mar 1790 (sp Jacob Eyer & Marg.)
 4711: MARIA  b 15 Nov 1792 (sp. Fred. Riema & Maria Bekker)
 4712: MARIA  b 2 Mar 1795 (sp. Johannes Rimah & Cath.)
```

HOCKSTATTER - 2nd Generation

4703: JOSHUA HOCKSTATTER (pr. a Woodert, not Hochstatter) - pr. born ca 1760 to 1770; m German Flats NY 30 Sep 1788 MARGARET RANCKIN pr. dau of JAMES RANCKIN. Subsequent baptismal records seem to confirm that the surname Hockstatter on the 1789 marriage record represents an entry mistake by the minister (see Joshua Woodert, page 322). This is the only case I know of in which a male surname entry error can be ascribed to the Rev. Rosencrantz. On the other hand, the Bellinger book and others have noted that Rev. Rosencrantz sometimes got the mother's names wrong on baptismal entries, all of which detracts not at all from the value of his records, which probably are ninety-eight percent accurate or better.

4702: ELISABETH HOCKSTATTER - born 1767; died Springville NY 31 Jan 1866; m 29 Dec 1789 FREDERICK AYER

4705: MARIA CATHERINE HOCKSTATTER - m German Flats (Ft.Herkimer Church) NY 31 Dec 1793 PETER RIEMA.

********** HOYER (Hayer) **********

4801: **PETER HOYER** - pr. born in Germany ca 1710 to 1730; liv. 1788 (will dated 6
May 1788, mentions two daughters and was wit. by John Christian Faks, John
Osterhout, & Jacob Crim) but died by May 1794 (when his widow was sponsor for GF
bp); m GF Jun 1750 ANNA MARIA HELMER pr. a dau of FREDERICK HELMER & MARIA BARBARA
KAST. Emigrated from Hesse Kessel Germany to New York about 1723 (Petrie book,
page 25). Peter & Anna Maria Hajer who were sponsors for bp Aug 1766 of Peter,
son of Adam Staring & Catherine (also believe this Cath. was a dau of Frederick
Helmer, and thus a sister of Peter Hoyer's wife). The home of Peter Hoyer & Marie
(Helmer) was on the route of Scout Adam F. Helmer's run to warn of the approach of
Brandt's warriors in Sep 1778.

                        surname HOYER
        4802: MARIA   b say 1750; m by 1784 GERRIT MILLER
       +4803: GEORGE FREDERICK   ca 1752-1816   m MARY STARING
        4804: dau (pr. ELISABETH)   b say 1754; liv. 1777 (spf Leiper bp)
                     ps. m by ca 1781 GRATES BULSON

                        HOYER - 2nd Generation

4803: **GEORGE FREDERICK HOYER** - born ca 1752; died Herkimer NY 25 May 1816 age
64; apparently m1 by 1770 MARGARET ... (she & he were sponsors for Mar 1770 bp of
Geo. Fred. Wallrath); m2 by 1776 MARIA ELISABETH STARING ("MARY STARING") pr. a
dau of Andrustown neighbor GEORGE STARING (as stated in Hatch Papers). Hatch
papers say he was one of the early settlers of Andrustown, and that when the Tory
Indian party attacked in July 1778, George and his family escaped. George Fr.
Hoyer was in Col. Bellinger's 4th Tryon Co. Revolutionary Regiment and on the 1790
German Flats census (2-2-4) next to Gradus Bolson & Jacob Crim.

        4805: MARY   b say 1774
       +4806: PETER   1776-1848   m 1797 EVE ANN PETRIE
       +4807: JOHN   b say 1780; m by 1804 CATHERINE PETRIE
        4808: HANNAH MARIA   b say 1782
        4809: CATHERINE   b GF 6 Sep 1787 (sp Adam Staring & Cath); pr d y
        4810: ANNA   b GF 13 Apr 1790 (sp. John Fox & Anna)
        4811: CATHERINE   b GF 15 Nov 1793 (sp John Osterhout & Cath.)
                     KATY liv. 1810 (spf Hoyer bp)

                        HOYER - 3rd Generation

4807: **JOHN HOYER** (aka John Hawyer) - pr. born ca 1778 to 1784; m by 1804 CATHERINE
PETRIE (b 15 Feb 1784) dau of Col. JACOB PETRIE. Here we have the two Hoyer
brothers marrying Petrie sisters. Children were George Frederick, Peter, Maria,
Anna, John, Byansa, Katie, & Mary (Petrie book page 25-6). Lived at Warren Ny in
1805 and later in 1835 moved to the far west.

4806: **PETER HOYER** - born pr. at Andrustown ca Jun 1776 (bp GF, sp. Peter Hajer &
Anna Maria); died 1 Feb 1848 (age 71-7-8); m 28 Feb 1797 EVE ANN PETRIE (b 1780, d
Warren NY 1823) dau of Col. JACOB PETRIE. Children include John (b 1800, d Aug
1803 age 3-7-20), Eve (b 1802), Anna (b ca 1804, d 1814 age 14), George Fred.,
Frederick, Jacob, Bally, Elisabeth, & Delia.

                              -143-

********** HUBER (Hoover) **********

4901: **HENRY HUBER** (Sr.) - pr. born ca 1710 to 1725 (over age 50 in 1776); m ...
Henry was on a Tryon Co. census ca 1776, in the northeast Herkimer area, listed
next to Henry Keller (pr. his son-in-law). His household then had an older man &
woman (over 50), 3 men & 2 women (ages 16-50), and 2 boys & 7 girls (see Penrose's
"Mohawk Valley in the Revolution", page 154).

surname HUBER
```
+4902: ps. JOHN    ca 1739-1840  ml by 1768 ELISABETH ...
 4903: ps. ADEL    b say 1742; liv. 1762 (spf Fehling bp <SAR>)
                   pr. m by ca 1760 HENRY KELLER
+4904: pr. HENRY   b say 1744; m by 1779 ELISABETH ...
+4905: pr. CASPAR  b say 1746; m ...
 4906: ps. URSALA (Huber?) b say 1748; m by 1775 JOHN MILLER jr.
+4907: pr. JACOB   b say 1750; pr. m by 1770 ...
 4908: ps. CATHERINE  b say 1752; m by 1773 GEORGE MILLER
 4909: ps. MARGARET   b say 1754; m ca 1777 JOHN ECKLER
 4909A ps. RACHEL     b say 1756; m by 1773 FREDERICK LEWIS
+4910: ps. ELISABETH  1761-1836  m by 1795 ADAM A. CRIM
```

HUBER - 2nd Generation

4905: **CASPER HUBER** - pr. born ca 1735 to 1746; m ...   Sponsored, with Maria
Frank, Nov 1777 bp of Susanna, dau of Henry Garter & Susanna. Caspar was at the
estate sale of Nicholas Smith's goods at Ft. Dayton in 1779. Presumably the same
Caspar who was a Tory on the United Empire Loyalist list (listed after the
Revolution), along with sons Henry & Jacob at Adolphstown Canada.

```
4911: pr. HENRY  b say 1762; Tory in Butler's Rangers
4912: pr. JACOB  b say 1764; Tory in Butler's Rangers
```

4904: Capt. **HENRICH HUBER** - pr. born ca 1735 to 1745; m ELISABETH ... Henry
Huber was a sponsor, with Susanna Keller, for Dec 1793 bp of Jacob, son of Jacob
Keller & Margaret. He was probably father of John Hen. Huber, and may have been
the Henrich, who with wife Elis., sponsored Nov 1791 bp of Henrich, son of John
Hen. Huber & Gert. Crim. Listed as Captain in Col. Bellinger's 4th Tryon Co.
regiment in Revol. On 1790 Herkimer census (1-5-3) near Henry Keller, John Huber,
& Jacob Huber. Lived at Schneidersbush in 1791.

```
+4913: pr. JOHN HEN.  b say 1766; m 1787 GERTRUDE CRIM
 4914: ps. MARIA  b say 1768; m 1784 DANIEL PETRIE
+4915: ps. ELISABETH  b say 1773; m by 1803 ROBERT SIXBERRY
+4916: ps. HENRY  b say 1776; m by 1793 MARGARET ...
 4917: JACOB   b GF 14 Feb 1779 (sp. Fred. Frank & Susanna)
 4918: ANNA    b GF 16 Mar 1781 (sp. John Huber & Anna Bellinger)
 4919: ADAM    b 1 Jan 1785 (sp. Adam Staring & Elis.)
 4920: PETER   b 13 Feb 1788 (sp Pet. Bellinger & Barb J. Keller)
 4921: DIETRICH  b SJR 20 Jul 1791 (sp Jac. Keller, Marg. Ka..)
```

4907: **JACOB HUBER** - pr. born ca 1735 to 1752; presumably m before 1770 ... Pr.
the Jacob Hoover in Col. Campbell's Revol. Regiment from the Canajoharie area and
the Jacob on 1790 Canajoharie NY census (2-2-2) living near Ecklers.

4902: Capt. **JOHN HOOVER** - born 1739 supposedly in Switzerland (Petrie book, pg 36); died Oct 1840; m1 by 1768 ELISABETH ...; m2 by 1770 CATHERINE ... Listed as a Captain in action at the Battle of Oriskany 6 Aug 1777 and ps. later the Johannes Hover on the list of Tryon Co. exempts (Book of Names, pg 175).

  +4922: ps. HENRY b say 1758; pr. m by 1779 ANNA ...
  +4923: ps. JACOB 1760-1847 m 1781 MARGARET EIGENBROD
  4923A ps. ANNA b say 1762; m by 1781 JACOB PHILIPS
  4923B ps. MARIA b say 1764; m by 1784 PETER MALLEN
  4924: SARA b SAR 1 Mar 1768 (sp Elis. Folts, Geo. Helmer)
        m Fonda NY Nov 1786 WIAGHT YALE
  4925: SUSANNA b SAR 7 Sep 1770 (sp. John Miller, Elis. Frank)
        m Fonda NY May 1786 WILLIAM SCHUT
  4925A ps. SOPHIA b say 1772; m FR 1789 WILLIAM JONES

HUBER - 3rd Generation

4922: **HENRY HUBER** - pr. born ca 1750 to 1760; m by 1779 ANNA ... Henry & Anna were sponsors for Sep 1781 bp of Elisabeth, dau of John Miller jr. & Ursala.

4916: **HENRY HUBER** - pr. born ca 1765 to 1777; m by 1793 MARGARET ...

  4926: DAVID b GF 15 Aug 1793 (sp Jacob Huber & Marg.)
        m HK 1816 LYDIA COX (dau of Fassette)

4923: **JACOB HUBER** (Hoover) - born Philadelphia PA 17 Apr 1760; died Little Falls NY 22 Jan 1847; m 1781 MARGARETHA EIGENBROD dau of PETER EIGENBROD & ELISABETH HELMER (DAR vol. 98 page 199). Jacob & Margaret were sponsors for Mar 1794 bp of Jacob, son of Bernard Minick & Debora. Pr. the Jacob on 1790 Herkimer census (1-2-1) living near Henry Huber & John Huber.

  4927: PETER b GF 19 Sep 1787 (sp. Geo. Eigenbrod, Elis. Huber)
  4928: WILHELM b 23 Aug 1789 (sp. Wilh. Vedder & Elis.)
        m by 1817 MARIA PETRY (dau of John M., Petrie book page 19)
  4929: JACOB jr. b GF 30 Oct 1791 (sp. Adam Stahring & Elis.)
        d 1852; m HK 1811 MAGDALENA H. KLOCK (1790-1835)
        (had five children, Dockstader book <page 159>)

4913: **JOHN HEN. HUBER** - pr. born ca 1755 to 1769 (son of Henry implied from mid. name); m at German Flats NY 6 Mar 1787 GERTRUDE JAC. CRIM pr. dau of JACOB CRIM & ELISABETH FRANK (though Petrie book, page 36, calls Gertrude dau of Paul Crim). John & Gertrude sponsored Dec 1790 SJR bp of Anna, dau of Adam Crim & Eliz. (Hoover). Pr. the John on 1790 Herkimer census (1-0-3), near Henry Huber & Jacob Huber.

  4930: ELISABETH b 11 Jun 1788 (sp. Adam Grim & Elis.)
  4931: ANNA bp SJR 24 Jan 1790 (sp Adam & Elis. Staring)
  4932: HENRICH b 21 Nov 1791 (sp. Hen. Huber & Elis.)
  4933: JOHANNES b 30 Sep 1794 (sp Con. Kessler & Cath.<Crim>)
  4934: JACOB J. b say 1800; m 1821 POLLY PETRY (Petrie book, pg 36)

4915: **ELISABETH HUBER** - m by 1803 ROBERT SIXBERRY. Had son Jacob Sixberry (b HK 9 Jan 1803, sp. Henr. Huber & w. Elis.). At Riemensniedersbush in 1803.

5001: GEORGE KAST Sr. - pr. born in Germany about 1679 (age 30 on 1709 London list of Palatines, with son age 8 <Book of Names page 93>); living at German Flats NY 1733 when he was a militia captain; m ANNA ... On NY Palatine subsistence list in 1710 (2A,3Y) & in 1712 (3A,3Y). He was naturalized at Albany NY 11 Oct 1715 but not on the 1717 Simmendinger census (that list has pr. unrelated "Casser" brothers Conrad, George, & John). In 1723 George received Burnetsfield lot #5 which was held by his grandson Frederick in 1791. He traded ammunition and trinkets to the Indians for valuable furs (Hardin's History, page 390) and a tradition exists that he also sold the Indians a keg of rum in exchange for 1,000 acres of choice land, title being confirmed by Great Britain in 1724. His only known Kast descendents were through his son George Jr. (see Kast ms. "Mohawk Valley Kasts and Allied Families" by Mrs Mildred Conrad & Mrs Ida House, Herk. Co. Hist. Soc. 1983). Compendium of American Genealogy (vol 6 page 65) has daughter Margaret as born 1703 and died 1791.

surname KAST

```
+5002: Johan GEORGE jr. (JURG)  b say 1701; m GERTRUDE ...
 5003: ELISABETH  b 1703; m NICHOLAS MATTICE
 5004: MARGARET  b say 1707; d 1791; m WILLIAM FOX Sr.
 5005: MARIA BARBARA  b say 1709;  m FREDERICK HELMER
 5006: SARAH  b say 1711; m TIMOTHY McGINNIS (d 1755)
 5007: DOROTHEA  b 13 Nov 1715 (sp. Christian Bauch & w.)
               pr. d before 1740;  m by ca 1732 HENDRICK HAGER
 5008: MARIA  b ca 1717; m GEORGE RICHTMYER
 5009: LODOWICK   b say 1719; will prep. 1753
```

KAST - 2nd Generation

5002: GEORGE KAST jr. (Johan Jurg) - pr. born ca 1701 (age 8 at London in 1709); m GERTRUDE ... (pr. liv. 1778 as widow on German Flats relief roll, Book of Names page 118). Mentioned in 1734 minster's visit to German Flats (Vosburgh's GF churchbook). Ps. he was the George naturalized 3 Jul 1759 or perhaps that was the "George Cass" (relationship to GF Kasts uncertain) who was at Stone Arabia by 1766 with wife Elisabeth (they had children Maria & George bp SAR 1766-8). Children named in the Kast book do not include a George or Anna, causing us to suspect the list below may be incomplete.

```
 5010: CATHERINE  ca 1721-1754   m AUGUSTINUS HESS
 5011: SARAH  b say 1723
 5012: GERTRUDE  b say 1725;  m DIETRICH STEELE
+5013: FREDERICK  1727-1817   m ELISABETH HELMER
 5014: DOROTHY  b say 1730
 5015: CONRAD  to England 1757 (Brit. Army); did not return
 5016: ELISABETH  b say 1745; d Perington NY 22 Feb 1843
```

KAST - 3rd Generation

5013: FREDERICK KAST - born 8 Apr 1727; died 3 Dec 1817; m ELISABETH HELMER. Was in 1769 German Flats militia and in Revol. service. Frederick had 5 adults & 4 children on 1778 GF relief and appears on the 1790 Herkimer census (3-1-2).

5017: ELISABETH b 1758; m Apr 1775/6 CHRISTIAN HESS
5018: MARGARET b SAR 2 Jul 1761 (sp Elis. Frey, Barb. Laux ...)
        m GF 1783 (fam. rec. has 7 Jul 1788) ANDREAS S. MILLER
5019: GERTRUDE b say 1763; m 1782 JACOB HEN. WEAVER
5020: CATHERINE b 25 Jul 1765 (sp. Elis. McKinnes, John Thomson)
        pr. m 1793 LORENTZ DORNBERGER
+5021: GEORGE 1767-1848 m 1791 ANNA SMITH
+5022: PETER b 1770-1849 m 1792 CATHERINE DORNBERGER
+5023: ps. SEVERINUS b say 1772; m by 1795 SABINA DORNBERGER
5024: ANNA b 8 Sep 1774 (bp Fonda NY, sp John Neef & Anna)

KAST - 4th Generation

5021: GEORGE KAST - born SAR 8 Oct 1767; died 19 May 1848; m1 29 Jan 1791 ANNA
SMITH (aka Nancy, b 1768, d 1836) dau of ADAM SMITH & SARAH HILTS; m2 20 Nov 1836
ANNA STAHRING widow of JOHN DOCKSTADER. Admin. for his estate in 1849 names
Conrad Kast (son), plus Anna Kast (widow), and children Mary Huyck (wife of
Martin), Lany Huyck (wife of Gerrit), Catherine Helmer (wife of Timothy Helmer),
Phoebe Helmer (wife of Luther Helmer), Peter Kast, Thomas Kast, Conrad Kast, all
of Herkimer; plus Elisabeth O'Rorke (wife of Constantine O'Rorke, liv. in
Illinois). Also his will lists kin as Helen Kast, Philo Helmer, Elisabeth Drake.

    5025: PETER b 1791 (sp. Pieter Kast, Elisabeth Ad. Smith)
        m 1814 LYDIA PORTER
    5026: GEORGE b 1792; m CATHERINE CHRISTMAN
    5027: ELIZABETH b 1794 (sp. Jacob Smidt, Marg. Helmer);
        m CONSTANTINE O'RORKE
    5028: MARIA b 1 Nov 1795 (Nic Hilts, Maria Smidt); m MARTIN HOUK
    5029: MAGDALENA b say 1797; m 1817 GERRIT HOUCK
  +5030: CONRAD b say 1799; m 1832 MARGARET HELMER
    5031: SARAH b 31 May 1802 (sp Andr. & Marg Schmit); d 28 Jun 1802
    5032: CATHERINE b 1803 (John Smith & w. Cath.); m TIMOTHY HELMER
    5033: DELIA (MATILDA) b HK 11 Apr 1807 (sp Jacob Herder & Marg.)
        d 1829; m LUTHER HELMER
    5034: THOMAS b Herkimer NY 1808 (sp. Thomas Bell & Anna)
        d 1881; m MARGARET SMITH
    5035: ANNA (NANCY) b say 1809; m 1826 JOSEPH SMITH
    5036: PHOEBE b 1811; m LUTHER HELMER

5022: PETER KAST - born 7 Feb 1770 (sp Geo. Steele, .. Dygert); died 3 May 1849; m
1792 CATHERINE DORNBERGER dau of FREDERICK DORNBERGER & ELISABETH HILTS.

    5037: THOMAS b GF 18 Oct 1792 (sp. Thomas Bell & w.)
    5038: pr. ELISABETH b GF 11 Aug 1794 (sp Lor. Dornberger & Cath.)
    5039: LYDIA b 17 Apr 1802 (sp. Thomas Bell & w.)
    5040: JACOB b HK 22 Dec 1803 (sp. Hen F Helmer, Cath. Weber)

5023: SEVERINUS KAST - born say 1772 (parentage uncertain, does not fit in 1778
or 1790 household count for Fred Kast); m by 1795 SABINA DORNBERGER.

    5041: GEORGE b GF 29 May 1795 (sp Thomas Bell & Anna)
    5042: MARIA b New Germany 2 Oct 1800 (sp M. Elis. Witrig)

********** KESSLER (Casler) **********

5101: JOHANNES KESSLER - Presumably the John bp in 1686 at Ebersbach Germany son
of a Hans Jacob & Magdalena (see Hank Jones´ "The Palatine Families of New York";
pr. living after 1760 (grandson Dietrich said to have remembered him); m pr. in
1710 MARIA MARGARET or ANNA MARGARET ... (a guess that she was ps. a dau of
George Laux & Eva Zout to explain Kessler selection as sponsors of later era Laux
baptisms). Casler tradition in America say that he immigrated, along with
Nicholas Kessler, from the Alsace area in Germany (Petrie book page 7). John was
on the NY Palatine subsistence list in 1710 (2A,0Y) & 1712 (2A,0Y) and by Hank
Jones´ findings seems to have been a brother of the ANNA MARIA KESSLER whose name
appears on the NY Palatine subsistence list in 1710 (1A,0Y) and in 1712 (1A,0Y).
This same John Kessler was a resident of the Queensbury camp when he volunteered
for the Canadian Expedition in 1711 and was naturalized at Albany NY 3 Jan 1716
(where his name appears in the list alongside that of John Miller). He was listed
on the 1717 Simmendinger census at Queensberg (in Schoharie NY) with wife Maria
Margaret & 3 children and in 1723 he received Burnetsfield Patent lot #45, next to
that of Nicholas Kessler.

Two of Johannes´ children, Catherine and John jr., have their baptisms in the
early church records of Rev. Kocherthal and another child, Eva, is established as
the wife of Marcus Petrie (Petrie book). Family traditions say that a John Jacob
born in the early 1720´s was a son of Johannes, so we have at least four children
without the "probable" qualifier. Assuming the Burnetsfield Patentee Nicholas was
a minor in 1723, we thus place the remaining second generation Kesslers under
Johannes (this seems the better guess, although one or more may belong to the
earlier immigrant Nicholas). We are merely guessing in placing below a daughter
Magdalena (on the basis that she was named for the paternal grandmother).

surname KESSLER

    5101A: ps. NICHOLAS b say 1713; liv. 1723 (Burnetsfield Patent)
    +5102: ps. GEORGE b say 1714; liv. 1765 (land deed date)
    5103: ANNA CATHERINE b 21 Nov 1715 (sp. Jost Snell, Cath. Grostler)
    +5104: JOHN jr. 1717- m by 1760 ANNA MARIA ...
    5105: ANNA EVA b say 1719; m pr. by 1738 Capt. MARK PETRIE
    +5105A: ps. HENRICH b say 1721; pr. m by 1745 ... (had son Jacob H.)
    +5106: John JACOB ca 1723-1811 m CATHERINE STEELE
    5107: ps. MAGDALENA (Kessler?) b say 1725; ps. m HENRY WOHLEBEN
    5107A: ps. MARGARET (Kessler?) b say 1727; <ps. m JOHN MILLER?>
    +5108: ps. PETER (Sr.) b say 1729;

5109: NICHOLAS KESSLER (situation uncertain) - pr. born ca 1685 (assuming he was
the Nicholas on 1709 London list of Palatines age 24, noted as a linen & cloth
weaver and of Lutheran faith). On NY Palatine subsistence list in 1710 (1A,0Y)
and in 1712 (2A,0Y). Despite Kessler tradition that a Nicholas immigrated with
the above Johannes, we suspect that the adult Nicholas of the 1709-10 London & New
York lists may have been of another family. The Nicholas of the 1712 Palatine
subsistence was apparently married by then but we think he may have departed
shortly thereafter as there is no Nicholas at the 1715-16 Albany naturalization
sessions or on the 1717 Simmindinger census. Probably then a younger Nicholas was
the one who in 1723 received Burnetsfield Patent lot #25 (a dependent´s area
property, as noted on page 327). The relatively low occurence of the name
Nicholas among the children of the next two generations seem further indication
that most Kesslers of German Flats descend from the immigrant Johannes.

Other probably unrelated Kesslers among the Palatines of 1709 were DAVID KESSLER who appeared on the NY Palatine subsistence list in 1710 (1A,OY) and in 1712 (2A,OY) and was naturalized at Albany NY 17 Jan 1716 and a PETER KESSLER, prob. born ca 1688 (a Lutheran given as age 21 on 1709 London list of Palatines) for whom no record has been seen in New York.

KESSLER - 2nd Generation

5102: **GEORGE KESSLER** - pr. born ca 1712 to 1721; liv. 16 Sep 1765 (name on land deed then); m ... Listed on land patent dated 14 Jun 1755, involving property near Burnetsfield lot #30 (originally assigned to Nicholas Wohleben), along with Rudolph Staley, Jost Herkimer jr., Thomas Shoemaker, Peter Bellinger jr, Frederick Orendorf, Michael Ittig jr, Hendrick Spohn, Augustus Hess, Nicholas Wohleben, Christopher Fox, Rudolph Shoemaker, Samuel Broughman, Jacob Ittig, Jacob Kessler, Nicholas Herkimer, and Dietrich Stahley (Vosburgh's HK records vol. 3, page 12).

+5113: ps. JACOB b 1734<?>-44; d 1816; m by 1760 MARIA DOROTHEA ...
            (Bellinger book says dau Delia J.G. m 1803 Geo. Bellinger)
 5114: ps. ELISABETH b say 1748; liv. 1761 (spf Simpson bp)
+5115: ps. ADOLPH b say 1755; liv. 1776 (spf Marg. Kessler bp)

5105A **HENRICH KESSLER** - pr. born ca 1712 to 1725; pr. died before 1760; m ... (ps. a Ittig?). Since amongst the 18th century Mohawk Valley Palatines the middle initial almost always referred to the father, we feel Henry's existence is established by the presence of Jacob H. Casler on the 1771 Burnetsfield Minister's support list (Vosburgh) and in Revolutionary service in Col. Bellinger's Regiment (Book of Names, page 166). However, there is no trace of a Henry when the church and militia records begin to pick up in the 1760's, so he perhaps he died in the 1757 assault on German Flats or in other French & Indian War fighting.

 5116: JACOB H. b say 1745; liv. 1771-77 (Revol. service)
+5117: ps. MICHAEL b say 1749; in GF militia 1767

5106: **John JACOB KESSLER** (Jacob Sr.) - apparently born ca 1721 (calc. from age at death in 1809); died Herkimer NY 31 Dec 1809 at age 88; m CATHERINE STEEL. Fits with Hardin & Willard "Herkimer Co." as father of Jacob who died in 1822. Family tradition (Casler file at Herk. Co. Hist. Soc.) says this Jacob had at least two sons and that his dates were born ca 1723 and died Jan 1811 (these dates give the same age of 88, but are shifted by two years and were perhaps based on confusion with another Jacob N. Casler who died in Dec 1811 at age 72). Children John, Jacob, & Dorothy are from Mrs. Laura Dwyer notes (1983). Pr. the Jacob Sr. on 1790 GF census (1-0-1).

 5117A pr. RUDOLPH b say 1743; May 1775 resident of German Flats NY
            (Penrose's Mohawk Valley in the Revolution, page 165)
+5118: ps. ADAM b say 1745; at Oriskany battle in 1777
 5119: pr. ELISABETH b ca 1747; m 1766 JOHN EYSAMAN
+5120: pr. MARGARET JAC. ca 1750-1829 m 1785 JOHN BURGHDORF
+5121: JOHN ca 1751-1816 m CATHERINE SHOEMAKER
+5122: JACOB 1753-1822 m ELISABETH MILLER
 5123: DOROTHY 1757-1831 m JOHN MARC. PETRIE
+5124: pr. DIETRICH ca 1760-1855 (grandson of immigrant John)
            (pr. enlisted 1781 as subs. for father Jacob)

5104: JOHN KESSLER - pr. the Johann born 5 Feb 1717 (son of immigrant John, as in Kochertal rec., bp sp. John Miller & Gert. Hetmann); ps. ml by 1737 MARGARET FOLTS (b 1721) dau of MELCHERT FOLTS (check Bell family also for possible marriage of that Margaret Folts!); m by 1757 ANNA MARIA ... (John & Maria sponsored Apr 1757 SAL bp of Maria Orlob). Pr. the John Kessler jr on the 1753 Burnetsfield Church building subscriber's List (name alongside that of Jacob Folts) and the Johannis in Capt. Frank's 1767 German Flats militia, next to Jacob Kessler & John Eysaman. Pr. the John Sr. on 1790 GF census (1-0-0). Notes of Mrs. Leonard Healton (33210 Bailey Park Dr, Sun City CA 92381) indicate that this John & Maria, rather than Jacob Joh. (of next generation), were the parents of Maria Elisabeth Kessler (b 14 May 1767, d Yates NY Dec 1813), wife of George Hausman.

+5125: pr. JACOB JOH. 1737-1830 m 1766 MARY CATHERINE PETRIE
+5126: ps. JOHN ca 1740-1805 m 1766 ELISABETH PETRIE
+5127: ps. MELCHIOR ca 1744-1819 m MARIA ELISABETH PETRIE
+5128: ps. PETER b say 1746; d 1781; m by 1777 MARGARET WOHLEBEN
+5129: ps. JOSEPH b say 1752; m MARGARET BRAUN in Revol. service
 5130: ELISABETH b 2 Jan 1761 (sp Elis. Ad. Laux, Wm H Merkel); d y
 5131: MARIA CATHERINE b 23 Oct 1763 (sp Cath Petri, Geo Herkimer)
 5132: ELISABETH b SAR 14 May 1767 (M Elis <Folts> & Dan Petri)
        Maria Elisabeth (b 1767) d Dec 1813; m 1785 GEORGE HAUSMAN

5101A NICHOLAS KESSLER (jr.?) - pr. born ca 1713 to 1720; m ... (ps. a dau of THOMAS SHOEMAKER?). The son Jacob N. (i.e. Jacob, son of Nicholas), born in 1739, seems the cornerstone for placing this Nicholas as a second generation Kessler (son of either immigrant John or Nicholas). A Kessler family tradition has Conrad as one of four brothers, the others being John, Jacob, and Nicholas (Casler file at Herk. Co. Hist. Soc.). Ps. the Nicholas Kessler in Capt. Frank's 1767 GF militia, listed near to John Simpson & Thomas Shoemaker.

+5133: ps. THOMAS b say 1737; m MARGARET KREMER GF militia 1757
+5134: JACOB N. 1739-1811 m by 1763 DELIA PETRIE
+5135: pr. JOHN jr. b ca 1741; d 1795; m 1763 GERTRUDE HELMER
+5136: pr. NICHOLAS b say 1745 (sup. brother of Conrad)
              in militia 1767 (spf 1769 bp); m by 1788 DELIA SALTSMAN
+5137: ps. CONRAD 1747-1818 m MARIA CATHERINE CRIM
 5138: ps. CATHERINE b say 1749; m 1766 JOST M. PETRIE
 5139: ps. ELISABETH b say 1753; liv. 1770 (spf Marg. Petrie bp)
              ps. m by 1786 BARTHOLOMEW BRODHACK
 5140: ps. MARY MARGARET ca 1763-1806 m HENRICH CRIM (b 1761)

5108: PETER KESSLER (existence uncertain) - an older Peter than the above placed son of John, with potential birthdate say between 1715 to 1735, is placed here as a prospective father of "John P." Kessler who was in Revolutionary service (Book of Names page 167).

KESSLER - 3rd Generation

5118: ADAM KESSLER - pr. born ca 1740 to 1760; liv. Aug 1777 (at Oriskany Battle in Bellinger's 4th Tryon Co. Regiment, Book of Names page 166) but pr. died soon after as there are no churchbook entries for an an Adam prior to 1787 (m 1787 Maria Sutz). We assume this Adam was older than the ones born in 1765, although ps. he could have been a youngster like "Black Jacob" Kessler (who, as a lad of say 10 or so, tagged along with the troops on the march to Oriskany).

5115: ADOLPH KESSLER - pr. born ca 1755 to 1761; pr. died during Revol. period; m
... His name ought to be a clue to his maternal ancestry as "Adolph" was rare in
German Flats families (but does occur in the Wallraths of Montgomery Co.). We see
no sign of this man after 1776 and so presume he died shortly thereafter, possibly
at Oriskany. Was sponsor, with Margaret Kessler for bp in 1776 of Margaret, dau
of Jacob Kessler, and also in Jun 1776, with Maria Elis. Nellis, for bp of George,
son of John Christman & Catherine. Elisabeth Adolph Kessler was a sponsor, with
Dorothy Eysaman, for Feb 1802 bp of Elisabeth, dau of Peter Klock & Anna Staring.

5142: pr. ELISABETH ADOLPH b say 1774; liv. 1802 (spf Klock bp)

5137: CONRAD KESSLER - born 21 Mar 1747; died 6 Aug 1818; m MARIA CATHERINE CRIM
dau of PAUL CRIM & LENA STEELE. Casler file (HCH) material has him as one four
brothers, the others being John, Jacob, & Nicholas (a Brig. Major), all of whom
served in the Revolution. Conrad was in the 1767 GF militia and in Bellinger's
Revol. Regm (Also a Conrad was in Klock's Regiment along with Melchert & Joseph).
Was sponsor for 1769 bp of Anna Eva Kessler dau of Jacob Jr & Delia (Petrie).
Conrad & wife Catherine sponsored Sep 1794 bp of John, son of John H. Huber &
Gertrude Grim. Conrad was on the 1790 GF census (1-2-4) and his will, dated 4 Jun
1818, names oldest son Jacob, son Richard, and daughters Magdalena, Margaret,
Catherine, Dorothy, Sally (wife of Joseph Bowers), & Eva.

    5143: MAGDALENA b GF 5 Jul 1779 (sp Jac. Kslr & M. Cath.<Petrie>)
                    pr. m JACOB SEYMOUR
    5144: MARGARET b GF 10 Aug 1780 (sp Christn Shell jr, Marg. Kslr)
    5145: CONRAD b GF 10 Jan 1782 (sp Con. Schaefer & Doro.<Crim>)
    5146: HENRICH b 4 Aug 1783 (sp Hen Crim & Marg.); pr. d. young
    5147: GERTRUDE b GF 10 Jul 1784 (sp Diet. Kessler, Gert. Crim)
    5148: JACOB b 27 May 1785 (sp Jac Kslr)
                    m 1807 SUSANNA EIGENAUR (dau of Conrad); liv. 1818
    5149: RICHARD b GF 27 Apr 1787 (sp Diet. Kesler, Cath. Rankin)
    5150: CATHERINE b 25 Apr 1789 (sp Cath. Jost Petrie)
    5151: ELISABETH b 4 Sep 1790 (sp Barth. Brdhack & Elis.)
    5152: MYNHARD b 18 Mar 1792 (sp Mynhart Wemple & Anna)
    5153: JOHANNES b GF 14 Feb 1793 (sp Joh Kesler, Maria Rsncrntz)
    5154: EVA b 28 Jan 1795 (sp Jac Kesler & Anna Eva); liv. 1818
    5155: DOROTHY b say 1797; liv. 1818
    5156: SALLY liv. 1818 (spf Kesler bp); m JOSEPH BOWERS
    5157: MARIA b 27 Jul 1804 (sp Philip Peter K...& w. M. Cath.)

5124: Major DIETRICH KESSLER - born ca 1760 (appar. grandson of immigrant
Johannes); died 1855 (age 95); pr. this Diet. Jac. m1 GF 15 Jan 1788 CATHERINE
RANCKIN presumably dau of JAMES RANKIN & ELISABETH MILLER; and perhaps m2 1799
MARGARET CASLER (b 1773 <? ps. 1780>, d 1860). Dates for second wife are from
DAR, but mention of a "son-in-law" Richard Kessler in 1818, in the will of Conrad
Kessler, suggests likelihood that second wife Margaret was the one born 10 Aug
1780 (dau of Conrad & Maria Catherine). Was a Revolutionary War veteran and among
Col. Wilett's force which pursued and slew the Tory raider Walter Butler in Oct
1781. On 1790 GF census (1-1-2). Supposedly was the elder of two Major Dick
Caslers; and could remember his grandfather Johannin (Casler family traditions in
Community Review of Ilion NY 2/11/1932).

    5158: JACOB b GF 12 Apr 1788 (sp Jac. Kesler, Anna Eva Kesler)
    5159: ELISABETH b GF 24 Aug 1789 (sp Jac Kessler & Anna Eva)
    5160: MARCUS b GF 10 Aug 1791 (sp Marc Kessler & Jenni Rankin)
    5161: MARIA CATHERINE b GF 18 Apr 1795 (sp Joh. Kessler & Maria)

-151-

5113: JACOB KESSLER - ps. born ca Jan 1734 (calc. from death date in 1816); if died Herkimer NY 27 Nov 1816 (age 82-10-); m by 1760 MARIA DOROTHEA ... Wife Dorothy sponsored May 1760 bp of Elisabeth, dau of John Simson & Elisabeth and Jacob & Maria Dorothea sponsored Aug 1769 SAR bp of Anna Maria, dau of Jacob Deek & Margaret. If the 1734 birthyear is correct then this was pr. a grandson, rather than a son, of one of the immigrants since the name Jacob seems to have been too important a Kessler name to come as late as 1734 for the immigrant's sons. There is a slot open for this Jacob to have been a son of either George or Henry, but the presumed children below provide no clue (choosing the former permits us to fold in a daughter Delia here). We do not think this was the Jacob jr. whose will admin. of Jul 1818 lists children Mathew, Joseph, Silvester & Betsy (Elisabeth) and executors Fred. Casler & Joseph Meyers jr. All the five Jacob Kesslers on the 1790 census of Montgomery Co. (incl. Herk. Co.) are accounted for without finding this Jacob, and yet the 1816 death record places him at Herkimer. Of course he may have been missed on the 1790 census, been living in someone else's household, or even out of the county then, although each of these alternatives strikes us as being of low probability. Another alternative is that the 1816 age of death is recorded incorrectly and refers instead to a later Jacob (born say 1754 to 1774, and thus age 42 to 62 at time of death), thus allowing us to speculate that the Jacob, who married Maria Dorothea, may (a) be the same as the early Jacob (b ca 1721), with Dorothy being a second wife after Catherine Steel; or (b) be a son of George or Henrich (of the previous generation) and presumably deceased before 1790 (there is no sign of an unplaced Jacob on the Montgomery Co. census).

 5162: ANNA MARIA b 8 Jul 1761 (sp. A. Maria, w of Joh. Ksslr)
      ps. m ca 1780 STEPHEN EYSAMAN
 5163: ADAM b GF 26 Dec 1765 (sp. Joh. Miller & w. Marg.)
 5165: ps. DELIA JAC. G. (? Bellinger book) m 1803 GEORGE BELLINGER

5125: JACOB JOH. KESSLER - born 1737 (DAR vol 134 page 46); died New York State 1830 (ibid.); m 16 Oct 1766 MARIA CATHERINE PETRIE (b say 1745, d 1835) pr. dau of MARCUS PETRIE & ANNA EVA KESSLER (as in Petrie book page 1). Possibly the Jacob J. in German Flats militia in 1767 and 1769. In Cmdr Bellinger's notes at Herk. Co. Historical Soc. there is a comment from a descendent of John Folts & Catherine (Kessler) giving parents of that Catherine as Jacob Kessler (born 1737 and felt to be a descendent of immigrant John). Identified as "Jacob Joh." on children's bp rec. in 1785 and 1790. Appears as Jacob J. on Tryon Co. census ca 1776 with 3 boys and no girls (under age 16), as given in "Mohawk Valley in the Revolution" (page 155). Jacob Joh. Kessler was listed on the 1790 German Flats NY census (2-1-8). His son Dietrich is difficult to distinguish from the earlier Dietrich Joh. (b ca 1760) with regard to which married Catherine Rankin in 1788 and Margaret Kessler in 1799.

 5166: RICHARD b SAR 4 Apr 1767 (sp Dietrich Petri, Elisabeth Folts)
       ps. m 1799 MARGARET CASLER
 5167: JOHN b SA 24 Nov 1770 (sp John Kesler & Elis. Frank)
+5169: ps. MARCUS b say 1773; m 1793 ELISABETH WAGGONER
+5170: JACOB b 11 Feb 1778 (sp. Jac. N Kesler & Delia <Petrie>)
     ps. m 1807 DOROTHY MEYER (b ca 1785)
 5171: MARIA b GF 9 Apr 1780 (sp. Stephn Eysaman & Maria)
 5172: CATHERINE 1782-1856 m JOHN FOLTS
 5173: DELIA b GF 15 Jan 1785 (sp. Henrich Crim & Margaret)
     ps. m 1803 GEORGE BELLINGER
 5174: child b GF 6 Jun 1787 (sp Barth. Brodhack & ...)
 5175: ANNA b 8 Mar 1790 (sp Melchior Keslr & M. Elis.)

5176: JACOB KESSLER jr. - m SAR 29 Jun 1763 DELIA DOCKSTADER. Rooney´s Dockstader book does not mention any early Delia Dockstader and we suspect the 1763 marriage record may be wrong and refer to the marriage of Jacob N. Kessler jr. & DELIA PETRIE. In this regard we note that no Dockstaders were baptismal sponsors for Jacob N. Kessler children and there is no other record for the marriage of Jacob Kesser to Delia Petrie. Ps. Sabina Dockstader resembled Delia Petrie, which may explain both the marriage entry error and the marked over entry of "Sabina" on the bp record for one of the children of Jacob Kessler & Delia (Petrie).

5134: JACOB N. KESSLER jr - born ca Nov 1739 (pr. son of Nicholas, Petrie book page 15); died Herkimer NY 8 Dec 1811 (age 72-0-22); m by 1763 DELIA PETRIE (aka Margaret Elisabeth, b ca 1742, d Mar 1804 age 61-4-22) dau of MARK PETRIE & ANNA EVE KESSLER. Called Jacob Jr. on 1765 GF bp record of son Nicholas. Ps. this Jacob was the father of the "Black Jacob" who was a youngster at the Battle of Oriskany (HCH Kessler file notes say Black Jacob´s father was a Jacob and his father had a brother John). On 1790 GF census (2-1-2).

+5177: NICHOLAS b SAR 3 Nov 1763 (sp Nic. Kesler, Cath. Petri, unm)
        ml 1782 GERTRUDE BELLINGER
+5178: MARCUS b 26 Apr 1766; m 1787-8 DELIA PETRIE
+5179: JACOB JAC. N. bp SAR 14 Sep 1768 (sp. Jac. Petrie & Eva)
        (pr. b ca 1767); m 1789 RACHEL VETTERLY
 5180: ANNA EVA b 28 Jan 1769 (sp. Eva Petrie, Conrad Kessler)
        liv. Mar 1791 (sp Woodert bp); m 1794 JOHN SCHELL
+5181: pr. PETER J. b say 1771; m by 1793 JEAN RANKIN
 5182: ps. CATHERINE b say 1773; m GF 1791 JAMES LAPDON
 5183: ps. MARGARET b German Flats 10 Jun 1776 (dau of Jacob)
        (sp. Marg. Kessler & Adolph Kessler)
+5184: DIETRICH b 1778; m 1803 ELISABETH KESSLER
        (sp. Adam Bellinger & Maria Elis.)
+5185: JOSEPH b 9 Sep 1783 (sp Jost Kayser & Mar.); m LANY MILLER
 5186: DELIA b GF 4 Nov 1786 (sp Col. Bellinger & Delia)
        m SAMUEL ABBOTT

5122: JACOB JAC. KESSLER - born German Flats NY 1753 (son of "John Jacob" <d 1811> as given in Hardin & Willard´s " History of Herkimer Co." page 73-4); died Herkimer NY Aug 1822 (age 69); m ELISABETH MILLER (DAR vol 31 page 307) pr. a dau of FREDERICK MILLER. His will mentions children Frederick, Jacob, Elisabeth and Polly (Maria). Hardin & Willard tie three generations together with John Jacob (d Jan 1811) as the father of Jacob (1753-1822) who was the father of Frederick Casler (died Oct 1849). On 1790 GF census (1-2-2).

 5187: pr. DOROTHEA b GF 21 Nov 1778 (dau of Jacob & Elisabeth)
        (sp. John M. Petrie & Dorothy <Kessler>)
+5188: FREDERICK b GF 13 Feb 1780 (sp. Jac Kesslr & Cath.)
        d 19 Oct 1849; m by 1802 MARGARET KLOCK
 5189: ELISABETH b 3 Feb 1785 (dau of Jacob Jac.)
        (sp John Eysaman & Elis.); m 1803 DIETRICH KESSLER
 5190: JACOB b GF 20 Mar 1788 (sp. Jac Eysaman & Anna Eva Miller)
        ps. m CATHERINE EYSAMAN (DAR v 64 pg 60)
 5191: ps. LENA b GF 26 May 1788 (sp John Kesslr, Lena Petrie)
 5192: DELIA b 13 Jun 1792 (sp Jac Kessler & Delia)
 5193: MARCUS b 19 Aug 1794 (sp Marcus Kesler & Elis.)
 5194: MARIA ("Polly") b say 1797; in father´s will
        ps. the Maria Jac. liv. 1811 (age 14 at HK confirm.)

5121: JOHN J. KESSLER (Casler) - born GF ca 1751 (birthyear calc. from death age, ps. 1755); died Herkimer NY 27 Mar 1816 (age 65); m CATHERINE SHOEMAKER (b ca 1761, d 21 Jul 1825 age 64-6-) pr. a dau of JOHN SHOEMAKER & CATHERINE GETMAN. At Battle of Oriskany (DAR vol 38 page 140). John & Cath. sponsored 1780 bp of Peter, son of George DeMuth & Anna. Admin. papers in 1816 mention wife Caty and sons John, Rudolph, Christopher, Richard, & Marks; also named was Caty, wife of John Shoemaker jr. John Jacob was on 1790 GF census (1-3-2).

> +5195: JOHN jr b 7 Feb 1777 (sp Joh. Petrie & Doro. <Kessler>)
>   m by 1804 MARY CASLER (DAR vol 139 page 177)
> 5196: pr. JACOB b 1 Feb 1779 (son of John & Cath.)
>   (sp. Jacob Kessler & Elisabeth <pr. Miller>)
> 5197: STOPHEL b GF Feb 1782 (sp Stofel Shoemaker & Elis.)
>   d 1822; m MAGDALENA UHLE
> 5198: DIETRICH b 20 Nov 1784 (sp Diet. J. Kesslr & Marg. Kesslr)
>   m 1809 ANNA HEN. WALLRATH
> 5199: pr. CATHERINE bp SJR Mar 1789; m 1811 JOHN SHOEMAKER jr
> 5200: JACOB b 7 Aug 1792
> 5201: RUDOLPH b 10 Oct 1794 (sp Lud. Shmker & Doro.)
> 5202: MARKS ca 1797-1830 m 1824 ELISABETH ROSENCRANTZ

5126: JOHN KESSLER - pr. born ca 1740 (calc. from age at death, assuming death rec. applies to him rather than wife); he died (mortuus) Herkimer NY 11 Feb 1805 age 65; m SAR 28 Aug 1766 ELISABETH PETRIE. Ps. the John with 2 adults & 4 children on 1778 German Flats relief and the John on 1790 Herkimer census (2-5-5). John and wife Elisabeth sponsored Jun 1778 bp of Peter, son of John Eysaman & Elis. (Kessler). Admin. of John Casler issued 2 Mar 1805 to Elizabeth Casler (pr. widow) and John Jr. (ps. son), with bond to Elis. Casler, John Casler jr., Ludwig Campbell, & Jacob Griswold.

> 5203: ps. JOHN b SAR 1 Aug 1769 (sp. Jost H.<M.?> Petrie)
> 5204: ps. ANNA b say 1774; m 1795 AARON BUTTERFIELD
> 5205: ps. DELIA b GF 15 Jun 1776 (dau of John, sp Jacob Keslr)
>   ps. m 1794 MARCUS CHR. SCHELL
> 5206: DIETRICH b GF 11 Oct 1777 (sp. John Eysaman & Elisabeth)
> +5207: pr. ADOLPH JOH. b 4 Aug 1779 (sp Bart. Brdhck, Elis. Keslr)
>   m by 1802 DOROTHY EYSAMAN
> 5208: HENRICH (twin) b GF 16 Feb 1781 (sp. Hen. Crim, Marg. Kslr)
> +5209: NICHOLAS (twin) b 1781 (sp. Nich. Kslr, Gert. Bellinger)
>   pr. m 1804 ELISABETH EIGENAUER
> 5210: ELISABETH b GF 16 Aug 1784 (sp Step. Eysaman & Anna Eva)
> 5211: DIETRICH b 16 Jun 1786 (sp Deitrich Petrie & Elis.)
> 5212: RUDOLPH b say 1790; m 1820 BOLLY G. ROSENCRANTZ

5135: JOHN KESSLER jr. - pr. born ca 1730 to 1745; died at Minden NY (DAR vol 116 page 149); m 1763 GERTRUDE HELMER dau of ADAM HELMER & MARGARET. Pvt. in Col. Bellinger's Revol. Regiment. John Kessler jr. & wife Gertrude sponsored Nov 1763 bp of Margaret, dau of Frederick Helmer & Barbara Elisabeth. Green's History of Ft. Plain has a John Casler as Revolutionary soldier (a John and Thomas Kessler were in Campbell's Rangers), resident of Minden NY, with children Jacob, Adam, Philip, Nicholas & Anna.

> +5213: NICHOLAS b GF 5 Mar 1764 (sp Nic. Kessler & Elis. Helmer)
> 5214: ADAM b 7 Oct 1765 (sp Adam Helmer & w. Maria <Barsh>)
>   pr. the ADAM died 1845; m MARIA SITTS (Sutz)

                    children of John & Gertrude cont.
+5215: JOHANNES JOH. b SAR 14 Jan 1768 (sp Con. Folts, Elis. Keslr)
              m 1788 CATHERINE G. NELLIS (Helmer book page 24)
   5216: CATHERINE b 15 Feb 1770 (sp Hen. Helmer, Cath. Shoemaker)
+5217: JACOB (twin) 1770-1857 m ANNA SITTS (Sutz)
   5218: pr. PHILIP JOH. b GF 29 Apr 1777 (sp Phil. Helmer, .. Harter)
   5219: ANNA b GF 16 May 1779 (sp. Fred. Helmer & Maria Elis.)

5129: JOSEPH KESSLER - pr. born 1745 to 1760; m by 1778 MARGARET BRAUN (her name
from 1789 St. Johnsville rec.). In Revolutionary service. Joseph & Marg. were
sponsors for Nov 1788 bp of Margaret, dau of Valentin Miller & Maria. Pr. the
Joseph on 1790 Palatine NY census (1-2-3), listed near Nicholas Kessler.

   5220: MARIA ELISABETH b 26 Aug 1778 (sp John Everts & M. Elis.)
   5221: JOHANNES b GF 25 Sep 1780 (sp. John Keslr & Cath. Elis.)
   5222: CHARLOTTE b GF 24 Aug 1783 (sp Dines Hollebold & Charlotte)
              pr m FPL 1805 ANDREW HERWICH
   5223: NICHOLAS b 14 Jul 1786 (sp Nic. Braun & Anna Bellinger)
   5224: FREDERICK bp SJR 23 Feb 1789 (sp Fr. Bellinger & Cath.)
   5225: JACOB bp 9 Apr 1792 (sp. Jac. Zimmerman & Magdalena)

5127: MELCHIOR KESSLER (Sr.) - born ca 1744; died Herkimer NY 10 May 1819 (age
75); m SAR 18 Feb 1766 MARIA ELISABETH PETRIE (b 1748, d 1839). In militia 1769
and in Col. Bellinger´s Revol. Regm. German Flats church records show a Delia,
dau of Melchior, who had a son Adam born 1 Jan 1787 (sp Dietrich Petrie & Elis.
Petrie) - that seems to have Melchert & Maria Elisabeth with two daughters named
Delia (one born ca 1771 the other in 1780). Possible alternatives are - (1) one
of the daughters is misnamed in the church record of 1780 or 1787 <seems most
likely>; or (2) a Melchert (Jr.), who may also have married a Maria Elisabeth is
the father of the second Delia (this seems less likely since no "Melchert Jr." is
seen designated as such. However it could be supported by the 1802 bp sponsors for
Abraham, son of John Melc. Kessler, who appear to be listed as "uncle and aunt").
Pr. the Mindert listed on 1790 Herkimer census (2-1-8).

   5226: ANNA b 4 Jun 1766 (sp. Anna Petrie, Joh. Eysaman)
              m 1788 NICHOLAS KEMPLIN
   5227: MARGARET b SA 7 Feb 1770 (sp Con. Kesler, Dan. Petrie)
              m 1786 JOHN WITHERSTINE
   5228: dau (DELIA ?) b say 1771; had child in 1787
   5229: pr. CATHERINE b say 1773; m GF 22 Nov 1791 THOMAS RANKIN
   5230: MARIA b 11 Apr 1776 (sp. Joh. Dietrich Petrie & Cath.)
+5231: JOHANNES b GF 16 Jan 1778 (sp Peter Keslr & Margaret)
              m by 1803 MAGDALENA SEGHNER
   5232: DELIA b 20 Mar 1780 (sp. Peter Folts & Barbara <Rasbach>)
   5233: DOROTHEA b GF 20 Dec 1782 (sp Conrd Schaefr & Doro.<Grim>)
   5234: MARIA ELISABETH b 14 May 1784 (sp Hen. Glock); pr. d y
   5235: ELISABETH b GF 14 May 1786 (sp Jac. Nic. Kessler & Delia)
   5236: MAGDALENA MELC. b say 1788; liv. 1805 (Hkmr Ch. Confirm.)
              ps. the Lena b GF May 1788 of "Jacob" & Maria Elisabeth
   5237: MARCUS b GF 19 Aug 1790 (sp John Kessler & Elis.)

5117: MICHAEL KESSLER - pr. born ca 1720 to 1749; in militia 1767.

   5239: ps. GERTRUDE b say 1769; m JESSE KIMBALL (dau Elis. b 1788)
+5238: ps. MICHAEL b ca 1771; liv. 1850 (age 79)

                              -155-

5136: NICHOLAS KESSLER - pr. born ca 1745 to 1752 (supposedly was a brother of Conrad, HCH Kessler file); m by 1788 DELIA SALTSMAN b 29 Dec 1759) dau of HENRICH SALTSMAN & MARIA ELISABETH WAGNER. A Nicholas was in 1767 GF militia and on 1790 Palatine NY census (1-1-3), next to Henry Saltsman.

     5240: ps. EVA b say 1775 (dau of Nich., Conn. Nutmegger, Dec 82)
               m Minden NY 1791 ELIAS GARLOCK (son of Carl)
     5240A DIETRICH b say 1777 (Leetham, "Families of The Mohawk Valley")
     5241: JOHN b SA 10 Aug 1788 (sp Fr. Godman & w Anna Eva)

5128: PETER KESSLER - pr. born ca 1737 to 1755; died as a Revolutionary soldier in the military ambush near Ft. Plain NY 18 Jul 1781; pr. m by 1777 MARGARET WOHLEBEN a dau of HENRICH WOHLEBEN (the Peter Casler killed in 1781 was named as a brother-in-law by Peter Hen. Wohleben). His widow m2 at German Flats 12 May 1784 DAVID SCHUYLER. A Peter was in Col. Bellinger´s Revol. Regm. and probably the same Peter was listed in Col. Campbell´s regiment as having died in action in the American Revolution (Book of Names, page 138).

     5242: ps. JOHN P. b say 1764; in Revol. service
     5243: ps. JACOB 1773-1854 m ELIZABETH JAC. WOHLEBEN (b 1787)
     5244: CONRAD b GF 3 Oct 1777 (sp. Conrad Kslr, Margaret Kslr)
     5245: JOHANNES b GF 20 Dec 1778 (sp. Hen. Wohleben & Margaret)
     5246: PETER b GF 14 Sep 1780 (sp. Geo. Laux, Elis. Herkimer)

5133: THOMAS KESSLER - pr. born ca 1734 to 1740; m pr by 1760 MARGARET KREMER (her surname on 1780 Schenectady bp rec., b 8 Feb 1743, d FPL Apr 1810, had 5 sons & 7 daughters). In 1757 Thomas was listed in the German Flats militia. Then in 1763 he was in Capt. Van Alstine´s militia unit and in 1767 in Capt. Mark Petrie´s GF Co. (name follows John and Joseph Cremer). On 1790 Canajoharie census (1-2-4).

     5247: pr. JOHN T. b say 1761; in Col. Bellinger´s Revol. Regm.
     5248: dau b ca 1763, d FPL Feb 1811; m Mr. YOUNG
     5249: pr. ELISABETH JOH. THOMAS b say 1765;
               m German Flats 18 Nov 1784 IMMANUEL TOOL
     5250: HENRICH b SAR 21 Sep 1767 (sp Hen. Kayser, Maria Jung)
               m SA 1791 ELISABETH SEEBER (1773-1807)
     5251: ANNA EVA THOM. b say 1772; m 1789 HENRY WIL. SEEBER
     5252: ps. PETER b say 1777; m by 1809 CATHERINE ... (FPL bp)
     5253: MARIA bp Schenectady 29 Oct 1780 (of Thom. & Marg.<Kremer>)
     5254: ANNA b GF 10 Nov 1783 (sp Jost Kramer & Anna Gilly)
     5255: ANNA b 27 Nov 1785 ; d SA 26 Jan 1790
     5256: ps. NICHOLAS b say 1787; m by 1809 CATHERINE ... (FPL bp)
     5257: ps. MARGARET (Peggy) b say 1789; m FPL 1807 JOHN COCHRAN

5132: ELISABETH JOH. KESSLER - pr. born ca 1750 to 1762; was sponsor, with Jacob Crantz, for bp Mar 1776 of Johannes, son of Jost Petrie & Catherine.

5120: MARGARET JACOB KESSLER - born ca 1750; died 20 Jul 1829 (age 79); m German Flats 22 Sep 1785 JOHANNES BURGDORFF (b Koenigsberg Ger. ca 1759, d Little Falls NY 7 Feb 1837 age ca 78). Possibly the Margaret who had a daughter Anna Eva born 14 Mar 1779 (bp. sp. Peter Flack & Sophia).

5214: ADAM KESSLER - born Oct 1765 (Morrison "Revol. Soldiers of Tryon County has birthyear as 1764 <pr. wrong as death age computes to 1765>, son of John & Gertrude); died 10 Mar 1846 (age 81); m German Flats NY 2 Oct 1787 MARIA SUTZ (b 1764, d 1848) dau of PETER SUTZ & JULIANA.   Ref. for dates and marriage is "Revolutionary Soldiers of Tryon County NY" by James F. Morrison jr.   Poss. also the Adam in service at Battle of Oriskany in 1777. Leetham ms. names wife and gives children as John A., Adam, Jacob, Nicholas, Isaac, Elisabeth, Anna, Peter A. (b 17 Jun 1797, m CATH. FOX), and Mary (b 21 Jun 1799).

5207: ADOLPH JOH. KESSLER - born 4 Aug 1779; pr. m by 1801 DOROTHY EYSAMAN dau of JOHN EYSAMAN & ELISABETH KESSLER.   Had Eva (b 1802, sp Cath. & Peter Eysaman), ps. Juhriel (1806, sp John Eysaman & Maria Elis.), John (1812, sp widow Elis. Casler <ps. Elis. Petrie, widow of the John Kessler who died in 1805>), Ira (1818, sp Melchior Rankin & w. Anna).

5197: CHRISTOPHER KESSLER - born 1782 (son of John J.); died 8 Aug 1822 age 40-6-; m Jun 1809 MAGDALENA UHLE dau of HENRY UHLE.   Had Luana (b 1812, sp John J. Casler & w Maria), John Sandford, Caty Maria, George Silvester, & M Magdalena.

5258: DIETRICH JACOB KESSLER - pr. born ca 1758 to 1770; m1 GF 15 Jan 1788 CATHERINE RANCKIN; ps. m2 1799 MARGARET CASLER.   This Dietrich, husband of Cath. Rankin, covered in prior generation.(believe he was grandson of immigrant John).

5180: DIETRICH KESSLER - born German Flats NY 29 Jul 1778 (son of Jacob & Delia and shown as son of Jacob N. on mar. record in 1803); died Little Falls NY 7 Oct 1833 (age 55-2-18); m Herkimer NY 1 Feb 1803 ELISABETH KESSLER (Casler) dau of JACOB J. KESSLER. Sponsors at marriage were Nich. Kessler (groom's brother) and Joh. Frederick Casler (bride's brother).

5259: DIETRICH KESSLER - pr. born ca 1770 to 1780; m by 1801 ANNA EVA SNELL.   Had dau Maria Elisabeth (b Herk. 23 Oct 1801, sp. Lena Kessler, John Burgdorf).

5179: JACOB JAC. KESSLER - pr. born ca 1766 to 1768 (bp SAR 14 Sep 1768); died by Mar 1809; m GF 3 Feb 1789 RACHEL VETTERLY pr. dau of HENRICH VETTERLY & EVA. Identified as "Jacob Jac." on 1789 bp record and as "Jacob J. N." on estate admin. records dated 6 Mar 1809 which give admin. to Rachel (pr. wife) and bond to Rachel Casler, Peter Fedderly, and John Bellinger.

> **5260:** JACOB b GF 28 Sep 1789 (sp Jac Kesler & Delia)
> **5261:** HENRICH b 10 Oct 1790 (sp Hen Walrad, M. Eva Vetterle widow)
> **5262:** NICHOLAS b 31 Jul 1792 (sp Nic. Keslr & Gertr.)
> **5263:** JAMES (Ciems) b 1 Jun 1794 (sp Jo Keslr, Maria Vetterly)
> **5264:** LEWI b 6 Feb 1806 (sp Jos. Casler, Magd. unm)

5170: JACOB KESSLER (Casler) - pr. born ca 1770 to 1785 (son of Jacob J. as given on mar. rec.); m Herkimer NY 22 Nov 1807 DOROTHY MEYER (b ca 1785, d 22 Jan 1815 age 30) dau of JOSEPH MEYER of Warren NY.   Possibly this was the Jacob Jr. whose estate admin. in 1816 lists children Matthew, Joseph, Silvester & Betsy and executors Fred. Casler and Joseph Meyer jr.

5217: JACOB KESSLER - born 1770; died Orleans (Jefferson Co) NY 18 Aug 1857 (age 87-6-3); m FPL 12 Nov 1793 ANNA SITTS (Nancy, pr. b ca 1764, d 26 Jun 1855 age 91), Leetham ms. says she was ANNA SUTZ (b 13 Sep 1767) dau of PETER SUTZ & JULIANA but 1767 SAR bp rec. gives the name Anna Eva. Children - John (b 22 Mar 1794, m MARY A. CASLER), Maria (b 21 Jun 1796, m JAMES BAUDER), Peter (b 12 Jan 1799), Jacob, ABRAHAM (1803-1856 m 1821 ELISABETH JORDAN <b 1802> DAR #115473), and Nicholas (b 18 Jun 1808, m MAGDALENA FOX).

5195: JOHN KESSLER - pr. the John Born 7 Feb 1777 (son of John J.); m by 1804 MARIA KESSLER. Had son Jost (bp HK 12 Aug 1804, sp. Diet. Caesler).

5215: JOHANNES JOHN KESSLER - pr. the John born 14 Jan 1768 (son of John); m GF 12 Jan 1788 CATHERINE G. NELLIS dau of GEORGE NELLIS & MARIA ELISABETH. Helmer book has him as son of John & Gertrude (Helmer) but Green's History has no adult son John for that John & Gertrude of Minden NY. Pr. the father of JOHN (b 2 Dec 1789, sp. Geo. Nellis & Mar. Cath.), ELISABETH (b ca 1796, dau of John J. Casler, age 16 at HK church confirmation in 1812) and JOHN (b ca 1800, son of John J., age 15 at HK confirmation in 1815).

5231: JOHANNES M. KESSLER - born GF 16 Jan 1778 (son of Melchior); m by 1803 MAGDALENA SEGHNER. Had Catherine (b Aug 1803, sp Thomas Rankin & Cath.), Maria Elisabeth (sp Melc. Casler & Maria Elis.), Abraham (1807, sp Conrad Seghner & Magdalena Pfeiffer, uncle & aunt), Magdalena (1810, sp James Rankin & Magdalena Casler), Melchior (1812, sp Th. Vetterle & w.), Maria Margaret (1817, sp F. Casler & w. Marg.), Eva (1819, sp Jost Eysaman & w. Anna), & Jacob (b 1823, d 1829).

5265: JOHANNES KESSLER - pr. born ca 1765 to 1774 (ps. the John born Nov 1770, son of Jacob Joh. Kessler); m GF May 1792 CATHERINE SEGNER dau of PAUL SEGNER & ELISABETH EYSAMAN. Had Elisabeth (b 4 Jan 1794, sp. Con. Segner & Marg.) and ps. George (b ca 1798, son of John, age 16 at HK confirmation in 1814).

5185: Johan JOST KESSLER - pr. the Joseph born GF 9 Sep 1783 (son of Jacob N. & Delia); m by 1802 MAGDALENA MILLER ps. dau of NICHOLAS MILLER. Had son Dietrich (b Jan 1802, sp. Diet. Kessler & Margaret Ryan), Delia (bp HK 10 Jun 1804, sp. Peter, Jacob, & Delia Casler), and pr. Nicholas (son of Jost & Lena, b FPL 7 Oct 1808, sp. Nich. Kessler & Gertrude). We presume the 1802 father was this Johan Joseph (i.e. ornamental Johan) rather than say a John, son of Jost.

5178: MARCUS JAC. KESSLER - born 26 Apr 1766; died 11 Sep 1841; m GF 8 Jul 1788 DELIA PETRIE (d ca 1800) dau of DIETRICH PETRIE & CATHERINE BELLINGER. On 1790 German Flats census (1-0-4). Children listed in Petrie book, page 18.

> **5266:** DELIA   1788-1854 m 1811 JOSEPH BELLINGER
> **5267:** CATHERINE b Little Falls NY; d 21 Mar 1876
> **5268:** DIETRICH b GF Sep 1791 (sp Stopel Bellinger, Cath. Diet. Petrie)
>   ps the RICHARD M. b 1793; liv. 1850 Little Falls NY
> **5269:** JOHANNES b GF 29 Jul 1794 (sp John Bellinger & Cath.)
> **5270:** pr. PETER M. b GF 31 Oct 1795 (sp. Peter Kessler & Jean)

5169: MARCUS KESSLER - pr. born ca 1765 to 1775; m Ft. Plain NY 1793 ELSABETH WAGGONER. Had son Abraham (b FPL 3 Jul 1810, sp. Melchior Bauder & Anna).

5238: MICHAEL KESSLER - pr. born ca 1771; liv. 1850 (age 79). Notes in Casler file at Herk. Co. Hist. Soc. indicate a Michael Casler had brothers Jacob and Conrad, and a sister who was in the 1778 Cherry Valley massacre. Pr. had son MICHAEL M. b ca 1809, d Oswego NY Feb 1877 (age 68)

5177: NICHOLAS KESSLER - born 3 Nov 1763 (pr. son of Jacob, not John as in Helmer book); died 21 Mar 1828; m1 1782 GERTRUDE BELLINGER (b 1764, d 5 Apr 1821) dau of Col. PETER BELLINGER & DELIA HERKIMER; m2 Herkimer NY 12 Dec 1821 POLLY MILLER dau of CALEB MILLER of Danube NY. Estate admin. in 1828 lists heirs as Peter P., Richard N., Robert, Nicholas N., Christopher B., John, Myron, Polly (wife of Henry Heath), & Lana (wife of Joseph Heath). Children from Petrie book, page 15. Pr. on Canajoharie NY census (1-1-2) next to H. Bell & P. Bellinger.

          5272: DELIA   b 28 Jan 1783 (sp Marc Petrie, Cath Petrie <widow>)
                         m 1811 JOST BELLINGER
          5273: PETER BELLINGER b GF 15 Jan 1785 (Pet. Bellinger & Christina)
                         m 1805 BETSY S. EYSAMAN
          5274: ANNA EVA   b 28 Jan 1787
                         (bp sp Jacob Kessler & Delia P. Bellinger)
          5275: LENA   b 26 Oct 1789 (dau of Nicholas Jac.); Confirmed 1804
                         Lena N. m HK 1807 JACOB VROOMAN
          5276: CATHERINE   b 14 Dec 1791 (sp Jost P Bellinger, Eva Gemmel)
                         ps. d 1819 (age 27) as wife of Mr. CRONKHITE
          5277: MARIA   b 17 Oct 1793 (sp Stophel Bellinger, Cath. Petrie)
          5278: RICHARD N.   b 1797; m JANE YOUNG
          5279: NICHOLAS jr b say 1800; m POLLY STARING
          5280: ROBERT   b GF 27 Sep 1802
          5281: CHRISTOPHER   b 10 Jun 1805
          5282: ESTHER   b 1806
          5283: JOHN P.   b 1807; m1 BETSY STEELE
          5284: MYRON   b say 1809; liv. 1818

5213: NICHOLAS KESSLER - born GF 5 Mar 1764 (son of John & Gertrude); pr. m by 1802 ANNA ...   Pr. the Nicholas who sponsored, with Anna, 1802 bp of son of Jacob Kessler & Anna (Sitts). Ps. the Nicholas John Kessler on 1790 Canajoharie NY census (1-0-2) next to Peter & Henry Sutz.

5209: NICHOLAS JOH. KESSLER - pr. born 16 Feb 1781 (son of John & Elis.); m 2 Jan 1804 ELIZABETH EIGENAUER dau of CONRAD EIGENAUER. Marriage wit. was Dietrich Kessler, and the same Jan 1804 date, a Nicholas Casler & wife Elizabeth sponsored bp of Aaron, son of Aaron Butterfield & Delia (Casler).

5285: NICHOLAS KESSLER - pr. born ca 1770 to 1787; m by 1808 ANNA EVA ... (b ca 1787, d 9 Mar 1808 age 21-0-11).

5181: PETER J. KESSLER - born say 1771; m GF 2 Oct 1792 JEAN RANKIN (Jenny).

          5286: DIETRICH   b 27 May 1793 (sp Diet. Kesler & Cath.)
          5287: JAMES   b GF Jun 1795 (sp Jac. Kessler & Rachel)
          5288: MARIA   b HK 19 Aug 1802 (sp Th. Rankin & Cath.)
          5289: BARENT   b HK 23 Jun 1804 (sp Anna Volzen, unm)
          5290: PETER   b HK 4 Jul 1806 (sp John Rasbach & w. Anna)
          5291: ELISABETH b HK 7 May 1808 (sp Pet. P Folts, Elis.Young, unm)
          5292: WILHELM   b 29 Apr 1810 (sp James Rankin & Delia)

5143: MAGDALENA KESSLER - b say 1775; m JACOB SAYMON. Had Isam (James?, b Manlius NY Sep 1800, sp John Dietrich Casler & Cath. Casler, both of GF).

********** KORSING (CURRING) **********

KORSING - 1st Generation

5301: RUDOLPH KORSING - born in Germany ca 1660 (age 50 in 1710, Book of Names page 121); liv. in New York 1721; m DELIA ... (b ca 1660, liv. 1721). He was from Hellstein, Duchy of Isenburg, Germany, as given in Bellinger book page 18. His family was called "Korning" on the 1710 list of Palatines remaining (hospitalized) at New York and included himself (Ludolph, age 50), Otilia (age 50), Catharina (age 16), Anna Dorothea (age 15) and Conrad (age 7). Appears as "Ludolph Coring" on Gov. Hunter's NY Palatine subsistence list in 1710 (6A,1Y) and in 1712 (3A,1Y) and he was naturalized as "Johan Ludolph Corning" at Albany on 31 Jan 1716. His name appears on the Sep 1721 minutes of the Albany council meeting preparatory to the Burnetsfield Patent grant, upon which he received lot#29 and his wife Delia received lot#13 (both on the south side of the Mohawk River).

surname KORSING
```
   5302: JOHANNA ELISABETH  b 1688; m CHRISTOPHER FOX
 +5303: CATHERINE  b ca 1694; m 1711 JOHANNES HESS
   5304: DOROTHY  b ca 1695; m ca 1714 THOMAS SHOEMAKER
   5305: CONRAD  b ca 1703 (age 7 in 1710)
```

KORSING - 2nd Generation

5303: Anna CATHERINE KORSING - born ca 1694 (age 16 in 1710, dau of Ludolst Curring); m 29 Aug 1711 JOHANNES HESS. Her marriage record ("Book of Names" page 43) gives her family's original location in Germany as Hellstein, earldom Isenburg.

LANT - 1st Generation

5351: VALENTINE LANT (var. Velte or Felte) - pr. born ca 1655 to 1675; pr. liv.
1709 and died enroute to NY in 1710; m ANNA CATHERINE ... We assume he was the
"Felte Lankr", with wife and five children, in the fifth party of Palatines
transported from Holland to England in July 1709 (Knittle's "The Early Palatine
Immigration" page 267). He and one or more children probably died on the ill-fated
Atlantic crossing and we find the widow Anna Catherine Lant as the only one of
this surname on the NY Palatine subsistence lists in 1710 (3A,1Y) and 1712
(5A,0Y). It appears from the dependent count in 1710 that she had three children
living with her then and by 1712 may have taken another in, or back. She is
missing from the 1717 Simmendinger census but apparently not due to remarriage
because by 1723 she appears, still as widow Anna Catherine Lant, in receipt of a
primary head of household lot (#13) on the Burnetsfield Patent, in the select
strip of properties on the north of the Mohawk River which constitute the present
town area of Herkimer New York. Also receiving a head of household lot (#3) in
this select strip was Johan Velde Lant. The third presumed member of this family
on the 1723 Burnetsfield Patent was Anna Velde Lant, probably wife of Johan Velde
Lant, who received a dependent area lot (#2), on the northern bank of the Mohawk
River, somewat west of the town area lots.

We assume the offspring include a son Valentine (i.e. the Burnetsfield
patentee Johan Velde) and probably daughters Christina (who married George Adam
Smith) and the Margaret Land who was a sponsor, with Nicholas Wohleben, for 1716
bp of Nicholas, son of Henrich Spohn & Catherine (Wohleben). There were not very
many Lant sound-alike Palatines but we will mention a "Christian Lang" who was
naturalized at Albany 17 Jan 1716 (near in list to Mathys Coens & Joh. George
Smith) who was perhaps related to the Magadalena Langin on the 1710 NY Palatine
subs. list.

surname LANT

5352: pr. CHRISTINA b say 1692; m ca 1712 GEORGE ADAM SMITH
+5353: Johan VALENTINE (Velde) b say 1695; m by 1722 ANNA ...
5354: pr. MARGARET b say 1701; liv. 1716 (spf Spohn bp)
ps. before 1723 m NICHOLAS WOHLEBEN

LANT - 2nd Generation

5353: Johan VELDE LANT - pr. born ca 1692 to 1700; liv. 1773 at Claverak NY
(will date then, probated 1791); pr. m1 by 1722 ANNA ... ; m (2nd?) ELISABETH
...(apparently liv. 1773). "Johan Velde Lant" received Burnetsfield lot #3 and we
think his first name was Valentine preceded by the ornamental Johan - this
assumption is based on a close reading of the names as transcribed on various
Burnetsfield maps (a recommended copy can be found in Vosburgh's Records of the
Reform Dutch of German Flats, vol. 3) and is very important to resolving the
identity of the various Lant patentees at Burnetsfield. We then conclude that he
was married to the "Anna Velde Lant" holding Burnetsfield lot# 2 (with the Velde
in her name referring to wife of, rather than daughter of, a Velde Lant). Our
basis for this conclusion is that female patentees seem to have been either wives
or widows (we do not know of any daughters receiving lots). Lant family
researcher Mrs. Emanuel <Laurel A.> Mussman (6 Winmar Crescent, New Hartford NY

13413) has found his name written later as Johannis Velte, which may have been his own alteration (there are other cases known of slight name changes amongst the early Palatines).

Children listed below are courtesy of Mrs. Mussman, who has found that the marriage records of two of the children below (Valentine and Catherina) have their birthplace as Burnetsfield, so evidently Johan Velde lived there with his family at least till about 1740. He must have moved back east shortly thereafter as two of his sons were married near Albany in 1746-7, these being Johannes jr., who married in 1746 at Loonenburg (Greene Co.) and Frederick, who married in 1747 at Germantown (Columbia Co.). We have retained the birthyear estimates as given by Mrs. Mussman, which she based on the order of children as listed in Johannes Velte's will, although we hold open the possibility for another early child (particulary a daughter, born say 1720 to 1725) to have reached maturity and married before the family left German Flats.

children of Johan Velde Lant
5355: FREDERICK b say 1724; m 1747 CHRISTINA SCHMIDT
5356: JOHANNIS jr (sic) b say 1726; m 1746 SARAH WINNE
5357: ELIZABETH b say 1729; m pr. ca 1754 JACOB KAERTER
5358: LAURENCE b say 1732; m 1761 CHRISTINA SCHULT
5359: VELTON (Valentine) b say 1735; m 1758 ELIZABETH PHILIP
5360: CATHARINA b say 1739; m 1758 JOHANNES ROORBACH
5361: MARIA b say 1742; m 1758 ANDRIES MARIS (Morris)
5362: JEREMIAS b say 1748; m 1768 CATHARINA MAUL
(later moved to Delaware Co. NY)

LANT - 3rd Generation

The Lant family appears to have remained till the late 1700's in the area of Claverack, Columbia Co., NY. Although there are closely similar names, such as Landman, Lentz, Lent, etc., in the Tryon Co. militia lists of the Revolutionary period, this Lant family does not not seem to figure further in the Mohawk Valley.

********** LEIPER (Lepper) **********

5401: JACOB LIPPER - born, pr. in Germany, ca 1679 (age 30 on 1709 London list of Palatines). Being Catholic, he pr. did not come to New York with the 1710 immigrants. No further record.

5405: PHILIP HERMAN LEPPER - pr. born in Germany before 1690 (name on 5th London list of Palatines in 1709); pr. died in 1710 Atlantic crossing ; m ... His widow was on NY Palatine subsistence in 1710 (1A,0Y) & in 1712 (2A,0Y).

LEIPER - 2rd Generation

5402: CONRAD LEIPER - pr. born before 1720; m MARGARET ... (Shults book page 29). Lepper file at Herkimer Co. Historical Soc. has notes relating Conrad as father of Honnes (pr. John) who married Elisabeth Barlet. Dockstader book (page 43) has Jacob and Wigand as brothers of Sophia (who married Jost Snell).

             surname LEIPER
    +5406: JACOB C. b say 1737; m 1761 SABINA DOCKSTADER
     5407: ps. ANNA b say 1739; m 1762 GEORGE DANNER
    +5408: JOHN (HONNES) b say 1741; m by 1773 ELISABETH BARLET
     5409: SOPHIA b ca 1743; spf Isaac Paris 1761 bp; d 1832 (age 88)
              m1 1766 JOST F. SNELL (d 1777); m2 JOHN HELWIG
    +5410: WIGAND 1746-1839 m1 1770 MARGARET GARLOCK

5403: FREDERICK LEIPER - pr. born before 1725; m1 ...; m2 SAR 24 Feb 1762 DELIA ... widow of Jost DeMuth. Early birthdate for this Frederick is needed for a father of Anna Fr. who had child in 1761. Pr. the Frederick, who with Paul Crim, was an early settler at Andrustown in the 1750´s.

    5411: pr. ANNA FR. b say 1743; had child bp SAR May 1761
    +5412: ps. JACOB b say 1757; m by 1783 ANNA ...

5404: JACOB LEIPER - born say 1730 (existence assumed as father of Fred. Jac.)

    +5413: FREDERICK JAC. b say 1755; m MARIA (b ca 1756)

LEIPER - 3rd Generation

5413: FREDERICK JAC. LEIPER - pr. born ca 1740 to 1757 (called Fred. Jac. on 1787 GF bp rec.); m by 1777 MARIA ... (pr. b ca 1756, age 24 in ca 1780). His wife Maria (age 24) & son Frederick (age 1 year) were taken captive in the Revolution (date uncertain but pr. about 1780 <Book of Names, page 114>). On the 1790 German Flats census (2-2-4) near Hen. Crim & Gratus Bulson.

    5414: JACOB b 9 Jun 1777 (sp Jacob Lepper, Elis. Hayger)
    5415: FREDERICK b say 1779; prisoner (at age 1) ca 1780
    5416: ps. CATHERINE b say 1781; m by 1807 HENRY BULSON
    5417: JOHANNES b GF 30 Apr 1787 (sp Thom. Shoemaker & Elis.)
    5417A MARGARET b GF 3 Jun 1791 (sp Hen. Crim & Margaret)
    5418: MARIA b 22 Nov 1793 (sp Geo. Fred. Hayer & M. Elis.<Starin>)

5406: JACOB LEIPER - pr. born ca 1740 to 1745 (son of Conrad, as given on mar. rec.); pr. the Jacob killed at Oriskany Aug 1777; m SAR 24 Feb 1761 SABINA DOCKSTADER dau of CHRISTIAN DOCKSTADER. Jacob, son of Conrad, sponsored Feb 1760 bp of Maria Catherine, dau of Fred. Miller & Maria Eva.

    5419: CHRISTIAN b SAR 5 Feb 1762 (sp Adam Emgie, Elis. Dockstader)
+5420: JOHN b SAR 22 May 1763 (sp John Walrath, Anna Dockstdr)
        m by 1778 MARGARET ROTNOUR
    5421: MARIA MARGARET b 26 May 1764 (sp Sophia Lepper, Jost Snell)
    5422: SOPHIA b say 1765; d Mar 1851; m 1787 GEORGE SALTSMAN
    5423: ANNA b 26 Jan 1767 (sp Anna Sabina & Wm Nellis)
    5424: CATHERINE ELIS. b 12 Mar 1768 (sp Cath. & Isaac Paris)
        m 1784 JOHN CASSELMAN
+5425: JACOB b SAR 30 Sep 1769 (sp John Lepper & Maria Getman)
    5426: ANNA MARGARET b SAR Jan 1771 (sp Wiand Lepper & w. Marg.)

5412: JACOB LEIPER - pr. born ca 1750 to 1760; m by 1783 ANNA ...

    5427: JACOB b GF 16 Feb 1783 (sp. Abrhm V Deusen, Anna Sillabach)

5408: JOHN LEIPER (Honnes) - pr. born ca 1735 to 1752; m by 1770 ELISABETH BARLET pr. dau of WOLFGANG BARLET & BARBARA of Canajoharie. Ps. the John on 1790 Fonda NY census (1-1-4) next to Henry Seber. Children (HCH Leiper file).

    5428: MARIA b Fonda NY 14 Jul 1770 (sp Jac. Leiper, Mar. Hoak)
    5429: CONRAD b Fonda NY 4 Jan 1773 (sp Geo. Ad. Dockstr & Eva)
        m 1799 AIGINETTE CRUMWELL
    5430: MARGARET b 12 Jun 1776 (sp. Hen. Seerver)
        m 1796 HENRY VANDERWERKEN
    5431: MARIA b 14 Jul 1779; m 1807 PETER V. PUTMAN

5410: WIGAND LEIPER - born GF 14 Mar 1746 (Martin's Snell book page 21); died 13 Jan 1839; m1 SAR 13 Mar 1770 MARGARET GARLOCK (liv. 1788); m2 MARGARET SNELL (bp 1751) dau of JOHN SNELL & MARGARET FINK and widow of JACOB F. SNELL (d 1777). Appears on 1790 Palatine NY census (3-5-2).

    5432: JOST b SAR 6 Sep 1786 (sp. John Shults & w. Elis.<Sutz>)
    5433: ADAM b 26 Aug 1788 (sp Fred. Godman & w. Anna Eva)

LEIPER - 4th Generation

5420: JOHN LEIPER - born 1763 (son of John, Dockstader book page 125); m Palatine NY 1 Apr 1778 MARGARET RATENAUER (b Aug 1761) dau of GOTFRID RATENAUER. Pr. the John Leiper who joined Col. Willet's Revol. troops at age ca 15. Had son JACOB (b 5 Dec 1782, sp. Stofel W. Fox & Elis.<Hess>)

5425: JACOB LEIPER - born SAR 30 Sep 1769; m by 1795 CATHERINE ... (b ca 1760, died Herkimer NY 26 May 1859 age 99-3-17). Wife mentioned in 1810 will of Catherine Joh. Diefendorf, widow of John Windecker (Dockstader book page 127).

    5434: MARGARET b Minden NY 21 Feb 1795 (sp. John Leiper & Marg.)
    5435: SABINA b Minden 13 Feb 1805 (sp. Fr. Schuls & w. Sowina)

********** LENTZ **********

5451: JOHN LENTZ Sr. - pr. born ca 1725 to 1740; killed in action in the
Revolution; m ... (pr. CATHERINE). Pr. immigrated to NY ca 1764 with
Hasenclever's group at New Petersburg (E. Schuyler) NY. Lentz soldiers in
Bellinger's Regiment were John, John jr., Peter, & Jacob (Book of Names page 167).

                    surname LENTZ
    +5452: ps. GEORGE b say 1754; sup. liv. 1780
    +5453: pr. JACOB b say 1756; ml by 1782 CATHERINE ...
     5454: pr. JOHN jr b say 1758; POW in 1780 (no further record)
     5454A pr. ELISABETH b say 1760; m by 1778 MICHAEL WITRIG
     5454B ps. ANNA (Lentz?) b say 1762; m by 1781 JACOB BIRCKY
    +5455: pr. PETER b say 1764; m 1788 MARGARET RIEMA
     5456: CATHERINE b say 1766; m 1784 CONRAD FOLTS jr.
     5457: SARA b say 1768; unm in 1787 (spf Witrig bp); pr m GEO RIEMA
     5458: pr. BARBARA b say 1770; liv. 1794 (spf F. Lentz bp)
    +5459: PHILIP b say 1772; m 1791 MARIA RINCKEL

                    LENTZ - 2nd Generation

5452: GEORGE LENTZ - Supposedly he & a son George jr. were captured in the 1780
Tory raid on New Petersburg (Hatch papers) but no sign of George is seen in church
or militia records (ps. a name mix-up and should be John & John jr.).

5453: JACOB LENTZ - pr. born ca 1755 to 1760; m CATHERINE...; pr. m2 GF 24 Jul
1794 ELISABETH RIEMA. Jacob Lentz & Catherine sponsored Jun 1791 bp of Cath., dau
of John Court & Latty. Jacob served at Oriskany in 1777 and was on the 1790
German Flats census (1-2-3) living near Henry Frank & Andrew Bell.

    5460: CATHERINE b 26 Dec 1782 (sp John Jukker, Cath. Lentz)
    5461: HENRICH b GF 29 Mar 1785 (sp Hen. Frank & Gertrude)
    5462: MARGARET b GF 8 Mar 1787 (sp Pet. Lentz, Marg. Riema)
    5463: ELISABETH b SJR 1 Aug 1791 (sp Mich. Witrig & Elisabeth)
               presumably by 2nd wife (Elisabeth)
    5464: JOHANNES b GF 11 Oct 1795 (sp Philip Lentz, Maria Lentz)

5455: PETER LENTZ - pr. born before 1772; m GF 15 Jan 1788 MARGARET RIEMA pr.
dau of JOHN RIEMA. On 1790 GF census (1-2-3, Frankfort area) near Conrad C Folts.

    5465: JOHN b GF 19 Apr 1790 (sp Philip Lentz, Elis. Riema)
               m 1814 MARIA H. MEYER
    5466: JACOB b GF 19 Apr 1792 (sp Jacob Bircky & Anna)
               m 1815 ELISABETH N. BAUMAN
    5467: CATHERINE b SJR 31 Oct 1793 (sp Pet. Riema, Cath. Hockstatr)
    5468: MARIA b say 1795; m 1814 DANIEL BREITENBACHER

5459: PHILIP LENTZ - b say 1772; m GF 25 Jan 1791 MARIA RINCKEL (wife listed as
Catherine on 1791 bp, pr. an error) pr. a dau of LORENTZ RINCKEL.

    5469: pr. CATHERINE b GF 4 May 1791 (sp Peter Lentz & Marg.)
    5470: JOHANNES b GF 29 Jul 1793 (sp Jac. D. Witrig & Cath Elis)
    5471: FREDERICK b GF 30 Dec 1794 (sp Fred. Riema, Barbara Lentz)

-165-

********** LIGHTHALL (Leithaal) **********

5501: ABRAHAM LIGHTHALL - pr. born ca 1690 to 1702; m by 1720 ANNA VAN DER
BOGART dau of CLAAS VAN DER BOGART. Lived at Schenectady NY (see Pearson´s "First
Settlers of Schenectady" page 105).

surname LIGHTHALL
     5502: ANNA bp Schenectady 18 Jun 1720
     5503: WILLEM bp 3 Feb 1722; m 1748 ELISABETH MARCELIS
+5504: NICHOLAS ("Claas") bp 7 Mar 1724
     5505: JACOB b 3 Jan 1726
+5506: ps. ABRAHAM 1735-1831 m CATHERINE BELLINGER
+5507: ps. GEORGE b say 1740; ml by 1777 MARGARET

LIGHTHALL - 2nd Generation

5506: ABRAHAM LIGHTHALL - born 14 Sep 1735; died 31 Dec 1831 age 96; m 12 Jul
1775 CATHERINE BELLINGER (b 1732, d 1843 age 110) dau of Capt. PETER BELLINGER.
Brothers Abraham, George & Nicholas were of a Schenectady family (Book of Names
page 171). On 1790 GF census (1-0-3). Children from Bellinger book page 34.

     5508: LENA 1776-1842 m DANIEL GIBBS (sp F. Bellinger & Lena)
     5509: ANNA MARGARET b 23 Jan 1783; m 1802 BENJAMIN HUNTLEY
     5510: ANNA ELISABETH b GF 15 Oct 1784 (sp. Fred Ittig, Elis. Frank)
     5511: CATHERINE b GF 2 Mar 1787 (sp. Peter Fr. Fox & Cath.)

5507: GEORGE LIGHTHALL - brother of Abraham.; ml MARGARET ...; m2 by 1788
CATHERINE ... On 1790 GF census (1-1-3).

     5512: MARIA b GF 21 Jun 1777 (sp Joh. Cunghm & Maria <Folts>)
     5513: MARIA BARBARA b GF 8 Jul 1787 (sp Lor. Ph. Harter & Barb.)
     5514: GEORGE b GF 24 Sep 1788 (sp Geo. Ittig & Delia <Petrie>)
     5515: ABRAHAM b GF 4 Jun 1793 (sp Abhm Leithal & Cath.)
     5516: CATHERINE b GF 11 Apr 1795 (sp Abhm A Wohleben, Lena Leithal)

5504: NICHOLAS LIGHTHALL - brother of Abraham; ps. the Nicholas bp Schenectady
NY 7 Mar 1724; m ca 1748 MARGARET EDICK (given as "Idich"). Nicholas Lighthall
Sr. had 2 adults & 1 child on 1778 German Flats relief (Book of Names page 117).

+5517: pr. NICHOLAS jr. b say 1750; pr. ml ELISABETH
     5518: JACOB bp Schenectady 14 May 1758
     5519: LANCASTER bp Schenectady 10 May 1761
     5520: WILLEM b say 1765; m SARAH MARCELIS

LIGHTHALL - 3rd Generation

5517: NICHOLAS LIGHTHALL - pr. born ca 1750 to 1760; ml by 1778 ELISABETH ...; m2
by 1790 CATHERINE ... Nicholas jr had 2 adults & 1 child on 1778 GF relief.

     5521: CATHERINE b GF 8 Mar 1778 (sp Tho. Gakkol & Cath.)
     5522: LENA b GF 9 Sep 1790 (sp Lud. Joh. Shmkr, Lena Joh. Bellngr)

********** MCGINNES (Magin) **********

5601: TIMOTHY MCGINNES ("Teddy") - pr. born ca 1705 to 1715 (son of William); died at Battle of Lake George in Sep 1755; m SARAH KAST (b 1713, d Fredericksburg Canada 9 Sep 1791) dau of GEORGE KAST Sr. & ANNA. He lived on the Sarah Maginnes patent, which extended from Oppenheim (Montgomery Co.) south to the Mohawk River and he held land in the Peter Winne Patent section of Herkimer Co. which he deeded to Simon Jacob Hilts. Timothy was engaged in fur trade with the Indians and his widow, who spoke the Iroquois language, continued to run his trading post with the help of her sons (HCH Kast ms.). This widow Sarah, being a Tory sympathizer, had her property confiscated and sold. In 1777, after being released from captivity at Fort Dayton, she fled to Canada and assisted in persuading the Indians to remain loyal to the British.

surname MCGINNES

5602: ANNA (Hannah) b say 1738; m HENRY WENDLE
5603: DOROTHY   b 1740; pr. m by 1761 JOHN THOMSON
5604: MARIA   b say 1742; m 1761 SIMON DEFOREST
5605: ELISABETH   b say 1746; liv. 1766 (spf Kast bp)
5606: CATHERINE   bp Albany NY 24 Apr 1748 (sp Rich & Sara Cartright)
         m 1770 ADAM JOS. STARING
5607: WILLIAM   bp Albany 1 Jun 1750; d ca 1777 in a fire (Kast ms.)
5608: MARGARET   bp Albany NY 28 Jun 1752
5609: GEORGE   bp Albany NY 12 Jun 1755; m by 1777 ANNA ...

5610: ROBERT MCGINNES - born ca 1710; died 22 Apr 1796 (age 86, NYGBR vol 106 page 113). Ps. the Robert who married at Kingston NY in 1736 Mary Brodhead. Robert, Richard, and John McGennis were brought before the Tryon Committee of Safety in October 1776 for making Loyalist statements. Robert's children include RICHARD (b ca 1745, d 1830 <age 84>, a Tory in Revol.), JOHN (b ca 1741, d 1833 age 92), and ALEXANDER. Ps. an earlier son was the man called William McGennis the Elder by the Tryon Co. Committee of Saftey in Oct 1776 when it ordered him and his sons to be apprehended as disaffected persons (Mohawk Valley in the Revolution, page 89).

5611: Capt. WILLIAM MCGINNES - pr. born ca 1705 to 1720; killed 7 Sep 1755 at the Battle of Lake George NY; m 21 Feb 1751 MARGARET VEEDER. Pr. a brother of the above Timothy & Robert. Only child was a son Alexander who died 13 Feb 1770 (Pearson's Schenectady book, page 109).

MCGINNES - 2nd Generation

5609: GEORGE MCGINNES - bp Trinty Church, Albany NY, 12 Jun 1755; m by 1777 ANNA... This was pr. the George (b 1751, d Bath, Ontario, Canada 1822) who m ANNA STARING (spouse and dates from "Loyalist Lineages of Canada", pg 436) and had children Timothy, William, Nancy, Cath., Mary, Sarah, George, Nicholas, Sarah, & Elisabeth. In 1775 his militia Captain, George Herkimer, was degraded for striking him. Despite his later Tory leanings we see him as pr. the Jurry McLonis in Col. Campbell's Regiment (Book of Names, pg 140) and the George supposedly wounded at the Oct 1780 Battle of Stone Arabia (Kast ms.).

5611: MARGARET   bp 25 May 1777 (sp Marg. Thomson, Hen. N. Staring)

5605: ELISABETH MCGINNES - pr. born ca 1745 to 1750; She sponsored, with John Thomson, 1766 bp of Catherine (b Jul 1765), dau of Fred Kast & Elisabeth (Helmer).

********** MCKOOM (Maccomb) **********

5701: **ANDREW MCKOOM** - born in Scotland ca 1740 (age 22 in 1762); pr. died Aug 1777 at Oriskany (Frank Duell assumption in 12 Jun 1929 E&N McCoombs article, based on absence of Andrew in later records); ps. ml ...; m2 SAR 13 Feb 1765 ANNA ELISABETH ... (pr. Hilts) widow of THOMAS BELL (ibid). On May 1762 Albany Co. militia enlistment he was described as a tailor, aged 22, stature 5 feet 4 1-2 inches, complexion fair, eyes blue, & hair black (ibid). In 1769 GF militia. Church marriage record in 1765 does not list Andrew as a widower so ps. Maria, wife of Jacob Weaver, was a sister rather than a daughter.

                           surname MCKOOM
        5702: pr. MARIA b say 1760; m ca 1776 JACOB G. WEAVER (b 1751)
                           by 2nd wife
       +5703: HELENA (Lena) b GF 23 Nov 1766 (sp Mar. Petrie, Geo. Hilts)
                      d 1833 (age 66-3-25); m 1789 JACOB F. HARTER
       +5704: GEORGE b 1768 (sp Geo. Hilts, Cath. Hilts); m ELIS. FOLTS
       +5705: SARA b Jun 1770 (sp. Sara <pr Hilts> & Smidt, mar. per.)
                      d 1839; m 1792 PHILIP L. HARTER
        5706: ANNA b say 1772; liv. 1785 (spf bp of Jac. G. Weber's dau)
       +5707: JOHN ca 1776-1849 m 1795 LENA FRANK

5708: **URIEL MCKOOM** - pr. born ca 1730 to 1745; died Aug 1777 at Oriskany; m SAR 9 Oct 1764 CHRISTINA FAILING. Mar. rec. says he was from New England.

       +5709: JOHN b say 1770; ml 1793 CATHERINE FRANK

5710: **MAGDALENA MCKOOM** - pr. born ca 1742 to 1749; m by 1768 LAWRENCE HARTER (b 1742, d 1815) son of LORENTZ HARTER (Harter book page 4). Perhaps Magdalena was a sister of the above Andrew as she seems too early to have been a daughter.

                           MCKOOM - 2nd Generation

5704: **GEORGE MCKOOM** - born 24 Jan 1768; died 1833; m 15 Dec 1789 ELISABETH FOLTS dau of JOST FOLTS & MARGARET BELLINGER (Bellinger book page 26). He was on the 1790 Herkimer census (1-0-1), near Hanyost Folts, and was ps. earlier at Brownsville (E&N of 6/12/1929). Sponsored Apr 1802 bp of Andreas, son of Jacob F. Harter & Helena. His children (15 May 1929 E&N article "The Third Scout") were ANDREW (b GF 31 May 1791, sp John Mckoom, Cath. Folts), MARIA (b 3 Jul 1793, sp Jacob G. Weaver & wife), JOST (b 8 Jun 1795, sp Jost Piper, Marg. Folts), JOHANNES (b 19 Oct 1804), MAGDALENA (b 16 Sep 1809), and MARGARET (b 15 Sep 1810).

5707: **JOHN MCKOOM** - born ca 1776; died 1849 age 73; m 27 Jan 1795 LENA FRANK. Was sponsor, with Maria Ad. Smith, for Jan 1793 bp of John, son of Jacob G. Weaver & Maria (McKoom). Had children George (b GF 11 Jun 1795, sp James Campbell & Elis. Frank), John, Appolonia (Abigail), Hannah, Andreas (b Frankfort NY 12 Jan 1802, sp Conrad Koch), Catherine (b 1804, sp Cath. Weber & John Clapsattle), Maria (b 1806), Sally (b 1808, sp Conrad Frank & w Sally Sletter), Wilhelm (b 1810, sp Fr. Meyer & w. Appolonia), George (b 1812, d Apr 1868), and Betsy (b ca 1814).

5709: **JOHN MCKOOM** - born say 1770; ml 4 Apr 1793 CATHERINE F. FRANK; m2 by 1800 MARGARET HERKIMER pr. dau of GEORGE HERKIMER & ALITA (ibid, Deuel). Had sons Patrick (b GF 7 Feb 1794) & Uriel (b 12 Jun 1800, sp Christina McCombs).

********** MEYER, Henry **********

5801: HENRICH MEYER - pr. born in Germany ca 1680 to 1690 (son of Johannes); m by 1711 ANNA KUNIGUNDA. No support seen for presumption in "Meyer Genealogy" by Helen M. Hills (117 High Street, West Chicago, Illinois; typed ms. seen at Herk. Co. Hist. Soc.) that he was a brother of the Christian Meyer who settled at Kingston NY (see Jones´ "Palatine Families of New York" for more, also Virkus´ Comp. of Amer. Genealogy, vol. 7, page 68). Of the two Henrichs on the NY Palatine Subsistence List, he was pr. the one in 1710 with (1A,0Y) and in 1712 (2A,1Y), which fits with a recent marriage and one child in 1711. Pr. the Henrich naturalized at Albany 28 Feb 1715 and on the 1717 Simmendinger census at New Queensberg (Schoharie) NY with wife Kunegunda & 3 children. He received Burnetsfield Lot #12 and Anna Meyer received Burnetsfield Lot #29. There were several other early Meyer (or Moyer) families in the Mohawk Valley, in addition to the family of this Henry, including that of Jacob Meyer (page 173), Peter Myer (came up from New Jersey, see page 176), and Solomon Moyer (many descendents in the Minden NY area, not covered in this book <unless inadvertently>).

surname MEYER

5802: ANNA MARIA   bp 31 Dec 1711 (sp. Joh. Shster, Jacob Berman)
+5803: Johan HENRICH   bp Schoharie NY 1715 (sp. Henrich Frey & wife)
m ANNA MARIA GETMAN
5804: CATHERINE
5805: PETER

5806: CHRISTIAN MEYER - born ca 14 Mar 1688; died Saugerties, Ulster Co., NY 5 Jan 1781; m GERTRUDE STEFANUS TONIUS (b 1690, d 1766) dau of STEPHAN TONIUS. On NY Palatine subsistence list in 1710 (2A,0Y) and in 1712 (2A,0Y) and 1717 Simmendinger census with wife Anna Gertrude & 2 children. Settled near Kingston NY and names in his will living sons William, John, & Benjamin; also Christian, deceased (ENCY. oF BIOG. OF NY vol 6 page 20). No sign of interaction with the German Flats line of Henry Meyer.

5807: MARIA ELISABETH   bp 1711 (sp. w. of Peter Oberbach, Geo. Obrbch)
5808: WILHELM   b 13 Feb 1714 (sp Wm Sneider,... Anna Maria DeMuth)
5809: PETER   b 5 Nov 1715 (sp. Pet. Bitzer, Geo. Snider, Anna DeMuth)
5810: ANNA CHRISTINA   b 26 Jul 1717 (sp. Christina Tonius, ...)
5811: CATHERINE   b 10 May 1719 (sp. Sybl Cath Kehl, Heir. Weller)
5812: JOHANNES   bp 30 Apr 1721 (sp. Joh. Emmerig, Griet. Snyder)
5813: CHRISTIAN jr.   b say 1722; m by 1747 MARIA SCHNEIDER
5814: CATRINA   bp Kingston 25 Dec 1724 (sp. Wm Snider, Mar. Overpag)
5815: STEPHANUS   bp Kingston 20 Aug 1727 (sp. Wm & Maria Smit)
5816: GEERTJEN   bp Kingston 30 Mar 1729 (sp Hend. Frelig ...)
5817: PETER   bp Kingston 23 Jul 1732 (sp. Jurg Snyder, Joana Swart)
5818: BENJAMIN   b say 1734; m LEA OSTERHOUDT

5819: FREDERICK MEYER - pr. born ca 1670 to 1685; On NY Palatine Sub. List in 1710 (3A,1Y) and in 1712 (4A,0Y).

Also on the NY Palatine Subsistence list were a Henrich Meyer in 1710 (1A,0Y) and in 1712 (1A,0Y) and an Elisabeth Meyer in 1710 (1A,2Y) and in 1712 (2A,0Y).

MEYER - 2nd Generation

5820: FELIX MEYER (Frederick?) - pr. born ca 1700 to 1710; died before 1784 (will of widow Appolonia at Fonda NY); ml ... ; m2 ca 1750 APPOLONIA ... (b say 1705) widow of ADAM BELLINGER (bp 1699, d by 1750). Bellinger book refers to will of Appolonia Mayer as listing numer. offspring (not seen). Felix Meyer & Appolonia Bellinger sponsored Sep 1751 bp of child of Peter Kilts & Maria. Felix was naturalized 3 Jul 1759 (same day as Gerlagh Meyer).

```
        +5821: ps. HENDRICK   b say 1740; m by 1762 MARGARETHA
         5823: ps. MARGARET   b say 1746; m 1766 JACOB JOH. N. WEAVER
        +5824: pr. JOHN F.    b say 1750; ml 1776 ERNESTINA HARTER
```

5803: HENRY MEYER - born 30 Oct 1715; ps. died Schoharie NY 1810 (Home Folks Book page 16, but ps. earlier if Mary on 1778 GF relief was his widow); m ANNA MARIA GETMAN (b 1721, d HK 16 Oct 1811 age 90) dau of FREDERICK GETMAN & MARY BIERMAN. Hendrich & wife Maria sponsored bp Jul 1766 of Maria dau of Jacob Weaver & Maria. See Beck's Home Folks Book (page 16) and Getman book (page 15).

```
         5825: ps. MAGDALENA (Meyer?)  b say 1739; m NICHOLAS H. WEAVER
         5826: MARGARETHA  b say 1741; m 11 Aug 1767 JOHN HELMER
         5827: MARIA   1743-1830 ml 1768 JACOB BELL m2 1785 JOHN G. HILTS
         5828: GERTRUDE  b say 1745; m 26 Aug 1765 CONRAD FRANK jr.
        +5829: ps. (?) JEHAVE GERLASH 1746-1773  m 1770 ELISABETH RASBACH
        +5830: FREDERCK H.  1748-1822 m ANNA MARGARETHA WEAVER
         5831: ANNA EVA   1752-1828  m ca 1774 FREDERICK CHRISTMAN
        +5832: JOHANNES  b say 1754;  m MARIA ELISABETH (Getman book)
        +5833: PETER H.  b 1757; died 1823 (age 66) unm
        +5834: Johannes NICHOLAS  1758-1843  m CAMELIA LAKE
        +5835: HENRICH H.  b 16 Oct 1760; d 1789  m CHRISTINA LEATHER
         5836: CATHERINE  b SAR 13 Jun 1767; m 1784 JOHN PHILIPS
```

MEYER - 3rd Generation

5830: FREDERICK MEYER - born 25 May 1748; died Herkimer Co. NY 18 Jul 1822; m ca 1772 ANNA MARGARET WEAVER (b 1753, d 1831; Comp. of Amer. Genealogy <v 4 page 368> say grandfather was Nich. Weaver) pr. dau of GEORGE WEAVER & BARBARA. Hills' Meyers book has wife as dau of P. J. Weaver. Was in Capt. Henry Tiebouts Co. in Revol. and on 1790 Herkimer census (2-3-6) next to Peter Myer.

```
         5837: CATHERINE F.  b 16 Sep 1774; m 1794 WILLIAM F. HELMER
         5838: MARIA  b 30 Jul 1776 (sp Jac. Bell & Maria); ps. m F WEAVER
                      (Meyer Genealogy has ml HEZ. TALCOTT & m2 NIC. STARING)
        +5839: HENRY F.  1778-1830 m 1803 ELISABETH P. GETMAN
        +5840: GEORGE F.  1781-1863  m CATHERINE SMITH
        +5841: FREDERICK F.  b say 1783; m 1804 ABIGAIL JOH. FRANK
         5842: MARGARET  b 1 Jun 1785; m 1804 HENRY H. STAHRING (Sterling)
        +5843: JOHN F.  b GF 24 Jun 1787 (sp. Fritz Weaver & Gertr.)
                      d 1867;  m ELIZABETH SMITH
         5844: EVA  b GF 8 May 1789 (Pet. Weber & Maria <Ittig>)
                      m 1806 HENRY F. HELMER
         5845: ELISABETH F.  b ca 1790; liv. 1810 (age 19, HK Confirm.)
         5846: MICHAEL b 27 Apr 1791 (sp Geo. Ittig?); m3 1826 CATH. DYGERT
         5847: DANIEL  ca 1792 (age 18, 1810); d 1832; m SUSAN ETHERIDGE
         5848: DAVID  b 21 Feb 1793 (sp Geo. Weaver Sr & Maria)
         5849: ANNA (NANCY)  b ca 1795;  m 1820 THOMAS ROBERTS
```

5835: HENRICH H. MEYER - born 16 Oct 1760 (sp Hen. And. Weaver, Elis. Con.
Frank); died 7 Jan 1789 (Getman book); m CHRISTINA LEATHER (b 1756, d 1855) dau of
JOHN LEDER & ELISABETH . His widow m2 1791 FREDERICK SMITH son of MARTIN SMITH.

    5850: HENRICH bp GF 6 Apr 1785 (sp. Hen. Helmer, Magd. Leather)
              m 1810 MAGDALENA PH. HERWIG
    5851: PETER bp GF 18 Feb 1787 (sp Peter H. Meyer, Maria Ledder)
              m 1809 SALLY STEVENS (dau of Simeon)
    5852: JOHANNES b GF 7 Jan 1789 (sp Philip Bell, Cath. Meyer)

5821: HENRICH MEYER - pr. born ca 1730 to 1743; m by 1762 MARGARETHA...; ps. as
widower m2 GF 5 Oct 1784 GERTRUDE HAUS, widow of J. BETTIN. Hendrich & Gertrude
sponsored Oct 1784 bp of George, son of John Steele & Maria Elisabeth.

    5853: NICHOLAS b SAR 4 Dec 1762 (sp Nic. Weber & Margaret)
  +5854: ps. PETER b say 1770; m by 1794 CHRISTINA ...
    5855: ps. CATHERINE H. ca 1773-1832 m 1793 PETER HARTER
    5855A ps. MARIA H. b say 1778; m1 1795 HEZEKIAH TALCOTT
              m2 1800 NICHOLAS STARING
    5856: FREDERICK bp GF 10 Oct 1781 (sp Fr. Windecker & Barbara)

5829: JEHAVE GERLASH MEYER (Johan GERLACH on mar. rec.) - born 1746; died 1773; m
SAR 2 Dec 1770 ANNA ELISABETH RASBACH. Gerlach name suggests link to the Mont.
Co. Solomon Meyer family. DAR (vol 30 page 341) has dau Maria born in 1775.

    5857: MARIA ca 1773-1860 m 1794 HENRY SCHELL

5824: Lt. JOHN F. MEYER - pr. born ca 1745 to 1755; m 7 Jun 1776 ERNESTINA HARTER
(aka CHRISTINA HARTER b 1760) dau of HENRY HARTER & CATHERINE PFEIFFER. Reported
dead in Sep 1778 combat with Indians, he was taken captive to Canada and returned
home after 1784 to find his wife Ernestina was married to Adam Stahring of
Andrustown. Without alerting Ernestina that he was alive, he went off again to
Canada and remarried there.

   +5858: HENRY J. b 1777 (sp. Hen. Meyer, Cath. Harter)
            d 1861; m1 ANNA HELMER

5832: JOHN MEYER - pr. born ca 1748 to 1752 (pr. son of Henrich); pr. m by 1776
ELISABETH ... (Getman book). A John Meyer & Elisabeth were sponsors for Jun 1776
bp of Elisabeth, dau of Jacob Bell & Maria H. Meyer.

    5859: pr. HENRICH JOH. b GF 20 Mar 1778 (sp Pet. Meyer, .. Bellingr)

5834: NICHOLAS MEYER - born Dec 1758 (son of Henrich, Home Folks Book, page 17);
died Utica NY 26 June 1843; m CAMELIA LAKE (or Cornelia, aka GEISJE LEICH, b 1756,
d 1852 age 96). Lived at Fort Schuyler according to Bellinger book (page 26).

    5860: JOHN NATHAN 1782-1863 m RACHEL SMITH
    5861: NICHOLAS b 1783; died young
    5862: CORNELIA (KEZIAH) b Mar 1785; m 1803 JACOB CHRISTMAN jr.
    5863: HENRY b 1787; m ELSIE POOL
    5864: TUNIS VAN ALEN (Thomas?) b 12 Dec 1789; m CORNELIA ...
    5865: FREDERICK b GF 1 Mar 1792 (sp Fr. H. Meyer & Marg.)
    5866: MARGARET (Polly) b 10 Jun 1794; m WILLIAM MASTERS
    5867: HANNAH b 19 Apr 1796; m Mr. PURDY
    5868: NICHOLAS b say 1798; m ANNA ...

5833: PETER MEYER - born ca 1757; pr. the Peter Myer who died Herkimer NY 2 Jun 1823 (age 66, unm). Tradition has account of Peter Meyer, brother of Frederick (both sons of Henry Meyer), who received a head wound in the Revolution and was incapacitated thereafter.

5869: MARY MYER - Pr. a widow of a Myer as she appears with 4 adults and 2 children (under age 16) on the 1778 German Flats relief. She may have been Anna Maria Getman, a widow of above Henry Meyer (which means the "Home Folks" book is wrong about the death date of 1810 for said Henry) and such assumption would fit the size of household described in 1778.

MEYER - 4th Generation

5870: FREDERICK F. MEYER - pr born ca 1782 to 1785 (son of Frederick as indicated on mar. record); m at Herkimer NY 1804 APPOLONIA FRANCK (bp 1785) dau of JOHN FRANK & APPOLONIA WEAVER.

5840: GEORGE F. MEYER - born Herkimer NY 23 Sep 1781; died Frankfort NY 8 Aug 1863; m 23 Aug 1802 CATHERINE SMITH (b 1783, d 1864) dau of FREDERICK SMITH & CATHERINE . Children were Catherine (b 1802), Benjamin, Felix, Isaac, Margaret, Elisabeth, George Frederick, Mary, Rhoda, and Charles. Family bible at HCH.

5839: HENRY F. MEYER - pr. born ca Oct 1777 (calc. from age at death); died Frankfort NY 2 Jan 1830 (age 52-2-16); m Herkimer NY 11 Jan 1803 ELISABETH GETMAN (b 1785; d 1831) dau of PETER GETMAN (son of Capt. Frederick Getman). Was a blacksmith and had daughter Margaret (b ca 1809, m 1830 Isaac Piper). Pr. also had a son Conrad who, as son of Henry "T" Meyer of Frankfort, died HK 9 Sep 1805 (age 1-10-10) after eating too many unripe cherries.

5858: HENRY J. MEYER - born 6 Apr 1777 (son of Lt. John & Ernestina); died 4 Apr 1861; m1 ANNA HELMER (b 1783; as wife of Henry J. Myer blacksmith, she died HK 8 Dec 1816 age 34) dau of PHILIP F. HELMER & ANNA MYERS; m2 ANNA HELMER (b 1790, d 1883) dau of Lt. GEORGE F. HELMER & MARGARET MYERS. Children by first wife were JOHN (b say 1801; m 1822 MARIA BELLINGER), PHILIP (b 7 Jan 1803, sp. Philip Helmr & w. Anna Myers; this Philip, son of blacksmith Henry, d HK 1 Sep 1805), ANNA (b 26 Feb 1804, sp. Nicholas Thumb & w. Marg.), PHILIP (b 1 Jul 1805, sp. Philip Helmer jr, Elis. Stahring unm), and ERNESTINA (b 30 Jul 1806). Children by second wife were GEORGE HENRY (1818-1878 m ELISABETH MCKENNAN), MARY CATHERINE (b 20 Nov 1820), PETER (b 16 Dec 1823), CINTHY (b 2 Nov 1826), and HELEN M. (b ca 1829, died 1832 age 3).

5843: JOHN F. MEYER - born Herkimer NY 24 Jun 1787 (bp there 1 Jul 1787 sp. by Fritz Weaver & wife Gertrude) son of Frederick & Anna Marg.; died Frankfort NY 14 May 1867; m ELISABETH SMITH (b 1793, d 1849) dau of FREDERICK SMITH & CHRISTINA LEATHER. Children were Margaret (b 1821), Elisazabeth, Matthew, Solomon, Asa, Felix, John, George, Sanford, and Mary Ann.

5854: PETER MEYER - pr. born ca 1750 to 1775; m by 1794 CHRISTINA ...

     5881: MARGARET b GF 5 Jul 1794 (sp Stofel Bellingr & Anna <Harter>)

********** MEYER, Jacob (Moyer) **********

Three Moyer brothers named Jacob, Joseph, and John emmigrated from Wurzburg Germany to the Mohawk Valley before 1760 (Henry Hudson Myers´ "Myers Genealogical Record", De Bary, Floria, 1955, which suggests Moyers came with Clapsaddles <in New York by 1737>). With these Moyers were most likely a younger Jacob and Joseph and a Margaret Moyer (born ca 1752, married in 1770 George F. Helmer). The family was settled on the south side of the Mohawk River at Burnetsfield by 1767 when Joseph Moyer, Joseph Moyer Jun´r, Jacob Moyer, and John Moyer appear in Capt. Frank´s GF militia (Book of Names, page 13). Some potential confusion exists with the Montgomery Co. Solomon Meyer family where there was a Jacob who married ca 1755 ANNA MARIA HAGER and another Jacob who married in 1767 CATHERINE WOHLEGMUTH. Most early records show the family as Moyer, but we use Meyer below to avoid having spelling differences be a criterion for grouping families.

5901A JACOB MEYER (Sr.) - pr. born in Germany ca 1725 to 1735; liv. Feb 1778 (spf Helmer bp) and Sep 1778 (GF relief list); m pr. before 1760 MARGARET ... pr. the Margaret (b ca 1732), who as widow of Jacob Meyer deceased, died at Herkimer NY 15 Mar 1806 (age 74). In 1771 a Jacob appears, along with Joseph Meyer, on the Burnetsfield Minister´s Support List and he was pr. the Jacob who had 4 adults & 6 children on the 1778 GF relief. We do not know when, after Sep 1778, that this Jacob died, but we don´t think he was the Lt. Jacob of Klock´s Regiment killed in action later in the Revolution. Jacob & Margaret are the parents listed on the 1766-67 SAR baptisms and they were sponsors for the Jul 1777 bp of Jacob, son of Joseph Meyer & Catherine, and the Feb 1778 bp of Jacob, son of George Helmer & Margaret (Meyer).

                        surname MEYER
    +5902: HENRICH   b GF 3 Aug 1766 (son of Jacob & Margaret)
                    (bp sp. Henry Meyer & w. Maria); m by 1796 CATHERINE BAUM
    +5903: JACOB   b SAR 8 Dec 1767 (sp Jos. Meyer, Anna Weber)
     5905: pr. CATHERINE JAC.   b say 1769; liv. 1793 (spf Campbell bp)
     5906: pr. JULIANA JAC.   b say 1772; m 1792 FRED. STOF. HILTS
     5907: ps. GERTRUDE JAC.   b say 1774; m 1790 PATRICK CAMPBELL
     5908: ps. ELISABETH JAC.   b say 1776; m 1792 PHILLIP MILLER

5901B JACOB MEYER (Jr.) - pr. born in Germany ca 1730 to 1747; pr. the Private Jacob killed at Oriskany 6 Aug 1777 (Book of Names, page 134, and son Ludwig´s testimony to Simms ca 1850 which notes that Jacob´s throat had been cut, pr. after being taken prisoner); pr. m1 before 1760 ... (mother of Ludwig); and m by 1766 CATHERINE MARGARET ... (b say 1746, listed as wife of Jacob on Jun 1770 SAR bp rec.), ps. the unnamed daughter of ANDREW WEAVER who married a Meyer 4 Jun 1765 (SAR). Hatch papers (page 16) say that Jacob Meyer´s wife was Catherine Weaver and puts her age at 11 when she was captured in the 1757 French attack on German Flats. Jacob´s widow m2 by 1 Apr 1778 HENRY SCHAEFFER (when Ludwig Meyer substituted in the military for his stepfather) and she was living in Nov 1793 when Henry Schaeffer & Catherine Margaret sponsored the baptism of Ludwig Meyer´s daughter Margaret. Ludwig Meyer informed Simms (Frontiersman of New York, vol. 2, pg 553) that his father Jacob came from Germany, and later settled near Hasenclaver´s Patent when Ludwig was a small boy (pr. ca 1767). About 1772, Jacob moved to the Royal Grant northeast of German Flats (now Fairfield NY). He appears amongst the Hasenclever men in Petrie´s 1769 GF militia (north of the Mohawk) and was naturalized 8 Mar 1773, next to Hen. Schafer (Book of Names, page 7).

    +5909: LUDWIG   b ca 1760; liv. 1850 (age 90); at Oriskany in 1777
     5909A pr. ANNA BARBARA   b say 1769; m 1785 CHRISTIAN CASSELMAN
     5909B pr. CATHERINE ELISABETH   b SAR Jun 1770 (sp Cath. Gruninger .)

5910: **JOHN MEYER** - pr. born ca 1725 to 1750 ("Myers Genealogical Record" has a John as a brother of immigrants Jacob & Joseph).; pr. died during the Revolution (Book of Names, page 167, has a John Moyer of Bellinger's Regiment as killed in action); ps. m ... Was in the GF militia in 1767 and on the 1771 Burnetsfield Minister's list, so he pr. lived south of the Mohawk River near Jacob Sr. Except perhaps for a daughter Maria Elisabeth Joh., who was the daughter of a John Meyer of Manheim NY in 1777 (Petrie book, page 11), we have no indications of family for this man and he may even have been unmarried. At the same time there were two John Meyers in the HENRY MEYER family (one married Ernestina Harter, another married an Elisabeth), a Capt. John who married in 1766 Maria Frank (pr. of the PETER MEYER family) and some younger Johns of the Montgomery Co. Solomon Meyer family.

<blockquote>
5911A ps. MARIA ELISABETH JOH. b say 1758; m 1777 JOST DYGERT
5911B ps. ADAM b say 1760; m CATH. DYGERT (see P. Meyer family)
</blockquote>

5912: **JOSEPH MEYER** (Sr.) - pr. born in Germany ca 1715 to 1735; liv. 1767 (in Capt. Frank's GF militia). This man may be the Joseph on the 1771 Burnetsfield Minister's List but we suspect he was pr. deceased by 1778 and that Joseph Jr. was the one appearing on the Sep 1778 GF relief.

5913: **JOSEPH MEYER** (Jr.) - born ca May 1746; died Warren NY 15 Apr 1812 (age 65-11-6); m by 1769 CATHERINE CLEPSATTLE (b 18 Nov 1748, d 3 Apr 1839 age 90-4-9) dau of ANDREW CLEPSATTLE. He had a wooden leg, supposedly received as a result of injuries in the French & Indian War (but his apparent presence as Joseph Jun'r. in the 1767 GF militia suggests the leg loss occurred later). Various accounts (Hatch papers, Simms, Myers Genealogical Record) tell of a Tory Indian raid near his farm on 2 Aug 1780 (pr. in the Minden NY area) in which his young daughter Eva was captured and taken prisoner to Canada. The young Eva was later identified there by a fellow prisoner, Peter Orendorf, based on her recollection that her father had a wooden leg and lived near a fort. In the same August 1780 raid, Joseph's young sons John and Jacob were killed by a Indian's knife while riding together on horseback. At the time, Joseph was away making bullets at nearby Fort Plank and his wife Catherine was working in a flax field where she hid as soon as she heard shots fired (Myers Genealogical Record). Joseph was listed with 2 adults & 5 children (under age 16) on the 1778 GF relief and moved after the Revolution to Orendorf Corners in Conradstown (now Columbia, Herkimer Co. NY). He was there for the 1790 German Flats census (2-2-6) living near Fred Christman, Conrad Orendorf, & Timothy Frank.

<blockquote>
5914: JOHN b 20 Oct 1769; killed by Tory Indians on 2 Aug 1780
5915: pr. MARIA JOS. b say 1771; m 1792 JOHANNES JOH. CAMPBELL
+5916: ANDRIES JOS. b 3 Jan 1772; m 1793 CATHERINE SCHERER
5917: EVA b 26 Oct 1774; captive to Canada 1780 (age 5 then)
    m1 1794 JACOB EYSAMAN; m2 LAWRENCE SHOEMAKER
5918: JACOB b GF 22 Jul 1777 (sp Jac. Meyer & Marg.); d 2 Aug 1780
5919: ELISABETH b GF 10 Apr 1782 (sp Wm Klepsattle)
    m GEORGE HENRY CAMPBELL
5920: DOROTHY ca 1785-1815 m 1807 JACOB KESSLER
5921: JOSEPH b 12 May 1787 (sp Mich. Meyer & Cath.)
    m JANETTE WINN
5922: JOHN b 16 Dec 1789; m1 NANCY SKINNER
5923: GERTRUDE (Charity) b 19 Jun 1791 (sp Geo Fred H*, Elis. Meyer)
    m RICHARD GETMAN
5923A DANIEL bp SJR 12 Jan 1794 (sp Dan. Petrie & Anna)
</blockquote>

5924: MARGARET MEYER - born ca 1752; died Columbia NY 1818 age 66; m SAR 8 Jan 1770 GEORGE F. HELMER (b 1739, d 1823) son of FREDERICK HELMER & MARIA BARBARA KAST. They had four children by the 1778 GF relief list including an Adam (b Nov 1770) and Jacob (b Feb 1778, sp. Jacob Meyer & Margaret). Later they had Barbara (1780), Margaret, Anna (1790, sp Joseph Meyr & Cath.), & Eva. An early son Jacob and the Meyer bp sponsors justify placing her in this family.

MEYER - 2nd Generation

5916: ANDRIES JOS. MEYER - born 3 Jan 1772; died Cedarville NY 29 Apr 1851 (age 79-3-26); m GF 15 Nov 1793 CATHERINE SCHERER (b 8 Sep 1773, d 4 Sep 1851 age 77-11-5) dau of CHRISTIAN SCHERER & MARGARET BELLINGER. At Conradstown in 1801.

> 5925: PETER b 7 Jul 1794 (sp Jac. Scherer, Cath. Meyer)
>   m CATHERINE CROUCH
> 5926: NANCY b 20 Oct 1797; m THOMAS WEAVER
> 5927: ABSALOM b 11 Jul 1799; d 1876; m CATHERINE EDICK
> 5928: CHRISTOPHER (or CHRISTIAN) b 5 Dec 1801 (sp Cath. Spohn)
>   m ALZINA ORENDORF
> 5929: JOSEPH b 30 Jan 1807
> 5930: MARGARET b 1 Jan 1809; m ALPHINS NORTON
> 5931: KATHEERINE b 14 Jan 1814
> 5932: JEREMIAH b 14 Sep 1817; m SOPHRONIA GETMAN

5902: HENRICH JAC. MEYER - pr. born ca 1760 to 1775; m ca 1795 CATHERINE BAUM (b ca 1768) dau of ABRAHAM BAUM & DOROTHY CUNINGHAM (Deuel notes at Oneida Hist. Soc., Hatch Papers have her as Cath. Boone!). Church records show that another Henry Jac. Meyer, probably from the Montgomery Co. Solomon Meyer family, married at German Flats Feb 1795 Barbara DeBus. Henry Meyer and Catherine Baum were sponsors for Jun 1795 bp of Catherine, dau of Jacob J. N. Weaver & Margaret (Baum). Children, as given in the Hatch Papers and the HCH Moyer file, were James (1796-1824, m POLLY SHOEMAKER), Anna (Nancy, b ca 1798, m 1834 NICHOLAS SMITH), Catherine (m 1836 FREDERICK REIS), Dolly (m Dinus Clepsattle), Jacob (had 5 children), Elisabeth (unm), Mary (m Dr. Palmer), and Margaret (m DANIEL DYGERT)

5903: JACOB MEYER - pr. the Jacob born SAR 8 Dec 1767 (son of Jacob); m by 1790 ANNA ...; m2 by 1794 DELIA ... Had daughters Maria Catherine (bp SJR 31 Aug 1790, sp Hen. Meyer, Maria Helmer), Elisabeth (b SJR 27 Aug 1792, sp. Jac. Wallrath & Elis.), and Delia (b GF 25 Jan 1794, sp. George Fr. Helmer, Cath. Meyer).

5909: LUDWIG MEYER (Moyer) - born ca 1760; liv. 1850 (age 90, according to Simms); m 1791 CATHERINE G. ETEL pr. dau of GEORGE ETEL. He was in Col. Bellinger´s 4th Tryon Co. Regiment and served at the Oriskany battle in 1777 (Book of Names page 167). On 1 Apr 1778 Ludwig Meyer of Kingsland entered military service as a substitute for his stepfather Henry Schaeffer (as seen in "Revolutionary Soldiers of Tryon County N.Y." by James F. Morrison Jr., 95 Lincoln St, Gloversville, NY 12078).

> 5933: JOST b GF 15 Jan 1791 (sp Jost Etel & Maria)
> 5934: MARIA MARGARET b GF 10 Nov 1793 (sp H. Schaefer & C. Marg.)
>   m 1814 JOHN DAVIS (son of Jacob)

********** MEYER, Peter (Myers) **********

6000: Lt. **PETER MEYER** - born at Michelfeld near Stuttgard, Wurtenburg, Germany
4 Nov 1714 (son of John Mayer); died Herkimer NY 29 Apr 1802 (age 87-5-25); m
1739 ...   He emigrated in 1734 from Germany to Philadelphia, settled in New
Jersey, and had 11 children.   "Home Folks Book of the Darius Myers Family" by
Violet M. Beck (1926) suggests that Peter was a brother of the 1710 immigrant
Henry Meyer of Burnetsfield and uses as support the account that when this Peter
Myers family came to the Mohawk Valley they first settled with 500 feet of the
Henry Meyer Grant (ibid, page 16).
                            surname MEYER
        6001: pr. CATHERINE b say 1745; m by 1770 JOHN HILLER
       +6002: pr. JOHN ca 1747-1815 m 1766 MARIA FRANK
        6003: pr. ANNA ca 1747-1829 m PHILIP F. HELMER
       +6004: MATTHEW b say 1748; killed at Johnston NY battle 1781
        6005: pr. MARGARET b say 1750; m JACOB JOH. N. WEAVER
        6006: pr. MARY 1753-1851 m by 1776 LAWRENCE FRANK
       +6007: MICHAEL 1753-1814 m CATHERINE HARTER
        6008: PETER b say 1755; killed 1779; a Tory
       +6009: ps. LORENTZ b say 1757; m by 1777 MARIA BARBARA ...
       +6010: JOSEPH 1759-1804 m ABIGAIL HARTER
        6010A ps. ELISABETH b say 1765; liv. 1790 (spf Cath. Meyer bp)

                          MEYER - 2nd Generation

6011: ADAM MEYER - pr. born ca 1745 to 1770; m by 1793 CATHERINE, said by Harter
book (page 23)to be CATHERINE DYGERT dau of PETER S. DYGERT. Ps. this Adam
descends from Mont. Co. family of Solomon Meyer. On 1790 Herkimer census
(1-2-3) Adam Myer is listed amongst the New Germantown residents (i.e. Witrig,
Riema, Brietenbacher, ...). Called Adam of Minden NY when daughter Elisabeth
married in 1806 Peter Harter (HK church rec.).

        6013: CATHERINE b GF 10 Dec 1788 (sp Jost Herkmr & Cath.)
        6014: ELISABETH 1789-1861 m 1806 PETER PH. HARTER
        6015: MARIA b 24 Dec 1793 (sp John Keller & Maria)

6002: Capt. **JOHN MEYER** - pr. born ca 1746 to 1747; looks like the John Myers
of GF who died HK 22 May 1815 (age 68); m 25 Oct 1766 MARIA FRANK (Maria, wife
of John Meyer, d HK 6 Mar 1811) dau of immigrant HENRY FRANK. Son Johannes
(i.e. son of John & Maria) had same baptism date in 1787 as child of Frederick
H. Meyer. Looks like the John with 2 adults & 6 children on 1778 German Flats
relief and pr. the ... Moyer on 1790 GF census (3-4-4) near in list to Getmans,
Piper, & Law. Frank. Was living at Frankfort NY in 1802 when his son Peter Joh.
was married.

        6016: pr. MARIA b say 1768; m 1785 JOHANNES JAC. WEAVER
        6017: pr. PETER JOH. b say 1771; m 1802 ELISABETH G. DEMUTH
        6018: pr. MICHAEL JOH. b say 1773; m 3 Feb 1795 EVA W. DYGERT
        6019: EVA ca 1776-1826 m NICHOLAS STEELE
        6020: pr. MARGARET b GF 20 Oct 1777 (sp Math. Meyer, Marg. Getman)
        6021: MARGARET b GF 25 Dec 1784 (sp Jos. Meyer & Maria)
        6022: JOHN bp GF 1 Jul 1787 (sp John Frank & Appolonia)
        6023: HENRICH bp SJR 30 May 1790 (sp. Hen. Frank, Eva Frank)
        6024: CATHERINE b GF 15 May 1792 (sp Michael Meyer)

                                  -176-

6010: JOSEPH MYER - born 15 May 1759; died Herkimer NY 15 May 1804 (note in
church death rec. says he was an innkeeper, too much addicted to strong
liquors); m ABIGAIL HARTER (b 1768, d 1829) dau of HENRY HARTER & CATHERINE
PFEIFFER. Was sponsor at 1778 bp of Peter M., son of Michael Myers and possibly
the Joseph who was sponsor with Elisabeth Lentz, for 1778 bp of Joseph, son of
Joh. Nicholas Weaver & Elisabeth. Pr. the Joseph on 1790 Herkimer NY census
(1-2-2), in the town area next to Henry Helmer and Adam A. Staring. Children
listed in Harter book (page 10).

   6025: CATHERINE b 19 Dec 1785; d 7 Apr 1796 (age 10)
   6026: MICHAEL J.H. b GF Aug 1787 (sp Mich. Meyer & Cath.)
              d 1813; m 1810 MERCY LEVALLEY (dau of Benjamin)
   6027: PETER   bp SJR 2 Feb 1790 (sp Peter Bellingr & Elis.)
   6028: HENRICH b 11 Dec 1791 (sp Hen. Harter, Maria Hiller)
   6029: JOSEPH b 27 Jan 1795; m LUCY FITCH
   6030: LAWRENCE b 3 May 1798 (sp Lor. Harter, Anna Myers)
   6031: MARGARET b 9 Aug 1802 (sp Jacob G. Weber & Marg.)
   6032: MATTHEW 1802-1884 m CHRISTINA (b 1808)

6009: LORENTZ MEYER - pr. born ca 1745 to 1761; ps. died soon after Nov 1777
(no mention in later records); m by 1777 MARIA BARBARA ... His daughter
Margaret was bp same date (23 Nov 1777) as Margaret, dau of John Meyer & Maria
(Frank).

   6033: MARGARET b GF 17 Nov 1777 (sp Jac. Weber & Marg.)

6004: MATTHEW MYER - pr. born ca 1740 to 1758; killed at Johnston NY battle
1781; Matthew Meyer, along with Elisabeth Pfeiffer, sponsored Aug 1776 GF bp of
Peter, son of Jacob Weaver & Anna Margaret (Meyer).

6007: Maj. Gen. MICHAEL MEYER - born Anville (or Elizabeth NJ) New Jersey 1
Feb 1753; died Herkimer NY 17 Feb 1814 (Harter Geneal. page 8); m by 1778
CATHERINE HARTER (b 1759, d 1840) dau of Capt. HENRY HARTER & CATHERINE
PFEIFFER. In 1781 he was seriously wounded at the Johnston NY battle in which
his brother Matthew died.

  +6034: PETER M. 1778-1815 m MARIA VAN SCHOONHOVEN
  +6035: HENRICH b GF 11 Mar 1780 (sp. Philip Harter & Elis. Helmer)
        d 1822; m MARIA BELL
   6036: ANNA (NANCY) 1782-1840 m1 JOAB GRISWOLD
  +6037: MATTHEW b GF 1784 (sp. Stophel Bellinger & Appolonia Harter)
        d 1864; m1 LUCIA RICHARDS
   6038: MARGRETHA b GF 17 Sep 1786 (sp. Geo. Helmer, Marg. Helmer)
        pr. died by 1801
   6039: Johan MICHAEL b 1 Oct 1788; m SARAH GRISWOLD
        (sp. Michael Joh. Meyer, Barbara N. Harter)
   6040: JOHN b 2 Oct 1789; unm; feeble
  +6041: CATHERINE b 1790 (sp. Lawrence Harter, Elis. Meyer)
        m 1808 ROBERT SHOEMAKER (1782-1838)
   6042: JACOB b ca 1799; d Apr 1804 (age 5-3-18)
   6043: MARGARETHA 1801-1860 m GEORGE H. FEETER
        (b 7 May 1801, sp. Peter Helmer & w. Marg.)

MEYER - 3rd Generation

6035: HENRICH M. MEYER - born 11 Mar 1780; died Frankfort NY 28 Aug 1822; m by
1801 MARIA BELL (ps. Anna, liv. 1838). Had Elisabeth (b ca Dec 1801, d 14 Aug
1804), Catherine (b ca Dec 1803, d Feb 1805), Anna (b 1803, m 1825 Ira Curtis),
Catherine (b 1807, m 1829 Lucas Doolittle), Lucia (b 1810, Math. Myers & w.
Lucia), John Michael (b 1812, sp Michael M. Myers & wife Sally), and Maria
Elisabeth (bp 1819, sp Lawrence Weaver & Elisabeth Staring).

6037: MATTHEW MEYER - born 14 Aug 1784; died 1 Aug 1864; ml 1 Oct 1809 LUCIA
RICHARDS (b 1791) dau of ALEXANDER RICHARDS & MARY; m2 ORPHA HORTON (b ca 1793, d
1853 age 60). Was a judge by 1811 (HK bp rec.). Had children by first wife
including Maria Richards (b 1811, sp Henry Meyer & w. Maria), Robert (m Louisa P.
Leland), Elisabeth Alsop, Catherina Ann, Margarette, and Michael Alexander (b
1822); and by his second wife he had F. Horton (b 1829, d 1833) and Clara Melinda
(1833-1900 Charles Ellis).

6018: MICHEL J. MEYER - pr. born ca 1760 to 1775; m 3 Feb 1795 EVA W. DYGERT dau
of WILLIAM DYGERT & MARGARET CUNINGHAM.

   6044: MARGARET b GF 5 Jun 1795 (sp Wm Dygert & Margaret)

6034: PETER M. MEYER - born 13 Mar 1778 (sp. Joseph Mayer & ... Harterin); died 28
Nov 1815 m MARIA VAN SCHOONHOVEN (b 1776, d GF 1838) dau of JACOB VAN
SCHOONHOVEN. Peter M. was a lawyer and had children Michael (b 1801, m 1826 Susan
Cornell) and Elisabeth (b 1803), as given in Harter book (page 21).

********** MILLER, Andrew (Muller) **********

MILLER, Andrew - 1st Generation

6101: ANDREW MILLER Sr. - born in Germany ca 1732 (Hatch Papers); died Columbia NY 4 Dec 1803 (age 71); pr. m MARGARET KETS (her surname from 1778 bp rec.); Margaret, widow of Andrew Miller was born ca 1743 and died HK 17 May 1816 (age 73). Supposedly Andrew came to America in 1760 (at age 28) and he may have seen action at the 1777 Battle of Saratoga, but he was not the husband of Sarah Ann Snyder (she was wife of a Capt. Miller of Orange Co.). Andrew lived until about 1790 at Greenwich (Renselaer Co.) NY when he moved his family in an oxen drawn cart to a wilderness glen near the headwater of the Unadilla River, in the present town of Columbia (Herkimer Co.) NY. There he and his six sons built and operated a saw mill and grist mill, known as Miller's Mills (Herkimer Evening Telegram article by P. Draheim, 9/9/1983). Information on children and descendents substantially based on "Descendents of Andrew Miller of Miller's Mills NY" by John H. & Doris Miller Schneider (1940) as expanded by 1984 findings of Miller family researcher Mr. Paul Munson (1009 S. 10th St, Laramie, Wyoming 82070).

                      surname MILLER
+6102: JOHN A. 1760-1838 m DOROTHY CARNER (Kerner)
 6103: MARGARET b 29 May 1762 (bp Churchtown NY)
+6104: HENRY A. 1764-1826 m by 1788 MAGDALENA VAN DEUSEN
+6105: ELISABETH b say 1766; m by 1787 WILHELM HANER
+6106: ANDREAS H. b say 1768; m 1793 GERTRUDE LOR. HARTER
+6107: WILLIAM b Oct 1773; m by 1802 CATHERINE EDICK
+6108: JONAS b say 1775; m by 1802 ELISABETH ISTEL
 6108A JACOB b Albany NY 11 Mar 1778 (sp. Jacob & Cath. Foorest)
                      pr. died young
 6109: JACOB b 23 Nov 1779; m SUSAN KILTS
 6110: CATHERINE 1783-1871 m HENRY GETMAN (1779-1873)

At least two other Miller (var. Mueller, Muller, ...) families of German origin settled earlier in the Herkimer County area than the family of Andrew Miller of Miller's Mills. One of these, that of Burnetsfield pateentee Johannes Miller, a 1710 Palatine immigrant, was established at German Flats by about 1725 (see page 181 for descendents) while the other family, that of Valentine Miller of New Petersburg, appears to have arrived about 1765 with Peter Hasenclever's group (see page 185).

                      MILLER - 2th Generation

6106: ANDREW MILLER - pr. born ca 1765 to 1772; m 6 Oct 1793 GERTRUDE LOR. HARTER dau of LORENTZ PHIL. HARTER & BARBARA DELANEY. Said to have moved to Manlius NY. Children given in Harter book page 20.

        6117: MARIA BARBARA b 10 Apr 1794 (sp Lor. Harter & M. Barbara)
        6118: MARGARET b 25 Mar 1796 (sp Andreas S. Miller & Marg.)
        6119: GERTRUDE b 4 Aug 1798 (sp Lor. Harter, Cath. Muller)
        6120: JOHANNES b Columbia NY 21 Jan 1803

6104: **HENRY A. MILLER** (seen also as GEORGE HENRY MILLER) - born 4 Aug 1764; died
Miller's Mills NY 23 Jan 1826; m Greenbush NY 1 Jan 1786 MAGDALENA VAN DEUSEN (b
24 Aug 1766, d 3 May 1848) dau of WILHELM VAN DEUSEN & CHRISTINA KITTEL (DAR#
70491 and HCH Miller file). Many descendents to Jamesville Wis.

      6121: CHRISTINA 1788-1863 m ISRAEL YOUNG
      6122: ANDREAS b GF 4 Jun 1791 (sp And. Miller & Marg.); d 1793
      6123: GEORGE HEN. bp GF 26 Jul 1793 (sp Geo. Hen. Bell & Cath.)
           d 1853; m SALLY WILLIAMS
      6124: ANDREAS bp GF 21 Aug 1795 (sp And. Miller & Marg.)
      6125: WILLIAM H. 1797-1836 m ELISABETH SMITH
      6126: MARGARET 1799-1830 m JACOB I. HANER
      6127: CORNELIUS bp Minden NY 7 Mar 1801; m SELINDA SMITH
      6128: JEREMIAH bp Columbia NY 13 Jul 1803
          d 1856; m 1828 JULIA ANN POTTER
      6129: CHRISTOPHER H. 1805-1849 m LAVINA JONES

6102: **JOHANNES MILLER** - born 1760; died Nov 1838; m 1784 ANNA DOROTHEA KERNER (b
29 Jan 1767, d 22 Nov 1848) dau of JOHN G. KERNER & SUSANNA MARGARETA

    +6130: ANDREAS 1784-1864 m 1810 MARIA GETMAN
     6131: SUSANNA b 11 Oct 1786; m PHILIP BARINGER
     6132: JOHN jr b 11 Mar 1789, d 1803, m REGINA ULINE
     6133: CATHERINE b GF 15 Oct 1791 (sp Geo H Bell & Cath.)
     6134: WILLIAM b 25 Sep 1796, d 1876, m NANCY HANER
     6135: NANCY b 1 Feb 1798, d 1875, m CALVIN CHAMBERLIN
     6136: CHRISTOPHER b 8 Feb 1802; d 1882, m 1826 REBECCA HANER
     6137: JACOB bp Herkimer 4 Nov 1804; m SOPHIA CHAMBERLIN

6108: **JONAS MILLER** - pr. born ca 1765 to 1778; died Columbia NY 17 Sep 1811; m
ELISABETH ISTEL. Children Maria (b 1801, d 1853, m JACOB J. HANER), Elisabeth (bp
Columbia NY 26 Nov 1802), James (b 30 Nov 1806, unm), Elias (b 1809, m ELISA
PUTNAM), Jonas (b 2 Oct 1810), and Margaret ("Peggy", unm).

6107: **WILLIAM MILLER** - born Greenbush NY 16 Oct 1773; died 18 Jul 1843; m1 by
1802 CATHERINE EDICK (Ittig); m2 1814 NANCY WALL (d 1852) dau of WILLIAM WALL of
Columbia NY. Children Katherine (m1 Peter Orendorf, m2 Joseph Milson), Jacob (bp
Columbia NY 22 Nov 1802, m BETSY HANER), John W. (b Mar 1804, d 1838 unm),
Margaret (m CALVIN LOWELL, moved to Missouri), Elisabeth (m NUNA P. WILLIAMS),
Maria (b 19 Feb 1811, m 1826 GEORGE HOYER), Jonas (b Apr 1819, m1 DOROTHY
CHAMBERLIN, m2 LOUISE MILLER dau of Jacob J.), Nancy (m MR. BRONSON), and William
Henry (b 1827, d 1901, m HELEN YAW).

6105: **ELISABETH MILLER** - born say 1766; m WILLIAM HANER (b Rhinebeck NY 23 Dec
1760, d Columbia NY) son of SAMUEL HEYHNER & REBECCA YELLER. Children were
Margaret (b Albany 10 Jun 1787, m George F. Getman), Jonas (b Greenbush NY Dec
1789), & Catherine (m 1812 Jacob Bargy).

MILLER - 3rd Generation

6130: ANDREAS MILLER - born 17 Dec 1784; died 26 Feb 1864 (Getman book page 25); m
HK 1 Jan 1810 MARIA GETMAN (b Jun 1786, d 1820) dau of JOHN GETMAN & MARGARET
LAUX. Children Anna (Nancy, bp Columbia NY Jan 1811), Dorothy, Margaret, & John.

6201: JOHANNES MULLER - pr. born at Rutershausen near Eversbach (Hesse) Germany ca 1680 to 1690; m in NY ca 1711 MARIA JACOBI widow of HENRY HAGER (Knittle´s "The Early Palatine Emigration" page 285). Of two John Mullers on the NY subsistence, he may have been the one listed in 1710 (2A,0Y) & in 1712 (2A,1Y), with the 1712 youngster ps. his stepson Henry Hager, son of his wife Maria by her first marriage (Petrie Book page 3). Researcher Hank Jones findings on Kessler origins in Germany (Jones "The Palatine Families of New York") show John Miller was a friend of Johannes Kessler and emigrated in 1709, as a single male, from the Kessler´s village of Ebersbach, Germany. Thus he was pr. the Johannis Miller naturalized at Albany NY 3 Jan 1716 (name alongside that of John Kessler) and on the 1717 Simmendinger census, with wife Maria & 4 children. In 1723 he received Burnetsfield lot #43.

In July 1749 he wrote a letter to relatives back in Germany in which he says that he had five sons (four of them married) and three daughters (two married) but he does not name them (letter provided by Hank Jones, translation by John A. Dahl). This letter was carried by his friend and neighbor Stephen Frank and includes greetings to his brothers Johannes Jacob, Helmes, Jacob, Hans Henry, & step-brother Ebert Jung. Except for a few offspring of his sons John & Frederick, there do not seem to be many Miller descendents of this Johannes in the German Flats area after the Revolution and tracing them elsewhere is made difficult by the numerous other Miller families in the Mohawk Valley region.

```
                     surname MILLER
     6202: dau   b say 1712; m by 1749 ...
    +6203: pr. CONRAD  b say 1715; in militia 1757
     6204: dau   b say 1718; m by 1749
    +6205: FREDERICK  b say 1721; m1 Jun 1749 MARGARET WOHLEBEN
    +6206: JOHN   b say 1724; m ANNA MARGARET ...
    +6207: ps. HENRY  b say 1726; pr. m by 1749 ...
                     died by 1784; m MAGDALENA ...
    +6208: pr. ISAAC  b say 1729
     6209: pr. ELISABETH  b say 1732; ps. unm in July 1749
              m by 1752 VALENTINE STAHRING
```

6210: JACOB MILLER - pr. born ca 1713 to 1720; ps. m1 by 1740 EVA ... ; pr. m2 SAR 18 Nov 1767 MAGDALENA REIS a widow (pr. MAGDALENA HELMER widow of Marc Reis). A Jacob Miller, pr. living in Montgomery Co., was noted in the 1755 Jost Petrie financial papers (Petrie book page 117). Pr. the Jacob who was naturalized 3 May 1755 and of a different family than the 1710 immigrant Johannes of German Flats. Ps. this man, or a son of the same name, was the Tory Capt. Jacob Miller living at the Durlach settlement in 1775.

Other early Miller families present in Montgomery Co. prior to the Revolution include a Daniel Miller (ps. related to a John Thomas Miller as both were naturalized on 3 Jul 1759), a Dionysius Miller (of Ft. Plain NY), a Garret Miller of Canajoaharie (supposedly from Connecticut and ps. related to Dionysius), a Capt. Henry Miller (Revolutionary officer, pr. of Palatine NY), plus a John Miller and Philip Miller of Fonda (both had children bp in 1760´s at Caughnawaaga).

MILLER, John - 2rd Generation

6203: CONRAD MILLER - pr. born ca 1712 to 1732; m ... In Capt. Mark Petrie's German Flats militia unit in 1757, listed near Fridrich Miller, George Fey, & Jost Demuth. Conrad appears also in Capt. Conrad Frank's 1767 GF militia, listed next to Johannis Miller & Nicholas Staring. Children from note in HCH Miller file.

> 6211: PETER b say 1745; ps. had dau Maria P. (bp SAL 1769)
> 6212: JOHN b say 1747; ps. m by 1766 ELISABETH ... (spf Spohn bp)
> 6213: KATIE
> 6214: GEORGE b say 1751; ps. liv. 1776 (spf C L Hilts bp)
> 6215: MARY b say 1757; ps. m by 1778 LORENTZ HILTS

6205: FREDERICK MILLER - pr. born ca 1713 to 1725; m1 GF 26 Jun 1749 MARIA MARGARETHA WOHLEBEN; and pr. m2 by 1760 MARIA EVA ... (pr. Hilts). In 1757 Frederick was in Capt. Mark Petrie's GF militia and in the 1769 GF militia he was listed next to Henry Miller & John Davis. The Tryon Co. census of ca 1776 has Frederick over age 50, with two girls under age 16, one male age 16 to 50, and three women age 16 to 50 (Mohawk Valley in the Revolution, page 153), and places him next to Melger Thum & Lorentz Hilts. It thus appears that Frederick lived north of the Mohawk River, perhaps as early as 1757 and almost certainly by 1769 to 1775 (which we feel ties in with the assumption that his second wife was a Hilts).

> 6216: ps. JACOB b say 1752; in Bellinger's Regiment (Staring's Co.)
> 6217: pr. ELISABETH b say 1754; m JACOB J. KESSLER (b 1753)
> 6218: ps. FREDERICK b say 1756; m by 1780 LENA WEAVER
> (had a son Fred. bp at Schenectady 11 Aug 1780)
> 6219: MARIA b say 1758; m 1777 GODFRID HILTS
> 6220: MARIA CATHERINE b 26 Feb 1760 (sp. M. Cath. dau of Stofel Hilts)
> (sp. also Jacob, son of Conrad Lepper)
> 6221: SUSANNA b 15 Jun 1763 (sp. Fred Frank & w. Susanna)
> d 1843; m 1784 JOHN HILTS
> 6222: ANNA EVA bp GF 4 Jun 1765 (dau of Fr. & Maria Elis.)
> (sp John Miller); m 1790 JACOB RYON
> 6223: pr. MARIA MAGDALENA b SAR 25 Nov 1767 (dau of Fred & Maria)
> (sp. Cath. Hilts, Jacob Bell, unm)
> 6224: ps. ANNA b say 1770; liv. Nov 1785 (spf Eva Hilts bp)

6207: HENRY MILLER - pr. born ca 1720 to 1745; died by Jan 1784; ps. m1 by 1769 DELIA ...; and m2 MAGDALENA ... (widow, Lena Miller m2 GF 2 Jan 1784 JOHN RYON). A Henry was in Capt. Frank's 1767 GF militia.

> +6225: ps. ANDREW b say 1764; m 1783 MARGARET KAST
> 6226: ps. JOHN b say 1766; m GF 1784 MARGARET NELLIS
> 6227: ps. JOST H. b SAR 2 Dec 1769 (sp. Geo. Miller & Gertrude)
> 6228: ps. MARIA b say 1771; m by 1795 HENRY FRANK

6208: ISAAC MILLER - pr. born before 1735; pr. died by 1760 (no sign in church or militia records thereafter); m .... Supposedly had two sons (HCH Miller file).

> +6229: CONRAD b say 1750; ps. m by 1782 CHRISTINA ...
> 6230: son b say 1754; a Tory (ps. Adam, in Canada 1800)

6206: JOHN MILLER Sr. - pr. born ca 1715 to 1735; m ANNA MARGARET ... His will dated at Burnetsfield 12 Jun 1780 (probated 30 Dec 1790) mentions wife Anna Margaret and son Nicholas - executors were Jacob Kessler and Johannes Eysaman. Listed with Conrad Miller in Capt. Conrad Frank's militia co. in 1767 and in

Bellinger's Revol. Regiment. His widow m2 GF 15 May 1787 FREDERICK GETMAN and she
was pr. the Margaret Getman, who with Nicholas Spohn & Jacob Bashor, sold some
Stahley Patent lands on 24 Feb 1792 to Henry Miller, Nicholas Miller & Cath. Hyers
for the sum of 10 pounds (HK deed book).

+6231: NICHOLAS b say 1742; in militia 1767
+6232: pr. JOHN jr. b say 1744; m URSALA in militia 1767
+6233: pr. HENRICH b say 1747; m by 1776 ANNA EVA (pr. Boshar)
 6234: ps. ANNA (Miller?) b say 1752; m by 1779 HENRY HUBER

MILLER - 4th Generation

6225: ANDREW MILLER - pr. born ca 1750 to 1765; m GF 7 Aug 1783 MARGARET KAST
(b Jul 1761) dau of FREDERICK KAST & ELISABETH HELMER. On 1790 Herkimer census
(1-1-3), living near Frederick Kast.

6235: pr. NICHOLAS AND. b say 1789; m 1807 CATHERINE LEIMBACH
6236: HENRICH b GF 12 Feb 1791 (sp "en. P. Dygert, Cath. Kast)
6237: CONRAD bp GF 14 Oct 1792 (sp Con. Koch, Sara McKoom)
6238: child b GF 28 May 1795 (sp Geo. Hilts, Maria Bell)
6239: PETER bp Herkimer 1802 (sp Elis. Smith unm, Pet. Harter)

6229: CONRAD MILLER - m by 1782 CHRISTINA ... Sponsored Sep 1791 bp of Magdalena,
dau of John Miller & Elisabeth and had ELISABETH (bp GF 14 Apr 1782, sp. Gerrit
Jung & Christina Bikkert) & pr. JOHN CON. (b GF 5 Mar 1784, sp. John Monck & Anna)
Pr. this Conrad belongs to a Montgomery Co. Miller family.

6233: HENRICH MILLER - pr. born ca 1743 to 1755; pr. m ANNA EVA BOSHAR dau of
JACOB BOSHAR (presumption based on baptismal sponsors and land transfers). Pr.
the Corporal of Bellinger's Revol. Regiment and ps. the Henry with 5 adults on 1778
GF relief. Henry was on 1790 German Flats census (2-3-2), next to Fred Christman,
George Jac. Edick, John Hess & Augustinus Hess. He lived at Warren NY in 1804 and
in 1805 received land from Jacob Boshar (HK Deed book).

+6240: ps. JOHN b say 1774; m by 1802 ELISABETH KILTS
 6241: ANNA MARGARET bp GF 1 Sep 1776 (sp Joh Miller & A. Marg.)
 6242: JACOB bp GF 16 Aug 1779 (sp Jacob Boshaar & Cath.)
        pr. liv. 1794 (spf Jac. Frieba bp)
+6243: FREDERICK bp GF 8 Sep 1782 (sp Fr. Christman & Anna Eva)
+6244: GEORGE bp GF 12 May 1788 (sp Geo. F Frieba, Eva Hess)
        pr. m by 1807 MARIA CATHERINE ORENDORF
 6245: SUSANNA b GF 31 Jan 1791 (sp Jac Christman, Sus. P Wohlben)
 6246: HENRICH b GF 8 Oct 1793 (sp Hen. Warner & Cath.)

6232: JOHN MILLER Jr. - pr. born ca 1740 to 1750; died by 1791; pr. m by 1777
URSALA ... (ps. Huber?). Listed with Nicholas Miller in Capt. Conrad Frank's 1767
militia co. and in Col. Bellinger's Revol. Regiment. Ps. the John Miller who
sponsored, with Elis. Frank, Sep 1770 SAR bp of Susanna, dau of John Huber
(Hoover) & Catherine. His widow Ursala m2 1791 CONRAD KROLL.

+6247: HENRICH bp GF 15 Mar 1777 (sp Hen Miller & Anna Miller)
 6248: ANNA bp GF 27 Mar 1779 (dau of John & Ursala)
        (bp sp Hen. Huber & Ursala <pr. should be Anna>)
 6249: ELISABETH bp GF 27 Sep 1781 (sp Hen. Huber & Anna)

6231: NICHOLAS MILLER - pr. born ca 1740 to 1750 (son of John, named in father's will); m MAGDALENA ... (ps. Davis?). In Capt. Conrad Frank's 1767 militia co. in 1767 and in Bellinger's Revol. Regiment. Nicholas sponsored Mar 1781 bp of Nicholas, son of Jacob Happle & Maria.

>   +6250: NICHOLAS (twin) b GF 14 Oct 1777 (sp. Peter Davis & Maria)
>   pr. m by 1803 EVA ORENDORF
>   6251: HENRICH (twin) b GF Oct 1777 (sp John Miller & Anna Marg.)
>   6252: LENA b GF 6 Sep 1781 (sp Jac Christman, Elis. Davis)

6253: PETER MILLER - pr. born ca 1740 to 1748; m by 1769 ... Ps. related to the Conrad and Jacob Miller who sponsored baptisms at the Stone Arabia Luth. Church just prior to 1770. Had MARIA (bp SAL 11 Jan 1769, sp Geo. Ruppert & w.). Ps. the father of John Miller (b ca Oct 1781, bp GF Jun 1795, age 13-8-).

6254: PHILIP MILLER - born say 1770; m GF 14 Feb 1792 ELISABETH JAC. MEYER

MILLER - 5th Generation

6243: FREDERICK MILLER - pr. the Fred. bp 1782 (son of Henry & Anna Eva); m by 1803 CATHERINE CHRISTMAN. Lived at Warren NY in 1804 (child's bp then was in Bashor's house).

>   6255: JACOB bp Columbia NY 20 Feb 1803
>   6256: FREDERICK bp HK 14 Jul 1804 (sp Hen. Miller & Anna Eva)
>   6257: CATHERINE bp Columbia NY 4 Apr 1813

6244: GEORGE MILLER - pr. born ca 1770 to 1789; m by 1807 MARIA CATHERINE ORENDORF pr. a dau of GEORGE ORENDORF & ELISABETH. Children include GEORGE (bp Herkimer NY 19 May 1807), ELISABETH (bp HK 1809), EVA (bp HK 30 Aug 1812), and HENRICH (bp HK 5 May 1816).

6247: HENRICH MILLER - pr. the Henry born 3 Mar 1777 (son of John & Anna, as seen in Hatch Papers page 234) and bp GF 15 Mar 1777 (sp Hen Miller & Anna Miller); m 1806 ELIZABETH WOHLEBEN (b 25 Feb 1785) dau of ABRAHAM WOHLEBEN & DOROTHY BELLINGER. Bellinger book page 37 has this Henry living at Warren NY.

6240: JOHN MILLER - pr. born ca 1760 to 1780; pr. the John who died Herkimer NY 23 May 1834 (age 59); m by 1802 ELISABETH KILTS pr. dau of NICHOLAS KILTS & CATERINE HILTS. John Miller & w. Elisabeth were sponsors for Feb 1803 bp of Elisabeth, dau of Nic. Spohn & Catherine (Kilts).

>   6258: CATHERINE bp Herkimer 8 Oct 1802 (of Jois & Elis. Kilts)
>   6259: JOHN b HK 28 Jul 1804 (sp Marc Staring & Anna)
>   6260: JACOB bp Herkimer NY 12 Jul 1809
>   6261: DAVID bp G. Flats 2 Jul 1815

6250: NICHOLAS MILLER - m EVA ORENDORF pr. dau of GEORGE ORENDORF & ELISABETH.

>   6262: GEORGE bp HK 20 Feb 1803 (sp Hen Miller, Marg. Orendorf)
>   6263: ELISABETH bp HK Aug 1804 (sp. Elis. Orendorf, widow)
>   6264: EVA bp HK 10 Aug 1806 (sp F. Orendorf & w. Barbara)

********** MILLER, Valentine **********

6300: **VALENTINE MILLER** - born in Germany 10 Mar 1740 (son of Andreas Muller &
Eva of Hettingen Germany, as seen in "The Valentine Miller Papers" by Reuben M.
Brockway); died Herkimer NY 27 Sep 1811 age 71-6-18; m in Germany 9 Jan 1766
ANNA MARIA MOREHOUSE (b 12 May 1736) dau of JOHN MEHRHAUS of Gernsheim Germany.
Valentine paid the amount of 71 pounds, 7 shilling, and 6 pence (New York money)
for passage with Peter Hasensclever´s group, which came to New York in 1766 and
located at the New Petersburg settlement (now E. Schuyler, NY). In the
Revolution, he was in Bellinger´s 4th Tryon Co. Regiment and in the Tory Indian
raid on New Petersburg in 1780 two of his children were taken prisoner (George,
returned in 1785, and Catherine, for whom there is no further record). On 1790
German Flats census (2-1-4). Other details in the "Valentine Miller Papers" (at
Herkimer Co. Hist. Society) include a note, dated 1772, specifiying 314 pounds
owed by Philip Clements of Petersburg to Valentine Miller.

                    surname MILLER
    6301: JACOBINA CATHERINE   bp SAR 23 Oct 1767 (Jac. Mohr & w. Cath)
                      m GF 9 Oct 1787 Johan ANDREES DYGERT ("Deger")
   +6302: GEORGE MATHEW   bp SAR 1768 (sp. Geo. Sneck & Barbara)
                      d 1802; m2 1801 ANNA CATHERINE BAKER
    6303: ANNA MARGARET   bp Palatine NY 25 May 1770
    6303A pt. ELISABETH b say 1772; m by 1797 CONRAD KRAMER
   +6304: VALENTINE V.   1775-1851 m by 1810 SARAH WITRIG
    6305: MARIA EVA b GF 4 May 1776 (sp Nich. Kolsch, M.Elis. Braun)
                      following dau were twins and bp GF 29 Nov 1778
    6306: ANNA CATHERINE   b 24 Oct 1778 (sp John Finster & A. Cath.)
    6307: MARGARET b 24 Oct 1788 (sp Jos. Kessler & Margaret <Braun>)

                    MILLER - 2nd Generation

6302: **GEORGE MATHEW MILLER** - bp Palatine NY 1768; died 26 Apr 1802; m1 ...;
m2 Herkimer NY 4 Oct 1801 ANNA CATHERINE BEKKER (mar. rec has Baker) dau of
DIEBOLD BEKKER of New Germany (E. Schuyler, NY).

    6308: VALENTINE
    6309: JOHN
    6310: MARY ("Polly")

6304: **VALENTINE MILLER** - born 1775; died 1851; m SARAH WITRIG (b 1791, d 1856,
dates from HCH Miller file), pr. (b Apr 1787) dau of MICHAEL WITRIG & ELISABETH.

    6311: NANCY m GEORGE WITRIG
    6312: ELISABETH   bp Schuyler NY 8 Apr 1810 (bp Herkimer Jun 1810)
                      m JACOB FINSTER
    6312A EVA   b HK 1 Sep 1812 (sp Joh. Dygert, Maria Witrig, unm)
    6313: MARY   m FREDERICK H ...
    6314: HULDAH   m HIRAM FINSTER
    6315: JANE   m Rev. CHARLES WITRIG
    6317: JAMES d. young
    6318: VALENTINE d. young
    6319: ADAM
    6320: MICHAEL   1826-1902 m PHILINDA FINSTER

********** MOAK (Moog) **********

6401: JOHANNES MOAK - pr. born in Switzerland ca 1700 to 1710; died ca 1800; m ... (his wife died at sea coming to America, as seen in Brown's Folts book page 2). Settled Bethlehem NY ca 1750. Presumably the Johannes Moak who immigrant from Switzerland was the ancestor to wives of the Rasbachs at German Flats (Mrs. Vera Eysaman notes) and was the same as the John Moak of Switzerland who was father of Jacob and was said to have come to Bethlehem NY ca 1750 ("American Ancestry" vol. 1 page 55).

                    surname MOAK
    +6402: pr. JACOB b say 1724; m2 1761 KATHERINE CLAUS
    +6403: BONOCRATIUS (Crotsy) ca 1726-1814 m ANNA CONRAD
     6404: SOPHRONIA (Veronica) 1732-1814 m Lt. MARKS RASPACH

                         MOAK - 2nd Generation

6403: CROTSY MOAK ("Bonocratius") - born in Switzerland ca 1726; died Herkimer NY 2 May 1814 (age 88); m ANNA CONRAD. In Capt. Mark Petrie's German Flats militia company in 1757. First lived at Schenectady NY (Mrs. Vera Eysaman notes, 1983), but apparently moved to Herkimer before 1790. His name was trouble for ministers and clerks and on the 1790 Herkimer census we see him as ".. nsom Mack" (1-0-3), listed next to Rasbach and Folts. Mrs. Eysaman's notes have Anna as Crotsy's daughter and the comment "a sister married a Mr. Francis" looks like it ties in Gertrude. Margaret seems to have been the youngest of Crotsy's three daughters who were married at German Flats NY between 1785 and 1792.

        6405: ANNA b SAR 29 Nov 1766 (dau of Erasmus Moog & Anna)
                    m GF 1785 JOHN M. RASBACH
        6405A HENRICH bp SAL 1 Apr 1769 (sp. Jacob Neff & w.)
        6406: GERTRUDE ca 1769-1843 ml GF Mar 1791 JOHN FRANCIS
                    m2 HENRY BAKER
        6407: MARGARET b Fonda NY May 1773 (sp John & Ger. Rechmeyer)
                    pr. m GF 1792 JOHN F. RASBACH

6402: JACOB MOAK ("Hannes Jacob Moogh") - pr. born ca 1720 to 1725; ml FRENA ... ; m2 21 Feb 1761 KATHERINE CLAUS or Claasen (b 1740, d 1821) of Holland as given in Pearson's Albany book (apge 80). Reportedly from Switzerland and settled at Bethlehem NY ("Amer. Ancestry" vol 1 page 55).

        6408: HENDRICK bp Albany 29 Jun 1740; pr. d. y.
        6409: ELISABETH bp Albany 22 Jan 1744 (sp Pet. & Christina Brad)
        6410: ARIANTJE bp Albany 16 Dec 1753 (sp Jac. Arnel, Aria. Lansing)
        6411: JACOB 1761- m MARY MCGHEE liv. at Sharon
        6412: SUSANNA bp Albany 14 Jan 1766; pr. m 1784 JOHN B. DILLENBACH
        6413: HENDRICK b 20 Nov 1771
        6414: JAMES 1776-1849 m MARTHA MCCLASKY

6415: JOHN MONCK (Monk) - m by 1781 ANNA ... Similar sounding name but pr. not related to Moak family. John Monk sponsored Mar 1784 GF bp of John, son of Conrad Miller. Two John Monks listed together on the 1790 Canajoharie NY census. Had son CONRAD MONCK (b GF 17 Dec 1781, sp. Con. Miller & Christina).

********** ORENDORF (Aherndarff) **********

ORENDORF - 1st Generation

6501: HENDRICK ORENDORF - pr. born in Germany ca 1675 to 1688; m ANNA MARGARTHA
... (tradition that wife was Jewish is apparently wrong, see H. Jones´ "Palatine
Families of New York"). Probably the Johan Hendrick Arendorff listed with wife
and one child on sixth sailing to England in Jul 1709. On NY Palatine subsistence
list in 1710 (2A,0Y) and in 1712 (2A,1Y). On 1717 Simmendinger census with wife
Anna Margaretha & 3 children and ca 1723 had Burnetsfield lot #39.

surname ORENDORF
```
        6502: child   liv. 1709; pr. died 1710
        6503: pr. child  b say 1711 (under 10 in 1712); ps. d. young
        6504: JANNETJE  bp Schenectady NY 3 May 1713; ps. m JOSEPH STARING
       +6503: CONRAD  b say 1715 (pr. eldest son)
        6505: MARIA ELIZABETH  b 1 Jun 1717 (Kocherthal rec.)
                   (sp. Martin Badorf, Maria Eliz. Walborn)
       +6506: pr. FREDERICK   ca 1720-1802  m ANNA EVA GETMAN
```

ORENDORF - 2nd Generation

6503: CONRAD ORENDORF - pr. born ca 1710 to 1718; poss. died 1757 to 1760 (not
seen as parent or sponsor in Church rec. of 1760´s); m ... Probably an eldest
son of immigrant Henrich to account for his receiving Burnetsfield lot #40, next
to Henrich Orendorf. The only hint as to this Conrad marrying is the presence of
two Henry Orendorfs in the 1780´s (i.e. Henry who married by 1787 Maria Crantz and
the Henry who married 1788 Anna Sternberger).

```
       +6507: ps. HENRY  b say 1747;  m by 1787 MARIA CRANTZ (b ca 1744)
        6507A ps. JOHN  b say 1750; liv. 1790 (war damages claimant)
        6507B ps. MARIA  b say 1753; liv. 1767 (spf Seghner bp)
```

6506: FREDERICK ORENDORF - born Canajoharie NY ca 1720; died Herkimer NY 8 Aug
1802 (age 82, HK church rec.); m1 ANNA EVA GETMAN dau of FREDERICK GETMAN (Getman
Genealogy); m2 GF 28 Nov 1786 the widow MARIA MARC. PETRIE, pr. widow of MARCUS J.
PETRIE. Sgt in Capt. Conrad Frank´s militia co. in 1767. Frederick Sr Orendorf
was in Col. Bellinger´s Revol. Regm. and on 1790 GF census (2-0-1) listed next to
Frederick Orendorf Jr. & Joseph Staring.

```
       +6508: CATHERINE   1741-1812  m 1760 MICHAEL EDICK
       +6509: pr. GEORGE  b say 1745; m by 1776 ELISABETH ... (pr. Fulmer)
       +6510: pr. CONRAD  b 1748; m 1770 CATHERINE SHOEMAKER
        6510A pr. MARIA (Orendorf?)  1750-1813  m JACOB D. PETRIE
       +6511: pr. PETER  b say 1753;  m CATHERINE PFEIFFER
       +6512: FREDERICK jr  1758-1830  m BARBARA FULMER
        6513: ELISABETH  b 28 Nov 1759 (sp. Elis. w of Nich. Fehling)
        6514: ANNA EVA  bp GF 17 Jul 1763 (sp Anna Eva & Christian Getman)
                   m by 1781 THOMAS SHOEMAKER
       +6515: HENRY FRED.  1765-1854  m 1788 ANNA JAC. STERNBERGER
        6516: ps. dau (?)  m Mr. EARL (as given in Hatch Papers)
```

6510: CONRAD ORENDORF - born 1748; died 4 Mar 1819 (age 71 yrs less 10 days); m 12 Jun 1770 CATHERINE SHOEMAKER (b 1748, d 24 Feb 1814 age 65-0-14) dau of Capt. RUDOLPH SHOEMAKER & GERTRUDE PETRIE.   Conrad Orendorf is said to have thrown Indian chief Joseph Brandt in a friendly wrestling match. Pr. the Conrad in Capt. Conrad Frank's militia co. in 1767 and later the Conrad listed in Col. Campbell's Revol. Regm. Conrad was on the 1790 GF census (2-2-5) and was an innkeeper at Columbia NY in 1819.

> 6517: GERTRUDE   ca 1773-1818   m 30 Jun 1793 JOHN OXNER
> 6518: ANNA EVA   bp GF 20 Mar 1778 (sp Anna Eva Orndrf, Rud. Shmkr jr)
>   m GF 1794 FRITZ PETRIE (pr. Fred Jac.)
> 6519: MARGARET   b GF 18 Feb 1781 (sp Marg. Cox, Nic. Rosencrantz)
>   m JOHN MIX
> +6520: HENRY   1783-1863   m MARY TUNNCLIFF
> 6521: ELISABETH   bp Aug 1785 (sp Geo Ittig, wid. Elis. Bellinger)
> 6522: CATHERINE   b 22 Aug 1790 (sp Mich. Ittig & Cath.)
>   m HENRY GRANTS (Crantz)

6512: FREDERICK ORENDORF ("Fritz") Jr - pr. born ca 1750 to 1757; m by 1778 LANNY BARBARA FULMER (b 1756, d 1830 gravestone, as in Myers Genealogy) pr. dau of CONRAD FULMER & LENA; ps. m after 1795 LUCY HELMER (Getman book, not other support seen). Bellinger book page 46 has daughter Catherine as wife of Michael Fox. Pr. the Frederick Jr. in Bellinger's Revol. Regiment and on 1790 German Flats census (1-2-6).

> 6523: FREDERICK   b GF 19 Aug 1778 (sp Fr. Ittig, Maria Piper)
> 6524: LENA   b GF 6 Aug 1780 (sp Conrad Volmer & Lena)
> 6525: EVA FRED.   b say 1782; m 1802 JACOB STAHRING
> +6526: HENRICH   b GF 23 Feb 1784 (sp Hen Orendorf, Cath. Fulmer)
>   m ANNA DEMUTH (Myers Genealogy)
> 6526A MARIA   b GF 19 Jul 1785 (sp ... Ittig & Maria)
> 6527: CATHERINE F.   bp GF 27 Jan 1787 (sp Wm Fulmer, Cath. M Petrie)
>   m1 1808 MICHAEL FOX; m2 1823 MICHAEL RICKERT
> 6528: CONRAD   b GF 20 Jun 1788 (sp Conrad Arndorf & Cath.)
> 6529: MARGARET   b GF 18 Jan 1790 (sp Ger. V Slyk, Maria M. Petrie)
>   m 1811 DANIEL HESS
> 6530: ANNA   b GF 8 Jul 1791 (sp. Mich. Ittig jr, Anna Hess)
> 6531: FREDERICK   bp GF 29 May 1793 (of Fritz & Barbara)
>   (sp Fred. Jac Ittig, Elis. Orendorf)
> 6532: GEORGE F.   b GF 6 Apr 1795 (sp John Shoemaker & Anna Eva)
>   m 1818 GERTRUDE BELL

6509: GEORGE ORENDORF - pr. born ca 1740 to 1755; died by Jun 1803; m by 1776 ELISABETH ...(pr. Fulmer). George was a sponsor for Oct 1765 bp of George, son of. Michael Edick & Catherine (Orendorf) and George & Elis. were sponsors for Jun 1777 bp of George, son of Jacob Petrie & Maria.

> 6533: ELISABETH   bp GF 6 Oct 1776 (sp Barb. Folmer, Jo. Fred Ittig)
> 6534: ANNA EVA   bp 2 May 1778 (sp Jacob Petrie & Maria)
>   pr. m by 1804 NICHOLAS MILLER
> +6535: HENRY   b say 1780; m by 1807 ELISABETH PETRIE
> 6536: GEORGE   bp GF Jan 1782 (sp John Hess & Marg.<Fulmer>)
> 6537: WILHELM   b GF 15 Sep 1783 (sp Wm Fulmer, Elis. Wohleben)
>   pr. m DOROTHY WERNER

6538: ANNA MARGARET bp GF 29 Sep 1785 (sp Geo. Ittig, Anna Hess)
            m 1803 ANSON KAPPEL (son of John, from Lebanon CT)
6539: CATHERINE (twin) b 1787 (Pet. Jo. Bellngr, Cath Fulmer) d.y.
6540: MARIA (twin) b GF 5 Aug 1787 (sp. Hend. Orendorf & Maria)
6541: CATHERINE G. bp GF Apr 1789 (sp Bill Delaney, Maria Petri)
            pr. m by 1807 GEORGE MILLER
    6542: GEORGE bp 1792

6507: HENRY ORENDORF - pr. born ca 1740 to 1750 (believed to son of Conrad); m by
1787 MARIA CRANTZ (b ca 1744, d GF 22 Jun 1818 age 74).

6515: HENRY FRED. ORENDORF - born 1765; died 1854; m at German Flats NY Jul 1788
ANNA JAC. STERNBERGER.

6511: PETER ORENDORF - pr. born ca 1740 to 1756; m by 1777 CATHERINE PFEIFFER dau
of PETER PFEIFFER & MARIA CATHERINE WEAVER. Listed with Fred Sr, Fred Jr and
George Ohrendorph in Col. Bellinger's Revol. Regiment. He was apparently the
Peter Orendorf who, while a prisoner of war in Canada in 1780, identified Joseph
Meyer's young daughter Eva. On 1790 German Flats census (2-2-3).

    +6543: ps. HENRY b say 1774; m by 1805 ELISABETH WOLF
    6544: FREDERICK   bp GF 14 Sep 1777 (sp. Fritz Orndf, Elis. Piper)
    6545: MARIA CATHERINE b GF 14 Apr 1780 (sp Mic. Ittig & Cath.)
    6546: ANNA EVA bp 4 Mar 1783 (sp And. Piper & Dor. Shoemaker)
    6547: MARGARETHA b GF 6 Aug 1785 (sp. H. Orendrf, Marg. Piper)
    6548: JACOB b 18 Nov 1787 (sp Jac. Chr. Ittig, Dor. Tooty)
    6549: MARIA b 4 Feb 1790 (sp Ludwig Campbell & Maria)
    6550: LUDWIG b 14 Feb 1791 (sp Ludwig Campbell & Maria)
    6551: JOHANNES b GF 3 Feb 1794 (sp Joh. Ochsner & Gertrude)

6508: CATHERINE ORENDORF - pr. born ca 1735 to 1740; m 1760 Capt. MICHAEL EDICK
(Ittig, b 1734, d 1806). Prob. the Catherine, dau of Fred., who was sponsor at Apr
1760 bp of Catherine, dau of Marcus Ittig.

ORENDORF - 4th Generation

6526: HENRY F. ORENDORF - born GF 23 Feb 1784; m 24 Feb 1805 ANNA DEMUTH.
Marriage witnesses were the groom's father Frederick Orendorf and John Petry.

    6551A MARIA b HK 25 Jul 1805 (sp Jac. Staring & Eva)
    6552: ELISABETH bp Hkm 21 May 1809; m CHRISTOPHER YATES
    6553: BARBARA bp 6 Jun 1813 (sp Fr. Orndorf & w. Barbara)

6535: HENRY ORENDORF - pr. born ca 1765 to 1785; m by 1807 ELISABETH PETRIE.
Sponsored bp Mar 1807 bp of Henry Orend., son of Jacob Petrie & Anna Eva Orendorf.

6520: HENRY SHOEMAKER ORENDORF - born German Flats NY 17 Jan 1783 (sp. Maj. Stofel
Yates & Maria); died 12 Oct 1863 (gravestone has born 1782, d 1863); m MARY
TUNNCLIFF (Hatch Papers page 179). Had son Conrad (b 1813, d Mar 1814).

6543: HENRY ORENDORF - pr. born ca 1760 to 1784; m by 1805 ELISABETH WOLF. Had
dau CATHERINE (bp HK 24 Feb 1805, sp Jac. Shoemaker & Cath.).

********** OSTERHOUT (Osteroth) **********

6595: **GUSTEV OSTHEHOUT** - m MARIA HESS (b 1715) dau of JOHANNES HESS. Gustev, along with Paul Crim, was an early grantee of land at Andrustown (Herk. Co. Deed Book v 12 page 348) and an early member of the Manheim Church, with Werner & Adam Schafer (Book of Names, pg 61). Daughter Anna, was raised by her grandmother Mrs. Katherine Hess, after the murder by Indians (pr. ca 1755-60) of her parents, four sisters, and a brother; there surviving only herself and brothers John & Frederick (Dann's "The Revolution Remembered" pg 268).

       surname OSTERHOUT
       6598: girl (ps. Delia) bp SAR Jun 1745 (Otila Shoemaker, Fred. Hess)
      +6601: JOHN b ca 1746
       6601A ANNA b 1747, liv. 1840 (age 83); m HENRY MOYER
      +6612: FREDERICK b say 1750; m by 1771 ELISABETH KLOCK

OSTERHOUT - 2nd Generation

6601: **JOHN OSTERHOUT** - born ca 1746; died Warren NY 22 Apr 1818 (will proved 27 Apr 1818); m by 1765 KATHERINE SPENCER. John was in Frank's GF militia in 1767 and in Revol. service in the 4th Tryon Co. Regiment. He had 2 adults & 5 children on the Sep 1778 GF relief. Hatch papers (page 183) say he settled early at Andrustown, and that during the July 1778 massacre there, he and his wife escaped carrying their infant children, but their son Nicholas was lost for three days in the woods before finding his way to the fort.

       6602: pr. NICHOLAS (oldest) b say 1768; liv. 1778; pr. d. by 1780
       6603: ANNA (Nancy) b say 1773; m 1794 JOHN AD. SCHAEFFER
       6604: LENA
       6605: pr. MARIA b say 1775; m 1794 WILHELM HAGADORN
       6606: ANNA EVA b 28 Dec 1777 (sp John Step. Frank & Anna Eva)
              liv. 1795 (spf Eva Hess bp)
      +6607: Johan NICHOLAS b GF 7 Nov 1780 (sp. John Bellinger & Maria)
       6608: JOHN b say 1783; m by 1808 CATHERINE
       6609: DENUS (Augustinus) b say 1784; liv. 1805 (spf Hagedorn bp)
       6610: CATHERINE b 19 Nov 1785 (Fred Hess & Bally); m JACOB GRANT
      +6611: FREDERICK b GF 20 Feb 1787 (sp Fred Fox & Elis.)
              m HK 1808 MARIE DEVOE dau of ANTHONY & HELEN (VANDENBERG)

6612: **FREDERICK OSTERHOUT** - pr. born ca 1740 to 1755; m by 1771 ELISABETH KLOCK. Fred. Osterhout & Elisabeth sponsored Jan 1771 SAR bp of Catherine, dau of George Kraus & Cath. On 1790 Palatine NY census (2-2-3).

       6613: PETER b GF 28 Jan 1782 (sp Peter Fox, Anna Bellinger)
       6614: JOHN b GF 3 Jan 1785 (sp John Glock & Anna Margaret)
       6615: EVA bp SJR 3 Jan 1789 (sp Con. Hillegas & Eva <Walrath>)
       6616: ELISABETH bp SJR 24 Oct 1792 (sp. Henry Mayer & Anna)

OSTERHOUT - 3rd Generation

6607: **NICHOLAS OSTERHOUT** - b 7 Nov 1780; m 1803 DELIA PETRIE (b 1784) dau of Col. JACOB PETRIE. Children (Petrie book, pg 25) - John (b 1808, sp. gr-parents John & Cath.), Nicholas, Daniel, Caty, Phoebe, Jacob, Elizabeth, & Polly.

********** PETRIE, Jost **********

6701: Johan JOST PETRIE - born ca 1620 to 1640; m CATHARINE ... Resident of
Breitscheid (a few miles south of Seigen) in Nassau Dillenburg, Germany. Material
on the Petrie ancestry in Germany is quoted, with permission of the author, from
"The Palatine Families of New York" by Mr Hank Jones (P.O. Box 8341, Universal
City, Ca 91608).

                            surname PETRIE
       +6702: JOHANNES bp Breitscheid Germ. 28 Feb 1664; m GERTRUDE
        6703: pr. LUDWIG b say 1670; spf 1697 bp of dau of Joh. & Gert.
        6704: pr. CATHERINE b say 1675; spf 1700 bp of dau of Joh. & Gert.

                          PETRIE - 1st Generation

6702: JOHANNES PETRIE <P1> - bp Breitscheid Germany 28 Feb 1664; died ca 24 Jun
1700 (buried at Breitschied as given in H. Jones findings). Note that Petrie
Genealogy gives his name as Johan Jost Petrie who was supposedly born at
Strassburg, Alsace, Germany (now France) and married ANNA GERTRUYD VON RINGH and
further states the tradition that he died in crossing the Atlantic and that his
wife was of noble descent. H. Jones findings that Johannes Petrie's widow of
Breitscheid had petition to emigrate to America at Weisbaden in 1709 seems to
clear matters in regard to the father of NY immigrant Johan Jost Petrie.
Johannes' widow Gertrude appears on NY Palatine subsistence list in 1710 (2A,1Y)
and 1712 (2A,1Y). Since her son Jost appears separately on the 1710-12
subsistence list, we suspect widow Gertrude's 1710 dependents were a daughter over
age 10 (ps. Elisabeth or Gertrude) and a younger daughter (pr. Catherine). In
1723 Widow Gertrude Petrie received Burnetsfield lot #17, which she subsequently
donated for use as a town area to be shared by all residents. Gertrude ultimatly
became known as "the mother of the Palatines". Identification numbers in brackets
<P..> are provided as a cross reference to identifications used in "The Mohawk
Valley Petries and Allied Families".

       +6705: Johan JOST (Joseph) 1686-1770 m CORDELIA DEMUTH
        6706: ANNA ELISABETHA bp 1691
        6707: JOST HENRICH bp 1693
        6708: a son (ps. PETER) bp 6 Jan 1695
        6709: ANNA GERTRAUD bp 1697 (sp. Ludwig Petrie son of Joh. Jost)
        6710: ANNA CATHERINE bp 5 May 1700; d 22 Dec 1700
        6711: pr. CATHERINE b say 1702; m JOST HERKIMER (1700-1775)

6712: CHRISTIAN PETRIE - pr. b ca 1650 to 1665; m ANNA OTTILIA... Christian Petrie
had a petition to emigrate to America at Weisbaden in 1709 (ref. H. Jones notes).

       +6713: Johann CONRAD bp Breitschied 1696 m MARIA CATHERINE ROSMAN

                          PETRIE - 2nd Generation

6705: **Johan JOST PETRIE** <P2> - bp Breithschied Germany 13 Oct 1689 (H. Jones´ book) but ps. born Strassburg Alsace 1686 (Petrie book); died German Flats NY 1770 (age 84, Petrie book); Petrie book has m in 1706 CORDELIA DEMUTH dau of JACOB DEMUTH (date seems early for Demuth connection). Jost was a volunteer in Col. Nicholson´s Canadian expedition in 1711 and on the NY Palatine subsistence list in 1710 (2A,0Y) & 1712 (2A,0Y). He and Conrad Rickert petitioned the Albany council in 1721 to secure a license for the Palatines to purchase the German Flats land and, later in 1757, he was town magistrate and taken prisoner that year in the French & Indian raid on German Flats (he appears to have been released with other prisoners in the Sep 1758 exchange, as noted in the Book of Names, page 112). His will in 1759 mentions sons Marcus, John, Daniel, Jost, & Dietrich, and daughters Catherine, Dorothy, Gertrude & Maria.

+6714: MARCUS   b say 1712; d 1776; m by 1737 ANNA EVA KESSLER
 6715: CATHERINE   1714-1799   m JACOB FOLTS
 6716: GERTRUDE   b 14 Dec 1715; m HENRY HAGER
 6717: DOROTHY   b say 1717; pr. m by 1735 PHILIP FOX
+6718: JOHANNES   b say 1718; d 1783; m MARIA ELIZABETH ...
+6719: ps. JACOB (?)   b say 1720; pr. died before 1759
+6720: DANIEL   b say 1721; killed 1782; m ELIZABETH FOLTS (b 1721)
+6721: Johan JOST   b say 1723; m bef. 1760 MARIA (pr. BELL)
+6722: DIETRICH   b say 1726; pr. m 1761 CATHERINE KLOCK
 6723: ANNA MARIA   b say 1728; ml 1748 ACKUS VAN SLYCK

6724: **JOHN CONRAD PETRIE** <P3> - born 1698; m MARIA CATHERINE ROSMAN dau of JOHAN ROSMAN & ELIZABETH. Bound out to Robert Livingston of Livingston Manor NY in 1710 and was naturalized 22 Nov 1715. He and his wife sponsored grandson´s bp (son of Christian & Lea) at Linlithgo, Columbia Co., NY in 1756.

 6725: ANNA CATHERINE   b 27 Nov 1720 (sp. Joh. Rosman & Elis.)
+6726: JOHANNES   b 7 Oct 1722; m LANY MUSCHER
 6727: CONRAD   b say 1724; m 1754 CATHERINE SCHRAM at Kingston NY
 6728: CHRISTIAN   b say 1726; m by 1756 LEA MUSCHER

PETRIE - 3rd Generation

6720: **Capt. DANIEL PETRIE** <P13> - pr. born ca 1715 to 1722; killed in combat 21 Jun 1782; m ELIZABETH CATHARINE FOLTS (b Dec 1721, d HK 3 Mar 1807 age 85-3-3) dau of MELCHERT FOLTS & MARGARET. Operated a mill with Gershom Skinner at Little Falls where he was butchered in a Tory Indian raid in 1782 (see page 230 for more). Daniel´s will in 1780 mentions sons Jost (oldest), Jacob, Marx, & Daniel.

+6729: JOST   b say 1738; pr. m by 1777 MARIA ELISABETH ZIMMERMAN
+6730: JACOB D.   1740-1823   m MARIA
 6731: ps. ANNA   b say 1746; liv. 1766 (spf Anna Melc. Kessler bp)
 6732: ps. MARIA ELISABETH   1748-1839   m by 1765 MELCHIOR KESSLER
+6733: MARKS   1750-1806   m MARGARET BELLINGER
 6734: CATHARINA   b say 1752; pr. m by 1776 FASIER COX
 6734A ps. JOHN   b say 1756; killed at Oriskany 1777
+6735: DANIEL   b say 1760; pr m by 1788 MARIA STAHRING
 6736: DELIA   b say 1766; m 1787 JAMES RANCKIN
 6737: ZIPPORAH   b say 1769; killed by Indians in summer 1782
 6738: CAROLINE   b say 1771; killed by Indians in summer 1782

6722: DIETRICH PETRIE <P15> - pr. born ca 1725 to 1740; died before 1770 (Petrie book); m 31 Mar 1761 CATHERINE KLOCK dau of JOHANNES KLOCK & MARGARET FOX. In 1757 GF militia and sponsored Sep 1760 bp of Elisabeth, dau of Christian Schell.

    6739: CATHERINE b 21 Dec 1761 (sp Cath. Jac. Foltz, John J. Klock)
  +6740: JOST b 14 Feb 1763 (sp. Jost M. Petrie)
          d 1822; m ANNA EVA BELLINGER
  +6741: JOHANNES 1765-1843 m GERTRUDE G. DEMUTH
    6742: ps. LENA DIET. b say 1768; liv. 1789 (spf Lena Klock bp)

6719: JACOB PETRIE (existence?) - born say 1720; died before 1759 (not named in Jost Petrie Sr.´s will). Another son of immigrant Jost Petrie seems needed as father for stray Petries (the name Jacob takes care of Jost´s father-in-law). A Henry Petrie, son of immigrant Jost, is also possible if one accepts the existence of the Jost H. Petrie sponsoring the Aug 1769 SAR bp of John Kessler.

    6743: ps. MARIA ELISABETH b say 1740; m by 1758 CHRISTIAN SCHELL
    6743A ps. ISAAC b say 1743; liv. Oct 1777 (Mohawk Val. in Revol.)
    6744: ps. JOST JAC. b say 1746; liv. 1775 (spf Jost Petrie bp, GF)

6718: JOHANNES PETRIE <P12> - pr . born ca 1712 to 1720; died 1783; m MARIA ELIZABETH ... His will in 1780 mentions wife Maria Elisabeth & three children.

  +6746: MARCUS J. b say 1740; d by 1783; m by 1764 ANNA MARIA ...
  +6747: DIETRICH b say 1742; m by 1766 ELIZABETH DYGERT
  +6748: JOST (Hanyost) b say 1743; d 1777; m 1769 BARBARA WINDECKER
    6749: ps. ELISABETH b say 1745; m SAR 1766 JOHN KESSLER
  +6750: JOHANNES b say 1747; liv. 1786; m BARBARA KLOCK (b 1751)
    6751: ps. NICHOLAS b say 1749; Sgt., killed at Oriskany Aug 1777
    6751A ps. DELIA (Petrie?) b say 1751; m by 1775 JACOB SCHUYLER
    6752: ps. MARIA J. b say 1759; liv. 1775 (spf Schuyler bp)
    6753: MARGARET JOH. b Jul 1761 (sp Marg., w. of Chrstian Ittig)

6726: JOHANNES PETRIE <P22> - born Oct 1722 (Conrad´s son); m LANY MUSCHEUR dau of JURY MOSSER of Albany. Pr. lived near Albany. Had 12 children - Christiana (b 1754), Maria (1756), Elizabeth (1757), Conrad (1759), Lydia (1760), Lany (1763), John (1765), Jacob (1767), Anna, Peter (1770), Jeremiah (1772), & Cath. (1774).

6721: JOST PETRIE jr. <P14> - pr. born before 1731; m1 12 Jun 1748 (Petrie´s son m by Rev. Somner to Bell´s daughter) MARIA BELL pr. dau of FREDERICK BELL; m2 by 1760 MARIA EVA ... (ps. a Hilts). Jost jr. was captured in the 1757 French raid on German Flats, and, with wife Maria & four children, was taken to Canada until released in Sep 1758. In 1766 Jost & wife Eva sponsored bp of Elisabeth, dau of Nic. Hilts. Pr. this Joseph Petry was the Tory in Canada in 1786 with a grandson Joseph Hilts (The Old United Empire Loyalist List).

    6754: ANNA b say 1749
    6755: MARIA b say 1751; ps. liv. 1770 (spf Maria Hilts bp)
    6756: JOHN JOST b say 1753; a Tory, liv. 1800 in Canada
    6757: ELIZABETH b say 1755; pr. liv. 1776 (spf P. Reyle GF bp)
          pr. m ca 1777 Mr. HILTS (father of Joseph Hilts)
                by 2nd wife
    6758: DELIA b 12 May 1760 (sp. Anna Merchel, Wm Coppernol)
          ps. m by 1776 JOHN REYLE
    6759: CATHERINE b 4 Nov 1763 (sp Cath. Harter, Geo. Fr. Helmer)
    6760: ps. GEORGE FREDERICK b say 1765; liv. 1784 (spf M W Petry bp)

6714: Capt. MARK PETRIE <P11> - pr. born ca 1712 to 1716 (called oldest son in father Jost's will); died 1776; m ANNA EVA KESSLER dau of JOHANNES KESSLER & ANNA MARGARET. Had Burnetsfield lot #14 and headed GF militia company in 1757. His will, dated 9 Apr 1776 , names only sons Jost (eldest) & John (excecutors - George DeMuth & Jacob Small). Petrie book has a child Margaret Elisabeth (m 1768 HENRY ZIMMERMAN) but Zimmerman book says she was a Bellinger.

```
+6761: JOST M.  b say 1736; m 1766 CATHARINE KESSLER
+6762: MARCUS jr  b say 1738; m by 1764 ELIZABETH (ps. Smith)
 6763: MARIA ELIZABETH  ca 1740-1808  pr. m Lt. ADAM BELLINGER
            (she was spf Sep 1760 bp of dau of Christian Schell)
 6764: ps. ANNA MARIA  b say 1741; m NICHOLAS SMITH (1739-1812)
 6765: DELIA  b 1742-3; d 1803; m JACOB KESSLER jr (son of Nich.)
 6766: ps. MARIA CATHERINE  b ca 1745; m 1766 JACOB JOH. KESSLER
 6767: ps. EVA  b say 1747; liv. Feb 1768 (spf Eva Jos M Petri bp)
            ps. m by Sep 1768 JACOB PETRIE (spf Kessler bp)
+6768: DIETRICH  b say 1749; m 1771 CATHERINE BELLINGER (b 1750)
+6769: JOHANNES MARC.  ca 1751-1823  m DOROTHY KESSLER (b 1757)
+6770: ps. JACOB MARC.  b say 1753; at Oriskany 1777
```

PETRIE - 4th Generation

6735: DANIEL PETRIE jr. <P66> - pr. born ca 1750 to 1765 (son of Daniel); pr. m1 German Flats NY 25 Jul 1784 MARIA HUBER ps. dau of HENRICH HUBER; pr. m2 by 1788 MARIA STAHRING (b ca 1759, d Little Falls NY 27 Mar 1837 age 77-5-7). Maria (born Stahring) was listed as the widow of Daniel Petrie on her death record at Little Falls in 1837. On 1790 Herkimer census (1-2-3).

```
6770A pr. DELIA  b GF Jul 1785 (sp. Jac. Perris <pr. Petri> & Mar.)
6771: CATHERINE  b GF 1 Oct 1786 (sp Danl Petrie & Cath. Kessler)
6772: ELISABETH  b 22 Apr 1788 (sp Joh. Adam Starin & Elisabeth)
            Elisabeth liv. 1804 (Herk. Church Confirmation)
6773: DANIEL  b 11 May 1790 (sp Dan. Jac. Petrie & Elis. Staring)
6774: CATHERINE  b 23 Jul 1792 (sp. Fasier Cox & Cath.<Petrie>)
```

6775: DANIEL PETRIE - m by 1794 DELIA <?> ... (ps. same as above Daniel jr.)

```
6776: DAVID  b GF 10 Oct 1794 (sp Marc Schell & Delia <Kessler>)
```

6768: DIETRICH M. PETRIE <P42> - pr. born ca 1735 to 1750; died at Oriskany battle 6 Aug 1777; m 1771 CATHERINE BELLINGER (b 1750) dau of Col. PETER BELLINGER.

```
6777: DELIA  b ca 1772; d ca 1800; m 1788 MARCUS JAC. KESSLER
6778: CATHERINE  1777-1854  m JOHN J. BELLINGER
```

6747: DIETRICH PETRIE <P53> - pr. born ca 1738 to 1745 (son of Johannes & Maria Elis.); m by 1776 ELIZABETH DYGERT dau of WARNER DYGERT & MAGDALENA HERKIMER; ps. m2 by 1805 CATHERINE FOLTS. Dietrich & Elisabeth sponsored Jun 1791 GF bp of Elis., dau of Wm Veeder Esqr. & Elisabeth. On 1790 Herkimer census (1-0-2).

```
6779: LENA  b 14 Jul 1776; ps. m GF 1794 GEORGE LAUX
6780: CATHARINA  b 18 Feb 1777 (sp. Jac. Kessler)
6781: ps. ELIZABETH  b 25 Dec 1805 (sp. Eliz. Petry)
```

6730: Col. JACOB D. PETRIE <P64/P78> - born 1740 (pr. son of Daniel <Petrie book has ps. step son of Jost Sr.>); died Petries Corners (Columbia) NY 1823; ps. ml by 1768 EVA ... (Petri?); m by 1772 MARIA ... (b ca 1750, d Columbia NY 8 Jun 1813; pr. an Orendorf). Was an ensign in the Revolution and a Colonel by 1795. Maj. Jacob sponsored 1792 bp of Jacob, son of John Fox & Anna (Frank). On 1790 Herkimer census (3-3-6) near Adam & Jacob Staring.

    6782: DANIEL J. b GF 14 May 1772; m 1791 ANN PAUL SEGNER
    6783: FREDERICK JAC. b say 1774; liv. 1791 (spf Jac. D. Petrie bp)
              pr. m 1794 EVA CON. ORENDORF
    6784: JOSEPH b 28 Sep 1775 (sp. Joh Jost Jac. Petrie)
              m by 1802 GERTRUDE SCHAEFFER
    6785: GEORGE b 20 May 1777 (sp Geo. Orendorf & Elis.)
              m MARGARET GETMAN
    6786: ps. JACOB jr. b GF 31 Dec 1779 (sp Jac. Small & Maria)
    6787: EVE ANN b 4 May 1780 (Hoyer rec.); m 1797 PETER HOYER
    6787A MARIA JAC. b say 1782; m GF Sep 1803 ABRAHAM JACOBSEN
    6788: DELIA (twin) b GF 15 Feb 1784 (sp. Jon. Wieth & Delia)
              ps. m NICHOLAS OSTERHOUT
    6789: CATHERINE (twin) b Feb 1784 (Mich. Ittig & Cath.<Orendorf>)
              m 1802 JOHN HOYER
    6790: ELISABETH JAC D b 1786 (sp John Eysaman & Elis.<Kessler>)
    6791: JACOB FREDERICK b 1794
    6792: CONRAD J. b 30 Jul 1795 (sp Conrad Orendorf & Cath.)
              m ANNA ELISABETH GETMAN

6770: JACOB MARC. PETRIE - ps. born ca 1740 to 1755; m by 1788 MARIA ... At Oriskany battle in 1777 according to a story that Jacob Marc. Petrie watched over the young "Black Jacob" Kessler on the Oriskany battlefield (HCH Kessler file). A Jacob Petri & Maria Hilts sponsored 1770 bp of Jacob, son of Conrad Folts & Cath. DeMuth. Was ps. the first grist miller at Little Falls NY. Baptism of Polly Maria in 1788 lists father as "Jacob M.", so she is placed here rather than under above Jacob D. There seems room for two Jacobs in this generation (ps. both with wives named Maria) and some of the children given under Col. Jacob D. may belong to this presumed Jacob M.

    6793: POLLY MARIA b 27 Apr 1788 (sp Melchior Vols & Marg.)

6741: JOHANNES DIET. PETRIE <P83> - born 17 Feb 1765; died 11 Aug 1843; m German Flats NY 26 Dec 1786 GERTRUDE G. DEMUTH pr. the Gertrude (bp 1768, d 15 Mar 1855 age 86-2) dau of GEORGE DEMUTH & ANNA. Children Joseph (b 1787), George (1788), Dietrich (1790), George, John, David, Aaron, Catherine, Anna, Gertrude, and Adam.

6750: JOHANNES PETRIE jr. <P52> - pr. born ca 1740 to 1752; m by 1774 BARBARA KLOCK (b ca Mar 1751, d 25 Feb 1807 age 55-11-7) dau of JOHN KLOCK & MARGARET FOX. On 1790 Herkimer census (3-1-3).

    6794: JOHANNES JOH. b 29 May 1774; m 1795 MARIA AD. BELLINGER
    6795: DIETRICH b 29 May 1774; m MARY ELISABETH EYSAMAN
    6796: ANNA ELISABETH b 13 Jul 1776 (sp. Geo. Zimmermn & Elis.)
    6797: DOROTHY 1779-1861 m MELCHIOR SMALL
    6798: CHRISTIAN b 14 May 1782 (sp. Henrich Joh. Klock & Maria)
              m 1806 ANNA FOLTS
    6799: MARIA ELISABETH b 22 Sep 1786
              (sp. Jac. Petrie & Maria, widow of Joh. Petrie)
    6800: MARY b say 1807; m SANFORD EYSAMAN

6769: JOHN MARC. PETRIE <P43> - pr. born ca 1751; died Little Falls NY 1823 (bur. Manheim NY); m DOROTHY KESSLER (b 1757, d 1831) pr. dau of JACOB KESSLER & CATHERINE STEELE. On 1790 Herkimer census (2-6-2).

6801: EVA b 30 Oct 1776 (sp. Joh. Eysaman & Elis.<Kessler>)
6802: JOHANNES b 10 Nov 1777 (sp. Joh. Kessler & Cath.)
6803: MARK b 26 Jul 1779 (Jac Kesler & w. Elis.)
6804: DELIA b 3 Mar 1781 (sp. Jac. Kessler & Delia)
6805: ADAM b 24 Nov 1782 (sp Adam Bellinger & Maria Elis. <Petri>) m SUSAN KEYSER
6806: JACOB b GF 20 Nov 1784 (sp Jac. Petrie & Maria); m ...
6807: DIETRICH b 9 Jul 1787 (sp Joh. Eysaman, Anna Segner)
6808: JOST b 15 Feb 1789 (sp. Jost Petrie, Eva Petrie)
6809: ELISABETH b 10 Jan 1791 (sp Wm Weaver <pr. Veeder> & Elis.)
6810: MARIA AGNES b 23 Aug 1793 (Marc C Schell, Maria A. Bellingr) m WILLIAM HOOVER
6811: SOLOMON b 12 Apr 1797; d 1868; m SABINA ARNOLD
6812: CATHERINE m SYLVANUS J. WATERS

6729: JOST D. PETRIE <P63> - born say 1737-55 (pr. son of Daniel); m by 1777 MARIA ELISABETH ZIMMERMAN pr. dau of LAWRENCE. On 1790 Herkimer census (1-2-5).

6813: DANIEL b 5 Nov 1777 (sp Dan. Petrie & Elis. Kessler) m by 1805 ELISABET BISHOP
6814: LORENTZ b GF 2 Sep 1781 (bp Dec 1781, sp Henry, Anna Zimmrmn)
6814A ELISABETH b GF 23 Feb 1784 (sp David Meyer, Cath. Zimmerman)
6815: MARGRET b 3 May 1786 (sp. Conrad L. Zimmerman & Marg.)
6816: DELIA b GF 3 Mar 1788; liv. 1804 (Herk. Ch. Confirm.)
6817: MARIA b GF 5 Apr 1790 (sp Maria Zimmermn, Fred Petrie)
6818: JACOB b GF 23 Aug 1791 (sp Maj. Jacob Petrie & Maria)

6740: JOST DIET. PETRIE <P82> - born 14 Feb 1763 (son of Dietrich Jos. Petrie); died Herkimer NY 14 Aug 1822 (age 59-5); m GF 17 Jul 1787 ANNA EVA BELLINGER (b 1767) dau of Lt. ADAM BELLINGER & MARIA ELISABETH PETRIE. Marriage record has him as "Johannes Deit. Petrie" but we have another Johannes Diet. Petrie (who married in 1786 Gertrude G. DeMuth) so we assume the church record is wrong and Jost was intended. Children Catherine (b 1788), Elisabeth (1789), ps. Jacob (1791), David (1792), ps. Sara (called Lany, b 1795), Isaac (1797), Moses (1800), Joram (1803), Mary (1805), Philo (1811), and Ulysses.

6748: Sgt. JOST PETRIE <P51> - pr. born ca 1740 to 1750 (son of John); died 30 Aug 1777 from Oriskany battle wounds; m SAR 24 Oct 1769 BARBARA WINDECKER. Jost had 2 boys & 1 girl (under age 16) on the Tryon Co. census ca 1776 (Mohawk Valley in the Revolution, page 154). Barbara Petri was on 1790 Palatine NY census (1-2-2) near Conrad & Fred Windecker.

6819: JOHANNES DEITRICH J. b 3 Oct 1777; m by 1805 MARGARET BISHOP

6761: JOST M. PETRIE <P41> - pr. born before 1745 (oldest son of Marcus); died by Oct 1789 (when widow Cath. J. Petri was spf bp of Cath. Steph. Eysaman); m SAR 5 May 1766 CATHERINE KESSLER. Jost M. was an officer in 1775 Tryon Co. militia.

6820: ANNA MARIA b 31 Aug 1766 (sp Maria <Petri> & Joh. Heering) d 1841; m HENRY RITTER
6821: ANNA EVA b SAR 29 Feb 1768 (sp. Jac. Petri, Anna Eva Petri) m 1785 STEPHEN EYSAMAN

6822: MARGARETHA b 5 Mar 1770 (sp. Elis. Kessler, Diet. Petrie)
        liv. 1786 (spf Ritter bp); pr. m 1789 LEONARD BEYER
6823: pr. MARCUS JOS. b say 1772; liv. 1790 (spf Jost L. Beyer bp)
6824: ps. CATHERINE b say 1774; m GF 1791 CONRAD BIKKERT
6825: JOHANNES b GF 6 Mar 1776 (sp Jac. Grantz & Elis. Joh. Kessler)
6826: JOST b 19 Jun 1777 (sp. Jac. Kessler & Delia <pr Petrie>)
        m 1797 POLLY STAHRING

6733: Major MARKS DAN. PETRIE <P65> - born Nov 1750; died 12 Feb 1806; m MARGARET
BELLINGER ("Peggy", b ca 1758, d ca 1830) dau of Col. PETER BELLINGER & DELIA
HERKIMER. In command of Ft. Herkimer during the Revolutionary War.

        6826A dau b say 1775; liv. 1776 (Tryon Co. census)
        6827: DANIEL b 14 Jan 1779 (sp. Daniel Petrie & Gertr. Bellinger)
                m DEBORAH YOUNG
        6828: PETER BELLINGER b GF 9 Oct 1781 (P. Bellinger & Delia); d 1862
        6829: ELIZABETH b 25 Jan 1784 (sp. Joh. Bellinger, Cath. Petrie)
        6830: MARGARET b 6 Sep 1785; m JOHN DYGERT
        6831: JOSEPH b 29 May 1788 (sp Joh. Jost Bellinger, Delia Petri)
        6832: JOHN b 9 Jun 1790 (sp. John P. Bellinger, Delia Bellngr)
        6833: CATHERINE b 30 Jul 1792 (Stopel Bellnger, Cath. Diet. Petry)
        6834: MARKS b 22 Mar 1795 (sp. Marc. Kessler & Delia)

6746: MARCUS J. PETRIE - pr. born ca 1735 to 1745; m by 1764 ANNA MARIA ... (ps. a
Frank?). Widow Maria m2 GF 28 Nov 1786 Fred. Orendorf, a widower.

        6835: CORDELIA b SAR 10 May 1764 (sp Cath. Folts, Jost Petrie)
                pr. the DELIA who m 1783 GEORGE MICHAEL ITTIG
        6836: ELISABETH bp 29 Mar 1766 (sp Elis. Petrie, Jac. Kessler)
                m1 1788 WILLIAM FULMER; m2 THOMAS T. SHOEMAKER
        6837: CATHERINE b SAR 14 Jul 1768 (sp John Petrie jr, Cath Crantz)
                m 1787 LORENTZ T. SHOEMAKER
        6838: pr. MARIA MARC. b say 1771; liv. 1789 (spf Edick bp)
        6838A pr. MARK M. b say 1776; m 1803 ANNA EYSAMAN

6762: MARCUS PETRIE jr <P45> - born say 1738; m by 1763 ELISABETH ... A guess
that wife was from the Montgomery Co. Smiths, who descend from 1710 immigrant
Henrich Schmit and came to Tillaborough NY from Greene Co. ca 1763.

        6839: HENRICK b SAR 15 Apr 1764 (sp. Nic. Schmit & w. Anna Marie)
                d 1852; m1 1789 MARIA P. LAUX (1768-1790); m2 MAGDALENA ...
        6840: CATHERINE M. b 1 Dec 1765 (sp. Cath. & Hen. Herkimer)
                m GF 1786 GEORGE YOUNG
        6841: JOHANNES b SAR 12 Mar 1768 (sp. Joh. Champel & Eva Meyer)
        6842: JOHANNES b 1 May 1770 (sp. Joh. Smit & Marg. Kasselman)

PETRIE - 5th Generation

6782: DANIEL JAC. PETRIE <P391> - born 14 May 1772; m GF 9 Apr 1791 ANNA SEGHNER
dau of PAUL SEGHENR & ELISABETH EYSAMAN. Had children JACOB (b GF Sep 1791,
father listed as Dietrich), ELISABETH (b Aug 1793), JOST (b Sep 1795, sp Jost Jac
Petri, Jany Segner), JACOB (d 1837, m1 POLLY CASE), RUDOLPH (m BETSY VROOMAN dau
of Teunis), ABRAM (m EVA CHRISTMAN dau of Barney), & EVA (m LORING MILLS).

********** PETRY, William **********

PETRY - 1st Generation

6901: Dr. **WILLIAM PETRY** - born Nierstein Germany 7 Dec 1733 (son of Jacob Andrew & Anna Maria); died Herkimer NY Aug 1806; m SAR 22 Dec 1766 MARGARET SALOME WOLF (b Wesselheim Germmany 1749, d Herkimer NY 1820) dau of JOHN WOLF, who came from Seeberg Germany in 1764 (Petrie book page 121).

After receiving his medical education at Manheim Germany, he came to New York in 1765 and was a surgeon of importance to the German Flats community during the Revolutionary War. His account of treatments at German Flats during the Revolution was printed in the Herkimer Democrat & Gazette (12 Feb 1875) and includes the following - 6 Aug 1777 Conrad Vols (wounded with a ball), 10 May 1779 the wife of Jost Smith and the wife of Henry Widerstyn (scalped), 9 Jul 1779 Jost Folts (wounded in thigh & arm) and Catherine Dornberger (scalped & stabbed with spear in five sundry places), 8 Aug 1780 John Dockstader and Conrad Vols (buckshot wounds), 1 Sep 1780 Jacob Ittig (wounded), 30 Sep 1780 Christian Schell, 29 Oct 1780 Adam Hartman and John DeMood (each with a ball), 6 Feb 1781 Peter Davis - three of his daughters wounded, 28 May 1781 Nath. Shoemaker (wounded with a ball through the breast), Oct 1781 Abraham Wohleben (scalped), 24 Jun 1782 Frederick Schell (wounded with a ball through the thigh).

Dr. Petry's family bible, with details on children, is amongst those kept at the Herkimer Co. Historical Society. Dr. Petry was pr. the William Petrie on 1790 Herkimer census (2-3-4) listed next to Henry Harter and Jacob G. Weaver.

surname PETRY

6902: CATHERINE b 1767; d HK 3 Feb 1814 (age 46-4-20) unm
6903: ANNA b SAR 19 Mar 1770 (sp Anna Weber, Jost Smidt); d y
6904: HENRY 1773-1861 unm
+6905: JACOB 1775-1851 ml MARIA SMITH
6906: FREDERICK 1777-1851 m CATHERINE THUM
6907: WILHELM b GF 12 Oct 1781 (sp Adam Smit & Sara); d 1783
6908: MARIA b GF 9 Dec 1784 (sp Geor. Fr. Petrie & w.)
           d 1840 m JOHN SMITH (son of John M.)
6909: ELIZABETH b GF 26 Jun 1787 (sp Peter F. Bellinger & Elis.)
           died 1870 unm
6910: MARGARET SALOMA 1791-1843 m JOHN EARL

PETRY - 2nd Generation

6906: **FREDERICK PETRY** - born 1777; died 1851; m 1 Jan 1803 CATHERINE THUM (b 1782, d 21 Jul 1846) dau of MELCHIOR THUM & ELISABETH. Children William (b 1805, m Fanny Shell), Nancy, Elizabeth, Mary, Melchert, Catherine, Frederick, Margaret, Simeon, Jacob Henry, and Jeremiah.

6905: JACOB PETRY - born 1775; died 1851; ml 17 Feb 1803 MARIA SMITH (b 1783, d 27 May 1808) dau of GEORGE SMITH; m2 28 May 1826 MARIA HAMLIN. Children Elizabeth (b 1803, m Charles Gray), Jacob, John, and Margaret.

********** PFEIFFER (Piper) **********

7001: **HENRICH PFEIFFER** - pr. born in Germany ca 1670 to 1690; pr. died ca 1710; m CATHERINA ... Widow Catherine appears on NY Palatine subsistence list in 1710 (2A,1Y) and in 1712 (2A,0Y). Probably this Catherine was the widow on 1717 Simmendinger census at Queensbury with 1 child.

surname PFEIFFER
+7002: pr. ANDREAS b say 1696; liv. 1712 (confirm. at Queensberg)

7003: MICHAEL PFEIFFER - pr. born in Germany ca 1650 to 1662; pr. died during Atlantic crossing in 1710; m CATHERINE ... Michel was on 1709 London list with wife & 2 children. Widow Catherine and son Michael were on NY Palatine subs. list in 1710 (2A,0Y) and in 1712 (2A,1Y).

+7004: MICHAEL b say 1678; m by 1711 ANNA MARIA

7005: SEVERIN PFEIFFER - His child on 1710 NY Palatine subs. list (0A,1Y)

PFEIFFER - 2nd Generation

7002: **ANDREAS PFEIFFER** (Piper) - pr. born ca 1692 to 1700; m ... (ps. ERNESTINA based on name appearance amongst grandchildren). Andreas Pfiester who was a new communicant at Queensberg camp on 23 Mar 1712 (Book of Names page 39). He drew lot #21 & #37 on the 1723 Stone Arabia Patent.

+7006: PETER b say 1723; m MARIA CATHERINE WEAVER
7007: pr. ELISABETH b say 1731; m 1749 JOHANNES BELL
+7008: pr. CATHERINE ca 1733-1807 m HENRY HARTER
+7009: JACOB b say 1740; m 1763 ELIZABETH FOLTS

7004: MICHAEL PFEIFFER (Pfester) - pr. born ca 1678 (son of Michael, age 32 in 1710, Book of Names page 122); m ca 1711 ANNA MARIA ... (b ca 1682, age 28 in 1710). On 1717 Simmendinger census at New York City with wife Anna Maria & 3 children. No sign of this family in the Mohawk Valley.

7010: HANNES b 1 May 1711 (sp Joh. Plank, Kunig. Wanamaker)
m2 1736 AGNETJE VAN HOORN
7011: Johannes MARCUS b 12 Oct 1713
7012: pr. ADAM b say 1715; m CATHERINE (had sons bp NYC 1746-8)

PFEIFFER - 3rd Generation

7013: JACOB PFEIFFER - pr. born ca 1730 to 1745 (brother of Peter); died by Oct 1802 (dec'd father of Anna on her mar. record); m 16 Mar 1763 ELISABETH FOLTS (b 1744, d 1827) dau of CONRAD FOLTS & CATHERINE DEMUTH. In 1769 GF militia.

7014: ERNESTINA b 1763 (bp 7 Nov 1763)
7015: JOST b 1765 (bp G. Flats 4 Dec 1765)
7016: PETER bp SAR 19 Jan 1768 (sp Pet. Weber, Maria Folts); d.y.
+7017: ANDREW JAC. b 15 Apr 1770; m ELISABETH BELLINGER
children cont. next page -->

children of Jacob & Elis. cont.

7018: CATHERINE 1773-1851 m 1793 GEORGE F. HARTER
7019: ps. JOHN b ca 1775; d GF 12 Apr 1811 age 35-9 a carpenter
7020: ELISABETH JAC. b ca 1778; m 1795 LAWRENCE FRANK
+7021: PETER bp GF 10 Mar 1781 (sp Pet. Orndorf & Cath.)
7022: MARGARET b GF 6 Mar 1783 (sp And. Piper, Marg. Folts)
m LAWRENCE L. HARTER
7023: ANNA bp GF 17 Sep 1786 (sp Lorentz Harter, Marg. Cuningham)
m 1805 JOHN CLEPSATTLE

7006: Johan PETER PFEIFFER - pr. born ca 1715 to 1730 (son of Andrew, as given in
St Johnsville Enterprise & News 23 Jul 1930); died 1786 (will probated 12 Aug
1786); ml pr. by 1750 MARIA CATHERINE WEAVER pr. dau of JACOB WEAVER Sr. &
ELISABETH; m2 GERTRUDE .... . He was taken prisoner in November 1779 and held at
the Seneca nation capitol of Canadaseago where he was said to be "of advanced age"
when conversing with a neutral Oneida Indian whose offer of escape he declined
(Campbell's "Annals of Tryon County" and Enterprise & News of 26 Mar 1930 page
98). In his will dated 20 Jun 1786 he mentions a brother Jacob and a bequest of
10 shillings to Henry Staring (husband of dau Elisabeth).

+7024: JACOB b say 1750; pr. died in Canada as POW
7025: ps. MARIA b say 1754; liv. 1778 (spf F. Orendorf bp)
7026: CATHERINE b say 1756; m by 1777 PETER ORENDORF
+7027: ANDREAS b 1760 (sp. Andr. Weaver & w.); m ELISABETH FOX
7028: ELIZABETH b 7 Mar 1763 (sp. Jost Shoemaker, Elis. Frank)
m HENRY NIC. STARING (ps. m2 ELLIS HENRY)
+7029: JOHN bp May 1763; m MAGDALENA DYGERT
7030: DOROTHY b say 1765; m Sep 1782 Ens. EMMANUEL TOOBY
7031: MARGARET P. b say 1767; m 23 May 1786 CONRAD SEGNER
7032: PETER b say 1770

7033: CATHERINE PFEIFFER - born ca 1733; died 1807; m HENRY HARTER (b 1731, d
1820) son of LORENTZ HARTER. Named second daughter Christina.

PFEIFFER - 4th Generation

7027: ANDREAS P. PFEIFFER - born 6 Jan 1760; died 5 Jun 1842; m 4 Jan 1785
ELISABETH FOX (bp 1766, d 1851) dau of FREDERICK FOX & ELISABETH FRANK. His
Revolutionary service included the Battle of Oriskany, scout duty, boat service
under Capt. Leffler in 1779, and Col. Willet's pursuit of Butler. In June 1782 he
was knocked down three times before being taken prisoner at the Little Falls mill
battle. He was held captive at Montreal, where he was out on bail for a brief
period in care of his uncle (pr. J. Weaver, ps. H. Dockstader), and in December
1782 he was exchanged at Boston (E&N 26 Mar 1930, Petrie book page 73).

7034: JACOB b GF 13 Jul 1785 (sp John Shoemakr, Elis. Fox); d.y.
7035: Johan FREDERICH b 17 May 1787; d Frankfort NY 1875
7036: ELIZABETH b 11 Sep 1788 (sp. Peter Fox & Elis.)
7037: PHILIP b 25 Oct 1790; m EVA AD. HAGADORN (1797-1873)
7038: MARIA CATHERINE b 24 Aug 1792 (sp. Peter Orendorf & Cath.)
7039: JOHN bp 25 Mar 1794 (sp Joh. Piper, Marg. Fox); d 1885
7040: JACOB b HK 5 Mar 1803 (bp 2 Jun, sp Jacob Fox & Marg. Frank)
7041: JAMES 1805-1863 m MARY ...
7042: EVA bp Herk. NY 10 Mar 1811 (sp. Jacob Weber & w. Eva Frank)

-200-

7017: ANDRES JAC. PIPER - born 15 Apr 1770; m ELISABETH BELLINGER (b 1774, d 1847) dau of FREDERICK BELLINGER & MAGDALENA WOHLEBEN (Bellinger book pg 64).

    7043: FREDERICK b 27 Sep 1795 (sp F. Bellinger ...); unm
    7043A JACOB A. b ca 1798; liv. 1813 (age 15 at HK confirm.)
    7044: ANDREW 1799-1888 m CATHERINE GROAT
    7045: CATHERINE unm
    7046: NICHOLAS b 1801; m DIANA VAN VALKENBURG
    7047: pr. MARGARETHA b 8 Oct 1802 (sp. Step. Frank & Marg.)
    7048: MAGDALENA b HK 7 Jan 1804 (sp John Clepsatle, Cath. Bellingr)
            m JOHN S. SHOEMAKER
    7049: DANIEL b HK 13 Nov 1805 (sp Geo. Harter & w. Cath.); m2 MARY
    7050: DOROTHEA b 1810; m1 ROBERT JONES
    7051: ELISABETH b 1813

7024: JACOB PFEIFFER - pr. born ca 1750 to 1762 (son of Peter) ; pr. m by 1769 ...
In November 1779 he and his father were taken prisonser by Tory forces and, as a result, his brother Andrew was released from colonial military service to care for the family (Enterprise & News of 3/26/1930). Subsequently we hear of an American prisoner named Jacob Piper (probably this man) who died from a flogging of 1000 lashes which was meted out by British captors in Canada as punishment after an unsuccesful escape attempt (see Jacob Witrig account).

    +7052: pr. PETER JAC. b say 1769; m 1791 MARGARET CLEPSATTLE

7029: JOHN PFEIFFER - bp 15 Mar 1763 (son of Peter & Maria Cath.); died by 1812; m MAGDALENA DYGERT (b 1775) dau of WILLIAM DYGERT & MARGARET CUNINGHAM (Harter book page 26). In 1812 Peter J.(age 16) & Jacob J. (age 15), sons of John dec'd, were confirmed at Herkimer.

    7053: PETER   1795-1855 m 1822 CATHARINE BAUMAN
    7054: JACOB   ca 1797-1819 m BETSY HILTS
    7055: ANNA b HK 27 Jun 1803 (bp 24 Jul, sp Geo. Clepsattle & w Anna)
            m 1823 RUDOLPH STEELE
    7055A MARGARET b HK 23 Jun 1805 (sp Marg. Shoemaker)
    7056: ISAAC bp Herkimer 8 Oct 1809 (sp Geo. Harder & Cath.)

7021: PETER PFEIFFER - pr. born ca 1770 to 1790 (ps. son of Jacob); m Herkimer NY 17 Jan 1813 DOROTHY WOHLEBEN dau of ABRAHAM WOHLEBEN & DOROTHEA BELLINGER. Had son Jacob (bp Columbia NY 10 Jun 1813).

PFEIFFER - 5th Generation

7052: PETER JAC. PFEIFFER - pr. born ca 1760 to 1770 (son of Jacob as given on 1791 mar. rec.); died by 1821 (Harter book page 26); m at German Flats NY 8 May 1791 MARGARET CLEPSATTLE (b ca 1769, d Ft. Herkimer NY 27 Jan 1827 age 58) pr. dau of AUGUSTINUS CLEPSATTLE. A Peter & Margaret were sponsors for Dec 1803 bp of Petrus, son of George Harter & Catherine Jac. Piper.

    7057: ELISABETH bp GF 8 May 1791 (sp And. Piper, Anna Klepsttle)
    7058: ps. MARGARET b 20 Feb 1794; m 1814 JOHN HARTER
    7059: MAGDALENA b 9 Mar 1802; m 1821 ADAM BOWMAN

********** RASBACH (Rasper) **********

7101: JOHANNES RASBACH - pr. born ca 1690 to 1705; died before 1789; m MARGARET BIERMAN dau of JOHANNES BIERMAN (V. Eysaman notes). About 1720 he emigrated from Berne Switzerland to Maryland and about 1726 he moved to New York State, settling on the old turnpike about one mile east of Ft. Dayton (ibid). He and son Johannes Jr were in Capt. Petrie's militia co. in Feb 1757. Harter book (page 2) gives genealogist Deuel as reference for daughter Elisabeth with husbands Peter Folts and later Frederick Harter, but her birthdate seems early (both with regard to arrival at Burnetsfield and dates for other children).

surname RASBACH

```
+7102: ps. ELISABETH (Raspach?)   b say 1724; m PETER FOLTS (b 1714)
 7103: JOHN jr.  b say 1730; killed in Fr. & Indian Wars
+7104: MARKS   1733-1799  m SOPHRONIA MOAK
 7105: LAWRENCE   b say 1735; killed in Fr. & Indian Wars
 7106: BARBARA   b say 1737; m by 1763 JOHN SCHELL (b 1734)
 7107: ANNA MARIA   ca 1739-1822 m1 HENRY HISER m2 HENRY WIDERSTINE
 7108: MARIA MARGARET   b say 1747; m 1771 VALENTINE STAHRING
+7109: FREDERICK   b ca 1749; m CATHERINE ...
```

RASBACH - 2nd Generation

7109: FREDERICK RASBACH - pr. born ca 1749 (H. Patrick notes); m CATHERINE ... His wife and son were taken prisoner in the Revolution. He settled in the Snell's Bush area (V. Eysaman notes) where he was a contributor to the Snell's Bush Church in 1805. On 1790 Palatine NY census (2-2-4) next to John J. Snell.

```
 7110: JOHANNES   1772-1863  m 7 Feb 1792 MARGARET MOAK
 7111: HENRY   b say 1781; pr. m HANNAH ... (b 1787, d 1830)
 7112: MARIA CATHERINE   b GF 13 Jan 1783
                 (sp Werner Joh. Dygert, Maria Cath. Dygert)
 7113: JOST   b GF Jun 1785 (sp. Jost Kayser & Maria)
                 d 1870; m MAGDALENA STEBER (or Bentz?)
 7114: ANNA EVA   b 1787 (sp. Diet. Fehling, Eva Snell)
                 m PHILIP GOURNAMENT⁴
+7115: JACOB   b say 1790; m1 NANCY HOUSE (b ca 1792, d 1848 age 57)
 7116: ps. MARIA   b say 1795; m by 1818 DAVID BASS
```

7104: Lt. MARKS RASBACH - born German Flats NY 17 Jun 1733; died Aug 1799; m SOPHRONIA MOAK (aka "VERONICA MOAK", b in Switzerland ca Mar 1732, d 13 May 1814 age 82-2-) dau of JOHANNES MOAK. Was wounded in battle of Oriskany in 1777.

```
 7117: ps. ANNA ELISABETH   b say 1751; m SAR 1770 Johan GERLACH MEYER
 7118: BARBARA   1759-1841  m PETER FOLTS (b 1750)
 7119: JOHANNES   b 6 Oct 1760 (sp. Joh. Raspe & Marg.); pr d. young
+7120: JOHN   1764-1828 m ANNA MOAK
 7121: FREDERICK   bp GF 16 Sep 1766 (sp. Fred Raspe, Elis. Folts)
+7122: MARKS   ca 1769-1822  m by 1778 ELISABETH DEVENDORF
 7123: ANNA   ca 1774-1855  m 1793 THOMAS FR. HARTER
 7124: MARGARET   b say 1776; m 1797 HENRY BALDE
+7125: ADAM   1778-1863  m MARGARET SMITH
```

7102: ELISABETH (ps. RASBACH ?) - pr. born ca 1714 to 1725; m PETER FOLTS (b 1714, d 1777). We don't agree with accounts which say this Elisabeth was the one (born ca 1724) who died Herkimer NY 24 Oct 1808 (at age 84) as the wife of Frederick Harter. Furthermore we feel Peter Folt's wife Elisabeth was a bit early to have been a Raspach and we lean to the Elisabeth Rasbach who married Gerlach Meyer as a probable daughter of immigrant Johannes Raspach.

RASBACH - 3rd Generation

7125: ADAM RASBACH - born GF 3 Mar 1778 (sp. Adam Stahle & Cath.), died 1863; m 1801 MARGARET SMITH (b 1781, d 1814) dau of GEORGE SMITH & MARIA BELLINGER. Children were Mary, Catherine (m Christian Sharer), Adam, John (m Cath. Dockstader), Mark, George (m Cath. Eysaman), David (m Mary Myers), and Elisabeth.

7115: JACOB RASBACH - pr. born ca 1780 to 1792; m1 NANCY HOUSE (b ca 1792, d Mar 1848 age 56-0-26). Snell's Bush Church manuscript (HCH).

7120: JOHN RASBACH - born 23 Jan 1764; died of sunstroke while mowing hay 4 Sep 1828; m German Flats NY 8 Nov 1785 ANNA MOAK dau of CROTSY MOAK (son of John) & ANNA CONRAD. Name of daughter Maria Catherine, born GF 1787, sometimes confused with a MAGDALENA (no daughter Lena known for this couple).

        7128: MARY CATHERINE   b 4 Aug 1787 (sp Nic Harter, M. Cath Frank)
                 m JACOB C. FULMER
        7129: MARGARET   b 1 Oct 1789 (sp John Schell, Marg. Moak)
                 m 1806 MIKE YOUNG (son of Barent)
        7130: MARIA   b ca 1791; liv 1810 (age 19 at HK Confirm.)
       +7131: MARK   1792-1855   m BARBARA ELISABETH HELMER
        7132: PETER   b 16 Dec 1794; died at age 16
        7133: ANNA NANCY   b 22 Apr 1797; m 1812 PETER C. HELMER
        7134: SOPHIA   m SOLOMON NELLIS
        7135: VERONICA (Fannie)   1800-1872   m HENRY HELMER (1797-1868)
        7136: EVA   b Jan 1808; d 21 Jan 1808 age 13 days
        7137: ELIZABETH   d age 10 months

7122: MARKS RASBACH - pr.   the Marx born ca 1769; died Fairfield NY 10 Aug 1822 (age 53-1-21); m Ft. Plain NY 31 Jan 1796 ELIZABETH DEVENDORF. Children include JOHN M. (b Nov 1801, m ROSANNA DELONG, went west), MARCUS (b ca 1804, d 1821), ADAM (m BETSY BALDE), and JACOB M..

RASBACH - 4th Generation

7131: MARK J. RASBACH - born in the old Rasbach house 8 Mar 1792; died Feb 1855 age 62-11-12 (buried Herkimer Cemetery, German St. Herkimer NY); m 1 Jan 1815 BARBARA ELIZABETH HELMER (b ca Feb 1796, d 15 May 1857 age 61-12-27 or died 15 May 1887 age 91-2-27) dau of CONRAD HELMER & ANNA FOLTS. Children were PETER (d 16 Jul 1816), JOHN (1819-1905 m1 1839 MELINDA SMITH, m2 ALZINA CHRISTMAN <Helmer book page 21>), WILLIAM CONRAD (1822-1916 m1 MARY HARTER), MARGARET (b Feb 1826, d. young), GEORGE HENRY (b Apr 1828, d. young), MARC (1831-1916, m NANCY MARIA SCHELL).

7201: CONRAD RICKARDT - born Hailer Germany ca 1680 (son of JOHANNES RICKER & EVA GRUEL, as in H. Jones "The Palatine Families of New York") & bp Neidermittlau Germany 4 Feb 1680; liv. 1722 (Burnetsfield Patentee); m1 25 Jan 1700 KUNIGUNDA FISCHER (d Sep 1703 age 22) dau of JOHANN FISCHER & MARIA; m2 Nieder-Grandau Germany 8 Jan 1704 SARA CATHERINE SCHIEFFER dau of ALEXANDER SCHIEFFER. Much more on German origins in the Isenburg area east of Frankfurt can be found in Jones' Palatine Families book. The Young book seems to suggest a wife in America named ELISABETH HANES but we think that she was the wife instead of Conrad Jr of the next generation. Conrad appears on the NY Palatine subsistence list in 1710 (2A,3Y) & in 1712 (3A,2Y) and was presumably the Conrad Richert, who along with Jost Petrie, petitioned the Council Meeting at Albany on 9 Sep 1721 for license to purchase land for the Palatines immigrants. The license was granted by NY Governor William Burnet's letter of 16 Oct 1721 and the site, which was to be along the Mohawk River not closer than 40 miles beyond Fort Hunter (i.e. 60 miles west of Albany), became known as Burnetsfield, where Conrad received lot #34 (but there is no indication that he settled there and he may have been amongst the Bellingers and Richards who remained at Schoharie NY).

                    surname RICHARDS
+7202: LUDWIG   bp Nov 1700; pr. m by 1723 CATHERINE
+7203: CONRAD   bp Feb 1703 (sp Con. Fischer)
            by 2nd wife
 7204: FERDINAND MAX. b 1 Oct 1704 (sp Fern. M. Schiffer)
+7205: pr. MARCUS b say 1712; m 1731 ELISABETH LAWYER (Cady)
+7206: ps. ELISABETH b say 1714; m1 1730 ADAM STERNBERGH

7207: HANNES REICHARD - pr. born in Germany about 1663; pr. died ca 1710; m ... Pr. the John Richardt on the second London Palatine list of May 1709 (age 46 and with sons age 14 & 3, and daughters age 19, 12, 9, & 6) and from Kirchberg, commune Marbach, duchy of Wuerttemberg Germany (as shown on daughter Maria's marriage record in 1711, Book of Names page 43). Our guess is that Hannes, his wife, and most of the young daughters perished in the 1710 trans-Atlantic crossing and that elder daughter Maria was in the household of relative Joseph in 1710.

  7208: ANNA MARIA b say 1690; m 1711 BERNHARD ZIPPERLIN
+7209: ps. JOHAN b say 1695; m by 1715 ELISABETHA CATHERINA BACKUS

7210: JOSEPH RICKERT - pr. born in Germany ca 1660 to 1675; m1 ... (d by 1710); m2 9 Jan 1711 ANNA MARIA ... widow of JOHANN TRABER (a wheelwright formerly of Woellstein, commune Kreuznach). On NY Palatine subs. list in 1710 (4A,0Y) & in 1712 (3A,0Y). His 1711 marriage rec. has him a widower of Kirchberg, commune Marbach, Germany so he was pr. a relative of the above Hannes Reichard. On 1717 Simmendinger census with wife Anna Maria & 2 children. Joseph & wife Maria sponsored Jun 1711 bp of Joseph, son of Franz Giller (Keller) & Barbara. Children Nicholas and Catherine seen in Cdmr. Bellinger's notes (which were from Cady's Book No. 4, marriages and births, page 144 <not seen>) and, lacking dates, may as well have been later offspring born in New York.

  +7211: ANNA CONSTANTIA b say 1694; m 1715 CARL NAEHER (Koch.)
   7212: NICHOLAS   b say 1697; pr. died by 1710
   7213: CATHERINE b say 1700; pr. died by 1710
   7214: BERNHARD   b 30 Dec 1711 (sp. Bern Zipperlin & w. Maria)
   7215: DAVID   b 17 Apr 1714 (sp. Bernhard Zipperlin)

7216: ANDRIES RICHTER - pr. born ca 1663 (age 46 in 1709); died by 1713; m ANNA
MARIA ... (b ca 1665, age 45 in 1710). Probably he was the John Andres Richter on
the 1709 London lists (Lutheran of age 46, with son age 14 & daughters ages 17, 7
and 3). On NY Palatine list in 1710 (3A,2Y) and in 1712 (3A,0Y). On NY City
hospital list including children Andreas (age 16) and Anna Barbara (age 9). His
widow Anna Maria married 7 Apr 1713 JOHANN FUEHRER and his son Andries appears on
the 1717 Simmendinger census at Beckmansland with wife Elisabeth & 1 child (pr.
John, born 21 Sep 1714, as given in Book of Names page 27).

RICHARDS - 2nd Generation

7203: CONRAD RICKERT (pr. Jr.) - bp Nieder Grandau Germany 28 Feb 1703 (H.
Jones' "Palatine Families of New York", though Cady, as given in Cdmr Bellinger
notes, has born in Germany 7 Feb 1707); m by 1724 ELISABETH ... (ps. ELISABETH
HANES). Based on the number of children born from 1724 to 1733, we question the
implication (as in Young book) that this was the same person as Conrad Sr.,
co-organizer of the Burnetsfield Patent. Records of St. Paul's Lutheran Church at
Schoharie NY show baptisms in 1728 for John (sp. John Scheffer & Maria) and in
1729 for George (sp George Zimmer, John Lawyer).

      +7217: JOHANNES b 1724 (bp SHH 19 May 1728, sp John Schaefer & Maria)
                       d 1809; m 1748 CATHARINE YOUNG
      +7218: GEORGE b say 1725 (bp SHH 7 Jul 1729, sp George Zimmer)
                       m 1750 EVE STAHRING
      +7219: MARCUS b say 1728; m 1761 ELISABETH KRAUSLER
       7220: CONRAD bp SHH 7 Jul 1729
       7221: ANNA EVA bp 5 Oct 1732 (sp Wm Vuchs <Fox> & Eva)
       7222: ELISABETH bp SHH 19 Mar 1733 (sp John Lawyer, Elis Schafer)

7209: JOHANN REICHART (or Reitz) - pr. born ca 1685 to 1697 (looks like a son of
John or Joseph); m by 1715 ELISABETHA CATHARINA BACKUS. Pr. with dependents of
Joseph for 1710 NY Subsistence. Parents of child Jacob bp 1737 at Schoharie were
listed as "Jan Ryckert & M. Catryn" (Vosburgh's Records of St. Paul's Luth. Ch.).

       7223: MATTEUS b 1 Mar 1715 (sp. Math. Jung, Cath. Rohrbach)
       7224: pr. JACOB bp SHH 1737 (sp. Jacob Borst & wife).

7202: LUDWIG RICHARDS - Ludwig Ehrenhard bp Nieder Grandau Germany 7 Nov 1700
(son of Conrad, as in H. Jones' findings, but Cady had birthdate as 9 Jan 1705);
ps. m CATHERINE ... Ludwig had Burnetsfield lot #19, a prime area, and perhaps
his wife was the Cath. Rickart who received Burnetsfield secondary woodland area
#3, north of the Mohawk River. Existence of an extra Ludwig here is assumed to
provide parent for the Ludwig who married Catherine Conrad (and had children 1757
to 1759), the Burnetsfield patentee Ludwig being presumably too old to have
children in the 1750's. This may be all wrong, particularly if the Burnetsfield
Ludwig was a youngster rather than an adult, when assiged lot #19 (but we assume
dependents did not get such primary lots). It is also feasible (but unlikely) that
a single Ludwig, born before 1710, had children into the 1760's.

      +7225: ps. LUDWIG b say 1720; m CATHERINE CONRAD
       7226: ANNA LUD. b say 1725; m SHH 1746 JACOB HANS
      +7227: CONRAD b say 1730; m 1751 ANNA SCHAEFFER

7205: MARCUS RICHARDS - pr. born ca 1705 to 1715 (H. Jones' findings have him as
son of Conrad, which is pr. OK in spite of Cdmr. Bellinger notes #2.11 at Herk.
Co. Hist. Soc. which have Marcus born West Camp NY 14 Oct 1711, son of Joseph, on
a date conflicting with Kocherthal record for birth of Joseph's son Bernard);
died 7 Sep 1784; m1 13 Dec 1731 ELISABETH LAWYER (d 9 Nov 1780). Had Burnetsfield
lot #6, which was in the dependents area on the south bank of the Mohawk River,
but we see in the Bellinger book (page 19) that he never lived there.

> 7228: ELIZABETH b 7 Oct 1731; m 1748 JACOB SCHAEFFER
> 7229: CATHERINE b 9 Feb 1732 (sic.); m 1758 NICHOLAS STERNBERGH
> 7230: SARAH b 14 Sep 1733; m MARTYNUS SCHAEFFER
> 7231: SOPHIA b 9 Apr 1735; m1 ADAM STERNBERG m2 JOHN DOMINICK
> 7232: JOHANNES b 7 Oct 1737
> 7233: ANNA MARIA b 19 Jun 1740; m 1758 JOHANNES BELLINGER
> 7234: ANATIA b 6 Sep 1742; m 1761 JOSEPH MATICE
> 7235: LENA b 12 Nov 1743; m 1762 CONRAD BROWN

7211: ANNA CONSTANTIA RICHARDS - b say 1694 (dau of Joseph of commune Marbach,
ducy of Wuerttemberg); m 11 Jan 1715 CARL NAEHER widower of Brickenfeld, commune
Trarbach Palatinate Germany (Kocherthal records as seen in Book of Names page 45).

7206: ELISABETH RICHARDS - pr. born ca 1700 to 1713 (birthdate of 16 Feb 1705 in
Cdmr Bellinger notes at HK Co. Hist. Soc but no source given); m1 1730 ADAM
STERNBERGH; m2 1748 HENDRICK HEEM

RICHARDS - 3rd Generation

7227: CONRAD RICKERT - born say 1730 (son of Ludwig); m Schoharie NY 26 Sep 1751
ANNA SCHAEFFER dau of HENRY SCHAEFFER. This Conrad of Schoharie may moved to
German Flats area by 1775 and sponsored, with his wife, the Nov 1775 GF bp of
Conrad, son of Johan Peter Buje & Cath. A Conrad Rickart was on the 1790 Palatine
NY census (2-1-2) at Sneidersbush near F Windecker, V Beyer, & J Buje.

> 7236: JACOB b SHH 13 May 1752
> 7237: MARIA b 21 Nov 1755; pr. d young
> 7238: EVA b SHH 19 Jul 1757 (sp Marx Rickert, Eva Sprecher)
> 7239: MARIA b 13 Jul 1759 (sp Hen. Becker, Maria Kniskern)
> +7240: LUDWIG b SHH 17 May 1761 (sp Ludwig Rickert & w.)
>   pr. m 1786 MARIA SEUFFER
> 7241: MARIA b SHH 3 Dec 1764 (sp Christian Schaefer & w.)
> +7242: pr. HENRICH CON. b say 1770; m 1791 CATHERINE SEUFFER

7218: GEORGE RICKERT - pr. born ca 1720 to 1730 (son of Conrad Rickert & Elisabeth
Haines); m 21 Sep 1750 EVE STAHRING dau of NICHOLAS STAHRING. Cady lists his wife
as EVA STERNBERG (b 6 Oct 1730, d 9 Feb 17.., Cady Schoharie rec., not seen).

> 7243: NICHOLAS bp 14 Sep 1752; m 1774 LEA G. HOMMEL
> 7244: GERTRUDE bp 5 Dec 1755; pr. died young
> 7245: CATRINA b 21 Sep 1759
> 7246: JACOB bp 2 Oct 1761
> 7247: GEORGE b 4 Jun 1763
> 7248: MARIA b 27 Mar 1764
> 7249: GERTRUDE b Albany NY 6 Apr 1766; m 1785 MARCUS RICKERT
> 7250: ANNA b 28 Oct 1768

7217: JOHANNES RICKERT - born 1724 (Young book page 39 has Johannes as son of Conrad & Elisabeth); died 1809; m 1748 CATHERINE YOUNG (Cady rec. at Schoharie).

+7251: ps. GEORGE b say 1752; m CATHERINE ... at Canajoharie 1790
+7252: ps. JOHN b say 1755; at Canajoharie NY 1790
 7253: CONRAD b 31 Mar 1762
 7254: JACOB b SHH 11 Oct 1767

7225: LUDWIG RICKERT - ps. born ca 1720 to 1730 (son of Ludwig?); m CATHERINE CONRAD (Getman book page 221).

+7255: ps. PETER b say 1747; m 1767 ELISABETH GERLACH
+7256: ps. JACOB b say 1751; liv. 1769 (spf J. Rickert bp)
+7257: LUDWIG b SHH 12 Sep 1757 (sp Ludwig Sneider, Cath. Rickert)
        m CATHERINE GETMAN (Getman book)
 7258: SARA b SHH 10 Mar 1759 (sp Mart. Schaeffer & w.)
        ps. m by 1785 JOHN HART
 7259: ps. ELISABETH b say 1764; m PETER GETMAN (b 1764)
+7260: ps. CONRAD b say 1766; m 1786 CATHERINE ECKER
 7260A ps. CORNELIA b say 1775; liv. 1794 (spf Getman bp)

7219: MARCUS RICHARDS - pr. born ca 1725 to 1735 (son of Conrad & Elis. <from Cady rec.>); died 9 Dec 1793; m 3 Mar 1761 ELISABETH KRAUSLER (Kriesler).

 7261: CATHERINE bp 7 Dec 1761
 7262: PHILIP b 31 May 1763
 7263: CONRAD b 1 Jan 1764
 7264: HEIRONYMUS b 12 Aug 1766
 7265: MARCUS bp SAL 1771 (sp Pet. Sommer, Marg. Creisler)

7266: PETER RICHARDS - pr. born ca 1730 to 1760; m MARIA ...

 7267: EVA b GF 23 Dec 1775 (sp Joh. Riemensndr & Eva)

RICHARDS - 4th Generation

7268: BARTHOLOMEW RICKERD - In Col. Klock's Revol. Regiment (Book of Names, page 151) and pr. a Pickert, not a Richards/Rickert. Descendents of Bartholomew Pickard, an Englishman who was at Schenectady by 1700, were early settlers of Montgomery Co. NY.

7260: CONRAD RICKERT - pr. born ca 1750 to 1770; m FNR 1 Jun 1786 CATHERINE ECKER. Children (Leetham ms., Fonda Lib.), were LUDWIG (b 16 Feb 1792), CATRENA (b 17 Mar 1796), CONRAD (b 19 Feb 1801), and WILHELM (b 17 Mar 1803).

7251: GEORGE RICHARDS (Rykard) - pr. born ca 1750 to 1765; m by 1784 CATHERINE ... Pr. the George Rickert on 1790 Canajoharie NY census (3-2-5) listed next to George Vetterly & John Rickart. Lived at Canajoharie NY in 1793 (SJR bp rec.).

        7269: HENRICH bp Gilead Luth. 13 Oct 1784
        7270: SAMUEL bp SJR 20 May 1793 (sp Sam Krank, Marg. Rykard)
        7271: GEORGE bp Minden NY 27 Nov 1795
        7272: PETER bp Minden 16 Feb 1805

7242: HENRICH CON. RICKERT - pr. born ca 1760 to 1772; m German Flats NY 24 May
1791 CATHERINE SEUFFER (b 1771) dau of JOHANNES SEUFFER & MARIA..

      7238A CONRAD   bp SJR 25 Dec 1791 (sp Con. Rikert, Elis. Rikert)

7256: JACOB RICHARD (ps. PICKERT?) - pr. born ca 1730 to 1760. Served in Col.
Klock´s 2nd Tryon Co. Revol. Regiment at Battle of Oriskany.

7252: JOHN RICKERT - pr. born ca 1750 to 1762; m by 1793 CATHERINE ... In Col.
Klock´s Revol. Regiment. A John Rickart appears on 1790 Canajoharie NY census
(1-3-3) listed next to George Rickart & Hendrick Cramer. Living at Sneidersbush
in 1793 (SJR bp rec.).

      7273: CATHERINE   b SJR 5 Aug 1793 (sp John Puyoux & Cath.)

7257: LUDWICK RICKERT - born 12 Sep 1757 (son of Ludwig & Catherine <Conrad> as
given in Getman book); died Palatine NY 11 Jan 1819 (age 61); m by 1780 CATHERINE
GETMAN (b 1761) dau of CHRISTIAN GETMAN & ANNA EVA ZIMMERMAN. Ps. the Ludwig in
Col. Klock´s 2nd Tryon Co. Regiment during the Revolution. Ps. the Ludwig Rickart
on 1790 Palatine NY census (2-2-2) living in general vicinity of Getmans (the
location looks right for this Ludwig but the census data seems short by 2 or 3
daughters!). Data on children is mostly from Getman book (page 221).

      7274: SUSANNA   b 5 Aug 1780; d 1802; m ROSWELL CLEVELAND
      7275: ANNA EVA   b 22 Jan 1782; m CASPER C. KOCH
      7276: JOHANNES   b GF 7 Oct 1783 (sp John Koch, Anna Eva Getman)
                  m MARGARET KEYSER
      7277: CATHERINE   b 28 Sep 1785; m ADAM VER PLANK
      7278: FREDERICK   b 5 Aug 1787 (sp F Getman);   m MARIA SNELL
      7279: ELIZABETH   b 19 Mar 1790 (sp Tho. Getman & w Elis.)
                  d 1827; m JOSEPH GETMAN
      7280: GEORGE   b SAR 20 May 1792 (sp John Hardt, Lena Rickert)
                  m MARGARET GROVE
      7281: LUDWIG (LEWIS)   b SAR 27 Nov 1793 (sp Ch. Getman & Maria)
                  m CATHERINE NELLIS
      7282: MARIA   b 12 Aug 1795; m 1812 WILLIAM H. SCHULTZ
      7283: DELIA   b 2 Jan 1798; m GEORGE WASH. WILLIAMSON
      7284: NAOMI   b 31 Mar 1805; m JOHN I. VROOMAN

7240: LUDWIG RICKERT - pr. born ca 1750 to 1766; m at German Flats NY 19 Mar 1786
MARIA SEUFFER (b 1766) dau of JOHANNES SEUFFER & MARIA. Birthdate of son Johannes
in 1787 marks this Ludwig as a separate person from the Ludwig who married
Catherine Getman. Lived at Sneidersbush in 1793 (SJR bp rec.).

      7285: JOHANNES   b GF 18 Dec 1787 (sp Hen. Rickert, Barbara Keller)
      7286: ANNA   bp SJR Sep 1789 (sp John Seuffer & Maria)
      7287: CONRAD   b SJR 30 Aug 1791 (sp Conrad Rikert)
      7288: PETER   b SJR 3 Aug 1793 (sp Peter Louks & Anna)

7255: PETER RICKERT - pr. born ca 1740 to 1750; m SAR 28 Apr 1767 ELISABETH
GERLACH. Ps. the same person as prior generation Peter, who had a daughter Eva bp
at GF in 1775.

      7289: JACOB   b SAR 14 Apr 1769 (sp Jac Rickert, Marg. Gerlach)

********** RIEGEL (Reals, Riehl, Ruehl) **********

7301: GODFRID RIEGEL <R1> - pr. born near Wetzler Germany ca 1681-82 (son of
Michael, Reals book); m1 Nuenheim Germany 1709 KATHERINE WEBER (she pr. died
enroute to New York); m2 by 1712 ANNA MARGARETHA ... (Margaret listed as mother of
child born Nov 1712); m3 by 1717 ANNA ELISABETH ... "The Reals Family
Descendents" by William J. Reals & Vivian Y. Brecknell presents Hank Jones
findings that Godfrid, son of Michael (pr. died Nov 1690), married on 10 Feb 1709
KATHERINE WEBER dau of PETER WEBER. Godfrid was on the NY Palatine subsistence
list in 1710 (1A,0Y) and in 1712 (2A,0Y) and was sponsor, with Eva Catharina
Manck, Elis. Jung, & Johan Balthasar Kuester, for Nov 1711 bp of Anna Maria, dau
of Peter Dibble & Catherine. In Jan 1716 he sponsored baptism of Johann Godfrid,
son of Leonard Helmer & Elisabeth. He appears on the 1717 Simmendinger census
with wife Anna Elisabeth & 2 children and in 1723 he drew Burnetsfield lot #15, on
the north side of the Mohawk. Possibly he was lived to an old enough age (say 81)
to have been the Godfray Regel on the 1763 list of Freeholders of Albany Co.
(Reals book, page 14).

                         surname RIEGEL
        7302: ANNA CATHERINE b 9 Nov 1712 (sp Hen Stubenrauch & wife)
       +7303: GODFRID jr b say 1715; liv. 1723 (Burnetsfield patent)
       +7304: pr. CHRISTIAN b say 1722; liv. 1769 (GF militia Sgt.)
        7305: pr. dau (Riegel?) b say 1725; believe m CHRISTOFEL HILTS Jr.
              <Stofel Hilts & wife, killed ca 1756, had a son Gotfrid>
        7306: pr. JOHN b say 1727; liv. 1757 (J. Raal in Dygert's militia?)
              (John Rickel, Revolutionary exempts; Book of Names, page 175)

7307: CHRISTOPHER RIEHL - pr. born in Germany before 1690. On NY Palatine subs.
list in 1710 (1A,0Y) and ps. was the Christopher of Bichenbach Germany listed as
father of Christian Riegel (1709 marriage record at London Eng.).

7308: CHRISTIAN RIEGEL - born ca 1689 (age 20 on 1709 London list); pr. the
Christian Ruhl (son of Christopher of Bichenbach Germany) who married in London
England 17 Jul 1709 ANNA CATHERINE CRAUS dau of JOHANNES CRAUS and pr. the
Christian Reger on 1717 Simmendinger census at Hackensack with wife & 2 children.

7301: NICHOLAS RUHL - pr. born ca 1670 to 1682; m ANNA DORTHEA MARGARET ...   On
NY Palatine subs. list in 1710 (2A,2Y) and 1712 (3A,1Y). Was sponsor for bp Jan
1716 of Niclaus, son of Hen. Fehling & M. Kunigunda. On 1717 Simmendinger census
at New Ansberg (Smitsdorf) with wife Anna Dorothea & 4 children. A Nicholas Ruell
moved to the Tulpehocken Valley in Penn. ca 1723. Known children include
CHRISTIAN WILHELM (bp Albany NY 25 May 1713, sp. Christian Wilh. Walborn & Anna
Doro. Marg. Roul) and ANNA CATHERINE (b WCL May 1717, sp. Johann Zoeller & w.).

                         RIEGEL - 2nd Generation

7304: Sgt. CHRISTIAN RIEGEL <R4a> - pr. born ca 1715 to 1734; liv. 1769 (GF
militia Sgt.). In May 1769 there was a Sgt. Christian Riegel, in addition to a
private Christian Riegel, in Capt. Petrie's German Flats militia unit (Book of
Names, page 13).

       +7309: ps. GODFRAY b ca 1759; m1 by ca 1794 CHARLOTTE FULMER

7303: **GODFRIED RIEGEL** jun'r <R3> - pr. born ca 1713 to 1721; pr. died before Dec 1759 (Fred. Riegel mar. record); ps. m MARGARET ... (an Anna Margaret Rils appears on roster of Manheim church ca 1750 <Book of Names, page 61>). His assignment of Burnetsfield lot #10 in 1723 marks him as a dependent, thus Godfrid jr. was presumably the eldest son of immigrant Godfrid. Church records have a "Godfrid" as father of Frederick, and we favor Godfrid jr as that father (rather than immigrant Godfrid, who would have been about age 56 by Frederick's supposed birthdate of say 1738). The child Marguerite Rill, who was amongst the New York prisoners held in Canada and recovered in 1758 (Book of Names page 112), possibly also belongs to this family.

```
    +7310: FREDERICK GODF.  b say 1738; m 1759 CATHERINE HELMER
    +7311: pr. CHRISTIAN  b say 1742; m 1763 MARGARET HELMER
     7312: ps. MARGARGET  b say 1745; liv. 1757 (prisoner in Canada)
```

Albany records show a Patrick Regil in 1742 (m Elisabeth Prys then) and a William Rhigel who married in 1765 Charlotta Phaff. There is no indication of a tie between the Albany Regils and the German Flats family.

RIEGEL - 3rd Generation

7311: **CHRISTIAN RIEGEL** <R4b> - pr. born ca 1735 to 1745; m SAR 15 Mar 1763 MARGARET HELMER dau of ADAM HELMER & MARGARET. In 1769 GF militia (ps. two Christians listed there, see Book of Names pages 13-14) and in Col. Bellinger's Revol. Regm. Was a first settler at Deerfield NY with Marc DeMuth and George Weaver in 1773 and returned there in 1784. Had 2 adults & 4 children (under age 16) on 1778 German Flats relief and appears on the 1790 Herkimer census (2-1-2), next to Jacob Edick and Peter Weaver jr. in what looks to be the Deerfield group. He later moved to Manlius, in Onondaga Co. NY (Reals book page 14).

```
     7313: FREDERICK  b 1 Jan 1764 (sp. Fr. Reigel & w. Cath. <Helmer>)
     7314: MARIA ELISABETH  bp GF 7 Jan 1766 (Maria Helmer, Godf Hilts)
    +7315: GODFRIED CHR.  b SAR Aug 1767 (sp. Godfrid Hilts, Cath. Folts)
              m 1789 GERTRUDE TH. FULMER
     7316: ps. MARIA  b say 1770 (Deuel notes, no other basis seen)
    +7317: CHRISTIAN  1772-1841 m by 1797 ELISABETH HISER
    +7318: JOHN  b ca 1778-80 m PEGGY ... (b 1786, d 1822)
```

7310: **FREDERICK RIEGEL** <R5> - pr. born ca 1730 to 1740 (son of Godfrid); m SAR 26 Dec 1759 CATHERINE HELMER dau of ADAM HELMER & MARGARET ... (Helmer book page 23). His father Godfrid was deceased at the time of Frederick's marriage in 1759 (SAR mar. rec. call Frederick the son of the "late" Godfrid). In militia in 1769 and in Col. Bellinger's Revol. Regiment. Children Christian & Godfrid bp at German Flats NY 1764-7. Had 2 adults & 5 children (under 16) on the 1778 German Flats relief and is listed on the 1790 Herkimer census (5-0-2) near Mark DeMuth and John Helmer.

```
     7319: MARGARET  b SAR 16 Oct 1760 (sp Marg. Ad. Helmer, Tm C. Frank)
    +7320: CHRISTIAN  bp GF 4 Feb 1763 (sp. Christian Riegel)
     7321: GODFRID  bp GF 4 Dec 1764 (sp Joh. Helmer, Marg. Bellinger)
     7322: CATHERINE  bp 29 Apr 1767 (sp. Maria Hilts, Hen Helmer)
    +7323: FREDERICK  b SAR 15 Jun 1769 (sp Fr. Helmer & w Phillippina)
              m by 1792 CATHERINE DEMUTH
    +7324: ADAM  b May 1770; m 1796 CATHERINE HUYSER
```

7309: GODFRAY RIEGEL <R6> - born ca 1759; died Ontario Co. NY after 1850 (Reals book, page 17); ml by 1794 CHARLOTTE FULMER (d 1818); m2 11 Dec 1831 Ms. PHILIPS (b ca 1769). Godfray was a hunter, Indian fighter and veteran of the War of 1812 (Reals book) and, based on his birthyear, was pr. the Godfray Regel in Col. Bellinger's Regiment during the Revolution. His children were Christian, Eva, John (b ca 1797), Charlotte (b 1798, d 1908), Catherine, Mary, and pr. another son and 3 other daughters (ibid).

RIEGEL (Reals) - 4th Generation

7324: ADAM F. RIEGEL <R17> - born May 1770; died Manlius NY 12 Dec 1836; m GF 19 Jan 1796 CATHERINE HISER (b ca 1777, d 18 Sep 1851) ps. dau of MATHEIS HISER & BARBARA (see Cath. M. Hiser, bp GF Aug 1777). Children Betsy (bp 1800), Fred. A. (1802-1834), Catherine (1800-1855 m DANIEL EATON), Jacob, George, William A. (b Minden 1816, m Cath. Folts), James, Mariah, Reuben A, & pr. others.

7320: CHRISTIAN F. RIEGEL <R13> - bp GF 4 Feb 1763 (son of Frederick); died by Feb 1819 (will probated then in Onondaga Co. NY); m by ca 1795 PEGGY ... Children were Catherine, Maria, and Peter (Reals book page 19).

7317: CHRISTIAN RIEGEL <R10> - born 1772 (son of Christian); died Manlius NY 6 Jul 1841 (Reals book page 18); m ELISABETH HISER (b 22 Feb 1770-77, d Jamesville NY 21 May 1863) dau of MARTIN HISER (Hauser). Children were Daniel (b 1797), George, John, Frederick, Christian, William (b 1810), Jacob (b 1813), Reuben, and Martin.

7323: FREDERICK F. RIEGEL <R16> - born 17 Jun 1769; died 7 Dec 1826 (or 1828, dates from cemetery inscription as given in Reals book page 19); m CATHERINE DEMUTH (b 1770, d 23 Sep 1850) pr. dau of GEORGE DEMUTH & ANNA. Daughter Hannah's marriage to Henry Harter identified in Harter book (page 21). Children (see Reals book for more detail) were George, Elizabeth, Matilda, Hanna, James, Frederick, Catherine, William (b ca 1808, m Gertrude), Henry, and Maria.

> 7325: GEORGE b 17 Dec 1792 (sp Joh. DeMuth, Cath. Riegel)
>   m 1813 CATHERINE HARTER
> 7326: FREIDRICH b GF 28 Jun 1794 (sp Godf Riegel, Cath. Hauser)
> 7327: HANNAH 1801-1852 m HENRY HARTER (b 1796)

7315: GODFRIED CHR. RIEGEL <R9> - born GF 1 Aug 1767; m 24 Nov 1789 GERTRUDE TH. FULMER dau of THOMAS FULMER & CATHERINE. Pr. the Godfrid on 1790 Herkimer census (1-0-1) at Deerfield, next to John Brodhack.

> 7328: CHRISTIAN GODF. bp GF 15 Sep 1790 (sp Chr. Folmer & Anna Eva)
> 7329: ELISABETH bp GF 26 Dec 1791 (sp Con. Fulmer & Elis.)
> 7330: CHRISTIAN bp GF 19 Jan 1794 (sp Chr. Regel, Cath. Regel)
>   d 1846; m BETSY HILTS

7318: JOHN RIEGEL <R11> - pr. born ca 1778 to 1780; died after 1840; m PEGGY... Children were John, Michael (b 1815), and pr. others.

7331: WILLIAM RIEGEL - pr. born ca 1790 to 1797; m by 1814 EVE... Had children Cornelius (1814), Elizabeth, Lena Maria (bp Minden 13 Mar 1817), Hannah B. (1820), Eva (1821), William Wash. (1824). Ps. related to the Cornelius Riegel on 1790 Canajoharie census (1-0-3).

RIEMA - 1st Generation

7401: JOHN RIEMA Sr. - pr. born in Germany ca 1715 to 1735; pr. died 1779-80; m by 1767 CATHERINE ...   John Riema was listed in the German Flats militia in 1769, was naturalized 8 Mar 1773, and was later in Revolutionary service.   John Sr. lived first at the New Petersburg (now Schuyler NY) settlement of the Peter Hasenclaver immigrants of 1766, along with the Ayer/Oyer, Finster, Lentz, Valentine Miller, and Witrig families.   Then later he apparently moved with several neighbors to the New Germantown settlement in the Reimensneider's Bush area northeast of Herkimer.   The Hatch Papers say John Reima was captured and shot during the Tory Indian raid of 1780, and at the same time his sons John jr, Frederick, & Jacob were captured.   However the aforementioned raid may have been in 1779 as in a petition (undated, but we think ca fall 1779), it is noted that widow Elisabeth Bowen's husband was killed by the Indians at German Town on the 2nd of August 1779 and widow Elisabeth Brown's husband (George Braun) was killed at the same time (Mohawk Valley in the Revolution, page 182-3).   That petition also refers to an old widow named "CATHERINE ROMAR", as mother-in-law of Mrs. Elisabeth Hiller, and so we have placed an early daughter Elisabeth below on the off chance that Romar was a spelling variant of Riema (see for example "Hannes Rimer" of this family in Book of Names, page 168).   Subsequently we presume that John Jr. became the head of household and was the John Riema on the 1790 Herkimer census (5-0-4), listed next to D. Bekker, Jacob Riema, and Peter & Jacob Bircky in what appears to be the E. Schuyer area northwest of Herkimer NY.

surname RIEMA

```
      7401A ps. ELISABETH (Romar) b say 1748; m by 1765 JACOB HILLER
     +7402: JOHN jr  b say 1752; in Revol. Service
                   apparently m by 1795 CATHERINE ...
     +7403: pr. GEORGE  b say 1756; m by 1790 SARA ... in Revol. service
     +7404: JACOB  b say 1760; m by 1787 DOROTHEA ...
      7403A FREDERICK  b say 1765; m 1795 MARIA BEKKER
     +7405: CHRISTIAN b SAR 14 Aug 1767 (sp Jac Mohr, Jac Hiller, Cat Rank)
                   m by 1789 MARGARET ...
      7406: pr. MARGARET  b say 1769; m Jan 1788 PETER LENTZ
     +7407: DEOBALD  b SAR 2 Dec 1770 (sp Geo Schiff, Maria Groonhard)
                   m 1795 MARGARET BREITENBACHER
     +7408: PETER  1772-1844  m 31 Dec 1793 CATHERINE HOCKSTATER
      7410: ps. CATHERINE  b say 1774; liv. 1794 (spf C. Riema bp)
                   (ps. the 1794 sponsor Cath. Riema was the widow)
```

RIEMA - 2nd Generation

7405: CHRISTIAN RIEMA - born, pr. at Hasenclever's New Peterburgs settlement (Herkimer) New York, 14 Aug 1770 (bp SAR Oct 1767); m by 1789 MARGARET ... Christian and Margaret were sponsors for Mar 1795 bp of Margaret, dau of Wm Gather & Lena.   On 1790 Herkimer census (1-0-1) near H. Bender, M. Witrig, Adam Meyer, & Baltus Breitenbacher at New Germantown area.

```
      7411: JOHN  b GF 10 Sep 1789 (sp Jac. Bircki & Anna)
      7412: CATHERINE  b GF 14 Aug 1792 (sp. Geo. Rima & Sara)
```

7407: DEOBALD RIEMA (Theobald) - born SAR 2 Dec 1770 (bp Jan 1771); m GF 3 Mar 1795 MARGARET BREITENBACHER pr. dau of BALTES BRIETENBACHER. Deobald and wife Margaret of Germantown sponsored the Feb 1804 HK bp of Eva, dau of Wilhelm Balde & Catherine (Breitenbacher).

   7413: CATHERINE b GF 26 Nov 1795 (sp John Rima, Cath. Bretnbachr)

7403A FREDERICK RIEMA - pr. born ca 1760 to 1775; m GF 17 Mar 1795 MARIA BEKKER pr. a dau of DIEBOLD BECKER. Was sponsor, with Maria Becker, for Nov 1792 bp of Maria, dau of Christian Hockstater & Maria Catherine.

   7414: LORENTZ b GF 25 Dec 1795 (sp Lor. Rinckel, Cath. Reima)

7403: GEORGE RIEMA - pr. born ca 1750 to 1764; m by 1790 SARA ... (pr. Lentz). In Revol. service in Bellinger's 4th Tryon Co. NY Regiment. Sponsored, with Cath. Elis. Rinckel, Oct 1784 bp of George, son of Christian Hockstater & Maria Cath., and, with Sara Lentz, Apr 1787 bp of Sara, dau of Michael Witrig & Elisabeth.

   7415: JOHN bp SJR 9 Jan 1791 (sp Christian Rima & Margaret)
   7416: GEORGE b GF 25 May 1793 (sp Mich. Witrig & Elis.)
   7417: ANNA b GF 21 Oct 1795 (sp Jac. Bircky & Anna)

7404: JACOB RIEMA - pr. born ca 1760 to 1770; m by 1787 DOROTHEA ...   Living at New Deutschland in 1789. On 1790 Herkimer NY census (1-1-3).

   7418: JOHN b GF 29 Feb 1788 (sp John Rima & Marg. Lentz)
   7419: CATHERINE b SJR 13 Sep 1789 (sp Geo. Rima, Sara Lentz)
   7420: ELISABETH b SJR 18 Jul 1791 (sp Fr. Rima, Elis. Meyer)
   7421: MARGARET b 19 Feb 1793 (sp Peter Lentz & Marg.)
   7422: JACOB b GF 19 Mar 1795 (sp Theobald Riema & Marg.)

7402: JOHN RIEMA jr - pr. born ca 1750 to 1763; m by 1795 CATHERINE ...   Served in Bellinger's Revol. Regiment. John & wife Catherine were sponsors for Mar 1795 bp of Maria, dau of Christian Hockstater & Maria Catherine.

7408: PETER RIEMA - born New Petersburg NY 18 Apr 1772; died 22 Mar 1844; m 31 Dec 1793 CATHERINE HOCKSTATER (bp 1776, d 1840) dau of CHRISTIAN HOCKSTATER. A story related in Arnold's Oyer book (page 14) says that during the Revolution, Tory Indians, having captured his young friends in a field while Peter hid in the woods, ordered the other children to call for him - instead they yelled in German "Peter, bleib wo du bist" (i.e. "Peter, stay where you are"). Children of Peter Riema & Catherine were Catherine (1794-1862), Mary Margaret (b 1796, m Jacob Witrig), Frederick (b 1798, m Elisabeth P. Oyer), Elisabeth (b 1800), Mary (b 1801, m Jacob P. Ayer), George, Eva, Lany, Sophronia, Peter jr., Philanda (1816-1902, m Lyman B. Ouderkirk), and Anna (1820-1842).

   7423: CATHERINE b GF 6 May 1794 (sp Jac. Hockstatr, Cath. Rima)

********** RIEMENSNEIDER **********

RIEMENSNEIDER - 1st Generation

7451: HENRY RIEMENSNEIDER - pr. born ca 1720 to 1730; m pr. before 1750 ANNA DOROTHEA ... Hendrick appears on the 1751 list of supporters for Rev. Wernig of the Stone Arabia Church. In 1757 he was in Lt. Severinus Dygert's militia unit, listed near Hen. Salsman, Stofel Schultz, George Shacke, & William Laux. Henry was naturalized on 20 Mar 1762, along with Nicholas Kiltz, Harme Schaeffer, and others (Book of Names page 6). He and his wife were sponsors for 1760 SAR bp of Henrich (born Dec 1759), son of John Pet. Ritter & Barbara, and in Jan 1763 they were sponsors for bp of Henry, son of George Etel & Maria Dorothea. In 1769 Henry Rieme Schneider's name appears, alongside those of John Ritter and George Etel, on the roster of Capt. Petrie's German Flats militia. In the list of Revol. soldiers in Col. Klock's 2nd Tryon Co. Regiment (Book of Names page 151) we find Henry Rumsnider, and the notation that he was a prisoner of war. He evidently was repatriated after the war as he and Anna Dorothea were sponsors for Mar 1784 bp of Anne Buje at German Flats. It does not seem likely, as given in the Book of Names (page 171) that Riemensneiders may have changed their name to Riema (i.e. that family descends from John Riema who immigrated with Peter Hansenclever about 1765).

surname RIEMENSNEIDER
```
7451A  ps. DOROTHY (Riemnsndr ?)  b say 1746; m by 1763 GEORGE ETEL
7452:  pr. ELISABETH  b say 1749; liv. Apr 1766 (spf Jost G Etel bp)
                       m Oct 1766 JOHN PURCK
+7453:  pr. JOHN  b say 1751; m by 1775 EVA ...
 7454:  child  b SAL 7 Dec 1755 (sp Rudolph Koch & Elis.<Dygert>)
 7455:  pr. CATHERINE  ca 1758-1839  pr. m JACOB DAVIS (1750-1836)
              (husband called Jost Henry Davis in Petrie book page 36)
```

RIEMENSNEIDER - 2nd Generation

7453: JOHN RIEMENSNEIDER - pr. born ca 1740 to 1755; m by 1775 EVA ... Since John first appears in 1770 as a sponsor for the bp of John, son of George Etel & Maria Dorothea, we assume he was a generation later than the above Henry. In Dec 1775 John & Eva were sponsors for bp of Eva, dau of Peter Rickert & Elisabeth. A John Riemensneider & Maria <pr. Eva> sponsored Jun 1778 GF bp of Jacob, son of Jacob DeBus & Catherine, and John Riemensneider & Eva sponsored Feb 1779 GF bp of Maria, dau of John Boye & Catherine. He served in Col. Klock's 2nd Tryon Co. regiment during the Revolution and appears on the 1790 census of Palatine NY (2-2-49), living near Frederick & Henry Ritter and a George "Cadle" (pr. Etel).

```
7456:  pr. JACOB  b say 1778; m CATHERINE ...
7457:  JOHN  b 7 Oct 1785 (GF sp Ludwig Rickert, Marg. Ritter)
7458:  ADAM  bp SJR 5 Sep 1790 (sp Henrich ..., Susanna ...)
7459:  ANNA ELISABETH  b GF 23 Feb 1793 (sp Joh. Peter Bouje & Cath.)
```

Note - Reimensneider's Bush, also known as Schneidersbush, was located north of Little Falls in the Township of Manheim, Herkimer Co., New York. The St. Johnsville Church bp records of 1790-5 note many families there.

********** RITTER (Reuter) **********

7501: Sgt. JOHANNES RITTER - pr. born in Germany ca 1720 to 1735; died at the Oriskany battle 6 Aug 1777; m by 1759 Anna BARBARA ... Petrie book (page 18) calls him John Peter Ritter from Sponheimethal Germany. Was a sponsor for 1762 bp of Barbara Frisch and for Jun 1764 bp of John, son of George Etel & Maria Dorothea. Lived at Riemensnider's Bush and in 1769 was in the GF militia listed, next to Henry Riemensneider & George Etel (Book of Names, page 14).

surname RITTER
7502: ps. JACOB   d Oriskany 6 Aug 1777 (Book of Names, pg 168)
+**7503:** HENRICH b 1759 (sp Hen Remnsnider & w. Doro); m MARIA PETRIE
+**7504:** pr. FREDERICK b say 1763; m 1786 ELISABETH SEUFFER
7505: MARIA CATHERINE   bp 14 Feb 1765 (sp Cath. Petrie, Geo Helmer)
          m GF 28 Sep 1784 BALTHAZER STRAUCH
7506: ANNA ELISABETH   bp 28 Apr 1767 (sp. Elis. & Johannes Purk)
          m 1786 HENRICH ANSTED
7506A pr. MARGARET b say 1769; liv. 1785 (spf Riemensneider bp)
7507: pr. JOHANNES b say 1771; had child bp GF Oct 1794
+**7508:** MATTHEUS b say 1773; liv. 1790 (spf bp of Joh. Ritter)
7509: ANNA MARIA b 30 Jan 1775 (sp. Joh. Schmid & w. Maria)

7510: HENDRICK REUTER - pr. born ca 1675 (age 34 in 1709); m Anna JULIANA. A Catholic huntsman, with girls 4 & 2 on 1709 London Palatine List. On NY Palatine subs. list in 1710 (2A,0Y) and 1712 (2A,2Y) and on 1717 Simmendinger census with wife Anna Juliana & 2 children. Children were JOHANNA ELISABETH (bp 8 Jul 1711, sp J E Werner, Joh. Hess), FREDERICK (b 16 Aug 1714, sp. Joh. Stahl, Fred. Maul), and EVA CATHERINE (b Dec 1717, sp Cath. Maul, Eva & David Muller). No known connection to the Ritter family of Sneidersbush in Herkimer Co.

RITTER - 2nd Generation

7504: FREDERICK RITTER - pr. born before 1770; m 11 Apr 1786 ELISABETH SEUFFER dau of JOHANNES SEUFFER & MARIA. On 1790 Palatine NY census (1-1-2).

          7511: MARIA b GF 15 Apr 1788 (sp Joh. Seuffer & Maria)
          7512: JOHANNES bp 15 Jun 1790 (sp. Math. Ritter, Cath. Senfer)
          7513: CATHERINE b SJR 6 Jul 1792 (sp Baldus Straub & Cath.)

7503: HENRICH RITTER - born 28 Dec 1759 (son of Johannes); died 7 Jun 1847 (age 87-5-12); m 1 Jan 1786 MARIA PETRIE (b 1766, d 1 Jul 1841 age 75-10-, buried at Riemensneders Bush) dau of JOST PETRIE & CATHERINE KESSLER. At Sneidersbush 1792. On 1790 Palatine NY census (1-1-2) near John Keller, F. Ritter, & Jacob Davis.

          7514: JOHANNES b 5 Nov 1786 (sp. Fred. Ritter, Marg. Petrie)
          7515: CATHERINE b 2 Aug 1788 (sp Hen. Etel, Cath. Petrie)
                    m1 DANIEL L. DAVIS (1788-1862); m2 BALTUS STROUGH
          7516: ANNA EVA b 15 Dec 1790 (sp. Stephen Eysaman & Anna Eva)
          7517: MARGARET bp SJR 30 Dec 1792 (sp John Bayer & Margaret)
          7518: JOSEPH b 1799; m BETSY KELLER

7508: MATHEUS JOH. RITTER - pr. born ca 1765 to 1774; m 19 Jan 1792 ANNA JOH. ADAM KLOCK (Glock). Had Catherine (bp SJR 22 Feb 1793, sp Adam Klock & Cath.) and John (b GF 14 Nov 1794, sp John Buje & Anna Klock)

7601: Rev. ROSENCRANTZ Sr.- pr. born ca 1680 to 1705; died ca 1752.. Vosburgh´s German Flats Church History, vol. 3 (1920), has this "Elder Rosencrantz" as pastor from 1751 to 1752. Vosburgh thought this family came from Germany, however then name is seen amongst the early settlers of Kingston NY.

surname ROSENCRANTZ

+7602: ABRAHAM 1728-1796 m MARIA HERKIMER

ROSENCRANTZ - 2nd Generation

7602: Rev. ABRAHAM ROSENCRANTZ - born ca 1728; died at Herkimer NY 29 Dec 1796; m 27 Apr 1758 (mar. rec. Dutch Reform Church of Kingston NY, 16 May 1758) ANNA MARIA HERKIMER dau of JOST HERKIMER & CATHERINE PETRIE. In 1752 he succeeded his father as pastor of the German Flats church at Burnetsfield. On November 12th 1757, he narrowly escaped the French & Indian attack on German Flats, being awakened and escorted across the Mohawk River by friendly Indians. Burnetsfield´s early octagonal shaped wood church was destroyed in that raid (sketch depicted on front of this book). Abraham went to New York City, then returned to occupy the parsonage at Stone Arabia from Sep 1759 to Jan 1772 (this constituting the earliest period for which records now survive). He apparently lived at the Sand Hill Church in Canajoharie from 1772 to 1781, succeeding Dominie John Caspar Lappius (those records were lost in the attack on Ft. Plain on 2 Aug 1780), and spent his last years at the Ft. Herkimer Church (where tradition has it that he is buried beneath the old pulpit). His diligence in the recording of marriages and baptisms form the basis for this genealogy.

    +7603: NICHOLAS b SAR 25 Aug 1760 (sp Nic Herkimer & w. Maria)
    7604: MARGARET b SAR 26 Apr 1762; m 1785 RUDOLPH R. SHOEMAKER
    +7605: GEORGE 1764-1838 m ANNA SCHNELL
    +7606: HENRICH JACOB b 13 May 1766 (sp Hen. Frey & Elis. <Herkimer>)
    7606A CATHERINE b SAR 23 Jul 1768 (sp Cath./w. of Andr. Fink)
    7607: pr. MARIA b say 1770; ml by 1802 Joh. JOST BELLINGER (b 1766)
    7608: pr. ABRAHAM jr. b 1778 (?); d 1829 m MAGDALINE FEETER
    7609: JOST b 28 Jul 1778 (sp Geo. Herkimer & w); m TRYPHET BIRD
    7611: ps. ELIZABETH

ROSENTCRANTZ - 3rd Generation

7603: NICHOLAS ROSENTCRANTZ - born 25 Aug 1760; m ... (see Petrie book page 6). He sponsored, with Margaret Kessler, Apr 1780 bp of Margaret, dau of Stephen Eysaman. Had a son HENRY (b say 1790).

7605: GEORGE ROSENCRANTZ - born GF 15 Mar 1764 (sp Jost Shoemaker, unm, & Capt. Frey´s w. Elis. <Herkimer>); died Fall Hill NY 21 Dec 1838; m 6 May 1792 ANNA SCHNELL (b 1770, d 1850) dau of JACOB SNELL. George was a judge of the Court of Common Pleas. Children (Petrie book page 17) were Catherine, Henry, Nancy, Abraham, Elisabeth, Maria, & Margaret.

7606: HENRICH JACOB ROSENCRANTZ - born 13 May 1766; m PATIENCE EASTERBROOK. Lived at Fall Hill NY. Children (Petrie book page 17) were Elizabeth, Peggi, Heneritta, Catherine, Beatie Ann, George Henry, and Nicholas.

7701: JOHN SCHELL - born Nassau-Dilenburg Germany 1734; died Herkimer NY of suffocation 1 Aug 1802; m SAR 16 Feb 1762 BARBARA RASBACH dau of JOHANNES RASBACH & MARGARET BIERMAN. Came to Philadelphia in 1752 and thence to the Mohawk Valley where he settled in the Schell's Bush road area (just east of the present town of Herkimer). He was naturalized on 20 Oct 1764. Later he was disabled from wounds received in Revolutionary War service (V. Eysaman notes, orig. from Mrs. Stanley Irene Sell of Waterloo NY). He and his wife adopted Mary Moyer (born 1775, m 1794 Henry Schell), daughter of Gerlach Majer (as on 1794 mar. rec.).

surname SCHELL

+7702: CHRISTIAN 1763- m CATHERINE HISER
+7703: MARK 1764- m CATHERINE ELIZABETH RAAN
7704: ANNA CATHERINE b 12 Apr 1766 (sp Cath. Bentz, Fr. Rasbach)
+7705: PETER J. 1768-1838 m CATHERINE HILTS
7706: ELIZABETH bp SAL 2 Mar 1771 (sp. Fr. Heine & w.)
+7707: JOHN b say 1773; m1 1792 MARGARET THUM m2 EVA CASLER
7708: ps. BARBARA b say 1775; m by 1803 MICHAEL KAISER jr

7709: Johan CHRISTIAN SCHELL - born ca 1725; killed in combat with Tory Indians at his blockhouse home Jul 1782; m MARIA ELISABETH PETRIE (b 1735, as in DAR# 29953) ps. a dau of JOST PETRIE & CORDELIA DEMUTH (Petrie book, page 3-4) but the naming of children below seems to hint that her parentage may lie elsewhere.

7710: JOHN CHRISTIAN jr 1758- m 1793 ELISABETH SEGNER
7711: MARIA ELISABETH b 21 Sep 1760 (Elis. M Petri, Diet. J Petri)
7712: AUGUSTINUS (DENIS) b SAR 17 Apr 1763 (sp Aug. Hess & w.)
d Jul 1782 (from blockhouse fight wounds)
+7713: FREDERICK b 1764 (sp. , Mar. Petri); m 1788 CATH. STARING
7714: EVA b ca 1765; m MR. PLANCK
7715: ANNA MARIA b GF 16 Feb 1766 (sp Joh Heering & Maria<Petrie>)
+7716: HENRY (twin) b 22 Sep 1770 (sp Hen Widerstn & Magd.<Hilts>
m 1794 MARY MOYER
7717: MARK (twin) b 22 Sep 1770 (sp Jac N Kessler & Delia <Petrie>)
7718: MARY CATHERINE b 1 Dec 1777 (sp Christian Hess & Elis.)
m ADAM KAISER

7719: ANNA SCHELL - pr. born ca 1720 to 1735; m ca 1754 AUGUSTINUS HESS

SCHELL - 2nd Generation

7702: CHRISTIAN SCHELL - born 6 Jan 1763; died Schell's Bush, Herkimer NY; m 8 Aug 1786 CATHERINE HISER (b 1768) dau of HENRY HISER & ANNA MARIA RASBACH.

7720: CATHERINE b GF 17 Dec 1787; m 1806 PETER C. FOLTS
7721: JOHN CHRISTIAN no children
7722: BARBARA b 1789 (sp John Shell & w); m 1804 HENRY WM. DYGERT
7723: HENRY b GF 9 Sep 1791 (sp Hen. Schell, Maria Meyer)
7724: MARIA b 25 Feb 1793 (sp Marc Staring, Maria Schell)
7725: JOHANNES b 29 Dec 1794 (sp John Witherstine & Margaret)
7726: EVA b 13 Nov 1802; m JAMES CASLER
7727: MOSES b HK 2 Jun 1805 (sp John Petry & w. Gertr.)
7728: ps. DOROTHEA b 1812

7713: FREDERICK CHR. SCHELL ("Fritz") - born 16 Dec 1764 (son of Christian, sp Fred Meyer & Maria Petrie); m Jul 1788 CATHERINE STAHRING. Lame from wound received in the 1782 blockhouse fight in which his father and brother died.

> **7729: CATHERINE** b GF 20 Mar 1790 (sp Nich. Thum & Maria)
> **7730: ANNA** b GF 4 Feb 1794 (sp Hen. Chr. Schell, Marg. Raspach)

7716: HENRY CHR. SCHELL - born 22 Sep 1770 (son of Christian); died Ingersoll Ontario Canada 1859 (Petrie book page 10); m GF 13 Apr 1794 MARIA GERLACH MEYER (ie MARY MOYER, b 1775, d 1860, DAR vol 30 page 341). Children Elisabeth (b 2 Oct 1794, sp Jacob Meyer, Elis. Schell) and Henry (b 1798, d 1881) married ELIZABETH LOONEN.

7707: JOHN JOH. SCHELL - pr. born ca 1765 to 1772; m1 GF 31 Jan 1792 MARGARET THUM dau of MELCHIOR THUM; m2 1794 ANNA EVA CASLER (b 28 Jan 1769, d 23 Mar 1844 age 75-1-25) dau of JACOB N. KESSLER & DELIA PETRIE. Later in life he was very much stooped over and walked with two canes (Wm U. Smith notes).

> **7731: JOHN** 1795-1880 m 1815 NANCY HILTS
> **7732: PETER I.** m MARY SCHELL
> **7733: JACOB J.** m ELISABETH MOYER
> **7734: MARK** m ELIZABETH FULMER
> **7735: ADAM** m 1822 DELIA FOLTS
> **7736: CATHERINE** b 8 Feb 1803; m JOHANNES CHRISTMAN
> **7737: MAGDALENA** b 2 Dec 1804; m CONRAD FOLTS
> **7738: MARGARET** b 5 Nov 1806; m DAVID WIEDERSTEIN
> **7739: MARY** b say 1807; confirmed 1819
> **7740: DELIA** b 7 Jan 1811 (sp Marc. Folts, Cath. Schell)
> **7741: ANNA** (or NANCY) b 1 Feb 1813

7703: MARCUS JOH. SCHELL - pr. the John born 1764 (son of John); m GF 25 Mar 1788 CATHERINE ELISABETH RYAN (Raan) dau of NICHOLAS RYAN.

> **7742: JOHANNES** b GF 29 Oct 1789 (sp John Schell, Maria Raan)
> **7743: MARIA** b GF 8 Feb 1792 (sp Godf. Hilts & Maria)
> **7744: ANNA** b GF 2 Aug 1794 (sp John Rasbach & Anna)

7705: PETER J. SCHELL - born 1768; died 4 Jan 1838; m 1790 CATHERINE G. HILTS (b ca 1770, d 6 Sep 1822 age 52) dau of GEORGE HILTS & ELISABETH FOLTS. Twin daughters Catherine and Delia were confirmed in 1813 at age 15 (Herk. Ch. rec.).

> **7745: ELISABETH** b GF 25 May 1791 (sp Nic Thum & Elis.); pr. d y
> **7746: PETER P.** b 2 Nov 1792 (sp Pet. Vols & Barb.); m MARY RASBACH
> **7747: ELISABETH** b 17 May 1794; d 10 Feb 1802 (age 7-9-6)
> **7748: ISAAC**
> **7749: ANNA** (Nancy) 1797-1868 m HENRY HARTER
> **7750: CATHERINE** (twin) b ca 1798; m 1815 CONRAD HELMER (b 1792)
> **7751: DELIA** (twin) b ca 1798; m CONRAD HARTMAN
> **7752: MARY** b ca 1801; m PETER I. SCHELL
> **7753: LEA** b say 1803; m 1823 CORNELIUS H. LEE
> **7754: BARBARA** b HK Mar 1805; m BENJAMIN FOLTS of Steuben NY
> **7755: FANNY** m WILLIAM PETRIE
> **7756: AMELIA** m JACOB CHRISTMAN
> **7757: LYDIA** m HIRAM LEE

********** SCHERER **********

SCHERER - 1st Generation

7801: CHRISTIAN SCHERER - pr. born ca 1735 to 1745; killed at Oriskany 6 Aug 1777; m Stone Arabia NY 2 Mar 1767 ANNA MARGARET BELLINGER (b ca 1750, d GF 19 Oct 1837 age 86-10-19) dau of Capt. PETER BELLINGER. His widow was listed with 2 children (under age 16) on the 1778 German Flats relief and she m2 WARNER SPOHN whose estate administration in 1826 lists wife Anna Margaret and her children as Peter Sharer, Margaret Illich (Edick), Anna Fox, and Catherine Myers; also a Jacob Illich son of George Illich. Christian was a sponsor, with Eva Frank, for Sep 1766 bp of Christian, son of Christian Ittig & Margaret (Bellinger book page 36). Was witness to a land transfer in 1773 amongst sons of Martin Smith.

                    surname SCHERER
        7802: ANNA MARGARET 1767-1821 m GEORGE JAC. EDICK
        7803: ANNA (Nancy) 1769-1845 m 1787 PETER FR. FOX
        7804: CATHERINE b say 1772; m 1793 ANDRIES JOS. MEYER
        7805: pr. JACOB b say 1774; liv. 1794 (spf Pet. A. Meyer bp)
       +7806: PETER 1776-1827 pr. m MARIA THUMB

SCHERER - 2nd Generation

7806: PETER SCHERER - born 1776; died 1827; m by 1804 MARIA THUMB (seen as Maria Dom). Was sponsor with, Elisabeth Bellinger, for Sep 1792 bp of Mary, dau of George Jac. Ittig & Margaret (Scherer). Peter Scherer and "Elisabeth" were sponsors for May 1795 bp of Peter, son of Henry Leimbach & Maria (Hiser). Brown's Folts book (page 5) has Mary, daughter of this Peter Scherer, as wife of Jacob P. Folts.

        7807: MARY 1799-1857 m JACOB P. FOLTS
        7808: CHRISTIAN b say 1801; m 1824 CATHERINE RASBACH
        7809: DAVID b HK 2 Apr 1803 (sp Widow Margaret Spohn)
        7810: MOSES bp HK 31 Dec 1811.

********* SCHUTT (Shute) *********

7901: **WILLIAM SCHUTT** ("Schott") - pr. born in Germany ca 1670 to 1685; m HELENA
... (she pr. d ca 1711); pr. m2 by 1717 GERTRUDE ..., assuming he was the "Wilhelm
Schuch" on NY Palatine subsistence list in 1710 (2A,1Y) and 1712 (1A,1Y) and on
the 1717 Simmendinger census with wife Gertrude & 3 children. Willam & Helena
were sponsors for bp Mar 1711 of Robert, son of Henric Chisom & Anna. Probably
related was a Margaret Schott who was sponsor for bp in Apr 1713 of Christina, dau
of Henrich Chisem & Annike.

surname SCHUTT
+7902: ps. APPOLONIA (Schutt?) b 1702; m LORENTZ HARTER
+7903: ps. CATHERINE b say 1708; liv. 1726 (spf Dieterich bp)
 7904: MARGARET b 9 Nov 1711 (sp. Hen. Chisem & Marg.)
+7905: ps. FREDERICK b say 1730; m by 1761 ELISABETH ...
+7906: ps. WILLIAM b say 1735; m 1764 CATHERINE HARTER

7907: **SALOMON SCHUTT** ("Schuett") - born Kingston NY pr. ca 1670 to 1685; m1 by
1710 JANNETJE SESUMS (Chisom?); m2 1 Sep 1712 MARIA ... (b Germany) widow of PAUL
MUNE. Wife Jannetje apparently sponsored bp at New York in Feb 1709 of her niece
Jannicke, dau of Michael Schuetze & Maria (Book of Names page 15) and was thus
apparently part of the small group of Germans who came early to New York in 1708.

+7908: pr. WILLIAM b say 1708; m by 1729 LENA FREER
 7909: HENRICUS b Aug 1710 (sp. Hen. Rison & Anna Risom)

SCHUTT - 2nd Generation

7905: **FREDERICK SCHUTT** - pr. born ca 1725 to 1740; believed to have m before
1761 ELISABETH WOHLEBEN dau of NICHOLAS WOHLEBEN.   In 1757 German Flats militia,
where his name appears alongside that of Peter Wohleben (Book of Names, page 8).
Presumably his wife was the Elisabeth, who was sponsor with Frederick at Jun 1766
bp of Appolonia, dau of William Schutt & Catherine (Harter).

 7909A MARIA b SAR 8 Apr 1761 (sp Werner Spohn, Maria Wohleben)
+7910: WILHELM b SAR 27 Mar 1763 (sp Wm Schot, Elis. Hess)
 7912: FRIEDRICH b SAR 16 Sep 1764 (sp. Fred. Shoemaker & Cath.)
 7912A CATHERINE b SAR 11 Mar 1768 (sp Cath ..., * Wohleben)
 7913: NICHOLAS b GF 5 May 1776 (sp. Nicol Weber & Cath.)
 7914: SUSANNA b GF 16 Aug 1778 (sp Tho. Shoemkr, Susanna Flagg)

7906: **WILLIAM SCHUTT** - pr. born ca 1720 to 1740; m Stone Arabia NY 30 Oct 1764
CATHERINE HARTER (b 1733) pr. dau of LORENTZ HARTER & APPOLONIA (Harter book page
1). Presumably the Wilgen Schott in 1757 German Flats militia and the Willem
Schut in Col. Bellinger's 4th Tryon Co. NY Revol. Regiment (Book of Names page
168). Had 2 adults & 3 children on 1778 GF relief and was ps. the William Schut
on 1790 Canajoharie NY census (1-0-3), near Abraham Gardner & Teunis Van Wagener.

 7915: MARIA CATHERINE (twin) b 20 Jun 1766
                        (sp. Anna Maria & Joh. Nicol Harter)
 7916: APPOLONIA (twin) b 20 Jun 1766 (sp. Elis. & Fred. Shut)
 7917: FRIEDRICH b SAR 17 Mar 1768 (sp. Fred. Frank & Maria Elis.)
 7918: ELISABETH b SAR 13 Jul 1769 (sp Sophia Wohleben, Fred Hess)
                        ps. m by 1806 HENRY HESS

7908: WILLEM SCHUT - pr. born ca 1690 to 1710 (ps. son of Solomon); m by 1729 LENA FREER and had children Wilhelm (bp Kingston NY 12 Jan 1729) and Soloman (bp Kingston 24 Dec 1732). Other Wilhelm Schutts at Kingston include one who married by 1725 Lena Cool (and had children Lea & Gertrude bp in 1725), another who married by 1729 Margaret Grieks (had dau Grietjen bp 26 Jan 1729), and another who married by 1739 Maria Dirks (and had children Maria & Cornelius bp 1739 to 1741). There is no indication of ties of this Schutt family at Kingston NY with that of the Mohawk Valley.

7902: APPOLONIA ... (Schutt?) - born 30 Jul 1702 (Harter book page 1); m LORENTZ HARTER (b 1698, d ca 1776). We do not see the early Schutt names such as William and Helena amongst the offspring of Lorentz Harder & Appolonia, although possibly the names were given to unaccounted for children who died young.

7903: CATHERINE SCHUTT (Schut) b say 1708; liv. 1726. Was sponsor at Nov 1726 bp (location uncertain, ps. New York City) of Catherine, dau of Christian Dieterich & Margareta (Book of Names, page 50).

                         SCHUTT - 3rd Generation

7918A PETER SCHUTT - pr. born ca 1740 to 1760; m by 1778 CATHERINE ...

        7918B ABRAHAM b SAL 6 Jul 1778 (sp Jos. Fink & Elisabeth)

7910: WILHELM SCHUTT (SCHOTT) - ps. the Wilhem born SAR 27 Mar 1763 (son of Frederich), though age at death computes to a birthyear of ca 1761); died Herkimer NY 24 Nov 1839 at age 78; m ANN BEDINGER and lived at Florida NY.

        7919A CATHERINE b ca 1793; age 18 in 1811 (Herk. Ch. Confirm.)
                   Cath., of Florida NY, d HK 18 Aug 1816 (age 23)
        7920: ANNA b say 1798; m 1816 NICHOLAS HILTS
        7921: OLIVE b say 1800; m 1818 NICHOLAS F. SMITH

7222: WILLIAM SCHUTT - pr. born ca 1750 to 1775; m Fonda NY 1786 SUSANNA HOVER (HUBER). Ps. the same William as the above man who married by 1793 Ann Bedinger.

        7223: REBECCA b FR 17 May 1787 (sp. Fred Lewis & Rachel <Hover>)
        7224: SOLOMON b FR 18 Jan 1792 (sp Jacob Philips & w. <Ann Hover>)

7924: MARIA SCHUTT - pr. born ca 1755 to 1773; m by 1790 JOSEPH COOPER. Had children LENA (b Fonda NY 29 Jul 1790, sp. Geo. Robertson & Lena Schut) and WILLIAM (b HK 14 Jan 1805, sp. Adam Staring & Ernestina <Harter>).

********** SCHUYLER **********

8001: DAVID P. SCHUYLER - bp Albany NY 26 Dec 1686 (son of Peter D. Schuyler &
Alita <Slechtenhorst>, as in Pearson's Albany book); died 1762; ml 17 Jul 1720
ANNA BRATT (bp 17 Dec 1694, d 24 Sep 1722) dau of ANDRIES A. BRATT & CORNELIA
TEUNISE; m2 ... Will of David of Canajohary, dated 3 Apr 1759, has children by
his 2nd wife as John, Adoniah, David jr., Philip, & Jacob and Anna, Margreta,
Alyda, & Catherine. Harvey Ingham's The Ingham and Schuyler Families (HI) offers
children's birthdates (his source not clear) and researchers Dr. Gilbert S. Bahn
and James O. Schuyler (HCH) provide good detail on the line of this David P., but
differ on placement of the two Jacobs (#8008 & #8021).

                          surname SCHUYLER
        8002: ALITA bp 12 Feb 1721; pr. d. young
       +8003: PETER D. b 1722; m ELISABETH BARBARA HERKIMER
                          by 2nd wife
        8004: JOHN b Jun 1726 (HI); liv. 1762 (estate adm.); to Madison Co.
       +8005: ADONIAH (ANTHONY) b Apr 1727 (HI); moved to Madison Co.
        8005A DAVID jr. b Feb 1728 (HI); to Madison Co. by 1790
       +8006: PHILIP b Mar 1730 (HI); d 1777; m pr. by 1762 ANNA ...
        8007: ANNA b Sep 1732 (HI)
        8008: JACOB b Mar 1734; ps. ml by 1755 EVA SWACKHAMER (d 1781)
        8009: MARGARET b Feb 1736 (HI)
        8010: ALIDA b Oct 1737 (HI); pr. d. young
        8010A CATHERINE b say 1742; ps. m by 1760 JOSEPH MEBIE
        8011: ALITA 1752-1830 m GEORGE HERKIMER

                    SCHUYLER - 2nd Generation

8005: ANTHONY SCHUYLER - pr. had children David, Alida (b 1765), Nicholas A.
(spf 1984 Schuyler bp), Adoniah jr., John A, & Peter A. (Dr. Bahn notes).

          +8012: DAVID ANT. b 15 Aug 1763; pr. m GF 1784 MARGARET WOHLEBEN
           8014: PETER ANT. b say 1769; m FPL 1789 CATHERINE WEIL (WILD)

8003: PETER D. SCHUYLER - born Albany NY 24 Sep 1722 (bp Mar 1723, son of David
& Anna); liv. 1783 (spf Schuyler bp); m 9 Jun 1743 ELISABETH BARBARA HERKIMER (b
1726, d 1800) dau of JOST HERKIMER & CATHERINE PETRIE. Sons Joist, Peter Jr., &
Nicholas were in Capt. Conrad's 1767 GF militia (Book of Names, pg 12).

          +8015: HAN YOST ca 1744-1810 m ANNA ... (widow of Phil. Schuyler)
          +8016: DAVID b say 1745; d unm ca 1762 (Petrie book, pg 14)
                          (guide to Col. Thomas to Otsego in the French War)
          +8017: PETER jr. b 1746; d bef 1822; m CATHERINE FREYMAUER
          +8018: NICHOLAS b ca 1749; m 14 Nov 1784 ELISABETH HERKIMER
           8019: CATHERINE ELISABETH ca 1751-1800 m JOSEPH HERKIMER
           8020: ANNA b ca 1754; pr. liv. 1785 (spf Schuyler bp)
          +8021: ps. JACOB b ca 1754; d 1825; m DELIA ...

8006: PHILIP SCHUYLER - killed at Oriskany 6 Aug 1777 (in Bellinger's Reg.); m
ANNA ... Had 2 boys & 2 girls on Tryon Co. census ca 1776, living near Petries &
Kesslers. Widow Ann had 4 children on 1778 GF relief.

           8022: DAVID PH. b say 1765; pr. m GF Oct 1790 HILLETJE SMIDT
           8023: MARGARET PH. b say 1767; liv. 1785 (spf Marg Schuyler bp)
           8023A ps. JOHN b say 1771; liv. 1792 (spf Schuyler bp)

8012: DAVID A. SCHUYLER - m MARGARET HEN. WOHLEBEN (1790 bp rec. calls her Wolaver
& him David A.). Pr. this man, not David Ph., m GF 12 May 1784 MARGARET
<Wohleben> P. KESSLER's widow. David A. on 1790 Canajohary census (1-3-2).

        8023A MARGARET b GF 23 Dec 1785 (sp Schylers, Nic. Ant & Marg. Ph)
        8023B NICLAUS bp SJR 5 Apr 1790 (sp John Wollever & Cath.)
        8023C LEA bp SJR 29 Jul 1792 (sp Pet. Wollever & Cath.)

8021: JACOB SCHUYLER - born 1754; died Chittenango NY 24 Sep 1825 (age 70); m
DELIA ... (b ca 1751, d 12 Jun 1831 age 80). He and Leonard Eckler were captured
23 Oct 1780 and held in Canada until 21 May 1783. About 1790 he moved to Sullivan
NY (near Chittenango). In addition to the 5 children below, he had Betsy, Mary,
David, Delia, Sarah, & Catherine (James O. Schuyler notes).

        8025: MARGARET b GF 10 Dec 1775 (sp Jost D Petri, Mar. J Petri)
        8026: JOHN J. b GF 3 Sep 1778 (sp Adam Stahl & Cath.)
        8027: PHILIP b GF 11 Mar 1781 (sp Joseph Mavi & Cath.)
        8028: JACOB b GF 31 May 1785 (sp Geo. Herkimer & Alita)
        8029: BARENT b GF 30 Jan 1788 (sp Dr. U. Wight, Cath. Wohleben)

8015: JOST SCHUYLER - born 1 Jan 1744; died 1810; m GF 14 Nov 1784 ANNA ... widow
of PHILIP SCHUYLER (Petrie book, pg 5-13). Lived an independent life in his
youth, much of it with the Indians. He and Tory Walter Butler were captured just
after the Oriskany battle and condemned to die. However General Benedict Arnold,
amidst the pleas of Jost's mother, spared his life on condition that Jost would
report to British Col. St. Leger that Arnold's forces were more numerous than
actual. Jost did so and became the hero of Arnold's strategem prompting St. Leger
to fall back to Canada (E&N 9/2/1936).

        8030: CATHERINE b 23 Jan 1787 (sp Jost H Herkmr, Marg. Ph Shuyler)

8018: NICHOLAS SCHUYLER - born 13 Apr 1748 (or 1749, Petrie book page 14); m 14
Nov 1784 his cousin ELISABETH HERKIMER (b 1764, d 1832 age 68) dau of HENDRICK
HERKIMER & CATHERINE DYGERT. Lived at Fall Hill, near Little Falls NY. Was on
1790 Canajoharie NY census (1-3-1), next to David A. Schuyler.

        8031: PETER DAVID b 19 Aug 1785 (sp P. Schyler jr, Anna Schuyer)
        8032: NICHOLAS b GF 22 Jan 1787 (sp Jost H Herkimer & Cath.)
        8033: HENRY bp SJR 26 Apr 1789 (sp Sev. Dygert, Magd. Herkimer)
        8033A JOST bp SJR 22 May 1791 (sp John Herkimer & Anna)
        8033B MARGARET b SJR 9 Jul 1793 (sp Nic. Herkimer & Marg.)
        8034: NICHOLAS jr 1796- m LYDIA GREEN
        8035: GEORGE ca 1796-1878 m ALIDA GREEN
        8036: AARON married and moved to Columbia NY

8017: PETER SCHUYLER jr. - born 28 Nov 1746 (Mrs. J. Spellman notes); died before
1822; m Schoharie NY 23 Jul 1776 CATHERINE FREYMAUER dau of JOHN FREYMEIER of
Cobleskill NY (no basis is seen for supposed marriage to a CATHERINE H. HERKIMER).
Children ELISABETH (b GF 7 Apr 1777, sp Marg. Rsncranz, Nic. Schuylr), ANNA (b GF
10 Jun 1779, sp Geo. Herkimer & Alita; m HK 1803 WILLIAM DYGERT), PETER (b SJR 3
Jul 1784, sp Pet. Schyler & Elis. Barbara; d Cazenovia NY), John, ABRAHAM (b SJR
29 Mar 1789, sp Abhm Mabie, Marg. Freymauer), JOSEPH (Petrie book, also E&N
3/24/1937). On 1790 Canajoharie NY census (1-3-4).

********** SEGHNER (Singer, Sickner) **********

8101: JOHANNES SICKNER - pr. born ca 1655 to 1666; pr. died 1710; m APPOLONIA
... (born ca 1666, age 44 in 1710). Widow Appolonia Signer/Sicknerin was on NY
City recuperation rolls in 1710 with sons John (deceased 1710 age 9) & Jacob (age
7). On NY Palatine list in 1710 (1A,3Y) and 1712 (1A,1Y). On 1717 Simmendinger
census at Hackensack with one child. Son JACOB SICKNER (b ca 1703) was pr. living
in 1717, but there is no hint of a tie to the Seghner family at German Flats.

8102: PAUL SEGHNER - pr. born ca 1730 to 1742 (ps. descendent of above
Johannes?); m 12 Mar 1762 ELISABETH EYSAMAN pr. dau of JOHANNES EYSAMAN. The
Seghner family was at German Flats by Nov 1757 when they reportedly fled across
the Mohawk River to escape capture during the French & Indian raid. Paul was a
Corp. in Capt. Conrad Frank's 1767 militia and on the 1790 GF census (1-2-7)
listed next to Conrad Seghner & Magdalena Ryan.

surname SEGHNER
```
     8103: ANTHONY  bp GF 6 Jan 1763 (sp Anth. Eysaman & Jannetje)
    +8104: CONRAD   b Nov 1764 (sp Con. Frank); m 1786 MARGARET PFEIFFER
     8105: LENA   b SAR 1 Mar 1767 (sp Maria Orendorf, Steph. Eysaman)
            liv. 1775 (spf Jacob Jac Petrie bp); ps. d by 1782
     8106: ANNA  b GF 17 Jan 1769; m 1791 DANIEL J. PETRIE
     8107: MARIA P.  b say 1771; m 1789 JOHANNES KELLER
     8108: ELISABETH P.  b say 1773; m 1794 CHRISTIAN SCHELL
     8109: CATHERINE  b say 1774; m 1792 JOHANNES KESSLER
     8110: ANTHONY  b 19 Aug 1776 (sp Jost Bell, Maria Bekker)
     8111: JANNETJE  b GF 16 Mar 1779 (sp John Eysaman, Jannetje)
     8112: JOHN  b say 1781; m 1804 ELISABETH NESH
     8113: child (ps. Lena?) b GF 19 Aug 1782 (sp P. Wohleben, Bolly Niers)
            ps. LENA who m JOHN M. KESSLER (children b 1803-23)
```

8114: VALENTINE SINGER - pr. born ca 1740 to 1766; m by 1787 ELISABETH ... Val.
& Elis. sponsored Jan 1787 GF bp of John, son of John Ekkerson & Elisabeth. A
guess that he was of an earlier generation than children listed below.

```
        8115: ps. CATHERINE  b say 1770; m GF 1788 NICHOLAS A. STARHING
        8116: ps. VALENTINE  b say 1772; m by 1791 MARIA  (spf Starin bp)
        8117: ps. ADAM  b say 1774; liv. GF 1792 (spf Adam N. Staring bp)
        8118: ps. JOSEPH  b say 1780; m by 1806 MARIA VETTERLE
```

SEGHNER - 2nd Generation

8104: CONRAD SEGHNER - born 23 Nov 1764; m 23 May 1786 MARGARET P. PFEIFFER dau
of PETER PFEIFFER & CATHERINE. On 1790 GF census (1-1-2).

```
        8119: MARIA CATHERINE  b GF Jan 1787 (sp Stephn Eysaman & Anna Eva)
        8120: JACOB  b GF 12 Sep 1788 (sp Jac. Eysaman, Anna Segner)
               d 1878; m ELIZABETH CROUCH
        8121: HENRICH  b GF 7 Feb 1791 (sp Hen. N. Staring & Elis.<Piper>)
        8122: ELISABETH  b GF 6 Dec 1793 (sp John Kessler & Cath.)
        8123: MARGARET  b HK Nov 1804 (sp Jac. Staring, Cath. Eysaman)
```

8124: MARIA SAEGER - b ca 1775; died HK 6 Jul 1822, age 47; m JOHN BODMAN.

********** SHOEMAKER (Schumacher) **********

SHOEMAKER - 1st Generation

8201: Lt. **THOMAS SHOEMAKER** - pr. born in Germany ca 1680 to 1690; living 1763
(he & wife Dorothy apparently sponsored 1763 bp of grandson Thomas, son of Sgt
Thomas); m1 ... (subs. list evidence that she pr. died 1711-12); m2 ca 1714 ANNA
DOROTHEA KORSING (b 1695, liv. 1763) dau of RUDOLPH KORSING & DELIA. On NY
Palatine subsistence list in 1710 (2A,1Y) and 1712 (1A,0Y) and was at the
Hunterstown settlement in July 1711 (Book of Names, page 126). Thomas was
naturalized at Albany NY on 22 Nov 1715 and listed on the 1717 Simmendinger census
at New Ansberg with wife Anna Dorothea and 1 child. Received lot #12 on
Burnetsfield Patent and is said to have settled first at Little Falls NY, and
later at Mohawk NY (Comp. of Amer. Gen.. vol. 7, page 881). As with other
Burnetsfield families where records are lacking, the children below have been
assigned birthyears based on their ages found or estimated later as adults. The
resulting pattern suggests possibility of other children born about 1720 (most
likely daughters).

                    surname SHOEMAKER
     8202: pr child b say 1707; pr. died ca 1711
                    by second wife
    +8203: RUDOLPH b say 1715; d 1778; m GERTRUDE HERKIMER
     8202A ps. dau (Shoemaker?) b say 1717; ps. m a KESSLER
    +8205: pr. FREDERICK JOST b say 1725; pr. m 1750 CATHERINE WOHLEBEN
    +8206: pr. JOHANNES 1727-1808 m CATHERINE GETMAN
     8207: pr. UTILIA b say 1729; m Jun 1750 GEORGE GETMAN
    +8208: THOMAS b ca 1731; m 1762 ELISABETH HARTER
    +8209: pr. CHRISTOPHER b say 1733; in militia 1757
     8210: pr. CATHERINE b say 1735; m1 MELCHERT BELL m2 FRED. YOUNG
     8211: ANNA MARGARETHA 1738-1818 m 1760 JOHANNES HEN. KLOCK
     8212: ps. (?) GODFRID b say 1740; liv. 1760 (spf Godf. Helmer bp)
                    (Godf. "Shoewaker" naturalized 11 Sep 1761, pr. diff. family)

8213: JACOB SHOEMAKER - pr. born in Germany ca 1670 to 1685; m ANNA BARBARA . On
NY subsistence list 1710 (3A,0Y) and 1712 (3A,1Y). Naturalized at Albany 22 Nov
1715 and listed on 1717 Simmendinger census with wife Anna Barbara and 1 child.
Wife Anna Barbara was sponsor, with Joh. Bernard and Joh. David Ifland, for bp in
1711 of Johan David, son of Matheus Cuntz & Anna Margaret. Jacob was sponsor for
bp in 1717 of Jacob, son of Johannes Straup & Maria Elisabeth. His descendents
appear to have settled in Greene Co. NY (Loonenburg Church area) by the 1740's.

    +8214: Johan PHILIP b say 1705; m 1730 ANNA MARTENA MILLER

8215: DANIEL SHOEMAKER - born ca 1680 (age 30 in 1710); m ANNA MARIA ... (age 36
in 1710). On NY Palatine list in 1710 (2A,2Y) and in 1712 (2A,2Y). On 1717
Simmendinger census at Rarendantz/Kniskerndorf with Anna Maria & 5 children.

     8216: NICHOLAS b ca 1702 (age 8 in 1710)
     8217: JOST b 29 Sep 1712 (sp Jost Bernard, Mi Huenschck, N. Basn)
    +8218: ps. GEORGE MICHEL b say 1715; m by 1744 CATHERINE

                    SHOEMAKER - 2nd Generation

8209: CHRISTOPHER SHOEMAKER (Stofel) - pr. born ca 1720 to 1735; pr. died before 1790 (not on census then); pr. m by 1776 CATHERINE ... Stofel listed in German Flats militia in 1757. A Stofel Schumacher & Catherine were sponsors for Apr 1776 bp of Philip, son of Lorentz Phil. Harter & Barbara (Delaney). Conceivably this Christopher died during the Revolution as there is no sign of him after 1776.

8205: FREDERICK JOST SHOEMAKER - pr. born ca 1720 to 1733; m at the Falls (GF) Jun 1750 CATHERINE WOHLEBEN (Vosburgh, Herk. Ch., vol 3 page 48). Was in Capt. Conrad Frank's 1767 GF militia company listed near Augustus Folmer & Joseph Meyer and on 1771 Minister's Support List near names of Rudolph Schumacher, Augustinus Clepsadel, and John & Joseph Meyer. Fred. Shoemaker & Catherine sponsored 1767 bp of Catherine, dau of Diet. Steele & Margaret (Wohleben).

> 8219: ps. DOROTHY 1753-1809 m GEORGE STEELE (b 1750)
> +8220: ps. THOMAS b say 1756; m by 1780 ANNA EVA ORENDORF
> 8221: ps. RUDOLPH b say 1756; m by 1776 DOROTHY ...(spf Bellingr bp)
> +8222: ps. NATHANIEL b say 1760; wounded in Rev. combat May 1781
> +8223: ps. HENRICH (? LDS) b say 1764; m by 1785 MARIA HERRIS

8215: GEORGE MICHAEL SHOEMAKER - pr. born ca 1700 to 1723; m by 1744 CATHERINE ... when they had a daughter ANNA MARGARET (bp Loonenburg 13 May 1744). Ps. the same couple as "Michel & Catherine" who had daughters Anna (bp Albany Mar 1754) & Dorothy (bp Loonenburg Apr 1759). No apparent tie to GF family of Thomas.

8204: JACOB SHOEMAKER - pr. born ca 1720 to 1750; m ELISABETH RICHTMEYER. The LDS (Mormon church) CFI shows a son ABRAHAM bp at Herkimer 1 Oct 1769, but this looks like a location error as that entry is not in Vosburgh's GF church records. Pr. a descendent of immigrant Jacob.

8206: JOHANES SHOEMAKER - born ca 1727; died German Flats NY 13 Jan 1808; m pr. by 1755 CATHERINE GETMAN (b ca 1737, d 23 Jun 1806 age 69) dau of FREDERICK GETMAN & MARIA. John Shoemaker and Cath. Getman sponsored Jul 1754 Stone Arabia bp of John, son of George Getman. Pr. the John Shoemaker in Revol. service who was a prisoner of war (Book of Names page 115) and the John whose will, dated 1799, names sons, Christopher (the eldest), Frederick, Rudolph, John, and daughters Maria Catherine & Dorothy (Bellinger book page 73). Ps. the ... Shoemaker Sr on 1790 German Flats census (4-1-3) listed near Fred. & Christopher Shoemaker.

> 8224: GEORGE b 30 Jan 1756 (sp Geo Getman & w. Utilia); pr d young
> 8225: pr. MARIA b ca May 1757; died HK 21 Mar 1831 (age 73-10-19)
> m by 1775 AUGUSTINUS HESS jr
> +8226: CHRISTOPHER b say 1759; m by 1779 ELISABETH EDICK
> 8227: CATHERINE b 23 Jan 1761 (sp. Cath. Wm Laux, Joh. Getman)
> pr. the Cath. (ca 1761-1825) who m JOHN J. KESSLER
> 8228: DOROTHY bp GF 6 Mar 1763; pr. m 1783 THOMAS SHOEMAKER
> +8229: JOHANNES b 19 Sep 1765 (sp. Joh. Glock & Anna Marg.)
> ps. d 1805-7 (Bellinger book); m ANNA ELISABETH FOX
> +8230: FREDERICK b SAR 7 Jul 1768 (sp. Fr. Getman, Maria Bell)
> m 1786 ELISABETH P. WOHLEBEN
> +8231: RUDOLPH b say 1770; m1 by 1790 ... m2 MARGARETHA ITTIG

8214: Johan PHILIP SHOEMAKER - pr. born ca 1710 to 1714 (son of Jacob); m 1730 ANNA MARTENA MILLER (Marlena) dau of SAMUEL MILLER (NY Lutheran Church records). Had daughters ANNA (bp Loonenburg NY 25 Aug 1743), DOROTHY (bp Loonenburg 31 Mar 1746) & ANNA BARBARA (bp Germantown NY 30 Apr 1749)

8203: Capt. **RUDOLPH SHOEMAKER** - pr. born ca 1715 to 1722; died 1788; m GERTRUDE
HERKIMER (b ca 1722, d 1806) dau of Johan JOST HERKIMER & CATHERINE PETRIE as in
Petrie book (page 4) and DAR (vol 23, page 338). Was a Captain in Revol. service.
Comp. of Amer. Genealogy (vol 1 page 827) seems wrong in giving wife as Maria
Herkimer (that Maria m 1758 Rev. Abraham Rosencrantz). Widow Gertrude appears on
the 1790 GF census (0-1-2), listed next to Yost, Rudolph, & Frederick Shoemaker.

```
    +8232: ANNA DOROTHEA   b say 1740; m1 1759 JOHANNES DYGERT
     8233: ANNA GERTRUDE   b say 1742; m1 Lt. MATHEW WORMUTH (d 1778)
              m2 Major JOHN FREY
    +8234: JOST (HAN YOOST)  1747-1800  m MARY SMITH
     8235: CATHERINE  b 25 Dec 1748; m 1770 CONRAD ORENDORFF
     8236: ELIZABETH  b say 1745; liv. 1764 (spf Geo. Rosencranz bp)
    +8237: RUDOLPH  1762-1830  m MARIA ROSENCRANTZ
```

8208: Sgt. **THOMAS SHOEMAKER** - born ca 1731 (Comp. Amer. Geneal. vol 6 page 66);
Johan Thomas Shoemaker widower of GF died Herkimer NY 24 Aug 1813 (age 82-4-); m
Palatine NY 16 Nov 1762 (SAR mar. rec. first marriage for both parties) ELISABETH
HARTER (b 1737, d 1805) dau of LORENTZ HARTER & APPOLONIA. In Revolutionary
service. Sponsors for baptism of their son Thomas in Aug 1763 were Thomas
Shoemaker & Dorothea (pr. the child's grandparents). On 1790 GF census (4-3-8).

```
    +8238: THOMAS jr  b 15 Aug 1763; m 1783 DOROTHY SHOEMAKER
    +8239: LORENTZ  b SAR 28 May 1767 (sp Lorentz Harter, Elis. Shmkr)
              m1 CATHERINA M.J. PETRY
    +8240: CHRISTOPHER T.  b say 1771; m 1794 MAR. CATH. BELLINGER
     8241: FREDERICK  b GF 10 Apr 1776 (sp Fr. Harter, Doro. Bellinger)
     8242: NICHOLAS  b 24 Aug 1778 (sp. Nic. Harter & Maria); pr. d. y.
     8243: NICHOLAS B.  b 18 Aug 1779; ps. m by 1803 ELISABETH ...
     8244: ELISABETH  b GF 5 Mar 1783 (sp Fred Frank & Elisabeth)
     8245: ELISABETH  1785-1866 m FREDERICK BELLINGER (1780-1863)
```

SHOEMAKER - 3rd Generation

8226: CHRISTOPHER SHOEMAKER (Stofel) - pr. born ca 1759 and the Christopher
Shoemaker, farmer of GF, who died HK 19 Mar 1831 (age 71-10-); m by 1779 ELISABETH
EDICK (b ca Dec 1758, d 1846) dau of CHRISTIAN ITTIG & MARGARET. Pr. the oldest
son named in 1799 will of John Shoemaker. Stofel & Elisabeth sponsored Sep 1779
bp of Elisabeth, dau of Augustinus Hess jr & Maria (Shoemaker) and Jul 1804 bp of
Christopher, son of Jacob Bassage & Catherine. On 1790 census (1-0-5).

```
    8246: MARGARET  b GF 20 Sep 1780 (sp Tho. Shmkr & Maria Frank)
              died Herkimer NY 27 Feb 1802 (Ch. rec.)
    8247: child  b GF 23 Jul 1783 (sp Con. Ittig, Dor. Shoemaker)
              pr. CATHERINE who m by 1804 JACOB BASHOR (Bassage)
    8248: pr. ANNA  bp GF 8 Nov 1785 (sp ... Shoemaker, Anna Ittig)
    8249: ELISABETH  b GF 22 Apr 1787 (sp F. Shoemakr & Elis.); pr d y
    8250: MARIA  bp SJR 26 Mar 1789 (sp Jac Shmkr, Mar. Elis. Frank)
    8251: ELISABETH  b 17 Feb 1791 (sp John Shmker & Elis.); pr. d y
    8252: ANNA  b 10 Aug 1793 (sp Lor. Shomaker & Cath.)
    8253: ELISABETH  b GF 30 Sep 1795 (sp John Ittig, Elis. Joh. Fox)
    8254: DELIA  b GF Jan 1802 (sp. Elis. Shoemaker)
```

8240: CHRISTOPHER T. SHOEMAKER - pr. born ca 1771 and died HK 24 Sep 1811 (age 39-10-); m GF 20 May 1794 MARIA CATHERINE BELLINGER (b 1770) dau of JOHN P. BELLINGER & MARIA DYGERT (Bellinger book page 35).

    8255: CHRISTOPHER b GF 6 Jan 1795 (sp Stophl Bellinger & Anna)
             d HK 23 Aug 1814 age 19-6-17 <month age at death should be 7>
    8256: THOMAS b 1798
    8257: JAMES b 1802; m 1825 MAGDALENA HESS

8230: FREDERICK SHOEMAKER - born Jul 1768; died HK 1 Apr 1836 (age 67-8-); m 1786 ELISABETH P. WOHLEBEN (b 1766) dau of PETER WOHLEBEN & CATHERINE. In Revol. service and pr. the Frederick on 1790 GF census (1-0-2).

    8258: ANNA bp GF 26 Jun 1787 (sp Ludol. Shmkr, Sus. Wohlebn); d y
    8259: ANNA bp GF 16 Nov 1788; liv. 1802 (Herk. Ch. Confirm.)
    8260: CATHERINE b GF 24 Feb 1793 (sp Gerrit V Slyk & Cath.)

8223: HENRICH SHOEMAKER - m by 1785 MARIA HERRIS (LDS). Ps. had children Elisabeth & Catherine bp GF (LDS CFI, but not found in Vosburgh's GF churchbooks).

8229: JOHANNES SHOEMAKER - born 19 Sep 1765 (Bellinger book page 73 lists him as "Johannes (Joh.) Shoemaker"); pr. died after 1807; m ANNA ELISABETH FOX (b 1768) dau of Lt. FREDERICK FOX & ELISABETH FRANK.

    8261: ELISABETH bp GF 28 Feb 1786; liv. 1802 (Herk Ch. Confirm.)
    8262: JOHANNES b 1788 (sp Rud. J. Schumacher, Marg. F. Fox)
    8263: CATHARINA b GF Aug 1792 (sp. Fred. Shoemaker & Elisabeth)
    8264: LENA b 23 Jan 1794 (dau of John & Anna)
                (sp Stophel T Shmkr, Lena Fox)
    8265: MARIA b HK Feb 1803 (sp Elis. Fox); m 1821 FREDERICK FOX
    8266: CATHERINE (twin) b 1807 (sp. Tho. Shoemaker & w Doro.)
    8267: GEORGE (twin) b 25 Mar 1807; d 10 May 1808 (age 1-1-16)

8234: Maj. JOST SHOEMAKER (Han Yost) - born 1747; died 1800; m 1771 MARY SMITH (Bolly, b in England ca 1752, d HK 21 Jul 1825 age 73) dau of the Tory ROBERT SMITH & MARY ILE (Ehle?) as in Comp. of Amer. Genealogy v 4 page 368. Was a Tory in Revolution. Pr. the Yost Shoemaker on 1790 German Flats census (1-3-3).

    8268: RUDOLPH J.   1776-1828 in State Assembly 1813
              m by 1805 MARGARET CLAPSATTLE
    8269: JOST b GF 13 Oct 1779 (sp Rud. Shoemaker & Gertrude)
    8270: ROBERT b GF 14 Oct 1782 (sp. Jost Stahl & Maria)
             d 1838; m 1808 CATHERINE MIC. MYERS
    8271: GERTRUDE b 3 Mar 1786 (sp Elis J P Bellingr, Wm Smidt)
  +8272: ELIZABETH 1790-1874 m NICHOLAS N. WEAVER
    8273: ps. MARIA (Bolly) ca 1798-1823 m JAMES MYERS

8239: LORENTZ SHOEMAKER - born 28 May 1767 (son of Sgt. Thomas); died HK 27 Jun 1834 (age 67); m1 1787 CATHERINE M. J. PETRY; m2 MARGARET BELLINGER (b 1776, d 1817, Bellinger book page 37) dau of FREDERICK BELLINGER & MAGDALENA WOHLEBEN.

    8274: CATHERINA b GF 12 Jan 1789 (sp Stofel Shmkr, Maria Petri)
    8275: THOMAS b GF 12 Jun 1790 (sp Tho. Shmkr & Doro.)
             d HK 5 Jun 1839; m 1813 CATHERINE BELLINGER
    8276: MARCUS b 16 Jan 1793 (sp George Ittig & Delia)
    8277: DIETRICH b GF 14 Sep 1795 (sp Nic. Shoemkr, Elis. Fox)

8222: NATHANIEL SHOEMAKER - pr. born ca 1740 to 1764; liv. 1781. He was wounded with a ball through the breast in Revolutionary fighting on 28 May 1781 (medical notes of Dr. William Petry).

8237: RUDOLPH SHOEMAKER - born 9 Oct 1762; m 26 Jun 1785 MARGARETH ROSENCRANTZ (b 26 Apr 1762) dau of Rev. ABRAM ROSENCRANTZ & MARIA HERKIMER. A Rudolph Shoemaker jr & "Dorothy" sponsored Aug 1776 bp of Nicholas, son of Peter Bellinger.

    8278: RUDOLPH   b GF 27 Jun 1786 (sp Marc Jac Kesler, Cath Rosencrnz)
                    died 16 Dec 1787
    8279: ABRAHAM   b 25 Aug 1787 (sp Nic Rosencrnz, Elis J P Bellngr)
    8280: RUDOLPH   b GF 6 Jan 1789 (sp Gertr., widow of Rud. Shmkr)
    8281: DANIEL WILHELM   bp GF 24 Oct 1790 (sp Con. Orendorf & Cath.)
    8282: MARIA CATHERINE b & d GF 12-5 Apr 1792 (sp Jost Shmkr & Maria)
    8283: CHARITY (Gertrude)   b GF 3 Oct 1793 (sp Jost Shoemakr & Maria)
                    m MICAL HELMER
    8284: BETSY
    8285: DOROTHEA   b German Flats NY 18 May 1802
    8286: MARY
    8287: CONRAD
    8288: ROBERT

8231: RUDOLPH JOH. SHOEMAKER - pr. born ca 1755 to 1775; m 25 Dec 1795 MARGARETHA CHRISTIAN ITTIG dau of CHRISTIAN EDICK.

    8289: MARGARET   b GF 30 Nov 1795 (sp Thomas Shoemkr, Marg. Fox)
    8290: EVA   bp Herkimer 2 Aug 1802 (sp. Fred Shmkr & wife Elis.)

8220: THOMAS SHOEMAKER - born ca 1757; died Columbia NY 11 Dec 1824 (age 67-5-2); m ANNA EVA ORENDORF dau of FREDERICK ORENDORF (Getman book page 15).

    8291: FREDERICH   bp GF 6 Jan 1781 (sp Fritz Orndorf & Barbara);
    8292: ANNA EVA   b GF 25 Nov 1783 (sp Joh. Jacob Petri & Maria)
    8293: JOHN   b Fonda NY (FR) 27 Mar 1785 (sp. Geo. Steel & Dorothy)
                    m Jan 1804 CATHERINE J. EYSAMAN
    8294: HENRICH   b GF 8 Nov 1786 (sp H. Orendorf, Delia Petrie)
                    died 10 May 1806 (age 19-6-15)
    8295: CATHERINA   bp GF 25 Dec 1790 (sp Geo. Stahl, Cath. Bellinger)

8238: THOMAS T. SHOEMAKER - born 5 Aug 1763 (son of Sgt. Thomas & Elis.); m 23 Dec 1783 DOROTHY SHOEMAKER (b ca 1763, d HK 4 Jan 1817 age 54 <her surname on 1803 bp rec., not DOROTHY SUTZ!>). Children in Harter bible (Bellinger book, pg 95).

    8296: CATHERINE   b 24 Sep 1784 (sp. Lor. Shoemkr, Elis. Fox)
                    liv 1802 (HK church confirm.)
    8297: FREDERICK   b 27 Mar 1786; d HK 20 Jun 1803
    8298: ELISABETH   b 23 May 1787 (sp Ludol Shmkr, Elis Petri)
    8299: DOROTHY   b 1 Jun 1789 (sp Stofel Shmkr, Doro. Steel)
    8300: ps. STOFEL   b GF 24 Jul 1792 (sp Stofel Shoemkr & Eva)
    8301: LENA   b GF 8 Sep 1793 (sp Fred Bellinger & Lena)
    8302: GERTRUDE   b HK 3 May 1803 (sp Chrsphr Shoemkr & w. Elis.)

8232: DOROTHY SHOEMAKER - pr. born ca 1735 to 1740; m1 at Palatine NY 29 Nov 1759 JOHN S. DYGERT; m2 WILHELM NELLIS

SKINNER - 1st Generation

8321: GERSHOM SKINNER - born ca 1750; died 1824 (age 74); m GF 30 Sep 1783 MARGARET GETMAN (b ca 1762, d 14 Sep 1840 age 78) dau of FREDERICK GETMAN & MARGARET as given in Lambeer´s "The Getman Family Genealogy". On June 21, 1782, just prior to the German Flats visit of Gen. George Washington (on June 30th), Gershom Skinner, Frederick Fox, Daniel Petrie Sr., and others were operating the only remaining grist mill in the area. According to the account in the Hatch Papers, an enemy raiding party of several hundred Tories and Indians from Canada attacked the mill at that time, after having bypassed the nearby settlement which they suspected to be too heavily manned based on the loud commotion arising from the marriage celebration of a Frederick Smith (this was probably an engagement celebration as the GF church record has Frederick Smith´s marriage in Sep 1782). During the ensuing hand to hand fighting with the Indians in the dark, Gershom Skinner received several tomahawk wounds to the head but was able to escape into the waters of Furnace Creek. Genealogist Frank D. Deuel, in a letter published in the St. Johnsville Enterprise & News issue of 26 March 1930, relates how various prisoners were taken by the Tories at this Little Falls Mill Battle and that, similar to the experience of Andrew Piper, most were presumably held in Canada and exchanged about six months later (the patriots captured included Capt. Frederick Getman, Lawrence Harter, Christian Ittig, Jacob Petrie, Andrew Piper & Thomas Shoemaker).

The children of Gershom Skinner are listed in the Hatch papers (page 209), but some of the dates are questionable. For example Hatch has daughter Margaret born Feb 1785 but does not mention the Margaret shown in GF church records as born 18 Mar 1784 (another birthdate of about 9 Mar 1785 for Margaret is obtainable by calculation from her age at death), and does not explain apparent proximity to the birthdate of son John, who by Hatch dates was born 23 Dec 1785.

surname SKINNER

    8322: MARGARET b GF 18 Mar 1784 (sp Fr. Getman & Cath.); pr. d y
    8323: MARGARET (Peggy) b 12 Feb 1785; d 31 Jan 1852 (age 66-10-22)
+8324: JOHN 1785-1863 m 1810 BETSY SHOEMAKER
    8325: ANNA b GF 18 Sep 1788 (sp Philip F. Helmer)
        (NANCY) m JOHN MEYER (Myers)
    8326: CATHERINE b GF 25 Jan 1790 (sp Geo. Jac. Weaver & Cath.)
           m SAMUEL BLOODGOOD
    8327: MARIE (Polly) b GF 28 Aug 1791 (sp Melc. Folts & Maria)
          m 1812 FREDERICK AUG. HESS
    8328: AMY b say 1794; m HENRY HESS (b 1790)

SKINNER - 2nd Generation

8324: JOHN SKINNER - born 23 Dec 1785 (birth rec. not seen, mar. rec. has John as son of Gershom); died 1863; m Herkimer NY 22 Apr 1810 ELISABETH SHOEMAKER dau of JOHN SHOEMAKER (as given on Herk. Church mar. rec.). Hatch states instead that wife of John Skinner was a "Betsy Fox", widow of a Shoemaker (i.e. presumably JOHN SHOEMAKER <died ca 1806>) and pr dau of FREDERICK FOX & ELISABETH FRANK as she is given in Hatch papers (page 209) as a granddaughter of Conrad Frank.

********** SMALL (Schmall) **********

SMALL - 1st Generation

8341: Capt. **JACOB SMALL** - pr. born in Germany ca 1730 to 1740; killed and scalped by Indians in the orchard of his home in New York's Mohawk Valley in the fall of 1783 (Petrie book page 19); m at Ringwood New Jersey 28 Jun 1772 SUSANNA BELTZER (d Herkimer NY 5 Apr 1822). In 1760 he was a mining smith at the copper mines of Neider Sommerfield Germany and lived at Thal Itter, Hesse Darnstadt. He supposedly immigrated, with two brothers, to New Jersey where he lived for a while before moving, about 1774, to Cherry Valley NY (ibid). In May 1775 Jacob Small was a German Flats NY resident, listed near Hess, Davis, & Flagg (Mohawk Valley in the Revolution, page 165). In 1779 Jacob Small and Maria (perhaps a mistaken entry for wife Susanna) sponsored bp of Jacob, son of Jacob Petrie & Maria. Widow Susanna Small appears on the 1790 German Flats census (0-3-6) near to Jost Herkimer, Peter Flagg, & Conrad Hess. Perhaps sons Melchior & Jacob jr. were twins as birthdates are both in Jan 1779 (but three days apart, as given in Petrie book!).

surname SMALL

```
8342: MARIA      1771-1842  m 1792 JACOB FR. CHRISTMAN
8343: ELISABETH  1773-1851  m NICHOLAS WOHLEBEN
8343A CATHERINE  b say 1775; m 1796 NICHOLAS KILTS
8344: pr. JOHN   b say 1777; liv. 1795 (spf Wohleben bp)
+8345: JACOB     b SAL 11 Jan 1779 (sp Melchior Thum & Elis.)
             m HANNAH POTTER
+8346: MELCHIOR  1779-1847  m DOROTHY PETRIE
+8347: FREDERICK 1781-1865  m 1806 MARGARET SMITH
```

SMALL - 2nd Generation

8347: **FREDERICK SMALL** - born ca Mar 1781 (son of Jacob indic. on mar. record); died Herkimer NY 19 Apr 1865 (age 84-0-22); m at Herkimer NY 2 Mar 1806 ANNA MARGARET SMITH (b 1785) dau of ADAM SMITH & SARAH HILTS. Children were David (b Oct 1807, d Dec 1807), Sarah Ann, Susanna, Lucia, Louisa, Eli, Jacob, and Cynthia (1828).

8345: **JACOB SMALL (jr.)** - born, pr. at German Flats NY, 11 Jan 1779 (SAL bp rec. and Petrie book, page 20); m 23 Jan 1799 HANNAH POTTER dau of WILLIAM POTTER (b Dec 1732) & SARAH.

```
8348: JACOB  b say 1800; m DELIA FEETER (b 1801)
8438A ELI    b HK 24 Oct 1807 (sp Jac. Christman & w. Maria of GF)
```

8346: **MELCHIOR SMALL** - born 14 Jan 1779 (Petrie book page 22, ps. a twin of brother Jacob); died 14 Dec 1847 at age 68; pr. m by 1800 DOROTHY PETRIE (b 1779, d 1861) dau of JOHANNES PETRIE & BARBARA KLOCK.

```
8349: MARIA      b say 1800; m 1819 PETER EYSAMAN jr.
8350: JACOB M.   b 30 Dec 1801; m 1821 ANNA PETRY (dau of Joh.)
8351: ELISABETH  1802-1864  m 1817 GEORGE HILTS (son of John)
8352: EVA        b 2 Mar 1804; m 1823 HENRY FALK
8353: DOROTHY    b 2 Apr 1806 (sp Nich. Kilts & Cath.)
             m 1825 GEORGE COLVIN
```

********** SMITH (Schmidt) **********

8401: GEORGE SMITH (called Johan Jurg or Yorry) - pr. born in Germany ca 1670
to 1685; made a will at Albany in 1730 (not seen) and was living in 1733 (logged
his grandson's birth in family bible); m by 1711 Anna ELIZABETH RICHARDS (her
surname from note with family bible, seen ca 1920 by Mrs. Vera Eysaman). Ps. he
came from Eisemroth, Nassau-Dillenburg, Germany (Mr. Hank Jones 1982 notes show a
Johan George Schmitt, with wife & 1 child, petitioned to emigrate from Eisemroth
in 1709). He appears on the NY Palatine Subsistence list in 1710 (2A,1Y) & in
1712 (2A,2Y) and in July 1711 was a volunteer from the Hunterstown camp for the
Canadian military expedition. By ca 1714, he was village leader of Smitsdorf at
Schoharie where he ran a hotel and gave refuge to Nicholas Bayard, the Dutch land
claimant, whom the Palatines had set upon in anger over their property rights.
George was naturalized at Albany on 31 Jan 1716, and was on the 1717 Simmendinger
census with wife Anna Elisabeth & 3 children. Supposedly he grieved for a brother
who disappeared in this country (ps. Martin, single adult on 1710 NY subs. list).
Less credible is another story that he had four brothers named John, Joseph,
Martin, & Adam, who came to New York in Oct 1722 (Barker's "Smith Descendents of
Herkimer NY").

Two other Smiths who had lots on the 1723 Burnetsfield Patent were Adam
Michael & son Ephraim, but they appear to have settled at Schenectady and are not
believed related to Johan George's family. The information source for his
children is his family bible, quotes from which, rather than original itself, are
among Cdmr. L. Bellinger's papers at the Herkimer Co. Hist. Society. These notes
say "Today Sept. 14 is my son Johan Marten born into the world; the 6th of Sept.
is my son George born into the world; the 22 Jul 1715 is my daughter Elisabeth
born; the 26 Nov 1717 is my daughter Anna Margaretha born; the 30 Jul 1733 is
Johan George the son of my son Marten born; the 22 Oct 1737 (sic) is Johan Velter
son of Marten born;" etc for the remaining sons of Martin (except Fredrich). With
regard to immigrant George's two daughters Elisabeth and Margaret, it seems likely
from the baptismal sponsorship evidence in later years that one or both survived
childhood and intermarried with the Weaver and Bauman families.

surname SMITH
```
+8402: MARTEN   b say 1705 (14 Sep); m by 1754 ELISABETH ...
 8403: GEORGE   b say 1707 (pr. 6 Sep as in bible entry)
 8404: pr. child  b ca Oct 1710; died soon (NY Hunter list)
+8405: GEORGE LUDWIG  b WCL Aug 1711 (sp Geo. Ludwig Koch & w. Maria)
 8406: ELISABETH  b 22 Jul 1715; ps. m ADAM BAUMAN jr.
 8407: Anna MARGARETHA  b 26 Nov 1717; pr. m NICHOLAS WEAVER jr.
```

SMITH - 2nd Generation

8405: GEORGE LUDWIG SMITH - born West Camp NY 23 Aug 1711 (bp Aug 26); liv.
1776; ps. unmarried. In 1769 he and Marten Smith's sons were in Capt. Petrie's
GF militia and in May 1775, as Ludwig Smith, he was a German Flats NY resident,
listed next to Peter & Jacob Folts (Mohawk Valley in the Revolution, page 164).
In 1776 he & Christian Schell were named executors in the will of Lorentz Harter,
with witnesses Georg, Johannes, & Friedrich Schmit (pr. Marten's sons). Ps. he
was the George L. whose name appears at the end of the estate settlement papers of
Nicholas Smith in Jan 1780. We think erroneous a story (pr. from Mrs. Lena Smith
Aney ca 1950), that a brother of Marten Smith had 3 children; vis. George (died
young), an unmarried daughter, & the Nicholas who married Marg. Bellinger.

8402: MARTEN SMITH - born 14 Sep .... (pr. in Germany ca 1702-08); died German
Flats NY ca 1769-72; m by 1733 ... (ps. a dau of ADAM BAUMAN Sr.) and by 1754 had
m ELISABETH ... (ps. a dau of NICHOLAS WEAVER Sr.). Since Marten's sisters pr.
married Bauman and Weaver husbands, and as Marten's sons appear mainly as
godparents for Baumans and Weavers from 1760 on, it is likely that Marten's wife
was also from one of those two families. The naming of Marten's early sons
slightly favors a Bauman wife, but if an Elisabeth was mother for all children, as
supported by the pattern of Marten's granddaughters, a Weaver seems likely (while
not known, an Elisabeth Weber, dau of immigrant Nicholas & Barbara, seems more
available than an Elisabeth Bauman). In 1768 Marten Smith purchased 350 acres of
land from Goldsboro Banyar in Schellsbush (now East Herkimer), and Marten seems to
have died by 1773 when some of this land exchanged amongst his sons. Wm Urias
Smith 1903 notes say Martin had two daughters, but he did not know their names as
Marten apparently ceased recording his children in the Smith bible with the birth
of John in 1748 (that bible has been missing since about 1950). Apparently Marten
was not popular with his children as only one grandson was named for him, some 20
years after his death (also Vosburgh notes an early attempt to deface the 1754 bp
record of daughter Elisabeth).

        8408: Johan GEORGE b 30 Jul 1733; pr d. young
        8409: PETER (Johan VETTER) b Oct 1734 (death record); d 1813 unm
        8410: Johan GEORGE b 11 Jan 1738; pr d. young
       +8411: Johan ADAM 1740-1824 m SARAH HILTS
       +8412: "JOHANNES" b 25 Apr 1742; (pr. renamed later as Jost)
              i.e. JOSEPH ca 1743-1811 m APPOLONIA HARTER
       +8413: Johan GEORGE 1744-1809 m MARIA BELLINGER
       +8414: NICHOLAS   1746-1779 m MARGARET BELLINGER
       +8415: JOHANNES   1748-1822 m CATHERINE GRAY
       +8416: FREDRICH   1750-1828 m1 CATARINA .. m2 CHRISTINA LEDER
        8417: ps. MARIA b say 1752; m by 1777 JOSEPH BELL
        8418: ELISABETH b SAL 23 Feb 1754 (sp John Leder & Elisabeth)

                         SMITH - 3rd Generation

8411: ADAM SMITH - born 29 Sep 1740; died Herkimer NY 21 Jan 1824; m SAR 4 Dec
1764 SARAH HILTS (b ca 1744, d HK 3 Jan 1802, age 58-7-10, from drinking bad
water) dau of JACOB HILTS. Family tradition says that Adam & his wife were taken
as prisoners to Canada in the Revolution. Adam was on the 1790 HK census (2-1-7)
listed next to Philip Bell & George Folts.

        8419: ELIZABETH b 8 Mar 1766 (sp. Cath. Hilts, Jost Smith)
              d Herkimer NY 26 May 1848 unm
        8420: ANNA (NANCY) b SAR 1 Jan 1768 (sp Pet. Smith, Anna Weber)
              m GEORGE KAST
       +8421: JACOB bp SAR 19 Nov 1769 (sp Fred. Schmidt, Cath. Bauman)
              d 1846; m MARGARET HELMER
        8422: CATHERINE b say 1771; m by 1790 MELCHERT FOLTS
        8423: MARIA AD. b say 1774; d 1834; m BALTHASAR FALK
        8424: ADAM b GF 7 Aug 1779 (sp Geo. Hiels & Cath.)
              d 1857; m MARGARET FOLTS
        8425: MAGDALENE b 5 Dec 1782 (sp Adam Bauman, Lena MacKoom)
              m 1802 HENRY HISER
        8426: Anna MARGARET b 19 Aug 1785 (sp. Con. Helmer, Marg. Folts)
              m FRED SMALL

                                 -233-

8416: FREDERICK SMITH - born German Flats 19 May 1750; died HK 11 Jun 1828 (bur. Oak Hill Cemetery); m1 GF 8 Sep 1782 Hilts´ widow CATHERINE ... (d ca 1790) pr. widow of GEORGE JAC. HILTS; m2 1791 CHRISTINA LEATHER (b 7 Apr 1756, d 2 Jun 1855 age 99) dau of JOHN LEDER & ELISABETH and widow of HENRY MYERS. Was in 1769 GF militia and in Col. Bellinger´s Revol. Regiment (Book of Names, page 168). Family notes have him at the Battle of Oriskany. On 1790 HK census (1-1-2).

   8427: CATHERINE b GF 5 Apr 1783 (sp John Smidt & Cath.)
         d 1864; m GEORGE F. MYERS
   8428: MARIE b 6 Apr 1785 (sp. Jacob Weaver, Elisabeth Smidt)
        m LEVI MOORHOUSE
   8429: ELIZABETH b 11 Nov 1787 (sp. Jac. Smidt, Sara MacKoom); d. y.
   8430: ELIZABETH b 20 Jun 1789 (sp. Geo. & Maria Smidt); d. y.
        by 2nd wife
   8431: MATHEW ca 1791-1868 m ELIZABETH NELLIS
   8432: MARTIN b 1 Dec 1792 (sp. Jac. Ad. Smith & Marg. Fr. Helmer)
   8433: ELIZABETH 1793-1849 m JOHN F. MYERS
   8434: child bp 27 Jul 1794
   8435: MARGARET ca 1798-1873 m TIMOTHY BARSH
   8436: John NICHOLAS b say 1799; d 1853; m 1818 OLIVE SCHUTT
   8437: ANNA b ca 1800; d 1838; m JAMES P. WEAVER
   8438: EVA b HK 3 May 1804 (sp. Cath. Weber, Nic. Smith, unm)

8413: Sgt GEORGE SMITH - pr. Martin´s son Johan George born 24 Mar 1744; died 16 Dec 1809 (age 65); m 16 Jul 1771 MARIA BELLINGER (b 14 Feb 1751, d 27 Jan 1848) dau of Capt. PETER BELLINGER & MARGARET HORNING (Bellinger book page 36). George was an artistic pensman who annotated many family bibles. He was in Bellinger´s Revol. Regiment and saw action at Oriskany & Otsego Lake (Pension W19064). On the 1790 HK census (2-1-3) next to Jost Smith.

   8439: PETER b GF 29 Mar 1779 (sp Adam Smidt & Sara)
        d 1865; m DOROTHY STEELE (b 1781, d 1869)
   8440: MARGARET (twin) b Oct 1781 (sp Marc Petri & Marg.<Bellinger>)
        d 1814; m Johan ADAM RASBACH
   8441: ELIZABETH (twin) b GF Oct 1781 (sp Adam Bauman, Elis. Smidt)
        m JOHN BELLINGER
   8442: MARY b GF 15 Oct 1783 (sp Nic. Harter, Maria Frank)
        d 1808; m JACOB PETRIE
   8443: child b & d 1786 (lived two weeks)

8415: JOHN M. SMITH - born 7 Mar 1748; died Herkimer 1822 (age 74); m CATHERINE GRAY (b ca 1752, d Herkimer NY 19 Apr 1825 age 73) pr. dau of ADAM GRAY & MARIA ELISABETH HORNING. Beers (History of Herkimer County page 263) says this John M. was son of Martin, the 1768 land purchaser, and that John M. was in flatboat service during the Revolution. Hardin´s History of Herkimer Co. has the grandfather (pr. great-gr-grandfather) of "Banker Bill" Smith (born 1814) as John George (who made will at Albany 1730). Was a farmer and on 1790 Herkimer census (1-3-1).

   8444: ADAM bp GF 29 Jul 1776 (sp. Geo. Smidt & Maria)
   8445: JOHANNES bp 14 Aug 1778 (sp John Bellinger, Elis. Harter)
        m 1805 MARIE PETRIE
   8446: NICHOLAS ca 1783-1851 m 1834 ANNA MYERS
   8447: PETRUS bp 26 Dec 1784; pr. died by 1790
   8448: GEORGE b GF 20 Nov 1785 (sp Geo. Smidt & Maria); d 1855 unm

8412: JOSEPH SMITH (Jost) - born ca 1743; died HK 19 Apr 1811 (age 68); m 17 Jan 1770 APPOLONIA HARTER (b 1750, d 1827) dau of NICHOLAS HARTER & MARIE. His wife was scalped in the May 1779 Tory raid near Ft. Dayton in which her brother-in-law Nicholas Smith (Bellinger book) was killed, and afterwards she was known as "the woman in the white cap" (worn to cover her bare head). On 1790 HK census (1-1-2).

    8449: CATHERINE b 13 Dec 1773
    8450: Johan GEORGE bp 17 May 1777 (sp. Geo. Smidt); pr d. young
    8451: MARIE bp APPOLONIA Feb 1781 (Lor. Harter, Apol. Harter)
           d 1832; m GEORGE N. SMITH
    8452: child bp GF 14 Jun 1783 (sponsors not given)
    8452A pr. ELISABETH JOS. b ca 1785 (bp 1792); adptd by G. Weaver
    8453: GEORGE b GF 3 Nov 1787 (sp. George Harter)
    8453A pr. MARGARET JOS. b ca 1788 (bp 1792); adptd by G. Weaver
    8454: Johan JOSEPH b 2 Nov 1792; d 1857; m CATHERINE HARTER
    8455: APPOLONIA b 25 Jun 1793

8414: Johan NICHOLAS SMITH - born 15 May 1746 (son of Marten, as given in the Smith bible); killed by Tory raiders at German Flats NY 10 May 1779; m SAR 20 Nov 1769 MARGARET BELLINGER (b ca 1748, d 19 May 1779) pr. a dau of JOHN PH. BELLINGER & ELISABETH BARBARA FOLTS rather than a dau of Capt. PETER BELLINGER (as in Bellinger book, page 35, where basis seems to have been an unsupported notion that wife Margaret was a sister of the Maria Bellinger who married brother Sgt. George Smith). The Bellinger book says he was the Nicholas born May 1746 and the choice of the name "Nicholas Marten" for a son of Col. Nicholas of Utica seems enough to tie him in as a son of Marten (descendents Charles S. & Lena G. Smith wanted him to be son of someone else!). Nicholas Smith was a farmer and in April 1778 he received 176 acres for "love and consideration" and five lbs currency from NICHOLAS WEAVER (a deed, seen amongst the Nicholas Smith estate papers in possession of Mrs. Edna Aney, shows that Nicholas Weaver jr. purchased the land in 1762 from Cornelius Cuyler). Here is where he had his farm, on the lowlands east of the West Canada Creek near the west end of Schell's Bush Road and where his son George N. Smith in 1790 built the Smith homestead, still owned in 1983 by a Smith descendent, Mr. Gary Richardson.

    In the 1777 Battle of Oriskany he and a relative, John Bellinger, are said to have assisted moving General Nicholas Herkimer, who had been shot from his horse, to a vantage point by a tree where Herkimer directed the battle to its close (Vera Eysaman notes). MacWethy's roster of Oriskany heroes in the Book of Names shows a Nicholas Smith Sr. who was a different man (i.e. the latter Nicholas Sr. was killed at Oriskany and most likely belongs to the Henrich Smith family of Tillaborough NY). On May 10th 1779 Nicholas Smith and his wife were slain and scalped by Tory Indians, after leaving Fort Dayton to go to their farm in the company of some 12 settlers, which included Henry Widerstine's wife, Henry F. Harter (age about 23) and Joseph Smith's wife. According to notes in the George N. Smith Bible, the attack occurred on the east side of West Canada Creek about one mile north from where creek empties into the Mohawk River. Their bodies were found about four weeks later by their little dog and a story survives of how their infant son Nicholas survived by being concealed in a hollow under a log at the attack onset by his aunt Appolonia (born Harter & wife of Joseph Smith).

    +8456: GEORGE N. 1771-1840 m MARIE SMITH
    8457: ELIZABETH b say 1775; m GEORGE STEELE
    +8458: NICHOLAS bp GF 25 Jan 1778 (sp. Adam Smidt & Sara)
           d 1864; m HANNAH CLARK

8421: JACOB SMITH - born 1768 (bp Palatine NY 19 Nov 1769); died Herkimer NY 1846;
m at German Flats NY 5 May 1795 MARGARETHA HELMER (b 18 Sep 1778, d 18 Apr 1844)
dau of HENRY HELMER & ELIZABETH. At age 7 he served on picket guard duty in Revol.
War (ref. "Yesteryears" vol. 10, No. 39, Mar 1967, page 162) and later served in
War of 1812.

      8459: ELIZABETH 1795-1877 m THOMAS HARTER
      8460: ADAM   b say 1798; d 1865; m BETSY HILTS
      8461: JACOB jr. pr b bef 1800; m by 1821 MARY LIVINGSTON
      8462: HENRY bp 17 Jan 1803 (Herkimer Church rec.); pr. d. young
      8463: HENDRIK b say 1806 (bp Herk. 31 May 1807)
      8464: LEA b 7 Apr 1807; m by 1825 HENRY CHRISTMAN
      8465: BENJAMIN 1809- m by 1832 MARIA HARTER to Monrovia NY
      8466: CATHERINE b 27 May 1811; m 1829 LEMANN CHRISTMAN
      8467: MARGARETHA b 21 Aug 1814; d Herkimer 17 May 1816 (age 1)
      8468: ANNA b 30 Jul 1816; d 5 Feb 1830 (age 13)
      8469: MARION b 26 Aug 1819
      8470: JOSEPH M. 1821-1909 m 1844 LOUISA CHRISTMAN

8456: GEORGE N. SMITH ("Han Yost") - born 17 Apr 1771; died 16 Jun 1840; m pr. ca
1797 his cousin MARIE SMITH (bp as "Appolonia" 1781, d 1832, H. Patrick notes) dau
of JOSEPH SMITH & APPOLONIA HARTER. In 1839 he conveyed to his son Nicholas (for
$3000) 96 acres of Herkimer land on the east side of the West Canada Creek . Most
of this land (88 acres) his father, John Nicholas Smith, obtained in 1778 from
Nicholas Weaver . Children's births listed in his Bible.

      8471: NICHOLAS G. 1797-1884 m CHARITY HELMER
      8472: ELIZABETH G. b 18 Feb 1801; d 16 Aug 1827 (age 27)
      8473: Johan JOSEPH 1803-1886 m1 ANNA KAST m2 SUSAN EASTMAN

8458: Col. NICHOLAS SMITH - born German Flats NY 21 Jan 1778 (bp 25 Jan, son of
Nicolas Smidt & "Elisabeth"); died Utica NY 29 Feb 1864; m at Utica 15 Sep 1813
HANNAH CLARK (b 1791, d 1863) dau of SILAS CLARK, a merchant, & MARY ANN HILL of
Goshen Conn. He was the infant hidden in the hollow log when Indians killed his
parents in 1779 and was raised by relatives, Major John Bellinger & Catherine
(Weaver). In 1788 they lived in a hut made of tree branches while his foster
father built the first frame house in Utica. Nicholas was adjutant of 134th NY
Regiment in the War of 1812 (rank of Capt., raised to Col. at war's end) and a
merchant, alderman, dep. sheriff, and overseer of the poor at Utica. His
education was modest and supposedly, when asked the meaning of "E Pluribus Unum"
on the sign over John Bellinger's inn, he replied "Dat means mon oncle keebs de
best tavern in Utica" (family notes). In 1839 he sold to his nephew Nicholas G.
Smith, for $200, 88 acres of his inherited land at Herkimer.

      8474: NICHOLAS CLARK bp May 1815; pr. d. young
      8475: JOHN W. b say 1817; d ca 1852
      8476: JOHN NICHOLAS bp 5 Nov 1820; pr. d. young
      8477: SILAS CLARK b 7 May 1822; d Utica NY 16 Nov 1852
      8478: WILLIAM BELLINGER 1824- m SARAH STARK
   +8479: MARGARET ELIZABETH 1826-1910 m GILES H.F. VAN HORNE
      8480: NICHOLAS MARTIN 1831- m LOUISE BINSOE

********** SPOHN (Spahn) **********

SPOHN - 1st Generation

8501: Johan HENRICH SPOHN - pr. born in Germany ca 1670 to 1688; m 20 Feb 1711
MARIA CATHERINE WOHLEBEN dau of the late WALLRATH WOHLEBEN. He was a stepson of
the furrier PHILIP MUELLER and appears on the NY Palatine subsistence list as
alias HENRICH MUELLER in 1710 (2A,1Y) & in 1712 (2A,1Y). He was not listed as a
widower on his marriage record so we suspect that the dependents in his household
in 1710-12 may have been say a brother & sister, which would account for Adam
Spohn (married in 1713) & Anna Margaret Spohn (born say 1700, liv. 1714 as spf
Marg. Ad. Spohn bp). With no other Spohns on the 1710-12 Palatine subsistence, we
feel this Henrich may have been the man Kochtheral lists as "Johan Peter", father
of Henrich in 1712. On the 1717 Simmendinger census Hendrick appears with wife
Maria Catherine & 3 children. He drew Burnetsfield lot #32 (south side of the
Mohawk River, near Wohleben´s lot #30) and presumably his son Henrich jr. was the
one who received dependent area Burnetsfield lot #7 (north of the Mohawk River).

surname SPOHN

+8502: pr. HENRICH jr. b say 1712; liv. 1723 (Burnetsfield lot #7)
+8503: pr. dau b say 1714; liv. 1717 (Simmendinger census)
8504: NICHOLAS b 19 Jan 1716 (sp. Nich. Wohleben, Marg. Land)

8506: ADAM SPOHN - pr. born ca 1680 to 1695 (listed as son of the late WERNER
SPOHN on marriage record in 1713); m 10 Feb 1713 ANNA MARIA SCHMID dau of HENRICH
SCHMID. Listed as a sexton at Manweiler, commune Kaiserlautern, on his marriage
record. Adam and his wife Anna Maria were sp. for bp in Mar 1716 of Anna
Elisabeth dau of Johan Wulfen & Anna Margaretha and at Kiskatom Church in Mar 1729
they were again sp. for Joh. Adam, son of Johan Wolf & Anna Marg. In 1729 their
daughters Margaret (age 16) and Maria Eva (age 14) appear in church records for
first communion. Probably he lived in Albany or Greene Co. NY as there is no
indication of his presence at German Flats.

8507: ANNA MARGARETHA b 8 Jan 1714 (sp Geo Schmid, A. Marg. Spohn)
8508: MARIA EVA b 23 Mar 1716 (sp. Wm Lehman & wife Maria Eva)
8509: MARIA ELISABETH b 6 Mar 1718
                   (sp. Nich. Smid, Maria Elis. Mueller)

8510: Johan PETER SPOHN (existence questionable) - m by 1712 MARIA CATHERINE ...
Undoubtably this "Johan Peter" was related to the above Henrich and Adam and there
seems some basis to suspect that the birth entry (Kochertal record as seen in Book
of Names, page 23) is possibly wrong with regard to the father´s name. There is
no Peter Spohn in the subsistence lists (nor room for one under another Spohn).
Since no record is seen of a Peter Spohn before or after this 1712 birth of son
Hendrick, we suggest that the child below may belong to the above Hendrick Spohn &
his wife Maria Catherine.

8511: Johan HENDRICH b 30 Jul 1712 (sp. Adam Spohn, Hen. Reiter)

8512: MARGARET SPOHN - b say 1700; m Kingston NY by 1716 JOHN WOLF (or Wolven, pr.
a relative of Gotfrid Wolven Sr. & Jr. of Kingston).

SPOHN - 2nd Generation

8502: **HENDRICK SPOHN** jr - pr. born ca 1710 to 1715; pr. liv. 1755 (deed involving Burnetsfield lot #30 list Henry Spohn next to Michael Ittig & Augustinus Hess). In 1723 he received Burnetsfield lot #7, on the North Side of the Mohawk River east of the West Canada Creek. We have no evidence that this Henry jr. ever married, and the children placed below may belong to Hendrick Sr.

> +8513: ps. JOHANNES b say 1730; in militia 1757
> +8514: ps. NICHOLAS H. b say 1733; m ELISABEH DIEVENDORF
> +8515: ps. WERNER b say 1735; in militia 1757
> 8516: ps. CATHERINE (Spohn?) b say 1737; m by 1776 JACOB BASHOR

SPOHN - 3rd Generation

8513: **JOHN SPOHN (Spawn)** - pr. born ca 1720 to 1740; liv. 1771 but pr. died by 1775 (he does not appear in the May 1775 German Flats list of residents or in any Tryon Co. regiment during the Revolution). "Hannes pahn" was in Capt. Petrie´s 1757 GF militia unit, listed next to Michel Itig & Jacob Bashor, and the John Spawn in Capt. Frank´s 1767 GF militia unit, listed next to Fred Fox & Conrad Frank <jr.>. John & Werner Spohn were on the 1771 Burnetsfield Minister´s Support list, in the proximity of Michel Itig, John Bellinger & Augustinus Hess.

8514: **NICHOLAS SPOHN** - pr. born ca 1715 to 1733 (son of Hendrick as given on land lease dated 13 Sep 1765, Vosburgh´s HK Churchbooks, vol 3 page 12); died by Aug 1817; m ELISABETH DIEVENDORF (b ca 1733, d Herkimer NY 30 Aug 1817 age 84) dau of JOHANNES DIEVENDORF & ELIZABETH KELLER. Nicholas was in Capt. Petrie´s 1769 GF militia unit, listed near Melchior Kessler & Barthy Pikert, and was in Col. Bellinger´s Revol. Regiment. He appears with 5 adults & 2 children (under 16) on the 1778 German Flats relief and on the 1790 Herkimer NY census (3-2-3) listed next to Conrad Eigenauer & Peter Davis. A Nicholas Spaan & Anna (pr. children of this Nicholas) sponsored May 1783 GF bp of Margaret, dau of Jacob Dievendorf & Catherine.

> 8517: pr. ELISABETH (Spohn?) b say 1758; m by 1781 PETER DAVIS
> 8518: ANNA b ca 1760; d Hk 1834 (age 74-5); m CONRAD EIGENAUR
> 8519: ANNA EVA b 18 May 1761 (sp. Anna Eva dau of Jos. Stahring)
>   (also sp. Jacob Dieffendorf)
> +8520: NICHOLAS jr. b SAR 8 Aug 1762 (sp Werner Spohn, Elis. Folts)
>   pr. the Nic. ca 1764-1839 m 1786 CATHERINE GIELS
> 8521: JOHANNES b GF 26 Jan 1765 (sp Joh Dievndrf, Cath. Hess)
> +8522: HENRICH b GF 8 Jun 1766 (sp Joh Miller & w. Elisabeth)
> 8523: CATHERINE b say 1768; m Jun 1786 NICHOLAS HOUSE
> 8524: SUSANNA bp SA May 1770 (sp. Fred. ... & w. Susanna)
>   m MR. DAVEY (Davis)

8515: **Johan WERNER SPOHN (Span)** - pr. born ca 1720 to 1740; In 1757 Werner was in Petrie´s GF militia, listed next to Gotlieb Camerdiner & Frederick Helmer jr., and in 1767 he was in Capt. Frank´s GF militia, next to Denis Clepsattle & Augustinus Hess. Werner Spohn appears on a land lease at German Flats dated 13 Sep 1765 (Vosburgh, HK vol 3 page 12), on the 1771 Burnetsfield Minister´s list, and, in May 1775, as a Germans Flats resident, listed next to Fred Dornberger & George Hilts jr. (Mohawk Valley in the Revolution, page 165). In the Revolution, Werner was in Col. Bellinger´s Tryon Co. Regiment. He sponsored, with Maria Wohleben, the Apr 1761 bp of Maria, dau of Fred Schutt & Elisabeth (Wohleben). On the 1790 GF census (2-0-3) listed next to Conrad & Fred Hess, and Michael Ittig.

8520: NICHOLAS SPOHN Jr (Spoon) - pr. the Nicholas born Aug 1762 (son of Nicholas); died HK 17 Apr 1830 at age 68-8 (determination of birthdate from death age gives b ca Aug 1761, which is exactly one year off and looks like a calculation error at the time of death); m at German Flats 20 Jun 1786 CATHERINE KILTS (aka CATHERINE GEILS, b ca 1765, d 1848 age 83) dau of NICHOLAS KILTS & CATHERINE STOF. HILTS. Alternate dates for this Nicholas appear in HCH Spohn file notes, which have him born ca 1764, based on death on 27 Apr 1839 at age 75. Served in Revol. (Bellinger book page 65). Nicholas owned land in Columbia NY where the Dutch Reform Church was later built and he gave land as a marriage portion to Susan Davy (pr. his sister). Children were Nicholas, John, Adam, George, Elisabeth, Catherine and Evaline as given in Spohn file at Herkimer Co. Hist. Society.

> **+8525:** NICHOLAS III b GF 27 Sep 1787 (sp. Peter Folts & Barbara)
>   d 1861; m 1812 ELISABETH DYGERT
> **8526:** JOHN b 17 Jan 1789 (sp. John Windecker & Cath.)
>   m 1812 ELISABETH HESS
> **8527:** ADAM b GF 7 Jul 1791; d 1874; m 1812 MAGDALENA BELLINGER
> **8528:** WERNER b GF 1 Apr 1794 (sp Werner Folts & Maria Elis.)
> **8529:** GEORGE N. b ca 1796; liv. 1813 (age 17 at HK confirm.)
>   pr. m by 1821 ELISABETH ZOLLER
> **8530:** EVE m JOSEPH MEYER
> **8531:** ELISABETH b HK 22 Jan 1803 (sp John Muller & w. Elis.)

8522: HENRICH SPOHN - born ca 1765 (based on age at death) and pr. the Johan Henrich born at German Flats NY 8 Jun 1766 (son of Nicholas); died 19 Aug 1855 (age 90); m GF 10 May 1791 MARGARET JOH. HILLER (b ca 1774, d 1853 age 79) dau of JOHN HILLER. Children were Henry, Simon, Warner, John, Nicholas, Margaret, and Elizabeth (Spohn file at Herk. Co. Hist. Society).

> **8532:** CATHERINE b GF 12 Feb 1792 (sp Nich. Spohn & Cath.)
> **8533:** MARGARET b 26 Jan 1793 (sp Peter Hiller, Marg. Frank)
> **8534:** child bp GF Jan 1795 (sp Peter Davis & Maria <Hiller>)

8535: WARREN F. SPOON (ps. Warner?) - pr. born ca 1730 to 1755; died by May 1803 (when widow Margaret Spoon sponsored bp of David, son of Peter Scherer); m as her second husband ANNA MARGARET BELLINGER (b 1750, d 1837) dau of Capt. PETER BELLINGER and widow of CHRISTIAN SCHERER (d 1777). The name Warren F. comes from the Bellinger book and may be a corruption of Werner, which raises the possibility that this man was perhaps the same Werner listed in the above generation.

8525: NICHOLAS SPOHN III - born 27 Sep 1787; died 9 Jun 1861; m 17 May 1812 ELIZABETH DEGERT (surname "Dygert" on 1812 mar. record, b 24 May 1788, d 1870) dau of ANDREW DEEGER & CATHERINE MILLER. He served at Sachets Harbor in War of 1812. Children were Daniel, Nicholas, Andrew, Warner, Jeremiah, and Catherine.

********** STAHRING (Staring, Sterling) **********

8601: **NICHOLAS STAHRING** - pr. born in Germany ca 1663 (son of Frederick of Wensheim as reported by Hank Jones´ Palatine Families of New York); ps. died German Flats NY 1759 at age 96 (William L. Stone´s "Starin Family"); m at Marnheim, ca 10 miles so. of Wensheim, Germany 17 Jul 1686 ANNA ELISABETH BARCKEY (bp 1659) dau of GEORGE BARCKEY & ANNA ELISABETH; m2 by 1711 MARIA CATHERINE ... Stone´s Staring book has Nicholas born 1763 in Guilderland Holland, however, the reader is advised that much of Stone´s pre-1800 genealogical material is bad. Nicholas Staringer was on the NY Palatine subsistence list in 1710 (3A,0Y) & in 1712 (4A,2Y) and was ps. the Nicholas Stickling naturalized at Albany NY 14 Feb 1716. He was a brickmaker (see 1711 bp of Margaret, Book of Names page 19). On the 1723 Burnetsfield Patent an adult male received a lot in his own name and another in the name of dependent, a pattern we have tried to use in analyzing the Staring lot assignments for relationship hints (n.b. some map versions erroneously show a Hendrick rather than Frederick on lot #24).

Stahring Name	Lot# at Burnetsfield and pr. relationship
Frederick	24 (N of Mohawk River); pr. adult (got town lot)
Adam	28 (N of Mohawk); married adult
Mary Eva	13 (Little Falls); wife of Adam
Nicholas	42 (S of Mohawk); pr. immigrant Nicholas
Joseph	41 (S of Mohawk); pr. son of Nicholas
Johanus Velde	6 (N & near River); pr. child (ps. adult?)
John Veld jr	1 (S of Mohawk); pr. son of Frederick

Stone´s Staring book says Nicholas came to NY in 1696 (should be 1710) with sons Frederick, Valentine, & Adam. The 1710 subs. list dependents allow for only two sons, so perhaps son Adam was off on his own and not recorded then. It would seem then that Nicholas was a widower without other young children in 1710 when he married his second wife Catherine. We see no basis for Stone´s claim of other early children incl. Tunis, Elisabeth, Rickert, Service, & Eve, all supposedly born 1700 to 1708. Stone has immigrant Nicholas as father of the Nicholas born in 1712 (died 1802), but even that is questionable since, unless there were twins, there seem too many children born from Aug 1711 to Apr 1714.

surname STAHRING

8602: PETER b Marnheim Germ. 20 Oct 1686 (H. Jones findings)
+8603: ADAM 1688-1778 m in NY 1712 ANNA MARIA ...
8604: ps. VALENTINE b say 1695; (1723 Burnetsfield lot #6 holder?)
        ps. named for mother´s brother, a Barckey (H. Jones)
+8605: pr. FREDERICK ca 1700-1774 m MARY GOLDMANN to Penn.
        pr. by 2nd wife (Maria Catherine)
8606: ANNA MARGARETHA b 7 Aug 1711 (sp. Philip Petrie & w. Marg.)
        pr. m HENRY CONRAD
+8607: pr. NICHOLAS ca 1712-1802 m ANNA ...
8608: CATHERINE bp Albany NY 11 Apr 1714 (sp Catryna Engelsprecken)
        she m by ca 1728 GEORGE ADAM DOCKSTADER
+8609: JOSEPH bp Albany 11 Apr 1714 (sp Jos. & Catr. Essching)
8610: GERTRUDE b 1717 (Stone´s "Starin Family")
        m at Schoharie NY 1738 JOHN SCHAEFFER
8610A EVA b say 1724; m Schoharie NY 1750 GEORGE RICKER

8603: ADAM STAHRING - pr. born in Germany ca 1688 (son of Nicholas of Wonsheim Germany, as seen on his marriage rec.); died 1778 (birth and death dates from Comp. of Amer. Geneal. vol 2 page 128); m in NY 2 Dec 1712 ANNA MARIA .... widow of BERNARD LIFENIUS; apparently m by 1723 MARIA EVA ... (as wife of Adam she got Burnetsfield lot #13 in Little Falls area). Adam was having children at the same time as immigrant Nicholas, and we feel justified in given him a large family as the name Adam is most prevalent in later years (despite Stone's rendering in the Staring book). Although not placed below we feel there is room for a son named Nicholas, ps. the one whose dates Stone gives as 1712-1802. Adam Starn was naturalized at Albany 31 Jan 1716 and was on the 1717 Simmendinger census with wife Anna Maria & 3 children (ps. one of these children was a foster son Christoper Listenius, born Aug 1711). Drew lot #28 on 1723 Burnetsfield patent.

```
    8611: MARIA CATHERINE  b 28 Sep 1715 (sp. Diet. Laux & wife)
    8612: ps ANNA ELISABETH  b say 1718; m by 1745 FRED. DOCKSTADER
   +8613: pr. PHILIP FRED. ADAM  b say 1720; ml ELISABETH EVERTSON
   +8614: ps. VALENTINE jr. b say 1722; m by 1752 ELISABETH MILLER
   +8615: pr. ADAM  b say 1724; m by ca 1752 CATHERINE (pr. Helmer)
   +8616: JACOB  b say 1727; m by 1761 CATHERINE ...
```

8605: FREDERICK STAHRING - pr. born ca 1700 (son of Nicholas, pr. named for paternal grandfather); died 1774; m MARY GOLDMANN (b ca 1703) dau of CONRAD GOLDMANN, as given in "A History of the Starnes Family" by H. Gerald Starnes & Herman Starnes (Gateway Press, 1983). Received Burnetsfield lot #24 but apparently he left the Mohawk Valley and moved south to Pennsylvania (ibid), perhaps just after the 1757 destruction of German Flats. "Starnes Family" book notes descendents settled in North Carolina and gives children as listed below.

```
    8618: VALENTINE  ca 1722-1761
    8619: FREDERICK  1724-1779  in GF militia 1757
    8620: LEONARD  ca 1726-1782
    8621: JOSEPH  ca 1730-1779  killed by Indians
    8622: ADAM  ca 1732-1816
    8623: THOMAS  ca 1734-1818
    8624: SARAH  ca 1738-1820
```

8609: JOSEPH STAHRING (Jost) - pr. born ca 1712 to 1714 (son of Nic., as in Virkus' Comp. Of Amer. Gen. <vol 7 page 6.) and bp at Albany 11 Apr 1714 (son of Nich. & Catryn); living at German Flats NY May 1775 (Mohawk Valley in the Revolution, page 166); m by ca 1735 ... (pr. an Anna based on descendent naming, ps. a Spohn or the Janetje Orendorf <bp 1713> dau of Henry). Drew lot #41 on 1725 Burnetsfield patent. In militia in 1757 and 1767, but not in Revol.

```
    8625: ps. NICHOLAS  b say 1736; at Oriskany 1777 (nephew of Nich.)
               ps. m MARIA BARBARA ... (spf Aug 1783 Staring bp, GF)
   +8626: ADAM JOSEPH  b say 1738; m 1770 CATHERINE MCGINNES
               in militia in 1767
    8627: ANNA EVA  b say 1741; liv. 1761 (spf Spohn bp)
               m 1764 ADAM STEELE
   +8628: HENDRICK J.  1743-1812  m 1764 ELISABETH HESS
   +8629: PETER J.  b say 1745; m MARIA ...  in militia 1767 & Revol.
    8629A ps. JOHN  b say 1747; m ... in 1767 GF militia
               captive 1780 with 2 sons & 4 dau. (Book of Names page 115)
    8630: MARIA  b say 1750; m FREDERICK HESS (1749-1795)
```

8607: NICHOLAS STAHRING - born ca 1712; died 1802 age 90 (Stone´s Staring book); m ANNA ... (ps. Dockstader or Kast?). Pr. the Nicholas in Capt. Frank´s 1767 GF militia and the Nicholas Sr in Bellinger´s Revol Regm. At Oriskany in 1777, when age 65, with his nephews Hendrick & Nicholas (Stone´s book).

+8632: ps. GEORGE b say 1738; in Col. Bellinger´s Revol. Regm.
+8633: ELISABETH b say 1741; m ca 1761 ARCHIBALD ARMSTRONG
+8634: ADAM NICHOLAS b say 1745; pr. m 1768 CATHERINE WEAVER
 8635: ps. MARIA EVA b say 1748; d 1779; m 1769 MELCHIOR FOLTS
 8635A ps. JOHN b ca 1750 (Green´s Gateway to the West)
 8636: CATHERINE b say 1752; m by ca 1772 PATRICK CAMPBELL
+8637: NICHOLAS N. b say 1754; m by 1774 MARIA ...
 8638: DOROTHY b say 1756; m by 1777 JACOB BRODHACK
+8639: HENRICH NIC. b say 1758; m by 1778 ELISABETH PFEIFFER

STAHRING - 3rd Generation

8615: ADAM STAHRING (Sr. in 1778) - pr. born ca 1715 to 1733; pr. died 1790 (will dated 1787/probated 1792); m by 1761 CATHERINE ..., pr. CATHERINE HELMER dau of FREDERICK HELMER & MARIA BARBARA KAST. Adam & wife Catherine sponsored 1761 bp of dau of Dietrich Steele. Adam Sr. was in Col. Bellinger´s Revol. Regiment along with an Ens. Adam A., Adam J., & Adam Staring. Adam Sr. had 2 adults & 4 children on the 1778 GF relief and was on 1790 GF census (3-2-2) next to Hoyer, Crim, & Osterhout. Pr. the Adam of Andrustown whose will (at Fonda NY, 1983 notes of Staring researcher Mr. Sterling Kimball, 4293 Lapeer Rd, Burton MI 48509) mentions wife Catherine, children Adam (oldest son), George, Peter, Jacob, Frederick, John, Maria Barbara & Catherine.

+8640: pr. ADAM 1752-1815 m 1784 ERNESTINA HARTER (b 1760)
 8641: pr. MARIA BARBARA bp 17 Mar 1762 (dau of Adam)
        (sp. Elis, dau of Pet. Folts; Philip, son of Fr. Helmer)
+8642: GEORGE b 1764 (sp Geo Helmer & Cath. Hess)
 8643: Johan PETER b GF 20 Aug 1766 (sp Peter Hoyer & w. Maria)
                    d 13 Aug 1836 (age 70)
 8643A ps. NICHOLAS A. b ...; m by 1787 ELISABETH (spf Brodhack bp)
 8644: CATHERINE b say 1770; liv. 1787 (father´s will)
 8645: JOHN b say 1773; liv. 1787 (father´s will)
 8646: pr. JACOB b 16 Jul 1778 (sp Adam Steel & Cath.<Crantz>)
 8647: pr. FREDERICK b GF 13 Dec 1781 (sp Fr Helmer & Barbara)

8626: ADAM JOS. STAHRING - pr. born ca 1735 to 1752; m SAR 3 Jul 1770 CATHERINE MACGINNES dau of TIMOTHY MCGINNES & SARAH KAST. In 1767 GF militia. Moved to Canada, near Kingston, Ontario, by 1800 (Mr. S. Kimball notes). Pr. the Adam on 1790 HK census (2-3-4) next to Peter Fox & David Baker.

+8648: ps. GEORGE AD. b say 1773; m GF 1792 MARGARET HAGEDORN
 8649: ANNA b GF 3 Oct 1776 (sp Hen. Staring & Elis.)
 8650: TIMOTHY b GF 17 May 1778 (sp Hen Staring & Elis.)
 8651: NANCY b 6 Sep 1780 (Sterling Kimball notes)
 8652: ps. ADAM b ca 1784; d 1835 (age 51); ps. m BETSY COX
 8653: pr. NICHOLAS b 6 Mar 1785 (sp. Nich. H Starin & Cath. Kinket)
                     pr. m ADELIA COX (b 1787)
 8654: SARA AD. JOS. b 20 May 1788 (sp Billy Dygert & Anna); pr. d y
 8655: SARA b GF 13 Sep 1790 (sp Marc Crantz & Elisabeth)

-242-

8634: ADAM N. STAHRING - pr. born ca 1735 to 1750 (son of Nicholas); m SAR 8 Nov 1768 CATHERINE WEAVER. In Capt. Frank's militia co. in 1767. On 1790 German Flats census (3-1-6) near Nich. Staring, ... Stephen Eysaman.

+8656: pr. NICHOLAS b 27 Feb 1770 (sp Nic. Weber & Cath.)
        pr. m GF 1788 CATHERINE SINGER
8657: ps. FREDERICK b GF 16 Jun 1776 (sp Fred. Bell & wife)
8658: pr. ADAM b GF Feb 1782 (sp Joh. Nic. Staring & Maria)
8658A pr. ANNA b GF 27 Jul 1784 (sp. Diet. Stahl, Anna Cuningham)
8659: CATHERINE b GF 30 Jun 1786 (sp Steph. Eysaman & Eva)
8660: ps. ELISABETH bp SJR Mar 1789 (sp Fred Gemmer, Cath. Staring)
        pr. same Elis. Ad. m 1809 JOHN N. STARHRING
8661: JOHN b 23 Mar 1791 (sp Val. Singer & Maria)
8662: CATHERINE b GF 28 Jun 1793 (sp Adam Campbl, Alita Staring)
8663: JACOB b GF 11 Mar 1795 (sp John Smidt & Barbara <Weaver>)

8632: GEORGE STAHRING - pr. born before 1738; ps. died by ca 1760 (no sign in records of 1760's or May 1775 GF residents list); m ... Hatch says George settled on Henderson Patent lands at Andrustown with Paul Crim.

8664: pr. MARIA ELISABETH b say 1755; m by 1775 GEO. FRED HOYER
8665: ps. MELCHERT b say 1757; in Col. Bellinger's Revol. Regm.
+8665A ps. MARIA ca 1759-1837 m DANIEL PETRIE jr.

8628: Lt. Col. HENDRICK J. STAHRING - born ca 1743; died Schuyler Town (Herk. Co.) NY 27 May 1808 at age 65; m SAR 2 Oct 1764 ELISABETH HESS (b 1743) dau of AUGUSTINUS HESS & CATHERINE KAST. His will (Herk. Co. probate #06596) names children Nicholas, George, Caty, Elisabeth, Nancy (w. of John Dockstader), Augustinus, Henry, Catrout (w. of John Fluskey), Adam, John, & Polly (w. of Wm Williams). He was in the 1767 GF militia and a Capt. in Bellinger's Regiment in the Revolution (at Oriskany with his uncle Nich.). On October 15th 1781 he was captured by the Indians who had scalped Abraham Wohleben, and later that same evening overheard that he was to be tortured to death the following morning. He freed himself from bonds during the night and escaped by wading through creek waters to throw off tracking by dogs (see Stone's Starin book and Hardin's Herkimer Co. history <page 83>). He was later a Herkimer County judge.

8666: HENRY b GF 9 Jul 1765 (sp Adam Staring, Cath. Hess); d y
+8667: NICHOLAS b 24 Mar 1767 (sp Nic. Staring & w. Anna); d 1813
        ml 1793 CUNIGUNDA DYGERT (Jane); m2 1800 MARIA MEYER
+8668: GEORGE b 11 Sep 1768 (sp Geo. Kast & Gertrude)
        m 1795 CATHERINE DOCKSTADER
+8669: CATHERINE bp 22 Mar 1770 (sp Maria Staring & Fred Hess)
        m 1790 GEORGE PHIL. HELMER
8670: ELISABETH b 1774; m 1795 HENRICH DEW. DYGERT
8671: ANNA H. b say 1775; ml GF 1795 JOHN DOCKSTADER
8672: AUGUSTINUS bp GF 23 May 1776 (sp Aug. Klpsttl & Barbara)
8673: HENRICH bp 23 May 1778 (son of Hen. J. & Elis.)
        Henry H. (Schuylertown) m 1804 MARGARET F. MEYER
8674: GERTRAUT b GF 26 Dec 1779 (sp. Hen. N. Staring & Elis.)
        d 1853; ml 1802 JOHN FLUSKEY
8675: ADAM b 27 Aug 1781 (sp Leon. Dckstdr ..); m MARY DAVIS
8676: JOHN b 5 May 1782; d 1872; m PHOEBE SHEAF
8676A ps. child b GF 10 Aug 1783 (sp Nic. Staring & Maria Barbara)
8677: MARIA b 14 Feb 1786; m by 1808 WILLIAM WILLIAMS

8639: HENDRICK NIC. STAHRING - born say 1758; m by 1778 ELISABETH PFEIFFER dau of
PETER PFEIFFER (see 1786 will) & CATH. WEAVER. Pvt., Bellinger´s Revol. Reg.

8678: MARIA CATHERINE b GF 7 Feb 1780 (sp Adam Staring & Cath.)
8679: NICHOLAS b 26 Feb 1785 (sp Nicol Nic. Staring, Marg. Piper)
8680: JACOB b GF 30 Apr 1787 (sp Jac. Chr Ittig, Anna J N Staring)
8681: ELISABETH b 27 Apr 1789 (sp Pet Orendorf & Cath <Piper>)
8682: CATHERINE b GF 28 Feb 1794 (sp Gen Patr. Chample & Cath.)
8683: JOHN b 28 Sep 1791; m 1810 CATHERINE FR. FOX

8616: JACOB STAHRING - born say 1726 (pr. son of Adam, as given in Staring book);
m by 1761 CATHERINE ... Jacob sponsored, with Dorothy Elisabeth Jung, Aug 1747 bp
of Elisabeth Joh. Hess and was in Col. Klock´s Revol. Regiment.

8684: JACOB bp SA 2 Aug 1761 (sp. Jac. Chrstmn, Elis. Laux)
+8685: GEORGE b SAR 29 May 1763 (bp 6 Jun 1763, no sponsors)
8686: ANNA b SAR 28 Mar 1765 (sp. Diet. Suts & w. Cath.)
8687: LENA JAC. b SAR 30 Aug 1766 (sp H. Dockstadr & Lena <Weber>)
        m GF Feb 1788 JOHN H. HAUSS
8688: ELISABETH b SAR 4 Apr 1768 (sp Elis. & James Billington)
8689: JOHN b SAL 29 Aug 1771 (sp John Dockstdr, Eva Coppernol)
8690: pr. SUSANNA JAC. b say 1774; m 1795 CONRAD STAHRING

8637: NICHOLAS N. STAHRING jr. - pr. born ca 1753 and the Joh. Nicholas, farmer of
GF, who died at HK 12 Nov 1816 (age 63); ml by 1776 BALLY ... (liv. 1780 bp rec);
m2 by 1785 MARIA ..., pr. MARIA CUNINGHAM (b 1766) dau of William (Stone gave 2nd
wife to Nich. Ph. Staring). In Revol. service & on 1790 GF census (3-2-4).

8691: NANCY 1774-1845 m (as Anna N. N.) 1792 JOHN P. BELLINGER
8692: NICHOLAS b GF 30 Jul 1776 (H. Starin, Maria J. Starin); d y
8693: ADAM b GF 4 Apr 1780 (sp Adam Staring & Cath.); ps d y
8694: EVA b GF 24 Aug 1785 (sp Diet. Steele, Anna Cuningham)
8694A WILLIAM N. b GF 20 Oct 1787 (sp Wm Cuningham & Margaret)
        lived at Utica NY; m 1810 CATHERINE S. EYSAMAN
8695: NICHOLAS b GF 20 Jan 1790 (sp Hen. N. Staring & Elis.)
8696: JOHANNES b GF 30 Dec 1791 (sp Col. Patr. Campbell & Cath.)
        m 1809 MARIA ELISABETH AD. STAHRING
8697: ELISABETH b 7 Feb 1794 (sp. Diet. DeMuth & Elis.<Cuningham>)
        (Elis. Nic. N.) m 1812 JAMES RANCKEN (rec. has Rincken)
8697A ps. CATHERINE N. b say 1796; m 1814 ROBERT KLOCK
8697B DANIEL b HK Aug 1805; liv. 1892 Clayton NY
8697C JONAS b 6 May 1809; m HANNAH DEVOE

8629: PETER JOS. STAHRING - pr. born ca 1740 to 1750; m MARIA ... (pr. MARIA
DIETERICH as in DAR ref. <not seen>). In 1767 GF militia.

8698: CATHERINE PIET. b say 1774; m 1795 DEOBALD HEN. DYGERT
8699: ANNA bp 14 Feb 1779 (sp Hen. Staring, Maria Staring)
+8700: JACOB PET. b say 1781; m 1802 EVE ORENDORF
8701: MARGARET PET. b 10 Jun 1783 (sp Deobald Deiterich & Marg.)
        m 1802 ABRAHAM A. WOHLEBEN
8702: MARIA b GF 26 Dec 1784 (sp Lor. Shmkr, Mar. Cath Steele)
8703: MARIA b GF 10 Dec 1786 (sp Nich. N Staring & Maria)
8704: DOROTHEA PET. JOS. bp 12 Apr 1789 (sp Jacob Brodhack & Doro.)
8705: EVA PET. JOS. b GF 6 Jan 1791 (sp. Lor. Shoemaker & Cath.)
8706: PATRICK b 18 Sep 1793 (sp Col. Pat. Campbell & Cath.)

8613: PHILIP STAHRING - pr. born ca 1715 (Starin book); living 1766; m1 ELISABETH
EVERTSON dau of JOHN EVERTSON (died Stone Ridge NY, ibid.); m2 (Stone says by
1765) ELIZABETH SIMMONS. In 1757 GF militia. Stone calls him Philip Frederick
Adam and says son William was born 7 Sep 1756 (pr. should be 1766) and died 1825.

```
     8707: FREDERICK   1744-  m ELISABETH FRANK (Stone's Staring book)
    +8708: NICHOLAS    1749-  m CATHERINE REICHMEYER
    +8709: ps. JOHN    1754-  m JANE WEMPLE
    +8710: pr. ADAM    1756-1812  m NELLY QUACKENBUSH
    +8712: PHILIP   born 1757-9; m by 1787
     8713: MARGARET  bp Jan 1760 (sp Marg. Ph Crommel, Henry Jac Muller)
     8714: ELISABETH CATHERINE (twin)  b SAR 20 Apr 1763
                          (sp. Elisabeth, wife of John Everts)
     8715: SARA (twin)  b 1763 (sp Sara Dockstdr, Jac Sternbergr)
     8716: ELIZABETH  b 1765 ("Starin Family" <birthdate questionable>)
    +8717: WILLIAM  b SAR 5 Oct 1766 (sp Wm Brentup & Cath.)
```

8614: VALENTINE STAHRING jr. - pr. born ca 1715 to 1723; m by 1752 ELISABETH
MULLER. Fallindein Staring was on the Tryon Co. census ca 1776, apparently in the
northeast Herkimer area, with 1 older man & woman over age 50, 3 men & 3 women
(ages 16-50), and 2 boys & 2 girls. Feltin seems to be in about the same place on
the 1790 HK census (2-0-2), next to Frederick Schell.

```
    +8719: pr. CONRAD V.  b say 1750; m by 1777 LENA ...
    +8720: Johan VALENTINE  bp Stone Arabia 25 Jun 1752; d 1782;
                     pr. m 1771 MARIA MARGARET RASBACH
     8720A pr. MARIA  b say 1754; m by 1771 MARTEN VAN SLYCK
    +8721: ps. ADAM  b say 1756; m by ca 1779 ELISABETH (pr. Gaks)
    +8722: JACOB  bp 1764 (sp Jacob Staring & w. Cath.)
                     m 10 Jan 1786 ELISABETH G. LAUX
     8723: ANNA ELISABETH  bp SAR 27 Sep 1767 (sp Elis. & Peter Sutz)
    +8724: CATHERINE  bp 20 Feb 1770 (sp Adam Staring & w Cath.)
```

STAHRING - 4th Generation

8640: ADAM STAHRING - born 1752 pr. son of Adam of Andrustown (Harter book page 9
supports an Andrustown Staring parent, while Stone's book seems off the mark with
a father of Henry); died 4 Nov 1815 (age 63); m 1784 ERNESTINA HARTER (b 1761, d
1835) dau of Capt. HENRY HARTER and widow of Ens. JOHN F. BELLINGER (killed by
Indians Jul 1780, Bellinger book page 52). Children given in Harter book page 8.
In Revol. service (ps. Ensign Adam A.) and later in 1792 was a Captain. Pr. the
Adam A. on 1790 HK census (1-1-4) next to Helmers & Joseph Meyer.

```
     8725: ANNA  b GF 30 Jun 1785; m FREDERICK COOPER
     8726: ERNESTINA  b 21 Oct 1787; m SIMON WILLIAMS
     8727: MARIA ELISABETH  b SJR 11 Apr 1790 (sp Ludwig Barsh & Marg.)
     8728: CATHERINE  b GF 27 Apr 1792 (sp Geo. Fr. Hoyer & Cath.)
                     m Herk. 1818 JOHN RULISON (b 1782, d 1885)
     8729: ADAM  b GF 2 Jun 1794 (sp Capt. Pet. Bellinger & Elis.)
                     d 1870; m 1810 MARY MAGDALENA HARTER (DAR v 102, page 243)
     8730: EVA  b Minden NY 1797 (sp Adam Helmer & w. Maria)
                     d 1878; m JACOB A. CRIM jr
     8731: JACOB  b 9 Apr 1801 (sp Peter Maag, Maria Cooper)
                     d Herkimer NY 27 May 1807 (age 6-1-18)
```

8732: ADAM STARING - born 1762 (Starin Family); died ca 1859; ml ca 1790 Ms.
STERLING. Had children Adam, Philip, Sylvanus Seamon (b 1807), Alexander, John,
Gilbert, Mary Ann, Elizabeth, Eleanor (m Daniel Smith), and Katherine.

8710: ADAM STAHRING - born 1756 (pr. son of Philip, not of Nicholas as guessed by
Stone); died 1812 age 56; m NELLY QUACKENBUSH. His will in 1812 names wife Nelly
and children Frederick, Philip, John, Henry, Betsy, Elly, Peggy, and Caty. Ps.
the Adam on 1790 Mohawk NY census (1-3-3).

   8733: FREDERICK b Fonda NY 2 Dec 1776 (sp Fred. Staring & Elis.)

8721: John ADAM STARING - pr. born ca 1745 to 1760; liv. 1813 (will, HK Co.
B-298); m by 1802 ELISABETH GAKS. An Adam & Elisabeth are listed as parents of
the Anna, Catherine, & Peter placed below. Pr. the Adam on 1790 HK census (1-0-4)
next to Jacob Petrie & Jacob Staring. Was at New Germantown in 1804.

   8734: ANNA b GF 3 Mar 1779 (Con. Staring & Lena); m PETER KLOCK
   8735: pr. CATHERINE b GF 31 Aug 1784 (sp Jac. Staring, Elis. Huber)
   8736: pr. PETER b GF 9 Jun 1793 (son of Adam & Elisabeth)
                 (sp. Jost Diet. Petrie & Anna Eva)
   8737: JOHN b 6 Jan 1802 (sp Jac. Hartman, Anna Gaks)
   8738: JOSEPH b 19 Mar 1804 (sp Adam Staring & Cath.)

8719: CONRAD V. STAHRING - born ca 1745 to 1755; pr. ml before 1777 LENA ...(ps.
MAGDALENA MOAK); m2 30 Aug 1795 SUSANNA JAC. STAHRING pr. dau of JACOB STAHRING &
CATHERINE. Pr. the Conrat in Bellinger's Revol. Reg. (Book of Names page 168).
Had 2 boys on the Tryon Co. census of ca 1776 (listed after Valentine, pr. his
father), as seen in Mohawk Valley in the Revolution (page 154).

   8739: DELIA bp GF 1 Jan 1778 (sp. Hen Keller & Adlheit); pr. d y
   8740: DELIA bp 22 Feb 1786 (sp Jacob Vett. Staring & Elis.)
   8741: JACOB bp GF 28 Sep 1788 (sp Jacob Keller & Elisabeth)
   8742: BENJAMIN bp SJR 8 May 1791 (sp Martin V Slyk & Maria)
              m 1712 BARBARA ELISABETH KLOCK (Dockstader book, pg 157)
   8743: MAGDALENA bp SJR 17 Jan 1794 (sp. Valentin Beyer & Marg.)

8707: FREDERICK STARING - born 1744; died 1 Apr 1826; m ELISABETH FRANK (b 1746; d
12 Nov 1835) a descendent of Stephen Frank according to Stone's Starin Family.
Was member of Dominie Van Horne's Caughnawaga Dutch Reform Church.

   8744: JOHN F. b 6 Jan 1774 (Fonda NY sp John Frank, Maria Grand)
              m HANNAH HUGHTNER
   8745: PHILIP F. b Charleston NY 12 May 1775; d 2 Aug 1798
   8746: JACOB F. b 20 Jun 1785; m HARRIET SCHERMERHORN

8642: GEORGE AD. STAHRING - ps. the George born 1764 (son of Adam A.); m GF 10 May
1795 ANNA WOHLEBEN. Bp in 1795 lists parents as "George Hel." Staring & Anna and
with Wohleben sponsor that child would seem to belong with this couple.

   8747: pr. ANNA b GF 25 Aug 1795 (John Wohleben, Anna Ad. Staring)

8648: GEORGE AD. STAHRING - pr. born ca 1765 to 1773; m GF 1792 MARGARET HAGEDORN.

8668: GEORGE H. STAHRING - pr. born ca 1760 to 1776; m GF 10 Feb 1795 CATHERINE
DOCKSTADER, pr. the Cath. (b 1778) dau of PETER DOCKSTADER. George was a sponsor,
with Elisabeth Miller, for Apr 1793 bp of Andreas, son of Richard Sharpp & Lea.

8685: GEORGE STAHRING - pr. the Geo. born May 1763 (son of Jacob); m GF 6 Jun 1786
ANNA ZIMMERMAN dau of HENRY ZIMMERMAN. On 1790 Palatine NY census (1-0-3) in
proximity to Jacob Staring. Lived at Schnellsbush in 1791.

    8748: DOROTHEA bp SJR 20 Sep 1788 (sp Dor. Zimmrmn, John Staring)
    8749: ANNA bp SJR 8 May 1791 (sp Adam Zimmrman, Maria V Slyk)
    8750: JACOB bp SJR 13 Oct 1793 (sp Jac. H Zimmerman & Maria)

8722: JACOB V. STAHRING - bp 1764; m GF 10 Jan 1786 ELISABETH G. LAUX dau of a
GEORGE LAUX. Lived at Sneidersbush in 1792.

    8751: GERTRAUD b GF 19 Feb 1787 (sp Geo H Laux & Gertr.)
    8752: ELISABETH bp SJR 4 Mar 1792 (sp Geo. Laux, Elis. Staring)
    8753: ANNA b GF 9 Jun 1795 (sp Jac. Laux, Anna Staring)

8700: JACOB P. STAHRING - m HK 16 Apr 1802 ANNA EVA ORENDORF dau of Frederick.

8709: JOHN STAHRING - ps. born Caughnawaga NY 31 Aug 1754 son of Philip (Stone´s
Starin book) or born 1750 son of Nicholas (Greene´s Gateway to the West); died
Fonda NY 19 Feb 1832 age 77-5-18; m 1780 JANE WEMPLE (b ca 1752, d Syracuse NY 4
Sep 1840 age 88-3-2) dau of HENDRICK WEMPLE (b 1720). Was an Indian interpreter,
in Revol. service, and a friend of George Washington. He kept an inn at
Fultonville NY on the Mohawk´s south bank.

    8754: HENRY b Kinderhook Falls NY 10 May 1781; m CHLOE GAYLORD
    8755: JOSEPH b 29 Apr 1783; m1 MARIA GROAT m2 CALISTA DIMICK
    8756: MYNDERT b 31 May 1786; m RACHEL SAMMONS (dau of Thom.)
    8757: EVELINA b 1 Aug 1789; d. single
    8758: JOHN born 1792; d unm
    8759: WILLIAM b 29 Mar 1793; unm
    8760: CHARLES HANSON b 18 Nov 1796; m ELIZA HENRIETTA BERGER
    8761: ELIZABETH b 20 Oct 1799; m THOMAS ROBISON

8708: NICHOLAS PH. STARING - pr. born 1749 (Stone´s Starin Family); m 1780
CATHERINE REICHMEYER (apparently liv. 1793). We think Stone has confused him with
Nicholas N. Staring of German Flats and Utica NY who married MARY CUNINGHAM by
whom he had children, ADAM (b 4 Apr 1781), MARIA, ELIZABETH, WILLIAM (b 1787,
lived at Utica NY), JOHN (of Utica), NICHOLAS (of Utica), DANIEL (liv. 1892 at
Clayton NY), & JONAS (b 1809, m HANNAH DEVOE). We suspect that this Nicholas (son
of Philip) resided in eastern Montgomery Co. sufficiently separated in distance so
that neither he nor the Nicholas (son of Nicholas) of German Flats were given a
middle initial for identification. Daughter Maria was married at Caughnawaga NY
in 1818 to George Dockstader (Dockstader book, page 120).

    8761A MARIA b Charleston NY 22 Mar 1793; m GEORGE G. DOCKSTADER

8656: NICHOLAS AD. STAHRING - presumably the Nicholas b 27 Feb 1770 (pr. son of
Adam N. & Cath.); m GF 26 Dec 1788 CATHERINE SINGER. He was noted as insane on
Sep 1810 HK bp record.

    8770: CATHERINE b 24 Apr 1789 (sp Adam Staring & Cath.)
    8771: MARIA b GF 27 May 1790 (sp Pet. Jos. Staring & Maria)
    8772: ADAM b GF 5 Dec 1792 (sp Adam Singer, Dor. Staring)
    8773: ANNA ELISABETH b GF 18 Jan 1794 (sp Val. Singer & Elis.)
    8773A CHRISTOPHER b 5 Apr 1805 (? year not clear)
              presented for bp HK 2 Sep 1810 (sp Christphr Bell)

8667: NICHOLAS H. STAHRING - born ca Mar 1766 (son of Col. Henry); died at
Herkimer NY 11 Feb 1813 (age 46-10-18); m1 FPL 22 Sep 1793 KUNIGUNDA DYGERT
(Jane); m2 ca 1800 MARIA H. MEYER widow of HEZEKIAH TALCOTT (note Talcot´s 1795 GF
mar. rec. has Bolly H. Meyer) so apparently she was a dau of a HENDRICK MEYER.
Nicholas H. Starin & Catherine Kinket sponsored May 1785 GF bp of Nicholas, son of
Adam Staring & Cath. Living at Schuylertown in 1802. Stone´s Starin book lists
children by second wife (Maria Meyer) as Abigail, Rhoda, Sarah, Maruerite, &
Nicholas H. (but omits Catherine whose 1802 bp is in Herkimer Church rec.).

> 8774: ELIZABETH   b Jan 1795 (sp Adam H Staring, Elis. H Staring)
> m JAMES CARDER
> 8775: MARY   m WARNER DYGERT
> 8776: HENRY N.   m MARGARET BETTINGER
> by 2nd wife
> 8777: CATHERINE   b 9 Jan 1802 (sp George Meyer)
> 8777A MARGARET   b HK 22 Sep 1803 (sp H Staring, Marg. Meyer, unm)
> 8777B SALLY   b HK Jul 1805 (sp Peter Herder & w. Cath.)

8643: PETER STAHRING - pr. born ca 1760 to 1780; m by 1801 EDWINA HELMER (listed
as "Sabina" on 1793 bp rec.) and pr. same person as the PETER AD. STAHRING who m
GF 5 Dec 1792 SABINA FR. HELMER. Living at Endrichstown NY in 1801.

> 8778: MARGARET   b GF 2 Jun 1793 (sp John Helmer, Marg. Harter)
> 8779: EDWINA   b ca 1797; liv. 1814 (age 17 at HK Confirm.)
> 8780: GEORGE FREDERICK   b 4 Dec 1801 (sp Geo Fr Hoyer)

8712: PHILIP STARING - pr. born ca 1757 to 1759 (Starin Family); m ... Had
children Adam (b 1 Aug 1787, m MARTHA WILLIAMS), Nicholas (m NANCY WILLIAMS),
Barney (unm), and Elizabeth (m Isaac Mansfield).

8720: VALENTINE STAHRING - pr. the Valentine bp Stone Arabia NY 25 Jun 1752 (son
of Valentine & Elisabeth); died 17 Jul 1782; m SAR Feb 1771 MARIA MARGARET RASBACH
dau of JOHANNES RASBACH & MARGARET BIERMAN. He was captured and tortured to death
outside Fort Herkimer by Sir John Johnson´s Tory Indian raiders.

> 8781: MARCUS   b GF 28 Nov 1775 (sp. Marc. Raspch & Veronica)

8717: WILLIAM STAHRING - born 5 Oct 1765 (bp SAR 15 Jan 1766 son of Philip &
Elis.); died Charlestown NY 25 May 1825; m Fonda NY 18 Aug 1785 DEBORAH PHILIPS (d
Root NY 1826, where her will names children Adam, Jennie, & Elisabeth) of
Schenectady.

> 8782: ADAM W.   ca 1786-1855   m MARTHA WILLIAMS
> 8783: MARY (Meritje)   b Mar 1787; ps. m 1811 JOHN I. QUAKENBOSH
> 8784: SUSANNA   b Fonda NY 24 Nov 1791
> 8785: ELISABETH   b FR 12 Dec 1793; pr. d. young
> 8786: BARNT (Barney)   b FR 25 Apr 1796
> 8787: JANNETJE   b FR 3 Aug 1798; m ABRAHAM VAN DEUSEN jr.
> 8788: ELISABETH (Betsy) b 12 May 1803; m ISAAC MAXWELL (Maxfield?)

8724: CATHERINE STAHRING - pr. the Cath. born 1770 (dau of Valentine); m GF 1788
FRED. CHR. SCHELL.

8665A MARIA STAHRING - born ca 1759; died Little Falls NY 27 Mar 1837 (age
77-5-7); m DANIEL PETRIE jr.

********** STEELE (Stahley) **********

STEELE - 1st Generation

8801: ROELOF STEELE (Rudolph) - pr. born in Switzerland (Deuel notes) or Germany ca 1675 to 1682; died ca 1770-71 (Steele family notes by Mildred Baker); m MARIA DOROTHEA ... . On NY Palatine subsistence list as Rudoph Stahl in 1710 (3A,1Y) and 1712 (2A,2Y) and was naturalized at Albany 11 Oct 1715. Also was listed on the 1717 Simmendinger census at New Heidelburg settlement with wife Maria Dorothea and 4 children. Maria Dorothea was sponsor for Jun 1717 bp of Maria Dorothea dau of Ludwig Wanner & Anna Barbara. Rudolph settled on Burnetsfield lot# 8 (on south side of Mohawk River present site of Ilion NY) which he had purchased from Peter Spies ("The Steele Family" manuscript by Mildred Baker in Steele file at Herkimer Co. Hist. Soc.). Baker manuscript says immigrant Rudolph had 4 children born in Germany and 6 in America, and that Adam was his oldest son. On the other hand Deuel lists as children only Dietrich (whom he calls the eldest son), Adam, Rudolph jr, Elisabeth, and Barbara (notes of Frank D. Deuel in Herkimer Evening Telegram of 4 Feb 1904).

surname STEELE
```
+8802: ADAM   b say 1705; liv. 1772
 8803: ELIZABETH  b say 1711
+8804: DIETRICH  b say 1713; liv. 1796; m MARGARET WOHLEBEN
+8805: RUDOLPH  b say 1715
 8806: BARBARA  b say 1719
```

8807: JOHANNES STAHL - pr. born ca 1670 to 1682; m ANNA URSALA ... On NY Palatine subsistence list in 1710 (3A,0Y) and in 1712 (3A,1Y). On 1717 Simmendinger census with wife Anna Ursala and 1 child. Johannes was thrice a baptism sponsor - (1) with Christian Meyer and Christina Tonius, for bp Nov 1713 of Johan Christian son of Peter Oberbach & Maria Christina; (2) with Fred Maul, for Aug 1714 bp of son of Henrich Reuter; and (3) with Elisabeth Duntzbach, for bp Aug 1717 of Elisabeth dau of Michel Hoenig & Magdalena.

```
+8808: ps. FREDERICK  b say 1700; ps. m by 1722 MARGARET DYGERT
 8809: ps. ELISABETH  b say 1710; m by 1727 ANDRIES RICKTER
 8810: ANNA MARIA  b 31 Oct 1711; ps m by 1730 WILLIAM ZUVELT
        (sp. Pet. Oberbach, Elis. Mueller, Maria dau of Wm Kuester)
+8811: HENRICH  b 19 Feb 1715 (sp. Fred. Maul)
        (sp. also Hen. Reuter, Anna Hartman)
```

8812: HENRICH STAHL - pr. born ca 1665 to 1680; A Henrig Stall appears with wife & 4 children on 5th London Palatine List of 15 Jul 1709. On NY Palatine subsistence list in 1710 (3A,1Y) and in 1712 (2A,0Y). An Elisabeth Stahl was sponsor, with Sibylla Cath. Kehl & Philip Mohr, for Jan 1712 bp of Cath., dau of Henrich Mohr & Margaret.

```
+8813: ps. ANNA ELISABETH  b say 1695; m by 1712 CONRAD BEHRINGER
 8814: ps. ANNA AGATHA  b say 1701; liv. 1714
        (was sponsor with Conrad Baringer for 1714 Roschman bp)
```

8815: JOSEPH STAHL - pr. born ca 1680 to 1690. On NY Palatine sub. list in 1710 (2A,0Y) and 1712 (1A,0Y).

8802: **ADAM STEELE** - pr. born ca 1700 to 1710; Pr. living 1755 or later as he was in service in the French & Indians Wars (Deuel in Herkimer Evening Telegram of 4 Feb 1904). Adam Steele, Ruldoph's oldest son, signed a release to his brother Dietrich in 1772, giving Dietrich sole title to Burnetsfield lot #8 (of Patentee P. Spies), whereupon Adam moved to Ft. Herkimer (note in Steele file at Herk. Hist. Soc.).

> +8816: pr. CATHERINE b say 1725; m John JACOB KESSLER
> 8817: ps. MAGDALENA b say 1731; d 1802; m 1750 PAUL CRIM

8804: **DIETRICH STEEL** Sr. - pr. born ca 1705 to 1716 (son of Roelof); liv. 9 Aug 1796 (date will prepared); m1 ca 1743 GERTRUDE KAST (b 1727, d Sep ...) dau of GEORGE KAST jr & GERTRUDE; m2 by ca 1760 MARGARET WOHLEBEN. In an indenture made 4 Jun 1793 Frederick Kast refers to three children of his dead sister Gertrude, naming them as Rudolph, George, & Gertrude (as in "Mohawk Valley Kasts") and Stone Arabia Reform Dutch Church records show Dietrich's wife as Margaret for the five children bp from 1761 to 1770. Hans Derich Stally deeded German Flats lots #45-47 to Peter Remsen on 26 Apr 1733 and built a grist mill and sawmill on Steele's Creek, south of the Mohawk River, where during an Indian attack he escaped capture by hiding in a sawdust pile. The Stahley Patent of 17 Jun 1755 granted land in the southern part of Herkimer Co. to Rudolph Stahley, Peter Bellinger jr, "Hans Dietrich Staley", and others. Steele family patentees living in 1795, who signed the 1755 petition, were Rudolph (pr. jr.), George, "Dietrich", and John. Dietrich was listed as a son of Rudolph on a Burnetsfield land lease dated 13 Sep 1765, was the Lt. Tiederich Steel in 1767 GF militia and at Oriskany in 1777. Pr. also the "Fiedrick Steale" who had 6 adults & 5 children on 1778 GF relief. The Baker manuscript has his children as Ruloph (oldest), second son George (m Dor. Shoemaker), then Gertrude (m Henry Crantz), Maria, Barbara, Elisabeth, Dietrich (m Cath. Bauman), Catherine (m George Dygert), John (m Catherine), and Nicholas (m Eva Meyer). Dietrich Stale was listed on the 1790 German Flats census (4-0-2), presumably his household consisting then of adult unmarried sons Dietrich, John, & Nicholas. The 1796 will of Dietrich Stehl of German Flats mentions wife living (but not named), sons Rudolph (oldest), Dietrich (received lot #8), John & Nicholas, and daughters Gertrude & Catherine ("now Dygert"). The younger sons John & Nicholas were designated to receive Burnetsfield lot #7 which Dietrich had purchased from Nicholas Harter (Harter book page 130).

> +8818: RUDOLPH 1744-1834 m ANNA MARIA WENTZ
> +8819: GEORGE D. 1750-1803 m 1774 DOROTHEA SHOEMAKER
> 8820: GERTRUDE b say 1752; liv. 1765 (spf Ger. Crim bp)
>   d bef. 1802; m by 1777 HENRY CRANTZ (Baker ms.)
> 8821: ps. MARIA b say 1754 (Baker ms.)
>   by 2nd wife
> 8822: MARIA BARBARA b 12 Mar 1761 (Adam Staring & w Cat.); d 1761
> 8823: ELISABETH b SAR 20 Apr 1762 (sp Nic Wohlen's wife M. Elis)
>   pr. liv. 1778 (spf Peter R. Stel bp) & dec'd by 1796
> +8824: DIETRICH D. b SAR 1 May 1765 (sp. Augustinus Hess & Barbara)
>   d 1826; m 1795 CATHERINE BAUMAN
> 8825: CATHERINE b SAR 22 Dec 1767 (sp Cath. & Fr. Shoemaker)
>   liv. 1796; m GEORGE DYGERT
> 8826: JOHN b SAR 19 Mar 1770 (sp John Thomson & Doro.)
>   liv. 1796; m by 1791 CATHERINE ...
> +8827: NICHOLAS b say 1773; liv. 1826; m EVA J. MEYER (b 1776)

8808: FREDERICK STEELE (existence questionable) - a "Frederick Staten" m by 1722 MARGARET DYGERT (Tiegert) and had a child MARITJE EVA (Maria Eva, bp Schenectady 30 Jun 1722).as given in Pearson's Schenectady book page 176. Ps. related to Henrich of Schenectady or of a different family.

8811: HENRICH STEELE - born 19 Feb 1715 (son of John); Schenectady branch?

       8828: ps. JACOB m by 1775 SUSANNA REYNEUS
       8829: ps. HARMANUS b say 1740; m by 1775 MARIA HOGEBOOM
       8830: ps. GEORGE m by 1775 JANE MACKALL
     +8831: ps. HENDRICK 1746-1835 m by 1777 RACHEL VAN HOESEN
       8832: ps. ROELOF m by 1784 ELISABETH CRAWFORD
       8833: ps. MATTHIAS m by 1784 SUSANNA SATTN.

8805: RUDOLPH STEEL jr. - pr. born ca 1700 to 1717; liv. 1795 (signer of 1755 Stahely patent); m ... His brothers Adam and Dietrich are identified on a 1772 land transfer, but only Deuel's notes single out this Rudolph.

       8834: ps. JOHN b say 1733; on Stahley Patent 1755
       8835: ps. BARBARA b say 1740; liv. 1764 (spf Deit. A Stele bp)
     +8836: ADAM RUD. b say 1742; m1 1764 EVA STAHRING
                      m2 1770 CATHERINE CRANTZ
       8837: ps. NICHOLAS b say 1745; liv. 1769 (spf Steele bp)
     +8838: ps. GEORGE b say 1750; m by 1778 MARIA

8813: ANNA ELISABETH STAHL - pr. born ca 1695; m by 1712 CONRAD BEHRINGER (Peeringer). Pr. was sponsor, with Joh. Mueller & Anna Julian Maul, for Nov 1711 Bast bp. Elisabeth & Conrad had Maria Elisabeth (b 1711, sp. Elis. Schlitzler), Hendrick (1714) and Marytjen (bp Kingston NY Aug 1722). Lived at Kingston NY.

STEELE - 3rd Generation

8836: ADAM STEELE - pr. born ca 1730 to 1745 (son of Rudolph, as on 1764 mar. rec.); m SAR 9 Mar 1764 EVA STARING dau of JOSEPH STARING ("The Staring Family" by Hubert A. Hess); according to Baker ms. notes in Steele file at Herkimer Co. Hist. Society, he m2 SAR 29 Jan 1771 CATHERINA CRANTZ (b ca 1750, died widow of Adam 19 May 1813, age 63). An Adam Stel was in the 1757 GF militia and later in Bellinger's Regiment were a George, Dietrich, & Adam Steele. Probably the Adam Steele on 1790 German Flats census (4-2-4), living near Thomas Shoemaker, Fred Orendorf Sr. & Jr., and Joseph Staring. Adam Stahl and wife Catherine were sponsors for 1778 bp of Adam, son of Marc Rasbach & Froena.

     +8839: DIETRICH b 9 Nov 1764 (sp. Diet. Wohleben & Barbara Stahl)
                 d Herkimer NY 1840; m ANNA JOH. CUNINGHAM
       8840: MARIA CATHERINE b SAR 12 Jun 1769 (sp Nic Stahl, Cath Starin)
                 d 1835; m 1786 GEORGE NELLIS
                    by 2nd wife
       8841: DOROTHY 1773-1850 m 1789 PETER J. BELLINGER (b 1768)

8824: DIETRICH D. STEELE - born 1 May 1765 (son of Dietrich & Marg.); died 22 Aug 1826 (age 61); m ca 1795 CATHERINE BOWMAN (b 1774, d 1841) dau of FREDERICK BAUMAN (Bauman book page 69). Had Rudolph (1796-1886 m1 Anna Piper), Dietrich (b Jan 1798), Elisabeth (b Nov 1802 sp Peter Steel, Elis. Bauman), Adam (1804, m Elis. Bauman), Daniel (1806), Maria (1810), James (ca 1815).

8819: GEORGE D. STEELE - born 16 Oct 1750 (son of Dietrich, implied by the middle
initial "D" seen on 1786 GF bp rec.); died 23 Nov 1803 (age 53-1-7); m pr ca 1774
DOROTHY SHOEMAKER (b ca 1753, d GF 28 Nov 1809 age 56, her death rec. said that 14
of her 15 children were alive then). Despite the fact that he did not name a son
Dietrich and was not named in the 1796 will of Dietrich Stehl, George D., for want
of another Dietrich, was still presumably the son of the Deitrich Stehl whose wife
was Margaret Wohleben, as given in the Folts/Steele ms. (15 page manuscript at
Utica Public Library, believe written ca 1920-50 by Folts researcher Mrs. F. D.
Callan of Frankfort NY). The Folts/Steele ms. had children's birthdates which
seem to agree with observed church records for the most part, but are questionable
for Catherine (ms. has b 2 Aug 1780) & Frederick (ms. has b 15 Apr 1796), whose
dates are too close to a subsequent child. Pr. the George Steele in 1769 GF
militia and the Sgt Geo. Steele in Revol. service. Pr. the George listed on the
1790 German Flats census (2-2-7) near John S. Frank & Ludwig Barsh.

```
     +8842: GEORGE    1775-1850  m ELISABETH N. SMITH (b ca 1775)
      8843: ELIZABETH  b Nov 1776; d 1864; m 1795 JACOB C. FOLTS
      8844: ADAM       b GF 1 Mar 1779 (sp. Adam Stahl & Cath.)
                       m ELISABETH DYGERT  dau of Capt. William
      8845: CATHERINE  b say 1780; died 1852 (Folts/Steele ms.)
      8846: DOROTHY    b 14 Feb 1781; d 12 May 1869;  m PETER SMITH
      8847: MARIA      1783-1864  pr. m 1802 CONRAD M. WITRIG
      8848: RUDOLPH    b GF 13 Aug 1785 (sp. Wm Klepsatle & Mar. Eliz.)
      8849: GERTRUDE GEO. D.  b GF 22 Dec 1786 (sp. Ludwig Barsh & Marg.)
                       pr. m 1811 ISAAC ANDERSON
      8850: MARIA BARBARA  b GF 11 May 1788 (Diet. Stahl & Maria Barbara)
                       m 1806 JACOB BURGHDORF
      8851: DELIA      bp SJR 13 Sep 1789 (sp Marx Kessler & Delia)
                       (Callan ms. has "Nella", b 22 Jul 1790)
      8852: JOHN       bp SJR 19 Jun 1791 (sp. John Stahl & Catherine)
                       m 1821 ELISABETH BURGHDORF
      8853: NICHOLAS   b 1 Dec 1792 (sp Nich. Steele, Eva Bayer)
                       m 1810 ANNA ANDERSON
      8854: FREDERICK  b say 1795 ; died 5 Jun 1796
      8855: MAGDALENA  b 4 Sep 1796; liv. 1813 (age 16 at Confirm.)
      8856: PETER      b 22 Jan 1798; liv. 1814 (age 16 at HK Ch. Confirm.)
```

8838: GEORGE STEELE - pr. born ca 1740 to 1757; living 1815 (as indicated on
daughters' confirmation record at Herkimer Dutch Reform Church); m by 1778 MARIA
... This George had distinctly different children than above George and was
living after 1803 (when the George who married Dorothy Shoemaker was deceased).
Family resided at Columbia NY in 1815 (dau's Confirm. rec.).

```
      8857: GEORGE    b 27 Jul 1778
     +8858: pr. PETER G.  1792-1882  m 1821 CATHERINE WEAVER
      8859: MARGARET  b ca 1797; liv. 1813 (age 16 at Confirm.)
      8860: DOROTHY   b ca 1799; liv. 1813 (age 14 at Confirm.)
      8861: ELISABETH b ca 1800; age 15 in 1815 (HK Ch. Confirm.)
```

8831: HENDRICK STAHLEY - born 13 Feb 1746; died 24 Jul 1835; m RACHEL VAN HOESEN
(d 7 Mar 1824). Pr. lived mainly at Schenectady NY. Ps. the Hendrick Staly on
1790 Mohawk NY census (1-2-4) near Ruoof Staly & Silvanus Staly. Children were
HENDRICK (1777-1835), ABRAHAM (1778-1780), ANNE (1781-1854 m Rev. THOMAS ROMEYN),
JACOB (1784-1862), SUSANNAH (b 22 Jan 1786), MARY (1788-1820 m BENJAMIN
CHAMBERLIN), HARMANUS (b 15 Mar 1793), and JOHN (1796-1863 m REBECCA DEVENPECK).

8862: JOHN STEELE (Stahl) - pr. born ca 1740 to 1763; m by 1784 MARIA ELISABETH
... Ps. the John Stahly on 1790 Canajoharie census (1-2-3) amongst House family.
Was a resident of Royal Grant area in 1792 (SJR bp rec.).

8863: GEORGE   b GF 27 Oct 1784 (sp Hen Meyer & Gertrude <Haus>)
8864: HENRICH   bp SJR 11 Nov 1792 (sp. Hen. Schaeffer & Anna)

8865: JOST STEELE - pr. born ca 1735 to 1761; m by 1782 MARIA ...   In Col.
Fischer's 3rd Tryon Co. Revol. Regiment were a George, Henry, "Joseph", & Roelof
Steele. Jost and Maria were sponsors for Oct 1782 bp of Robert, son of Jost
Shoemaker & Mary (Smith).

8827: NICHOLAS STEELE - born say 1773; m EVA MEYER (b ca 1776, d 1826 age 50) dau
of Capt. JOHN MEYER. In 1797 Nicholas & Rudolph Steel were deacons at the
Herkimer Reform Church and in 1826 Nicholas was at state prison in Auburn NY
(wife's death rec., supposedly he had killed a man). Children include Richard (b
ca 1796; age 19 at 1815 HK confirm.), Michael (b HK 12 Jul 1803, sp John Meyer of
Frankfort), Rudolph (b HK 25 Jul 1805, sp Rud. Steele & Marg.), Peter (b Sep 1807,
sp Hen. Meyer of Frankfort), Robert (b Jan 1809), Maria Margaret (bp 1814) &
Elizabeth (m Sylvester Joslin of Frankfort NY, as in Baker ms. <HCH Steele file>).

8818: Lt. RUDOLPH D. STEELE - born German Flats NY 1 May 1744; died 1834; m 6 Nov
1770 ANNA MARIA WENTZ (Kast book), ps. m2 MARGARET WENZ (b ca 1747, d GF 20 Jul
1820, age 72-11-12). Had 2 adults & 2 children on 1778 GF relief. Lt. Rudolph
was at Oriskany battle and resigned from service in 1779 (Bellinger book, page
60). Listed on 1790 GF census (1-1-3) next to Jost Shoemaker.

8866: Johan PETER b GF 17 Jun 1778 (sp Pet Getman, Elis. Steel)
                   d 1840 (age 62); m 1806 ELISABETH WITRIG
8867: REBECCA   bp Schenectady 3 Mar 1782 (mother Marg. Wierts)
                pr. m by Apr 1808 JONATHAN DEY (had child bp HK then)
8867A ps. CATHERINE L. b say 1785; m by 1809 JOHN GETMAN
8867B pr. RUDOLPH b ca 1797; d 1834 (age 37, bur. Mohawk NY)

STEELE - 4th Generation

8839: DIETRICH A. STEELE - born Nov 1764; died German Flats NY 29 May 1840; m 3
Nov 1785 ANNA CUNINGHAM (b ca 1763, d 20 Nov 1815 age 52) dau of JOHN CUNINGHAM.

8868: DIETRICH b GF 26 Feb 1786 (sp Diet. Demuth & Elis.)
                pr. m by 1808 ELISABETH STAHRING
8869: JOHN   b GF 31 Dec 1787 (sp John Delene, Doro. Steele)
8870: EVA   b GF 6 Jul 1790 (sp Nic. N Staring & Maria)
8871: ADAM   b ca 1792; d Jun 1874; m HK Nov 1808 FANNY JAC. LINK

8842: GEORGE STEELE jr. - born 20 Sep 1775; d 1850; m by 1802 ELISABETH SMITH (b
ca 1775) dau of NICHOLAS SMITH & MARGARET BELLINGER. Children were Dorothy,
Margaret, Gertrude (b 1802, sp H. Shoemaker & Gert. Steele), Catherine (1805, sp
Conrad M. Witrig & w. Maria), Appolonia, Nicholas, George, and Eva.

8858: PETER G. STEELE - born 22 Jan 1792; died 18 Apr 1882; m 15 Nov 1821
CATHERINE WEAVER (1799-1844) dau of GEORGE MICHAEL WEAVER & CATHERINE HARTER

8901: ADAM THUMB - born in Wurtenburg Germany ca 10 Dec 1734, died St.
Johnsville NY 24 Apr 1814 aged 79-4-14; m 1755 CHRISTINA MEYER (d 1798).
Immigrated to America in 1754 probably with a younger brother Nicholas and sister
Agnes. Lived at the old Thumb farm about four miles north of St. Johnsville and
had eight children (Cdmr. Bellinger's notes at Herk. Co. Hist. Soc., file #3.32).
Adam Tum appears on 1790 Palatine NY cenus (1-1-2) next to Henry Hees, David
Nellis, & Christian Nellis.

surname THUMB

```
+8902: ps. AGNES   b say 1759; m 1777 WILLIAM DYGERT
+8903: CONRAD MELCHIOR   1761-1811   m ANNA HOUSE
 8904: JACOB   pr. d. young
 8905: MARGARETH   b say 1768; pr. liv. Nov 1784 (spf J. Thum bp)
+8906: DEBALD   b say 1771; liv. 1787 (spf Anne Thum bp)
 8907: ADAM jr.   b 26 Aug 1775 (sp. Fred. Hess & w. Cath. (Nellis))
```

8908: MELCHIOR THUMB - pr. born ca 1745; died 23 Apr 1804 (age 59-5-); m by 1770
ELISABETH ... (b ca 1745, d 11 Feb 1828 age 83). Just a guess that wife was ps. a
dau of GEORGE HILTS Sr. In 1754 Melchior apparently immigrated with Adam and
Nicholas Thumb, as the three were naturalized together on 8 Mar 1773 (Book of
Names page 7). Melchior was sponsor, with Anna Weber, for Dec 1765 bp of Anna,
dau of John Weaver & Ernestina, and in the 1769 GF militia was listed next to John
Weber & George Hilts Sr. Melchior was sponsor, with wife Elisabeth, for Mar 1777
bp of Elisabeth, dau of George Hilts & Elisabeth (Folts).

```
+8909: ps. NICHOLAS   b say 1770; m by 1802 MARGARET HELMER
                ps. the child b SAR Oct 1770 (sp Nic. Weber & Margaret)
 8910: MARGARET   b say 1772; m 1792 JOHN JOH. SCHELL
 8911: BARBARA   b 1774; m 1793 RUDOLPH DIEVENDORF
 8912: ELISABETH MELC.   b say 1776; m 1796 GEORGE HELMER
 8913: MARIA   b 14 Mar 1778 (sp Godf. Hilts & w. Maria <Miller>)
                pr. died young
 8914: CATHERINE   b 4 May 1782 (sp Wm Dygert & Agnes <Thum>)
                d 1846; m 1803 FREDERICK W. PETRY
 8915: MARIA   b GF 1 Jan 1785 (sp. Peter S. Dygert, Anna Hufnagel)
                pr. m PETER SCHERER (b 1776)
```

8916: NICHOLAS THUMB - pr. born ca 1740 to 1748; m by 1767 ELISABETH DYGERT
("Betsy", liv. 1789). Nicholas Tunn was on 1790 Palatine NY census (1-2-6) listed
near Adolph Walrath, Adam Philips, Henry Hees, & Adam Thumb.

```
 8917: ELISABETH   bp 27 Jun 1767 (sp. Elis. Wagner, Peter Dygert)
 8917A MARGARET   b 16 Nov 1768 (Deuel ms.); pr. d. y.
+8918: NICHOLAS   b 2 Sep 1769 (SAL bp sp. Joh. Reber)
 8919: CHRISTINA   b 11 Jan 1770 (sp. Adam Dum & wife)
 8920: ANNA b SAL 18 Jan 1773 (sp Hen Saltsman jr, Marg. Walrath)
 8921: BARBARA   b SAL 10 Dec 1777 (sp. John Fink, Anna Hufnagel)
 8922: MELCHIOR   b 3 Oct 1779 (Hen Wallrath & Cath.)
 8923: MARGARET   b GF 3 May 1781 (sp Cath. Smidt, Christn Hufnagel)
 8924: MARIA   b 17 Feb 1783 (sp Sev. Koch & Cath.)
 8925: GERTRUDE   b SAR 29 Jun 1789 (sp. Gertrude V Slyck)
 8926: MAGDALENA   bp SJR 9 Feb 1794 (sp Christian Fink, Elis. Dygert)
```

8903: CONRAD MELCHIOR THUMB - born Stone Arabia NY 27 Dec 1761 (bp. sponsors
Conrad Frank & w. Elis.); died 20 Apr 1811 (age 49-5-1); m ANNA HOUSE pr. a dau of
a JOHN HOUSE. Conrad & Anna sponsored Nov 1791 SJR bp of Anna, dau of John Haus &
Magdalena of Palatine NY. Conrad was the father of seven sons and one daughter,
as noted on his death record (Vosburgh's "Records of Stone Arabia Luth. Trinity
Church" vol 2 page 350). Pr. the Conrad Tum on 1790 Palatine NY census (2-2-2).

> 8927: JOHANNES   b GF 21 Nov 1784 (sp. Joh. Joh. Haus, Marg. Thumb)
> 8928: ANNE   b 3 May 1787 (sp. Debold Thumb, Appol. Bellinger)
> 8929: ADAM   b 1 May 1790 (sp. Adam Thumb & Christina)
> 8930: JACOB   b 17 Jun 1792 (sp. Joh. Helmer, Magd. Helmer)

8906: DEBALD THUMB (Theobald) - pr. born ca 1765 to 1775 (son of Adam); m by
1792 EVA ...   Lived at Palatine NY in 1792.

> 8931: JOHANNES bp SJR 23 Sep 1792 (sp. Adam Thum, Maria Kring)

8909: NICHOLAS THUMB - pr. born ca 1765 to 1775 (looks like a son of Melchior
based on bapt. sponsorships); m by 1802 MARGARET HELMER pr. a dau of PHILIP HELMER
& ANNA. A Nicholas and wife Margaret were sponsors for Apr 1802 HK bp of
Melchior, son of George Frederick Helmer & Elisabeth (Thum) and for Feb 1804 bp of
Anna, dau of Henry J. Meyers & Anna Helmer (dau of Philip Helmer & Anna).

> 8932: ELISABETH b HK 23 May 1807 (sp Philip Helmer & w. Anna)

8918: NICHOLAS THUMB - ps. the Nicholas born 2 Sep 1769 (son of Nicholas &
Elis.); m ANNA ACKLEY.

> 8933: LAURA b say 1823; m 1843 AARON HISER

8902: AGNES THUMB - pr. born between 1740 and 1767; m by 1787 WILLIAM DYGERT.
She was probably either a sister or a daughter of immigrant Adam Thumb.

********** WEAVER (Weber) **********

9001: JACOB WEAVER - pr. born in Germany ca 1680 to 1690; living 1769 at German Flats NY; m MARIA ELISABETH ...; ps. m2 after 1717 CATHERINE HARTER (? Comp. of Amer. Geneal. v 4 page 368). He was on the NY Palatine subsistence list in 1710 (2A,1Y) & 1712 (2A,0Y) and lived at the Queensbury camp near the Hudson River in 1711 when he and Nicholas Weber volunteered for Col. Nicholson´s Canadian campaign (Book of Names page 125). These two Webers were naturalized at Albany on 11 Oct 1715. The 1717 Simmendinger census has Jacob with wife Maria Elisabeth & 2 children and about 1723 he received Burnetsfield lot #10, which was supposedly inherited by his sons George J. and Peter (Edick Family Record page 5). Immigrant Jacob built a grist mill at German Flats in 1733 which he and son George sold in 1769 to Dr. William Petry (Hardin, page 317).

             surname WEAVER
     9002: child   b say 1708, pr. d by 1712
    +9003: JACOB Jr.   b say 1713; m by ca 1735-40 MARGARET ...
    +9004: PETER   b say 1715; m MARGARET DYGERT (b say 1715)
    +9005: pr. NICHOLAS   b say 1718; m by 1737 ELISABETH at Schenectady
    +9006: pr. JOHN JACOB   b say 1724; in GF militia 1767-69
     9007: pr. CATHERINE   b say 1727; m by ca 1750 PETER PFEIFFER
    +9008: GEORGE J.   b say 1729;   m 1754 ELISABETH DUBOIS
     9008A ps. MAGDALENA   b say 1734;   m 1758 HENRY DOCKSTADER (the Tory)

9009: NICHOLAS WEAVER - pr. born in Germany ca 1680 to 1692; believed living at German Flats NY in 1779 (as "Old Nicholas" at Nich. Smith estate sale); m BARBARA ... . Was on the NY Palatine subsistence list in 1710 (2A,0Y) & 1712 (2A,1Y) and listed on the 1717 Simmendinger census with wife Barbara & 2 children. He received Burnetsfield lot #16 which he sold in 1754 to his son Jacob.

    +9010: ANDRIES   b say 1712; m pr. by 1737 ...
     9010A pr. CATHERINE   b say 1714; m by 1749 HENDRICK DOCKSTADER
    +9011: HENRICH NIC.   b say 1716; m pr. by 1736 ANNA MARGARETHA ...
    +9012: NICHOLAS jr.   b say 1718;   m MARGARET ... (pr. Smith)
     9012A ps. ELISABETH (Weaver?)   b say 1720; ps. w2 of MARTEN SMITH
    +9013: GEORGE   b say 1723; m by 1745 MARIA BARBARA ... (pr. Edick)
    +9014: pr. JOHN NIC.   b say 1725; in GF militia 1769
    +9015: JACOB N.   b say 1727; m by 1750 CATHERINE ... (Dockstader?)
     9017: pr. MARIA MAGDALENA   b say 1731; m GEORGE DOCKSTADER (b 1728)
     9018: ps.? MARGARET (Weaver?)   b say 1734; m CHRISTIAN ITTIG

9019: HENRICH WEBER - Listed on NY Palatine subs. in 1710 (2A,1Y) & 1712 (2A,1Y) and on 1717 Simmendinger census w. wife Christina & 3 children. Ps. related to Wigand Weber (single adult on 1710 NY subs. list).

9020: JACOB WEBER - born ca 1678 (age 30 in 1708); m ANNA ELISABETH (b ca 1683, 25 in 1708). Came to Newburgh NY with Kocherthal in 1708 and had EVA MARIA (b ca 1703), EVA ELISABETHA (1707), & pr. JOHN (bp Newburgh NY Apr 1710). Perhaps the ancestor of MICHAEL JAC. WEAVER (son of Jacob of Philipsburg Manor, Westchester, NY who m 1749 ANTOINETTE PALMATIER, Comp. of Amer Genealogy v 3 page 457)

9021: VALENTIN WEBER - pr. born ca 1678 (if the Valentin Weber, Refm. tailor, with son age 2 on 1709 London list). On NY Palatine list in 1710 (2A,0Y) and 1712 (2A,0Y). Also on 1717 Simmendinger census 1717 with wife Charlotte & 2 children.

9010: ANDRIES WEAVER - pr. born ca 1710 to 1715 (absence of naturalization for him suggests a NY birth); apparently living in 1767 south of the Mohawk at German Flats NY (Capt. Frank´s militia unit <Book of Names, pg 12>); m .... . He received dependent area Burnetsfield lot #11 on the south side of the Mohawk River, which seems to fix him as an eldest son of a patentee Nicholas Weaver (the other Weaver patentees, Jacob Sr. & Jr., being matched up). Andrew was either a bit independent and/or lived way out, since his kin seldom show up near other Weavers on various militia and resident lists (note absence of Jacob or Nicholas offspring). By 1790, none of his line can be spotted in the Herkimer area census (or anywhere in Montgomery Co.for that matter). We suspect his sons may include the Andrew at Van Buren NY (Onandanga Co.) in 1832 and the Adam at Ellisburg NY in 1818.

    +9022: pr. CATHERINE MARGARET b say 1733-47; m 1765 JACOB MEYER
           (SAR 1765 rec says only a dau of And. Weber mar. a Meyer)
    +9023: ps. GEORGE A. (?) b say 1735; ps. Lt. in Revol.
    9024: HENRICH b say 1738; liv. 1760
    9025: BARBARA b say 1740; m 1762 MARCUS ITTIG (widower)
    9026: MARIA MARGARETHA b say 1743; liv. 1761 (spf Getman bp)
           ps. m 1764 JACOB DEEK
    9027: ELIZABETH b say 1745; had child 1763 by JAMES MACGNOT
    +9028: ADAM ANDR. b say 1750; liv. 1787 (spf Adam Ad. H. Weaver bp)
    9028A ps. ANDRIES b say 1756; liv. 1832 (pension applic. rejected)

9008: Lt. GEORGE J. WEAVER (aka "George John") - pr. born ca 1720 to 1733 (son of Jacob); died at Herkimer NY 2 Aug 1811; m Jan 1754 ELISABETH DUBOIS of Livingston Manor NY (ps. the Elisabeth, b 1737, dau of PETER DUBOIS & ANNETJE TER BOS); ps. m2 by 1793 MARIA ... (A George Weber Sr. & Maria sponsored Feb 1793 bp of David, son of Fr. Meyer). Of the three George Webers on the 1769 GF militia list, this one was pr. "George Jun." assuming the "George" was a son of immigrant Nicholas and the "George Jacobs" was a son of Jacob jr. Thus we surmise that George J. was a jr. in 1769 (ps. being younger than his cousin George N.), but just "George" later in the Revolution and in 1790. George was supposedly a Lieutenant in 1778 (DAR vol 23 page 338), but we see only a Lt. "George A." in the Book of Names (page 165). To help sort out the George Weavers we offer the following -

ID#	1769 GF Militia	Birth Year	Pr. father	wife
9013	George	1724	Nich. Sr.	Barbara
9008	George Jr.	1729	Jacob Sr.	Elisabeth
9029	George Jac.	1747	George (?)	Catherine

About 1773, our George J., along with Marc DeMuth & Christian Reigel, settled in the wilderness area of Deerfield NY (now Utica), but in 1776 was forced to pull back to more protected areas, having been warned by a friendly Indian of an imminent raid by British and Indians. George J. was later captured during the Revolution and suffered bad treatment for two years as a prisoner in Canada & England, before gaining freedom via an exchange (ENCYCLOPEDIA OF BIOGRAPHY OF NEW YORK, vol 7 page 105). George returned permanently to Deerfield about 1784 and, with related Weavers, had a primary role in Oneida County growth. His children are not well established. Despite tradition we do not think he was the father of Henry Van Renselaer Weaver (b 1782), who was pr. his grandson, via

George G. of the next generation, based on family bible notes (1980 Vivian Brock
letter to Mrs. Elis. Hull, 37 N. Howard St., Gettyburg PA 17325). As to other
children, the Edick Family Record by Nellie Horne Rhodes in 1911 says that
Elisabeth was George J.'s only daughter and that she had two brothers, George
Michael & Nicholas. The three children noted by Rhodes are the ones verifiable in
church records but to these we feel should be added the the Frederick G. Weaver in
Revolutionary service and the John George named executor by Jacob Weaver Jr.
(however we see no basis to assume John G. married a Mary Riegel, as in Deuel
notes at Oneida Hist. Soc.). Johannes George and Frederick G. were executors for
the 1793 will of Jacob Weaver jr., an understandable arrangement if John G. &
Frederick G. were say Jacob's eldest nephews in the area. This George J. looks to
be the George on the 1778 German Flats relief who was living at a distance from
Fort Dayton with 5 adults & 1 child in his household.

children of George J.

```
+9029: ps. GEORGE G.  ca 1747-1819  m CATHERINE
 9030: pr. JOHN G.  b say 1755; pr. liv. 1793 (will of Jacob jr.)
+9031: pr. FREDERICK G.  1757-1813  pr. m by 1784 CATHERINE
 9032: ELISABETH (dau of Geo.)  1760-1847  m 1777 JACOB EDICK
          pr. child bp SA 7 Aug 1760 (of Geo. & Elis., sp. Elis. Frank)
+9033: NICHOLAS G.  1762-1838 m 1785 GERTRUDE DYGERT
+9034: GEORGE MICHAEL  1763-1832  m 1788 CATHERINE HARTER
```

9013: **GEORGE NIC. WEAVER** - pr. born ca 1720 to 1728 (son of NICHOLAS); pr. died
before 1790 (not on census); pr. m by 1747 MARIA BARBARA EDICK (Ittig) ps. dau of
JACOB MICHAEL EDICK or MICHAEL EDICK. He is fixed by the 1760 bp record which
lists "Georg Nic." & wife Barbara as parents of George Michael Weber. It is
possible that the 1760 George Nic. Weber was a son of Nicholas jr., but we feel
that the number and age spread of the children below suggests a large family based
on an older George, probably a son of immigrant Nicholas (Sr.). Placing Jacob G.
Weaver as a son of this George hangs on the mention of Jacob G. as a "friend",
rather than a cousin, in the will of Peter Jac. Weaver. Margaret Weaver, wife of
Fred Meyer, was by one account a child of George N. (Comp. of Amer. Gen. v 7 page
68) but Deuel places her as a sister of the George Michel Weber of Deerfield who
died 1832 (E&N of 10 Jul 1929), a choice which gets support in her naming of an
early Meyer daughter as Elisabeth. Accepting her 1753 birthyear, we place her
below (as the above George J. presumably had no children before his 1754 marriage
to Elisabeth DuBois). Deuel and others have not distinguished between the various
George Michaels (i.e. the ones born in 1760, 1763, and 1764), but at least two of
them were at the 1779 Nicholas Smith estate sale and we think the George Michael,
son of this George N., pr. died during the latter years of the Revolution, so the
remaining George Michael (d 1832) then needed no further identifier.

```
+9035: ps. NICHOLAS   b say 1744; ps. m1 by 1770 CATHERINE
            m by 1777 ELISABETH
 9036: ps. BARBARA ELISABETH  b say 1748; m 1767 STOPHEL STROBEL
 9037: ps. CATHERINE  b say 1750; m 1768 ADAM N. STARING
+9038: pr. JACOB G.  1751-1820 m1 MARIA MCKOOM; m2 MARG. HELMER
 9039: pr. ANNA MARGARETHA  1753-1831  m 1772 FREDERICK MEYER
 9040: pr. MICHEL  b say 1758; in Revol. serv. (Book of Names)
            pr. liv. 1794 (spf Ittig bp) and m MARIA
 9041: GEORGE MICHAEL  b 7 Oct 1760 (sp Marc Ittig & w Marg); pr d y
 9042: pr. GEORGE MICHAEL  b 9 Feb 1764 (SAR sp Mich Ittig & w)
            liv. 1779 (N. Smith sale); pr. died 1780-2
 9043: pr. GERTRUDE GEO.  b say 1767; m 1786 PETER W. DYGERT
```

9011: HEINRICH NIC. WEAVER - pr. born ca 1712 to 1718; liv. 1769; m ANNA MARGARETHA ... (mother of Jacob in 1762). John Dockstader's land deed to Jacob N. Weber in 1754 notes that Henderik, son of Niclas Weber, lived nearby. Pr. the Henry in 1769 GF militia listed next to John DeMuth & Nicolas Hen. Weber.

+9045: NICHOLAS H. 1736-1824 m1 LENA ..; m2 CATH. FRANK
 9045A ps. BARBARA ELISABETH b say 1742; m 1769 JOHN CAMPBELL
+9046: MARGARET H. b say 1744; spf Bauman bp 1764 with Adam Smit
 9047: ps. HENRY b ca 1746; d Minden NY 23 May 1816 (age 69-10-5)
 9048: CATHERINE H. b say 1750; liv. 1786 (spf Cath. Barsh bp)
+9048A ps. ANNA b say 1752; liv. 1768 (spf Anna Smith bp)
        ps. the Anna who m by 1786 DUNCAN MCDOUGAL
+9049: ADAM H. b say 1755; m by 1787 CATHERINE ...
+9050: JACOB bp May 1762 (sp Geo Ecker & w.); m 1782 GERT. KAST

9003: JACOB WEAVER jr. - born say 1713; died 1793; m1 MARGARET ... (mother of John in 1760); pr. m2 MARIA ... (mother of Maria in 1766). In 1723 he had Burnetsfield lot #15 south of the Mohawk River. In 1793 he and Jacob N. Weaver both owned land in Cosby Manor lot #11 in Schuyler NY. His will dated 20 May 1793 lists children as Nicholas (eldest), George, Frederick, John, Peter (whose dau Elisabeth was to get a lamb), Appolonia (wife of John Frank) & Margaret (wife of George Jac. N. Weaver); executors were Johannes George Weaver & Frederick G. Weaver. Referred to as Jacob Weber "late" of Schuylertown in a 4 Sep 1793 bond between John Weber (pr. his son) and Jacob N. Weber.

+9052: JACOB JAC. b say 1740; m 1767 CATHERINE HESS (b 1744)
+9053: NICHOLAS J. b say 1743; pr. m 1764 GERTRUDE DEMUTH
+9054: GEORGE JACOBS (ps. adopted) m by 1778 CATHERINE (pr. Getman)
+9055: PETER JAC. b say 1748; m 1769 MARY CATHERINE FRANK
+9056: FREDERICK J. ca 1750-1826 pr. m1 GERTRUDE BELLINGER
 9057: APPOLONIA ca 1753-1817 m by 1776 JOHN FRANK
 9058: MARGARET b say 1758; m by 1777 GEORGE JAC. N. WEAVER
+9059: JOHN b SAR Dec 1760 (John Stphn Frank, Elis. N. Rittmans)
        Johannes Jac. m 1785 MARIA MEYER
 9060: pr. MARIA bp GF Apr 1766 (sp. Hen & Maria Meyer)

9015: JACOB N. WEAVER - born say 1727; liv. Deerfield NY 1810; m by 1750 CATHERINE ... (mother of Peter James) ps. a dau of GEORGE DOCKSTADER. On 16 Oct 1753 Niclas Weber, by his mark, sold Burnetsfield lot #16 to his son Jacob for 20 pounds currency (deed wit. by Fred Bell & Johannes Wever) and on 4 Apr 1754 Jacob Niclas Weber was deeded part of lot #21 from John Dockstader. Jacob N. was on the German Flats Committee of Safety in 1775 and in Feb 1779 sponsored bp of John, natural child of Margaret F. Bellinger. Jacob & Catherine sponsored Dec 1782 bp of George, son of John Dockstader & Cath. (Bellinger). On the 1790 HK census (2-2-2) and in 1791 he owned Burnetsfield lot #16 and half of lots 18 & 21 (formerly Geo. Dockstader land). An 1803 land note lists Jacob N.'s sons as George, Jacob, & Peter. In 1793 Jacob N. purchased 400 acres of Cosby Manor lot #11, part of which he sold on 10 Mar 1810 to Peter Weaver.

+9062: PETER JAMES b 1750; m 1780 MARY EDICK (pr. b ca 1748)
 9063: ps. ELISABETH b ca Apr 1754; d 1842; m JACOB BELL
+9064: GEORGE JAC. N. b say 1756; m by 1777 MARGARET JAC. WEAVER
+9065: JACOB JAC. N. 1760-1852 m 1786 MARGARET BAUM
 9066: CATHERINE b GF 8 Jan 1764 (sp Nic H Weber, Cath. Dockstader)
        d 1802 (childbirth neglect); m LORENTZ F. HARTER

9014: JOHN NIC. WEAVER - pr. born ca 1718 to 1738; pr. died 1770-77; m by 1757 ERNESTINA BELLINGER (aka Christina, b say 1738) dau of ADAM BELLINGER & APPOLONIA. John & Ernestina sponsored 1761 bp of Nicholas, son of George Adam Bauman & Elisabeth. A "John Nic. Weber" was in the 1769 GF militia, listed between Henry & Nicholas H. Weber and Henry & Fred Meyer (Book of Names page 13). This John seems gone before Sep 1778 as he is not mentioned on or after the German Flats relief.

   9067: GERRIT bp Schenectady 3 Dec 1757
   9068: MARGARETHA bp Schenectady 25 May 1760
   9069: NICHOLAS b GF 29 Jun 1763 (sp Nic Jac Weber & Ern. Bellngr)
   9070: ANNA b 17 Dec 1765 (sp. Anna Weber & Melchior Thum)

9006: JOHN JACOB WEAVER - pr. born ca 1718 to 1727; pr. m by ca 1743 MARIA ... Pr. the "Johannes Wever" who, with Frederick Bell, witnessed a 1753 deed in which immigrant "Niclas Weber" sold Burnetsfield lot #16 to his son Jacob N. (we think a transaction witness would not be so close a relation as a brother). John Wiver, Maria Wiver & child Margaret (wife & daughter?) were taken prisoner in the Nov 1757 French & Indian raid on German Flats and held in Canada until the fall of 1758 (Book of Names page 112). This man may have immigrated in the early 1750's and been the Johannis Weaver, who, with Christian & John Schell, was naturalized on 20 Dec 1763 (Book of Names page 6). "John Jacob Weavour" appears, adjacent to Henry Frank Jr. and John Wallrath, in the 1767 GF militia co. of Capt. Frank (Book of Names page 13) and in the 1769 GF militia he looks to be the "John Weber" listed next to Jost Petrie & Melchior Thum. In 1771 we note a John Weaver on the Burnetsfield Minister's support list near the Schells. Despite mention of "John Jacob Weber" on the Tryon Co. Committee of Safety in September 1775 (Mohawk Valley in the Revolution, page 42), we think this John became the Tory "Hannes wever" by 1776 (ibid, page 183) and probably was the "uncle" in Montreal who assisted patriot prisoner Andrew Pfeiffer in 1782. Weavers named as Tories in The United Empire Loyalist List include a Frederick, John, Peter, Nicholas & Christy (all of whom served in the British Royal Regiment for New York).

  +9071: ps. FREDERICK b say 1744; m by 1768 MARIA ...
   9072: ps. MARGARET b say 1746; taken captive to Canada 1757
   9072A ps. PETER b say 1750; liv. 1786 (Tory in Canada)
   9073: ps. CHRIS b say 1752; liv. 1776 (N. Smith acct book, HCH)
   9074: ps. NICHOLAS b say 1755; liv. 1786 (Tory in Canada)

9005: NICHOLAS WEAVER - born say 1718 (pr. son of JACOB); m by 1737 ELISABETH ... Joh. Nich. Weber & Anna Elisabeth were members of Schenectady Church 1737. Hieronymus (Jeronimus) and others appear later at Schoharie.

  +9075: ps. JERONIMUS b say 1735; m ELISABETH at Schenectady
   9076: ps. HENRICH b say 1737; liv. 1773 (Schoharie NY)
   9077: ps. ANNATJE b say 1744; m bef 1775 JACOB WESTVAAL of Schn.
   9078: ps. NICHOLAS b say 1746; Revol. service (Fisher's Reg.)
  +9079: ps. JACOB b say 1748; of Schenectady; m GEERTJE VAN VLIET

9012: NICHOLAS WEAVER jr - pr. born ca 1715 to 1720 (pr. son of NICHOLAS); m by 1760 MARGARET ..., who was pr. the ANNA MARGARETHA SMITH (b 1717) dau of GEORGE SMITH. A Nicholas (either he or his father) received lot #4 at Burnetsfield in 1744 from Ephraim Smith (L. Bellinger's notes at HCH). In 1762 Nicholas Weber jr. bought land along the West Canada Creek from Cornelius Cuyler of Albany, which he sold for a low price in 1778 to Nicholas Smith (Marten's son), who we suspect was his nephew and/or godson (see appendix pages 333-6 for role of Weavers in Nicholas Smith estate auction). Nicholas & his wife Margaret sponsored the Aug 1760 bp of

Nicholas, son of Augustinus Hess & Anna (Schell).   Nicholas Jr. was in the 1757
GF militia and in the 1769 GF militia we think he was the "Jo⌐n Nicholas" listed
near Adam Helmer's four sons, George Weaver, & John Ph. Bellinger).   Tradition of
a Jacob Weber with three brothers (John, Nicholas, and George) killed in the
French & Indian War, seems to fit as sons of this Nichoals.

      9080: pr. CATHERINE b say 1734; m FREDERICK P. BELLINGER (b 1727)
      9081: pr. GEORGE b say 1736; ps. killed in Fr. & Indian War
      9082: pr. ELISABETH b say 1738; m by 1758 GEORGE ADAM BAUMAN
      9083: pr. NICHOLAS b say 1740; ps. killed in Fr. & Indian War
      9083A ps. JOHN b say 1742; ps. killed in Fr. & Indian War
      9084: pr. MARGARET (Weaver?) b say 1744; m by 1762 HENRY MEYER
      9084A ps. ANNA (Weaver?) b say 1746; m by 1766 GEORGE DEMUTH
    +9085: pr. JACOB JOH. N. b say 1748; d 1779; m 1766 MARGARET MEYER
      9086: ps. APPOLONIA b say 1750; liv. 1766 (spf Bauman bp)

9004: PETER WEAVER - pr. born ca 1711 to 1718; m MARGARETHA DYGERT (b 1715) dau
of PETER DYGERT & ANNA ELISABETH FOX (Bellinger book page 15).   Widow Margaret m2
WILLIAM FINK. Pr. the Ens. Peter in Col. Herkimer's 1767 militia co. and the
Peter who had children Frederick, Peter, Henry, & Nicholas, all admitted to first
communion at Stone Arabia on 3 Aug 1788.

    +9089: ps. ELISABETH (existence?)   ps. m 1767 JOHN PURCK
      9090: BARABARA ELISABETH b 7 May 1755 (G Dckstder,Barb Tygert ..)
                     pr. m JOHN F. DOCKSTADER.
      9059: MARGARETHA bp SA 5 May 1757 (sp Wm Dygert & w. M. Elis.)
    +9091: ps. NICHOLAS b say 1759; m ELISABETH ZOELLER
      9092: ps. HENRICUS b say 1761; in Revl. (Porr DAR ref., not seen)
      9093: PETER   b SAR 14 Jan 1764 (sp. Peter Dygert & w. Barbara)
      9094: FREDERICK b SAR 28 Jan 1766 (sp F. Getman, Elis. Emige)
                   pr. m by 1806 MARGARET ...
      9095: CATHERINE b say 1767; m JACOB PLANCK (Mrs. E. Hull notes)
          (ps. the child bp SAR 11 Sep 1768, sp. Hen. Dockstader)

WEAVER - 3rd Generation

9028: ADAM AND. WEAVER - pr. born ca 1740 to 1760 (son of Andries); pr. m by 1787
MARIA ... Adam Andr. & Maria were sponsors for Jun 1787 bp of Adam, son of Adam
H. Weaver. Not seen in Herkimer area on 1790 census. Ps. the Adam Weaver (b ca
1757) of Ellisburg NY in 1818 (age 61 then, pension application courtesy of Mrs.
Arthur Kelly, Box 129, RD 1, Rhinebeck NY 12572).

9049: ADAM HEN. WEAVER - pr. born ca 1740 to 1765 (son of Henry Nic.); m by 1787
CATHERINE ... ; pr. m2 by 1794 GERTRUDE ...(ps. Hess). Adam Weaver & wife
Catherine, parents of Adam & Conrad, were sponsors for Jul 1786 bp of Anna Eva,
dau of John Campbell & Barbara Elisabeth (Weaver). Pr. the Adam on 1790 German
Flats census (1-2-1), living near widow Barbara Campbell, R. Furman, & Ludwig
Campbell.

      9096: ADAM b 28 Jun 1787 (sp. Adam Andr. Weaver & Maria)
      9097: Johan CONRAD b 22 May 1791 (sp. John Cample & Cath. Klein)
               by 2nd wife (Gertrude)
      9098: CHRISTIAN b 3 Jun 1794 (sp Christian Hess & Elis.<Kast>)

9031: FREDERICK G. WEAVER - ps. the Frederick born ca 1757 (calc. from death age); died German Flats 6 Jun 1813 age 56 (ch. death rec. says he was blacksmith at GF); m by 1784 CATHERINE ... Frederick & Catherine sponsored Jan 1784 bp of Catherine, dau of Peter James Weaver & Maria (Edick), plus Oct 1788 bp of Catherine, dau of Jacob Ittig & Elis. (Weaver), plus Aug 1794 bp of Elisabeth, dau of George Michael Weaver & Catherine, and Oct 1794 bp of Wilhelm, son of Nicholas G. Weaver & Gertrude (Dygert). Frederick G. was in Col. Bellinger's Revol. Regiment but not on the 1778 GF relief (ps. still in the household of his father George then). He appears on the 1790 Herkimer census (2-0-2, Deerfield group). If he was not much older than we have projected (i.e. assuming we have matched the right dates with this Frederick), then the absence of church baptismal entries we think is a good indication that he had no children. This leads us to speculate that the other male and female in his 1790 household may have been adopted.

9056: FREDERICK JAC. WEAVER - born ca 1750; died Deerfield, Oneida Co., NY 16 Mar 1826 age 75 (HK Ch. rec.); pr. m GERTRUDE JOH. BELLINGER (b ca 1761) dau of JOHN BELLINGER & ELISABETH BARBARA FOLTS (see Bellinger book page 25 and First Settlers of Schenectady page 294); pr. m2 by 1791 MARIA ... . In the 1769 GF militia he looks to have been the Friederik listed just before Jacob (pr. father) & Nicholas Jun. (pr. brother, see Book of Names list, page 13). Fritz Weaver & wife Gertrude sponsored Jul 1787 bp of John, son of Fred. Meyer & Margaret. A Frederick J. Weaver was on the 1790 Herkimer census (1-2-2) and we think he resided then in the Herkimer town area, perhaps on Burnetsfield lot #19 (1791 property list).

+9099: FREDERICK   b GF 4 Mar 1779 (sp Cath Bellingr, John Bellingr)
  9100: ELISABETH   bp Schenectady 25 Jan 1781
          ps. m by 1805 ANDREW CLAPSADDLE jr
  9101: JOHANNES   bp GF 4 Jul 1785 (sp John Weaver & Maria)
          pr. by 2nd wife (Maria)
  9102: pr. DANIEL   b GF 19 Mar 1791 (sp Peter Weaver & Maria)

9071: FREDERICK WEAVER - pr. born ca 1740 to 1747 (ps. son of John); ps. died before 1790 (not on HK area census); m by 1768 MARIA ...; ps. m2 by 1776 ELISABETH ... (a Fritz & Elisabeth had dau then). He & Maria sponsored 1768 SAR bp of Nicholas, son of Jacob Weaver & Margaret. Either this man or the above Fred. Jac. Weber was pr. the F. Weber, widower, at Jul 1777 bp of Jacob, son of Peter Jac. Weber. On the other hand, this Frederick may have moved his residence, or perhaps have died in Revolutionary War combat, between 1776 and 1778 as he seems absent from the 1778 GF relief and from the 1779 Nicholas Smith estate sale. As the oldest Frederick seen we have put under him the Bellinger Regiment soldier "George F. Weber". Was pr. the Frederick who appears in the 1769 GF militia list separate from the other Weavers and near John & Christian Schell. A possibiltiy exists that this man went to Canada during the Revolution and was the Frederick Weaver who fought on the Tory side, along with a John and Peter Weaver, in the Royal Rangers unit (The Old United Empire Loyalists List).

  9103: pr. GEORGE F.   b say 1763; in Revol. service
          ps. by 2nd wife (Elisabeth)
  9104: ps. ELISABETH F.   b GF 7 May 1776 (sp. Geo. Orendorf & Elis.)

9023: Lt. GEORGE A. WEAVER (existence questionable, initial "A" implies son of Andries) - Book of Names (page 165) has him a Lieut. in Col. Bellinger's Revol. Regiment, but we think that may be a mistaken reference to Lt. George J. Weaver. No George A. appears elsewhere in militia or church records. A more likely descendent in the line of Andries was the Andrus Weaver of Van Buren (Onondaga Co.) NY whose Revolutionary War pension application was rejected ca 1832.

9029: GEORGE G. WEAVER - pr. born ca 1747 (calc. birthyear from death age); died
Deerfield NY 9 Jul 1819 (HK Ch. rec. which gives him as "George Weber", a farmer
age 72); m CATHERINE ... (b ca 1745, d 18 Jan 1829 age 84, from Mrs. Elis. Hull
notes), pr. CATHERINE GETMAN dau of Capt. FREDERICK GETMAN (Getman book has
Frederick's daughter Catherine marrying a George Weaver, but date info is bad).
They were pr. married by 1768 as a George Weaver & Catherine sponsored the Jan
1768 bp of Catherine, dau of Nicholas Christman & Susanna. The middle initial "G"
has not been seen with any George Weaver in the early militia, church or census
(1790) records. But then in a note lending money to Lorentz P. Harter, dated 3
Aug 1793, he appears as "George G. Weaver" of Schuyler Town (witness to the note
was "Gorg i Weber"). Subsequently in family bible notes and other papers held by
descendents there are references to "George G." (Vivian Brock letter of 18 Sep
1980 to Mrs. Elis. Hull, Gettysburg PA) which seem to indicate that he had
children John G. (b May 1776, d 3 Sep 1835 age 59-3-12), Catherine (m John Hicks),
and Henry V.R. (b 1782). In 1811 John G. Weaver & wife Margaret purchased Trenton
Road cemetery land near Utica where burial plots seem to link John G. and Henry
V.R. as sons of George G. (Mrs. Elis. Hull notes). The GF Church records show a
George Weaver & Catherine had a son John, b May 1776, who fits exactly the John G.
(d 1835), whom Weaver descendents believe was a son of George G. From 1776 to
1779, Getmans appear as sponsors for each of three children born at GF to George
Weaver & Catherine, thereby establishing the tie to Catherine Getman, mentioned as
wife of George Weaver in the will of Frederick Getman. George, as father, was
listed as "George Jac." on the 1778 bp record of daughter Catherine, which could
have been a minister's error, but we feel instead that it may be a clue to the
hypothesis that George G. and George Jac. were the same person. Pr. was the
George who had 2 adults & 1 child on the 1778 GF relief and the George on the 1790
Herkimer census (1-3-5, Deerfield group). A Margaret & Elizabeth Smith, young
daughters of Joseph Smidt & Appolonia (Harter) were bound out to George Weaver &
Catherine in 1792 (GF Ch. rec.).

    9105: JOHANNES   b 18 May 1776 (sp. John Weaver & Margaret Getman)
            pr. the John G. d 3 Sep 1835 age 59-3-12; m MARGARET
            ps. the John Jr of Schuyler who m WHS 1796 MARGARET WEAVER
    9106: pr. CATHERINE b GF 26 Jun 1778 (dau of Geo. Jac. & Cath.)
            (sp. Peter Getman, Cath. Herkimer); pr. d. young
    9107: CATHERINE b 26 Aug 1779 (sp. Gert. Bellinger, Peter Getman)
            m JOHN HICKS (ment. in George G. Weaver will)
  +9108: HENRY V.R.   1782-1822 m by 1804 ELISABETH BAUMAN

9054: GEORGE JAC. WEAVER - pr. born ca 1740 to 1750; name in records from 1769 to
1793; m by 1778 CATHERINE ... (wife of George Jac. Weber who had daughter
Catherine b GF Jun 1778). In the 1769 GF militia we have George Jacobs Weber
listed just after Jacob Jacobs Weber & Peter Weber, in what seems to be a cluster
of the children of Jacob Weber jr. Later in the 1793 will of Jacob Weber jr.
mention is made of a son George (pr. middle aged then). We have searched in vain
for evidence of this George Jac. on the 1778 GF relief, the 1779 Nicholas Smith
estate sale, and the 1790 census, but the only unaccounted for George on such
records seems to fit the above George G. Weaver. It is possible of course that
there were two George Weavers, of about the same age, who both had wives named
Catherine. However, we feel the indications point more likely to a single person
who was known mostly as just George before 1793 (only occasionally as George Jac.)
and as George G. thereafter. This has lead us to the assumption of a single George
(b ca 1747, son of George), who was perhaps adopted by Jacob Weber Jr. (thus
listed as his son in the 1793 will) and, after the 1793 death of Jacob Weaver jr.,
became known as George G. Weaver.

9034: GEORGE MICHAEL WEAVER - born 17 Nov 1763 (son of Lt. George J.); died
Deerfield NY 4 Dec 1832 age 69 (bur. Trenton Rd Weaver Cem., later moved to Forest
Hill Cem.); m GF 1 Jan 1787 CATHERINE HARTER (b 17 Nov 1765, d 1846) dau of
FREDERICK HARTER & APPOLONIA BELLINGER as in DAR vol 114 page 311. Was a fifer in
the Amer. Revolution. His son George (aka George Mich. jr) was the first white
male born at Deerfield NY (E&N 29 Aug 1934). On 1790 Herkimer census (1-1-1).

```
        9109: Johan GEORGE   b 15 Jan 1788; m 1813 DELIA BELLINGER
        9110: ABIGAIL   b 6 Sep 1790 (sp. Nic Weaver); m ADAM BOWMAN
        9111: FREDERICK GEORGE   b 16 Jul 1792 (sp. Fred. Weaver & Cath.)
                      d 1862; m 1817 MARGARET P. F. BELLINGER
        9112: ELISABETH b 16 Aug 1794 (sp. Phil. Harter & Elis.); unm
        9113: THOMAS   b say 1797;   m NANCY CRIM
                      ps. m2 by 1822 ANNA MEYER
        9114: CATHERINE   b 4 Nov 1799; d 1844; m PETER G. STEELE
        9115: JACOB GEORGE   1802-1886   m CAROLINE WELLS
        9116: EVA   b 10 Apr 1805; m (as 2nd wife) ADAM BOWMAN
```

9064: GEORGE JACOBS NIC. WEAVER - pr. born ca 1755 to 1759 (pr. son of Jacob N. &
Cath.); m by 1777 MARGARETHA WEAVER dau of JACOB WEAVER jr.   A George J. N. Weber
had 2 adults on 1778 GF relief.   On 1790 Herkimer census (2-2-5, Deerfield group).

```
        9117: ANNA MARGRETHA   b 27 Sep 1777 (sp Peter Jac. Weber); pr. d y
        9118: JACOB   bp GF 3 Jul 1779 (sp. Jac. Weaver & Cath.)
        9119: GEORGE   bp 4 Jan 1781 (sp. Geo Mich. Weaver, Cath. Weaver)
                      ps. m by 1810 ELISABETH CHRISTMAN (b 1784)
        9120: MARGARET   b 14 Jul 1782 (sp. Peter Weaver & Maria)
        9121: CATHERINE   bp 15 Jun 1786 (sp. Joh. Dockstader & Cath.)
        9122: GERTRUDE   bp 23 Jan 1788 (sp. Fred. Weaver & Gert.)
        9123: APPOLONIA   b SJR 11 Jun 1791 (sp F. Riegel, Cath. Weber)
        9124: MARIA   b SJR 11 Dec 1792 (sp Peter J N Weber & Maria)
```

9038: JACOB G. WEAVER   ("King" Weaver) - born Sep 1751; died 28 Nov 1820 (age
69-2-); m1 by 1774 MARIA MCKOOMS dau of ANDREW MCKOOMS (E&N of 10 Jul 1929); m2
MARGARET HELMER (b 28 Oct 1763, d 30 Nov 1831 age 68) dau of FREDERICK HELMER &
BARBARA ELISABETH HOMAN. His birth year before 1754 and early naming of child
Barbara support descent from George Nic. & Barbara, even though in 1791 he owned
immigrant Jacob's Burnetsfield lot #10. Had 2 adults & 2 children on 1778 GF
relief and was on 1790 Herkimer census (2-0-3). He went into the fur business
with J. Astor and amassed lots of property (Bellinger book pg 76). Children below
marked as "pr." have the parents listed only as Jacob (no middle initial G.) &
Maria; see earlier Apr 1766 bp of Maria, dau of Jacob (Jr.?) & Maria.

```
        9125: MARIA BARBARA   bp GF 2 Jan 1779 (sp Mel. Folts & Eva)
        9126: pr. CATHERINE   b GF 8 Jan 1780 (sp Thomas Bell, Cath. Weaver)
        9127: GEORGE MICHEL   b 11 Dec 1780 (sp Geo Mic Weber, Lena McKoom)
        9128: pr. THOMAS   b GF 4 Feb 1782 (sp Jacob Bell & Elis.)
        9129: CONRAD   b 7 Jul 1783 (sp. Conrad Vols & Anna Marg.)
        9130: ELISABETH   b 25 Jun 1785 (sp Phil. Harter, Anna MacKooms)
        9131: GEORGE   b 20 Nov 1786 (sp. Geo. P. Weaver, Sara McKooms)
        9132: CATHERINE   b 24 Sep 1787 (sp. Geo. Hen. Bell & Cath.)
                      pr. the Cath. 1785(sic)-1857 m FRED DOCKSTADER
        9133: JOHANNES   b 7 Jan 1793 (sp. John McKoom, Marie Ad. Smith)
                      by second wife
        9134: MARY BARBARA   1798-1874 m FRED P. BELLINGER
        9135: ANNA MARGARET   1801-1872 m CHRISTOPHER C. BELLINGER
```

9050: JACOB H. WEAVER - born SAR 22 May 1762; m GF 17 Feb 1782 GERTRUDE KAST dau of FREDERICK KAST & ELISABETH HELMER. On 1790 GF census (1-1-3). Pr. the Jacob & Gert. of Frankfort who sp. 1807 bp of John, son of John Baum.

        9136: ANNA MARGARET   b 10 Jun 1782; m 1823 CHRISTP. BELLINGER jr
        9137: ELISABETH   b 26 Aug 1784; m 1802 GEORGE WITRIG (Weiderich)
        9138: PAUL   b 1 Oct 1786 (sp. George Kast, Eliz. Smidt)
        9139: PETER   bp SJR 18 Jul 1790 (sp Peter Hayer, Cath. Kass)

9052: JACOB JAC. WEAVER - pr. born ca 1735 to 1748; pr. died 1776; m SAR 19 Nov 1767 CATHERINE HESS (b 1744, d 1821) dau of JOHN HESS jr & MARGARET YOUNG. Was in 1769 GF militia and had 5 children (E&N 12 Feb 1930, "Hess Family"). His widow m2 by 1782 CHRISTOPHER PH. FOX. Pr. the soldier Jacob Weaver who was hit by Capt. Winn for insubordination and died soon after, as reported to the Tryon Co. Committee of Safety in Nov 1776.

       +9140: JACOB   bp GF 28 Aug 1768; ps. m 1791 MARGARET FRANK
        9141: ps. DANIEL   b say 1770; liv. 1790 (spf Eva Hess bp)
        9142: ps. MARGARET   b say 1772; liv. 1792 (spf L. Weaver bp)

9065: JACOB JAC. NIC. WEAVER - born 17 Mar 1760; died 9 Mar 1852 (Deuel's cemetery inscriptions have Jacob as died at Adams NY 9 Mar 1853 age 94); m German Flats 24 Jul 1786 MARGARET BAUM ("Boom", b 1763, d Adams NY 9 Jul 1855 age 92 <sic, death age computes to birthyear 1760>) dau of ABRAHAM BAUM & DOROTHY CUNINGHAM. Was sponsor for Jan 1786 bp of Jacob, son of Johannes Jac. Weber & Maria Meyer. A Jacob & Margaret sponsored Oct 1795 bp of Eva, dau of John Hiller & Cath.

        9143: JACOB   b 17 Mar 1787 (sp. Lorentz Harter &)
        9144: ABRAHAM   bp SJR 3 Mar 1789 (sp John Delany, Gert. Baum)
        9145: PETER   b 1 Feb 1793 (sp Pet. Weber jr, Maria Weber)
        9146: CATHARINA   b 27 Jun 1795 (sp. Hen. Meyer & Cath. Baum)
        9147: JOHN   b 1802; liv. 1853 (Adams NY)

9079: JACOB WEAVER - pr. born ca 1742 to 1755; m GEERTJE VAN VLIET. A guess that Jacob descends from the GF Weavers (ps. son of Nicholas in immigrant Jacob's line). Children, all bp at Schenectady NY, were BENJAMIN (bp 16 May 1779), LYDIA (bp Mar 1781), ZACHARIAS (bp 24 Dec 1786), & BLANDINA (bp Mar 1789).

9085: JACOB JOH. N. WEAVER - born say 1746; killed by Tory raiders ca 1779 while gathering in his crops (1982 notes of Mrs. W. E. Gronberg, 313 N. Dixon Ave, Dixon Illinois 61021); m SAR 13 Apr 1766 MARGARET MEYER a sister of JOSEPH MEYER and Judge Meyer (ibid), thus dau of PETER MEYER. Traditon is that he had brothers John, Nicholas, & George, all of whom were killed in the French war (ibid). A Jacob & Margaret sponsored Nov 1777 bp of Marg., dau of Lorentz Meyer. Gronberg notes say son John went to Schenectady, had 2 children, and died a young man.

       +9148: JOHANNES   b SAR 6 Jun 1767 (sp. John Meyer & Maria)
                  pr. m by 1789 MAGDALENA KELLER
       +9149: Johan NICHOLAS   bp SA 1 Sep 1768 (sp. Fred. Weber & Maria)
                  d Illinois ca 1844 (age 76); m BARBARA KELLER
        9150: HENRICH   b SAR 29 Nov 1769 (sp Hen Harter & Cath.); ps. d y
       +9151: JACOB   b say 1771; m by 1803 EVA FRANK
       +9152: MICHEL   b 1774; d 1842; m 1800 GERTRUDE FRANK
       +9153: PETER   b GF 17 Aug 1776 (sp Math. Meyer, Elis. Piper)
                  m 1797 MERCY SAILES
        9154: MARGARET   b GF 29 Jul 1779 (H. Harter,); m 1795 JOHN SMITH

-265-

9075: JERONIMUS WEAVER - pr. born ca 1735 to 1740; m ELISABETH. Two children were baptised at Schoharie (SHH) and we think a tie is likely to the Henry Weber and Jacob Weber, both married, who were sponsors for children of William Laux at Schoharie from 1773 to 1775.

> 9155: CATHERINE   b 31 Jan 1758 (SHH sp Jacob Zimmer & w.)
> 9156: CATERINA   bp Schenectady NY 6 Oct 1762
> 9157: EBERHARD   b Hellenberg 22 Aug 1784 (SHH sp Ebrhd Burgele & w).

9059: JOHANNES JAC. WEAVER - pr. the Johannes born SAR 20 Dec 1760 (son of Johan Jacob & Anna Margaretha); killed in War of 1812 (see Enterprise & News 29 Aug 1934); m German Flats 28 Mar 1785 MARIA MEYER pr. dau of JOHN MEYER & MARIA H. FRANK. This John looks like the son of Jacob jr. whose 1793 will mentioned children of his son John as Jacob, Maria, Margaret, and Catherine (fits with children below if Catherine was child bp 1792). Probably the John Weaver on the 1790 German Flats census (2-1-2) in the Frankfort area with Law. Frank & Moyer nearby. A guess that the extra adult male in his 1790 household was an orphaned son of brother Jacob.

> 9158: JACOB   b 27 Jan 1786 (sp Jacob Jac. N. Weaver, Elis. Meyer)
> 9159: MARIA   b 13 Jan 1788 (sp. Peter Jac. Weaver & Maria)
> 9160: MARGARET   b SJR 31 Jan 1790 (sp Geo. Weber, Marg. Weber)
> 9161: child (pr. Cath.) bp 29 Jul 1792 (sp. Majer)
> 9162: JOHANNES   b 28 Jan 1795; m SALLY KELLOGG
>   (sp. Capt. John Meyer & Anna Maria)
> 9163: EVA
> 9164: ELISABETH   (see Enterprise & News 29 Aug 1934)

9033: NICHOLAS G. WEAVER - bp Stone Arabia 5 Apr 1762 (son of George & Elisabeth, bp. sp. Nicholas son of Jacob Weber Sr. & Catherine dau of Lorentz Harter); died 1838; m 1785 GERTRUDE DYGERT (b 1767, d 1851) dau of WILLIAM DYGERT & MARIA ELIZABETH ECKER. Sponsors for baptism of children were George Michel Weber & Cath. (1791), Fred. Weaver & Cath. (1794), Rudolph Shoemaker & w. Marg. (1804), and Hen. Meyer & w. Eva of Herkimer (1808). Nicholas G. Weaver was on the 1790 Herkimer census (1-1-2, Deerfield group). The will of Nicholas of Deerfield dated 16 May 1837 mentions wife Gertrude, sons Amasa (pr. Amos), Jeremiah, & Nicholas, and dau Elisabeth.

> 9165: ELISABETH N.   b 13 Mar 1787 (sp Geo Klepsattle & Anna)
>   m AMASA ROWE (Jeremias Weber was spf Rowe bp 1812)
> 9166: JEREMIAS   b 2 Oct 1788 (sp Geo. Jac. Weber & Cath.)
>   m MARIA TYLER
> 9167: NICHOLAS N.   1791-1853 m ELIZABETH SHOEMAKER
> 9168: WILHELM   b 17 Oct 1794; m HANNAH P. JAMES
> 9169: ISAAC   b Shyler 11 May 1804; ps. d. young
> 9169A AMOS   b Deerfield 6 Nov 1808; m LYDIA BELLINGER

9035: NICHOLAS WEAVER - pr. born ca 1740 to 1754; ps. m1 by 1770 CATHERINE ... (a Nich. Weber & Catherine were sponsors for Feb 1770 bp of Nicholas, son of Adam Staring & Catherine <Weaver>); m by 1778 ELISABETH ... The existence of a separate Nicholas here is not well established (info may be composite from other Nic. Weavers).

> +9170: ps. GEORGE N.   b say 1774; m by 1795 MARGARET
> 9171: JOSEPH   b 2 Feb 1778 (sp. Joseph Meyer, Elis. Lentz)

9045: NICHOLAS H. WEAVER - born German Flats 1736 (son of Hen.); died Deposit NY 1824; m1 by 1769 LENA ... (poss. Meyer?); m2 1772 CATHERINE FRANK (b 1731, d 1824) widow of JACOB EDICK as in DAR vol. 129, page 192-3. This Nicholas was badly wounded at the Battle of Oriskany as related in Parson´s "Mohawk Valley Edicks". He was a sponsor, with Cath. Dockstader, for 1764 bp of Catherine, dau of Jacob Weaver & Catherine. Later he appears on the 1778 German Flats relief with 2 adults and 7 children (3 or 4 of whom were pr. Ittigs from wife´s first marriage) and in 1792 he and his wife moved to Deposit NY, near Tompkins in Sullivan Co., along with their younger children Catherine and Henry (ibid).

                    surname WEAVER
      9172: JOHANNES b 19 Aug 1769 (sp. Joh. Smidt, Anna Eva Mayer)
      9173: FREDERICK b SAR 9 Jan 1771 (sp. Fr. Meyer, Anna Weber)
                  by 2nd wife
      9174: CATHERINE 1774-1852 m JOHN WHITAKER
      9175: JOHN NICHOLAS bp Jul 1777 (sp Joh. Nich. Franck & Marg.)
      9176: HENRICH bp GF 6 Jun 1779 (sp Hen Meyer, Cath. Weber)

9053: NICHOLAS JAC. WEAVER - pr. born ca 1735 to 1743; m SAR 18 Dec 1764 GERTRUDE DEMUTH (her 1832 will mentions dau Charity and a John Bellinger, ps. her grandson). Probably the son of Jacob Weber Jr. who was a sponsor, with Catherine Harter, for Apr 1762 bp of Nicholas, son of George Weber & Elisabeth. Then a "Joh. Nich. Joh. Jac Weber" was sponsor, with Ernestina Bellinger, for 1763 GF bp of Nicholas, son of John Weaver & Ernestina. Finally he found the right girl and we see "Nicol. Joh. Jac. Weaver" as a sponsor, with Gertrude Demuth, at Jul 1763 bp of Gertrude, dau of George Dockstader & Magdalena (Weaver). Ps. the Nicholas Weber jr. in 1769 GF militia and the Nicholas who had 2 adults & 4 children on 1778 GF relief. He was pr. father of Catherine P. Weaver, who married John Bellinger of Utica, even though her middle initial seems wrong on the GF church record. Was on 1790 Herkimer census (1-1-4), Deerfield group.

     +9177: CATHERINE b 29 Aug 1765 (sp Cath. Dockstdder, Jac. Weber)
             pr. m GF 1785 Maj. JOHN BELLINGER
     9178: pr. ELISABETH JOH. N. b say 1772; m 1794 CHRISTIAN SILLEBACH
     9179: ANNA J. NIC. b say 1774; liv. 1851; m 1794 JOHN DEMUTH
     9180: MARGARET b 27 Feb 1776 (George Jac N Weber, Margaret Weber)
             ps. m WHS 1796 JOHN WEAVER jr
     9181: GERTRUDE b 21 Sep 1778 (sp. Joh. Bellinger, A. Marg. Demuth)
             "Charity" (made will 1851); m PETER WEAVER jr.
     9182: JOHANNES b 3 Aug 1781 (sp. Peter Weber & Maria); liv. 1851

9182A: NICHOLAS WESER (Weiser or Wafer, not GF Weaver family!) - born say 1751; m by 1781 MARGARET WALLRATH. Nicholas Weser & Margaret Wallrath sponsored the Aug 1771 SAL bp of Josias Freth and pr. were married by 1774 (had child Elisabeth Weser, bp SAL Sep 1774, sp. Adolph H. Wallrath ...). Children shown below as they appear in Rosencrantz GF churckbook and have similar name to Weber.

     9183: CATHARINE b GF 19 Mar 1781 (sp. Jacob Wallrath & Cath.)
     9184: Johan PETER b 8 Jan 1783 (sp. Joh. Peter Wallrath & Rachel)

9055: PETER JAC. WEAVER - pr. born ca 1740 to 1750; died by 1800 (will executed then); m Palatine NY 7 Feb 1769 MARIA CATHERINE FRANK dau of CONRAD FRANK. In 1769 GF militia and ps. the Peter J. at 1777 Oriskany battle. His wife was listed as Anna on the Jul 1777 bp of son Jacob P. and then Peter Jac. & Anna sponsored Sep 1777 bp of Margaret, dau of George J. N. Weaver & Margaret (Jac. Weaver). Pr. the Peter with 4 adults & 3 children on 1778 GF relief and the Peter J. Weaver on the 1790 Herkimer census (2-3-2), apparently in the town area, and we think this was the same person who was half owner of Burnetsfield lot #10 in 1791. His will in 1800 names sons Peter (eldest), Jacob, & John, and daughter Elisabeth Griffin; executor was "friend" Jacob G. Weaver.

children of PETER JAC.

9185: GEORGE b SAR 3 Jul 1769 (sp Geo. Weber, Anna Frank)
  pr. died bef. 1800 (not in father´s will)
+9186: PETER P. b say 1775; m 1802 ELISABETH BODMAN
+9187: JACOB P. bp GF 20 Jul 1777 (sp Fr. Weber widower, E. Ittig)
  d 1864; m CATHERINE BELLINGER
9188: ELISABETH b 18 Nov 1780 (sp. Joh. Nicolas Weber & Gertrude)
  m1 Mr. GRIFFIN (Russel?); m2 1805 GEORGE L. HARTER
9189: JOHN b 11 Mar 1784 (sp Joh. Weaver, Cath. Weaver)
  d HK 9 Dec 1805, age 21, "constantly intoxicated"

9062: PETER JAMES WEAVER - born 1750 (son of Jacob N. & Katherine, as in Cdmr. Bellinger´s HCH files); m 1780 MARIA EDICK (pr. b ca 1748 if she was the widow of Petri Weber who died at Herkimer NY 30 Dec 1825 age 77). Peter was wounded at the Oriskany battle and while recovering he carved bowls out of the knot of an ash tree and made a hutch table still owned by Weaver descendents (Weaver History ms. by Mich. J. Lonergan, 1978). He lived on the farm on what is now Richardson Drive in North Utica (ibid). On 1790 HK census (1-2-3), Deerfield area.

9190: JACOB bp GF 31 Dec 1781 (sp Jac. Weber & Gert. Demuth)
9191: CATHERINE b GF 9 Jan 1784 (sp. Fritz Weaver & Cath.)
9192: PETER jr b 1786; m by 1813 GERTRUDE WEAVER
9193: ELISABETH bp SJR 15 Feb 1789 (sp Jac. Ittig, Elis. Weber)
9194: MARGARET b 22 Apr 1791 (sp. Marcus Ittig & Cath. Meyer)
9195: MARKS b SJR 7 Oct 1793; m by 1817 ABIGAIL BARNARD
9196: MARY b 1796; spf 1813 Gris. Weber bp; m HENRY VAN BUREN
9197: JOHN m MARY NORTHRUP (Mrs. E. Hull notes, 1983)

9044: WILLIAM WEAVER Esqr. (pr. should be Veeder, not Weaver) - He & Elisabeth sponsored Jan 1791 GF bp of Elis., dau of John M. Petrie & Dorothy.

9048A ANN WEAVER - m by 1786 DUNCAN MCDOUGAL. Lived at Schenectady NY (Pearson´s Schenectady book, pg 109). Duncan was at the 1779 Nicholas Smith estate sale.

9089: ELISABETH WEAVER (?) - b say 1748; m SAR 29 Apr 1767 JOHN PURCK. Another John Purck may have married Elisabeth Riemensneider in Oct 1766 (see Purck under Other Families). Another Elis. Weber m SAR 29 Apr 1767 STOPHEL STRUEL (Strobel).

9198: MARGARET WEAVER (?) - supposedly m 1769 Capt. HENRY MILLER (DAR vol 88 page 286), pr. mistake for Marg. Crommel.

WEAVER - 4th Generation

9099: FREDERICK WEAVER - pr. the Fred. born 4 Mar 1779 (son of Fred. Jac.); m by 1802 MARIA MEYER. HK Church has 1802 confirmation of Maria Meyer, wife of "Henry" (pr. should be Frederick) Weaver, which we think is a mistake in the husband´s name by the new minister (Spinner). Childrens baptisms to 1813 show him as Frederick, then in 1813 as Fred. Jr., and in 1814 as Fred. Ja. (Herk. Co. Hist. Soc. Weber file). Children were Henry (1802), John (1804), Elisabeth, Magdalena, Margaret (bp 1813, sp. Daniel Weber), & Christopher (1814).

9170: GEORGE N. WEAVER - pr. born ca 1765 to 1775; m by 1795 MARGARET

    9199: CATHERINE b GF 14 Nov 1795 (sp Pet P Weaver, Elis Frank)

9108: HENRY VAN RENSELAER WEAVER - born 7 Dec 1782 (father given as George G. in
Mrs. Elis. Hull's family notes but as George J. in Ency. of Biography of New York,
v 7 page 105); died 28 Jan 1822 age 39-1-21; m by 1804 ELISABETH BAUMAN (b 1788, d
9 Nov 1838 age 50) dau of FREDERICK BAUMAN & DELIA FOLTS. Children were Henry H.
(1804-1841), Abram (1805-1889), Elisabeth, Garret (b 4 Dec 1810), George Frederick
(b 10 Oct 1815), Catherine (b 31 Nov 1818), Susan, and Delia (b 11 Jan 1822).

9140: JACOB J. WEAVER - pr. bp GF 28 Aug 1768; m GF 6 Nov 1791 MARGARET FRANK dau
of JOHN FRANK. Lost father in Revol. and possibly raised by Lorentz Frank.

    9200: LORENTZ b SJR 13 Oct 1792 (sp Lor. Frank, Marg. Weber)

9187: Lt. Col. JACOB P. WEAVER - born GF 17 Jul 1777 (son of Peter Jac. & Anna);
died Herkimer NY 25 Oct 1864 (age 87, bur. HK Reform Churchyard); m CATHERINE
BELLINGER (b 1782, d 1837) dau of PETER F. BELLINGER & ELIZABETH HARTER. Children
were Elisabeth (b ca Feb 1804, d 1805), Mary (b 9 Dec 1805, sp. Maria Weber, widow
& grandmother of infant), Peter (b Mar 1808, Pet. F. Bellinger & w. Elis.),
Margaret (b Nov 1813, sp Patrick Mahon & Marg. Bellinger unm), Jacob Henry (b Feb
1815, sp. Peter P. Weber & w. Elisabeth); and Anna Catherine (b Sep 1820, sp.
George A. Clepsattle & w. Anna Bellinger).

9151: JACOB WEAVER - pr. born ca 1760 to 1775; m by 1803 EVA FRANK (b 1770)
supposedly dau of TIMOTHY FRANK & ANNA ELISABETH BELLINGER (Bellinger book, page
34) and ps. a widow of Lawrence H. Harter (a lookup of the Timothy Frank will <not
seen> is advised). Jacob sponsored, with wife Eva, Feb 1808 bp of Eva, dau of
John Smith & Margaret Weaver. Children from Mrs. Gronberg notes were Lawrence and
Margaret (twins), Betsy, Katherine, Isaac, James, Eva, Benjamin, Mary, Matthew,
and Lucretia. Lived on a farm in Frankfort NY and later moved to Ashford,
Cattaraugus Co., NY.

    9201: ELISABETH b 21 May 1803 (sp Andr. Piper & Elis.<pr. Fox>)
    9202: CATHERINE b HK 30 May 1804 (sp. Cath. Steel, Hen. Frank unm)
    9203: ISAAC JACOB b Herkimer NY 9 Mar 1805
                (sp. Hen. Keller jr & w. Barb. Elis. of Sneidersbush)
    9204: JAMES bp Herkimer NY 1 Jan 1808

9148: JOHN WEAVER - born 1767; pr. m by 1789 MAGDALENA KELLER (had child bp then).
Pr. this was the son of Jacob Joh. N. Weaver & Margaret (Meyer) and sponsors for
Sep 1789 bp were perhaps his brother and a cousin.

    9205: JACOB bp SJR 13 Sep 1789 (sp Jac. Weber, Elis. Meyer)

9206: JOHANNES WEAVER - pr born ca 1760 to 1772; m by 1790 BARBARA ...

    9207: CATHERINE bp SJR 30 May 1790 (sp Jac. Weber, Cath. Keller)

9208: JOHN WEAVER - pr. born ca 1780 to 1790; m by 1810 GERTRUDE CHRISTMAN (b Oct
1789) dau of JACOB CHRISTMAN & ERNESTINA BELLINGER (Deuel notes at Oneida Hist.
Soc.). Living at Ellisburg, Jeff. Co., NY in 1812. Had sons William (b 13 Jul
1810) and George (b Mar 1812, bp HK 5 Feb 1813, sp. George Weber & Elisabeth <pr.
Christman> of Ellisburg NY).

9152: MICHAEL WEAVER - born 7 Aug 1774; died Springfield NY 1842; m 11 Mar 1800 GERTRUDE FRANK (b 1782, d 13 Dec 1869) dau of HENRY FRANK. From age 5, when his father died, until his marriage, Jacob reportedly lived with his uncle Judge Meyer of Herkimer (Mrs. Gronberg notes). Children Henry (1800-1872), Barbara (bp HK Apr 1802, sp Nic. Weber & Barbara), Margaret (b 19 Feb 1804), Appolonia (b 17 Aug 1805), Maria (b 19 Nov 1806), Sara (b 27 Jun 1808), Charlotta (b 10 Jun 1810), Elizabeth, Jacob, Peter, Joseph, Irene, Katherine, & William.

9149: NICHOLAS WEAVER - born 1 Sep 1768; died in Illinois ca 1844 age 76; m by 1793 BARBARA KELLER (b ca 1768, d 3 Jun 1813 age 45). Nich. and w. Barbara were sp. for bp Feb 1805 of Elisabeth, dau of John Smith & Margaret Weaver. Lived at Frankfort NY until about 1841 when he moved to Illinois (Mrs. Gronberg notes).

> 9209: SUSANNA b 2 Mar 1793 (sp. Pet. Weaver, Susanna Keller)
> m by 1808 PATRICK CAMPBELL jr.
> 9210: JOSEPH b 6 Jul 1802 (sp. Stephen Frank & w. Marg.)
> 9211: MARGARET b 19 Dec 1804 (dau of John "Mich." & Barb. Keller)
> (bp sp. Hen Keller & w. Marg. of Sneidersbush)
> 9212: ELISABETH b 2 Oct 1807 (sp. Werner Folts & w. Elis.)
> 9213: ABRAHAM b Frankfort 7 Jun 1810 (sp Jac. Keller & w. Marg.)

9091: NICHOLAS WEAVER - pr. born ca 1760 to 1775; died 15 Nov 1824; m by 1794 ELISABETH ZOELLER (d 18 Mar 1841). Children Gertrude, Margaret (b SAL May 1792, sp Fred Weber, Marg. Zeller), Elisabeth (b SA 20 Jul 1794, sp John Dckstdr & w Barb. Elis.), Joh. Jacob (1797), Margaret, pr. Peter, & pr. Adam.

9153: PETER WEAVER - born GF 17 Aug 1776 (son of Jacob Joh. N.); died Allegany Co. NY; m WHS 18 Feb 1797 MERCY VERSAILES (Seyl). Was a blacksmith of Frankfort NY when married and later moved to Peterborough (Madison Co.) NY. Had sons William (a minister) and Peter (b 31 Mar 1806, sp Jac. Weber, uncle, & w. Eva, aunt). Son Peter moved to Adams Co. Wis. in 1855, where he died in 1879.

9186: PETER WEAVER - born say 1775; m by 1802 ELISABETH BODMAN (Putman) pr. dau of DAVID PUTMAN & CATHERINE.

> 9214: MARIA CATHERINE b 21 Feb 1802 (sp. Maria Cath. Weber, widow)
> 9215: ELISABETH b 8 Jul 1803 (sp. Elis. Griffin, father's sister)
> 9216: ANNA b 26 Mar 1805 (sp. ... Cath. Bodman)
> 9217: GEORGE b 27 Jul 1807 (sp. Thomas Bell & w. Anna)
> 9218: CATHERINE b 11 Sep 1809 (sp Cath. & David Bodman)
> (sponsors noted as aunt & uncle <ps. they were grandparents>)
> 9219: ELISABETH b 12 Jan 1812 (sp. Geo. L. Harter & w. Elis.)

9177: CATHERINE WEAVER - pr. born 29 Aug 1765 (dau of Nicholas & Gertrude); died Utica NY 29 Aug 1812 age 90 (age at death pr. wrong, should be ca 47); m 29 Nov 1785 Major JOHN BELLINGER (b ca 1760, d 1815 age 55) son of JOHN BELLINGER & ELISABETH BARBARA FOLTS. She and her husband were early settlers of Utica NY about 1788 and had adopted Nicholas Smith, the orphaned son of Nicholas Smith & Margaret. We think there is an error in the 1785 GF Church marriage record which lists her as "Catherine P.", causing the Bellinger book (page 25) to make her "Catherine (Nic. P.)" so as to get her back under Nicholas Weaver & Gertrude (Demuth). An 1815 deed of Nicholas Jac. Weber (Oneida Co. book #27, page 400) mentions an Elisabeth Bellinger and a Hannah Bellinger which we think refer to daughters born to John Bellinger & this Catherine in 1788 and 1792. Also mentioned in the 1815 deed was a John Ostrom, ps. a tie to the Joshua Ostrom who married Catherine Bellinger (b 1786) dau of John Bellinger & this Catherine.

********** WENTZ **********

WENTZ -1st Generation

9251: **GEORGE WENTZ** - pr. born ca 1715 to 1723; pr. died before 1790 (no Wentz surnames on 1790 Mont. Co. census); m by 1763 BARBARA ... (ps. an Ittig based on proximity to Ittigs in various lists and names of children below). Listed as a Lt. in Jost Herkimer's 1767 Grenadiers unit next to Jacob Folts & Fred. C. Frank (Book of Names page 12) and was a member of the German Flats Committee of Safety and a soldier in the Bellinger's 4th Tryon Co. Regiment during the American Revolution (Book of Names page 182). George & Barbara were sponsors for Sep 1763 bp of George Michel, son of Jacob Ittig & Sara.

George apparently lived south of the Mohawk River and appears in Capt. Conrad Frank's 1767 militia company, listed next to Joseph Staring & Rudolph Shoemaker, and on the 1771 Burnetsfield Minster's Support list next to Christian Ittig, Schells, & Fulmers. Lacking evidence of later presence, we presume his son Jacob were deceased by 1778, leaving George Wents with 4 adults & 3 children (under age 16, ps. grandchildren) on 1778 German Flats relief. A George Wentz sponsored, with Dorothea Elisabeth Kayser, May 1782 GF bp of Dorothea Elisabeth, dau of Andreas Werner & Anna Maria (Kurn).

surname WENTZ

+9252: pr. BARBARA b say 1743; m 1763 AUGUSTINUS CLEPSATTLE
+9254: JACOB b say 1745; liv. 1761 (spf Mary Getman bp)
+9255: pr. MARGARET b say 1747; liv. 1765 (spf John Delaney bp)
          pr. m (as his 2nd wife) RUDOLPH STEELE
9256: pr. ANNA MARIA b say 1749; liv. 1764 (spf Elis. Fulmer bp)
          m 1770 RUDOLPH STEELE
9257: ps. CATHERINE (Wentz?) b say 1751; liv. 1766 (spf Schell bp)

WENTZ - 2nd Generation

9254: **JACOB WENTZ** - pr. born ca 1735 to 1745; liv. 1761. Was identified as son of George when appearing as sponsor, with Maria Margaret Weaver, for bp of Mary, dau of Frederick Getman & Margaret. Jacob was listed in Capt. Conrad Frank's 1767 GF militia company, next to John Campbell & Augustus Folmer.

9252: **BARBARA WENTZ** - pr. born ca 1735 to 1746 (pr. dau of George); m 1763 AUGUSTINUS CLEPSATTLE (b 1727, d 1777). The marriage date in 1763 comes from Stone Arabia Reform Church records and helps place Barbara, and her father, agewise.

9255: **MARGARET WENTZ** - pr. born ca 1747; died Herkimer NY 20 Jul 1820 (age 72-11-12, as wife of Rudolph Steele); apparently m by 1782 RUDOLPH STEELE (Rudolph & Marg. had child bp at Schenectady in Mar 1782) pr. her brother-in-law and widower of Margaret's sister Maria. Margaret sponsored, with John Cuningham, Sep 1765 bp of John, son of Patrick Delaney & Maria Barbara.

9261: HENRY WITHERSTINE - born ca 1727; died Herkimer NY 5 Apr 1811 (age 84); m1 by 1762 CATHERINE ... (ps. SCHELL); m2 SAR 17 Jun 1766 MAGDALENA HILTS. (scapled by Indians 10 May 1779); m3 GF 1787 ANNA MARIA RASBACH (b ca 1739, d 1822 age 83) of JOHANNES RASBACH & MARGARET BIERMAN and widow of HENRY HISER. Pr. related to the Valentine Witherstine on 1753 Stone Arabia Church list. Henry was in Capt. M. Petrie's 1757 GF militia unit and sponsored, with wife Magdalena, 1770 bp of Henry, son of Christian Schell. Dr. W. Petry's records show he treated Henry's wife for scalping on May 10th 1779, so she was one of the 12 in the West Canada Creek massacre that included Smiths and Harters. The March 3, 1875 Herkimer Democrat says that Henry was great grandfather of the paper's editor C.C. Witherstine and Henry's daughter was the mother of Col. Honicle Smith of Utica (Smith info has mother as Margaret Bellinger, not Witherstine). Henry appears on 1790 Herkimer census (2-1-4) near Schells, John Hilts Jr., and George Hilts.

surname WITHERSTINE

+9262: JOHN (twin) b SAR Jul 1762 (sp. John Schell & wife Barbara)
          d 1835; m 1786 MARGRETH KESSLER
 9263: ANNA (twin) b 12 Jul 1762 (sp Aug. Hess' w. Anna <Schell>)

WITHERSTINE - 2nd Generation

9262: JOHANNES WITHERSTINE - born SAR 12 Jul 1762; died 19 Jun 1835 (age 72-11-23); m German Flats NY 1 Aug 1786 MARGRETH KESSLER dau of MELCHERT KESSLER (Casler) & MARIA ELISABETH PETRIE. Note absence of other Witherstines (except Henry Sr in 1786) among sponsors for children.

 9264: HENRICH b 2 Nov 1786 (sp. Hen. Widderstein, Elis. Schell)
         m 9 Mar 1809 BARBARA JOHNSON (dau of Elisha)
+9265: pr. CATHERINE b ca Oct 1787; d 1876; m 1806 GEORGE FULMER
+9266: JOHANNES b 5 Oct 1790 (sp. Hen. Schell, Gert. Thumm)
 9267: ANNA b 19 Feb 1793 (sp. Joh. Dietrich Petrie & Anna)
 9268: MARGARETHA b 1 Feb 1795 (sp. Fred. Schell & Cath.<Staring>)
 9269: ANNA EVA b ca 1797; d 11 Jul 1812 (age 15)
 9270: MELCHIOR b 6 Oct 1801 (sp. Joe. Kessler)
+9271: DAVID b 19 Dec 1803 (sp. John Rasbach & w. Anne <Moak>)
 9272: ABRAHAM b 26 Feb 1807 (sp. John Folts & w. Cath.); liv.1825
 9273: MARIA ELISABETH b 29 May 1809 (sp Melc. Casler & w Mar. Elis)
 9274: PETER b ca Jul 1812; d 11 Jan 1813 (age 6 months)

WITHERSTINE - 3rd Generation

9266: JOHN WITHERSTINE - born 5 Oct 1790; died 1881; m Herkimer NY 10 Dec 1811 CATHERINE HARTER (b 1791, d 1854) dau of PHILIP HARTER & CATHERINE PHILIPS. Lived at Steuben, Oneida Co, NY (Harter book page 23) with 12 children.

9271: DAVID WITHERSTINE - born 1803; died 1864; m 1847 MARGARET PETRY (b 1819) dau of FREDERICK PETRY & CATHERINE THUMB. Children Charles, Horace, William, Margaret, Isabella, and Martha (Petrie book page 122).

********** WITRIG (Wiederich) **********

9281: Maj. GEORGE WITRIG - born Wurtenburg Germany 1740; died Frankfurt NY 1830;
pr. m1 MARIA ELISABETH BENDER (b ca Jun 1759, d 25 Mar 1802 age 42-9-25);
apparently m2 NANCY SANFORD (as given in DAR #55358) Was a Private in Col.
Goosen Van Schaick's 1st NY regiment (DAR #55358) and was probably the George
Witrig, listed with Michel, Jacob, and Conrad, as Witrigs in Revolutionary service
in Col. Bellinger's 4th Tryon Co. regiment (Book of Names page 169). Listed as
Major George Witrig on 1794 GF bp rec. (wife given as "Maria" there).

surname WITRIG

 9282: CATHERINE b 17 Jun 1777 (sp. Adam Hartman & Maria Cath.)
+9283: GEORGE b say 1780; m 1802 ELIZABETH WEAVER
 9284: MARIA ELISABETH b 10 Sep 1782 (sp Christn Hockstr & M. Elis.)
+9285: JOHANNES b 1784; m MARIA CHRISTMAN
 9286: HENRICH b GF 14 Aug 1786 (sp. Hen. Staring & Elis.)
 9287: ELISABETH b GF 15 May 1788 (sp Hieron. Bender, Cath. Staring)
 9288: CONRAD b GF 28 Jul 1790 (sp Con. Witrig, Maria Koch)
 9289: MARIA b 23 Oct 1792 (sp Adam A. Staring, Elis. H. Staring)
 9290: MICHAEL b GF 7 Aug 1794 (sp. Mich. Witrig & Elis.)
 9291: MAGDALENA b 25 Mar 1802 (sp Wm Clepsattle & M. Elis.)

9292: MICHEL WITRIG Sr. - pr. born ca 1720 to 1735; pr. died by 1790 (will
issued 1796); pr. m1 by 1771 MAGDALENA ... and m2 by 1776 AMELIA CATHERINE ...
Pr. his widow was the Catherine Witrig on the 1790 Herkimer census, with one male
over 16 in her household (ps. unm son Conrad). Michel was in a German Flats
militia company in 1769 and was at the Battle of Oriskany in 1777. He was a
sponsor, with Amelia Catherine, for bp Jan 1776 of Maria Catherine, dau of
Christian Hockstatter & Maria Catherine. From Michel's will, bond issued to
George and Jacob Witrig and administration by Peter Fox and Adam Stahring.

 9293: MARIA CATHERINE b say 1750; m ca 1766 CHRISTIAN HOCKSTATER
+9294: ps. MICHEL b say 1756; m pr. by 1778 ELISABETH LENTZ
+9295: ps. CONRAD b say 1760; m liv. 1790 (spf Witrig bp)
 9296: EVA CATHERINE b SAR Jan 1771 (sp Lor. Rinckel, Marg. Keller)
+9297: ps. PHILIP b say 1775; m by 1802 MARIA ELISABETH MEYER
 9298: MARIA SYBILLA b 21 Oct 1779 (sp John Dunches & M. Sybilla)

9299: JACOB WITRIG - born Mohawk Valley NY 1754 (DAR); died Herkimer Co. NY
1844; m GF 31 Jan 1786 CATHERINE ELISABETH RINCKEL (b 1767) dau of LORENTZ
RINCKEL. Jacob sponsored bp Feb 1779 of Jacob, son of Christian Hockstatter &
Maria Catherine. He was taken to Canada as a prisoner of war in the Amer.
Revolution and served as a waiter for a British officer who interceded on Jacob's
behalf when Jacob was sentenced to a flogging of 1000 lashes for attempting escape
(Jacob Witrig was thus spared the punishment which resulted in the death of fellow
prisoner Jacob Pfeiffer). Listed on 1790 Herkimer census (2-1-3). Listed as Jacob
D. Witrig when sponsor for Aug 1793 bp of John, son of Philip Lentz & Maria.

 9300: JACOB b GF 21 Aug 1786 (sp. Conrad Witrig, Maria Rinckel)
 9301: GEORGE JAC. b say 1788; liv. 1804 (HK Ch. Confirm.)
 9302: MARGARET b GF 16 Sep 1789 (sp Geo. Rima, Maria Becker)
 9303: JACOB b GF 9 May 1791 (sp Jac. Clements & Cath.); pr. d y
 9304: JACOB b GF 10 Feb 1792 (sp Jac. Bircky & Anna)
 9305: LORENTZ b GF 9 Jul 1795 (sp Lor. Rinckel, Cath. Witrig)
 9306: ELIZABETH 1799-1880 m PETER MULTER jr.

9295: CONRAD WITRIG - pr. born ca 1750 to 1765. Conrad Witrig was sponsor, with Maria Koch, at 1790 bp of Conrad, son of George Witrig and also a sponsor, with wife Cath. Ad. Stahring, for bp Mar 1791 of Conrad, son of Adam Hartman & Mary Catherine.

9283: GEORGE WITRIG jr. - pr. born ca 1765 to 1783; m at Herkmer NY 19 Dec 1802 ELIZABETH WEAVER dau of JACOB H. WEAVER. Ref. Harter book (page 31).

> **9307: GEORGE G.** b ca 1804; m 1827 EVA HARTER

9285: JOHANNES WITRIG - born 17 Sep 1784 (son of George, bp sp John Finster & Maria Shneck); m MARIA CHRISTMAN (b 1786) dau of JACOB CHRISTMAN & ERNESTINA BELLINGER (Bellinger book page 26). Had dau MARGARET (m CALVIN DEWITT LEONARD).

9294: MICHEL WITRIG (jr ?) - pr. born ca 1754 to 1763; apparently he had died by Oct 1802 (when widow Elisabeth's son Michel was confirmed at Herkimer Dut. Reform Church); m by 1780 ELISABETH LENTZ (DAR Patriot Index). Apparently the Michel who was a sponsor, with wife Elisabeth, for Dec 1787 bp of Michael, son of Christian Hockstater, and for May 1793 bp of Michael, son of Adam Hartman & Mary Catherine. Was living at New Germany settlement in 1789 (St. Johnsville Church bp rec.).

> **+9308: ps. CONRAD MIC.** b say 1778; m 1802 MARIA STEELE
> **9309: MICHEL** b GF 12 Nov 1780 (sp Christn Hockstr & M. Cath.)
> m 1809 SUSANNA LONES
> **9310: ELISABETH** b GF 15 Mar 1783 (sp Jac. Countryman, Elis. Walrth)
> **9311: SARA** b GF 15 Apr 1787 (sp Geo. Rima, Sara Lentz)
> **9312: ELISABETH** bp SJR Mar 1789 (sp Jac. Lentz, Elis. Hockstatter)
> **9313: MARIA** b GF 2 Mar 1793 (sp Capt. Geo. Witrig & Maria)

9297: PHILIP WITRIG - pr. born ca 1770 to 1783; m by 1802 MARIA ELISABETH MEYER. Was living at New Germany in 1802.

> **9314: MICHEL** b 16 Feb 1802 (sp Jacob Witrig, Anna Clark)

9308: CONRAD MIC. WITRIG - pr. born ca 1770 to 1783 and ident. as son of Michel (dec'd) on 1802 mar. record; m 1802 MARIA STEELE (b 16 Aug 1783, d 15 Apr 1864 as given in Folts/Steele ms. at Utica Public Library) dau of GEORGE STEELE.

Witrigs on 1790 Herkimer Census (adult males - males under 16 - females) were a George (2-2-4), a Jacob (2-1-3), a Catherine (1-0-1, pr. a widow), and a Michel (1-2-4).

********** WOHLEBEN (Woolever) **********

WOHLEBEN - 1st Generation

9315: WALLRATH WOHLEBEN (Walrab) - bp Saarbrucken Germany 20 Oct 1648 (Jones´ Palatine Families of NY); died before 1711; m 1676 ANNA CATHERINE BAUMAN dau of PETER BAUMAN of Bacharach Germany (ibid.). Wallrath was the bride´s deceased father at 1711 marriage of Henrich Spohn. Wife Anna Catherine appears on the NY Palatine subsistence list in 1710 (5A,0Y) and in 1712 (7A,0Y) and as a widow with 2 children on the 1717 Simmendinger census at New Queensberg (Schoharie NY). The baptismal sponsorship links amongst most early Wohlebens suggest all may have been related. Walrab´s widow Catherine at the same New Queensberg settlement as her son-in-law Hendrick Spohn, and it seems likely she went also to Burnetsfield rather than following the other Wohlebens (i.e. Peter, Philip, & Valentin, who were at Beckmansland in 1717 and later lived near Kingston NY).

surname WOHLEBEN

9316: MARIA CATHERINE bp Dec 1685; m 1711 HENRICH SPOHN
9316A SARAH CATH. bp 1691; m ca 1711 GEORGE MARTIN DILLENBACH
+9317: NICHOLAS bp Feb 1698; liv. 1716 (spf Spohn bp)
9318: ps. MARIA ELISABETH b say 1700; liv. 1717 (spf Orendorf bp)

9319: CHRISTOPHER WOHLEBEN - NY Palatine sub. in 1710 (2A,0Y) & 1712 (2A,0Y)

9320: MICHAEL WOHLEBEN - pr. born ca 1675 to 1690; m ... Hans Miggel in 5th party from Holland in 1709 with wife & 1 ch. (Knittle´s Palatine Emigration). On NY Palatine subs. list in 1710 (1A,0Y) & 1712 (1A,0Y), but no record later.

9321: PETER WOHLEBEN - pr. born ca 1670 to 1680; m ANNA ROSINA VORSTER (liv. 1720); pr. m2 by 1725 MARGARET VINK. On NY Palatine subsistence list in 1710 (2A,2Y) and in 1712 (2A,0Y). On the 1711 list of inhabitants at West Camp NY with 1 boy age 9-15 (pr. Jacob), 1 boy under age 8 (? Henrich, b 1711), 1 woman (wife), & girl age 9-15 (ps. Margaret). On 1717 Simmendinger census with wife Anna Rosina & 5 children. Settled near Kingston NY.

+9322: pr. JACOB b say 1700; m 1720 MARIA ELISABETH SWIDSELAAR
9323: ps. MARGARET b say 1702; m 7 Aug 1722 CHRISTIAN BERG
9324: Johan HENDRICK bp 4 Nov 1711 (sp. Hen. Spaan, Gert. Kramer)
9325: SUSANNA bp 27 Dec 1713 (sp. Valent. Woleven & Susanna)
9326: ANNA BARBARA bp 8 Jan 1716 (sp. Frans Keller, Anna Barbara)
9327: CATRINA ELISABETH bp 12 Jan 1718 (sp. Philip Velliger)
        (sp. also Catrina Elisabeth Rouw)
9328: ANNA MARIA bp 23 Oct 1720 (sp. Hans Mic. Wyle, Maria Wyle)
        by second wife
9329: JOHANNES bp Kingston 14 Mar 1725 (sp. Hen. Kip, ...)

9330: PHILIP WOHLEBEN - pr. born ca 1680 to 1690; m ca 1712 ANNA MARGARETHA GEBEL. He was on NY Palatine list in 1710 (1A,0Y) and 1712 (3A,0Y), but Anna Marg. Gebel was listed separately in 1710 (2A,1Y) and 1712 (1A,2Y). Seen living at West Camp NY in 1711 (no dependents then) with Valentin & Peter Wohleben, and with these two men also on the 1717 Simmendinger census at Beckmansland. Perhaps was the Philip Volland (Wohleben?) who wed at Kingston NY Oct 1724 EVA SWITSELAAR

9331: ANNA MARGARETHA b 12 May 1714 (sp. Veltin Woh., Marg Caputz)

9332: VALENTIN WOHLEBEN - pr. born ca 1675 to 1690; m SUSANNA ... Hans Veltin on 5th London List of Palatines, July 1709, with wife and 3 children. On NY Palatine list in 1710 and 1712. On 1717 Simmendinger census with wife Susanna. Was sponsor, with John Lammert & Dorothea Veltin, for Kingston NY Jan 1730 bp of Veltin, son of Laterus Thom & Margaret.

> 9333: ANNA MARIA DOROTHEA b 10 Jan 1715; m by 1740 PETER KRELLER
> (1715 sp. Jos. Reichart, Carl Naeher & w. Dorothea Caputz)
> 9334: ANNA MARGARETHA b 14 Apr 1717 (Jos. Reichart, Marg. Caputz)

WOHLEBEN - 2nd Generation

9322: Johan JACOB WOHLEBEN - pr. born ca 1690 to 1700 (pr. son of Peter & Rosina, as indicated by name & sponsors selected for first child Rosina); m at Kingston NY 31 May 1720 MARIA ELISABETH SWIDSELAAR. His children with baptisms recorded at Kingston NY include ANNA ROSINA (b Rhinebeck NY Jan 1721, sp P. Whlbn & w Rosina), ELISABETH (bp 1 Jul 1722, sp. Hen. Swiselar, Elis. Bruye, and EVA (bp 30 Mar 1729, sp. Phil. Holland, Eva Swiseler). Nothing has been seen to connect this family of Jacob with the Herkimer County descendents of Nicholas Wohleben.

9317: NICHOLAS WOHLEBEN - bp in Germany 9 Feb 1698 (Jones´ Palatine Families); liv. in NY Jun 1711 (had first communion, Book of Names, pg 39); pr. died ca 1774-77 (Benton has Nicholas dying two years before the Revolution, as noted in Book of Names, page 172); ps. m1 say before 1720 MARGARET LANT dau of widow ANNA CATHERINE LANT; but presumably he later married second a daughter of NICHOLAS FELLER, ps. a Catherine or an Anna (Bellinger book, page 37, refers to a Wohleben bible photostat in claiming that Magdalena Nic. Wohleben, born 1755, was a granddaughter of Nicholas Feller). About 1716-17 Nicholas Wohleben was probably one of the two children listed by Simmendinger in Catherine Wohleben´s household at New Queensberg and Nicholas was apparently unmarried when he & Margaret Lant were sponsors at the Jan 1716 bp of Nicholas, son of Henrich Spohn & Catherine (Wohleben). On the Burnetsfield Patent of 1723 he received a head of household lot (#30), an unusual aspect of which is the fact that there was no comparable dependent lot given to a Wohleben wife or son. To explain this we suggest that he may have been the dependent designee of widow Anna Catherine Lant (as a son-in-law!?) and say after some swapping (perhaps with Frederick Bell?), Nicholas ended up with his lot in a primary area on the south side of the Mohawk River, located it would appear near that of his brother-in-law Hendrick Spohn. Benton´s "History of Herkimer County" names his 6 sons as Henry, Peter, Richard (i.e. Dietrich), John, Abraham, & Jacob, and his 6 daughters as Catherine, Mary, Sophia, Elizabeth, Hannah & Lany. However Benton seems to have missed the Maria Margaret Wohleben who married Frederick Miller at the Falls in 1749 (Vosburgh´s German Flats church records).

> +9335: ps. NICHOLAS (Jr. ?) b say 1720; liv. 1777 (Oriskany battle)
> m MARIA ELISABETH ....
> +9336: HENRY b say 1724; m1 by 1760 MAGDALENA ...
> +9337: ps. JACOB b say 1726;
> 9338: pr. MARIA MARGARET b say 1730; pr. d before 1760
> m 1749 FREDERICK MILLER
> 9339: CATHERINE b say 1732; m 1750 FREDERICK SHOEMAKER
> 9340: MARIA ca 1735-1816; liv. 1761 (spf Maria Schutt bp)
> 9341: pr. ELISABETH N. b say 1740; m by 1761 FREDERICK SCHUTT

9336: HENRICH WOHLEBEN - pr. born ca 1720 to 1728; m1 by 1760 MAGDALENA ...; m2 by Nov 1763 MARGARET ... Henry & Margaret sponsored Nov 1763 bp of Elisabeth, dau of George Laux & Gertrude (Dygert). His son Peter H. spoke of "his brother-in-law" Peter Casler who was killed, along with Nicholas Wohleben, in the skirmish with Tories & Indians on 18 Jul 1781.

> **9343: MARGARET** b say 1754; m1 PETER KESSLER (d 1781)
> m2 GF 1784 DAVID SCHUYLER (pr. son of Anthony)
> **9344: NICHOLAS** b say 1756; killed in combat 18 Jul 1781
> **9345: ps. ANNA** b sa 1758; m by 1780 JOHN SUTZ
> **+9346: JOHANNES** b 13 Sep 1760 (sp. Debld Dygrt & w. Kunig.<Laux>)
> by 2nd wife
> **+9347: PETER HEN.** b SAR 27 Nov 1764 (sp Peter Laux, Cath. Laux)
> m 1785 CATHERINE JAC. SNELL
> **9348: ADAM** b SAR 1767 (sp Adam Laux & Cath. Elis.); d soon
> **9349: JACOB** b SAR Sep 1769 (sp Jac Ecker, Marg. Fink)

9337: JACOB WOHLEBEN - pr. born ca 1690 to 1730; Presumably an adult about 1750-55 as the Jacob Wollaber who was supposedly an early settler of Andrustown with Paul Crim´s group (Herkimer Evening Telegram article "Boulder-Monument Andrustown Reminder", issue of July 16, 1977). Ps. this Jacob was an early son Nicholas Sr., but we think it more likely he came from the Kingston NY Wohlebens (see Jacob of previous generation, husband of Elisabeth Swidselaar). Ps. he died by 1760, as Jacobs are not seen in GF records till much later.

> **9349A ps. MARGARET** b say 1740; m by 1760 DIETRICH STEELE
> **9349B ps. MARIA BARBARA** b say 1742; liv. 1762 (spf N Harter dau)

9335: NICHOLAS WOHELBEN - pr. same man as prior generation Nicholas (bp 1698) although we have split between the two generations to show the possibility of a Nicholas jr. (father of Peter below) who reportedly died after Aug 1777 (son Peter´s death notice says he escaped the Oriskany battlefield "with his father", as noted in Book of Names, page 172); m by 1761 MARIA ELISABETH ... (listed as mother of Jacob on 1761 bp record). The 1761 wife Maria Elisabeth, was not likely to have been a Feller since there already existed alive then a Maria Elisabeth (Nic.) Feller who was the wife of George Hilts Sr. Nicholas & wife Maria Elisabeth sponsored May 1766 GF bp of Maria Elisabeth, dau of Peter Wohleben. The will of Nicholas Wohleben of Burnetsfield, dated 23 Feb 1773, mentions wife Maria Elisabeth, and children, Henry, Dietrich, Johannis, Abraham, Jacob, Sophia, Catherine, Elisabeth, Magdalena, Anna, and Anna Maria (executors were daughter Anna Maria, Jacob Boeshorn, and Dietrich Steele <Fernow´s wills #2017>).

> **+9350: PETER N.** 1736-1829 m 1765 CATHERINE FLAGG
> **+9352: DIETRICH N.** b say 1748; d 1777; m 1770 ELISABETH DYGERT
> **+9353: JOHN** b say 1750; killed at Oriskany 1777
> **9354: SOPHIA** b say 1753; m pr. by 1773 PETER FLAGG
> **9355: MAGDALENA** 1755-1829 m FREDERICK BELLINGER (b 1752)
> **+9356: ABRAHAM** 1756-1819 m DOROTHEA BELLINGER
> **9357: ANNA (HANNAH)** bp Loonenburg 1759 (sp Theunis Hess & Anna)
> m JOHN EMPIE (A Tory, went to Canada)
> **+9358: JACOB** b SAR 10 Jan 1761 (sp. Jacob Boshaar & wife Cath.)
> m SUSANNA FLAGG

9356: ABRAHAM WOHLEBEN - born 26 Dec 1756; died Herkimer NY 6 Feb 1819 (age 62-2-11); m 25 Jan 1778 DOROTHEA BELLINGER (b 1755, d 1847) dau of Capt. PETER BELLINGER. Abraham was taken prisoner, tomahawked and scalped 15 Oct 1781 on Shoemaker Hill. His feet were frostbitten as he lay for two days in the snow and he was reportedly confined nearly two years recovering from his wounds. In August 1783 he helped defend Ft. Herkimer in the "last battle" of the Revolution, after peace was declared (Bellinger book page 38).

> **9359:** ABRAHAM   b GF 23 Mar 1783 (sp Abraham Rosencrantz & Maria)
> m 1802 MARGARETHA STARING (dau of Peter)
> **9360:** ELISABETH   b GF 28 Feb 1785 (sp Peter Fox, Elis. Wohleben)
> m 1806 HENRY MILLER (son of John)
> **9361:** DOROTHEA   b 28 Feb 1787 (sp Peter Joh Bellingr, Dor. Steele)
> m 1813 PETER PIPER
> **9362:** Johan PETER   b 12 Apr 1789 (sp F. Bellinger & Lena)
> **9363:** Johan DIETRICH   bp 26 Jan 1791 (sp Diet. Steele & Anna)
> **9364:** JOHANNES   (twin)   b 9 May 1793   (sp John Bellinger & Cath.)
> **9365:** NICHOLAS   (twin)   b 9 May 1793 (sp Abhm Leithal & Cath.)
> **9366:** JEREMIAS   bp 7 Oct 1795 (sp And. Piper & Elis.<pr. Bellingr>)

9352: DIETRICH WOHLEBEN - pr. born ca 1735 to 1744; killed at Oriskany battle 6 Aug 1777; m SAR 8 Mar 1770 ANNA ELISABETH DYGERT ("Maria" on 1771 bp rec.). Sponsored, with Barbara Steel, Nov 1764 bp of Dietrich, son of Adam Steel & Eva.

> **9367:** KUNIGUNDA   b Jan 1771 (SA sp Kunigunda & Debald Dygert)
> **9368:** ps. ANNA   b say 1774; m by 1795 GEORGE AD. STAHRING

9358: JACOB WOHLEBEN - born 10 Jan 1761 (sp. Jacob Boshaar & wife Cath.); died Auriesville NY 1827, m SUSANNA FLAGG (b 1756, d 1850) as in DAR# 139177, ps. a sister of PETER FLAGG. A Private in Revol. under Capt. Frank & Capt. Bikebread.

> **9369:** CATHERINE   b GF 12 Feb 1783 (sp Tho. Shomker & Cath Delene)
> **9370:** LENA   b GF 25 Oct 1784 (sp Fred Bellinger & Lena)
> **9371:** ELISABETH   b GF 26 Oct 1786 (sp Nic Wohleben, Elis M Petri)
> d 1871; m JACOB CASLER (1773-1854)
> **9372:** JACOB   b GF 18 Feb 1790 (sp Jac. Christman, Gert. L. Harter)
> **9373:** MARGARET   b 13 Nov 1792 (sp Stophl T. Shmkr, Marg. F Bellngr)
> **9374:** NICHOLAS   b GF 20 Aug 1795 (sp Nich. Shoemaker, Dor. Flack)

9346: JOHN WOHLEBEN - born 13 Sep 1760 (son of Henrich); died 13 Aug 1838; m 14 Jan 1781 CATHERINE MCNAUGHTON. Taken prisoner on 18 Jul 1781 and held captive at Rebel Island in Canada (Morrison's Revolutionary War Soldiers of Tryon Co.).

> **9375:** NICHOLAS   b GF 15 Sep 1780 (sp Nic. Herkimer, Margaret Snell)
> **9376:** MARIA   b GF 16 Sep 1783 (sp Petr Wohlbn & Christina)
> **9377:** JOHANNES   b GF 16 Sep 1785 (sp John Snell & Elis.)
> **9378:** HENRICH   b GF 4 Jul 1787 (sp H Rosencrntz, Cath Wohlebn)
> **9379:** DANIEL   b Oct 1791 (sp Dav Schuyler & Marg.); d 1792
> **9380:** CATHERINE   bp SJR 3 Mar 1793 (sp John Mayer & Cath.)

9353: JOHN WOHLEBEN - pr. born ca 1740 to 1752; killed at Oriskany 6 Aug 1777. Pr. the Johannes Wohleber listed as a German Flats resident in May 1775 (Mohawk Valley in the Revolution, page 165).

9347: Sgt. PETER HENR. WOHLEBEN - born SAR 27 Nov 1764; died 13 Sep 1843; m German Flats NY 10 Jul 1785 CATHARINE JAC. SNELL (ps. b ca Oct 1756, d 10 Jan 1844 age 87-3-16); Martin´s Snell book (page 39) gives her later dates (b 1 Jul 1763, d 31 Oct 1851, age 87) and lists her as dau of JACOB SNELL & GERTRUDE MATTHEES. On July 18, 1781 while this Peter H. was on military duty near Ft. Plain NY, his unit was ambushed by a Tory war party, and in the ensuing battle he was wounded in the right thigh. In this same skirmish his oldest brother Nicholas and his brother-in-law Peter Casler were killed and his brother John Wholeben was taken prisoner (see Morrison´s "Revolutionary War Soldiers" page 31). Probably he was the Peter Wolever on 1790 Canajoharie NY census (1-1-3) listed near the Schuyler family.

  9381: MARGARET b GF 21 Feb 1786 (sp John Wohleben & Cath.)
  9382: GERTRUDE b GF 20 Jun 1788 (sp Joh. Dakker & Gert.)
  9383: HENRICH bp SJR 1 Aug 1790 (sp H. Zimmerman, Anna Snell)
  9384: pr. EVA b GF 25 Feb 1792 (sp F. Christman & Anna Eva)
  9385: ELISABETH bp SJR 1 Apr 1793 (sp John Snell & Elis.)
        pr. m JACOB ANSTEAD
  9386: ps. NICHOLAS b ca 1800; d Dolgeville NY 2 Jul 1886 (age 85)

9350: PETER WOHLEBEN - born ca Mar 1736; died Herkimer NY 26 Nov 1829 (age 93-8-7); m SAR 17 Jul 1765 CATHERINE FLAGG. In 1777 Tory Indian Chief Joseph Brant told Peter to vacate the farm which he was renting from Brant at Manheim or get tomahawked (Peter moved right away to a neighboring fort). Peter was wounded slightly at the Battle of Oriskany where he fought along with his father and brothers (Dietrich & John who were killed there). Was sponsor for May 1768 bp of Catherine, dau of Henry Hiser & Anna Maria (Rasbach). According to Benton´s "History of Herkimer County", Peter was the first shoemaker in German Flats and had sons Nicholas, John, & Henry who reached adult age. Notes of Arthur J. Dunckle (1971, Wohleben file at HCH) list wife as CATHERINE GREY (b 1734) and children as John, Henry, Catherine, Susan, Anna, Mary, Eva, Margaret & Elisabeth (Dunckle says m JACOB ANSTEAD). On 1790 GF census (2-2-4) near R. Furman, Adam Weaver, Ludwig Campbell, & Jacob Bashor.

  9387: MARIA ELISABETH b GF 1 Apr 1766 (sp Nic. Wohlebn & M. Elis.)
       pr. the ELISABETH P. who m 1786 FRED. SHOEMAKER
  9388: CATHERINE PET. b SAR 28 Mar 1768 (sp Cath. & Mich. Ittig)
       m 1793 GERRIT JOH. VAN SLYCK
 +9389: NICHOLAS b SAR Aug 1770; died 1861; m ELISABETH SMALL
  9390: SUSAN 1770-1820 m JACOB C. EDICK (b 1764)
 +9391: JOHN b say 1772 (listed as son by Benton)
  9392: ANNA b GF 29 Jan 1776 (sp. Geo. Feyl & Anna <Flack>)
       m Mr. FURMAN (Dunckle notes)
  9393: PETER b GF 12 Apr 1779 (sp. P. Flack & Sophia <Wohleben>)
  9394: JACOB b FNR 3 Sep 1781 (sp Jacob Burns, Susanna Vlack)
  9395: MARY m MR. WHITE
  9396: EVA m STANTON FOX
  9397: pr. HENRICH b GF 17 Jun 1786 (sp Jac. Wohleben & Susanna)
  9398: MARGARET b GF 24 May 1789 (Joh Hess & Marg.); m JOE LEPPER

9391: JOHN P. WOHLEBEN - pr. born ca 1770 to 1784 (listed as son of Peter by Benton); pr. m by 1804 ANNA FRANK. Had son Benjamin (bp HK 15 Aug 1804, sp. Anna Forman of Manlius NY).

9389: NICHOLAS P. WOHLEBEN - born 1 Aug 1770 (SAR); died 2 Aug 1861; m 19 May 1792 ELISABETH SMALL (b 1773, d 1851) dau of JACOB SMALL (Harter book page 36). Lived at Herkimer in 1810 (dau Elisabeth's confirm.) and 1814. Children were ANNA ELISABETH (b GF 24 Sep 1792, sp. F. Shoemaker & Elis.), DANIEL (b GF 4 Oct 1795 <sp. John Small, ... Wohleben>, and liv. 1814 <age 18 at HK confirmation>), JACOB (1797-1847, m CATHERINE HELMER), EVA (b HK 11 Jan 1802, sp. Susanna Small), DELIA (b HK 9 Mar 1804, sp. Melc. Small & w. Doro.), ANNA (b HK 8 Feb 1806, sp. Jacob Small & w. Anna), and JOSIAH (1813-1898, m MARGARET HARTER).

9401: HANS ADAM (Adami) - pr. born ca 1730 to 1755; m by 1780 MARIA CATHERINE
... Ps. related to the Peter Adami who served in Campbell's Tryon Co. Revol.
Regiment (from the Canajoharie NY area, Book of Names page 138) and perhaps also
to the Maria Adamy who married at Ft. Plain NY 1792 Martin Simon.
> surname ADAM
>> 9402: ps. CATHERINE b say 1766; m GF 1783 CONRAD SMIDT
>> 9403: ps. HENRICH b say 1768; liv. 1784 (spf Smidt bp)
>> 9404: JOHN b GF 2 Feb 1779 (sp. John Dinges)
>>> pr. m by 1805 ELISABETH CLEMENT
>> 9405: GEORGE b GF 21 Apr 1780 (sp Geo. Witrig & Maria Elis.)

9406: JAMES ADAMS - pr. born ca 1730 to 1755; m by 1777 APPOLONIA ...
> surname ADAMS
>> 9407: DANIEL b GF 10 Jul 1777 (sp Thomas Shaw, Elisabeth)

9408: ELISA ANDERSON - pr. born ca 1730 to 1755; m MARIA
> surname ANDERSON
>> 9409: ELISABETH b GF 30 Oct 1775 (sp. Joh. Ritter & Barbara)

9410: NICHOLAS ALDRIDGE - born say 1740; died by Mar 1817 (dau's mar. rec.); m
GF 5 Jun 1787 EUNICE HUTCHERSON a widow. A merchant, on 1790 GF census (3-0-4),
and in 1791 held part of Burnetsfield lot# 3 (owned in 1833 by J. Aldridge). In
1804 Nicholas & wife "Mary" sold Lot #29 land (s. of Mohawk River).
> surname ALDRIDGE
>> 9411: pr. JACOB ca 1778-1838 m WHS 1799 ABIGAIL HASTINGS
>>> wife pr. the Abigail Aldridge (b 1778, d HK 1867)
>> 9412: CLARISSA b say 1798; m HK 1817 NATHANIEL CRANDALL

9413: HENRICH ANSTED (Amsted) - born say 1760; m GF 5 Jun 1786 ELISABETH RITTER
(b 1767) dau of JOHN PETER RITTER. Lived at Reimensneiderbush in 1790 and on 1790
Palatine NY census (1-2-1), listed next to Jacob Louks.
> surname ANSTED
>> 9414: HENRICH b GF 10 Aug 1787 (sp Balt. Strauch & M. Cath.)
>> 9415: JACOB bp SJR 15 Jun 1790 (SJR sp Jac. Loucks & Cath.)
>> 9416: CATHERINE b GF 22 Jul 1795 (sp Jac DeBus & Cath.)

9417: BILLY ARNOLD - m by 1792 MARTYTJE ...
> surname ARNOLD
>> 9418: HOLYDAY b GF 20 Mar 1792 (sp Hen. Rosencrntz, Delia Bellingr)

9419: PHILIP AUSMAN - pr. born ca 1740 to 1750; m BARBARA ELISABETH ... (b ca
1747, d Warrentown NY 30 May 1811 age 64). On the 1790 German Flats census
(1-1-2) and was a schoolteacher at Columbia, Herk. Co., NY in 1796. A guess that
most Ausmans of Herkimer belong to this Philip.
> surname AUSMAN
>> 9420: pr. CONRAD b say 1782; m by 1803 LISIAE WILLIAMS
>> 9421: pr. MARGARET b say 1788; m PETER H. BELLINGER
>> 9422: pr. JOHN 1790-182x m CATHERINE ... (1792-1874)
>> 9423: pr. JACOB b say 1792; m MARIA H. BELLINGER
>> 9424: pr. HENRY b say 1795; m ELISABETH H. BELLINGER

9425: ICABOD BAANY - pr. born ca 1720 to 1740 (son of Joseph, Helmer book page 5); m SAL 30 Sep 1760 ELISABETH MARGARETHA HELMER dau of ADAM HELMER & MARGARET
surname BAANY
  9426: MARIA ELISABETH b 14 Jan 1762
       (sp Maria Elis. Helmer, John Folts both unm)
  9427: MARIA MARGARETHA b 12 Aug 1764 (sp. M Marg Weber, Joh. Helmer)
  9428: JOHANNES b 9 Jul 1766 (sp. Joh. Kesslr & Gert.<Helmer>)
  9429: ANNA b 10 Oct 1770 (sp Anna Frank, Hen. Helmer)

9430: HENRY BACUS (Bakkes) - pr. born ca 1730 to 1755; m ...
surname BACUS
  9431: HENRICH b GF 10 Oct 1794 (sp Hen. Etel & Cath.)

9432: JACOB BACUS - pr. born ca 1755 to 1774; m by 1792 JULIANA ... . Pr. from a Stone Arabia family. A George Bacus & Susanna and a Henrich Bakkes also appear in the GF churchbook in the 1790´s but pr. did not live in Herkimer Co..
surname BACUS
  9433: HENRICH b GF 6 May 1792 (sp Al Malthaner, Elis. Gutbrod)
  9434: BALTES b GF 26 Apr 1795 (sp Bernhard Meneck & Maria)

9435: JOHN BACUS (Backus) - born 9 Jun 1750; died Stark NY 5 Jun 1823 (age 73); m 1772 LENA DOCKSTADER (bp 1755, d 1846) dau of CHRISTIAN DOCKSTADER & CATHERINE NELLIS. Dockstader book (page 44) gives children as Anna (m Henry Louis), Frederick, Catherine (b 1781), John (b 1784), Christian (b 1786, liv. 1846, Livingston Co. NY), William, Magdalena, Elizabeth, Maria (b 1802).

  9435A CATHERINE b GF 7 Jul 1781 (sp Barth Kasselman, Maria Ecker)
  9436: JOHN b GF 10 Apr 1784 (sp. John Dockstader, Gert. Hahn)
  9437: CHRISTIAN b GF 21 Mar 1786 (sp. Jost Klock & Cath.)

9438: HENRY BALDE - born Umstadt Frankfort Germany 14 Nov 1769; died Ilion NY 1855 (Harter book page 20); m 1797 MARGARET RASBACH (wife of Henry, 1803 bp rec.) dau of MARKS RASBACH & SOPHRONIA MOAK. Was a tanner and brought the first piano to Herkimer NY. A Wilhelm Balde, ps. a brother, died HK 12 Nov 1810.
surname BALDE
  9439: WILLIAM H. b ca 1799; liv. 1813 (age 14 at HK Confirm.)
  9440: ELISABETH b ca 1801; liv. 1815 (age 14, HK Ch. confirm.)
  9440A DAVID b HK 3 Nov 1803 (sp Peter Folts & Barbara)
  9441: MARY 1808-1886 m BENJAMIN HARTER

9442: JOHN BARRY - pr. born ca 1735 to 1750; m CHRISTINA ...
surname BARRY
  9443: JOHN bp GF 9 May 1776 (sp. John Thompson & Dorothea)

9444: GEORGE BAUER - born say 1745; pr. died ca 1779-80; m SAL 24 Jan 1769 MARIA ELISABETH N*** (rec. not legible). Was in the 1769 GF militia and a resident of German Flats in May 1775, in both cases listed with the Hasenclever group. We suspect the widow Elisabeth Bowen (Bower misread as Bowen?), whose husband was reported killed at German Town on 2 Aug 1779, may belong here (Mohawk Valley in the Revolution, pg 182). If so they had five children ca 1779, ages given as 10, 8, 6, 4, and 2 (op. cit.); however, the Feb 1780 bp record should then indicate a posthumous child (which it does not).
surname BAUER
  9445: pr. ANNA EVA G. 1778-1844 m ADAM FR. BELL
  9446: GEORGE b SAL 25 Feb 1780 (sp John Keller & Christina)

9447: CHRISTIAN BECKER - pr. born ca 1765 to 1770; m by 1786 CATHERINE ...;
apparently m2 by 1790 BETSY ... Living at Canajoharie in 1790 (SJR bp rec.) and
on 1790 Canajoharie census (1-0-2).

    9447A RACHEL b GF 17 Apr 1786 (sp. John Smidt, Rachel Davis)
    9447B THOMAS bp SJR 5 Sep 1790 (sp John & Elisabeth Connikum)

9448: DIEBOLD BECKER - pr. born ca 1730 to 1750; m by 1770 ELISABETH ...;
apparently m2 by 1786 CATHERINE ... In 1769 GF militia, next in list to Val.
Miller and John Collsh. Theobald Bekker & "Catherine" were sponsors for Dec 1786
bp of Catherine, dau of Philip Bettinger & Margaret, and for Oct 1787 bp of
Theobald, son of Adam Hartman. Pr. the David Baker on 1790 Herkimer census
(2-1-3) in New Germantown group (Witrig, Riema ...)
surname BECKER

    9449: child b SAR 1 Jan 1770 (sp .. Barb. Snek, Chrstn Hostater)
    9450: pr. MARGARET b say 1772; m by 1790 JACOB AYER
    9450A pr. MARIA b say 1775; m 1795 FREDERICK RIEMA
    9451: CATHERINE b say 1782; m HK 1801 GEORGE MATTHEW MILLER

9454: HENRICH BECKER - pr. born ca 1738 to 1758; m by 1778 ANNA EVA ...
Sponsors and naming of children strongly point to wife being ANNA EVA COUNTRYMAN
(Gunterman) pr. dau of MARCUS COUNTRYMAN & CATHERINE AD. BELLINGER. In Col.
Bellinger's Revol. Regiment. A Henrich was sponsor for Aug 1770 SAR bp of
Henrich, son of Christian Hockstater.

    9455: CATHERINE b GF 25 Dec 1778 (sp Joh. Guntermn, Marg. Becker)
    9456: ps. MARCUS b say 1780; m by 1817 ELISABETH KNAUZ
    9457: HENRICH b 25 Oct 1782 (sp Adam Snell, Appol. Gunterman)
    9458: ELISABETH b GF 2 Jul 1784 (sp Jac Huber, Eva Bellinger)
    9459: CONRAD b GF 7 Jul 1786 (sp Adam Bellinger & Elis.)
    9460: MAGDALENA b GF 4 Dec 1791 (sp Pet. Bellinger & Elis.)
    9461: ANNA b GF 7 May 1795 (sp Peter Ad. Bellinger & Elis.)

9462: HENRY BECKER - pr. born ca 1740 to 1764; m by 1781 MARGARET ... Seems
distinct from the above Henry on the basis of difference in wives' names, plus the
fact that each had a child born in 1795 (different months). Ps. the Henry Baker
(b ca 1763) who died in the poor home at Herkimer NY 10 Jan 1838 (age 74-4-27,
noted as a soldier from Germany with Burgoine <in Revol.>) and/or the Henry Bekker
on 1790 Palatine NY census (1-3-4) near Sillebach, Brame, Dockstader, Reese,
Shults, & Kilts.

    9463: ps. HENRICH b GF 6 Sep 1781 (sp Adam Gielty <Kilts> & Cath)
    9463A ANNA b SAL 17 Mar 1795 (sp John Sillebach & Elis.<Dygert>)

9464: WILLIAM BENDER - pr. born ca 1720 to 1735; m by 1767 CATHERINE ... Pr. a
Hasenclever immigrant as William was listed next to Hieronymus Spies & Jacob Meyer
in the 1769 GF militia and next to George Bauer on the May 1775 list of German
Flats residents (Mohawk Valley in the Revolution, pg 166).
surname BENDER

    9465: ps. CATHERINE b say 1753; liv. 1769 (spf Molter bp)
    9466: pr. MARIA ELISABETH ca 1759-1802 m GEORGE WITRIG
    9467: pr. JACOB b say 1761; in Revol. service
    9467A ps. JOHN b say 1763; m by 1789 ELISABETH (spf Bottingr SJR bp)
  +9468: pr. PETER b say 1765; m 1793 ELISABETH EDICK
  +9469: HIERONIMUS bp 1767 (sp Heir. Spies,Arn. Steinwax,Mar. Meyer)

9469: HIERONIMUS BENDER (Henrich) - born SAR 26 Mar 1767; m MARIA ELISABETH ...
(pr. Multer, b 1769, dau of Peter). On 1790 HK census (1-0-1).

> 9470: ELISABETH b GF 6 Sep 1792 (sp Capt. Geo Witrig & M. Elis.)
> 9471: pr. child b GF 16 Oct 1794 (sp Theo. Molter, Cath. Witrig)

9468: PETER BENDER - m GF 8 Jan 1793 ELISABETH EDICK widow of JOHN DINGES. Had
a son GEORGE (b GF 26 Nov 1793, sp Geo. Witrig & M. Elis.<Bender>)

9473: Johan ADAM BENSON - pr. born ca 1730 to 1755; m ELISABETH
> surname BENSON
> 9474: LENA b GF 5 Jul 1777 (sp Jacob Hillenbrand)

9475: HENRY BERKHOFF - pr. born ca 1715 to 1730. In 1769 GF militia, listed
amongst Hasenclever group and next to Arnold Steinwax & Wm. Klein.
> surname BERKHOFF
> 9476: pr. CHRISTIAN b say 1748; liv. 1765 (spf Steinwax bp)

9477: PHILIP BETTINGER - pr. born ca 1740 to 1754; m by 1778 MARGARET ... On
May 1775 list of German Flats residents, next to Jacob Tines (Dinges).
> surname BETTINGER
> 9477A ps. WILLIAM b say 1770; m by 1789 MARGARET ... (SJR bp rec.)
> 9478: PHILIP b GF 19 Jul 1778 (sp Nic. Kolsh & Mar. Fredrica)
> 9479: GEORGE b GF 12 Sep 1784 (sp Michel Witrig & Elis.)
> 9480: CATHERINE b GF 13 Dec 1786 (sp. Deobald Bekker & Cath.)
> 9480A PETER b GF 6 Nov 1794 (sp John Finster & Maria)

9481: HENRICH JOH. BEYER - pr. born ca 1755 to 1774; m GF 21 May 1793 SARA
MISSELES. From the Stone Arabia family of Leonard Beyer and John Beyer who were
in Severinus Dygert's militia co. in 1757. Martin's Snell book (page 53) says the
Beyers came to the Mohawk Valley from Germany ca 1760.
> surname BEYER
> 9482: HENRICH b GF 9 Jan 1794 (sp John Beyer & Anna)
> 9483: MARIA b GF 20 oct 1795 (sp Lenhard Beyer & Maretha)

9484: JOHN BEYER (Bajer) - pr. born ca 1750 to 1770 (ps. the son of John, b SAR
Oct 1761); m GF 9 Mar 1788 MARGARET RITTER. Pr. he or his father was the John
Beyer on 1790 Palatine NY census (4-2-7) in the Sneidersbush area. Had a son JACOB
(b GF Jun 1794, sp H. Riemensndr, Nancy Newman)

9486: LEONARD BEYER (Bajer) - pr. born ca 1755 to 1770; m GF 1 Jan 1789 MARGARET
JOST PETRIE pr. dau of JOST M. PETRIE & CATHERINE KESSLER.

> 9487: JOST b GF 20 Feb 1790 (sp Marc Jos. Petri, Anna Bajer)
> 9488: ELISABETH b GF 23 Feb 1792 (sp John Beyer & Elis.)
> 9489: CATHERINE b GF 7 Apr 1794 (sp Jost Petri, Cath. Getman)
> m HK 1813 JOHN JOH. HOUSE
> 9490: SALLY b SAL 16 Aug 1811 (sp John M Petri & Doro.)

9491: ROBERT JOH. BEYER - pr. born ca 1750 to 1770; m GF 23 Aug 1789 MARIA
CATHERINE VAL. BEYER. Lived at Schneidersbush 1790

> 9492: CATHERINE bp 1 Jan 1790 (SJR sp John Beyer, Marg. Beyer)
> 9493: HENRICH b GF 4 May 1791 (sp Hen. Beyer, Susan Beyer)
> 9494: MARGARET bp SJR 21 Apr 1793 (sp Dines Beyer & Marg.)
> 9495: DAVID b GF 30 Jan 1795 (sp Hen. Garter & Susanna)

9496: VALENTINE BEYER - pr. born ca 1740 to 1753; m SAL 19 Feb 1770 MARGARET FRANK (she was pr. related to Susanna Frank, wife of Hen. Garter). In 1769 GF militia and on 1790 Palatine NY census (1-1-2) listed near Conrad Rickert & John Buye in the Sneidersbush area.

> 9497: CATHERINE b say 1771; m 1789 ROBERT JOH. BEYER
> 9498: ELISABETH b GF 6 Sep 1779 (sp H. Huber & Elis.)
> 9499: ADAM b GF 10 Jun 1784 (sp Adam Bellinger, Cath. Frank)

9500: JOHANNES BIERMAN - pr. born in Germany ca 1665 to 1680; pr. m MARY ... Was on the NY Palatine subs. list in 1710 (1A,2Y) & in 1712 (3A,1Y). Was naturalized at Albany NY 22 Nov 1715, listed next to Fred Kietman & Thomas Shoemaker, and on the 1717 Simmendinger census at New Ansberg (Schmidsdorf) with wife & 3 children. John received Burnetsfield lot #26 and Mary Beerman lot #11.
> > surname BIERMAN
> 9501: MARY b say 1700; m by 1721 FREDERICK GETMAN
> 9502: MARGARET b say 1702; m by ca 1725 JOHANNES RASBACH

9503: JACOB BIRCKY (Bargy) - pr. born ca 1710 to 1720; m ... (b ca 1718, widow of Jacob Bircky died HK 1813 age 95). Pr. one of the Peter Hasenclever workmen who settled ca 1765 at New Petersburg, near Herkimer NY.
> > surname BIRCKY
> 9504: ps. MARIA CATHERINE b say 1740; m PETER GOERNTER (b 1736)
> +9505: pr. JACOB b say 1745; m ANNA ...
> +9506: ps. PETER JAC. b say 1755; m 1790 ELISABETH YOUNG

9507: PETER BIRCKY Sr. - pr. born ca 1720 to 1740; Existence assumed as the Peter Bircky Sr. who served at Oriskany and was in Col. Bellinger's Revol. Regiment (Book of Names page 166). Ps. the Peter on 1790 HK census (1-0-1).

> 9508: ps. BARBARA b say 1760; liv. 1777 (spf Rinckel bp)
> +9509: ps. JACOB b say 1770; m by 1795 ...

9505: JACOB BIRCKY (Bargy) - pr. born ca 1740 to 1750; m ANNA ... (pr. Lentz). Pr. this Jacob was the one in the 1769 GF militia and later in Bellinger's Regiment during the Revolution (with Peter Berci Sr & Peter Jr.). Living at New Germany in 1802. Jacob appears on 1790 Herkimer census (1-2-3)
> > surname BIRCKY
> 9510: PETER b 2 Jan 1782 (sp Pet. Birki, Cath. Lentz); confrm 1802
> 9511: ELISABETH b 1 Sep 1784 (sp Mich. Witrig & Elis.<Lentz>)
> 9512: CATHERINE b 17 Aug 1787 (sp Jac. Lentz & Cath.)
> 9513: JACOB b 25 Dec 1789 (GF sp Jac Witrig & Cath.)
> -   m 1812 CATHERINE WIL. HENNER
> 9514: ANNA b GF 15 Aug 1792 (sp. Peter Lentz & Margaret)
> 9515: SARA b GF 17 Nov 1794 (sp George Riema & Sara)

9509: JACOB BIRCKY - pr. born ca 1760 to 1776; m by 1795 ... This Jacob appears distinct from the Jacob who had child born in Nov 1794. Had child MARIA (b GF 23 Jan 1795, sp Fred. Riema, Maria Becker)

9506: PETER BIRCKY - pr. born ca 1750 to 1772 (son of Jacob); m Ft. Plain NY 14 Sep 1790 ANNA ELISABETH YOUNG (Jung) dau of Joh. CHRISTIAN YOUNG.

> 9517: JACOB b GF 8 Jul 1792 (sp. Jac. Bircky & Anna)
> > m 1811 DOROTHY H. FRANK
> 9518: pr. PETER jr b say 1794; m POLLY (ca 1794-1818)

9518A **FREDERICK BONNSTACK** (Pumpstade) - pr. born ca 1740 to 1775; m GF 25 Nov 1783 MARIA ELISABETH ... On 1790 Canajoharie NY census (1-3-2).
             surname BONNSTACK
        9518B MARIA   b GF 20 Aug 1784 (sp Hen. Walrath & Maria <Bell>)
        9518C EVA   bp SJR 25 Sep 1792 (sp John Dillnbach, Eva Knieskern)

9519: **HENRICH BORDER** - pr. born ca 1740 to 1775; m by 1794 CATHERINE
             surname BORDER
        9520: HENRICH   b GF28 Feb 1794 (sp Nic Armstrong, Anna H Starin)

9521: **CHARLES BORROWS** - m GF 18 Aug 1782 MARGARET FRIEBER ps. a dau of FRANTZ FRIEBA.
             surname BORROWS
        9522: ANNA   b GF 7 May 1783 (sp. Gerrit Walrath & Anna)

9523: **DAVID BOTMAN** (Bodman) - see Putman

9524: **GEORGE BRAUN** - pr. born in Germany ca 1730 to 1745; pr. killed by Indians in German Town (Herk. Co.) NY Tory raid 2 Aug 1779; m by 1767 ELISABETH MARGARET ... Was in 1769 GF militia, amongst Hasensclever group. An Elisabeth Braun, pr. George's wife, was sponsor for May 1776 bp of Eva, dau of Valentin Miller. In Dec 1779 an Elisabeth Braun, possibly a daughter, had a child Maria Sybila (bp at GF, sp Jacob Dinges & Maria Sybila, father noted as PETER ZANG). A Nicholas Braun was living at Palatine NY in 1790. His widow was pr. the Elisabeth Brown petitioning for aid ca 1779 with children then ages 15, 17, & 9 (Mohawk Valley in the Revolution, page 183).
             surname BRAUN
        9525: ps. MARGARET   b say 1759; m by 1778 JOSEPH KESSLER
        9525A ps. ELISABETH   b say 1762; had a child in 1779
        9525B ps. NICHOLAS   b say 1764; liv. 1786 (spf Kessler bp)
        9526: PHILIP JACOB   b SAR 10 Oct 1767
                  (sp. Phil Clements, Jac Bircky, Elis. Keller)
        9527: pr. child   b say 1770; liv. ca 1779 (age 9)

9528: **BALTES BREITENBACHER** - pr. born 1740 to 1750; m SAL 26 Dec 1768 JULIANA SCHNEK pr. dau of GEORGE SCHNEK Sr. Baltes was amongst the Hasensclever immigrants in the mid 1760's and in the 1769 GF militia (listed there with an Abraham Breitenbacher). Was naturalized on 5 Mar 1773. He was wounded during the Tory raid on the New Petersburg settlement in 1780. Supposedly was a self-styled "witch doctor" who advised Henry Harter that his fortunes would improve if he burned down a building with a live pig inside (Papers Presented before the Herkimer Co. Hist. Soc., vol 1, 1896). On 1790 Herkimer census (1-5-4) near Adam Meyer & Valentine Miller and in 1802 was at New Germany (E. Schuyler).
             surname BREITENBACHER
        9529: MARLENA   b 14 Feb 1770 (SAR sp M. Witrig & Maria Marlena)
        9530: pr. GEORGE   b say 1772; m by 1802 ANNA BRODHACK
        9531: JULIANA   b say 1774; m PHILIP BELLINGER (b ca 1773)
        9532: pr. MARGARET   b say 1776; m 1795 THEOBALD RIEMA
        9533: pr. CATHERINE   b say 1777; liv. 1795 (spf Riema bp)
                  m by 1804 WILHELM BALDE (d HK 1810)
        9534: WILHELM   b 7 Apr 1779 (sp John Klein & Maria); ps. d y
        9535: WILLIAM   1782-1842   m 1802 ELISABETH JOS. PETRIE (b 1784)
        9536: JACOB   b 4 Sep 1787 (sp Jac. Eirer & Anna Schnek)
        9537: DANIEL   b 1 Jan 1790 (sp Dan. Weiss & Elis.)
                  m 1814 MARIA LENTZ (dau of Peter)
        9538: HENRICH   b 8 Jan 1793 (sp. Hen. Frank & Barbara)

9539: JOHN BUJE (Boye, Bouje) - pr. born ca 1740 to 1760; by 1779 CATHERINE ...
May be the "John B. Buyie" listed in Klock's Revol. Regiment (Book of Names page
145). Pr. lived in the Riemensneiderbush area (a guess from bp sponsors). Was
sponsor for Dec 1795 bp of James, son of John Rows & Susanna <pr. Beyer>. On 1790
Palatine NY census (2-1-5) in Sneidersbush area.

> surname BUJE
> 9540: MARIA b GF 22 Feb 1779 (sp John Riemensneider & Eva)
> 9541: ANNA b GF 17 Mar 1784 (sp H. Reimensndr & Doro.)
> 9542: ANNA EVA b GF 16 Sep 1786 (sp Ludwig Rickert, Eva Bellinger)

9543: Joh. PETER BUJE - pr. born ca 1740 to 1758; m by 1775 CATHERINE ...
Presumably we see here an ornamental Johan preceding the first name of Peter
(rather than a John, son of Peter).

> 9544: CONRAD b 27 Nov 1775 (sp Conrad Rickert & w.)

9545: GRATES BULSON (Boelson, Bolzer) - pr. born ca 1750 to 1765; living 1800
(spf Helmer bp); m by 1784 ELISABETH ... (ps. Hoyer?). Presumably related to the
Frederick Bulson who lost wife and child at the Andrustown massacre in 1778 (Hatch
papers). On 1790 German Flats census (1-3-3) listed near Henry Crim & George F.
Hoyer. Sons Henrich and Peter were both confirmed at the Herkimer Reform. Church
on 29 Sep 1802. Gradus Bohlson & wife Elisabeth were sponsors for 1800 bp of Eve,
dau of Adam Helmer & Anna (Bellinger).

> surname BULSON
> 9546: HENRICH b say 1783; m by 1807 CATHERINE LEIPER
> 9547: PETER b GF 9 Mar 1785 (sp Pet. Hoyer & Maria <Helmer>)
> 9548: CORNELIS b 13 May 1787 (sp F. Fox); liv. 1812
> 9549: ELISABETH b GF 24 May 1790 (sp Thomas Shoemkr & Elis.)
> 9550: pr. LENA b GF Aug 1792 (sp. Adam Staring & Ernestina)

9551: JOHN BURGDORF - born Koenigsberg Germany ca 1759, died Little Falls NY 7
Feb 1837 (age ca 78); m German Flats NY 22 Sep 1785 MARGARET JAC. KESSLER (b ca
1750, d Danube NY 10 Jul 1829 age 79) dau of JACOB KESSLER & CATHERINE STEELE. On
1790 GF census (1-2-2) listed next to Conrad Kessler & Jacob Jac. Kessler.

> surname BURGDORF
> 9552: JOHANNES b 8 Jan 1786 (sp John Jac. Kessler & Cath.)
>   m 1807 DOROTHY AUG. HESS
> 9553: ELISABETH b Oct 1787 (sp Jac. Kessler jr. & Elis.)
> 9554: JACOB b 8 Jun 1789 (sp Jacob Eysaman &)
>   m 1806 BARBARA GEO. STEELE
> 9555: CATHERINE b 28 Dec 1794 (sp John Joh. Kessler, Cath Meyer)

9556: AARON BUTTERFIELD - pr. born ca 1770 to 1777 (ps. son of Levy who was on
1790 HK census <1-1-2>); m GF 11 Oct 1795 ANNA KESSLER; pr. m2 by 1801 DELIA
KESSLER . Pr. two wives, unless Anna and Delia were same person, and a guess,
based on bp sponsors, that wives were daughters of JOHN KESSLER & ELISABETH
PETRIE. Children were Maria (b HK Aug 1801, bp Jan 1804, sp Mich. Young, Elis.
Casler), Aaron (b 1803, sp Nich. Casler & w. Elis.), Catherine (b 1810, sp John
Casler & w. Cath.), & John (b 1812, sp John J. Petry & w. Maria)

9569: **GOTLIEB CAMERDINGER** - m MAGDALENA MARXWARDEN. In 1757 GF militia.
surname CAMERDINGER
9570: JOHANNES bp Schenectady NY 19 Feb 1758 (Pearson book)

9571: **GEORGE CARL** (Carrol, Kessler) - pr. born ca 1740 to 1760 (ps. son of
the Fredrich Carl in 1757 GF militia); m by 1782 MARGARET ... The surname
KESSLER was entered on the 1782 bp record, which we think may be a hint that
he was raised by a Kessler family. Was just "George Carl" on baptism rec.
from 1784 to 1788. On 1790 GF census (1-4-2).
surname CARL
9572: PETER b GF 23 Apr 1782 (sp Hen. Joh Walrth, M Cath Dygert)
9573: MARIA b 10 Apr 1784 (sp Geo Hausman, Mar. Elis. Kessler)
9574: HENRICH b 1 Apr 1786 (sp Jacob Kessler & Elis.)
9575: JOHANNES b GF 4 Jun 1788 (sp John Kessler, Barb. Hausser)
9576: DEITRICH b 4 May 1790 (sp Diet. Kesslar & Cath.)
9577: MARGARET b 1 Feb 1792 (sp Adam N. Staring & Cath.<Weaver>)

9578: **CHRISTIAN CASSELMAN** - pr. born ca 1750 to 1765; m GF 11 Jan 1785 ANNA
BARBARA MEYER pr. dau of JACOB MEYER.
surname CASSELMAN
9579: LUDWIG b GF 2 Oct 1788 (sp Ludw. Meyer, Lena Petri)
9580: HENRICH b GF 24 Jan 1790 (sp Hen. Meyer, Cath. Klock)
9581: PETER b GF 29 Jun 1791 (sp Fritz H<iels> & Juliana)
9582: CATHERINE MARGARET b 2 Sep 1792 (sp Caspar Zoller, Marg. Meyr)
9583: MARIA b GF 20 Dec 1794 (sp Joh. Riema, Maria Math...)
m 1814 HENRY N. DOCKSTADER

9584: **JOSEPH CHAPMAN** - m by 1790 ELIZABETH ...
surname CHAPMAN
9585: MARIA b GF 19 Feb 1790 (sp. James Woodert & Cath.)

9586: **ARCHIBALD CLARK** - pr. born ca 1735 to 1760; m by 1782 MARY ... A Mr.
Clark had a daughter Nancy Stone (bp GF 13 May 1792).
surname CLARK
9587: JOHN b GF 6 Aug 1782 (sp H. Witherstine, Maria Stevens)

9588: **JACOB CLEMENTS** - pr. born ca 1748 to 1760; m by 1781 EVA CATHERINE
... (ps. Keller, b ca 1760, d HK 25 Sep 1833 age 73). Pr. related to the
Matthew Clemons in 1769 GF militia (Hasenclever group <Math. Clements was
over age 50 on Tyron Co. census ca 1776>) and Philip Clements in Bellinger's
GF Regiment. Jacob served at Oriskany (Arnold's Ayer book). Sons Michael &
Daniel wit. the 1815 marriage of Cath. Clements. Mr. Clements was on 1790 HK
census (1-2-3) near Chr. Hockstater & Fred. Ayer, New Germantown area.
surname CLEMENTS
9589: JACOB b GF 6 Aug 1781 (sp Geo. Fehling & Cath.<Walrath>)
9590: APPOLONIA b GF 21 Feb 1783 (sp John Klock, Appol. Keller)
9591: MARGARET b GF Oct 1784 (sp H. Wohleben & Margaret)
9592: MICHAEL b GF 19 Jan 1788 (sp Mich. Witrig & Elis.)
m by 1811 CATHERINE LENTZ
9593: JOHN b 19 Sep 1789 (sp John Keller & Maria)
9594: GEORGE b GF 25 Aug 1792 (sp. Jac Witrig & Cath. Elis.)
9595: CATHERINE b GF 5 Aug 1794 (sp Jac. Witrig & Cath. Elis.)
m 1815 JOSEPH GREIMS
9596: DANIEL b say 1796; liv. 1815 (wit. Cath. Clements mar.)

9597: **JOHN CLINE** (Klein) - pr. born before 1740; died by 25 Oct 1790 (will probated); ml by 1768 KUNIGUNDA ELISABETH ... (liv. 1778); ps. m2 by 1780 MARIA .... (may be a separate John Klein). Was "Joh. Wilh. Klein" on 1768 bp rec. (with wife Kunigunda), which we think means John son of Wilhelm. A John Cline was on the 1790 Mohawk NY census (3-0-5).

surname KLEIN
```
     9597A ps. MARTIN  b say 1757; m by 1779 NEELTJE VAN HORNE
     9598: ps. WILLIAM  b say 1762; m GF 1782 widow CATHERINE RICKERT
     9599: ps. CATHERINE  b SAR 7 Feb 1768 (sp Cat. Keller, H. Bekker)
     9600: GERTRUDE  b GF 25 Jun 1776 (sp Joh. Kolsch, Gert. Steinway)
     9601: ANNA AMELIA CATHERINE  b SAL 28 Mar 1778 (of John & Kun. Elis)
                 (sp Nic. Keltesch, Anna Amelia Cath. Steinwax)
     9602: JOST HERKIMER  b GF Dec 1780 (sp Jost Herkimer & Cath.)
```

9603: **WILLIAM CLINE** (Klein) - born in Holland 1736 (DAR vol 66 page 123); died NY State 1814; m MARIA ... DAR has mother of Joseph (b 1783) as MARIA ... (b 1740, d 1827). Had 2 adults & 5 children on 1778 German Flats relief. On 1790 Caughnawaga NY census (3-5-5).

surname CLINE
```
     9604: ps. MARTHA  b say 1770; m by 1791 FRANS RASCHER (SJR bp)
     9605: WILLIAM  b GF 21 Oct 1775 (sp John Ruff & Maria)
     9606: JOHANNES  b GF 8 Mar 1778 (sp John Frank & Anna Eva)
     9607: JOSEPH  1783-1849  m EVELINE LENGENFELTER
     9608: ANNA  bp SJR 30 Jul 1790 (sp Jacob & Cath. Mender)
     9609: JEMS (James)  bp SAL 20 May 1793 (sp John Streher)
```

9610: **Capt. ESAU COLE** - born 15 Jan 1733 (son of Seth); m SUSANNA ... Was a Capt. in the Revolution, serving at the Battle of Bunker Hill (Beers History of Herkimer Co., page 261). About 1790 he moved from Swansea Mass., where most of his children were born ("The Descendents of James Cole of Plymouth" by Ernest Byron Cole), to Fairfield (Herk. Co.) NY.

surname COLE
```
     9611: MARY  b 20 Oct 1768
     9612: JOSEPH  b 9 May 1700
     9613: MARSY  b 24 Jul 1773; m 1797 Mr. TABOR
     9614: SETH  b 16 Apr 1776
     9615: JAMES  b 4 May 1778; m 1821 MARGARET PUTMAN
     9616: GILBERT  b Swansea MA 16 May 1780
     9617: SUSANNAH  b 6 Nov 1782; m 1803 CONRAD M. FOLTS
     9618: JAMES  b 21 Apr 1785
     9619: JOANNA  b 24 Mar 1788
     9620: ANNA G.  b 12 Feb 1791; m PETER M. FOLTS
```

... **COLSH** - see Kelsch.

9621: **FREDERICK COOPER** - m ANNA STAHRING (b 1785) dau of ADAM. Son Nicholas (b HK Jun 1803, sp Jos. Cooper & w. Mar. Schutt) d HK 1807.

9622: **JOHN COURT** - m by 1791 ...
surname COURT
```
     9623: CATHERINE  b GF 2 Apr 1791 (sp Jac. Lentz & Cath.)
```

9624: **Col. EBENEZEER COX** - pr. born before 1735; died at Oriskany 6 Aug 1777; m Stone Arabia NY 7 Feb 1769 ELISABETH KLOCK (MARGARET in DAR# 43157, b 1750) dau of GEORGE KLOCK & MARGARET CATH. WALLRATH. Prior to the Oriskany ambush, most accounts say he pressured Gen. Herkimer to proceed with haste rather than caution, resulting in the disasterous surprise ambush at Oriskany (in which Col. Cox reportedly was amongst the first to fall).

surname COX

9624A ps. ANNA   1765-1851   m JOHN J. FAILING (Fehling book)
9625: EBENEZEER   1775-1847   m NANCY KELLER

9626: JOHN COX - m by 1763 ANNA ... Was sponsor at bp Nov 1762 of dau of George Whileing (Whitting). Also sp. at son Thomas' bp were William & Bally Queen.

9627: THOMAS   b GF 6 Jan 1763 (sp. Geo. Whitting ...)
9628: ANNA   b SAR 28 Oct 1769 (sp Anna <Nellis> & Jacob Geo. Klok)

9629: FASIER COX - born 1744; died N. Gage NY 5 Feb 1802; m 1775 CATHERINE PETRIE dau of DANIEL PETRIE & CATHERINE ELISABETH FOLTS (S. Kimball notes). Fasset Cox was listed on the 1790 Herkimer census (1-3-6).

9630: JOST   b 20 Sep 1776 (sp Jost Petrie & M. Elis.)
9631: ELISABETH   b 22 Apr 1778 (sp Pet. Bellinger, Delia Petrie)
9632: CATHERINE   b 29 Jan 1780 (sp Patrick Gimmel & Cath.)
9633: HENNA   b 1 Dec 1781 (sp Dan Petrie, Mar. Elis. Kessler)
9633A CIEMI (James) b GF 24 Aug 1783 (sp John Petri, Anna Kessler)
9634: MARGARET   b 13 Jul 1785 (sp John Burghdorf & Marg. Kessler)
9635: DELIA (Adelia)   1787-1877   m NICHOLAS AD. STARING
9636: DANIEL   b 12 Apr 1789 (GF sp Jac Petri, Cath. Kessler)
9637: MARIA   b SJR 20 May 1791 (sp Jacob Weber & Maria)
9638: LYDIA   b 21 Nov 1794 (sp Geo. Folts & Christina)
           m 1816 DAVID H. HUBER

9639: HENRY CRANTZ - pr. born ca 1740 to 1750; pr. m1 GERTRUDE STEELE (b say 1745) dau of DEITRICH STEELE; m2 GF 5 Sep 1802 ANNA MARIA FULMER (b ca 1762, d 1830 age 68) widow of FREDERICK HESS (Vosburgh's HK book, vol 1 page 302). Henry was in Revol. service in Bellinger's Regiment and pr. related to the JACOB CRANTZ, who was a GF resident in May 1775 and who sponsored 1776 bp of John Petrie, and to CATHERINE CRANTZ (b 1750) who married ADAM STEELE.

surname CRANTZ

9640: JACOB   1777-1837   m1 ANNA HESS (ca 1787-1811)
             m2 1812 CATHERINE JOH. OSTERODE (Osterhout)
9641: ELISABETH   b 27 Mar 1785 (sp Marc Crantz, Cath. Steele)
             m 1808 PETER BELLINGER (son of John Fred.)
9642: DOROTHY HEN.   b 2 Jul 1786 (sp Geo. Steele & Doro.)
             liv. 1803 (HK Ch. confirm.); m 1808 FREDERICK HESS
9643: ELISABETH   ca 1787-1864   m PETER F. BELLINGER
9644: MARCUS   bp SJR 31 Jan 1790 (sp Marc Kessler & Delia)
9644A MICHAEL   b HK 25 Jun 1803 (sp Pet. Bellinger & Dorothy)

9645: Rev. MARCUS CRANTZ (Grant) - pr. born ca 1748 to 1760; m 29 Nov 1785 CATHERINE DYGERT (Getman book page 369) dau of Capt. WILLIAM DYGERT & MARIA ELISABETH ECKER; m2 28 Apr 1805 CATHERINE HOUSE (b 1768, d Sep 1851). Children by his first wife were HENRICH (b GF 12 Jul 1786, sp Hen. Crantz & Gertr.), WILHELM (b GF 1 Nov 1787, sp. Wm Dygert & Marg., m 1812 REBECCA HENNER), ELIZABETH (1789-1856, m 1811 BARTLETT BROADHACK GETMAN), MARC (b SJR 4 Aug 1791, sp. Wm Helmer, Eva Dygert, m 1815 EVA G. HELMER), HENRICH (b GF 2 Dec 1793, sp Hen. Crantz & Gertr.), JOHN (b GF 5 Nov 1795, sp John Pfeiffer & Lena), CATHERINE b 1796, CONRAD (b 1798), and DAVID (b 1800). By his second wife Marcus had PETER (b 1806), EVA (b 14 May 1808, sp. Hen. Helmer & Eva), and ABRAHAM (b 21 Nov 1809, sp. Tho. Shoemaker & Cath.).

9652: MICHEL CRANTZ (Grantz) - m by 1780 CHRISTINA ... (ps. Davis).

9653: MARIA b GF 18 Jan 1780 (sp Peter Davis & Maria)

9654: GEORGE CRONHART - pr. born ca 1740 to 1750, liv. 1790; m by 1769 ANNA
MARIA ... Was in 1769 GF militia within Hasenclever group, next to Henry
Schaeffer & Georg Brown. Maria Cronhart was sponsor for Jan 1771 bp of Deobald,
son of John Riema. Pr. the George Grownhart on 1790 GF census (2-2-3). A George
Cronhart was sponsor, with Elis. Miller, for Sep 1790 SJR bp of George, son of
Joseph Diker & Margaret of German Flats.
                    surname CRONHART
    9655: GEORGE b SAR 1 Jan 1770 (sp Geo Schiff, Cath Rima)
    9609: pr. ELISABETH b say 1773; m GF 1793 JOHN FOSTER
    9656: HENRICH b GF 16 May 1784 (sp Hen Wohleben & Margaret)

.... CROUCH - see Kreid.

9657: Capt. GEORGE DACKSTETER - pr. born ca 1735 to 1740 (son of Cornelius & his
wife, a Mohawk Indian); dec'd by 1807; m SARA MARTIN (b ca 1738, d 1833 age 95).
A descendent of Palatine immigrant George Dockstader, he was a Capt. in the
Revolution and a leader of the Oneida Indian tribe. In Jan 1807 his widow Sara
applied for a pension and land ownership rights. George & Sara, noted as Indian,
were sponsors for May 1787 GF bp of Sara, dau of John Tenny (Deny) & Dorothy.
                    surname DACKSTETER
    +9658: JACOB ca 1755-1832 m LEA ...
    9659: CORNELIUS b ca 1758; d 1814; was an Oneida Chieftain
                    killed at Battle of Chippewa in the War of 1812
    9660: DOROTHY (Dolly) b say 1764; m by 1787 JOHN DENY
    9661: PETER b ca 1767 (age 65 in 1832); m Ms. STOCKBRIDGE

9658: JACOB DACKSTETER - born ca 1755; died 1832; m LEA ... An Indian.

    9662: DOROTHY b GF Dec 1785 (sp John Deny & Doro.); pr. d y
    9663: GEORGE b GF 25 Feb 1787 (sp Geo. Smarth & Cath.)
                    m POLLY MYTOP (b 1785, a Delaware Indian)
    9664: DOROTHY bp GF 26 Jan 1790 (sp John <Deny> & Dorothy)
    9665: MARTINUS b GF 16 Aug 1791

9666: FRANK DAYTON - m ... Had son JOHN WEMPLE DAYTON (b GF 24 Jun 1792)

9667: HENRICH DEBUS - m CATHERINE ... Pr. related to the Barbara who married by
1795 Henry Jac. Meyer. Ps. the Henry Dabush on 1790 Canjoharie census (1-2-4)
listed near Monks, Dievendorf, & Henry S. Meyer.
                    surname DEBUS
    9668: ELISABETH b GF 4 Jan 1778 (sp Wm Emgie & Maria Margaret)

9669: JACOB DEBUS - m CATHERINE ... Pr. the Jacob Dabush listed in Col.
Bellinger's Revol. Regiment (Book of Names page 166). Was a sponsor for Jun 1793
bp of Etel girl and Jacob DeBus & Catherine were sponsors for Jul 1795 bp of
Catherine, dau of Henrich Ansted & Elisabeth (Ritter).
                    surname DEBUS
    9670: JACOB b GF 19 Jun 1778 (sp John Riemnsneidr & Maria)
    9671: LUDWIG b GF Jul 1785 (sp Ludwg Rickert & Elis. Ritter)
    9672: DANIEL b GF 14 Jul 1788 (sp Geo. Etel & Maria)
    9673: JOHANNES b GF 30 Jan 1791 (sp Ludwig Meyer & Cath.<Etel>)

9674: ANDREAS DEEGER (Dygert?) - born in Germany ca 1751 (fr. death rec.); died Herkimer NY 1830; m by 1787 CATHERINE MILLER (name given as Anna Miller on 1804 ch. rec. for son´s death) dau of VALENTIN MILLER. Pr. the Andrew Dygert on 1790 HK census (1-1-2) near Wm Dygert Jr, Peter Dygert & Thomas Fulmer. His surname is close to Dygert, but his birth in Germany seems to separate him from the early Mohawk Valley Dygerts.

surname DEEGER
9675: ELISABETH b GF 24 May 1788 (sp Phil. Bettinger, Elis. Weis)
          m 1812 NICHOLAS SPOHN jr.
9676: JOHANNES ANDREAS b GF 20 Sep 1789 (sp Jac Ejer, Elis Miller)
9677: CHRISTIAN b GF Mar 1792 (sp Chrstn Hockstr & Cath.)
9678: ANNA CATHERINE b SJR 30 Jan 1794 (sp Val. Miller & Maria)
9678A JOHN b say 1798; m 1816 MARGARET SPOHN
9679: GEORGE FRED. b ca 1801, d HK Oct 1804
9679A VALENTIN b 31 Dec 1802; m 1833 CATH. SHOEMAKER
9679B CATHERINE b 8 Jun 1806 (Joh Folts & Cath); m 1823 JACOB HERDER
9679C ANNA b Herkimer NY Jun 1812

9680: JACOB DEEK - pr. born ca 1715 to 1745 (ps. son of Andreas Deek who was an early church of the Manheim Lutheran Church ca 1745, as in Book of Names pge 61); m SAR 15 Nov 1764 ANNA MARGARET WEAVER ps. a dau of ANDREAS WEAVER. Parents of children baptised in 1771 were listed as Jacob Deg & Margareth (pr. this couple).

surname DEEK
9681: ANDREAS b 21 Mar 1766 (sp. Jac. Petrie, Barb. Elis. Weber)
9682: CATHERINE b SAR 11 Oct 1767 (sp Cath. Weber, Jac Bauman)
9683: ANNA MARIA bp SAR Aug 1769 (sp Jac Kessler & Mar. Doro.)
9684: pr. ADAM bp SAL 1771 (sp Adam Jung & w.)
9685: pr. GEORGE bp SAL 1771 (sp Geo. Meyer & w.)

9686: PETER DELANEY - pr. born ca 1720 to 1740; m ... Apparently an early resident of German Flats area, but none of this surname can be seen on 1790 Gf/HK census. See Harter book (page 7).

surname DELANEY
9687: BARBARA b say 1755; m by 1775 LORENTZ PHIL. HARTER

9688: PATRICK DELANEY - pr. born ca 1720 to 1740; m MARIA BARBARA CUNINGHAM. Also have in German Flats Church records (Vosburgh) bp of Catherine (b 1 Dec 1765, sp. Hen. Herkimer & w. Cath.)

9689: ANNETJE bp Schenectady NY 4 Oct 1760
9690: CATHERINE b 10 Jun 1763 (sp. Fred. Getman & w. Cath.)
          pr. m by 1785 FREDERICK ITTIG
+9691: JOHANNES b 24 Sep 1765 (sp. Joh. Cuningham, Marg. Wentz)
9692: WILHELM b SAR May 1768 (sp Geo. Herkimer, Marg. Cuningham)

9692A JAMES DELANY - m by 1792 ALIDA ... Lived at Canajoharie in 1792.

9292B MARIA bp SJR 23 Dec 1792 (sp Dines Krankheit & Bally)

9691: JOHANNES DELANEY - born 24 Sep 1765; m by 1792 ELISABETH ...

9693: ELISABETH b SJR 21 Dec 1792 (sp Deit. Demuth & Elis.)
9694: ANDREAS b GF 23 Nov 1794 (sp John Dockstader & Cath.)

9695: PETER DELANEY - pr. born ca 1760 to 1778 (ps. a son of Patrick); m by 1795 MARGARET ... pr. MARGARET HESS (her surname on 1803 bp record). Pr. the Peter Delaney who was a sponsor, with Maria Leithal, for Jul 1794 bp of Catherine, dau of Lorentz Ph. Harter & Barbara (Delaney).

      9696: PATRICK b GF 5 May 1795 (sp Wm Delaney, Marg Harter)
      9696A pr. GERTRUDE b HK 22 Jan 1803 (sp Jac. Crantz, Maria Folmer)

9697: JOHN DENY - pr. born ca 1750 to 1765 (son of LOUIS DENY a Frenchman and his wife, a Mohawk Indian); m by 1787 DOROTHY DACKSTETER (d 1833) dau of GEORGE DACKSTETER & SARA. An Indian.
                 surname DENY
      9698: LUIS b GF Dec 1785 (sp. Maj. Pet. Schuyler & wife)
      9699: SARA b GF 6 May 1787 (sp Geo. Dackstaeder & Sara, Indian)
              pr. m by 1807 JOHN GERLACH
      9700: ABRAHAM bp GF 26 Jan 1790 (sp Abhrm & Cath., Indians)
      9701: JOHN b GF 2 Oct 1792 (sp David <Indian> & Mary Deny)
      9702: MARIA b GF Sep 1793 (sp Abhm Rosencrantz & Maria)

9703: THEOBALD DIETERICH (Dewald Dieterich) - pr. born ca 1750 to 1762; liv. 1807; m by 1783 MARGARET ... (b ca 1762, d Herkimer NY 4 Nov 1807 age 45 as wife of Dewald Deiterich). Debald Dietrich & Margaret sponsored Apr 1783 bp of Margaret, dau of Debald Meyer. On 1790 German Flats census (2-3-5).
               surname DIETERICH
      9704: CATHERINE b GF 1 Sep 1783 (sp John Armstrong & Cath.)
      9705: THEOBALD b GF 7 Aug 1785 (sp Pet. J. Starin & Maria)
      9706: JACOB b GF 22 Feb 1787 (sp Wm Klepsattle)
      9707: HENRICH b GF 1 Sep 1788 (sp Henry Jos. Starin & Elis.)
           liv. Frankfort NY 1808 (wit. for Ittig mar.)
      9708: JOHANNES b SJR 5 Sep 1790 (sp John Connikum & Maria)
      9709: DANIEL b GF 24 May 1792 (sp Hen. Dygert & Maria)
      9710: NICHOLAS b GF 5 Aug 1794 (sp Nich H Staring & w.)

9711: JACOB DINGES (Tynges) - pr. born ca 1730 to 1750; m by 1767 MARIA SYBILA ... Jacob Tynges was listed with the Hasenclever men on the 1769 GF militia. Jacob Dinges was a sponsor, with Michel Seitzer & Susanna Margaret, for Aug 1767 SAR bp of Jacob, son of Nicholas Ryan & Elisabeth. Jacob Dines & Maria Sybila were sponsors for Nov 1770 bp of a dau of Lorentz Rinckel. In Revol. service in Bellinger's Regiment (Book of Names page 168).
               surname DINGES
  +9712: pr. JOHN b say 1766; m 1785 ELISABETH MARC. ITTIG
      9713: ps. MARGARET b say 1770; liv. 1786 (spf Munterbach bp)
      9714: ps. ELISABETH JAC. b say 1772; liv. 1792 (spf Munterbach bp)

9715: JOHANNES DINGES (Tynges) - pr. born ca 1760 to 1767; died by Sep 1791; m 1785 ELISABETH MARC. EDICK. His widow Elisabeth m2 1793 PETER BENDER. Lived at New Germany (E. Schuyler) in 1789. In Revol. service in Col. Bellinger's Regiment.

      9716: ADAM b GF 1 Jul 1786 (sp Johan Adam Hartman & Cath.)
      9717: ELISABETH b SJR 11 Oct 1789 (sp Christphr Strubel & Elis.)
      9718: EVA b SJR 11 Sep 1791 (posthumous)
              (sp Hen. Meyer, Eva Sallie)

9725: JOHN EARL - born ca 1785; died Herkimer 21 Mar 1830 (age 45); m MARGARET PETRY (b 1791, d 1843) dau of Dr. WILLIAM PETRY & MARGARET WOLF. Was a blacksmith.
surname EARL
    9726: SAMUEL   an attorney in Herkimer
    9726A WILLIAM b ca 1819; d 21 Jul 1825 (age 6-6-)
    9727: ROBERT 1824-1902 m 1852 JULIET WILKINSON

9728: JOHN EASTOL (Istol) - m by 1786 MARIA .. Ps. the John Astel & Elisabeth who had a daughter Elisabeth bp GF Jan 1782 (sp Peter Getman). Pr. the John Isdale on 1790 GF census (3-1-4).
surnam EASTOL
    9729: ANNA b GF 4 Jan 1786 (sp John Frank & Appolonia)
    9730: JAMES (Ciems) b GF 15 Jul 1789 (sp Ciems Nasch & Anna)
        m 1812 ANNA ORENDORF (ca 1791-1835)

9731: CONRAD EIGENAUER - born ca 1748; died 27 Apr 1812 age 64; m ANNA SPOHN (b ca 1760, d 31 Oct 1834 age 74-5-15) dau of NICHOLAS SPOHN & ELISABETH DIEVENDORF. On 1790 Herkimer census (2-2-2).
surname EIGENAUER
    9732: ELISABETH b 23 Sep 1785; m 1804 NICHOLAS JOH. KESSLER
    9733: JOHANNES b GF 17 Dec 1786 (sp John Frank & Appolonia)
    9734: JACOB b 24 Dec 1787 (sp Jac. Bashor & Cath.)
        m 1812 BOLLY SMITH (dau of John)
    9735: SUSANNA b GF 29 Aug 1789 (sp Hen. Spohn, Sus. Wohleben)
    9736: CATHERINE (twin) b 13 Jan 1791 (sp Nic. Spohn & Cath.)
    9737: ANNA (twin) b 1791; m 1814 JOHN NASH
    9738: CONRAD b GF 24 Sep 1792 (sp Geo. Hausman & M. Elis.)
    9739: JOST b GF 1 Dec 1794 (sp Jost Petri, Lena Kessler)
    9740: pr. MARIA ca 1799-1839 m DEIDRICK SHOEMAKER

9741: Major JOHN EISENLORD - pr. born ca 1730 to 1745; killed at Oriskany 6 Aug 1777; m SAR 8 Jan 1767 ELISABETH CRIM dau of PETER CRIM (Shults book page 53). John was naturalized 20 Mar 1762 and early in the Revolution was a leader in the Tryon Co. Committe of Safety
surname EISENLORD
+9742: JOHN 1768-1838 m 1795 CATHERINE STRAYER
    9743: CHRISTOPHER b 13 Feb 1770 (sp Chrstphr Shults jr, Cath. Crim)
    9744: PETER b SAL 19 Apr 1772 (sp Pet. Crim jr, Christina Walrth)
    9745: CATHERINE b SAL 10 Oct 1774 (sp Isaac Paris & w. Cath.)

9742: JOHN EISENLORD jr. - born SAR 20 Jan 1768; died 1838; m 1795 CATHERINE STRAYER (b 1770, d 1840) dau of JOHN BURKHARD STRAYER & MARIA SHULTS. Was sheriff of Montgomery Co. in 1817 (Mohawk Valley in the Revolution, page 240).

    9746: JOHN 1795-1880 m MARIA JAC. FOX

9747: GEORGE ETEL - pr. born ca 1720 to 1745; m by 1763 MARIA DOROTHEA ...
surname ETEL (Edel)
+9748: HENRICH b 6 Jan 1763 (sp. Hen. Riemnsnider & w.)
    9749: JOHANNES b 11 Jun 1764 (sp. Joh. Ritter & W. Anna Barbara)
+9750: JOST b 6 Apr 1766 (sp. Joh. Jost Petrie, Elis. Riemensndr)
+9751: pr. JOHANNES bp 2 Apr 1770 (sp Joh Riemnsndr, Gert. Wndecker)
    9752: pr. CATHERINE G. b say 1772; m 1791 LUDWIG MEYER
    9753: GEORGE b 27 Jul 1778 (sp Valtn Bajer & Anna Marg.)

9748: **HENRICH ETEL** - born 6 Jan 1763; m 2 Apr 1793 CATHERINE CONR. KLOCK. Had a dau SUSANNA (b GF 1794 (sp. George Backus & Susanna).

9751: **JOHANNES ETEL** - pr. the John bp Apr 1770 (son of George); m GF 9 Mar 1788 MARIA BEYER (presume d before 1793); then JOHANNES G. ETEL m (2nd) GF 3 Feb 1793 LENA KLOCK. Lived at Sneidersbush in 1793.

    9755: pr. JOST bp SJR 16 Sep 1792 (sp Hen. Etel, Anna Bayer)
                by 2nd wife
    9756: JOHN b SJR 6 Aug 1793 (sp John Petri, Anna Klock)
    9757: MARIA b GF 30 May 1795 (sp Jost Etel & Maria)

9750: **JOST ETEL** - born 6 Apr 1766; m by 1790 GERTRUDE ...

    9758: ANNETJE b GF 24 Jan 1790 (sp Joh. Bayer & Anna)

9759: **CHRISTIAN ETX** - born 11 Nov 1713; died Ft. Plain NY 7 Nov 1789; m 7 Nov 1730 MARIA SPIES. Will probated 1812 lists children as Christian, William, Elisabeth, Mary, Catherine, & Gertrude.
               surname ETX
    9759A ELISABETH b say 1747; m SAR 1767 JOHN WALLRATH
    9759B ps. ADAM b say 1749; liv. 1769 (spf Hutmacher bp)
    9760: pr. MARIA b say 1751; m SAR 30 Oct 1770 PETER LAUX
    9760A WILLIAM b say 1758; m FPL 1792 ELISABETH BROWN

9761: **BALTHASAR FALK** - born ca Feb 1760, died Herkimer NY 8 Apr 1838 (age 78-2-3); m1 SARA ...; m2 by 1801 MARIA AD. SMITH (b say 1773; d HK 17 Sep 1834) dau of ADAM SMITH & SARAH HILTS. Baltas Falk was a shoemaker.
               surname FALK
    9762: WILHELMINA b say 1790; m 1810 GODFRIED HILTS
    9763: DOROTHY b say 1794; m 1814 JOHN HELMER (son of John)
    9764: HENRY b say 1798; m 1823 EVA SMALL (dau of Melchior)
                by 2nd wife
    9765: ADAM b 25 Dec 1801; m 1824 ELISABETH SPOON
    9766: JACOB b 4 Oct 1806; m 1831 MAGDALENA CHRISTMAN
    9767: SARAH ANN b 10 Jan 1811; d 28 Aug 1830 age 19-7-18
    9768: DANIEL b 18 Jul 1813; m SARAH ANN HISER

... **FEDDERLY** - see Vetterly.

9769: **JOHN FINSTER** - born 23 Apr 1760; died 9 Nov 1855; m1 MARY FREDERICA SCNECK (b ca 1766, d 25 Aug 1816 age 50); m2 MARGARET BEKKER widow of JACOB AYER. Came to America in 1764 with his step-father Frederick Ayer (Oyer) and settled at Hasenclever's New Petersburg area. Living at "New Deutschland" in 1789 (SJR bp rec.). John was a weaver, farmer, held several town offices, and built two saw mills ("Frederick Oyer and His Descendents" by Phyllis Oyer).
               surname FINSTER
    9770: MARY (Polly)
    9771: JOHN b GF 4 Jun 1787 (sp Balt. Breitnbchr & Jul.); d 1877
    9772: GEORGE bp SJR 3 Mar 1789 (sp Fred Ayer, Elis. Hofsttr)
    9773: PETER b GF 2 May 1791 (sp Pet. Eier, Marg. Beyer)
    9774: PHILIP b GF 4 Dec 1793 (sp Phil. Bettinger & Marg.)
    9775: CATHERINE 1795-1855 m PETER F. AYER
    9776: JACOB
    9777: WILLIAM

9778: **PAUL FLAGG** - pr. born ca 1705 to 1725; Was a GF resident in May 1775.
surname FLAGG (Flack, Vlack)
9778A ps. HENRICH b say 1743; m SAR 1762 DOROTHY ROHRIG
9779: ps. CATHERINE b ca 1747; d HK 29 Dec 1825 (age 78-8-9)
m 1765 PETER WOHLEBEN
9779A ps. JOHN b say 1749; liv. Jan 1778 (spf Fyles bp)
9779B ps. ANNETJE b say 1751; m by 1772 GEORGE FYLES (Feyl)
9780: ps. PETER ca 1753-1844 m SOPHIA WOHLEBEN
9781: ps. MARIA b say 1755; liv. 1770 (spf Wohleben bp)
9782: ps. SUSANNA 1756-1850 m JACOB WOHLEBEN

9780: **PETER FLAGG Sr.** - pr. born ca 1753; died 25 Jun 1844 (age 91, cemet.
rec.); m1 SOPHIA WOHLEBEN (b say 1754) dau of NICHOLAS WOHLEBEN; ps. m2 ABIGAIL
... (b ca 1764, d 24 Apr 1813 age 49, HCH cemet. rec.). Had 2 adults & 2 children
on 1778 GF relief. Hardin (Herk. Co. page 361) says that in July 1778 Peter
Flagg, Thomas Van Horne, and Richard Wohleben (sic.) took after the Andrustown
Tory raiders and were able to rescue a woman and her child from their Indian
captors. Pr. the Peter Flagg, age over 45, on 1800 Herkimer NY census.

9783: ps. DOROTHY 1773-1853 m MICHAEL ITTIG (b 1771)
9784: JACOB b Nov 1780 (sp Fred. Bellingr & Lena)
9785: PETER b GF 4 Sep 1783 (sp Wm Wohlgemuth, Marg. Leip); d 1861
9786: JOST b GF 12 Sep 1785 (sp Jost Herkimer & Cath.)

9787: **JOHN FONGIE** - pr. born ca 1735 to 1760; died by Jul 1785; m by 1781 LENA
... Widow Lena m2 GF Jul 1785 John Neuhoff.
surname FONGIE
9788: LENA b GF 21 Jan 1781 (sp Marg. Rosencrantz, John Neuhoff)
9789: ANNA b GF 21 Sep 1782 (sp John Bigbread & Anna)

9790: **JAMES FORBES** ("Ciems Forbes") - m GF 2 Feb 1784 MARGARET NELLIS. Name
appears as Varbos in GF church records of the 1780´s. The Forbes family
apparently lived east in Montgomery Co., as none appear on the 1790 GF/HK census.
Pr. the James on 1790 Palatine NY census (1-3-2) listed next to John Nellis.
surname FORBES
9791: ELISABETH b GF 14 Mar 1786 (sp Jac C Nellis, Elis G Nellis)
9792: JAMES bp SJR 23 Jan 1791 (sp Jacob Klock, Elis. Nellis)
9793: MARIA b 19 Jan 1794 (sp John C. Nellis, Maria G Nellis)

9794: **RUSSEL FORMAN** (Furman) - m by 1789 SARA ...; pr. m2 ANNA WOHLEBEN. On
1790 GF census (1-6-1). Russel Forman & Anna were sponsors for Aug 1804 bp of
Russel, son of Ger. Van Schlaik & Catherine Wohleben.
surname FORMAN
9795: pr. ROBERT b say 1782; m by 1805 MARIA WOHLEBEN
9796: HENRICH b GF Mar 1788 (sp Hen. N Staring & Elis.<Piper>)
9797: RUSSEL b GF 23 Dec 1789 (sp John Smidt & Maria Elis.)
9798: MARIA ELISABETH b GF 13 Aug 1791 (sp Jost Shoemkr & Maria)
9799: JAMES (Ciems) b GF 13 Jan 1793 (bp 1794, Ludwg Cmpbl & Maria)

9800: **JOHN FRANCIS** - pr. born ca 1750 to 1770; died by 1815; m GF 1 Mar 1791
GERTRUDE MOAK (b ca 1769, d 1843) dau of BONOCRATIUS MOAK & ANNA CONRAD.
surname FRANCIS
9801: ANNA b SJR 21 Aug 1791 (sp Marx Rasbach, Marg. Mauch)
9802: JOHANNES b GF 27 Sep 1793 (sp John Raspach & Anna)
9802A BARBARA b say 1795; m HK 1815 SAMUEL N. CHRISTMAN
9803: MARGARET b say 1797; m 1816 JOHN WIEDEN

9804: **FRANTZ FRIEBA** - pr. born ca 1730 to 1740; m by 1776 ANNA MARGARET ... Ps. the Francis Freaveau on 1790 GF census (1-1-0).
surname FRIEBA
 9805: MARGARET b SAR 23 Mar 1762 (sp Len. Bayer´s wife Barbara)
 9806: JACOB b GF 14 Nov 1776 (sp Jac. Boshar & Cath.)
 +9807: pr. GEORGE b say 1768; m 1793 ANNA CHRIST. ITTIG

9807: **GEORGE FR. FRIEBA** - pr. born ca 1750 to 1774 (pr. son of Frantz); m 29 Jan 1793 ANNA CHRIST. ITTIG dau of CHRISTIAN ITTIG & MARGARET. Was sponsor for May 1788 bp of George, son of Henry Miller & Anna Eva. Lived at Otsego NY in 1804.

 9808: FRANTZ b 28 Mar 1793 (sp Stofel Shmkr & Elis. <Ittig>)
 9809: JACOB b 27 Apr 1794 (sp Jac Miller, M. Elis. Ittig)
 9810: CATHERINE b HK 29 May 1804 (sp. Henry Werner & w. Cath.)

9811: **THOMAS GACKEL** (Gakkol) - born say 1740; m CATHERINE ... (ps. Wentz?).
surname GACKEL
 9812: WILHELM b GF 16 Jun 1776 (sp Wm Klepsttle, Maria Wentz)
 9813: GEORGE b 26 May 1778 (sp Stofel Shmaker & Cath Klepsttle)
 9814: MARIA BARBARA b 21 Aug 1779 (sp Lor. Phl. Harter & Barb.)
 9815: HENRICH b GF 26 May 1787 (sp Hen Werner, Cath L. Steel)
 9816: ANNA b GF 23 Aug 1789 (sp Lud Shoemkr, Anna Klepsattle)
   m 1812 PETER WOHLEBEN
 9817: PETER b GF 13 Feb 1792 (Pet. Orendorf & Cath.)

9818: **HENDRICK GARTER** - pr. born ca 1740 to 1760; m by 1777 SUSANNA FRANK. Hendrick & John Garter were pr. sons of Robert Garter (who was a sponsor, with wife Elisabeth Crommel, at Stone Arabia Reform Church in Mar 1754).   On 1790 Palatine NY census (3-0-6) and lived at Schneidersbush in 1792.
surname GARTER
 9819: SUSANNA b GF 30 Nov 1777 (sp Caspar Huber, Maria Frank)
   m by 1801 NICHOLAS SMITH
 9820: ELISABETH b GF 29 Jan 1780 (sp John Garder)
 9821: CATHERINE b GF 11 Mar 1782 (sp Mich. Bater, M. Cath Frank)
 9822: ANNA b GF 7 Apr 1786 (sp John Keller & Barbara)
 9823: MARIA b GF 6 Mar 1788 (sp. Sus. Frank)
 9824: ROBERT b GF 11 Apr 1790 (sp Robt Bayer & M. Cath.)
 9825: ADAM b SJR 4 May 1792 (sp Hen. Beyer & Margaret)

9826: **JOHN GARTER** - pr. born ca 1740 to 1750; m SAR 26 Nov 1765 GERTRUDE BAYER dua of LEONARD BEYER & BARBARA of Stone Arabia in Montgomery Co..

 9827: ROBERT b SAR 26 Mar 1766
 9828: LEONARD b Aug 1770 (sp Len. Bayer & Barbara)

9829: **ADAM GETHER** - m LENA ...
surname GETHER
 9830: JACOB b GF Oct 1784 (sp. Jac. Vorbus & Margaret)
 9831: GEORGE b GF 22 Aug 1786 (sp. Geo. Dieffendorf & Win.)
 9832: BARBARA b GF 18 Jan 1788 (sp. Chrstn Casselman & Barbara)

9833: **CHARLES GORDON** - m MARIA ... Mary Gordon on 1790 GF census (0-1-*).
surname GORDON
 9834: MARIA b GF Aug 1776 (sp Gen. Nic Herkimer & Maria)

9834A PETER GORTNER (GEORNTER) - born Germany 1736 (DAR vol 58 page 130); died Canajoharie NY 1813 (Ft. Plain); m MARY CATHERINE BARGY. Was in Col. Bellinger´s Regiment at Oriskany (Book of Names page 133 & 167). Peter Gortner appears on 1790 Canajoharie NY census (2-0-1).

surname GORTNER
9834B RACHEL   b say 1760; m JOHN HERM. EHLE (b 1756)
9834C GEORGE   b say 1770; m 1791 CATHERINE P. WESTERMAN

... **GRANT(s)** - see Crantz.

9835: JOHN GRINDEL- m by 1786 MARGRETHA ...
surname GRINDEL
9835A JOHANNES   b GF 9 Oct 1786 (sp James Yuel & Marg.)
9835B CATHERINE   b GF 3 Dec 1789 (sp John Stoph. Fox, Cath F ...)
9836: SUSANNA   b GF 27 May 1792 (sp Fr. Christman & Susanna)

9837: GERRIT GROESBECK - m DEBORA ... Gerrit & Debora were sponsors for May 1793 bp of Elisabeth, dau of Ciems Falkenburg & Elisabeth. Gerrit Groesbeck on 1790 Canajoharie census (1-2-2) listed near Richard Young and Peter Adimy (Adami?).

surname GROESBECK
9823: GERTRUDE   b GF 23 Feb 1794 (sp John Koom, Anna Arnoll)
9838: PETER   b GF 13 Oct 1795 (sp Peter Weaver & Maria)

9839: LORENTZ GRONINGER - pr. born ca 1730 to 1748; m by 1765 EVA CATHERINE ... (pr. same wife as listed as EVA MARGARET on 1769 bp rec.). On 1769 GF militia, near in list to Mich. Witrig & Geo. Snek jr. Widow Catherine L. Groninger m2 GF 23 Dec 1792 DIERCK JANSON.

surname GRONINGER
9840: EVA   b SAR 24 Dec 1765 (sp Eva & Henrich Frank)
9841: pr. JOHN   b say 1767; liv. 1784 (spf Welch bp at GF)
ps. John Kroninger, m by 1790 DELIA ...
9842: CATH. MARGARET   b SAR 3 Nov 1769 (sp Jac Meyer & w Cath Marg)

9841: JOHN GRONINGER (Grinninger) - m by 1790 DELIA ... Pr. the John Graneger on 1790 Canajoharie NY census (1-1-5) listed near Herkimers, John House, & Nic. Forbes. Of Minden NY in 1809

9843: DELIA   b SJR 24 Jan 1790 (sp H Dygert, Cath Kraninger)
9844: CATHERINE   bp SJR 26 Feb 1792 (sp John Young & Cath.)
Caty Joh. m HK 1809 WILLIAM W. FINK

9846: **FREDERICK HAACK** - born say 1745; m SAR 3 Jan 1770 ELISABETH YOUNG (Jung); ps. m2 MARGARET SCHAEFFER (Albany 1787 bp rec.). Sponsored 1764 bp of Margaret, dau of Marc Ittig. Pr. related to Mary Eva Haack (m 1764 FREDERICK BELL) & George Haak (spf Sep 1771 bp of George, son of James Billington & Elisabeth (Christman)).

9847: **GEORGE HANER** (Haine) - pr. born ca 1745 to 1760; m GF 7 Dec 1784 ANNA SOPHIA PIER, pr. the Sophia (bp 1751) dau of PHILIP PIER & LENA HELMER. George Hajny married Sophia Pier at the same time as Sophia Maria Hajny marrried Ernest Pier (ps. Haner brother & sister joining same from Piers).
surname HANER
9848: GEORGE b SAR 20 Jul 1787 (sp Bart. Schafer & Dor. <Haine>)
9849: JOHN b SAR 5 Nov 1789 (sp Jellis Miller, Elis. Eigenbrod)

9850: **JACOB HAPPLE** (Epply) - m by 1776 MARGARET ... (mother of child Maria bp 1776); ps. m2 by 1778 MARIA ... (mother of child Jacob bp 1778). Pr. a different man than the Jacob Epply who married 19 Dec 1769 (SAR) Elisabeth W. Laux and was reportedly killed in combat in Apr 1779.
surname HAPPLE
9851: MARIA b GF Sep 1776 (sp Peter Davis & Maria)
9852: JACOB b GF 27 Nov 1778 (sp Jac. Small & Susanna)
9853: NICHOLAS b GF 27 Feb 1781 (sp Nich. Miller & Lena)

9854: **DANIEL HARTH** (Hart) - pr. born ca 1745 to 1760; m GF 5 Feb 1786 CATHERINE GERLACH. Pr. the Daniel Hart on 1790 Palatine NY census (1-0-3) in Sneidersbush area, listed next to John Hart & Adam House.
surname HARTH
9855: MARLENA b GF 25 Jun 1788 (sp Geo. G. Laux, Marlena Harth)
9855A DANIEL bp SJR 26 Jan 1791 (sp John Adam Gerlach & Magd.)

9856: **JOHN HARTH** - pr. born ca 1740 to 1755; m by 1787 SARA ... Pr. the John Hart on 1790 Palatine NY census (1-3-6) in Sneidersbush area and listed next to Jacob Stauring & Daniel Hart.

9857: HENRICH b GF 2 May 1785 (sp. Jac. Rickert, Marg. Hardt)
9858: LUDWIG b GF 22 Oct 1787 (sp. Ludwig Rickert & Maria)
9858A MARIA bp SJR 10 Apr 1791 (sp. John Markel & Elis.)
9858B JACOB bp SJR 9 Feb 1794 (sp. Hen Hart & Anna Eva)

9859: **CASPER HASENCLEVER** - pr. born 1725 to 1750. Was a sponsor for Sep 1767 bp of Caspar, son of Adam Steinwax & Gertrude, and was presumably a son or close relative of Peter Hasenclever, entrepreneur and organizer of the New Petersburg settlement at Schuyler NY. Pr. went back to Europe with Peter Hasenclever at the onset of the American Revolution.

9860: **DANIEL HATCOCK** - pr. born ca 1740 to 1758; m by 1778 LENA ... Was living at Palatine NY in 1790 (SJR bp rec.).
surname HATCOCK
9861: LENA b GF 6 Oct 1778 (sp John Hatcock & Marg.)
9862: CATHERINE b GF 15 Sep 1782 (sp Peter H Nellis, Sophia Pier)
9863: ELISABETH b GF 15 Jul 1784 (sp John Con. Klock, Elis Meyer)
9864: JACOB b GF 13 Nov 1786 (sp Jacob Joran & Cath.)
9865: DANIEL (twin) bp SJR Aug 1790 (sp Sol.Yuker, Cath. Klock)
9866: MARIA (twin) bp SJR Aug 1790 (sp Conrad Klock, Elis. Joran)

9867: **JOHN HATCOCK** - pr. born ca 1725 to 1745; m by 1766 MARIA MARGARET HELMER dau of LEONARD HELMER & ELISABETH (Helmer book). A John Hatcock had land on th Klock & Nellis Patent in 1754 (map in Bellinger book page 89).

    9867A JOHN b GF 2 Apr 1779 (sp Danl Hatcock & Lena)
    9868: ANNA b 26 Jun 1781 (sp Adam Hauss & Anna Helmer)
    9869: JOST b GF 17 Mar 1783 (sp Jost Nellis & Marg. Helmer)
    9870: JACOB b GF 20 Mar 1785 (sp Jac. Joran & Cath.)
    9871: NICHOLAS b GF Apr 1787 (sp. Thom. Hatcock, Cath Ra..)
    9872: DANIEL b GF 8 Jun 1789 (sp Jacob Ryan, Anna Miller)
    9873: MARGARET b GF 10 Mar 1791 (sp John Keller, Maria Rahn)
    9874: WILLIAM b GF 17 Oct 1795 (sp Harpar V. Brockel & Anna)

9875: **JOHN HAUCK** - pr. born ca 1750 to 1770; m by 1791 LENA ...
          surname HAUCK
    9876: DOROTHY b GF 22 Jun 1791 (sp H. Dygert & Margaret)

9877: **GEORGE HAUSMAN** - pr. born ca 1750 to 1765 (son of GEORGE HOUSEMAN, who died in Revol. service 15 Jan 1778 <1984 notes of descendent Mrs. L. Healton, 33210 Bailey Pk Dr, Sun City CA 92381>); died Ridgeway NY ca 1817; m GF 3 May 1 MARIA ELISABETH KESSLER (b 14 May 1767, d Yates NY 1813). On 1790 GF census (1-1-2). Ps. had son Jacob (adult in 1818, Mrs. Healton notes).
          surname HAUSMAN
    9878: MARIA b GF 14 Feb 1786 (sp Joh. Diet. Kessler, Maria Nellis)
    9879: LENA b GF 28 Apr 1787 (sp. Barthol. Broadhaer & Elis..)
    9880: JOHANNES b GF 19 Jan 1790 (sp. John Kessler & Lena Ryon)
    9881: GEORGE b GF 7 Oct 1792 (sp Pet. Vetterle, Marg. Jac. Kessler)

9882: **JOHN HEERING** - son of Andrew; m SAR 2 Mar 1762 MARIA PETRIE dau of JOST PETRIE & widow of ACUS VAN SLYCK. John & wife sponsored Feb 1766 GF bp of Mari dau of Christian Schell & Elisabeth and Aug 1766 bp of Maria, dau of Jost M. Petrie & Catherine. John Sr. was in Fisher's Revol. Reg. (Fonda NY).
          surname HEERING
    9883: pr. ELISABETH 1766-1814 m 1788 HENRICH SMITH

9884: **HENRY HEES** - pr. born ca 1755 to 1760 (pr. son of John); m 1776 CATHERINE BELLINGER pr. dau of FREDERICK BELLINGER & ANNA ROSINA WALLRATH (Bellinger book page 11). Was living at German Flats in 1793 and at Palatine NY in 1805.
          surname HEES
    9885: JOHN b GF 3 Jun 1782 (sp John Bellinger, Anna Bellinger)
    9886: JACOB H. b say 1784; m by 1805 GERTRUDE RHOERIG
    9887: CATHERINE b say 1786; m by 1805 JACOB FOLTS
    9888: MAGDALENA b SJR 21 Dec 1792 (sp John Hees & Eva)
    9889: FREIDRICH b GF 27 May 1795 (sp Pet. Snell, Maria Kringing)

9890: **JOHN HELD** - m ANNA MARIA ...
          surname HELD
    9891: ANNA b GF 20 Jun 1791 (sp. Mynard Wemple & Anna)
    9892: EVA b GF 27 Jul 1793 (sp. H. Rosencrntz, Anna Eva Bauer)

9893: **WILLIAM HERD** - m by 1803 BARBARA HISER. Lived at Herkimer in 1814.
          surname HERD
    9894: MARIA b ca 1794; liv. 1814 (age 20, HK confirm.)
    9895: WILHELM b HK 3 May 1803 (sp Chrstn Schell & w. Cath.)
    9896: JACOB b HK 7 Jul 1805 (sp Hen. Deuchert & w. Barbara)

9897: **ELIJAH HILL** - m GF 6 Sep 1789 ELISABETH ENTER. 1790 HK census (2-0-1)

9898: **JACOB HILLER** - pr. born ca 1730 to 1745; killed at Oriskany Aug 1777; m by 1766 ELISABETH ROMAR (pr. RIEMA). Ages of her children ca Fall 1779 were 13, 14, 9 & 7 <Mohawk Valley in the Revolution, pg 183>. Jacob sponsored, with Jacob Mohr, the Oct 1767 SAR bp of Christian, son of John Riema & Catherine.

surname HILLER
```
       9899: pr. ELISABETH   b say 1765; m GF 1783 CHRISTIAN LAEMM
       9900: FREDERICK   b SAR 13 Aug 1766 (sp Fred Helmer & Sabina)
       9901: JOHN   b say 1772; m 1791 MARY HORNING
       9902: JACOB   b 9 Aug 1776 (sp Christian Hockstr & Cath); pr. d.y.
```

9903: **JOHN HILLER** - pr. born ca 1740 to 1750; m by 1770 CATHERINE MEYER. On 1790 Herkimer census (1-2-6). His wife was pr. the Catherine Hiller who sponsored Jul 1770 bp of Cath. Elisabeth, dau of Jacob Meyer & Cath. Margaret.

```
       9904: MARIA JOH.   b say 1767; m 1792 PETER DAVIS widower
       9904A pr. PETER   b say 1769; liv. 1793 (spf A. Davis bp)
       9905: CATHERINE ELISABETH   b SAR Jan 1771 (sp Elis. Becker, ...)
       9906: MARGARET JOH.   b say 1773; m 1791 HENRICH SPOHN
       9908: JOHANNES   b 8 Apr 1776 (sp John Meyer & Maria)
                 pr. m GF 1796 ELISABETH STEPH. FRANK
       9909: MICHEL JOH.   b FR 5 Nov 1780 (sp Mich. Myers, Catrina Myers)
                 m 1803 CATHERINE MUNTERBACH
       9910: SIMON   b GF 8 Mar 1791 (sp Lor. Frank & Maria <Meyer>)
       9911: EVA   b GF 3 Sep 1795 (sp Jacob Weaver & Margaret)
```

9912: **BENJAMIN HINMAN** - m ANNA ... On 1790 Herkimer census (1-2-1).
surname HINMAN
```
       9913: BENJAMIN   b GF 27 Jan 1794
```

9914: **SEBASTIAN HOFFMAN** - m by 1762 ELISABETH ... Bastian was in Capt. Petrie's German Flats militia unit in Feb 1757 (Book of Names page 8) but apparently settled east in Montgomery Co. shortly thereafter.
surname HOFFMAN
```
       9914A HENR. SEBASTIAN   b SAR 14 Apr 1762 (sp Hen. Wohleben & w.)
       9915: PETER   b SAR 10 Nov 1763 (sp Peter Dygert & Sara)
       9916: BARBARA   b SAR 7 Aug 1765 (sp Barbara & Jacob Cammerlin)
       9916A ELISABETH BARBARA   b SAR 1 Nov 1767 (Barb. Sch**, Wm Gutbrod)
```

9917: **JOHN HOGSLY** - m by 1767 NANCY ... (ps. Anna Dan. Petrie?). Was in 1769 GF militia, listed next to Melc. Kessler, and had a son Jacob (b SAR 8 Nov 1767, sp. Jac. Petrie & Cath. Crantz).

9918: **PETER HOMAN** - born in Germany ca 1731; died Herkimer NY 6 Dec 1813 (age 82, a widower); m .... In Sev. Dygert's militia in 1763. Peter sponsored 1768 bp of Peter, son of Frederick Ad. Helmer & Barbara Elisabeth (Homan, ps. a sister of Peter (she supposedly came to America in 1754).

9919: **JOHN HUYK** - pr. born ca 1750 to 1760; m ELISABETH KLAU (b ca 1757, d a widow HK 2 Mar 1838 <age 81> & buried at house of her son Andrew, a grocer).
surname HUYK
```
       9920: ANDREW   b say 1778; liv. 1838 (had a son And. <d HK 1819>)
       9921: ps. CATHERINE   b say 1780; m by 1809 ADAM BARSH
       9922: ps. GERRIT   b say 1785; m 1817 MAGDALENA KAST
       9923: ps. MARTIN   b say 1792; m 1819 MARIA KAST
```

9924: **MICHAEL J. KAYSER** (Keyser) - pr. the Michael born SAR 26 Jan 1764 (son of Capt. John); m GF 27 Apr 1788 MAGDALENA KELLER pr. dau of HENRY KELLER & ADELI. Ps. another MICHAEL KAYSER jr. m by 1803 BARBARA SCHELL.
surname KAYSER
 9925: HENRICH b GF 26 Sep 1788 (sp Jac. Keller, Marg. Kayser)
 9926: SUSANNA b GF 6 Oct 1790 (sp John Keller, Susanna Keller)
 9927: MARIA b GF 7 May 1793 (sp Barent Kayser & Maria)
 9928: MARGARET b GF 24 Jun 1795 (sp Capt. John Kayser & Marg.)

9929: **PHILIP PETER KAUDER** - born ca 1761 (from Erlenbch Germany acc. to death rec.); died GF 15 Aug 1816 (age 55); m GF 13 Jan 1796 CATHERINE JAC. CRIM (b 1778, d HK 1809 age 31) dau of JACOB CRIM & ELISABETH FRANK.
surname KAUDER
 9929A PHILIP PETER b Minden NY 18 May 1797 (Jacob Grim & w. Elis.)
 9930: JACOB b ca 1799; liv. 1815 (age 16 at HK Confirm.)
 9931: JOHN b ca 1800; liv. 1815 (age 15 at HK Confirm.)
 9932: ELISABETH b HK 19 Mar 1803 (sp And. Pfiefer & w. Elis.)

9933: **NICHOLAS KELLER** - born say 1720; m ... Appears in 1769 GF militia (amongst Hasenclever men) and naturalized May 1773 (Book of Names, pg 7).
surname KELLER
 9935: pr. CATHERINE b say 1750; liv. 1768 (spf Klein bp)
+9936: JOHN b say 1752; naturalized May 1773
   m1 by 1780 CHRISTINA; m2 MARIA P. SEGHNER
 9937: pr. MARGARET b say 1754; liv. 1770 (spf Witrig bp)

9934: **GEORGE NICHOLAS KELLER** (pr. the same man as the above Nicholas!) - pr. born ca 1715 to 1725 (age over 50 in 1776); m1 by 1767 EVA MARGARET ...; m2 by 1769 GERTRUDE ... On Tryon Co. census ca 1776 (male over 50, 2 females (age 16-50), plus 2 boys (under 16) & 3 girls (Mohawk Valley in the Revolution, page 154). In Bellinger's Regiment and a prisoner of war.
surname KELLER
 9937A ps. MARIA ELISABETH b say 1758; liv. 1783 (spf Keller bp)
 9937B ps. EVA CATHERINE (Keller?) 1760-1837 m JACOB CLEMENTS
 9938: ps. APPOLONIA b say 1765; liv. 1783 (spf Clements bp)
   m GF 1786 JOHN C. KLOCK (aka John Klock jr.)
 9939: JULIANA MARGARET b SAR 25 Sep 1767 (sp Marg. Elis. Snek)
 9940: JACOB b GF 21 Nov 1769 (J Birky, Elis. Klein, Anna M Harter)
   pr. liv. 1792 (spf Cath. Klock bp)
 9940A ps. MARIA b say 1771; m 1788 JOST KLOCK

9936: **JOHN KELLER** - pr. born ca 1750 to 1764; m1 by 1780 CHRISTINA ... ; m2 GF as a widower 28 Jun 1789 MARIA P. SEGHNER pr. dau of PAUL SEGHNER & ELISABETH EYSAMAN. Pr. the John Keller jr. naturalized 8 May 1773 in list of Hasensclever men and just after Nicholas Keller (Book of Names page 7). He & Christina sponsored Feb 1780 SAL bp of George, son of George Braun & Elisabeth, and John Keller & Maria were sponsors for 1793 bp of Maria, dau of Adam Meyer. On 1790 Herkimer census (1-2-2) listed near Hockstater, Ayer, & Clements.

 9941: JOHN b GF 7 Aug 1783 (sp Geo. V Slyck, Appolonia Keller)
 9942: MARIA EVA b GF 12 Feb 1785 (M. Elis & Eva Marg. Keller)
 9943: CHRISTIAN b GF 10 Dec 1786 (sp Christn Hockstatr & Cath.)
   by 2nd wife
 9944: CATHERINE b GF 30 Oct 1790 (sp Jac. Clements & Eva Cath.)
 9945: MARGARET b SJR 7 Aug 1792 (sp Peter Ayer, Marg. Keller)

9946: JOHN KELSH Sr. (COLSH) - pr. born ca 1720 to 1740; m by 1767 CATHERINE
... In 1769 GF militia and in Col. Bellinger's Revol. Regiment.
                        surname COLSH
      9947: pr. JOHN jr. b say 1760; in Revol. service
      9948: MARIA CATHERINE b SAR 3 Mar 1767 (sp Theo. Bekker)
                        (1767 other sp. Cath. Witrig, Maria Sybila Dinges)
      +9949: pr. PHILIP (Kelsh) b say 1770; m 1788 MARGARET WOLF

9950: NICHOLAS KELSH (COLSH) - pr. born ca 1750 to 1760; ml by 1778 MARIA
FREDERICA ...; apparently m2 by 1788 ANNA ... (mother of child bp 1788). Nicholas
& Maria Frederica were sponsors for Jul 1778 GF bp of Philip, son of PHILIP
BETTINGER & Maria. Was taken prisoner to Canada in the Revolution.

      9951: JOHN b SAL 6 Aug 1788 (sp John Kelsh, Elis. Lepper)

9949: PHILIP KELSH - m GF 1788 MARGARET WOLF. At Frankfort NY 1807.
                        surname KELSH
      9952: JOHN b GF 21 Sep 1788 (sp John Smith & Maria Elis.)
      9953: ELISABETH b GF 29 Nov 1789 (sp Wm Petry & Salome <Wolf>)
      9954: JOHANNES b GF 7 Jan 1792 (sp John Christman & Cath.)
      9955: CATHERINE b GF 2 Apr 1794 (sp John Helmer & Maria <Wolf>)
      9955A SOPHIA b HK 21 Aug 1807 (sp Jacob Petrie & w. Maria)

9956: NICHOLAS KEMPLIN - m GF 1788 ANNA KESSLER dau of MELCHIOR KESSLER. His
wife Anna appears to have had a child bp GF Jan 1792.
                        surname KEMPLIN
      9957: JOHN b GF 21 Apr 1789 (sp Joh Petri, Cath. Kessler)

      ... **KLEIN (KLEYN)** - see Cline.

9958: HENRICK JOH. KLOCK - born 7 Sep 1749 son of John Klock & Margaret (Fox);
died Herkimer NY 21 Jun 1810 age 60-10-14; m MARIA MARGARETHA WAGNER (b 1755, d
1836) dau of Lt. Col. PETER WAGNER (Waggoner) & BARBARA ELISABETH DOCKSTADER
(Klock book page 15). On the 1790 Herkimer census (1-3-6).
                        surname KLOCK
      9959: ps. GEORGE b say 1771; m by 1789 MARGARET OFFENHAUSER
      9960: PETER 1778-1873 m ANNA STARING (dau of Adam & Elis.)
      9961: CATHERINE b say 1780; m by 1798 PETER EYSAMAN
      9962: JOSEPH b 19 Oct 1782 (sp Jost Petry, Anna Wagner)
      9963: MARGARET b 1782; m FREDERICK CASLER (Kessler)
      9964: JOHN b 18 Aug 1784; m 1806 MARGARET G. HELMER
      9965: ELIZABETH 1786-1843 m 1806 JACOB HELMER (son of Geo. F.)
      9966: BARBARA ELISABETH   b 1788 (sp Melchior Thum & Elisabeth)
                   d 1850; ml HENRY KELLER; m2 1812 BENJAMIN STARHING
      9967: MAGDALENA b 26 Oct 1789; m 1811 JACOB HUBER jr
      9968: ROBERT b 7 Oct 1791; ml 1814 CATHERINE STARING
      9969: ANNA b GF 23 Oct 1794 (sp Ludol. Diefendorf & Barbara)

9969A JOST KOCH - pr. born ca 1735 to 1750 (presumably son of Caspar Koch of
Stone Arabia); m by 1770 GERTRUDE ... Pr. the Joel Koch in 1757 GF militia, listed
next to Thomas Kessler & Jacob Kessler, and the Joist Cock in Capt. Frank's GF
militia company in 1767. On 1790 Herkimer census (1-1-3) listed near Joseph
Klock, Philip Bellinger (Bettinger?), & John Finster.
                        surname KOCH
      9969B CATHERINE b 9 Jan 1771 (sp Cath. Schuyler, Jost Bell)

9970: **FRANK KREID** (Crouch) - born ca 1767; died Herkimer NY 26 Feb 1816 age 49; m GF 28 Jul 1789 MARIA BARBARA N. HARTER as in Harter book page 5.
surname CROUCH
    9971: FREDERICK b 20 May 1790 (sp Jost Smid & Apolonia <Harter>)
    9972: ELISABETH 1792-1869 m JACOB SEGHNER
    9973: CATHERINE ca 1794-1877 m PETER JOS. MEYER
    9974: MARY m CHARLES BATES

9977: **HANS LUDWIG KRING** - pr. born ca 1735 to 1758; m MARY GETMAN (b 1756) dau of GEORGE GETMAN & UTILIA SHOEMAKER. Green's Gateway to the West (page 354) lists early settlers of "Kringsbush" in Montgomery Co. as Matthias Smith, Leonard Helmer, Joseph Davis, and his brother in law John Kring.
surname KRING
    9978: MARIA b SAR 31 May 1793 (sp John Spnknebel & w Elis.)

9979: **CONRAD KROLL** (Knoll) - m GF 11 Jan 1791 URSALA ... widow of JOHN MILLER.
surname KROLL
    9980: CATHERINE b GF 3 Mar 1792 (sp Jac. Bashar & Cath.)
    m 1813 ALEXANDER M. VAN BROCKLIN

9980A **GUY LAKY** - m by 1776 JANNETJE ... He & Jannetje sponsored May 1776 GF bp of Jannetje, dau of James Rincken. A Mr. Leeky was a GF resident in May 1775, listed next to James Rankin.

9981: **JAMES LAPDON** - born say 1770; m GF 13 Nov 1791 CATHERINE KESSLER. A Daniel Lapdon on the 1790 Canajoharie census (3-3-6) was pr. a relative.
surname LAPDON
    9982: CATHERINE b 16 Mar 1793 (sp Marc Kessler & Delia)
    9983: ELISABETH b GF 4 Sep 1794 (sp John Kessler & Elis.)

9984: **ZADOCK LAPDON** - pr. born ca 1750 to 1773; m by 1793 NANCY ...

    9985: DOROTHY b GF 25 Dec 1793 (sp. Diet. Kessler & Doro. Petry)
    9986: ps. ALICE b ca 1795; d 1825 (age 30); m Dr. JACOB ABRAMS

9987: **GEORGE LEERS** - pr. born ca 1700 to 1720; dec'd by 1761 (widow's mar. rec.); m ELISABETH ... His widow m2 SAR 1761 JOSEPH HERDIN. In 1761 his family lived at the Falls (GF or Little Falls area).
surname LEERS
    9988: pr. LENA b say 1735; m by 1754 PETER LEWIS

9990: **HENRICH LEIMBACH** - pr. born ca 1745 to 1760; m GF 12 Nov 1785 MARIA H. HISER dau of HENRY HISER & MARIA RASBACH. On 1790 German Flats census (1-1-2).
surname LEIMBACH
    9991: CATHERINE b GF 10 Sep 1786 (Christn Schell & Cath.<Hiser>)
    m 1807 NICHOLAS AND. MILLER
    9992: JACOB b say 1787; m 1806 MAGDALENA COOPER
    9993: ANNA ELISABETH b 13 Aug 1788 (sp Jacob Joh. Kesler & M Cath.)
    9994: GEORGE b GF 23 Sep 1790 (sp Geo. Carl & Margaret)
    m 1812 DELIA GARLOCK
    9995: HENRICH b GF 2 Nov 1792 (sp Hen. Witherstine & Maria)
    9996: PETER b GF 13 May 1795 (sp Peter Scherer & Elis.)
    9997: MARIA b HK 19 Jan 1803 (sp Hen. Deuchert, Cath. Steel)
    9998: ISAAC b HK 30 Jan 1805 (sp. Fred. Petry & w. Margaret)

10011: JAMES MACGNOT (McNutt, MacDal) - born say 1740; m by 1786 ELISABETH
BARBARA ... Was a British soldier stationed in the Mohawk Valley in 1763 when son
James born (out of wedlock) by ELISABETH BARBARA WEAVER dau of ANDREAS WEAVER.
Lived in the Susquahanna River area in July 1775 (Mohawk Valley in the Revolution,
pg 169). Assume he, rather than a son, was father of children from 1786 to 1794.

          surname MACGNOT
+10012: JAMES   b SAR 30 Apr 1763 (sp Geo. Dackstader & w.)
 10013: CHRISTOPEL   b GF 15 Sep 1786 (sp Hen Meyer, Elis Bekker)
 10014: ELISABETH   b GF 23 Mar 1788 (sp Jac Meyer, Elis Hockstater)
 10015: DEBALD   b GF 19 Nov 1789 (sp Theobald Bekker & Cath.)
 10016: MARGARET   b GF 2 Apr 1792 (sp Theo. Dieterich & Margaret)
 10017: MICHAEL   b GF 23 Jul 1794 (sp Mic. Meyer, Maria Bekker)

... **MARTIN** - see Smarth.

10018: STEPHEN MARCH (Marchtz) - pr. born ca 1730 to 1750; m 1771 MARGARET KLOCK
dau of Col. JACOB KLOCK & ELISABETH BELLINGER.
          surname MARCH
 10019: JOHANNES   b SAL 1771 (sp Jacob Klock & w.)
 10020: HENRICH   b GF 18 Jun 1782

10021: PETER MARSH - pr. born ca 1750 to 1765; m GF 25 Nov 1783 DOROTHY MEBIE.
On 1790 Canajoharie NY census ((1-2-2), next to Albert Mebie.
          surname MARSH
 10022: ANNA MARIA   b GF 18 Jun 1784 (sp. Jost Laux & Marg.)
 10023: JOHN   b GF 13 Nov 1786 (sp. Joh. Herkimer, Cat. Mabee)
 10024: STEPHAN   bp SJR 10 Aug 1788 (sp Abm Mebie, Rach. Fetterly)
 10025: PHILIP   bp SJR May 1790 (sp Ph. Schafer, Maria Mebie)
 10026: JAMES   b GF 13 Jan 1791 (sp. James Yuel & Margaret)
 10027: ELISABETH   bp SJR 26 Feb 1792 (sp Geo. Schmid, Elis. Eker)
 10028: CATHERINE   bp SJR 2 Mar 1794 (sp Nic. Sternberger & Cath.)

10029: PHILIP PETER MARZ (Martz) - m by 1788 ELISABETH BARBARA ... Was on 1790
German Flats census (1-2-3) and living at Warren NY in 1811.
          surname MARZ
 10030: PETER   b say 1784; m 1805 MARIA CATHERINE JOH. FOX
 10031: DOROTHY   b say 1786; liv. 1802 (HK Ch. Confirm.)
 10032: CATHERINE   b ca Jun 1788; d 17 Aug 1806 (age 18-2-2)
 10033: MARGARET   b say 1790; m HK 1811 ABRAHAM PH. HARWICH

10034: DANIEL MACDOUGAL - born ca 1756; died ca 1786; m by 1782 MARIA ... (DAR
has m EVA SOMMER, as seen in Mohawk Valley in the Revolution, pg 283). In 1775 he
was at Palatine NY and on the Tryon Co. Committee of Safety.
          surname MACDOUGAL
 10035: MARIA   b GF 30 Oct 1782 (sp John Kayser & Margaret)
 10036: DANIEL   b GF 28 Nov 1784 (sp Geo. Fox & Maria)

10034A DUNCAN MACDOUGAL - born 1744; died 25 Aug 1795 (DAR); m ANNA WEAVER
(Pearson´s Schenectady book, pg 109). On the Tryon Co. Comm. of Safety at German
Flats 1775-79. Had Daniel (bp Schenectady Mar 1786) & Margaret (bp Sep 1794).

10037: DANIEL MACGUY - m by 1787 ELISABETH ...
          surname MACGUY
 10038: JACOB   b GF 16 Nov 1787 (sp Jac Meyer, Marg. Klepsattle)

10039: LEVI C. MOREHOUSE - born ca 1782 (son of JOHN MOREHOUSE & MARIA); died 22 Aug 1851 (age 69); m Herkimer NY 27 Mar 1803 MARIA SMITH (b 6 Apr 1785, d 11 Sep 1851 age 67) dau of FREDERICK SMITH & CATHERINE.

surname MOREHOUSE

10040: ROXANNA   b ca 1804; d Manheim NY 20 Apr 1831 age 27-4-5
10041: CHARLES   b 1 Dec 1805; d 2 Feb 1861 age 55-2-1
10042: MARIA   bp 19 Jun 1808
10043: CATHERINE ELISABETH   bp 8 Apr 1810
10044: MARTHA JANE   b ca 1811; d 21 Sep 1833 age 21-0-21
10045: ps. ZABODIE   b say 1820; m 1841 ASA WEAVER
10046: JACOB WEBER   b 1825; d 24 Aug 1826 age 1-0-3

10047: PETER MULTER (Molter) - pr died by 1790; m by 1769 MARGARET AYER. In 1769 GF militia and, with Jacob Multer, in Bellinger's Revol. Reg. Margaret (pr. widow) appears on 1790 HK census (1-1-2) next to Jacob Moulder.

surname MULTER

+10048: JACOB PET.   b say 1764; m 1789 MARIA G. SCHIFF
10049: ELISABETH BARBARA   b SAR 22 Sep 1767 (sp Elis. Bekker ...)
10050: ELISABETH   b SAR 18 Jun 1769 (Elis Becker, Cat Bender, Geo Snek)
10051: pr. THEOBALD   b say 1775; liv. 1795 (spf Multer bp)
10052: MARGARET   b GF 16 Jan 1778 (sp John Munterbach & Elis.)

10048: JACOB PET. MULTER - pr. born ca 1760 to 1768; m GF 29 Dec 1789 MARIA G. SCHIFF dau of GEORGE SCHIFF. On 1790 Herkimer census (1-0-1).

10053: ELISABETH   bp SJR 8 Jan 1791 (sp Hier. Bender & Maria Elis.)
10054: CATHERINE   b GF 24 Feb 1795 (sp Theob. Molter, Cath. Koch)
10055: PETER   b GF 9 Nov 1795 (sp John Schiff & Eva)
       pr. m ELIZABETH WITRIG (b 1799)

10056: JOHN MUNTERBACH - m ELISABETH ...   In Bellinger's Revol. Regiment. On 1790 German Flats census (2-2-4), next to Jacob Dinges.

surname MUNTERBACH

10057: pr. MARGARET   b say 1775; m by 1803 JOHN HELMER
10058: JOHN   b GF 10 Nov 1778 (sp John Riema & Anna Cath.)
10059: pr. ANNA   b say 1781; m ADAM HARTMAN
10060: CATHERINE   b GF 12 Apr 1783 (sp John Kelsch, Cath. Lentz)
       m HK 1803 MICHEL JOH. HILLER
10061: JACOB   b GF Jul 1786 (sp Jacob Molter, Margaret Dinges)
10062: HENRICH   b GF 31 May 1792 (sp Hen Meyer, Elis. Jac. Dinges)

10063: JOHN MUTH - pr. born ca 1740 to 1760 (son of John, as given on mar. rec.); m SAL 3 Nov 1788 MARGARET ECKER dau of ABRAHAM ECKER. Had son ABRAHAM (b GF Oct 1783, sp. And. Werner, Maria Vetterle).

10065: JAMES NASH (Nesch) - pr. born ca 1754; died GF 10 Sep 1823 (age 69); m by 1784 ANNA ...(pr. Hess). James & Anna sponsored Sep 1785 GF bp of Anna, dau of Jost Hess & Elis. In Bellinger's Revol. Reg. and on 1790 GF census (1-1-4).

surname NASH

10066: ANNA CATHERINE   b GF 7 Mar 1784 (sp John Osteroth & Cath.)
10067: ELISABETH   b GF 8 Aug 1786 (sp Geo. Orendorf & Elis.)
       m 1804 JOHN SEGHNER (son of Paul)
10068: FREDERICK   b GF 9 May 1788 (sp Fred. Aug. Hess & Maria)
10069: JOHN b GF 30 1792 (John Fox & Elis) m 1814 ANNA C. EIGENAUER
10070: DANIEL   b GF 4 Oct 1795 (sp Con. Hess & Margaret)

10071: **GEORGE NELLIS** - pr. born ca 1720 to 1743 (son of Christian); m by 1761
MARIA ELISABETH...(b ca 1726, d Herkimer NY 21 Apr 1806 age 79-8-, ps. a
Christman). George & wife Maria Elisabeth sponsored 1766 bp of Catherine, dau of
Marcus Demuth & Catherine. His dau was pr. the sponsor, with Adolph Kessler, for
1776 GF bp of George, son of John Christman & Cath. George had 5 adults & 1 child
(under age 10) on 1778 German Flats relief and was on the 1790 Herkimer census
(3-1-4) near Andrew Nellis, F. Cox, C. Eigenauer, & Nicholas Spohn.
surname NELLIS

   10072: ps. MARIA ELISABETH b say 1759; liv. 1776 (spf Christman bp)
   10073: ANNA MARIA b 15 Jan 1762 (sp. Maria Meyer, Joh. Chrstman)
+10074: GEORGE b GF 27 Aug 1765 (sp. Geo. Dkstdr & M. Magdalena)
          m ca 1786 MARIA CATHERINE STEELE (ca 1769-1835)
   10075: CATHERINE G. b say 1768; m 1788 JOHN JOH. KESSLER
   10076: WINA b SAR 14 Jan 1770 (sp. Sabina & Joh. Fred. Helmer)

10074: **GEORGE NELLIS jr.** - born GF 27 Aug 1765; m GF 17 Jan 1786 MARIA AD.
CATHERINE STEELE (b ca 1769, d 1835) dau of ADAM STEELE. A Herkimer NY in 1806.

   10077: JOHN b GF 13 Apr 1787 (sp. Geo. Ittig, Maria Nellis)
          m 1806 CATHERINE P. FOLTS
   10078: EVA b GF 16 Dec 1791 (sp Peter Bellinger & Doro.)
          m 1810 PETER JOH. DOCKSTADER
   10079: ELISABETH b GF 9 Feb 1794 (sp Adam Harter & Cath.)
          ps. the Elis. (ca 1792-1866) m 1815 MATTHEW SMITH
   10079A ADAM b say 1800; m 1823 MARGARET HESS

10080: **GEORGE OGH** - pr. born ca 1730 to 1745; m SUSANNA ... In 1769 GF militia
near Jacob Bircky & Lorentz Rinckel in Hasenclever group.
surname OGH

   10081: ERNESTINA CATHERINE b SAR 14 Mar 1766
          (sp. Ernestina & John Bellinger)
   10082: PETRUS b GF 15 Mar 1767 (sp. Peter Weber & Anna Weber)
   10083: MARIA BARBARA b 1 Aug 1776 (sp. Geo. Sneck & Maria Barbara)
   10084: HENRICH b GF 27 Mar 1779 (sp Hen. Schaffr & Cath Marg.)

10085: **NICHOLAS OXNER** (Oschner) - pr. born ca 1730 to 1750; died in action in
Revolution pr. by Sep 1778; m SAR 6 Jan 1767 MARIA FOX (b ca 1747) dau of
CHRISTOPHER FOX & CATHERINE BELLINGER (Bellinger book page 47). Mary Oxner (pr.
widow) had 1 adult & 4 children (under age 16) on 1778 German Flats relief.
surname OXNER

+10086: JOHANNES b SAR 16 Aug 1767 (sp John Bellinger & w. Maria)
          pr. m 1793 GERTRUDE CON. ORENDORF
   10087: NICHOLAS b 14 May 1768; pr. m CATHERINE HESS
   10088: PETER b 9 Oct 1778 (sp. Joh. Fox & Anna)

10086: **JOHANNES OCHENER** - born 16 Aug 1767; m 1793 GERTRUDE ORENDORF (b ca 1773,
d HK 1818 age 45) dau of CONRAD ORENDORF.

   10070: ELISABETH b GF Aug 1794 (sp Fr. Petri, Eva Orendorf)

10089: **SIMEON PARKER** - pr. born ca 1750 to 1765; m by 1787 MARGARET ...
surname PARKER
   10090: JOST b GF 17 Mar 1787 (sp. John Joh Campbell, Eva Campbel)
   10091: PATRICK b GF 16 Nov 1793 (sp Col. Ptrk Campbell & Cath.)

10092: **HENRY PHILIPS** - pr. born ca 1750 to 1765; m by 1787 MEIMY ... (also seen as Je Myme ...). Pr. related to the Philips family of the Fonda NY area of Montgomery County.
                            surname PHILIPS
        10093: EVA b GF 18 Feb 1787 (sp H. Rosencrantz, Gert. Philips)
        10094: RICHART b GF 17 Jan 1788 (sp (sp Adam Bell, Lena Philips)

10095: **JOHN PHILIPS** - pr. born ca 1750 to 1765; m GF 21 Nov 1784 CATHERINE HEN. MEYER pr. dau of HENRY MEYER & MARIA GETMAN. John Phillips appears on the 1790 GF census (1-2-*), pr. living in the Columbia NY area.

        10096: ELISABETH b GF 14 Apr 1786 (sp John DeMuth & Elis.)
        10097: HENRICH bp GF 29 Aug 1787 (sponsors not listed)
        10098: JOHN b GF 19 Sep 1789 (sp John Hilts & Maria <Meyer>)
        10099: PETER b GF 12 May 1793 (sp Pet. H. Meyer, Marg. F. Meyer)

10100: **JOHANNES POENRADT** - pr. born ca 1670 to 1690; m GERTRUDE ... Looks like the Johannes Bonroth on the NY Palatine subsistence list in 1710 (1A,0Y) & in 1712 (4A,0Y), who pr. married ca 1711 a women with two older children. He and his wife received Burnetsfield lots #46 and #9 (north of the Mohawk River).

10101: **ALEXANDER PORTER** - m by 1790 MARGARET ... On 1790 German Flats census (1-1-2) living near John Armstrong & Diewald Dietrich.
                            surname PORTER
        10102: child b GF 24 Feb 1790 (sp Adam Armstrong, Cath. Staring)

10103: **JOHN PORTEUS** - pr. born ca 1730 to 1745; died by 1801 (Pearson's Schenectady book page 145). Was a merchant in Schenectady in 1774 and subsequently in Herkimer in 1794. On 1790 Herkimer census (5-0-3) living near Starings, H. Barker, E. Hall, & Petries. Had twins Thomas & William (bp SJR 20 Feb 1792, mother not listed, no sponsors).

10104: **JOHN POST** - born Schenectady NY 1 Jan 1749 (son of ELIAS POST & MARIA VAN EPS, as given in Pearson's Schenectady book, page 145); died Manlius NY 10 Dec 1830; m1 DEBORAH CONYNE; m2 7 Jan 1779 MARGARET BELLINGER (b 1756, d 1836) dau of FREDERICK P. BELLINGER & CATHERINE WEAVER (see Bellinger book page 52, Hanson's Schenectady page 129, & Beers Herkimer County page 153). Ran a tavern at Utica NY in 1790 where his wife handled drunken customers with an iron bar and a chair. Formed a partnership of Post & Hamlin with his son-in-law but they were financially wiped out by a fire at their Utica store in Feb 1804 (Utica Morning Herald, 22 Nov 1871).
                            surname POST
        10105: REBECCA m Mr. STORM of Schenectady
                            by 2nd wife
        10106: JOHN b 19 Feb 1779; d 12 Jan 1806; m 1801 POLLY WARD
        10107: MARIA b Schenectady 8 Jan 1786; m1 GILES HAMLIN
                            m2 1826 JACOB W. PETRY
        10108: FREDERICK b Schenectady 9 Aug 1787 (Pearson's book)
        10109: CATHERINE b 27 Oct 1788; liv. 1843 Syracuse; unm
        10110: DEBORAH b 6 Mar 1792; m HEZEKIAH H. GEER
        10111: CATLINA b 1793; m JEREMIAH BETTS at Galena Illinois 1841
        10112: ELISABETH b 18 Aug 1795; m Rev. HENRY GREGORY
        10113: dau m Mr. ROSE of Geneva NY (Utica M. Hrld, 22 Nov 1871)
        10114: HELEN b 1800; liv. 1841; m JACOB GILLETT

10115: **NICHOLAS POST** - pr. born ca 1745 to 1760; m by 1779 ELISABETH ... Ps. the Nicholas Poss on 1790 Palatine NY census (1-2-5).
surname POST
   10116: ANNA b SAL 21 Mar 1779 (sp Hen. Krim & Anna)
   10117: CHRISTINA b GF 28 Sep 1785 (sp John Chr Nellis, Anna J Klock)
   10118: CATHERINE b SAL 14 Jan 1791 (sp John Nellis & Anna)

10119: **FRANCIS POSTLE** (Postill) - m by 1791 MARIA ... On 1790 Herkimer census (1-2-3) amongst Weavers in the Deerfield area. Had a son FRANCIS FREDERICK POSTLE (bp GF Mar 1792, sp Fr. Riegel & Cath.).

10121: **ROBERT PURCHES** - m by 1788 RACHEL ...
surname PURCHES
   10122: ELISABETH b ca 1788 (bp GF Feb 1793, sp John Hess & Marg)
   10123: NANCY (twin) b Oct 1792 (sp H. Miller & Eva)
   10124: SAMUEL HENRY (twin) b 1792 (sp M. Rockwel, Anna Hess)

10125: **DAVID PUTMAN** (Bodman) - born ca 1750 (pr. the David bp Stone Arabia NY Feb 1751 son of David Putman & Elisabeth <Lehr>); died Herkimer NY 14 Aug 1824 (age 74); m CATHERINE LEDER. (b ca 1757, d HK 26 Apr 1822 age 65) dau of JOHN LEDER. A David, David jr. and Frederick Putman were listed on the 1790 list of Revolutionary War damage claimants. Pr. the David Putman on 1790 Canajoharie census (1-1-5). David lived at Canajoharie in 1792 (SJR bp rec.).
surname PUTMAN
   10126: DAVID b FNR 18 May 1775
   10127: ELISABETH b FNR 22 Dec 1776; m by 1802 PETER WEAVER
   10127A JOHN b SAL 24 Mar 1779 (sp John Lederer, Cath Graf)
              m by 1812 MARIA SEGERT
   10128: CATHERINE b GF 31 Mar 1782 (sp Thom. Siele, Elis. Leder)
   10129: MARIA b GF 3 Jul 1784 (sp Abhm Herkimer, Maria Leder)
   10130: ANNA DAV. b GF 20 Jun 1787 (sp John Pader, Anna Bellinger)
              d HK 4 Oct 1804 (age 16-3-22)
   10131: MAGDALENA bp SJR 12 Feb 1792 (sp Geo Kern, Lena Walter)

10132: **JOHN PURCK** (Burk on 1780 Albany bp rec.) - pr. born ca 1730 to 1747; m SAR 28 Oct 1766 ELISABETH RIEMENSNEIDER pr. a dau of HENRY RIEMENSNEIDER. John Purck appears still married to Elisabeth Riemensnieder in 1780 so pr. another John m SAR 29 Apr 1767 ELISABETH WEAVER.
surname PURCK
   10133: ANNA b SAR 18 Jul 1767 (sp Anna & Peter Ten Broek)
   10134: ANNA MARTHA b GF 18 Feb 1778 (sp John Riemensdr & Doro.)
   10135: MARGARITA b Albany 4 Nov 1780 (sp Fred Wals, Marg Kerker)

10136: **JAMES RANKIN** - pr. born ca 1730 to 1740; apparently died at Battle of Oriskany 6 Aug 1777; m ELISABETH MILLER (b ca 1730, age 76 in 1806). In GF militia in 1767. Widow Elisabeth had 1 adult and 2 children on 1778 GF relief.
surname RANKIN
  +10137: JAMES jr. b say 1763; m 1787 DELIA PETRIE
   10138: ELISABETH bp SAR 7 Dec 1765 (sp. Arch. Armstrng & Elis.)
              m BARENT YOUNG
   10139: CATHERINE b SAR 29 Mar 1768 (sp Jost Dygert, Cath. Bellingr)
              m 1788 DIET. JAC. KESSLER
   10140: pr. MARGARET b say 1770; m 1788 JOSUA HOCKSTATTER
  +10141: pr. THOMAS b say 1772; m 1791 CATHERINE KESSLER
   10142: JANNETJE (Jane) b GF 31 May 1776 (sp. Guy Laky & Jannej)
              m 2 Oct 1792 PETER KESSLER

10137: JAMES RANKIN jr. - pr. born ca 1760 to 1765; m GF 22 Jan 1787 DELIA DAN.
PETRIE dau of DANIEL PETRIE & CATHERINE ELISABETH FOLTS. James Rancan was on 1790
Herkimer cenus (1-1-1).
> children of James Rankin jr.
> **10143: JAMES** b GF 22 Jan 1788 (sp Danl Jac Petri, Marg. Rankin)
> (aka Ciems); m 1812 ELISABETH NIC. N. STARING
> **10144: DANIEL** b GF 26 Nov 1790 (sp. Fasier Cox & Cath.)
> m 1813 CATHERINE HEN. N. STARING
> **10145: ELISABETH** b GF 28 Dec 1792 (sp Diet. Kessler & Cath.)
> **10146: DELIA** b GF 14 Feb 1794 (sp Jac. Small, Elis. Cox)

10141: THOMAS RANKIN - m 22 Jan 1791 CATHERINE KESSLER pr. a dau of MELCHIOR
KESSLER & MARIA ELISABETH PETRIE. Thomas sponsored, with Anna Eva Jac. Kessler,
Apr 1791 bp of Elis. Whoddert.

> **10147: MELCHIOR** b GF 20 Mar 1792 (sp Melc. Kessler & M. Elis.)
> m 1813 ANNA STEPH. EYSAMAN
> **10148: JOHANNES** b GF 9 May 1794 (sp John Withrstn & Marg <Keslr>)
> **10149: PETER** b GF 2 Jan 1802 (sp Peter Kessler)
> **10150: MARGARET** b HK Jan 1804 (sp Diet. Kessler & w. Margaret)

10151: ADAM REESE (Reis/Reid) - pr. born ca 1735 to 1759; m by 1783 ANNA BELL (b
ca 1759, d Manheim NY 10 Mar 1833 age 74-3-0). On the 1790 German Flats census
(3-2-4) and pr. of the Reese family which settled at Andrustown before the
Revolution. Adam Reis sponsored Mar 1793 GF bp of Samuel, son of Assam (i.e.
Gershom) Smidt & Helena (Reis).
> surname REESE
> **10151A JOHN** b FR 4 Sep 1783 (sp. John Young, Elis. Rees)
> **10151B MELCHERT** b FR 17 May 1785 (sp. Samuel Rees, Anna Rees)
> **10152: CATHERINE** b GF 14 Sep 1789 (sp Geo. Hen. Bell & Cath.)
> **10153: FREDERICK** b GF Aug 1792 (sp John Osteroth & Cath.)

10153A CHRISTOPHER REUBY - On 1790 German Flats census (1-1-1). Possibly his
wife or daughter was the Phebe Ruby who had a child Febe Fox (<no father given>
child bp GF Aug 1792, sp. Fred. Fox & Elis.)

10154: BILL RICHARDSON - m GF 1784 CHRISTINA ... widow of HENRICH NELLIS.
> surname RICHARDSON
> **10155: DAVID** b GF Oct 1784 (sp. David Mabee, Sally Sneider)

10156: LORENTZ RINCKEL - born in Holland in 1747 (DAR #55358); killed at the
Battle of Oriskany 6 Aug 1777; m CATHERINE ... John Runkel was a German Flats NY
resident in May 1775. His widow Catherine petitioned for assistance ca 1779
giving children's ages then as 15, 13, 8, & 2 (Mohawk Valley in the Revolution, pg
182). A Cath. Rinckel sponsored Jan 1786 bp of Conrad, son of Adam Hartman.
> surname RINCKEL
> **10157: CATHERINE** b ca 1764; m 1784 JOHANNES JUKKER
> **10158: CATHERINE ELISABETH** b ca 1766; m 31 Jan 1786 JACOB WITRIG
> **10159: MARIA SYBILLA** b SAR 14 Nov 1770 (sp Jacob Dines & Mar. Sybila)
> (aka MARIA) m 1791 PHILIP LENTZ
> **10161: LORENTZ** b 8 Dec 1777 (sp John Dinges, Barb. Birckin)
> m by 1812 CATHERINE YOUCKER

10162: NICHOLAS RITTMANS - pr. born ca 1700 to 1720; His daughter ELISABETH (b
say 1740) sponsored Jan 1761 bp of John, son of Joh. Jacob Weber & Margaret and
also sp. May 1763 bp of Peter, son of John Bellinger & Elis. Folts.

10163: **JOHN HASTEIN ROBERTSON** - Pr. born ca 1740 to 1758; m ... Pr. related to the Robert Robertson who was at Ft. Stanwix in the 1760´s.
surname ROBERTSON
    10164: JOHN BAFFLE b GF 7 Nov 1778 (Capt Pet. Bellinger & Christna)

10165: **JOHN ROBERTSON** - m by 1778 BALLY ...

    10166: DANIEL b GF 4 Jun 1778 (sp Nic. Varbos & Sara)

10167: **PETER ROBERTSON** - m GF 5 May 1783 widow CATHERINE RATTENAUER, presumably widow of GOTFRID RATTENAUER (he died at Oriskany 1777).

10168: **ROBERT ROBERTSON** - m SAR 16 Oct 1768 MARGARET BEALY. Vosburgh (GF rec.) has Robertson, Ruff & Campbell as soldiers at Ft Stanwix, early 1760´s.
surname ROBERTSON
    10164: ROBERT b GF 1 Sep 1776 (sp. Joh. Smidt & Anna Eva)

10169: Capt. **JOHANNES ROOF** ("Ruff") - born Baden Germany 1730; died Canajoharie NY 1798; m 1759 ANNA MARIE LEONARD. His son´s wife Mary was dau of NICHOLAS DUNKLE (b Germany 1758, d Canajoharie 1841) - see DAR# 115473.
surname ROOF
    10170: JOHN jr ca 1762-1847 joined mil. at Canajoharie 1778
    10171: NICHOLAS b GF 28 Aug 1762 (sp. Nic Herkimr & w. Maria)
    10171A SUSANNA b say 1770; m 1790 ANDREW FAILING
    10172: MARIA b GF 23 Mar 1777 (sp Maria, w of Gen. N. Herkimer)
    10173: DANIEL b 4 Mar 1779 (sp Maj. Stofel Yates & Maria)
    10174: MARGARET b 17 Jan 1781 (sp Marg. Cox, Math. Gerhard)
    10175: MARTIN b GF 5 Apr 1783 (sp Chrstn Laemum & Anna Elis.)
    10176: ANDREW b say 1785; d 1861; m 1806 MARY DUNKLE

10177: **NICHOLAS RYAN** (Rein) - pr. born ca 1720 to 1725; m by 1767 MARIA ELISABETH .... Living at New Petersburg in 1770. Nicholas Raan sponsored Mar 1785 bp of Maria Eva, dau of Johannes Keller & Christina. Nich. Kein (Rein) was on Tryon Co. census ca 1776, in the Royal Grant area (near Fairfield NY), with 1 male (over 50), two women (age 16-50), 1 boy & 2 girls.
surname RYAN
   +10178: pr. JOHN b say 1760; m 1784 MAGDALENA ...
   +10179: JACOB b SAR 17 Aug 1767 (sp Jac. Dinges, Mich. Sietzer,...)
                m 1790 ANNA EVA MILLER
    10180: EVA CATHERINE b 29 Jun 1770 (SAR sp Cath.... Gruning)
    10181: CATHERINE ELISABETH b say 1772; m 1788 MARC JOH. SCHELL
    10182: pr. MARIA b say 1774; liv. 1789 (spf Schell bp)

10178: **JOHN RYAN** - pr. born ca 1740 to 1762; m 1784 MAGDALENA ... widow of HENRY MILLER. In Bellinger´s Revol. Regiment. Magdalena Ryan (pr. wife) was sponsor for Aug 1806 bp of Magdalena, dau of John Young & Margaret (Ryan).

    10183: MARGARET b 8 Nov 1784 (sp Diet. Petrie & Elis.<Dygert>)
               m 1805 JOHN BAR. YOUNG

10179: **JACOB RYAN** - born SAR 17 Aug 1767; m GF 19 Jan 1790 EVA FR. MILLER.

    10184: MARIA b GF 17 Oct 1790 (sp Godf Hilts & Maria <Miller>)
    10185: JACOB b GF 16 Nov 1791 (sp Jac. Windecker, Maria Ryan)
    10186: NICHOLAS b 7 Mar 1793 (sp Marc. Schell & Cath.<Ryan>)
    10187: SUSANNA b GF 12 Sep 1794 (sp John Hilts, Susanna Christman)

10201: **HENRY SALJE** (called Henry Sallie on 1793 SJR bp. rec.) - pr. born ca 1730 to 1750; m1 BARBARA ... (liv. 1789); pr. m2 by 1793 CATHERINE ... Henry Salje & Barbara sponsored Nov 1789 bp of Henry, son of Jacob J. Edick & Elis. (Weaver). Henry Salyea was at Deerfield, with George DeMuth, and he sold land there in 1787 to John Post. Pr. Henry was on 1790 GF census (2-1-1) listed near Benj. Ballow & Wm Cuningham. The Utica Morning Herald (22 Nov 1871) tells of early settler Henry Salyea, who sold land to Mathew Hubbl and who was a straggler in the town, "like the remnant of a captured tribe domiciled amongst his captors".
surname SALJE
     10202: SARA H. b say 1773; m Dec 1793 ADAM ARMSTRONG
     10203: MARGARET b SJR 20 Sep 1793 (sp Adam Sallie, Elis. Stahli)

10204: **JOHN SCHAAD** - pr. born ca 1730 to 1750; m ... In 1769 GF militia, listed amongst Hasenclever group. A Margaret Elisabeth Schaad was sponsor for Oct 1767 SAR bp of Julianna Margaret Keller.

10205: Lt. **CONRAD SCHAEFFER** - pr. born ca 1745 to 1755; m by 1782 DOROTHY CRIM dau of PAUL CRIM & MAGDALENA STEELE and widow of FREDERICK BELL (d 1778).
surname SCHAEFFER
     10206: GERTRUDE b GF 18 Feb 1784 (sp Gert. Crim, Geo. Hausman)

10207: **HENRY SCHAEFFER** - pr. born ca 1730 to 1750; m by 1779 CATHERINE MARGARET ... (widow of Jacob Meyer). Was stepfather of Ludwig Meyer, who substituted for Henry in 1778 military enlistment at Kingsland, Tryon Co. Pr. the Henry listed with the Hasenclever men in the 1769 GF militia and the one naturalized 8 Mar 1773 along with Nich. Keller, John Keller jun., Jacob Meyer, & Adam Hartman.

10208: **CASPER SCHELLENBERG** - m by 1791 MARIA ...
surname SCHELLENBERG
     10209: ANNA b GF 9 May 1791 (sp Nich. J Kessler & Gert.)

10210: **GEORGE SCHEWMAN** (Scheurman) - m by 1785 ELISABETH ... German Flats' church records show a George Scheurman, a married man, had a daughter Margaret (b GF 27 Feb 1781) out of wedlock, the mother being the wife of BENJAMIN MAKKIS.
surname SCHEWMAN
     10211: HENRICH b GF 23 Sep 1785 (sp Henry Uhly & Helana)

10212: **JOHN SCHEWMAN** (Schauerman) - m by 1781 ANNA ELISABETH ...
surname SCHEWMAN
     10213: ANNA GERTRUDE b GF 9 May 1779 (sp John Bierhausen & Elis.)
             d 1805; m HENRY H. HARTER
     10214: GEORGE b GF 2 Jan 1781 (sp Geo. Herkimer & Alita)

10215: **GEORGE SCHIFF** Sr. - pr. born ca 1715 to 1725; m by 1767 MARIA CATHERINE ... Pr. the George Schiffen who died in action in the Amer. Revolution (Book of Names page 168). In 1769 GF militia where his name is amongst the Hasenclever group (Witrig, Bircky ...) and in Col. Bellinger's Revol. Regiment. On Tryon Co. census ca 1776 he was over age 50 with 3 boys & 2 girls.
surname SCHIFF
  +10216: GEORGE jr. b say 1763; m 1784 CHRISTINA VORBUS
   10217: MARIA MARGARET b say 1765; liv. 1782 (spf Hartman bp)
   10218: CHRISTIAN b SAR 22 Mar 1767 (sp Geo Hilts & M. Elisabeth)
   10219: MARIA G. b say 1769; m 1789 JACOB P. MULTER
  +10220: pr. JOHN b say 1771; m by 1793 EVA ...

10216: GEORGE SCHIFF jr. - b say 1763; m GF 13 Jan 1784 CHRISTINA VORBUS.

    10221: JACOB b GF 29 Mar 1785 (sp Jac Forbes, Marg. Schiff)
    10222: GEORGE b GF 24 Jul 1788 (sp Geo. H. Herkimer & Maria)
    10223: ALITA bp SJR Aug 1790 (sp John Meyer & Alita)
    10224: EVA b GF 1 May 1793 (sp John Schiff & Eva)

10220: JOHN SCHIFF - b say 1771; m by 1793 EVA ... Had dau ELISABETH (b GF 17 Dec 1793, sp. Christian Schiff, Elis. Miller).

10226: FRANCIS SCHIMMEL - pr. born ca 1720 to 1743; m ELISABETH .. On 1790 Canajoharie NY census (4-2-4) listed next to And. Smith and Conrad Shemell.
                surname SCHIMMEL
    10227: ELISABETH b 7 Jan 1763 (sp. Conrad Frank & Elis.)
             m 1783 CASPAR MILLER
    10227A pr. DIETRICH b say 1765; liv. 1778 (SAL confirm.)
    10227B pr. CONRAD b say 1769; m by 1799 MARIA ... (spf Dillnbch bp)
    10228: SOPHIA b SAL 2 Dec 1771 (Jost Haus & w.)
    10228A pr. MAGDALENA b 1773; d 1862; m JONAS DILLENBACH

10229: MICHAEL SCHNEIDER - pr. born ca 1735 to 1745; died by 1813 (will dated 1810, probated 1813); m 27 Nov 1764 ELIZABETH ECKLER (b 1746) dau of HENRY ECKLER & MARGARET YOUNG. Was a neighbor of Henry Eckler at the Chyle settlement in Warren NY, as given in the Eckler book by A. Ross Eckler (page 122). On the 1790 Canajoharie NY census (2-1-3) listed near Henry Murphy and Godfry Young.
                surname SCHNEIDER
    10229: ANNA MARGARET b 10 Sep 1765
    10230: ELIZABETH b 30 Mar 1767
    10231: MAGDALENA b 15 Jan 1769
    10232: ANNA MARIA bp SAL May 1771 (sp Gotlib Schneidr, Otila Resner)
    10233: JOHN b say 1773; liv. 1810; m ANNA
    10234: JACOB M. b say 1774; m SUSANNA (b ca 1774)
    10235: GEORGE b say 1777; m CHRISTINA
    10236: PETER b 17 May 1782; pr. died young

10237: GEORGE SCHNEK Sr. - pr. born ca 1710 to 1725; pr. m LENA ... Among the Hasenclever men in 1769 GF militia and in Bellinger's Revol. unit. George Shenk & Lena sponsored Sep 1767 SAR bp of George, son of Geo. Ecker & Susanna, and May 1768 SAR bp of child of John Smith & Barbara.
                surname SCHNEK
   +10238: pr. GEORGE jr. b say 1740, in Revol. service
    10239: ps. MARGARET ELISABETH b say 1750; liv. 1767 (spf Keller bp)
    10240: pr. JULIANA b say 1753; m 1770 BALTES BREITENBACHER

10238: GEORGE SCHNEK Jr. - pr. born ca 1730 to 1743; pr. m by 1767 BARBARA ... (b ca 1743; age 37 in 1780 when taken prisoner <Book of Names, pg 110>). In 1769 GF militia. George jr. & Barbara sponsored 1767 SAR bp of Jacob, son of Fred Ayer, and Aug 1776 GF bp of Barbara Ogh. Had 2 boys & 2 girls (under 16) on Tryon Co. census ca 1776 (Mohawk Valley in the Revolution, page 154).

    10241: pr. MARY FREDERICKA ca 1766-1816 m JOHN FINSTER
    10242: MARGARET b SAR 8 Nov 1767 (sp Marg. Frank, John Smith)
             liv. 1780 (age 13 when taken prisoner)
    10243: JACOB b SAR 15 May 1770 (sp Jac. Hiller & Elis.)
    10244: CHRISTINA b ca 1779; liv. 1780 (age 9 mos. when POW)
    10245: pr. BARBARA b GF 6 Aug 1780 (sp Peter Bircky, Cath Rinckel)

10245A MICHAEL SEITZER - With Hasenclever men in 1769 GF militia (no more!)

10246: JOHANNES SEUFFER Sr. - pr. born ca 1738 to 1746; m SAR 8 Dec 1765 MARIA BETTLI. The parents of the girls Anna and Barbara born 1791-93 are listed in the Church records as John & Maria, which could be either John Sr. or Jr. Pr. the John on Palatine NY census (2-1-5) next to John Keller.

          surname SEUFFER

    10247: ANNA MARIA   b 5 Jul 1766 (sp. Maria, w. of Nic. Herkmer)

+10248: JOHN jr.   b SAR 19 Jun 1768 (sp Werner Dygert & Lena)

          m by 1793 MARIA ...

    10249: ELISABETH   b SAR 16 Mar 1770 (sp Nich. Herkimer & w Maria)

          m 1786 FREDERICK RITTER

    10250: MARIA CATHERINE   b 4 Sep 1771 (sp Maria Herkmr, Jost Schyler)

          m HENRY CON. RICKERT

+10251: pr. ANDREAS   b say 1773; m 1795 MARIA ZOLLER

    10252: MARGARET   b 17 Sep 1779 (sp John Van Sleik & Marg.)

    10253: ps. ANNA   b GF 14 Jun 1791 (sp Cobus Van Slyk & Gertr.)

    10254: ps. BARBARA   b GF 21 Jun 1793 (sp F. Windecker, Barb. Keller)

10251: ANDREAS SEUFFER - born say 1770; m GF 13 Sep 1795 MARIA ZOLLER. Vosburgh copy of 1795 mar. rec. has his surname "Lauffer".

    10255: ANDREAS   b GF 30 Nov 1795 (sp Caspar Zoller & Christina)

10248: JOHN SEUFFER jr. - born ca Jun 1768 (son of John); m by 1793 MARIA ...

    10256: pr. ELISABETH   b GF 6 Nov 1786 (sp G. Zimmerman & Elis.)

    10257: MARIA   b GF 21 Dec 1793 (sp John Seuffer Sr & Maria)

    10258: pr. SUSANNA   b GF 4 Oct 1795 (sp Caspar Zoller & Susanna)

10259: DANIEL SHAW - pr. born before 1755. Was a soldier at Fort Dayton and one of the buyers at the Nicholas Smith estate sale in 1779. Ps. related to Thomas Shaw who sponsored Jul 1777 GF bp of Daniel, son of James Adams & Appolonia.

10260: RICHARD SHARPP - m LEA ...

          surname SHARPP

    10261: ANDREAS   b ca 1790 (bp GF 1793, sp Geo H Starin, Elis Miller)

    10262: MARIA   b ca Jan 1793 (bp GF Apr 1793)

10263: CHRISTIAN SILLEBACH - born ca 1762 (pr. son of Arnold of Stone Arabia); died Herkimer NY 28 Oct 1807 (age 45); pr. m1 by 1787 MAGDALENA LEDER; m GF 8 Jan 1792 ELISABETH JOH. N. WEAVER. Christian Syllebach and Magdalena (Leder) were sponsors for SAR Aug 1787 bp of Henrich, son of Hen. Fritscher & Elis. (Bayer). On 1790 Herkimer census (1-0-0). Was a blacksmith and widower in 1807.

          surname SILLEBACH

    10264: JOHN   b SJR 16 Aug 1792 (sp John Imhof, Anna Weber)

    10265: DIETRICH   b ca 1796; liv. 1812 (age 16 HK Ch. Confirm.)

10266: JOHN SIMSON - pr. born ca 1715 to 1740; ps. m1 at Schenectady 1758 CATRINA CAMPBELL; m by 1760 ELISABETH ... In 1767 GF militia listed next to Adam Steele & Thomas Shoemaker.

          surname SIMPSON

    10267: ELISABETH   bp May 1760 (sp. Maria Doro., Jac. Kessler's wife)

    10268: LENA   bp 3 Apr 1762 (sp. Lena <Herkimer> w of Werner Dygert)

    10269: MARIA   b 25 Feb 1764 (sp Elis. Kesslr, Jost Petrie, unm per.)

    10270: JOHANNES   b 27 Feb 1766 (sp. Joh. Gemmel, Marg. Bellinger)

10271: **GEORGE SMARTH** (Martin) - m by 1787 CATHERINE ...   Geo. Smarth & Cath.,
both Indians, sponsored May 1787 GF bp of George, son of Jacob Dacksteder & Lea.
surname MARTIN
  10272: pr. JOHN b GF 24 Jun 1788 (sp John Hess, Indian)

10273: **GEORGE SMITH** - pr. born 1735 to 1755; m by 1781 ANNA ...

surname SMITH
  10274: THOMAS bp 1781 (sp. Jacob Christman & Anna)
  10275: ELISABETH bp GF 8 Feb 1783 (sp Jac. Shill & Elis. <Smith>)
  10276: HENRICH bp SAL 10 Apr 1793 (sp Hen Smit, Elis. V. Lunen)
  10277: pr. JOHN (son of George) b say 1796; liv. 1811 (HK confirm.)

10278: **GEORGE ADAM SMITH** (Joh. Adam on 1791 bp rec.) - pr. born 1735 to 1755; m
by 1789 ANNA ... Two Geo. Smiths, pr. both of Montgomery Co. Henrich Schmid
family, had children bp in 1793. Lived at Canajoharie in 1793.

  10279: RUDOLPH bp SJR 8 Oct 1789 (sp Jos. Smith, Elis. Clerk)
  10280: pr. EVA bp SJR 20 Nov 1791 (sp Hen. Richtmeyr & Maria)
  10281: GASTINA bp SJR 17 Feb 1793 (sp Hen. Richtmyer & w.)

10282: **JOHN SMITH** - pr. born ca 1735 to 1745; m by 1775 ANNA EVA ...   (ps. a
Haus or Van Slyck. Parents of George, bp 1778, listed as John & Catherine. Pr.
the Johannis who was in Capt. Klock's militia co. in 1763, listed near Gerrit Van
Slyke & Conrad House.

  10283: MARIE CATHERINE bp 28 Jul 1776 (sp. Geo Hauss & w. Maria)
  10283A ps. GEORGE b SAL 28 Nov 1778 (sp Nic. Dygert, Anna Reuter)
  10284: NICHOLAS bp GF 24 Jun 1781 (sp Nic. Dygert, Engeltje Vn Slyk)
      ps. m ELIZABETH ECKER (1781-1851)
  10285: JOHN b GF 16 Jun 1785 (sp. Joh. House & w. Lena <V Slyck>)

10286: **Lt. JOHN SMITH** - pr. born ca 1730 to 1745; m MARIA ELIZABETH ... (notes
of V. Eysaman say Maria English); as widower m2 at Herkimer NY 25 Dec 1792 BARBARA
ELISABETH WEAVER widow of JOHN CAMPBELL. Was an Ensign in Capt. Eisenlord's co.
of militia in 1775 (Benton's "History of Herkimer" page 184). Prob. the John who,
with wife Elisabeth, was sponsor for 1778 bp of Elisabeth, dau of Rudolph
Wallrath, and the John & Maria Elis. who sponsored May 1785 bp of John, son of
John Fox & Anna Frank (Bellinger book page 47). Children, except Catherine (dau of
John & Maria), bp at Herkimer Reformed Church. Pr. this was the John Smith on the
1790 Census of German Flats NY (4-4-6).

  10287: ps. CATHERINE bp SAR 30 Sep 1770 (sp Cath & Isaac Paris)
  10288: MARIA ELIZABETH bp 13 Jul 1777 (sp. J. Fred. Helmer & Elis.)
  10289: GEORGE b GF 2 Apr 1780 (sp. Geo. Herkimer & Alita)
  10290: ALITA b 9 Jan 1782 (bp 1784 sp. Geo. Herkimer & Alita)
  10291: MARGARITHA b 16 Jun 1784 (sp Joh. Jost Hess, Cath. Nelles)
  10292: BALLY (Mary) b GF 30 May 1786 (sp Caleb Morrel, Maria Nelles)
      pr. m Mar 1812 JACOB EIGENAUER
  10293: JOHANNES bp 1788 (sp. Ludwig Chamble)
  10294: pr. HANNA b GF Apr 1791 (dau of John, merchant & M. Elis.)
      (sp John Portious, Eun. Nic. Aldrige)
      by 2nd wife
  10295: pr. BARBARA b GF 23 Oct 1793 (sp Ludwig Itol & Marg.)

10296: JOHN SMITH jr. - pr. born ca 1760 to 1775; m by 1795 MARGARET WEAVER (b 1779) dau of JACOB WEAVER & MARGARET MEYER. Had ten children (not incl. Luis bp 1795) - Margaritta, Henry, Betsy, Michael, Eve, John Nancy, Cynthia, Jacob, and Peter (as given in 1982 notes of Mrs. W. Gronberg, Dixon, Ill.).

> **10297: LUIS** bp GF 14 May 1795 (sp. Thomas Bell)
> **10298: ELISABETH** bp HK 8 Feb 1805 (sp Nic Weber & w Barbara)
> **10299: EVA** bp HK 2 Feb 1808 (sp Jacob Weber & w. Eva)

10300: PETER SMITH - born <Tappan> Rockland Co. NY 1768; died Schenectady NY 17 Apr 1837; m ELISABETH LIVINGSTON dau of Col. JAMES LIVINGSTON as given in Utica Morning Herald of 22 Nov 1871. Aprenticed at age 16 <ca 1784> in the importing house of Abraham Heering which he left after three years <ca 1787> to set up trade at Fall Hill in Little Falls NY for a year, then <ca 1790> set up a store at old Ft. Schuyler. Peter finally moved his store in 1792 to the present Utica NY corner of Main & 3rd Streets.

> **10301: dau** b 1792; m Capt. COCHRANE
> **10302: CORNELIA** b GF Jan 1793
> **10303: GERRIT** b Utica NY 1797

10304: PETER ABRAM SMITH - m SALOME BRONNER and moved to Herkimer Co. NY in 1790 (DAR rec.). The DAR record reference here may be to the same man as the above Peter (who married Elisabeth Livingston). No Peter appears on the 1790 census at German Flats or Herkimer however there were two Peter Smiths on the Canajoharie census then (the family sizes give little clue as to whether they are this Peter or some offspring of the Henrich Smidt family of Montgomery Co.).

> **10305: ABRAM** 1798-1880

10306: ROBERT SMITH - m by 1776 GRACE ... (pr. Braithwaite or Brave). He was pr. the son of Ephraim Smith of Schenectady and grandson of Burnetsfield Patentee Adam Michael Smith. Robert was probably only briefly in German Flats ca 1776 when his son Johannes was born.

> surname SMITH
> **10307: JOHANNES** b GF 30 Oct 1777 (sp Col Petr Bellinger & Delia)

10308: ROBERT SMITH - born in Yorkshire England ca 1726; died GF 12 Jun 1822 (age 95-6-); m MARY EHLE (surname?). Pr. immigrated after 1752, as daughter Mary´s death record has her born in England, and was a Tory in the Revolution.

> surname SMITH
> **10309: MARY** ca 1752-1825 m 1771 JOST SHOEMAKER
> **10310: ps. WILLIAM** b say 1755; liv. 1786 (sp Shoemaker bp)

10310A THOMAS SMITH - born ca 1715 to 1735; Was a trader at German Flats in 1757 when Sir Johnson´s papers indicate he was implicated (but not tried) in the murder of two Oneida Indians. He is not easily placable in the the Schmid family of George of Herkimer or Henrich of Montgomery Co. and we suspect he was of either Dutch or English ancestry. Ps. the same Thomas Smith who was a Tory and delivered the plans for Ft. Stanwix to the British at the start of the Revolutionary War.

10310B HENRICH SCHNICT - pr. born before 1740. In 1757 he was in Capt. Petrie´s GF militia unit, listed next to John Raspach jr. & Peter Foltz. The Schnict name does not appear in later records, but the spelling could have gone various ways and ps. this was Henry Snook (of Fisher´s Fonda area Revol. Regiment) or even Henry Sixth (of Stone Arabia ca 1742).

10311: PETER SPIES - pr. born ca 1670 to 1690; m pr. ca 1713 ELISABETH ... On NY Palatine subsistence list in 1710 (1A,OY) & 1712 (1A,OY) and on 1717 Simmendinger census at New Heesberg with wife Anna Elisabeth. He had Burnetsfield lot #38 and his wife Elisabeth received lot #8, located on the south side of the Mohawk, which was sold before 1772 to Adam Steele.
surname SPIES

     10312: ps. MARY b say 1713; m 1730 CHRISTIAN ETX (1713-1789)

10313: HIERONYMUS SPIES - pr. born ca 1730 to 1750; m by 1767 BARBARA ... In 1769 GF militia, listed near Hasenclever men Peter Multer & Wm Bender.

     10314: MARIA b SAR 1 Jul 1767 (sp Elis. & Wm Dygert)

10315: PHILIP STEINMETZ - pr. born ca 1740 to 1760; m by 1780 MARIA ... In Col. Campbell's Revol. Regimen.
surname STEINMETZ

     10316: MARIA ELISABETH b GF 3 Jun 1780 (sp John Bierhausen & Elis.)
     10317: MARIA b GF 14 Mar 1782 (sp Math. Bekker, Maria Schaffer)

10318: Sgt. ARNOLD STEINWAX - pr. born ca 1730 to 1750; killed at Oriskany battle 6 Aug 1777 (Book of Names page 168); m by 1765 MARIA CATHERINE ...; apparently m2 by 1767 GERTRUDE ... The widow Steinwax had 1 adult and 4 children on 1778 German Flats relief. A Gertrude Steinwax was sponsor for Jun 1776 bp of Gertrude, dau of John Klein. Anna Amelia Steinwax and Catherine Steinwax were sponsors for Mar 1778 bp of Amelia Cath. Klein, dau of John.
surname STEINWAX

     10319: CATHERINE b SAR 5 Dec 1765 (sp Cath Dockstdr, Chrn H Berkoff)
by 2nd wife
     10320: CASPAR b SAR 17 Sep 1767 (sp Caspar Hasenclever, John Schaad)
     10320A pr. ANNA AMELIA b ca 1769; liv. 1778

10321: FREDERICK STEVENS - died at Oriskany battle Aug 1777; m MARY GETMAN dau of FREDERICK GETMAN. His wife m2 MELCHERT FOLTS and his son lived with his stepfather's family (note in Stevens file at Herk. Co. Hist. Soc.).
surname STEVENS

     10322: FREDERICK b say 1775; m by 1802 ANNA LANTHORN (Lender)

10322A PHILIP G. STOWITZ - killed at Oriskany 6 Aug 1777 (Bellinger's GF Regiment, Book of Names, page 134); m by 1765 MARLENA... He had sons Michael P. (m 1790 ELISABTH BELLINGER) & GEORGE (b 1765, m MARGARET DIEVENDORF.

10323: BALTHASAR STRAUCH - m MARIA CATHERINE RITTER (b 1765).
surname STRAUCH

     10324: HENRICH b GF 17 Jul 1784 (sp Hen. Ritter, Maria Petri)
     10325: pr. BALTUS b 1787; m CATHERINE RITTER (Petrie book pg 36)
     10326: ANNA b GF 12 Apr 1794 (sp John Riemnsnider & Eva)

10327: CHRISTOPHER STROBEL (Stofel Truble) - pr. born ca 1730 to 1750; liv. 1796; m SAR 29 Apr 1767 ELISABETH WEAVER. Ps. related to the John Stroble in 1757 GF militia. Stofel was in Frank's GF militia co. in 1767 and served in Bellinger's Revol. regiment. Stofel & Barb. Elisabeth sponsored Feb 1768 SAR bp of Barbara Elisabeth, dau of Marx Ittig & Barbara (Weaver). Had 3 adults on 1778 GF relief and was on 1790 German Flats census (2-1-3). In 1796 he was listed as an executor in the will of Abraham Baum of Utica NY.

10401: **HEZEKIAH TALCOTT** jr. - pr. born ca 1740 to 1760; died by 1800; ml ... ;
m2 GF 14 Jun 1795 MARIA H. MEYER (Bolly) dau of a HENRY MEYER (most Meyer
references have Maria as dau of FREDERICK MEYER & MARGARET WEAVER, but the middle
initial "H." in her mar. rec. seems to refute that). Was on 1790 Herkimer census
(3-2-7). His widow m2 ca 1800 NICHOLAS H. STAHRING. Had sons Alpheus (m 1804 PATY
VEAZEE) & Asa G. (b say 1798; m 1821 ASENATH CASWELL)

10402: **PETER TEN BROEK** - pr. born ca 1720 to 1730; died 1804; m 3 Mar 1750 ANNA
HERKIMER dau of JOST HERKIMER & CATHERINE PETRIE. Was a Tory Capt. in Butler's
Rangers during the Revolution. Children from Petrie book page 5.
surname TEN BROEK
    10403: CHRISTINA b say 1757 (bp Jul 1760)
             ml NICHOLAS BELL; m2 PETER BELLINGER (1760-1851)
    10404: ANNATJE b say 1759 (bp 5 Jul 1760)
    10405: JACOB b SAR Dec 1761 (sp Jost Herkimer & Cath.)
    10406: JOHN bp SAR 26 Oct 1764 (John Herkimr, Maria Wm Dygert); d y
    10407: CATHARINE m GEORGE FORSYTH
    10408: ANN b 8 Feb 1769; m THOMAS BUTLER
    10409: GERTRUDE bp SAR 7 Feb 1769 (sp Gert. & Rud. Shoemaker)
    10410: NICHOLAS b 1771; m 1792 DELIA BELLINGER
    10411: JOHN b 10 Jan 1780

10412: **JOHN THOMPSON** - born 1738 (Mohawk Valley in the Revolution, page 330); m
by 1761 DOROTHEA... (b 1740, pr. McGinnes). In 1769 GF militia. Sponsored 1776
GF bp of John, son of John Barry. Became a Tory and served in the King's Royal
Regiment in 1779. John & Dorothy lived at Niagara Canada in Dec 1783.
surname THOMPSON
    10413: MARGARET b 23 Aug 1761 (sp Sara, w of Pet. Dygert)
    10414: TIMOTHY b SA 23 Jul 1763 (sp. Wm Laux & w. Marg.)
    10415: ps. JOHN b say 1767; m GF 1787 GERTRUDE H. PHILIPS

10416: **EMMANUEL TOOBY** - pr. born ca 1740 to 1763; m GF 8 Sep 1782 DOROTHY
PFEIFFER dau of PETER PFEIFFER. Had dau MARIA CATHERINE (b GF 20 Dec 1782, sp.
Lor. Shoemaker, Marg. Piper).

10418: **HENRICH UHLE** - born in Germany 14 Sep 1755; died 12 Jun 1813 (buried Fall
Hill, Little Falls NY); m GF 9 Sep 1784 MAGDALENA WERNER DYGERT (b 1763) dau of
WERNER DYGERT & MAGDALENA HERKIMER. Was sponsor, with Lena, at bp Feb 1794 of
Catherine, dau of Abraham Herkimer & Dorothea. In the American Revolution, he was
a Hessian soldier with the British Army but, upon learning that he had to fight
against his former German countryman, he defected seeking refuge at the house of
Werner Dygert where he was taken in (Petrie book page 13). On 1790 German Flats
census (1-0-4), near Rev. Rosencrantz & John Hilts.
surname UHLE
    10419: DOROTHY b 1 Dec 1785 (sp Sev. W. Dygert, Doro. P. Dygert)
             m ADAM GRAY
    10420: WARNER b 13 Dec 1786 (sp Jost Dygert & M. Elis.); pr d y
    10421: MAGDALENA b 31 Dec 1787; m CHRISTOPHER CASLER
    10422: MARIA b 17 Apr 1790; m WALTER MCCHESNEY
    10423: ANNA b 18 Feb 1793 (sp Conrad Folts & Anna)
    10424: HENRICH b 7 Apr 1796; m CATHERINE CASLER
    10425: CATHERINE b 28 Feb 1799
    10426: GEORGE b 11 Oct 1801; ml SALLY MAXWELL
    10427: JOHN b 17 May 1804; m ANNA EVA BELLINGER

10428: **DANIEL ULLENDORF** - pr. born ca 1740 to 1760; m by 1783 CATHERINE ... (b
ca 1760, age 20 in 1780 when taken prisoner). Name is similar to Orendorf but no
other basis is seen for connection to that German Flats family. Daniel was pr. a
later immigrant to the Mohawk Valley, ps. arriving about the time of the
Revolution. Daniel & Catherine were sponsors for Oct 1782 bp of John, son of John
Eckler & Margaret (Huber). On 1790 German Flats census (1-2-5). Had dau
ELISABETH (b GF 3 Sep 1783, sp Elis. Huber, Fred. Jung).

10429: **THOMAS VAN HORNE** - born Hunterdon Co. New Jersey 14 May 1748 (son of
Mathias Van Horne & Nelly Crumm); died Springfield NY 26 Feb 1841; m Caughnawaga
NY 21 Oct 1779 MARIA FREDERICK dau of PHILIP FREDERICK & SOPHIA SALTZ. A Lt. in
the Col. Frederick Fischer's 3rd Tryon Co. militia in the Revolution. Other Van
Hornes in Fischer's unit include an Abram, Cornelius, Henry, and John. Thomas
lived at Otsego Co. NY and his children were baptised at St. Paul's Luth. Church
in Minden, NY. Had fourteen children, as given in Van Horne book, Mathias, Leah
(bp 1781, m ROBERT DAVIS), philip (b 1784, m MARGARET ECKLER), Sophia (b 1786, m
JOHN ECKLER), Eleanora (b 1788, m GEORGE SHAUL), Eve (b 1789, m JACOB I YOUNG),
Anna (b 1791, m JOHN G. SHAUL), Cornelius (b 1793, m CATHERINE SHANHULTZ),
Magdalena (b 1795, m JOHN E. ECKLER), Elizabeth (b 1797, m WILLIAM VAN HORNE,
Abram (b 1799, m1 DOROTHY SHANHULTZ), Thomas (b 1802, d.y.), Maria (b 1804, m JOHN
WYCKOFF), and Francis (b 1809, d.y.).

10430: **JAMES VAN HORNE** - presumably born before 1750; m ... . According to
Beers History of Herkimer Co., James ran the first general trade store at German
Flats and in his account book are mentioned persons such as Duncan McDougal
(1775), John N. Casler (rum & grog purchases 1776-1784), and George Weaver (who he
calls brother-in-law). However, James Van Horn has not been seen in any of the
Revolutionary era Tryon Co. militia or church records or on the 1790 census of
Montgomery Co. NY. The Van Horne book mentions an early James (b 1740, m Eliz.
Selight), but that one seems to have resided in Marlboro NJ (where his children
were bp between 1761 and 1781).

10431: **HENRICH VETTERLY** - pr. born ca 1730 to 1745; m EVA ... Widow Eva was a
sponsor for 1791 bp of Henrich, son of John Vetterly & Gertrude. Eva Fedderly
appears on 1790 Herkimer census (0-2-2) along with Thomas and John Fedderly and
near in list to F. Getman, Skinner, and Moulder.
                          surname VETTERLY
    +10432: ps. THOMAS   b say 1763; m by 1786 MARGARET SCHIFF
    +10433: ps. HENRICH b say 1767; m 1792 EVA HITSHMAN
     10434: pr. RACHEL   b say 1770; m 1789 JACOB KESSLER
    +10435: ps. PETER   b say 1775; m by 1803 ELISABETH FOX

10433: **HENRICH VETTERLY** - born say 1767; m GF 3 Jun 1792 EVA HITSHMAN
                          surname VETTERLY
     10436: HENRICH   b GF Jun 1794 (sp Fritz Getman, Maria Vetterle)

10437: **JOHN VETTERLY** Sr. - pr. born ca 1715 to 1735; m MARGARET ... His widow
Margaret m2 Stone Arabia NY 6 Aug 1761 JOHN BAART a widower.

    +10438: pr. JOHN jr.   b say 1754; m by 1784 GERTRUDE CASSELMAN
     10439: ps. ROBERT   b say 1756; m FPL 1793 ANNA RATTENAUER
     10440: ps. ANNA   b say 1758; m FPL 1793 CHRISTIAN BRUNNER
     10441: pr. GEORGE JOH. b say 1760; m FPL 1791 ANNA JOH. DYGERT

10438: JOHN VETTERLY - pr. born ca 1750 to 1765; m by 1784 GERTRUDE CASSELMAN. On 1790 Herkimer census (1-0-5).

> **10442: EVA** b 15 Aug 1784 (sp Joh. Bickert, Rach. Vetterle)
> **10443: MARIA** b SAR 24 Jan 1788 (sp Tho. Vetterle & w. Marg.)
> **10444: child** b GF 7 Mar 1790 (sp Jac. Brodhack & Doro.)
> **10445: HENRICH** b GF 29 Dec 1791 (sp Eva Vetterle, widow of Hen.)
> **10446: JOHANNES** b GF 14 Jan 1794 (sp Fritz Meyer & Marg.)

10447: JOHN VETTERLY - m by 1782 MARIA ... John & Maria were sponsors for GF Nov 1784 bp of Nicholas, son of Nicholas Stenzel & Margaret. Had son JOHANNES (b GF Jul 1782, sp. Wm Wohlgemuth, Maria Vetterle)

10435: PETER VETTERLY - born say 1775; m by 1803 ELISABETH FOX. Children bp at Herkimer Dutch Reform Church incl. Elisabeth (b 13 May 1803, sp. Christopher Fox & w. Marg.) and Maria Catherine (b 3 Apr 1805, sp. Geo. Rosencrantz & w. Anna).

10449: ROBERT VETTERLY - m Ft. Plain NY 27 Jan 1793 ANNA RATTENAUER pr. a dau of GODFRID RATTENAUER. Had son JOHANNES (b GF 16 Oct 1793, sp. Joh. Lepper & Marg.).

10432: THOMAS VETTERLY - pr. born ca 1755 to 1768; m GF 10 Jan 1786 MARGARET SCHIFF. They sponsored 1812 bp of Melchior, son of John M. Casler. On 1790 Herkimer census (1-2-2).

> **10451: HENRICH** b GF 26 Sep 1786 (sp Hen. Vetterly, Dolly Mebie)
> **10452: EVA** bp GF 21 Jul 1790 (sp Eva Vettrly, Fr. Getman)
> **10453: ADAM** b GF 20 Nov 1791 (sp Adam Hartman & Maria Margaret)
> **10454: PETER** b GF 17 Jul 1793 (sp Pet. Vetterly, Marg. Kessler)

10454A HENRICH VOGT - pr. born before 1750. Listed next to a Michael Vogt, in 1769 German Flats militia (Book of Names, page 14), amongst Hasenclever group of men. Ps. of the New Jersey family of Voughts and perhaps returned to New Jersey prior to the Revolution (no further record of Vogt surname in German Flats area).

10455: JOHANNES VROOMAN - pr. the Johannes born 5 Mar 1754 son of Johannes Symonse Vrooman & Volkje Wemple (Vrooman book); m GF 15 Oct 1781 ANNA SCHAEFFER.

10456: EDWARD WALKER - pr. born ca 1740 to 1760; m by 1790 GERTRUDE ...; ps. m2 by 1794 CATHERINE ... Lived at Lake Otsego in Jun 1790 (SJR bp rec.) and was on 1790 German Flats census (2-2-3). Parents of Gertrude, bp 1786, are given as "Nath. Waaker und Gertrude" (perhaps Nath. should be Edward?).
> surname WALKER
> **10457: ps. GERTRUDE** b GF 23 Feb 1786 (sp. Hen. Miller & Anna Eva)
> **10458: ANNA EVA** bp SJR 27 Jun 1790 (sp Adam Ecker, Marg. Ecker)
> **10459: ELISABETH** b GF 13 Oct 1792 (sp Geo. Friba & Anna <Ittig>)
> **10460: ALITA** b GF 20 Apr 1794 (dau of Edward & Catherine)
> (bp sp John Ittig, Anna Staring)

10456A EDWARD WALL - pr. born ca 1730 to 1750; m FNR 6 Jul 1772 DEBORA BUTLER (Mohawk Valley in the Revolution, page 343). Edward resigned from the Tryon Committee of Safety in 1775 and apparently later joined the Tory cause (various Loyalist wives, including Mrs. Wall, were ordered confined at Johnston NY in Aug 1777).

10461: HENRY JOH. WALLRATH - born 3 Apr 1760 (son of John & Amelia, bp sp. Hen Wallrath & Cath.); died after 17 Jul 1823; m 14 Jan 1783 MARIA BELL (b 1763) dau of GEORGE HENRY BELL & CATHERINE HERKIMER. Pr. the Henry Wallrath of Col. Bellinger's Regiment who was noted as having been a prisoner of war in the Revolution. Not on 1790 census for GF or Hekimer but was living at German Flats in 1792 (SJR bp rec.). Was sponsor, with Maria Catherine Dygert, for GF Apr 1782 bp of Peter, son of George Carl & Margret.

surname WALLRATH

    10462: DIETRICH   b GF 9 Apr 1786 (sp Diet Petrie & Elis.)
    10463: CATHERINE   b GF Feb 1788 (sp. Geo. Hen. Bell & Cath.)
    10464: ANNA   b GF 29 Aug 1789 (sp Peter Waggoner & Anna)
    10465: HENRICH   b GF 28 Aug 1791 (sp H Rosencrantz, Eva Campbell)
    10466: JACOB   b SJR 22 Jun 1792 (sp Pet. Bauman, Marg. Gerlach)
    10467: MARIA   b GF 23 Aug 1793 (sp John G. Wolrad, M. Rscrntz)
    10468: JOHANNES   b GF 18 Mar 1795 (sp John Sweeding, Abig. How)

10469: CONRAD WALS - pr. born ca 1715 to 1740; m by 1770 GERTRUDE ... Conart Wals was in Capt. Petrie's 1757 GF militia co. and pr. later settled east in Montgomery Co., there being a Conrad Waltz listed as a tenant of Sir William Johnson (pr. ca 1770 <Book of Names, page 178-9>). A Conrad, Conrad jr. and Jacob Walse were in Col. Campbell's Canajoharie area Revolutionary Regiment and the 1790 Canajoharie census lists two Conrad Walts, a Jacob Walts, & a Peter Walts.

surname WALS

    10470: pr. JACOB   b say 1761; m by 1788 MARGARET ... (SAL bp)
    10470: pr. CONRAD jr.   b say 1763; in Revol. service
    10471: PETER   b say 1765; m 16 Oct 1785 ANNA DAVIS
    10472: ps. WILLIAM   b say 1767; m by 1790 ELISABETH KELLER
    10473: JOHN   bp SAL 16 Jun 1770 (sp John Lederer & w.)
    10474: HENRICH   bp SAL 29 Aug 1772 (sp Joh. Kaiser, Marg. Dillenbach)
    10475: CATHERINE b SAL Sep 1774 (sp Joh. Warmuth & w.)
    10476: MARIA   b GF 9 Sep 1776 (sp Barth. Bikert & M. Cath.)

10477: CHARLES WARD - born Chester NY 24 Jan 1758 (son of Stephen Ward); died Fairfield (Herk. Co.) NY 18 Apr 1809; m Fredericksburg NY 1783 MARY PELL. Had 12 children (DAR Magazine, 1927, page 781).

10478: RICHARD WELCH - pr. born ca 1735 to 1760; m by 1784 MARGARET ... Ps. connected to the Richart Wheltz who married Eva Catherine and had child bp at GF 4 Jan 1776. Richard Welsh was on the 1790 Canajoharie NY census (1-2-2) listed next to John Frynler & Dolly Mebie.

surname WELCH

    10479: JOHN   b GF 20 Sep 1784 (sp John Gruninger, Delia Mabee)

10480: DANIEL WEISS - pr. born ca 1745 to 1760; m by 1782 ELISABETH ...
surname WEISS

    10481: ELISABETH   b GF 25 Jan 1782 (sp Geo. Saltsman, Mar. Straub)
  +10482: DANIEL   b GF 4 Mar 1783 (sp Chrstn Zimmerman & Eva)
    10483: JOHN   b GF 24 Sep 1786 (sp John Rima, Elis Hofstater)
    10484: PETER   bp SAL 8 Aug 1790 (sp Peter Ries, Maria Straub)
    10485: HENRICH   bp SAL 26 Jun 1792 (sp Henry Bekker & Margaret)
    10486: WILHELM   bp SAL 31 Jul 1793 (sp H. Straub, Maria England)

10486A JOHN WEISGERBER - pr. born before 1750. Appears in 1769 GF militia, listed amongst Hasenclever men (no further record).

10487: ANDREAS WERNER - born ca 1726; died Herkimer NY 30 Oct 1818 (age 92-6-); m SAL 24 Dec 1769 MARIA KIRN. Doro. And. Werner was liv. 1803 (HK Confirm.).

surname WERNER

+10488: HENRY bp SAL 30 Jun 1770; m CATHERINE EDICK
10489: ANNA EVA b SAL 24 Feb 1778 (sp Geo. Stamm & w.)
10490: DOROTHY ELISABETH b GF 12 May 1782 (G Wentz, Dor. El Kayser)
pr. the Doro. who d HK 1821 (age 36) & m WILLIAM ORENDORF

10488: HENRY WERNER - bp 30 Jun 1770 (son of Andrew); m 1 Jun 1789 CATHERINE CHR. ITTIG (b 1770) dau of CHRISTIAN ITTIG & MARGARET WEAVER. On 1790 GF census (1-0-2) next to Rudolph Steele.

10491: MARGARET b GF 25 Aug 1789 (John Mahon, Anna Ittig); pr d y
10492: pr. ANDREW b SAL Jan 1791 (sp And. Werner & Maria)
liv. 1808 (wit. mar. Anna Werner)
10493: ANNA b say 1792; m HK 1808 JACOB C. ITTIG
10494: MARGARET b GF 22 Oct 1794 (sp Con. J. Frank, Marg Ittig)
10495: DOROTHY b 4 Nov 1803 (HK sp Dor. Werner, Nich. Youl, unm)
10496: FRANCISUS b 24 Mar 1806 (sp Franc. Crautsh & w. Barbara)
10497: CATHERINE b 22 Jun 1808 (sp Con. Ittig & w Cath.)
10498: JAMES b GF 31 Jul 1812 (sp James Gemmel & w Anna)

10499: PETER WESTERMAN - born in Germany 1741; died Ft. Plain NY 15 Nov 1791 (Church rec.); m 15 May 1767 MARIA ELISABETH DUNCKLE. On 1790 Canajoharie NY census (2-1-3).

surname WESTERMAN

10500: CATHARINE b say 1772; m Ft Plain 1791 PHILIP GEORGE GORDNER
10501: PETER jr. b say 1774; m 1794 ANASTACIA EHLE
10502: HEINRICH b 28 Jun 1779; d Ft. Plain NY 1 Jul 1788
10503: ANNA MARIA b GF 8 Nov 1783 (sp And. Haens & Anna Maria)

10504: SIMON WILLIAMS - pr. born ca 1760 to 1785; m by 1804 ERNESTINA STAHRING (b 1787) dau of ADAM STARHING. Children incl. Adam (b HK 21 Dec 1804, sp. John Bellinger & w. Eva) and George (born & died Herkimer NY 1807).

10505: JOHANNES WIRTH - m by 1764 DOROTHEA ...

surname WIRTH

10506: NICHOLAS b GF 20 Jun 1764 (sp Nic. Brodhauer & w. Marg.)

10507: JAMES WOODERT - pr. born ca 1740 to 1765; m by 1790 CATHERINE HAUS. A James Woodward was on 1790 German Flats census (1-0-*), listed next to Conrad House. Was living at Schuyler Lake in 1790 (SJR bp rec.).

surname WOODERT

10508: ANGELIQUE bp SJR 26 Dec 1790 (sp Conrad Haus & Angelique)
10509: MARIA bp SJR 10 Feb 1793 (sp Geo Haus & Maria Lisa)

10510: JOSHUA WOODERT - pr. born ca 1745 to 1767; m GF (church marriage rec. has his name as JOSHUA HOCKSTATER) 1788 MARGARET RANKIN pr. dau of JAMES RANKIN & ELISABETH.

surname WOODERT

10511: MARIA b GF 1 May 1789 (sp James Rankin & Delia)
10512: ELISABETH b GF 26 Mar 1791 (sp Tho. Rankin, Eva Jac. Kessler)
10513: JOSHUA b GF 26 Aug 1792 (sp Nic. Wohlebn, Elis. Small)
10514: AMOS b GF 2 Feb 1794 (sp Bernhard Young & Elis.)

10515: GEORGE MICH. WOLF - m by 1772 ELISABETH ... Had daughter Magdalena (bp SAL 31 Mar 1772, sp. Peter Jung & wife). Ps. this was same man as the Michael Young who married Elisabeth Neer Raussin.

10516: JACOB WOLFF - m by 1782 MARGARET ...
surname WOLFF
    10517: CATHERINE b GF 12 Jun 1782 (sp John Gunterman, Barb. Nellis)
    10518: MARIA b GF 27 Sep 1784 (sp Caspar Miller & Maria Magdal.)

10519: JOHN WOLFF - pr. born in Germany ca 1710 to 1725; m ... Came from Seerbury Germany in 1764 and was father-in-law of Dr. William Petry (Petrie book page 121). Immigration date and place in 1769 GF militia suggest that he was one of Hasenclever's group at New Petersburg. Daughter Margaret was born at Wesselheim Germany (ibid). Resident of GF in 1775.
surname WOLFF
  +10520: pr. MICHEL b say 1745; m 1768 ELISABETH NEER RAUSSIN
  10521: MARGARET SALOMA 1749-1820 m 1766 Dr. WILLIAM PETRY

10520: MICHEL WOLFF - pr. born ca 1742 to 1750 (pr. son of John); m SAR 19 Jan 1767 ELISABETH NEER RAUSSIN. Michel and John Wolff were listed in the German Flats militia in 1769.

    10522: MARY b 1768; m 1786 JOHN P. HELMER
    10523: MARGARET SALOME b SAR 19 Oct 1767 (sp Marg Sal. & Wm Petry)
                m 1788 PHILIP KELSCH
    10524: VALENTINE b 2 Aug 1770 (SAR sp Val. Miller & w. Maria)
    10525: CATHERINE b SAL 22 Aug 1774 (sp Diet. Suts & w.)
    10526: child bp GF 13 Jul 1777
    10527: ps. ELISABETH b say 1780; m by 1803 HENRY ORENDORF

10527A ADAM YOUNG (Jung) - pr. born ca 1725 to 1745; m by 1776 ... Listed as a Lieut. in Jost Herkimer's 1767 Granadier co. from Burnetsfield (Book of Names, apge 12). Had a child bp GF 17 Jun 1776 (sponsors not named). Ps. this was the Adam Young jr., who with wife Margaret, sponsored Jul 1762 SAR bp of Adam, son of Caspar Bauer & Elisabeth Catherine.

10528: GEORGE YOUNG (Jung) - m GF 8 Jan 1786 CATHERINE M. PETRIE pr. dau of MARCUS PETRIE & ELISABETH.
surname YOUNG
    10529: JOHN b GF 17 Jan 1787 (sp Hen. Petrie, Elis. Casp. Koch)

10530: BARENT YOUNG (Jung) - pr. born ca 1750 to 1767 (pr. the Barent b SAR Aug 1766, son of John & Margaret); m Albany NY 14 Jun 1785 ELISABETH RANKIN (bp 1765) dau of JAMES RANKIN & ELISABETH. Wife's full name appears on 1803 Herkimer bp record. A Bernhard Young & Elisabeth were sponsors for Jul 1794 bp of Amos, son of Joshua Woodert & Margaret (Rankin).
surname YOUNG
    10531: JOHN bp Albany NY 15 May 1786 (sp John Young & Delia)
                m 1804 MARGARET JOH. RYAN
    10532: MICHAEL b GF 1 Oct 1787 (sp Mich. Young, Cath. Rankin)
                m 1806 MARGARET JOH. RASPACH
    10533: ELISABETH BAR. b say 1790; m 1809 PETER P. FOLTS
    10534: MARGARET bp SAL 3 Aug 1792 (sp John Koch, Bezi Seber)
    10535: MARIA b GF 6 Nov 1794 (sp James Rankin & Delia); liv. 1810
                pr. the "Polly" who m 1812 JOHN S. EYSAMAN
    10536: JULIUS b HK 28 Apr 1803 (sp Jos Klock, Cath. Eysaman)

10537: JAMES YUEL - born in Ireland pr. ca 1745 to 1760; m 12 Sep 1779 MARGARET CHRISTMAN (b 28 Dec 1758/59, d Danube NY 25 Feb 1837) dau of NICHOLAS CHRISTMAN (E&N 8 Mar 1939). James Youhe was on 1790 GF census (1-4-2), near Jacob Bashor & John <C.> Frank.

surname YUEL

10538: JAMES b 12 Sep 1780 (sp Jacob Bashor & Cath.)
10539: MARGARET b 4 Sep 1782 (sp Jacob Christman, Marg. Getman)
10540: NICHOLAS b 4 Nov 1784 (sp Fr. Fox & Elis.)
10541: JOHN b 9 Aug 1787 (sp John Smidt & Mar. Elis.)
10542: GEORGE b GF 28 Jun 1788 (sp Geo. Nellis & M. Elis.)
          m 1813 CATHERINE HOYER (dau of Geo. Fred.)
10543: CATHERINE b 2 Oct 1791 (sp Jacob Bashor & Cath.)
10544: JACOB b GF 3 Oct 1793 (sp Jac. Christman & Maria)
10544A MARY b 1796; m JOHN JORDAN (DAR v 58, pg 136)
10545: ELISABETH b 31 Aug 1800 (bp HK 1804, sp Elis. Gemmel)

10546: GEORGE YUKER - m by 1785 ELISABETH SCHALL (SHOLL). On 1790 Palatine NY census (1-4-5).

surname YUKER

10547: MARGARET b GF 2 Nov 1785 (sp Solomon Yucker, Marg. Schell)
10547A JOHANNES bp SJR 8 Feb 1789 (sp Nic. Shaffer & Anna)
10548: ELISABETH b SJR 7 Aug 1791 (sp Peter Schaffer, Cath. Joran)

10549: JACOB YUKER (Jucker) - m GF 16 Sep 1781 MAGDALENA DUSSLER pr. dau of JACOB DUSSLER & ANNA. Appears on 1790 Palatine NY census (1-2-3) and was living there in 1791 (SJR bp rec.).

10549A ELISABETH b GF Oct 1781 (sp Wm Dussler, Elis, Jucker)
10550: JOHN b GF 6 Feb 1785 (sp John Snell & Elis.)
10550A MARIA bp SJR Apr 1789 (sp And. Scheffer, Maria Walrath)
10551: ANNA bp SJR 3 May 1791 (sp Jac. Dussler & Anna)

10552: JOHANNES YUKER (Jucker) - pr. born ca 1745 to 1765; m 1784 CATHERINE RINCKEL (Ringel) pr. dau of LORENTZ RINCKEL. Child's mother named as Anna on 1790 bp record. John was on 1790 Palatine NY census (1-3-2) and lived at Palatine NY in 1793 (SJR bp rec.).

10553: ANNA b GF 27 Mar 1785 (sp Solomon Yuker, Marg. Schall)
10554: JOHANNES bp SJR 17 May 1789 (sp. Joh Shafer, Elts. Schall)
10555: GEORGE bp SJR 20 Jul 1790 (sp Geo. Yuker & Elis.)
10556: CATHERINE bp SJR 29 Jan 1793 (sp Fr. Bellinger & Cath.)

***** APPENDIX *****

Smidt's Log of 1710 Palatine Immigration

A diary-style log, written in German on both sides of a single sheet of very old and yellowed paper, was found by this author (Barker) in 1982 amongst the Nicholas Smith estate papers, most of which bore dates of 1779 and 1780. The papers had for years been held by Mrs. Edna Aney of Herkimer New York, who had inherited them from Smidt relatives. The log itself was undated, untitled, and unsigned, its text being unknown until a translation in 1982 by Mrs. Lesley Nowakowski of Shelton Connecticut showed it to be a firsthand account of the Palatine exodus from Germany to America, beginnng with their arrival in England in 1709. Judging from the fine quality of penmenship, the log may have been a copy. Nonetheless, we feel the original was probably written sometime after 1712 (since it alludes to the Schoharie settlements) and was most likely the work of Johan George Smidt, a known 1710 Palatine immigrant and the grandfather of the Nicholas Smidt of 1779. The translation (comments in parenthesis are the present author's) follows:

"And so we came up out of our Deutschland to the town of London where the people knew us by our old clothing. We lay then a long time. They promised us much goods but instead many of us would die once they threw us into the ships. In these we had to suffer much hunger and pain. We proceeded on to No pords (Newport?) where the men treated us badly and our spirits were pulled down in misery and dispair. Praise that God has mercy for afterwards when we got to sea how the lice and fleas did bite us. And thus we traveled by day and night. Some starved. The largest and smallest of us rotted and some lost wife and child. When they would take us up to the church place (on deck) it was to toss us by arm and leg into the sea. There we would swim on the water and the fish would come to gobble us up. So have we come upon this expedition and are never more to see our Deustchland. We arrived at New York in ... (August?), stopping outside the city. All were greatly undernourished and a number were put in a hospital. ... The others had to go up river on the sail boats. There they pitched the tents and issued us 600 rifles. Now this is the way we learned our exercises - first one makes left and then one makes right - the officer does this too! Many became so sick that the officer did not dare to go their door. Nobody knew what was going on ... this was hardly an army standing in the field. We were assembled before the (officer's) horse and had to stand up straight. During a night watch we went down to New York and stole some bread. They found out who it was and put us on the Lion Rock. There we lay in prison and had to suffer hunger and thirst. From the prison they let us go to take part in the Canada expedition. We had to trek through water and mud, dragging ... (carts?) over branches and rocks. Some injured arms and legs. An officer from New Georgeland whose name was quite well known to us was supposed to travel with us to Canada, but it was far too long for him. So we arrived at our destination but then had to turn around and go back to Albany. Here they took the rifles from us and swiftly discharged us, advising us to fend for ourselves. And so we are reunited with our wives and hope that we can stay with them. Important men came to us from Albany with promise of daily wages, but no money was to be seen. Moving camps to New George seemed in order but would take a long time. Eventually we set up camp below the town of Albany. There we had to keep watch all day. We were not allowed to move from there and did not know how to keep body and soul together. We put up our huts. We had only water to drink and no beer. Finally we were brought before Commissioner Frans. ..."

The Burnetsfield Patent

On the ninth of July 1722, New York's Governor William Burnet authorized the Palatines of the Schoharie Valley to purchase from the Indians about ten thousand acres along the Mohawk River, in the vicinity of the present town of Herkimer N.Y., for the purpose of providing a settlement for many of the German immigrants of 1710 then living on disputed lands in the Schoharie Valley (see Albany NY council minutes beginning with Sep 1721). By 28 March 1723, surveyors Philip Verplanck and Nicholas Schuyler had charted this area and prepared a "Map of Burnet's Field" showing the boundaries of 92 lots, of 100 acres each, and the name of each lot purchaser (these patentees are listed in Vosburgh's Church Records of German Flats and Herkimer, vol. 3, pages 1-8). An early rendering of this map is preserved under glass and on display at the Herkimer Historical Society, but it is both faded and torn, and quite difficult to read. The rectangular shaped outlines of some of the lot boundaries have been lightly sketched on the map of Herkimer County at the front of this book to provide an approximate fix as to their location; however, we prefer to use the tabular format of the following pages for our analysis.

Vosburgh (op. cit.) has the best written listing of the 92 persons from 37 families who were the 1723 Burnetsfield patentees, and researchers are advised to watch for minor differences present in copies of the Burnetsfield map, such as in the Petrie book (page 113) and Mr. Boyd Ehle's version in the Book of Names (page 190). We have generally followed Vosburgh's order in our listing on page 328, although we have added sub-titles, such as "Little Falls area" for various lot groups. We have also placed the letter N or S after the lot# (to designate whether the lot was North or South of the Mohawk River) and an optional second letter (such as W or E to indicate if the lot was near the West or East end of the tract). It seems that qualified Palatines, such as heads of households, were able to receive a single lot of 100 acres in size, in their own name, and a second lot, also of 100 acres, in the name of a dependent (normally a wife or eldest son). To support this assumption we have used the material of this book to project the patentee's status under the column marked "S" in the table on page 328 (husbands are coded "h", wives "w" and children "c").

To explain the lot numbering system, we assume a process in which the heads of households drew the first 46 lot numbers (possibly randomly) beginning with the town area lots (1N-24N), then eastward across the W. Canada Creek to lots 25NE thru 28NE, then south across the Mohawk River to lots 29S thru 45S, and finally back across the Mohawk to Johannes Poonradt's lot #46. Then a block of 29 dependent area lots were allocated south of the Mohawk (lots 1SW-23SW, 24S, 25SE-27SE, then reverse direction to 28SE and 29SW) and finally 17 dependent lots north of the Mohawk were assigned (i.e. lots 1NW-6NW, 7NE-9NE, 10NE-13NE, then reverse direction to 14NE, 15NE-16NE and ending with Gertrude Petrie's town lot 17NC). Assuming that the widows Coens and Lant had head of household status, the only apparent exceptions in which dependents appear in head of household lot strips, or vice versa, involve lots 40S and 41S, assigned to Conrad Orendorf and Joseph Staring (both believed to have been children at the time) and the assignment of Frederick Bell (a known head of household then) to lot 16NE. These exceptions do not seem significant enough to discard the assumed basis for lot allocation, and they may in fact have been simply the result of a limited amount of swapping permitted after the allocations were first made. For those individuals whose condition at the time is uncertain (status marked as "?"), we feel the lot numbering system provides a reasonable predictor of their status.

Ln#	Name (Last, First)	S	Lot#	Acres
	Little Falls area			
BU001	STARING, MARY EVA/Adm´s	w	13NE	100
BU002	TEMOUTH, JOHN JOST	?	12NE	100
BU003	BEERMAN, MARY	w	11NE	100
BU004	HESS, AUGUSTINUS	c	10NE	100
	East, near L. Falls			
BU005	BOWMAN, JACOB	?	27SE	100
BU006	FOX, XTOPHER<Christpher	?	26SE	100
BU007	KESLAER, JOHANNES	h	45SE	100
BU008	KESLAER, NICOLAS	?	25SE	100
BU009	DACKSTEDER, ANNA/Jurg´s	w	28SE	100
BU010	POUNRADT, JOHANNES	h	46NE	100
BU011	POONRADT, GERTRUY/Joh´s	w	9NE	100
BU012	HEGER, HENRY	c	8NE	100
BU013	HELMER, ELISABETH/Len´s	w	14NE	100
	E. of W. Canada Creek			
BU014	SPOON, HENDRICK JUNR.	c	7NE	100
BU015	STARING, JOHAN ADAM	h	28NE	100
BU016	PARES, LODWICK	h	27NE	100
BU017	BEERMAN, JOHANNIS	h	26NE	100
BU018	HELLMER, PHILIP	h	25NE	100
BU019	PELL, FREDERICK	h	15NE	100
BU020	PELL, ANNA MARY	w	16NE	100
	Town area (now Herkimer)			
BU021	KOENS, MARY CATHARIN/wid.		1N	100
BU022	FFOLS, MELGERT	h	2N	100
BU023	VELDELANT, JOHAN	?	3N	100
BU024	SMITH, ADAM MICHELL	h	4N	100
BU025	KAST, JOHAN JURGH SR.	h	5N	100
BU026	HELMER, JOHAN ADAM	h	6N	100
BU027	FELLER, NICOLAS	h	7N	100
BU028	WEVER, JACOB	h	10N	100
BU029	SMITH, JOHAN JURGH	h	9N	100
BU030	PETRIE, JOHAN JOST	h	8N	100
BU031	MEYER, HENDRICK	h	11N	100
BU032	SHOEMAKER, THO.S	h	12N	100
BU033	LANT, ANNA CATHARENA/wid.		13N	100
BU034	BOWMAN, JOHAN ADAM	h	14N	100
BU035	REELE, GODFREE	h	15N	100
BU036	WEVER, NICOLAS	h	16N	100
BU037	TEMOUTH, TEDRIGH	h	17N	100
BU038	DACKSTEDER, JURGH	h	18N	100
BU039	RICKERT, LODWICK	h	19N	100
BU040	PELLINGER, JOHANNES	h	20N	100
BU041	HELMER, LENDERT	h	21N	100
BU042	KAST, JOHAN JURGH	h	22N	100
BU043	PELLINGER, PETER	h	23N	100
BU044	STARING, FREDERICK	h	24N	100
BU045	PETRIE, GERTRUY/J Jos´s	w	17NC	86
	NW riverbank area			
BU046	STARING, JOHANES VELDEN	?	6NW	100
BU047	EDIGH, ELIZABETH	w	5NW	100
BU048	PELLINGER, MARG.<Petr´s	w	4NW	100
BU049	RICKERT, CATHERINE	w	3NW	100
BU050	VELDELANT, ANNA	?	2NW	100
BU051	HELMER, FREDRICH	c	1NW	100
	S. Central area			
BU052	ERGHEMAR, JURG	h	44S	100
BU053	MILLER, JOHANNES	h	43S	100
BU054	STARING, NICOLAS	h	42S	100
BU055	STARING, JOSEPH	c	41S	100
BU056	ORENDORF, CONRADT	c	40S	100
BU057	ORENDORF, HENDRICK	h	39S	100
BU058	SPEIS, PETER	h	38S	100
BU059	HERTER, LOWRENS	h	37S	100
BU060	ERGHEMAR, JOHAN JOST	h	36S	100
BU061	PELLINGER, FFREDRICK	h	35S	100
BU062	RYCKERT, CONRADT	h	34S	100
BU063	EDIGH, JOHAN MICHALL	h	33S	100
BU064	SPOON, HENDRICK	h	32S	100
BU065	HESS, JOHANNES	h	31S	100
BU066	WELLEVEN, NICOLAS	h	30S	100
BU067	KORSING, LUDOLPH	h	29S	100
BU068	ERGHEMAR, MADALENA	w	24S	100
	SW (dependents´ area)			
BU069	MAYER, ANNA	w	29SW	100
BU070	PEARS, CATHERINE	w	23SW	100
BU071	PELLINGER, MARG.<John´s	w	22SW	100
BU072	EDICH, JACOB	?	21SW	100
BU073	EDITCH, MICHAELL	?	20SW	100
BU074	FFELMORE, HANS CONRAD	c	19SW	100
BU075	FFELMORE, CHRISTINA	?	18SW	100
BU076	SHOEMAKER, LUDOLPH	c	17SW	100
BU077	FELLER, MARY/ Nicholas´	w	16SW	100
BU078	WEVER, JACOB JUNR.	c	15SW	100
BU079	PETRIE, MARK	c	14SW	100
BU080	KORSING, ODELIA/Ludl.´s	w	13SW	100
BU081	HELMER, A MARGARET/Ad´s	w	12SW	100
BU082	WEVER, ANDRIES	?	11SW	100
BU083	REELE, GODFREY JUNR.	c	10SW	100
BU084	SMITH, EPHRAIM	c	9SW	100
BU085	SPEIS, ELIZABETH/Petr´s	w	8SW	100
BU086	HERTER, APPOLONIA	w	7SW	100
BU087	RYCKERT, MARK	?	6SW	100
BU088	ERGHEMAR, CATHERINE	w	5SW	100
BU089	SMITH, MARTE	c	4SW	100
BU090	FFOLS, JACOB	c	3SW	100
BU091	KONES, LUDWIG	c	2SW	100
BU092	STARING, JOHN VELDE JR.	?	1SW	100

ALPHABETIZED 1723 BURNETSFIELD LIST (Names Standarized)
(People in household estimated under column P)

Name (Last, First)	Lot#	P	Ln#	Name (Last, First)	Lot#	P	Ln#
(Pears)				KESSLER, Johannes	45SE	7	BU007
BARSH, Catherine	23SW	1	BU070	KESSLER, Nicholas	25SE	4	BU008
BARSH, Ludwig	27NE	5	BU016	KORSING, Delia<Rud.´s w	13SW	1	BU080
BAUMAN, (Johan) ADam	14N	7	BU034	KORSING, Rudolph	29S	1	BU067
BAUMAN, Jacob	27SE	1	BU005	(Veldelant)			
BELL, Anna Mary	16NE	1	BU020	LANT, (Johan) Veldelant	3N	1	BU023
BELL, Frederick	15NE	7	BU019	LANT, Anna Catherine/wid.	13N	1	BU033
BELLINGER, Frederick	35S	6	BU061	LANT, Anna Veldelant	2NW	1	BU050
BELLINGER, Johannes	20N	1	BU040	MEYER, Anna	29SW	1	BU069
BELLINGER, Marg.<John´s w	22SW	1	BU071	MEYER, Hendrick	11N	4	BU031
BELLINGER, Marg.<Petr´s w	4NW	1	BU048	MILLER, Johannes	43S	6	BU053
BELLINGER, Peter	23N	1	BU043	ORENDORF, Conrad	40S	1	BU056
BIERMAN, Johannis	26NE	3	BU017	ORENDORF, Hendrick	39S	5	BU057
BIERMAN, Mary	11NE	1	BU003	PETRIE, (Johan) Jost	8N	7	BU030
COENS, Ludwig	2SW	1	BU091	PETRIE, Gertrude	17NC	1	BU045
COENS, Mary Catherine/wid	1N	3	BU021	PETRIE, Mark	14SW	1	BU079
DEMUTH, Dietrich	17N	1	BU037	POENRADT, Gertruy<Joh´s w	9NE	1	BU011
DEMUTH, John Jost	12NE	3	BU002	POENRADT, Johannes	46NE	1	BU010
DOCKSTADER, Anna<Geo.´s w	28SE	1	BU009	RICKERT, Catherine	3NW		BU049
DOCKSTADER, George	18N	7	BU038	RICKERT, Conrad	34S		BU062
EDICK, Elisabeth	5NW	1	BU047	RICKERT, Ludwig	19N		BU039
EDICK, Jacob	21SW	1	BU072	RICKERT, Mark	8SW		BU087
EDICK, (Johan) Michael	33S	3	BU063	(Reele)			
EDICK, Michael	20SW	1	BU073	RIEGEL, Godfrid	15N	3	BU035
FELLER, Mary<Nich.´s w	16SW	1	BU077	RIEGEL, Godfrid Jr.	10SW	1	BU083
FELLER, Nicholas	7N	5	BU027	SHOEMAKER, Rudolph	17SW	1	BU076
FOLTS, Jacob	3SW	1	BU090	SHOEMAKER, Thomas	12N	3	BU032
FOLTS, Melchert	2N	6	BU022	SMITH, (Johan) George	9N	5	BU029
FOX, Christopher	26SE	1	BU006	SMITH, Adam Michael	4N		BU024
(Felmore)				SMITH, Ephraim	9SW		BU084
FULMER, Christ<ina>ian	18SW	1	BU075	SMITH, Marten	4SW	1	BU089
FULMER, Hans Conrad	19SW	1	BU074	SPEIS, Elizabeth<Petr´s w	8SW	1	BU085
HAGER, Henry	8NE	1	BU012	SPEIS, Peter	38S	1	BU058
HARTER, Appolonia	7SW	1	BU086	SPOHN, Hendrick	32S	5	BU064
HARTER, Lorentz	37S	1	BU059	SPOHN, Hendrick Jr.	7NE	1	BU014
HELMER, (Johan) Adam	6N	1	BU026	STARING, (Johan) Adam	28NE	4	BU015
HELMER, Elisabeth<Len´s w	14NE	1	BU013	STARING, Frederick	24N	3	BU044
HELMER, Frederick	1NW	1	BU051	STARING, Johannes Velden	6NW	1	BU046
HELMER, Lendert	21N	4	BU041	STARING, John Velde Jr.	1SW	1	BU092
HELMER, Marg.<Adam´s w	12SW	1	BU081	STARING, Joseph	41S	1	BU055
HELMER, Philip	25NE	2	BU018	STARING, Mary Eva<Adm´s w	13NE	1	BU001
(Erghemar)				STARING, Nicholas	42S	4	BU054
HERKIMER, Catherine	5SW	1	BU088	WEAVER, Andries	11SW	1	BU082
HERKIMER, George	44S	1	BU052	WEAVER, Jacob Jr.	15SW	1	BU078
HERKIMER, (Johan) Jost	36S	2	BU060	WEAVER, Nicholas	16N	4	BU036
HERKIMER, Magdalena	24S	1	BU068	WEAVER, Jacob	10N	4	BU028
HESS, Augustinus	10NE	1	BU004	(Welleven)			
HESS, Johannes	31S	7	BU065	WOHLEBEN, Nicholas	30S	1	BU066
KAST, (Johan) George	22N	3	BU042				
KAST, (Johan) George Sr.	5N	8	BU025	Population estimate in 1723: 203			

-329-

Burnetsfield Town Lot Property Descent, 1723 to 1791

The table includes information assembled about 1981 by Mrs. Jane Bellinger of the Herkimer County Historical Society (Herkimer N.Y.) and shows the pattern of ownership change, over about a two generation interval, for selected Burnetsfield Patent town lots. The time span is a bit too long for the data to be directly used for inheritance analysis, nonetheless patterns of property retention within a family are evident and provide clues to descendency of individuals.

An interesting mixing of apparently unrelated Smiths occurs in case of Burnetsfield lot #4, which was sold by patentee Adam Michael Smith in 1744 to Nicholas Weber (whose wife was believed to have been a daughter of immigrant George Smith) and was thereafter transferred at some point to the 1791 Smith owners (patentee George Smith's line and believed unrelated to Adam Michael Smith).

Town Lot	1723 Patentee	1791 Owner
1	Maria Cath. Coens	
2	Melchert Folts	George Folts & others
3	John Veldelant	Jacob G. Weber, Nic. Aldridge
4	Adam Mich. Smith	Fred & John Smith
5	George Kast	Frederick Kast
6	Adam Helmer	Fred. & Henry Helmer
7	Nich. Feller	Nich. Hilts
8	Jost Petrie	Hezek. Talcott
9	George Smith	Hezek. Talcott
10	Jacob Weber	Peter & Jacob G Weber
11	Henry Meyer	Dr. Wm Petry
12	Tho. Shoemaker	Henry & Lor. Harter
13	Anna Cath. Lant	Nicholas Harter
14	Adam Bauman	John Bowman (Bauman)
15	Godfrid Reale	Fred. Meyer & others
16	Nich. Wever	Jacob N. Weber, Mich. Meyer
17	Dedrick DeMuth	John DeMuth, John Bellinger jr.
18	Geo. Dockstader	Jacob N. Weber, Jacob G Weber
19	Ludwig Rickert	Jacob Weber Jr, Fred. Weber
20	John Bellinger	
21	Lendert Helmer	Geo. Dockstader, Jacob N Weber
22	George Kast	Widow Elisabeth Helmer
23	Peter Bellinger	Peter Bellinger, Peter F. Bellinger

Population Projection for German Flats in November 1757

Following the attack on German Flats by the French & Indians at 3 AM on November 12th 1757, the French commander, Lt. M. de Bellestre, reported that 40 of the inhabitants were killed and 150 taken prisoner. We have assumed that his count of the prisoners included only those actually taken away to places of captivity (in Canada or in northern New York Indian camps) and that there were another 30 to 60 of the seriously wounded, aged, and very young who were probably also captured but then released upon departure of the attack force. We further speculate that some 40 to 100 town residents escaped capture entirely, under the presumed conditions of darkness and general confusion. Adding Le Bellestre's figures to our range estimates for released and escaped gives a population projection of 260 to 350 living in the town area on the north side of the Mohawk River. This projection range seems consistent with the composite population estimate of 331 below, a figure based upon the known family members believed living then (as taken from the individual sections of this book).

Family	Men	Boys	Women	Fam. Size	Estimated Killed	Pris.
Bauman	2	4	3	9	1	5
Bell	6	5	4	15	3	8
Bellinger	6	8	16	30	4	17
Christman	4	5	8	17	2	5
Coens	1	1	2	4	4	0
Demuth	5	5	5	15	3	6
Dockstader	3	3	4	10	2	8
Folts	4	8	8	20	1	10
Frank,H.	3	3	5	11	2	9
Harter	4	5	10	19	2	13
Helmer	8	3	7	18	0	14
Hilts	7	7	11	25	3	13
Kast	3	0	2	5	1	3
McGinnes	1	1	3	5	1	4
Meyer,H.	2	4	5	11	1	0
Moak	1	0	0	1	0	0
Petrie	8	8	14	30	1	16
Riegel	4	1	2	7	2	2
Rosencrantz	1	0	0	1	0	0
Schutt	3	0	0	3	1	0
Seghner	2	0	1	3	0	0
Smith	5	5	3	13	1	5
Weaver	12	13	23	48	3	10
Witherstine	1	0	1	2	0	0
Other	6	0	3	9	2	2
North side	102	89	140	331	40	150

The above figures represent only those families believed to have been living in the town area, which was north of the Mohawk River and west of the West Canada Creek. As to those estimated as killed or taken prisoners, for the most part we are simply guessing with regard to the breakdown by family. Nonetheless we have support from the individual family records for there having been prisoners amongst the Bellinger, Dockstader, Henry Frank, Harter, Helmer, Hilts, Petrie, and Weaver families.

Completing our population projection for German Flats on November 12th 1757, we include below an estimate of the size of families living to the south of the Mohawk River and to the east of the West Canada Creek (a few families are believed to have had members living on both sides of the Mohawk River and therefore appear again in the following table). From the accounts of the French and Indian raid, the attackers apparently did not cross either the Mohawk River or the West Canada Creek, and so we presume that the families below had no fatalities or captives at that particular time.

Family	Men	Boys	Women	Fam. Size
Barsh	2	2	5	9
Bashor	1	2	2	5
Bell	3	3	5	11
Clapsaddle	2	3	3	8
Crim	1	1	2	4
Edick	7	1	5	13
Eysaman	2	1	2	5
Folts,P.	1	2	7	10
Fox	2	2	3	7
Frank,C.	5	5	8	18
Fulmer	4	0	3	7
Getman	1	1	3	5
Harter	1	2	3	6
Herkimer	4	4	6	14
Hess	2	6	4	12
Hoyer	1	1	2	4
Kessler	8	12	9	29
Leiper	1	1	2	4
Miller	3	7	6	16
Orendorf	2	4	3	9
Pfeiffer	1	1	3	5
Rasbach	4	1	6	11
Schell	2	0	1	3
Shoemaker	5	3	11	19
Spohn	4	0	2	6
Staring	8	5	9	22
Steele	4	5	4	13
Weaver	2	3	2	7
Wohleben	3	2	8	13
Smith,T.	1	0	0	1
Other	5	0	3	9
South side	92	80	130	300
Total GF	194	169	270	631

The reader should be reminded here that there was no actual census or count of family members taken at the time of the French raid in 1757. The population projection on this and the preceding page represent merely a recap of the findings obtained by research into the separate families, as reported earlier in this book.

NICHOLAS SMITH ESTATE PAPERS 1779-80

LIST 1 - "Public Vantue helt at Fort Dayton the 18th of May 1779
The Effects of Nicholas Smith late deceased" (list has purchaser, item,
and price <in pounds & shillings, about 2.5 NY dollars to a pound> and a
postscript says John Meyer was paid four dollars as auctioneer).

John Smith	1 mare paid by D. Macdougall	105- 0
George J. Weaver	a mare	52- 0
Duncan MacDougal	a calf	41- 0
Duncan MacDougall	2 cows	59- 0
Adam Smith	1 harrow	13- 0
John Smith	a wagon	30- 0
John Smith	a sleigh	12- 0
Peter Dockstader	a wood sleigh	2-16
John Smith	1 cow bell	1- 0
Peter Dockstader	1 dog	1- 4
George Dockstader	collar & plow	4- 0
Frederick Moyer		3- 4
Frederick Smith	1 line with bits	2-12
Adam Smith	1 neck yoke	2-16
Nicholas Weaver	2 collars	6- 0
William Cline	1 large Iron	13- 0
Daniel Shaw	1 Bits small	4- 0
Michael Mayer	Do. (Bits)	5- 0
Frederic Weaver	Do. (Bits)	5- 0
John Smith	1 frying pan	2-12
Frederick Moyer	1 Jingtel	1-12
William Cline	2 brooms	0-11
Daniel Shaw	1 tup	1- 0
Jost Smith	1 hand saw	1- 4
Phillip Helmer	1 tub	1- 0
Frederick Weaver	1 milk tub	0-14
Daniel Shaw	1 fyer stuffel (fire shovel)	2- 0
George Smith	1 fire tongs	2-13
Adam Smith	1 lamp	0-12
Frederick Hoyer	1 bag bolts	2- 0
George Hilts	1 bag bolts	1- 0
Nicholas H. Weaver		1- 5
Jacob Bell	1 hoe	3- 0
Jacob Bell	Shuffel	0- 4
William Shutt	1 iron bolt	0- 9
Frederick Meyer	1 bearle	1- 4
Philip Helmer	1 milk tub	1- 0
Frederic Weaver	knife & forks	0-16
Adam Smith	sundries	0-12
Daniel Shaw	1 stove cream pot	2-10
Daniel Shaw	1 stove cream pot	2- 8
George Weaver	1 cream pot	1-16
J. John Frank	1 pail	0-14
Jacob Weaver	1 grater	0-13
Jacob N. Weaver	2 chairs	2-11
Daniel Shaw	1 chair	1- 6
Frederick Weaver	1 bag with vinegar	2-11
John Frank	1 bag with molasses	3-12
John Meyer	1 broad axe	4- 0
Jacob G. Weaver	1 axe	2- 0
William Cline	1 axe	0-16

LIST 2 - This list, undated, was written primarily in German (with "Schmit" and "Weber" spellings) and the handwriting is more ornate than the other lists, which may suggest the writer was Sgt. George Smith, the expert pensman who illustrated many family bibles at that time. The sale probably occurred not too long after the death of Nicholas Smith in May 1779 since foodstuffs such as fat ("Speck") and sugar ("Zueker") as well as livestock (sheep and hogs) are involved.

		L- S- D
Nicholas Weaver	ein ammen mit feelt	1-10- 6
Nicholas H. Weaver	ein Sens	2- 4-12
Frederick Meyer	ein leinge	0- 5- 4
John Meyer	ein Sip vor	1-14- 0
Frederick Meyer	flacks und werck und korl	1-13- 6
Nicholas Weaver	ein Segel ge Sehms	6- 7- 2
Hendrich Harter	ein fesgen mit Sals	5-12- 0
Frederick Harter	ein rack vor	4-16- 0
Ludwig Barsh	ein fet kiewel vor	4- 9- 0
George Hilts	4 bund Speck und half y das pund	
Lorens Harter	pund Speck	2- 2- 0
Frederick Meyer (?)	ein flas ga wel for	0-11- 6
George J.N. Weaver	1 pund Speck und vercil vor	1-13- 4
Henrig Harter	hem hol vor	2-16- 0
"Nicholas Weaver	er wes vor"	0-10
George J.N. Weaver	haber vor	1- 1- 0

Nicholas Schmit vor du di emfangen   7- 0 - 0
(apparently a contribution to Nicholas Smith's estate)

Michael Mayer	to 1 ax	5-14- 0
William Petry	1 churn	1-12- 0
"do." (Wm Petry)	ein spinnen wel	8- 6- 0
Frederick Weaver	1 troff	0- 6- 0
Frederick Meyer	1 troff	0- 8- 0
John Smith	1 hogg	3-16- 0
Henry Meyer	1 hogg	3-12- 0
Old Nicholas Weaver	1 hogg	5- 8- 0
Jacob Bell	1 hogg	8- 4- 0
Jacob G. Weaver	for a sheep	7- 4- 0
John Smith	for a sheep	6-16- 0
George Smith	for 2 sheep	8- 0- 0
Henry Harter	for a sheep	6-16- 0
Michel Meyer	73 bund Zueker	10- 2- 0
Johan Schmit j	barl	0-14- 0
John Bauman	8 bund Zucker	3- 4- 0
George J. Hilts	ein kiewel vor	0-10- 0
Nicholas Weaver	ein par wilde Schu vor	2-16- 0
Michael Meyer	1 pr Leather Mitts	1- 6- 0
Hendrick Meyer	1 pr Milln & galine	0- 5- 0
Michael Meyer	1 Deer skin 39 Dollars	15-12- 0
Frederick Bowman	1 Sugar Bos	0- 5- 4
Hendrick Harter	1 pr Indian shoe & leather	0-17- 0
Peter Dockstader	1 Smoothing Iron	0-10- 0

LIST 3 -"Eim Vontu Von Nicolas Schmit Seimen Guth   December 11, 1779

Ein Rent Wedges Nicholas Weber Gekaufft		
hat fur Zwey und Siebendrig Punt		72- 0- 0
John Schmit	ein Rend fur	16- 0- 0
John Schmit	ein Gebibs	2- 0- 0
Georg Schmit	Das Dengel gehher	4- 2- 0
Peter Dachsteter	ein Schleeff Stein	7- 4- 0
Frid. Schmit	ein Rothhack	3- 4- 0
Michel Mayer	ein Gakeul fur	1-12- 0
Georg Dachsteter	ein kameShol	28- 8- 0
Lorens F. Herter	ein Pahr Buckse	49- 8- 0
Hannes Kesler	ein Kuchel Tack	
Henry Herter	ein bundig Lamp	16- 0- 0
Melger Fols	ein Pahr Stremps	
Melger Fols	ein pahr Stremps	16- 0- 0
Michel Mayer	ein Pahr Stemps	9-12- 0
Hanes Bellinger Ju.	ein Shorn Ste mander	3- 4- 0
Philip Helmer	entege fur	5- 6- 4
Michel Mayer	entege fur	4- 0- 0
Michel Mayer	im Peffer Base	4- 0- 0
George fols	Piffer fur	3- 0- 0
Henry Harter	Allaun fur	2- 8- 0
Jacob Bell	ein Chatus Base	1-12- 0
Michel Mayer	Invwen fur	1-14- 8
Frid. Weber	Stromp bennel fur	2- 8- 0
Peter bellinger	Stromp bennel fur	5- 4- 0
Jacob Weber Jun:	Dek fur	3-16- 0
Fred. G. Weber	Chartun fur	3- 8- 0
Hans Bellinger	Sieslade fur	1-12- 0
Frid. G. Weber	Nodele fur	2- 0- 0
John Meyer	Schewbel fur	0-16- 0
Michel Meyer	ein mefser	1- 8- 0
Michel Meyer	ein mefser	1- 9- 4
Michel Meyer	ein mefser	2-10- 8
Michel Meyer	ein Dek base	0-16- 0
Hendrich Mayer	ein Pahr Shnale	2- 4- 0
Hendrich Mayer	ein mifser	2- 8- 0
Melger fols	ein mifser	1-12- 0
		260- 7- 0
Georg Schmit	ein Schen fur	2- 0- 0
Nicolas Weber	ein Sack	* 2- 4- 0
Michel Mayer	ein Sack	1-16- 0
John Moyer	ein Sack vor	3- 4- 0
George fols	vor polwer	0-12- 0
Michel Meyer	Zwo kleile keebe	0- 8- 0
George Fols	din de pulwer	0-16- 0
Georg Fols	vor Spelden	0-16- 0
Georg Fols	vor Siede und einige Saehen	1- 2- 4
Johannes Kessler	ein koffert vor	0- 9- 0
		11- 3- 4
		260- 7- 0
(* all items were marked as paid except N Weber's 2- 4)		271-10- 4

LIST 4 - "Eim Vontu Von Das Nicolas Schmit Seimen Guth   January 22, 1780
                                                                Th

Georg M. Weber	ein Strick		0-15- 0
Georg M. Weber	ein Strick		0-10- 8
Henrich Mayer	ein Strick		1- 0- 0
Henrich Mayer	ein Strick		0-12- 0
Henrich Mayer	ein Strick		0- 2- 8
Georg M. Weber	ein haben Sack		0-16- 0
Frid. Weber	ein weibs Rack	45	
Henrich Harter	ein Rebert	51	
Henrich Herter	ein Borstauck	16	
Georg M Weber	ein Nachtrack	6.5	
Frid. Weber	ein Nachtrack	10.5	
Frid. Weber	ein Nachtrack	5	
Hannes Bellinger	ein Schwartzer rack	62	
Georg Schmit	ein Nachtrack	46.5	
Casper Huber	ein Leibge	31	
Georg M. Weber	ein Huth	102.5	
Frid. Schmit	ein mans Rock	117	
Nicholas Weber	ein lebinell	14	
Georg Schmit	Lacke fur	10.5	
Michael Meyer	ein The han	15	
Georg M. Weber Ju.	ein Hals tag	17	
Nicolaus Herter	ein Schirt	37	
Michel Meyer	ein Deller	14	
Ludwig Bersch	ein deller	15	
Georg M. Weber	ein Nuhtrn bucky	2.5	
Michel Mayer	knefs for	2	
Georg Dachsteter	parhr Johnn	12	
Jacob Weber	ein pahr Schmaddel	12	
Nicholas Herter	ein spirtgs	14	
Frid Weber	parh Strop ermil	5.5	
Kasper huber	ein hempt	3	
Georg M. Weber	ein hempt	10	
Jacob G. Weber	ein Schemesakl	6	
Lorens F. Herter	ein korp	10.5	
Hannes Bellinger	ein packebuch	17.5	
Lorens f. Herter	Livez barell	12	
Michel Mayer	Fivez barll	6	
Georg Schmit	Ein Korse	5	
Februi. 22th			
Georg Dachsteter	Ein part gekuft		110- 0 -0
Jacob N. Weber	ein bruh	3.5	
Frid. Mayer	ein Schledeback	12.5	

Von Diesem Gelb Haben wir An Jacob Weber Jr.
Geben fur Das tus vussen in der Voontu Die sumn
Zwey und DreySick Sthater

Georg L: S. 4

1790 RESIDENTS OF GERMAN FLATS & HERKIMER
(from list order on 1790 NY Census)

Tw Ln#	NAME (Last/1st)	Tw Ln#	NAME (Last/1st)	Tw Ln#	NAME (Last/1st)
	<German Flats>	GF 048	CAMPBELL,Ludwig	GF 098	SEGHNER,Paul(SAGNER)
GF 001	UNDERWOOD,Joseph	GF 049	WOHLEBEN,Peter	GF 099	RYAN,Magdalena
GF 002	HOPKINS,Micah	GF 050	BASHAR,Jacob	GF 100	DRISSELMAN,Christian
GF 003	MABEE,David	GF 051	YOUHE(Yuel),James	GF 101	BRODHACK,Barth.
GF 004	WALKER,Edward	GF 052	FRANK,John	GF 102	KESSLER,John Sr.
GF 005	FREAVEAU,Francis	GF 053	FOX,Frederick	GF 103	HAUSMAN,George
GF 006	THARE,Pheneas	GF 054	SHOEMAKER,Frederick	GF 104	KESSLER,Dietrich
GF 007	HOUSE,Conradt	GF 055	SHOEMAKER,Christophe	GF 105	KESSLER,Jacob John
GF 008	WOODWARD,James	GF 056	SHOEMAKER,...	GF 106	KESSLER,Conrad
GF 009	GORDON,Mary	GF 057	FRANK,Frederick	GF 107	BURGHDORF,John
GF 010	FISK,Jonathan	GF 058	FANSHOR,Eaton	GF 108	KESSLER,Jacob Jacob
GF 011	ALLEN,Seth	GF 059	WILCOCKS,Joseph	GF 109	KESSLER,John Jacob
GF 012	HYNES,Joseph	GF 060	ALDRIDGE,Nicholas	GF 110	KESSLER,Jacob Sr.
GF 013	LIGHTHALL,Abraham	GF 061	ISDALE,John	GF 111	ROSENCRANTZ,Abraham
GF 014	WOHLEBEN,Abraham	GF 062	CASE,Gabriel	GF 112	OELEY(Uhle),Henry
GF 015	ETICK,Frederick	GF 063	CASE,Aseph	GF 113	HILTS,John
GF 016	HESS,Jost	GF 064	REUBY,Christopher	GF 114	KESSLER,Jacob J N
GF 017	EATON,Ebenezer	GF 065	CASE,Elijah Jr.	GF 115	KESSLER,Jacob N
GF 018	HAWKS,Daniel	GF 066	HERKIMER,George	GF 116	BELLINGER,Peter Sr.
GF 019	HITCHINS,John	GF 067	HERKIMER,Jost	GF 117	STARING,Henry N
GF 020	MARTIN,John	GF 068	SMALL,Susannah	GF 118	DURELL,Dorothy
GF 021	MARTIN,Robert	GF 069	FLAGG,Peter	GF 119	SMITH,John
GF 022	MARTIN,Nathan	GF 070	NASH,James	GF 120	MOYER(Meyer),Henry
GF 023	MARTIN,Samuel	GF 071	HESS,Conrad	GF 121	CONANT, elner (?)
GF 024	BAYLEY,Oliver	GF 072	HESS,Frederick	GF 122	ODELL, Luke (?)
GF 025	OLENDORF,Daniel	GF 073	SPOHN,Warner	GF 123	GELLASPLE,Thomas
GF 026	TUSLER,Mark	GF 074	EDICK,Michael	GF 124	LOGAN(?),Thomas
GF 027	CHAPMAN,Joseph	GF 075	LIGHTHALL,George	GF 125	WERNER,Henry
GF 028	FINK,John/ECKER,Chp.	GF 076	BELLINGER,John	GF 126	STEELE,Rudolph
GF 029	BELLINGER,Philip	GF 077	BELLINGER,Frederick	GF 127	SHOEMAKER,Jost
GF 030	HILL,William	GF 078	FOX,John	GF 128	SHOEMAKER,Gertrude
	<Old Andrustown group>	GF 079	SHOEMAKER,Thomas	GF 129	SHOEMAKER,Rudolph
GF 031	LEAPER,Frederick	GF 080	STALE(Steele),Adam	GF 130	SHOEMAKER,Frederick
GF 032	GRIM(Crim),Henry	GF 081	ORENDORF,Fredrick Jr		<GF/Frankfort area>
GF 033	BULSON,Grates	GF 082	ORENDORF,Fredrick Sr	GF 131	SHOEMAKER,...
GF 034	HOYER,George F	GF 083	STARING,Joseph	GF 132	CASLER(Kessler),Marc
GF 035	CRIM,Jacob	GF 084	STARING,Nicholas	GF 133	GRANTZ(Crants),Henry
GF 036	STARING,Adam Sr.	GF 085	CAMPBELL,Patrick	GF 134	CLEPSATTLE,Andrew
GF 037	OSTERHOUT,John	GF 086	ELWELL,Ebenezeer	GF 135	CLEPSATTLE,William
GF 038	REESE,Adam	GF 087	CAMMERON,Even	GF 136	CLEPSATTLE,George
GF 039	MARTZ,Philip Peter	GF 088	ELWELL,Samuel	GF 137	STEELE,Dietrich
	<German Flats cont.>	GF 089	HULL,William C	GF 138	LYON(?),Henry
GF 040	GETHAN,Conrad	GF 090	PETRY,Nathan	GF 139	DYGERT,William Sr.
GF 041	ORENDORF,Peter	GF 091	HATCH,Peter	GF 140	FOLTS,Jacob Sr.
GF 042	CONANT,Amos	GF 092	STARING,Adam N	GF 141	FOLTS,Conrad J
GF 043	ONEAL,John	GF 093	PETRIE,Catherine	GF 142	GETHAN,Peter
GF 044	ETICK,Christian	GF 094	EYSAMAN,Stephen	GF 143	GETMAN,John
GF 045	CAMPBELL,Barbara	GF 095	LEIMBACH,Henry	GF 144	MOYER(Meyer),...
GF 046	FURMAN,Russel	GF 096	CORAL(Carl),George	GF 145	PIPER,...
GF 047	WEAVER,Adam	GF 097	SEGHNER,Conrad	GF 146	FRANK,Lawrence

1790 RESIDENTS OF GERMAN FLATS & HERKIMER
(from list order on 1790 NY Census)

Tw Ln# NAME (Last/1st)	Tw Ln# NAME (Last/1st)	Tw Ln# NAME (Last/1st)
GF 147 WEAVER,John	GF 196 FULMER,William	HK 245 STIFFORD,Samuel
GF 148 WEAVER,Nicholas	GF 197 AUSMAN,Philip	HK 246 RUSSEL,Samuel
GF 149 LENTZ,Peter	GF 198 ORENDORF,Conrad	HK 247 KRENNEL,John
GF 150 FOLTS,Conrad C.	GF 199 HYSER(Hiser),Jacob	HK 248 RIEGEL,Christian
GF 151 MUNTERBACH,John	GF 200 FRANK,Timothy	HK 249 EDICK,Jacob
GF 152 TINUS(Dinges),Jacob	GF 201 UNDERWOOD,Parker	HK 250 WEAVER,Peter Jr.
GF 153 FRANK,Henry	GF 202 BALL,Nathaniel	HK 251 BENNET,Andrew
GF 154 LENTZ,Jacob	GF 203 RAMSAY,Ebenezeer	HK 252 PARKER,Henry
GF 155 HUCK(?),John	GF 204 BAKER,Joel	HK 253 SPENCER,Rufus
GF 156 BELL,Andrew	GF 205 SNOW,Elijah	HK 254 BAKER,Nathan
GF 157 FINK(?),Conrad	GF 206 ANDREWS,John	HK 255 BETHOOM,William
GF 158 CRIM,Adam	GF 207 EVERITT,John	HK 256 WILLIS,Aseph
GF 159 DEDERIK,Diebald	GF 208 DAY,Ithamy	HK 257 WILLIS,Caleb
GF 160 PORTER(?),Alexander	GF 209 DAY,Joseph	HK 258 NICHOLS,Thomas
GF 161 ARMSTRONG,John	GF 210 HITCHCOCK,Ebenezer	HK 259 DOCHETY,Charles
GF 162 BRADLEY,John	GF 211 MCCARTHY,John	HK 260 WOOD,John
GF 163 BROWN,David	GF 212 MCCARTHY,George	HK 261 NIGHT,John
GF 164 DAVIDSON,John	GF 213 GREGG,James	HK 262 GARDNER,Westcoat
GF 165 GROWNHART,George	GF 214 ALLEN,Moses	HK 263 ANDREW,David
GF 166 STROBEL,Christopher	GF 215 VINTON,Benomi	HK 264 BRICKS,Eliakim
GF 167 GREEN,Jedediah	GF 216 GILLETT,Eli	HK 265 CORNISH,Stephen
GF 168 DOWELL(?),Jeremiah	GF 217 SWEET,Jonathan	HK 267 AUSTEN,Abel
GF 169 BOOM(Baum),Abraham	GF 218 MERRY,Samuel Jr.	HK 267 HENDERSON,Daniel
GF 170 SALIS,William	GF 219 MILLER,Samuel	HK 268 RIEGEL,Godfrey
GF 171 DYGERT,Peter	GF 220 JONES,William Clark	HK 269 BRODHACK,John
GF 172 CUNINGHAM,John	GF 221 MERRY,Samuel Sr.	HK 270 STIFFORD,Richard
GF 173 BOWMAN,Frederick	GF 222 STICKNY,Joseph	HK 271 STIFFORD,David
GF 174 ..TELE,John D	GF 223 FRANK,John S.	HK 272 STIFFORD,Jacob
GF 175 SALVEA,Henry	GF 224 STEELE,George	HK 273 BRODHACK,Jacob
GF 176 BALLOW,Benjamin	GF 225 BARS(Barsh),Ludwig	HK 274 HELMER,Philip F.
GF 177 CUNINGHAM,William	<HK/Deerfield area>	HK 275 GETMAN,Frederick
GF 178 DEMUTH,Anna	HK 226 DEMUTH,Mark	HK 276 SKINNER,Gershom
GF 179 HESS,Christian	HK 227 RHEEL(Riegel),Fred.	HK 277 FEDDERLY,Thomas
GF 180 WEAVER,Jacob H.	HK 228 HELMER,John	HK 278 FEDDERLY,John
GF 181 WOHLEBEN,Jacob	HK 229 WEAVER,Nicholas J	HK 279 FEDDERLY,Eve
GF 182 HARTER,Lawrence P.	HK 230 HILTS,Lawrence	HK 280 MOULDER,Margaret
GF 183 BENEDICT,Elias	HK 231 WEAVER,George Michel	HK 281 MOULDER,Jacob
GF 184 BENEDICT,Avery	HK 232 POSTLE,Francis	HK 282 KLOCK,Joseph
GF 185 HELMER,Adam	HK 233 WEAVER,Jacob	HK 283 BELLINGER,Philip
<GF/Columbia area>	HK 234 WEAVER,George	HK 284 KOCH,Joseph
GF 186 MILERD,Robert	HK 235 WEAVER,Frederick G.	<New Germantown area>
GF 187 SHURMAN,Samuel	HK 236 WEAVER,George J	HK 285 FINSTER,John
GF 188 MOYER(Meyer),Joseph	HK 237 WEAVER,George J.N.	HK 286 EYRE(Ayer),Elizabeth
GF 189 HELMER,George	HK 238 WEAVER,Nicholas G.	HK 287 HENDERSON,Cornelius
GF 190 PHILLIPS,John	HK 239 DEMUTH,Dederick	HK 288 JONES,Richard
GF 191 CHRISTMAN,Frederick	HK 240 SPENCER,John	HK 289 OWER(Ayer),John
GF 192 MILLER,Henry	HK 241 GLASGOW,Hugh	HK 290 STARING,Henry
GF 193 EDICK,George Jacob	HK 242 HARTER,Nicholas	HK 291 WITRIG,George
GF 194 HESS,John	HK 243 JAMES,Howard	HK 292 FOX,Peter
GF 195 HESS,Augustinus	HK 244 JAMES,Abel	HK 293 STARING,Adam

1790 RESIDENTS OF GERMAN FLATS & HERKIMER
(from list order on 1790 NY Census)

Tw Ln#	NAME (Last/1st)	Tw Ln#	NAME (Last/1st)	Tw Ln#	NAME (Last/1st)
HK 294	BAKER,David	HK 343	SMITH,Adam	HK 392	PETRIE,Marks
HK 295	RIEMA,John	HK 344	FOLTS,George	HK 393	PETRIE,Daniel
HK 296	RIEMA,Jacob	HK 345	FOLTS,Melchior	HK 394	KESSLER,Minert
HK 297	BIRCKY,Peter	HK 346	SMITH,Frederick	HK 395	CASLER(Kessler),John
HK 298	BIRCKY,Jacob	HK 347	KAST,Frederick	HK 396	DEVENDORF,John
HK 299	HARTMAN,Adam	HK 348	MILLER,Andrew	HK 397	DEVENDORF,Isaac
HK 300	WITRIG,Jacob	HK 349	BELLINGER,Peter F	HK 398	FARMER,...
HK 301	WITRIG,Catherine	HK 350	HARTER,Nicholas	HK 399	ICEMAN(Eysaman),John
HK 302	BENDER,..mumus	HK 351	HARTER,Lawrence	HK 400	KLOCK,Henry
HK 303	WITRIG,Michael	HK 352	HARTER,Henry	HK 401	RANCAN,James
HK 304	RIEMA,Christian	HK 353	PETRIE,William	HK 402	NELLIS,Andrew
HK 305	MYER,Adam	HK 354	WEAVER,Jacob G.	HK 403	COX,Fasset
HK 306	BREITENBACHER,Baltes	HK 355	HILTS,Nicholas	HK 404	NELLIS,George
HK 307	MILLER,Elton (Valtn)	HK 356	FULMER,Conrad	HK 405	EIGENAUER,Conrad
HK 308	HOCKSTATTER,Christn	HK 357	TALCOT,Hezekiah	HK 406	SPOHN,Nicholas
HK 309	AYER(Eyre),Frederick	HK 358	HELMER,Frederick A.	HK 407	DAWAY(Davis),Peter
HK 310	CLEMENTS,...	HK 359	HELMER,Henry	HK 408	STARING,Valentine
HK 311	KELLER,John	HK 360	MYERS,Joseph	HK 409	SCHELL,Frederick
	<Central Herkimer area>	HK 361	STARING,Adam A.	HK 410	SHELL(Schell),Marks
HK 312	CRANTZ,Mark	HK 362	STOUGHTON(?),Amasa	HK 411	HILTS,John Jr.
HK 313	DYGERT,William Jr.	HK 363	WEAVER,Peter J.	HK 412	HILTS,George
HK 314	DYGERT,Peter W.	HK 364	BAUMAN,John A.	HK 413	WITHERSTINE,Henry
HK 315	FULMER,Thomas	HK 365	BAUMAN,Adam A.	HK 414	SCHELL,John
HK 316	DYGERT,Andrew	HK 366	HELMER,Frederick F	HK 415	SCHELL,Marks Sr. (?)
HK 317	HARTER,Lawrence F.		<East Herkimer>	HK 416	SCHAFER,Henry
HK 318	HARTER,Frederick Sr.	HK 367	HELMER,John F.	HK 417	THUMM,Melchior
HK 319	SMITH,George	HK 368	SILLEBACK,Christian	HK 418	HILTS,Godfrey
HK 320	SMITH,Yost (Joseph)	HK 369	SMITH,John M.	HK 419	EDICK,George
HK 321	RICHMOND,Daniel	HK 370	HILLER,John		<North Herkimer>
HK 322	DORNBERGER,Frederick	HK 371	RASPACH,Marc	HK 420	WHARRY,Evans
HK 323	BELLINGER,Christian	HK 372	MAKE(Moak),...ratom	HK 421	THRASHER,George
HK 324	FOLTS,Jost (HanYost)	HK 373	FOLTS,Peter	HK 422	THRASHER,Stephen
HK 325	MCCOMBS,George	HK 374	FOLTS,Conrad	HK 423	PETRIE,Jost Jr
HK 326	BELL,Jacob	HK 375	MYER,Michael	HK 424	PETRIE,John M.
HK 327	BAUMAN,Jacob	HK 376	HURDER(Harter),Adam	HK 425	KELLER,Henry
HK 328	MYER,Frederick	HK 377	HARTER,Philip	HK 426	HOVER(Huber),Jacob
HK 329	MYER,Peter	HK 378	DEACON,Joseph	HK 427	ARNOLD,Edward
HK 330	DEMUTH,John	HK 379	BEECH,Gershom	HK 428	NICHOLS,William
HK 331	WEAVER,Jacob N	HK 380	BEECH,Moses	HK 429	HUVER(Huber),Henry
HK 332	DOCKSTADER,George	HK 381	MACK,John	HK 430	HUVER(Huber),John
HK 333	WEAVER,Frederick J	HK 382	HOLLEDAY,Robert	HK 431	EATON,John
HK 334	BELLINGER,Christophr	HK 383	PETRIE,Jacob	HK 432	EATON,Elisha
HK 335	PIPER,Jacob	HK 384	STARING,Adam	HK 433	KNAP,Elijah
HK 336	ANDREES,John	HK 385	STARING,Jacob	HK 434	BENTSLEY,David
HK 337	SEAMORE,Ebenezer	HK 386	BARKER,Henry	HK 435	BUCKLAND,William
HK 338	HILL,Elijah	HK 387	PORTEOUS,John	HK 436	BUCKLAND,John
HK 339	CHRISTMAN,John	HK 388	HALL,Eldin	HK 437	COLE,Ebenezer
HK 340	BELL,Thomas	HK 389	PETRIE,Richard	HK 438	CARPENTER,Stephen
HK 341	HILTS,John	HK 390	PETRIE,John	HK 439	BROWN,Nathaniel
HK 342	BELL,Philip	HK 391	PETRIE,Jost(HanYost)	HK 440	BROWN,David

1790 RESIDENTS OF GERMAN FLATS & HERKIMER
(from list order on 1790 NY Census)

Tw Ln#	NAME (Last/1st)	Tw Ln#	NAME (Last/1st)
HK 441	BENTSLEY,Joseph	HK 491	LATHAM,Peter
HK 442	ROWN,Nicholas	HK 492	LATHAM,David
HK 443	SMITH,Noah	HK 493	LATHAM,Benjamin
HK 444	WHIPPLE,William	HK 494	MANLY,Thomas
HK 445	GOFF,Calvert	HK 495	UNDERHILL,David
HK 446	MANN,Abijah	HK 496	HENMAN,David
HK 447	FORD,Benomi	HK 497	POTTER,Jeremiah
HK 448	GRISWOLD,Francis	HK 498	COE,John
HK 449	GRISWOLD,Edward	HK 499	COE,Andrew
HK 450	TEAL,Joseph		
HK 451	CHATFIELD,Cornelius		
HK 452	MOTTONER,John		
HK 453	POLLARD,Jeremiah		
HK 454	GOODBROADT,William		
HK 455	VAN BRACKLE,Herbert		
HK 456	SMITH,Clark		
HK 457	PARKER,Daniel		
HK 458	SCRIBNER,Aaron		
HK 459	MILLER,John		
HK 460	COE,Amos		
HK 461	MANN,Abel		
HK 462	REED,Curtis		
HK 463	FEETER,William		
HK 464	CHURCHILL,Isaac		
HK 465	NIELSON,Ball		
HK 466	COFFIN,Edward		
HK 467	HEDRINGTON,Isaac		
HK 468	HENNEX,Barnhart		
HK 469	RIED,Abner		
HK 470	HINDMAN,Benjamin		
HK 471	HADCOCK,John		
HK 472	DODGE,Nathaniel		
HK 473	STACKWEATHER,Elijah		
HK 474	JOHNSTON,Isaiah		
HK 475	BYINGTON,John		
HK 476	STANDARD,Oliver		
HK 477	EMPIE,John		
HK 478	LOBDEN,Joseph		
HK 479	BOWEN,Benjamin		
HK 480	PAINE,Philip		
HK 481	JOHNSTON,William		
HK 482	HAWKINS,Christopher		
HK 483	WHIPPLE,Nicholas		
HK 484	WHIPPLE,Levy		
HK 485	AVERY,Sarah B.		
HK 486	WATSON,Jud		
HK 487	WATSON,Nathan		
HK 488	WATSON,Samuel		
HK 489	BUTTERFIELD,Levy		
HK 490	COMMINGS,Francis		

ALPHABETIZED PORTION OF 1790 MONTGOMERY CO. NY CENSUS
(As relates to Herkimer Co. families)

Name (Last/1st)	M	B	F	Tw	Ln#	Name (Last/1st)	M	B	F	Tw	Ln#
..TELE,John D	1	1	2	GF	174	BELLINGER,Christopher	1	1	2	HK	334
ADIMY,Peter	1	0	3	CJ	381	BELLINGER,Frederick	1	2	5	GF	077
ALDRIDGE,Nicholas	3	0	4	GF	060	BELLINGER,Henry	2	1	7	PL	633
ALLEN,Moses	4	0	3	GF	214	BELLINGER,Henry	1	2	4	PL	662
ALLEN,Seth	1	3	2	GF	011	BELLINGER,John	2	2	3	GF	076
ANDREES,John	1	1	2	HK	336	BELLINGER,John L.	1	1	1	PL	636
ANDREW,David	1	6	4	HK	263	BELLINGER,Joseph	1	3	3	MK	550
ANDREWS,John	1	1	1	GF	206	BELLINGER,Peter	1	2	2	CJ	301
ARMSTRONG,John	1	2	1	GF	161	BELLINGER,Peter	1	0	3	PL	637
ARNOLD,Edward	1	2	3	HK	427	BELLINGER,Peter F	2	1	5	HK	349
AUSMAN,Philip	1	1	2	GF	197	BELLINGER,Peter Sr.	4	0	2	GF	116
AUSTEN,Abel	1	3	3	HK	267	BELLINGER,Philip	1	4	1	HK	283
AVERY,Sarah B.	1	0	3	HK	485	BELLINGER,Philip	2	0	2	GF	029
AYER,Elizabeth (Eyre)	1	0	3	HK	286	BELLINGER,William	2	4	5	CJ	114
AYER,Frederick (Eyre)	1	0	1	HK	309	BENDER,..mumus	1	0	1	HK	302
AYER,John (OWER)	1	2	2	HK	289	BENEDICT,Avery	1	1	+	GF	184
BADER,Ulrich	2	4	6	PL	641	BENEDICT,Elias	1	2	2	GF	183
BAKER,David	2	1	3	HK	294	BENNET,Andrew	2	0	0	HK	251
BAKER,Joel	2	0	0	GF	204	BENTSLEY,David	1	2	2	HK	434
BAKER,Nathan	1	1	3	HK	254	BENTSLEY,Joseph	1	3	1	HK	441
BALL,Nathaniel	1	0	0	GF	202	BETHOOM,William	1	2	3	HK	255
BALLOW,Benjamin	5	0	1	GF	176	BIRCKY,Jacob	1	2	3	HK	298
BARKER,Henry	1	2	5	HK	386	BIRCKY,Peter	1	0	1	HK	297
BARSH,Adam	2	2	2	PL	632	BOSHARR,Margaret	2	0	2	CG	524
BARSH,Ludwig (Bars)	1	1	2	GF	225	BOWEN,Benjamin	1	3	4	HK	479
BARSH,Rudolph	1	1	2	PL	628	BOWMAN,Frederick	1	1	4	GF	173
BASHAR,Jacob	2	1	2	GF	050	BRADLEY,John	1	0	0	GF	162
BASHASHA,Hannah	+	+	4	CJ	008	BREITENBACHER,Baltes	1	5	4	HK	306
BAUM,Abraham (Boon)	2	1	4	GF	169	BRICKS,Eliakim	1	2	1	HK	264
BAUM,Hendrick	1	0	1	CJ	324	BRODHACK,Barth.	2	1	3	GF	101
BAUM,Philip	1	0	2	CJ	063	BRODHACK,Jacob	1	3	4	HK	273
BAUMAN,Adam A.	1	2	1	HK	365	BRODHACK,John	1	1	1	HK	269
BAUMAN,Jacob (Beauman)	1	2	3	HK	327	BROWN,Adam	1	1	1	CJ	161
BAUMAN,John A.	4	0	2	HK	364	BROWN,Christian	1	1	7	CJ	159
BAYER,John	4	2	7	PL	661	BROWN,David	1	0	1	HK	440
BAYER,Valitine	1	1	2	PL	653	BROWN,David	1	2	2	GF	163
BAYLEY,Oliver	1	2	2	GF	024	BROWN,Nathaniel	1	0	0	HK	439
BECKER,Christian	1	0	2	CJ	319	BROWN,Simon	1	0	3	CJ	162
BEECH,Gershom	3	0	2	HK	379	BUCKLAND,John	1	2	3	HK	436
BEECH,Moses	1	0	2	HK	380	BUCKLAND,William	1	1	1	HK	435
BEKKER,Henry	1	3	4	PL	608	BULSON,Grates	1	3	3	GF	033
BELL,Andrew	1	2	3	GF	156	BURGHDORF,John	1	2	2	GF	107
BELL,Hendrick	2	2	2	CJ	302	BUTTERFIELD,Levy	1	1	2	HK	489
BELL,Jacob	1	1	4	HK	326	BUYE,John	2	1	5	PL	654
BELL,Philip	1	0	1	HK	342	BYINGTON,John	1	0	3	HK	475
BELL,Thomas	1	1	1	HK	340	CAMMERON,Even	1	0	1	GF	087
BELLINGER,Adam	3	1	5	PL	655	CAMPBELL,Barbara	2	3	3	GF	045
BELLINGER,Adam A.	2	2	2	PL	642	CAMPBELL,Ludwig	1	4	2	GF	048
BELLINGER,Adam B.	1	2	3	CJ	242	CAMPBELL,Patrick	2	2	6	GF	085
BELLINGER,Christian	1	1	4	HK	323	CARL,George (Coral)	1	4	2	GF	096

Name (Last/1st)	M	B	F	Tw	Ln#
CARPENTER,Stephen	1	0	1	HK	438
CASE,Aseph	1	0	0	GF	063
CASE,Elijah Jr.	1	2	2	GF	065
CASE,Gabriel	1	1	3	GF	062
CASSELMAN,John J	1	0	3	PL	607
CAUSSELMAN,John	2	1	2	PL	589
CHAPMAN,Joseph	1	0	2	GF	027
CHATFIELD,Cornelius	1	3	2	HK	451
CHRISTMAN,Frederick	1	1	5	GF	191
CHRISTMAN,Jacob	1	5	3	PL	600
CHRISTMAN,Jacob	1	1	5	CJ	426
CHRISTMAN,John	2	2	3	HK	339
CHRISTMAN,John	2	3	3	PL	598
CHRISTMAN,John	1	2	3	CJ	460
CHRISTMAN,Nicholas	1	4	2	PL	643
CHURCHILL,Isaac	1	2	3	HK	464
CLEMENTS,...	1	2	3	HK	310
CLEPSATTLE,Andrew	2	2	4	GF	134
CLEPSATTLE,George	2	2	5	GF	136
CLEPSATTLE,William	1	3	3	GF	135
CLINE,John	3	0	1	MK	571
COE,Amos	1	0	0	HK	460
COE,Andrew	1	0	0	HK	499
COE,John	1	2	2	HK	498
COFFIN,Edward	1	4	2	HK	466
COLE,Ebenezer	1	1	2	HK	437
COMMINGS,Francis	1	2	5	HK	490
CONANT, elner (?)	1	0	4	GF	121
CONANT,Amos	1	1	2	GF	042
CORNISH,Stephen	1	1	2	HK	265
COX,Fasset	1	3	6	HK	403
CRANTZ,Henry (Grants)	1	2	3	GF	133
CRANTZ,Mark	1	1	2	HK	312
CRIM(Krams),John	1	2	1	PL	591
CRIM,Adam	1	0	1	GF	158
CRIM,Henry (Grim)	1	3	1	GF	032
CRIM,Jacob	1	3	4	GF	035
CROMMELL,Philip	2	4	6	CG	502
CUNINGHAM,James	1	1	3	HP	537
CUNINGHAM,John	1	2	3	CJ	251
CUNINGHAM,John	1	0	1	CH	531
CUNINGHAM,John	2	0	5	GF	172
CUNINGHAM,William	2	0	5	GF	177
CUNINGHAM,William Jr.	2	0	1	PL	617
CUSSELMAN,William	1	1	2	CG	500
CUSTLEMAN,John	1	1	1	CG	513
DAVIDSON,John	1	2	2	GF	164
DAVIS,Jacob	1	5	1	PL	659
DAVIS,John	1	1	1	MK	572
DAVIS,John	1	1	3	CJ	173
DAVIS,Mary (Davy)	0	1	5	CJ	325
DAVIS,Peter (Daway)	1	1	5	HK	407
DAVIS,Thomas	1	2	4	CG	528
DAY,Ithamy	3	1	6	GF	208
DAY,Joseph	1	0	1	GF	209
DEACON,Joseph	1	1	1	HK	378
DEDERIK,Diebald	2	3	5	GF	159
DELYNE,Benjamin	3	1	1	CG	526
DEMUTH,Anna	1	3	5	GF	178
DEMUTH,Dederick	1	0	3	HK	239
DEMUTH,John	1	1	2	HK	330
DEMUTH,Mark	3	2	3	HK	226
DEVENDORF,Isaac	1	0	2	HK	397
DEVENDORF,John	1	0	3	HK	396
DIVENDORPH,Jacob	2	1	4	MK	543
DOCHETY,Charles	1	1	7	HK	259
DOCKSTADER,Christian	3	1	3	CJ	343
DOCKSTADER,Elizabeth	2	0	3	CG	516
DOCKSTADER,Frederick F	3	0	2	CG	518
DOCKSTADER,Fredrick II	2	2	5	CG	515
DOCKSTADER,George	4	6	6	HK	332
DOCKSTADER,George	2	2	3	CG	514
DOCKSTADER,Jacob	1	2	1	CG	505
DOCKSTADER,John	1	2	3	CG	509
DOCKSTADER,John	1	4	1	PL	609
DOCKSTADER,Leonard	2	2	7	CG	503
DOCKSTADER,Marcus	2	0	2	CG	504
DOCKSTADER,Nicholas	2	2	5	CG	517
DOCKSTADER,Nicholas	2	1	5	CJ	195
DOCKSTADER,Nicholas II	1	2	3	MK	549
DODGE,Nathaniel	1	1	4	HK	472
DORNBERGER,Frederick	1	0	3	HK	322
DOWELL(?),Jeremiah	1	3	2	GF	168
DRISSELMAN,Christian	1	0	0	GF	100
DURELL,Dorothy	0	0	3	GF	118
DYGERT,Andrew (Tygert)	1	1	2	HK	316
DYGERT,Nicholas	1	3	2	CJ	363
DYGERT,Peter	5	0	6	GF	171
DYGERT,Peter H.	1	2	4	CJ	462
DYGERT,Peter S.	3	0	1	CJ	289
DYGERT,Peter W.	1	2	2	HK	314
DYGERT,Severinus	3	1	4	PL	602
DYGERT,Severinus I	2	2	4	PL	604
DYGERT,William Jr.	1	3	3	HK	313
DYGERT,William Sr.	3	0	4	GF	139
EATON,Ebenezeer	1	0	0	GF	017
EATON,Elisha	1	0	1	HK	432
EATON,John	4	2	2	HK	431
ECKLER,Hendrick	1	+	2	CJ	017
ECKLER,Henry	1	3	5	CJ	002

Name (Last/1st)	M	B	F	Tw	Ln#	Name (Last/1st)	M	B	F	Tw	Ln#
ECKLER,John	1	6	2	CJ	001	FOX,William	1	1	2	CJ	316
ECKLER,Leonard	1	1	2	CJ	016	FOX,William	2	2	5	PL	620
ECKLER,Peter	1	3	3	CJ	005	FOX,William W.	2	2	3	PL	619
EDICK,Christian	2	4	3	GF	044	FRANK,Adam	2	2	6	MK	568
EDICK,Conrad	1	1	2	HP	536	FRANK,Andrew	1	2	3	MK	566
EDICK,Frederick	2	0	3	GF	015	FRANK,Frederick	1	2	3	GF	057
EDICK,George	1	1	3	HK	419	FRANK,Henry	3	0	7	GF	153
EDICK,George Jacob	1	3	2	GF	193	FRANK,John	3	1	8	GF	052
EDICK,Jacob	1	4	2	HK	249	FRANK,John S.	3	1	7	GF	223
EDICK,Michael	3	0	4	GF	074	FRANK,Lawrence	2	4	3	GF	146
EIGENAUER,Conrad	2	2	2	HK	405	FRANK,Michael	1	2	1	CJ	065
ELWELL,Ebenezeer	1	0	0	GF	086	FRANK,John	1	0	3	GF	200
ELWELL,Samuel	1	0	3	GF	088	FRANK,Timothy	1	0	3	GF	200
EMPIE,John	2	1	3	HK	477	FREAVEAU,Francis	1	1	0	GF	005
ETEL(Cadle),George	2	1	3	PL	657	FULMER,Conrad	1	3	1	HK	356
EVERITT,John	2	0	0	GF	207	FULMER,Thomas	3	3	5	HK	315
EYSAMAN,John (Iceman)	2	2	6	HK	399	FULMER,William	1	1	5	GF	196
EYSAMAN,Stephen	1	1	3	GF	094	FURMAN,Russel	1	6	1	GF	046
FANSHOR,Eaton	2	2	1	GF	058	GARDNER,Westcoat	2	4	3	HK	262
FARMER,...	1	0	2	HK	398	GELLASPLE,Thomas	1	0	3	GF	123
FEDDERLY,Eve	0	2	2	HK	279	GETMAN,Conrad	1	1	2	GF	040
FEDDERLY,John	1	0	5	HK	278	GETMAN,Frederick	1	2	3	HK	275
FEDDERLY,Thomas	1	2	2	HK	277	GETMAN,Frederick	2	1	5	PL	594
FEETER,William	1	4	3	HK	463	GETMAN,John	1	1	2	GF	143
FINK(?),Conrad	1	3	3	GF	157	GETMAN,Peter	1	1	2	GF	142
FINK,Joh	1	1	4	GF	028	GETMAN,Peter	1	0	3	PL	586
FINSTER,John	1	3	2	HK	285	GILLETT,Eli	1	1	1	GF	216
FISK,Jonathan	3	1	1	GF	010	GLASGOW,Hugh	2	0	4	HK	241
FLAGG,Peter	1	2	3	GF	069	GOFF,Calvert	1	2	3	HK	445
FLANDER,John	4	0	4	PL	578	GOODBROADT,William	1	1	2	HK	454
FOLTS,Conrad	1	1	3	HK	374	GORDON,Mary	0	1	+	GF	009
FOLTS,Conrad C.	1	3	1	GF	150	GRAY,Adam	4	1	4	PL	606
FOLTS,Conrad J	2	4	3	GF	141	GRAY,John	2	1	2	PL	588
FOLTS,George	2	2	3	HK	344	GRAY,Samuel	1	6	2	PL	595
FOLTS,Jacob Sr.	1	0	2	GF	140	GREEN,Jedediah	1	4	3	GF	167
FOLTS,Jost (HanYost)	2	2	4	HK	324	GREGG,James	1	0	0	GF	213
FOLTS,Melchior	1	3	2	HK	345	GRISWOLD,Edward	1	1	3	HK	449
FOLTS,Peter	1	2	3	HK	373	GRISWOLD,Francis	1	0	0	HK	448
FONDA,John	1	4	2	CG	507	GROESBECK,Garrit	1	2	2	CJ	380
FORD,Benomi	1	3	4	HK	447	GROWNHART,George	2	2	3	GF	165
FOX,Christopher	4	4	+	PL	625	HADCOCK,John	3	5	3	HK	471
FOX,Daniel	2	2	+	PL	624	HALL,Eldin	2	1	8	HK	388
FOX,Frederick	2	3	5	GF	053	HARTER,Adam (Hurder)	1	1	2	HK	376
FOX,George	3	0	3	PL	616	HARTER,Frederick Sr.	4	0	3	HK	318
FOX,John	2	2	5	GF	078	HARTER,Henry	3	0	2	HK	352
FOX,Jost (HanYost)	1	1	3	PL	626	HARTER,Lawrence	4	3	5	HK	351
FOX,Peter	1	0	3	HK	292	HARTER,Lawrence F.	1	2	3	HK	317
FOX,Peter	4	3	4	CJ	405	HARTER,Lawrence P.	1	2	5	GF	182
FOX,Philip	3	2	3	CJ	340	HARTER,Nicholas	3	1	3	HK	350
FOX,Philip	1	1	2	PL	627	HARTER,Nicholas	3	0	2	HK	242
						HARTER,Philip	1	1	2	HK	377

Name (Last/1st)	M	B	F	Tw	Ln#	Name (Last/1st)	M	B	F	Tw	Ln#
HARTMAN,Adam	1	5	2	HK	299	HILTS,John	1	2	3	HK	341
HATCH,Peter	2	2	3	GF	091	HILTS,John Jr.	1	2	3	HK	411
HATCOCK,Daniel	1	1	6	PL	638	HILTS,Lawrence	1	5	2	HK	230
HAUSMAN,George	1	1	2	GF	103	HILTS,Nicholas	3	1	3	HK	355
HAWKINS,Christopher P.	1	0	3	HK	482	HINDMAN,Benjamin	1	2	1	HK	470
HAWKS,Daniel	4	2	5	GF	018	HISER,Jacob (Hyser)	1	0	2	GF	199
HEDRINGTON,Isaac	1	0	0	HK	467	HITCHCOCK,Ebenezer	1	0	0	GF	210
HEES,William	2	0	3	PL	645	HITCHINS,John	3	2	0	GF	019
HELMER,Adam	2	1	5	GF	185	HOCKSTATTER,Christian	1	4	2	HK	308
HELMER,Frederick A.	3	1	2	HK	358	HOLLEDAY,Robert	1	1	3	HK	382
HELMER,Frederick F	2	1	3	HK	366	HOOVER,Jacob	2	2	2	CJ	003
HELMER,George	3	2	5	GF	189	HOPKINS,Micah	2	0	2	GF	002
HELMER,Henry	1	4	4	HK	359	HOUSE,Christian	2	2	6	PL	639
HELMER,John	1	1	3	HK	228	HOUSE,Conradt	1	3	2	GF	007
HELMER,John F.	1	0	0	HK	367	HOYER,George F	2	2	4	GF	034
HELMER,John G.	1	1	3	PL	621	HUBER,Henry (Huver)	1	5	3	HK	429
HELMER,John P.	1	3	3	HK	635	HUBER,Jacob (Hover)	1	2	1	HK	426
HELMER,Jost (HonYost)	1	0	2	PL	622	HUBER,John (Huver)	1	0	3	HK	430
HELMER,Leonard	1	3	4	PL	590	HUCK(?),John	1	2	5	GF	155
HELMER,Philip	2	4	4	PL	634	HULL,William C	1	0	1	GF	089
HELMER,Philip F.	3	3	6	HK	274	HULTS,John	2	2	2	HP	533
HELMER,Philip L.	1	2	4	PL	629	HYNES,Joseph	3	2	4	GF	012
HENDERSON,Cornelius	1	2	2	HK	287	ISDALE,John	3	1	4	GF	061
HENDERSON,Daniel	3	6	3	HK	267	JAMES,Abel	1	1	1	HK	244
HENMAN,David	2	0	1	HK	496	JAMES,Howard	1	0	2	HK	243
HENNEX,Barnhart	1	0	1	HK	468	JOHNSTON,Isaiah	4	0	2	HK	474
HERKIMER,Abraham	1	2	1	CJ	299	JOHNSTON,William	1	1	3	HK	481
HERKIMER,Alita	2	1	6	CJ	291	JONES,Richard	2	2	2	HK	288
HERKIMER,Catherine	0	0	3	CJ	279	JONES,William Clark	1	0	0	GF	220
HERKIMER,George	1	0	4	GF	066	KAST,Frederick	3	1	2	HK	347
HERKIMER,Henry	1	0	2	CJ	278	KELLER,Henry	2	2	4	HK	425
HERKIMER,Jost	2	0	6	GF	067	KELLER,John	1	1	1	MK	541
HERKIMER,Nicholas	1	0	1	CJ	277	KELLER,John	1	2	2	HK	311
HERRING,John	1	0	1	MK	569	KELLER,Rudolph	8	0	2	MK	544
HESS,Augustinus	1	5	4	GF	195	KESSLER(Cesler),Nichol	1	1	3	PL	593
HESS,Christian	1	2	3	GF	179	KESSLER,Adam (Casler)	2	0	2	CJ	365
HESS,Conrad	2	1	3	GF	071	KESSLER,Conrad	1	2	4	GF	106
HESS,Daniel	1	2	4	PL	621	KESSLER,Dietrich (Ric)	1	1	2	GF	104
HESS,Frederick	2	3	4	PL	623	KESSLER,Jacob J N	1	0	1	GF	114
HESS,Frederick	2	2	4	GF	072	KESSLER,Jacob Jacob	1	2	2	GF	108
HESS,Henry	2	1	3	CJ	425	KESSLER,Jacob John	2	1	8	GF	105
HESS,John	1	5	4	GF	194	KESSLER,Jacob N	2	1	2	GF	115
HESS,John	2	0	1	PL	630	KESSLER,Jacob Sr.	1	0	1	GF	110
HESS,Jost	1	2	3	GF	016	KESSLER,John (Casler)	2	5	5	HK	395
HILL,Elijah	2	0	1	HK	338	KESSLER,John (Casler)	2	0	2	CJ	369
HILL,William	2	4	2	GF	030	KESSLER,John	1	1	3	CJ	124
HILLER,John	1	2	6	HK	370	KESSLER,John Jacob	1	3	2	GF	109
HILTS,George	2	1	4	HK	412	KESSLER,John Sr.	1	0	0	GF	102
HILTS,Godfrey	1	3	3	HK	418	KESSLER,Marc (Casler)	1	0	4	GF	132
HILTS,John	1	1	3	GF	113	KESSLER,Minert	2	1	8	HK	394

Name (Last/1st)	M	B	F	Tw	Ln#	Name (Last/1st)	M	B	F	Tw	Ln#
KESSLER, Nich. I	1	1	2	CJ	303	MEYER, Michael (Myers)	2	4	5	HK	375
KESSLER, Nicholas John	1	0	2	CJ	476	MEYER, Peter (Myer)	1	0	1	HK	329
KESSLER, Thomas	1	2	4	CJ	419	MILERD, Robert	1	0	2	GF	186
KILTS, Adam	1	4	5	PL	613	MILLER, Adam	1	1	1	MK	552
KILTS, Peter N.	1	1	2	PL	611	MILLER, Andrew	1	1	3	HK	348
KILTS, Philip	1	2	7	PL	612	MILLER, Elton (Valtn)	2	1	4	HK	307
KLOCK, Henry	1	3	6	HK	400	MILLER, George	1	5	3	CG	508
KLOCK, Joseph	1	1	1	HK	282	MILLER, Hendrick	2	1	2	MK	570
KNAP, Elijah	1	1	1	HK	433	MILLER, Henry	2	3	2	GF	192
KOCH, Joseph	1	1	3	HK	284	MILLER, Henry	2	2	2	PL	587
KRENNEL, John	1	1	2	HK	247	MILLER, John	1	3	2	CG	523
LAPER, John	1	2	1	CG	519	MILLER, John	1	3	4	HK	459
LAPPER, Jacob	1	5	3	CG	512	MILLER, Philip	4	1	7	CG	525
LASHER, Gerrit	3	2	5	PL	614	MILLER, Samuel	1	0	0	GF	219
LATHAM, Benjamin	1	0	0	HK	493	MOAK,..ratom (MAKE)	1	0	3	HK	372
LATHAM, David	1	0	1	HK	492	MONK, Johannes	1	5	3	CJ	199
LATHAM, Peter	1	2	1	HK	491	MONK, John	1	3	5	CJ	200
LEAPER, Wyant	3	5	2	PL	592	MOTTONER, John	3	0	3	HK	452
LEIMBACH, Henry	1	1	2	GF	095	MOULDER, Jacob	1	0	1	HK	281
LEIPER, Frederick	2	2	4	GF	031	MOULDER, Margaret	1	1	2	HK	280
LENTZ, Jacob	1	2	3	GF	154	MOYER, David	2	1	4	PL	647
LENTZ, Peter	1	2	3	GF	149	MUNTERBACH, John	2	2	4	GF	151
LIGHTHALL, Abraham	1	0	3	GF	013	MYER, Jacob	1	1	3	MK	545
LIGHTHALL, George	1	1	3	GF	075	MYERS, Christian	1	1	+	MK	558
LOBDEN, Joseph	1	0	3	HK	478	MYERS, John	1	1	3	MK	559
LOGAN(?), Thomas	2	1	4	GF	124	NASH, James	1	1	4	GF	070
LYON(?), Henry	1	0	1	GF	138	NELLIS, Andrew	1	4	2	HK	402
MABEE, David	1	1	2	GF	003	NELLIS, George	3	1	4	HK	404
MACK, John	1	1	2	HK	381	NICHOLS, Thomas	2	1	3	HK	258
MANLY, Thomas	1	1	1	HK	494	NICHOLS, William	1	2	3	HK	428
MANN, Abel	1	0	0	HK	461	NIELSON, Ball	1	3	3	HK	465
MANN, Abijah	1	1	2	HK	446	NIGHT, John	1	0	1	HK	261
MARSH, Peter (Nash?)	1	2	2	CJ	270	ODELL, Luke (?)	1	0	2	GF	122
MARTIN, John	2	0	1	GF	020	OLENDORF, Daniel	1	2	5	GF	025
MARTIN, Nathan	1	1	3	GF	022	ONEAL, John	1	2	3	GF	043
MARTIN, Robert	1	0	1	GF	021	ORENDORF, Conrad	2	2	5	GF	198
MARTIN, Samuel	1	1	1	GF	023	ORENDORF, Frederick Jr	1	2	6	GF	081
MARTZ, Philip Peter	1	2	3	GF	039	ORENDORF, Frederick Sr.	2	0	1	GF	082
MCCARTHY, George	+	+	+	GF	212	ORENDORF, Peter	2	2	3	GF	041
MCCARTHY, John	1	0	0	GF	211	OSTERHOUT, Cornelius	1	2	5	MK	546
MCCOMBS, George	1	0	1	HK	325	OSTERHOUT, Frederick	2	2	3	PL	640
MCNUTT,...	1	3	2	CG	522	OSTERHOUT, John	2	3	5	GF	037
MERRY, Samuel Jr.	1	0	2	GF	218	PAINE, Philip	2	1	3	HK	480
MERRY, Samuel Sr.	5	2	3	GF	221	PARKER, Daniel	1	0	4	HK	457
MEYER,... (Moyer)	3	4	4	GF	144	PARKER, Henry	1	1	1	HK	252
MEYER, Adam (Myer)	1	1	3	HK	305	PETRIE, Barbara	1	2	2	PL	651
MEYER, Frederick (Myer)	2	3	6	HK	328	PETRIE, Catherine	2	0	1	GF	093
MEYER, Henry (Moyer)	2	0	3	GF	120	PETRIE, Daniel	1	2	3	HK	393
MEYER, Joseph (Moyer)	2	2	6	GF	188	PETRIE, Jacob	3	3	6	HK	383
MEYER, Joseph (Myers)	1	2	2	HK	360	PETRIE, John	3	1	3	HK	390

ALPHABETIZED PORTION OF 1790 MONTGOMERY CO. NY CENSUS
(As relates to Herkimer Co. families)

Name (Last/1st)	M	B	F	Tw	Ln#	Name (Last/1st)	M	B	F	Tw	Ln#
PETRIE,John M.	2	6	2	HK	424	ROWN,Nicholas	2	0	2	HK	442
PETRIE,Jost (HanYost)	1	2	5	HK	391	RUSSEL,Samuel	2	0	0	HK	246
PETRIE,Jost Jr	2	0	3	HK	423	RYAN,Magdalena	0	1	3	GF	099
PETRIE,Marks	1	4	2	HK	392	SALIS,William	4	1	2	GF	170
PETRIE,Richard	1	0	2	HK	389	SALVEA,Henry	2	1	1	GF	175
PETRIE,William	2	3	4	HK	353	SCHAFER,Henry	3	0	4	HK	416
PETRY,Nathan	1	0	0	GF	090	SCHELL,Frederick	2	0	2	HK	409
PFEIFFER,Andrew	1	0	1	PL	601	SCHELL,John	4	0	6	HK	414
PHILLIPS,John	1	2	+	GF	190	SCHELL,Marks (Shell)	1	0	0	HK	410
PICKARD,Nicholas	1	4	2	CN	532	SCHELL,Marks Sr. (?)	1	1	1	HK	415
PIPER,...	1	2	2	GF	145	SCHUT,William	1	0	3	CJ	105
PIPER,Jacob	4	1	6	HK	335	SCHUYLER,Clmon	3	0	1	MK	560
POLLARD,Jeremiah	2	1	2	HK	453	SCHUYLER,David A.	1	3	2	CJ	255
PORTEOUS,John	5	0	3	HK	387	SCHUYLER,David P.	1	0	1	CJ	258
PORTER(?),Alexander	1	1	2	GF	160	SCHUYLER,Jacob	2	2	2	MK	564
POSTLE,Francis	1	2	3	HK	232	SCHUYLER,Lear	1	1	1	CJ	293
POTTER,Jeremiah	4	2	3	HK	497	SCHUYLER,Nicholas	1	3	1	CJ	256
PUMPSTADE,Frederick	1	3	2	CJ	193	SCHUYLER,Peter	4	0	1	PL	618
PUTMAN,David	1	1	5	CJ	311	SCHUYLER,Peter D.	1	0	3	CJ	259
PUTMAN,Frederick	2	3	3	MK	547	SCHUYLER,Peter P.	1	3	4	CJ	253
PUTMAN,Victor D	1	4	1	MK	548	SCRAMLIN,David	1	2	3	OT	574
RAMSAY,Ebenezeer	1	0	0	GF	203	SCRAMLIN,George	2	2	3	OT	575
RANCAN,James	1	1	1	HK	401	SCRAMLIN,Henry	5	0	4	OT	573
RASPACH,Marc	3	1	3	HK	371	SCRIBNER,Aaron	1	3	1	HK	458
REED,Curtis	1	2	2	HK	462	SEAMORE,Ebenezer	1	1	4	HK	337
REES,Peter	3	0	2	PL	610	SEBEER,James	1	1	2	CJ	411
REESE,Adam	3	2	4	GF	038	SEGHNER,Conrad	1	1	2	GF	097
REESE,Jonas	2	1	3	PL	615	SEGHNER,Paul (Sagner)	1	2	7	GF	098
REID,John	1	2	1	PL	599	SHILL,Jacob	1	2	1	PL	603
REMENSNEIDER,John	2	2	4	HK	656	SHOEMAKER,...	2	2	2	GF	131
REUBY,Christopher	1	1	1	GF	064	SHOEMAKER,... SR.	4	1	3	GF	056
RICHMOND,Daniel	1	1	6	HK	321	SHOEMAKER,Christopher	1	0	5	GF	055
RICHTER,Nicholas	2	2	5	PL	577	SHOEMAKER,Frederick	1	0	2	GF	054
RICKART,Conrad	2	0	3	MK	551	SHOEMAKER,Frederick	0	0	0	GF	130
RICKART,Conrad	2	1	2	PL	652	SHOEMAKER,Gertrude	0	1	2	GF	128
RICKART,John	1	3	3	CJ	012	SHOEMAKER,Jost	1	3	3	GF	127
RICKART,Ludwig	2	2	2	PL	597	SHOEMAKER,Rudolph	2	2	2	GF	129
RICKER,Peter	1	2	5	MK	567	SHOEMAKER,Thomas	4	3	8	GF	079
RICKERT,George	3	2	5	CJ	011	SHOLL,George	1	4	3	CJ	006
RIED,Abner	1	0	0	HK	469	SHOLL,.John	1	3	1	CJ	014
RIED,Conrad	1	2	3	MK	561	SHOLL,Matice	1	2	1	CJ	020
RIEGEL,Christian	2	1	2	HK	248	SHURMAN,Samuel	2	1	2	GF	187
RIEGEL,Fred. (Rheel)	5	0	2	HK	227	SILLEBACK,Christian	1	0	0	HK	368
RIEGEL,Godfrey	1	0	1	HK	268	SKINNER,Gershom	1	1	4	HK	276
RIEMA,Christian	1	0	1	HK	304	SMALL,Susannah	0	3	6	GF	068
RIEMA,Jacob	1	1	3	HK	296	SMITH,Aaron	3	1	3	CG	521
RIEMA,John	5	0	4	HK	295	SMITH,Adam	2	1	7	HK	343
RITTER,Fredrick	1	1	2	PL	658	SMITH,Baltus	1	3	2	PL	583
RITTER,Henry	1	1	2	PL	660	SMITH,Clark	1	1	2	HK	456
ROSENCRANTZ,Abraham	3	1	3	GF	111	SMITH,Conrad	1	0	3	CH	530

Name (Last/1st)	M	B	F	Tw	Ln#	Name (Last/1st)	M	B	F	Tw	Ln#
SMITH,Cornelius	1	2	4	CG	501	STEELE,Rudolph	1	1	3	GF	126
SMITH,Edward	2	0	2	HP	534	STICKNY,Joseph	1	0	0	GF	222
SMITH,Frederick	1	1	2	HK	346	STIFFORD,David	1	0	4	HK	271
SMITH,George	2	4	4	PL	580	STIFFORD,Jacob	1	1	2	HK	272
SMITH,George	2	1	3	HK	319	STIFFORD,Richard	1	2	3	HK	270
SMITH,Hendrick	1	1	4	PL	585	STIFFORD,Samuel	2	1	4	HK	245
SMITH,Hendrick J.	1	1	1	PL	582	STOUGHTON(?),Amasa	2	0	0	HK	362
SMITH,Henry	2	1	3	PL	579	STROBEL,Christopher	2	1	3	GF	166
SMITH,Jeremiah	1	1	2	PL	584	SWEET,Jonathan	1	0	0	GF	217
SMITH,John	4	1	6	GF	119	TALCOT,Hezekiah	3	2	7	HK	357
SMITH,John M.	1	3	1	HK	369	TEAL,Joseph	1	1	2	HK	450
SMITH,Jost (Yost)	1	1	2	HK	320	THARE,Pheneas	1	1	2	GF	006
SMITH,Nicholas	2	1	5	PL	581	THRASHER,George	3	2	2	HK	421
SMITH,Noah	1	0	0	HK	443	THRASHER,Stephen	1	0	1	HK	422
SMITH,Thomas	1	2	2	MK	555	THUMM,Melchior	2	1	7	HK	417
SNOW,Elijah	1	2	4	GF	205	TINUS(?),Jacob	2	1	3	GF	152
SPENCER,John	1	0	3	HK	240	TUSLER,Mark	1	0	3	GF	026
SPENCER,Rufus	1	2	3	HK	253	UHLE, Henry (Oeley)	1	0	4	GF	112
SPOHN,Nicholas (Spoon)	3	2	3	HK	406	UNDERHILL,David	1	0	0	HK	495
SPOHN,Warner	2	0	3	GF	073	UNDERWOOD,Joseph	3	1	4	GF	001
STACKWEATHER,Elijah	1	1	4	HK	473	UNDERWOOD,Parker	1	0	3	GF	201
STALE,Anthony Jr	1	0	1	CG	529	VAN BRACKLE,Herbert	1	1	1	HK	455
STALL,Joseph	4	1	8	CG	506	VAN HORN,Hendrick	1	0	2	MK	557
STALY,Hendrick	1	2	4	MK	565	VAN SLYK,Jacob	1	3	4	PL	650
STALY,Jacob	2	1	1	CG	527	VETTERLY(Fed..),George	3	+	4	CJ	010
STALY,Ruoof	1	2	4	MK	563	VINTON,Benomi	2	0	0	GF	215
STALY,Slivanus	1	6	6	MK	562	VROOMAN,Clmon	1	2	1	MK	542
STANDARD,Oliver	1	0	3	HK	476	VROOMAN,John	1	3	2	MK	538
STARING,Adam	1	0	4	HK	384	WALKER,Edward	2	2	3	GF	004
STARING,Adam	1	3	3	MK	556	WALLRATH,John II	1	3	1	CJ	015
STARING,Adam	2	3	4	HK	293	WATSON,Jud	1	0	2	HK	486
STARING,Adam A.	1	1	4	HK	361	WATSON,Nathan	1	0	0	HK	487
STARING,Adam N	3	1	6	GF	092	WATSON,Samuel	1	3	2	HK	488
STARING,Adam Sr.	3	2	2	GF	036	WEAVER,Adam	1	2	1	GF	047
STARING,Conrad	1	2	4	PL	649	WEAVER,David	1	4	2	PL	596
STARING,Fredrick	2	2	2	MK	554	WEAVER,Frederick G.	2	0	2	HK	235
STARING,George	1	0	3	PL	646	WEAVER,Frederick J	1	2	2	HK	333
STARING,Henry	3	4	5	HK	290	WEAVER,George	1	3	5	HK	234
STARING,Henry N	1	2	3	GF	117	WEAVER,George J	1	0	1	HK	236
STARING,Jacob	2	0	3	PL	648	WEAVER,George J.N.	2	2	5	HK	237
STARING,Jacob	1	0	2	HK	385	WEAVER,George Michael	1	1	1	HK	231
STARING,John	1	3	2	MK	540	WEAVER,Jacob	2	1	3	HK	233
STARING,Joseph	2	2	7	GF	083	WEAVER,Jacob G.	2	0	3	HK	354
STARING,Nicholas	3	2	4	GF	084	WEAVER,Jacob H.	1	1	3	GF	180
STARING,Philip	1	3	3	MK	553	WEAVER,Jacob N	2	2	2	HK	331
STARING,Valentine	2	0	2	HK	408	WEAVER,John	2	1	2	GF	147
STARING,William	1	1	3	MK	549	WEAVER,Nicholas	1	0	2	GF	148
STEELE,Adam (Stale)	4	2	4	GF	080	WEAVER,Nicholas G.	1	1	2	HK	238
STEELE,Dietrich	4	0	2	GF	137	WEAVER,Nicholas J	1	1	4	HK	229
STEELE,George	2	2	7	GF	224	WEAVER,Peter	1	2	1	CG	520

Name (Last/1st)	M	B	F	Tw	Ln#
WEAVER,Peter J.	2	3	2	HK	363
WEAVER,Peter Jr.	1	2	3	HK	250
WEBBER,Christopher	2	0	4	OT	576
WERNER,Henry	1	0	2	GF	125
WESTERMAN,Peter	2	1	3	CJ	446
WHARRY,Evans	1	3	3	HK	420
WHIPPLE,Levy	1	2	1	HK	484
WHIPPLE,Nicholas	1	1	2	HK	483
WHIPPLE,William	2	3	2	HK	444
WICK,John	3	1	4	PL	605
WILCOCKS,Joseph	1	1	2	GF	059
WILLIS,Aseph	1	0	0	HK	256
WILLIS,Caleb	1	0	0	HK	257
WITACER,Squire	2	3	2	HP	535
WITHERSTINE,Henry	2	1	4	HK	413
WITRIG,Catherine	1	0	4	HK	301
WITRIG,George	2	2	4	HK	291
WITRIG,Jacob	2	1	3	HK	300
WITRIG,Michael	1	2	4	HK	303
WOHLEBEN,Abraham	1	2	3	GF	014
WOHLEBEN,Henry	2	3	3	PL	644
WOHLEBEN,Jacob	1	1	4	GF	181
WOHLEBEN,Peter	2	2	4	GF	049
WOHLEBEN,Peter	1	1	3	CJ	254
WOOD,John	1	2	1	HK	260
WOODWARD,James	1	0	+	GF	008
WORMWOOD,Abraham	1	0	1	CG	510
WORMWOOD,Matthew	1	3	2	CG	511
YUEL,James (YOUHE)	1	4	2	GF	051

Note: The alphabetized listing on this and preceding pages is not the complete
Montgomery County census of 1790 as it includes only German Flats, Herkimer, and a
small selection of residents from other towns whose surnames are similar to the
early Herkimer area families. Census count of individuals in a household is the
sum of M (males age 16 and over), B (boys below age 16), and F (females). The
following two-letter codes represent towns listed under Montgomery Co. in the 1790
census of New York State. Some of these, such as German Flats & Herkimer, were
later split into separate counties (i.e. such as modern day Herkimer Co.).

        CG: Caughnawaga (now Fonda) NY
        CH: Chemung NY
        CJ: Canajoharie NY
        GF: German Flats (see Ln# on pages 337-340 for neighbors)
        HK: Herkimer (see Ln# on pages 337-340 for neighbors)
        HP: Harpersfield NY
        MK: Mohawk NY
        OT: Otsego NY
        PL: Palatine NY

BIBLIOGRAPHY

... , **The Old United Empire Loyalists List.** Toronto, 1885 (repr. Baltimore: Genealogical Publishing Co. Inc., 1976).

BAGG, Moses M., **The Pioneers of Utica.** Utica: Curtis & Childs, 1877.

BAKER, Mildred, **The Steele Family** (ms. at Herkimer Co. Historical Soc.).

BARKER, William V. H., **Smith Descendents of Herkimer, N.Y.** (1982 ms. of W. Barker, 3999-A Valley Ct, Winston-Salem, N.C. 27106).

BECK, Violet M., **Home Folks Book of the Darius Myers Family.** 1926.

BEERS, F. W., **History of Herkimer County, N.Y.** New York: F.W. Beers & Co., 1879.

BELLINGER, Lyle F., **Genealogy of the Mohawk Valley Bellingers and Allied Families** (indexed by Hazel Patrick, publ. Herkimer Co. Historical Society, Herkimer, N.Y., 1976). <Bellinger book>.

BENTON, Nathaniel, **A History of Herkimer County, Including the Upper Mohawk Valley.** Albany: J. Munsell, 1856.

BROWN, Charles P., **The Descendants of Peter Folts** (1974 ms. at Herkimer Co. Historical Soc.).

CAMPBELL, William W., **Annals of Tryon County; or, the Border Warfare of New York During the Revolution.** New York: J. and J. Harper, 1831.

COOKINGHAM, Henry J., **History of Oneida County, N.Y.** Chicago: S.J. Clarke Pub. Co., 1912.

CONRAD, Mrs. Mildred and Ida House, **Mohawk Valley Kasts and Allied Families** (1983 ms. at Herkimer Co. Historical Soc.). <Kast book>.

COWEN, Phoebe Strong, **The Herkimers and Schuylers.** Albany: J. Munsell's Sons, 1903.

EARL, Robert, "The Mohawk Valley in History" **Herkimer County Historical Society Papers.** Herkimer N.Y., 1896.

DEUEL, Frank Dygert, **Dygert Charts.** (Utica, N.Y., 1948). Ms. at Montgomery County Dept. of History and Archives, Old Court House, Fonda N.Y. 12068.

ECKLER, A. Ross Jr., **The Eckler Family of the Mohawk Valley** (1949 ms. at Herkimer Co. Historical Soc.).

ELLSWORTH, W.W., "The Palatines in the Mohawk Valley" **New York State Historical Association Proceedings,** vol. XIV, 1915.

GREEN, Nelson, **History of the Mohawk Valley, Gateway to the West 1614-1925.** 4 vols. Chicago: S.J. Clarke Pub. Co., 1925.

HALLENBECK, Elsie O., **Our Van Horne Kindred** (ca 1940, no publisher given; copy at Herkimer Co. Historical Soc.).

HARDIN, George A., **History of Herkimer County**. Syracuse: D. Mason & Co., 1893.

HATCH, Mrs. Alice Griffin, **The Hatch Papers** (ms. at Herkimer Co. Historical Society).

HILLS, Helen M., **Meyer Genealogy** (ms. at Herkimer Co. Historical Soc.; Publ. H. Mills, 117 High St., Chicago, Illinois).

HISLOP, Codman, **The Mohawk (Rivers of America series)**. New York: Rinehart & Company, 1948).

JOHNSON, William, **The Papers of Sir William Johnson**. Albany: University of the State of New York, 1921.

JONES, Hank, **The Palatine Families of New York** (priv. published 1985 by H. Jones, P.O. Box 8341, Universal City, CA 91608).

KNITTLE, Walter A., **The Early Eighteenth Century Palatine Emigration**. Philadelphia: Dorrance and Co., 1937 (repr. Baltimore: Genealogical Publishing Co., Inc., 1965).

KOFMEHL, Marion and Hazel Patrick, **The Mohawk Valley Harters and Allied Families**. Herkimer Co. Historial Soc., Herkimer, N.Y., 1981. <Harter book>.

LAIMBEER, William, **The Getman Family Genealogy 1710-1974** (publ. ca 1975 <publisher not given>, copy at Herkimer Co. Historical Soc.). <Getman book>.

LEETHAM, Rosabell G., **Families of the Mohawk Valley**. Ms. at Montgomery County Dept. of History and Archives, Old Court House, Fonda N.Y. 12068.

MACWETHY, Lou D., **The BOOK of NAMES, Especially Relating to THE EARLY PALATINES And the First Settlers in the MOHAWK VALLEY**. St. Johnsville, N.Y.: Enterprise & News, 1933 (repr. Baltimore: Genealogical Pub. Co., 1969).

MARTIN, David Kendall, **THE EIGHTEENTH CENTURY SNELL FAMILY OF THE MOHAWK VALLEY**. Priv. published 1982 by David K. Martin, Mouse Hill, West Chazy, N.Y. 12992.

MORRISON, James F., **Index to Revolutionary Soldiers of Tryon Co. N.Y.** (copy at Herkimer Co. Historical Society).

MYERS, Henry Hudson, **Myers Genealogical Record** (1955 ms. at Herkimer Co. Historical Soc., Herkimer, N.Y.).

O'CALLAHAN & Fernow, **Documents Relating to the Colonial History of the State of New York**. 15 vols. Albany: Weed Parsons and Co., 1853-1887.

OYER, Phyillis Smith, **Frederick Oyer and His Descendants** (ms. copy at Herkimer Co. Historical Soc.).

PARSON, ..., **Mohawk Valley Edicks** (1983 ms. at Utica Public Lib., Utica, N.Y.).

PEARSON, Jonathan, **First Settlers of Schenectady.** Albany, 1873 (repr. Baltimore: Genealogical Publishing Co., Inc., 1976).

PENROSE, Maryly B., **MOHAWK VALLEY IN THE REVOLUTION.** Publ. Liberty Bell Associates, P.O. Box 51, Franklin Park NJ 08823, 1978.

PENROSE, Maryly B., **Baumann/Bowman Family of the Mohawk.** Publ. Liberty Bell Associates, P.O. Box 51, Franklin Park NJ 08823, 1977. <Bauman book>.

POTTER, John B. Jr., **HERKIMER/SCHUYLER & Allied Families** (Published by J. Potter, 61 E. Main St, Mohawk, N.Y.).

PRINDLE, Paul W., **The Van Derwerken Family.** St. Johnsville, 1966.

REALS, William J. and Vivian Y. Brecknell, **The Reals Family Descendents of Gottfried Ruhl** (Published by Dr. W. J. Reals, 706 Stratford Road, Wichita, Kansas 67206; sold through Herkimer Co. Historical Soc., Herkimer, N.Y.).

REYNOLDS, Cuyler, **Hudson-Mohawk Genealogical and Family Memoirs.** 4 vols. New York: Lewis Pub. Co., 1911.

ROONEY, Doris Dockstader, **The Dockstader Family** (priv. published 1983, Mrs. D. D. Rooney, 1918 LaMesa Drive, Dodge City, Kansas 67801). <Dockstader book>.

RUPP, Prof. I. Daniel, **A Collection of Upwards of Thirty Thousand Names of German ... Immgrants in Pennsylvania from 1726 to 1776.** Philadelphia 1876 (repr. Baltimore: Genealogical Publishing Co., Inc., 1965).

SIMMS, Jephth R., **Frontiersman of New York** 2 vols. Published 1882.

STAEHLE, Mrs. Metta, May L. Petrie, and Raymond C. Petrie, **The Mohawk Valley Petries and Allied Families** (Edited by Hazel Patrick, Herkimer Co. Historical Soc., Herkimer N.Y., 1979). <Petrie book>.

STARNES, H. Gerald, **A History of the Starnes Family.** Baltimore: Gateway Press, 1983.

STONE, William L., **Starin Family.** Albany, 1892. <Staring book>.

VOSBURGH, Royden W., **Records of the Reformed Protestant Dutch Church, German Flats.** 2 vols. (New York. 1918) <ms. copies at Herkimer Co. Historical Soc., Conn. State Lib. at Hartford, Lib. of Congress>.

VOSBURGH, Royden W., **Records of the Reformed Dutch Church of Stone Arabia, New York.** 2 vols. (New York. 1916).

VROOMAN, John J., **Forts and Firesides of the Mohawk Country.** Philadelphia: Elijah Ellsworth Brownell, 1943.

WARD, Christopher, **The War of the Revolution.** 2 vols. MacMillan Co., 1952.

WILLIAMS, Pascoe, **The Helmer Family** (repr. from Enterprise & News, St. Johnsville, N.Y., 1931-32). <Helmer book>.

Name ID#	Name ID#	Name ID#

Name	ID#		Name	ID#		Name	ID#